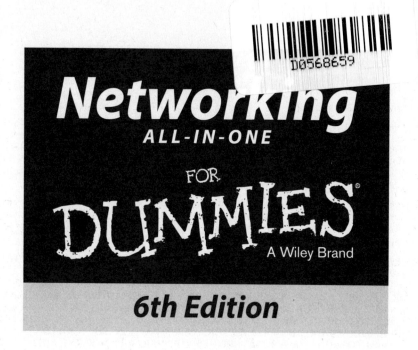

Networking

ALL-IN-ONE

FOR

DUMMIES

A Wiley Brand

6th Edition

by Doug Lowe

Networking All-in-One For Dummies®, 6th Edition

Published by: **John Wiley & Sons, Inc.,** 111 River Street, Hoboken, NJ 07030-5774, www.wiley.com

Copyright © 2016 by John Wiley & Sons, Inc., Hoboken, New Jersey

Published simultaneously in Canada

For general information on our other products and services, please contact our Customer Care Department within the U.S. at 877-762-2974, outside the U.S. at 317-572-3993, or fax 317-572-4002. For technical support, please visit www.wiley.com/techsupport.

Wiley publishes in a variety of print and electronic formats and by print-on-demand. Some material included with standard print versions of this book may not be included in e-books or in print-on-demand. If this book refers to media such as a CD or DVD that is not included in the version you purchased, you may download this material at http://booksupport.wiley.com. For more information about Wiley products, visit www.wiley.com.

Library of Congress Control Number: 2015960607

ISBN 978-1-119-15472-3 (pbk); ISBN 978-1-119-15473-0 (ebk); ISBN 978-1-119-15474-7 (ebk)

Manufactured in the United States of America

10 9 8 7 6 5 4 3 2

Contents at a Glance

Introduction *1*

Book I: Planning a Network *5*

Chapter 1: Understanding Networks 7
Chapter 2: Planning a Network 23
Chapter 3: Installing Network Hardware 41
Chapter 4: Setting Up a Server 53
Chapter 5: Configuring Windows Clients 63
Chapter 6: Mac Networking 73
Chapter 7: Configuring Other Network Features 81
Chapter 8: Setting Up a Wireless Network 89

Book II: Network Administration *119*

Chapter 1: Help Wanted: Job Description for
  a Network Administrator 121
Chapter 2: Security 101 135
Chapter 3: Managing User Accounts 145
Chapter 4: Firewalls and Virus Protection 153
Chapter 5: Blocking Spam 165
Chapter 6: Managing Network Software 177
Chapter 7: Solving Network Problems 189
Chapter 8: Backing Up Your Data 205
Chapter 9: Disaster Recovery and Business Continuity Planning 217

Book III: Protocols *225*

Chapter 1: Understanding Network Protocols and Standards 227
Chapter 2: Introduction to TCP/IP and the Internet 249
Chapter 3: Understanding IP Addresses 257
Chapter 4: Using DHCP 275
Chapter 5: Using DNS 291
Chapter 6: Using FTP 317
Chapter 7: TCP/IP Tools and Commands 339

Book IV: Going Virtual 365

Chapter 1: Introducing Virtualization............................367
Chapter 2: Working with Hyper-V 377
Chapter 3: Working with VMware 395
Chapter 4: Virtualizing Your Desktops 405

Book V: Remote Networking 413

Chapter 1: Managing Mobile Devices 415
Chapter 2: Working with VPN for Remote Access 429
Chapter 3: Using Remote Desktop Access......................435
Chapter 4: Using Remote Assistance............................447

Book VI: Cloud Networking..................... 455

Chapter 1: Cloudy with a Chance of Gigabytes...............457
Chapter 2: Using Essential Cloud Services 467
Chapter 3: Administering Office 365............................477
Chapter 4: Using SharePoint Online 485

Book VII: Windows Server 2016 Reference 497

Chapter 1: Installing and Configuring Windows Server 2016 499
Chapter 2: Managing Windows Server 2016 513
Chapter 3: Dealing with Active Directory 529
Chapter 4: Managing Windows User Accounts 541
Chapter 5: Managing a File Server 563
Chapter 6: Using Group Policy 577
Chapter 7: Troubleshooting..589
Chapter 8: Windows Commands..................................601

Book VIII: Using Other Windows Servers.................... 629

Chapter 1: Using Internet Information Services...............631
Chapter 2: Managing Exchange Server 2016 641
Chapter 3: Using SQL Server 2014 659

Book IX: Managing Linux Systems 675

Chapter 1: Installing a Linux Server 677
Chapter 2: Getting Used to Linux................................689
Chapter 3: Basic Linux Network Configuration...............701
Chapter 4: Running DHCP and DNS 713

Chapter 5: Doing the Samba Dance 723
Chapter 6: Running Apache 737
Chapter 7: Running Sendmail 749
Chapter 8: Running FTP 759
Chapter 9: Linux Commands 765

Appendix A: Directory of Useful Websites *793*

Appendix B: Glossary *801*

Index *829*

Table of Contents

Introduction *1*

About This Book 2
Foolish Assumptions 3
Icons Used in This Book 3
Beyond the Book 4
Where to Go from Here 4

Book 1: Planning a Network *5*

Chapter 1: Understanding Networks 7

Defining a Network 7
    Network building blocks 8
    Seeing the benefits of networking 10
Comparing Clients and Servers 11
Understanding Dedicated Servers and Peers 12
Seeing Networks Big and Small 13
Looking Closer at Servers 13
    What's important in a server 14
    Components of a server computer 15
    Server form factors 16
    Operating systems for server computers 18

Chapter 2: Planning a Network 23

Making a Network Plan 23
Being Purposeful 24
Taking Stock 25
    What you need to know 25
    Programs that gather information for you 27
To Dedicate or Not to Dedicate: That Is the Question 28
Considering Server Roles 28
    File servers 29
    Print servers 29
    Web servers 29
    Mail servers 29
    Database servers 30
    Application servers 30
    License servers 30

Choosing a Server Operating System..30
Considering Cable 31
Surmising Switches 32
Planning the Network Topology 35
Planning the TCP/IP Implementation..36
Drawing Diagrams 36
More Questions Your Network Plan Should Address.....................38

Chapter 3: Installing Network Hardware.....................41

Working with Cable 41
Cable categories..41
What's with the pairs?..42
To shield or not to shield 43
When to use plenum cable 43
Sometimes solid, sometimes stranded 44
Installation guidelines 44
Getting the tools that you need 46
Pinouts for twisted-pair cables 47
Attaching RJ-45 connectors...48
Wall jacks and patch panels 49
Installing Switches..50
Daisy-Chaining Switches 51

Chapter 4: Setting Up a Server.............................53

The Many Ways to Install a Server Operating System...................53
Full install versus upgrade...53
Installing over the network...55
Gathering Your Stuff...55
A capable server computer 55
The server OS...56
Other software 56
A working Internet connection..56
A good book..57
Making Informed Decisions 57
Final Preparations 58
Installing a Server Operating System...59
Phase 1: Collecting information 59
Phase 2: Installing Windows 60
Configuring Your Server 60

Chapter 5: Configuring Windows Clients....................63

Configuring Network Connections 63
Joining a Domain 69

Chapter 6: Mac Networking **73**

Basic Mac Network Settings 73
Joining a Domain 77
Connecting to a Share 79

Chapter 7: Configuring Other Network Features **81**

Configuring Network Printers 81
Adding a network printer 81
Accessing a network printer using a web interface 84
Mapping Network Drives 85

Chapter 8: Setting Up a Wireless Network **89**

Diving into Wireless Networking 90
A Little High School Electronics 91
Waves and frequencies 91
Wavelength and antennas 92
Spectrums and the FCC 93
Eight-Oh-Two-Dot-Eleventy Something? (Or, Understanding Wireless
Standards) 94
Home on the Range 95
Wireless Network Adapters 96
Wireless Access Points 97
Infrastructure mode 98
Multifunction WAPs 99
Roaming 99
Wireless bridging 100
Ad-hoc networks 100
Configuring a Wireless Access Point 100
Basic configuration options 101
DHCP configuration 102
Connecting to a Wireless Network 103
Paying Attention to Wireless Network Security 105
Understanding wireless security threats 105
Securing your wireless network 109
Troubleshooting a wireless network 114

Book II: Network Administration *119*

**Chapter 1: Help Wanted: Job Description for
a Network Administrator** **121**

Knowing What Network Administrators Do 121
Choosing the Part-Time Administrator 123
Establishing Routine Chores 124

Managing Network Users 125
Patching Up Your Operating System and Software 126
Discovering Software Tools for Network Administrators 126
Building a Library 128
Getting Certified 129
    CompTIA 130
    Microsoft 131
    Cisco 131
Gurus Need Gurus, Too 132
Helpful Bluffs and Excuses 132

Chapter 2: Security 101 135

Do You Need Security? 136
Considering Two Approaches to Security 137
Physical Security: Locking Your Doors 137
Securing User Accounts 139
    Obfuscating your usernames 139
    Using passwords wisely 140
    A password-generator For Dummies 141
    Securing the Administrator account 142
Hardening Your Network 142
    Using a firewall 142
    Disabling unnecessary services 143
    Patching your servers 143
Securing Your Users 143

Chapter 3: Managing User Accounts 145

Exploring What User Accounts Consist Of 145
Looking at Built-In Accounts 146
    The Administrator account 146
    The Guest account 147
    Service accounts 147
Assigning User Rights 148
Controlling User Access with Permissions
    (Who Gets What) 149
Assigning Permissions to Groups 150
Understanding User Profiles 150
Automating Tasks with Logon Scripts 151

Chapter 4: Firewalls and Virus Protection 153

Firewalls 153
The Many Types of Firewalls 155
    Packet filtering 155
    Stateful packet inspection (SPI) 157
    Circuit-level gateway 157
    Application gateway 157

The Built-In Windows Firewall 158
Virus Protection 159
What is a virus? 159
Antivirus programs 161
Safe computing 162
Using Windows Action Center 162

Chapter 5: Blocking Spam **165**

Defining Spam 166
Sampling the Many Flavors of Spam 167
Using Antispam Software 168
Understanding Spam Filters 169
Looking at Three Types of Antispam Software 172
On-premises antispam 172
Antispam appliances 173
Cloud-based antispam services 174
Minimizing Spam 175

Chapter 6: Managing Network Software **177**

Understanding Software Licenses 178
Using a License Server 180
Options for Deploying Network Software 182
Deploying software manually 182
Running Setup from a network share 182
Installing silently 183
Creating an administrative installation image 185
Pushing out software with group policy 185
Keeping Software Up to Date 186

Chapter 7: Solving Network Problems **189**

When Bad Things Happen to Good Computers 190
Fixing Dead Computers 191
Ways to Check a Network Connection 192
A Bunch of Error Messages Just Flew By! 193
Double-Checking Your Network Settings 193
Using the Windows Networking Troubleshooter 194
Time to Experiment 195
Who's on First? 196
Restarting a Client Computer 196
Booting in Safe Mode 198
Using System Restore 198
Restarting Network Services 200
Restarting a Network Server 202
Looking at Event Logs 203
Documenting Your Trials and Tribulations 204

Chapter 8: Backing Up Your Data 205

    Backing Up Your Data 205
    Where to Back Up Your Data 206
    Backing Up to Tape 206
    Backup Software 207
    Types of Backups 208
        Normal backups 209
        Copy backups 210
        Daily backups 210
        Incremental backups 210
        Differential backups..211
    Local versus Network Backups....................................212
    How Many Sets of Backups Should You Keep?...........213
    A Word about Tape Reliability....................................215
    About Cleaning the Heads 216
    Backup Security 216

Chapter 9: Disaster Recovery and Business Continuity Planning. . .217

    Assessing Different Types of Disasters.......................218
        Environmental disasters 218
        Deliberate disasters..219
        Disruption of services 219
        Equipment failure 220
        Other disasters..220
    Analyzing the Impact of a Disaster.............................220
    Developing a Business Continuity Plan 221
    Holding a Fire Drill..222

Book III: Protocols **225**

Chapter 1: Understanding Network Protocols and Standards......227

    Understanding Protocols...227
    Understanding Standards...229
    Seeing the Seven Layers of the OSI Reference Model............229
        The Physical layer 231
        The Data Link layer...232
        The Network layer 233
        The Transport layer 236
        The Session layer..238
        The Presentation layer..238
        The Application layer 239
    Following a Packet through the Layers 239

The Ethernet Protocol 240

Standard Ethernet..242

Fast Ethernet 242

Gigabit Ethernet 243

The TCP/IP Protocol Suite..244

IP 245

TCP 246

UDP 247

Other Protocols Worth Knowing About 247

Chapter 2: Introduction to TCP/IP and the Internet 249

What Is the Internet?...249

A Little Internet History...251

TCP/IP Standards and RFCs 252

The TCP/IP Protocol Framework..254

Network Interface layer...254

Network layer 255

Transport layer 255

Application layer..256

Chapter 3: Understanding IP Addresses 257

Understanding Binary...257

Counting by ones 257

Doing the logic thing 259

Working with the binary Windows Calculator 260

Introducing IP Addresses 262

Networks and hosts...262

The dotted-decimal dance 262

Classifying IP Addresses 263

Class A addresses 265

Class B addresses 267

Class C addresses 267

Subnetting..267

Subnets 268

Subnet masks..269

Network prefix notation 270

Default subnets 271

The great subnet roundup..271

IP block parties 272

Private and public addresses..273

Network Address Translation...273

Chapter 4: Using DHCP 275

Understanding DHCP 275

Configuration information provided by DHCP 275

DHCP servers...276

How DHCP actually works 276

Understanding Scopes 278
  Feeling excluded? 279
  Reservations suggested 279
  How long to lease? 280
Working with a DHCP Server 281
  Installing a Windows Server 2016 DHCP server 281
  Configuring a new scope 282
How to Configure a Windows DHCP Client 287
  Automatic private IP addressing 287
  Renewing and releasing leases 288

Chapter 5: Using DNS 291

Understanding DNS Names 291
  Domains and domain names 292
  Fully qualified domain names 294
Top-Level Domains 294
  Generic domains 294
  Geographic domains 295
The Hosts File 297
Understanding DNS Servers and Zones 300
  Zones 300
  Primary and secondary servers 302
  Root servers 303
  Caching 305
Understanding DNS Queries 306
  A real-life DNS example 307
Zone Files and Resource Records 308
  SOA records 309
  NS records 310
  A records 311
  CNAME records 311
  PTR records 312
  MX records 312
Reverse Lookup Zones 313
Working with the Windows DNS Server 314
How to Configure a Windows DNS Client 315

Chapter 6: Using FTP 317

Discovering FTP 317
Configuring an FTP Server 318
  Installing FTP 318
  Creating an FTP site 318
  Changing the FTP site properties 321
  Adding content to your FTP site 323
Accessing an FTP Site with a Browser 324

Using an FTP Command Line Client 325
FTP Command and Subcommand Reference 328
    The FTP command 328
    ! (Escape) 329
    ? (Help) 329
    append 329
    ascii 329
    bell 329
    binary 330
    bye 330
    cd 330
    close 330
    debug 330
    delete 331
    dir 331
    disconnect 331
    get 331
    glob 332
    hash 332
    help 332
    lcd 332
    literal 333
    ls 333
    mdelete 333
    mdir 333
    mget 334
    mkdir 334
    mls 334
    mput 334
    open 335
    prompt 335
    put 335
    pwd 335
    quit 336
    quote 336
    recv 336
    remotehelp 336
    rename 337
    rmdir 337
    send 337
    status 337
    trace 338
    type 338
    user 338
    verbose 338

Chapter 7: TCP/IP Tools and Commands **339**

Using the arp Command 339
Using the hostname Command 340
Using the ipconfig Command 340
    Displaying basic IP configuration 341
    Displaying detailed configuration information 342
    Renewing an IP lease 342
    Releasing an IP lease 343
    Flushing the local DNS cache 343
Using the nbtstat Command 344
Using the netstat Command 345
    Displaying connections 345
    Displaying interface statistics 346
Using the nslookup Command 349
    Looking up an IP address 349
    Using nslookup subcommands 350
    Displaying DNS records 350
    Locating the mail server for an email address 352
    Taking a ride through DNS-Land 352
Using the pathping Command 355
Using the ping Command 357
Using the route Command 358
    Displaying the routing table 358
    Modifying the routing table 361
Using the tracert Command 362

Book IV: Going Virtual *365*

Chapter 1: Introducing Virtualization **367**

Understanding Virtualization 367
Understanding Hypervisors 368
Understanding Virtual Disks 370
Understanding Network Virtualization 373
Considering the Benefits of Virtualization 373

Chapter 2: Working with Hyper-V **377**

Understanding the Hyper-V Hypervisor 377
Understanding Hyper-V Virtual Disks 378
Enabling Hyper-V 379
Getting Familiar with Hyper-V 380
Creating a Virtual Switch 381
Creating a Virtual Disk 384
Creating a Virtual Machine 387
Installing an Operating System 391

Chapter 3: Working with VMware **395**

Looking at vSphere...395
Getting Started with VMware Player..396
Creating a Virtual Machine...398
Installing VMware Tools...402

Chapter 4: Virtualizing Your Desktops **405**

Introducing Desktop Virtualization...405
Considering Two Approaches to Desktop Virtualization....................407
Looking at VMware's Horizon View 408
Looking at Citrix XenApp...409

Book V: Remote Networking *413*

Chapter 1: Managing Mobile Devices **415**

The Many Types of Mobile Devices 416
Considering Security for Mobile Devices 417
Managing iOS Devices..418
Understanding the iPhone..418
Understanding the iPad 419
Integrating iOS devices with Exchange 419
Managing Android Devices..425
Looking at the Android OS..426
Perusing Android's core applications..427
Integrating Android with Exchange..427

Chapter 2: Working with VPN for Remote Access **429**

Understanding VPN...429
Looking at VPN Security 431
Understanding VPN Servers and Clients 432

Chapter 3: Using Remote Desktop Access **435**

Enabling Remote Desktop Connection 435
Connecting Remotely...436
Using Keyboard Shortcuts for Remote Desktop................................439
Configuring Remote Desktop Options 440
Setting the Display options...441
Setting the Local Resources options...442
Setting the Programs options...443
Setting the Experience options 444
Setting the Advanced options 444

Chapter 4: Using Remote Assistance 447

Enabling Remote Assistance 447
Inviting Someone to Help You via a Remote
    Assistance Session 449
Responding to a Remote Assistance Invitation 452

Book VI: Cloud Networking 455

Chapter 1: Cloudy with a Chance of Gigabytes. 457

Introducing Cloud Computing 457
Looking at the Benefits of Cloud Computing 458
Detailing the Drawbacks of Cloud Computing 460
Examining Three Basic Kinds of Cloud Services 461
    Applications 461
    Platforms 462
    Infrastructure 462
Public Clouds versus Private Clouds 462
Introducing Some of the Major Cloud Providers 463
    Amazon 463
    Google 464
    Microsoft 465
Getting into the Cloud 465

Chapter 2: Using Essential Cloud Services 467

Sharing Files in the Cloud 467
    Google Drive 468
    Microsoft OneDrive 469
    Dropbox 469
    Box 470
Hosting Meetings in the Cloud 470
    GoToMeeting 471
    WebEx 471
Creating a Company Social Network 472
    Yammer 473
    Socialcast 474

Chapter 3: Administering Office 365 477

Looking at the Features Provided by Office 365 477
Using the Admin Center 479
Creating a New User 480
Editing a User Account 482
Considering Other Important Administrative Tasks 483

Chapter 4: Using SharePoint Online 485

What Is SharePoint? 485
Connecting to SharePoint Online 486
Adding a Part 487
Adding and Removing Announcements 491
Adding Apps 492

Book VII: Windows Server 2016 Reference 497

Chapter 1: Installing and Configuring Windows Server 2016 499

Planning a Windows Server Installation 499
Checking system requirements 499
Reading the release notes 500
Deciding whether to upgrade or install 500
Considering your licensing options 501
Thinking about multiboot 501
Planning your partitions 501
Deciding your TCP/IP configuration 502
Choosing workgroups or domains 503
Before You Install 503
Backing up 504
Checking the event logs 504
Disconnecting UPS devices 504
Running Setup 504
Adding Server Roles and Features 509

Chapter 2: Managing Windows Server 2016 513

Using the Administrator Account 513
Using Remote Desktop Connection 514
Enabling remote access 514
Connecting remotely 515
Using Microsoft Management Console 517
Working with MMC 517
Taking an overview of the MMC consoles 518
Customizing MMC 520
Adding snap-ins 521
Adding taskpads 521

Chapter 3: Dealing with Active Directory 529

What Directories Do 529
Remembering the Good Ol' Days of NT Domains 530
PDCs and BDCs 530
Trusts 531
NetBIOS names 531

Active Directory to the Rescue..532
Understanding How Active Directory Is Structured 532
    Objects 532
    Domains 533
    Organizational units 534
    Trees..535
    Forests...535
Creating a New Domain..536
Creating an Organizational Unit 537

Chapter 4: Managing Windows User Accounts 541

Understanding Windows User Accounts......................................541
    Local accounts versus domain accounts.............................541
    User account properties 542
Creating a New User...542
Setting User Properties..545
    Changing the user's contact information 546
    Setting account options 546
    Specifying logon hours..548
    Restricting access to certain computers 549
    Setting the user's profile information 549
Resetting User Passwords 550
Disabling and Enabling User Accounts......................................551
Deleting a User..552
Working with Groups 552
    Group types 553
    Group scope 553
    Default groups 554
    Creating a group..556
    Adding a member to a group...557
Working with User Profiles..558
    Types of user profiles..559
    Roaming profiles 559
Creating a Logon Script 561

Chapter 5: Managing a File Server 563

Understanding Permissions 563
Understanding Shares..565
Managing Your File Server 566
    Using the New Share Wizard 566
    Sharing a folder without the wizard 572
    Granting permissions 573

Chapter 6: Using Group Policy...............................577

Understanding Group Policy...577
Enabling Group Policy Management on Windows Server 2016............578

Creating Group Policy Objects 579
Filtering Group Policy Objects.. 585

Chapter 7: Troubleshooting 589

Working with the Event Viewer 589
  Using the Event Viewer 589
  Setting event log policies 591
Monitoring Performance... 592
  Using the Reliability and Performance Monitor........................... 592
  Creating performance logs 595
Using the Computer Management Console.................................... 598
Working with Services 599

Chapter 8: Windows Commands 601

Using a Command Window 601
  Opening and closing a command window................................. 602
  Editing commands 602
  Using the Control menu 603
Special Command Tricks 603
  Wildcards.. 603
  Chaining commands 604
  Redirection and piping... 605
  Environment variables 606
  Batch files 607
The EventCreate Command 608
Net Commands... 609
  The Net Accounts command 610
  The Net Computer command 611
  The Net Config command 611
  The Net Continue command.. 612
  The Net File command 612
  The Net Group command 613
  The Net Help command 615
  The Net Helpmsg command 615
  The Net Localgroup command... 615
  The Net Name command 617
  The Net Pause command 617
  The Net Print command 618
  The Net Send command 619
  The Net Session command 620
  The Net Share command.. 620
  The Net Start command 621
  The Net Statistics command 622
  The Net Stop command... 623
  The Net Time command... 623

The Net Use command 624
The Net User command 625
The Net View command 627
The RunAs Command 627

Book VIII: Using Other Windows Servers 629

Chapter 1: Using Internet Information Services 631
Installing IIS 631
Understanding the Default Website 634
Creating Websites 636

Chapter 2: Managing Exchange Server 2016. 641
Creating a Mailbox 641
Managing Mailboxes 644
Enabling mailbox features 644
Creating a forwarder 645
Setting mailbox storage limits 647
Configuring Outlook for Exchange 651
Viewing Another Mailbox 654

Chapter 3: Using SQL Server 2014 659
What Is a Database? 659
What Is a Relational Database? 660
What Is SQL? 661
SQL dialects 661
SQL statements 662
Using the select statement 662
Using SQL Server 2014 Management Studio 664
Creating a New Database 665
Creating Tables 667
Editing Tables 670
Working with Queries 671
Working with Scripts 672

Book IX: Managing Linux Systems 675

Chapter 1: Installing a Linux Server 677
Planning a Linux Server Installation 677
Checking system requirements 677
Choosing a distribution 678
Going virtual 680
Deciding on your TCP/IP configuration 680
Installing Fedora 22 680

Chapter 2: Getting Used to Linux **689**

Linux: It Isn't Windows 689
X Window 689
Virtual consoles 690
Understanding the file system 690
On Again, Off Again 692
Logging on 692
Logging off 693
Shutting down 693
Using GNOME 693
Getting to a Command Shell 694
Enabling the SUDO Command 695
Managing User Accounts 697

Chapter 3: Basic Linux Network Configuration **701**

Using the Network Configuration Program 701
Restarting Your Network 704
Working with Network Configuration Files 704
The Network file 705
The ifcfg files 706
The Hosts file 707
The resolv.conf file 708
The nsswitch.conf file 708
The xinetd.conf file 710
Displaying Your Network Configuration
with the ifconfig Command 711

Chapter 4: Running DHCP and DNS **713**

Running a DHCP Server 713
Installing DHCP 714
Configuring DHCP 714
Starting DHCP 716
Running a DNS Server 716
Installing BIND 716
Looking at BIND configuration files 717
Restarting BIND 721

Chapter 5: Doing the Samba Dance **723**

Understanding Samba 723
Installing Samba 724
Starting and Stopping Samba 725
Using the Samba Server Configuration Tool 726
Configuring server settings 727
Configuring Samba users 729
Creating a share 730
Editing the smb.conf File 732
Using the Samba Client 734

Chapter 6: Running Apache **737**

Installing Apache 737
Starting and Stopping Apache 737
Confirming That Apache Is Running 738
Using the HTTP Configuration Tool 740
Allowing or Restricting Access to an Apache Server 741
Configuring Virtual Hosts 742
   Configuring the default host 743
   Creating a virtual host 745
Manually Editing Apache's Configuration Files 746
Creating Web Pages 747

Chapter 7: Running Sendmail **749**

Understanding Email 749
Installing Sendmail 750
Modifying sendmail.mc 751
   Enabling connections 752
   Enabling masquerading 752
   Setting up aliases 753
Using SpamAssassin 753
   Installing SpamAssassin 753
   Customizing SpamAssassin 754
   Blacklisting and whitelisting email addresses 755
Using the Mail Console Client 755
Using Evolution 757

Chapter 8: Running FTP **759**

Installing vsftpd 759
Starting the vsftpd Service 759
Configuring FTP 760

Chapter 9: Linux Commands **765**

Command Shell Basics 765
   Getting to a shell 766
   Editing commands 767
   Wildcards 767
   Redirection and piping 768
   Environment variables 768
   Shell scripts 769
   Running a command with root-level privileges 770
Directory- and File-Handling Commands 770
   The pwd command 771
   The cd command 771

The mkdir command 771

The rmdir command.. 772

The ls command.. 772

The cp command 773

The rm command.. 774

The mv command 775

The touch command 775

The cat command 776

Commands for Working with Packages and Services 777

The service command 777

The yum and dnf commands 779

Commands for Administering Users 779

The useradd command 779

The usermod command 781

The userdel command 781

The chage command 781

The passwd command 782

The newusers command 782

The groupadd command.. 783

The groupdel command 783

The gpasswd command 783

Commands for Managing Ownership and Permissions......................... 784

The chown command 784

The chgrp command 785

The chmod command 785

Networking Commands... 786

The hostname command 787

The ifconfig command... 787

The netstat command 788

The ping command 789

The route command 790

The traceroute command 791

Appendix A: Directory of Useful Websites.................... *793*

Certification.. 793

Hardware 793

Home and Small-Business Networking 794

Linux... 794

Magazines 795

Microsoft... 795

Network Standards Organizations 796

Reference 797
Search 797
TCP/IP and the Internet 798
Wireless Networking 799
Smartphones 799

Appendix B: Glossary 801

Index 829

Introduction

*W*elcome to the sixth edition of *Networking All-in-One For Dummies,* the one networking book that's designed to replace an entire shelf full of the dull and tedious networking books you'd otherwise have to buy. This book contains all the basic and not-so-basic information you need to know to get a network up and running and to stay on top of the network as it grows, develops problems, and encounters trouble.

If you're just getting started as a network administrator, this book is ideal. As a network administrator, you have to know about a lot of different topics: installing and configuring network hardware and software, planning a network, working with TCP/IP, securing your network, working with mobile devices, virtualizing your servers, backing up your data, managing cloud services, and many others.

You can, and probably eventually will, buy separate books on each of these topics. It won't take long before your bookshelf is bulging with 10,000 or more pages of detailed information about every imaginable nuance of networking. But before you're ready to tackle each of those topics in depth, you need to get a bird's-eye picture. This book is the ideal way to do that.

And if you already own 10,000 pages or more of network information, you may be overwhelmed by the amount of detail and wonder, "Do I really need to read 1,000 pages about Bind to set up a simple DNS server?" or "Do I really need a six-pound book to show me how to install Linux?" Truth is, most 1,000-page networking books have about 100 or so pages of really useful information — the kind you use every day — and about 900 pages of excruciating details that apply mostly to networks at places like NASA and the CIA.

The basic idea of this book is that I've tried to wring out the 100 or so most useful pages of information on nine different networking topics: network basics, building a network, network administration and security, troubleshooting and disaster planning, working with TCP/IP, home networking, wireless networking, Windows server operating systems, and Linux.

So whether you've just been put in charge of your first network or you're a seasoned pro, you've found the right book.

About This Book

Networking All-in-One For Dummies, 6th Edition, is intended to be a reference for all the great things (and maybe a few not-so-great things) that you may need to know when you're setting up and managing a network. You can, of course, buy a huge 1,000-page book on each of the networking topics covered in this book. But then, who would you get to carry them home from the bookstore for you? And where would you find the shelf space to store them? In this book, you get the information you need all conveniently packaged for you in between one set of covers.

This book doesn't pretend to be a comprehensive reference for every detail of these topics. Instead, this book shows you how to get up and running fast so that you have more time to do the things you really want to do. Designed using the easy-to-follow *For Dummies* format, this book helps you get the information you need without laboring to find it.

Networking All-in-One For Dummies, 6th Edition, is a big book made up of several smaller books — minibooks, if you will. Each of these minibooks covers the basics of one key element of network management, such as setting up network hardware, installing a network operating system, or troubleshooting network problems. Whenever one big thing is made up of several smaller things, confusion is always a possibility. That's why *Networking All-in-One For Dummies,* 6th Edition, is designed to have multiple access points (I hear an acronym coming on — MAP!) to help you find what you want. At the beginning of the book is a detailed table of contents that covers the entire book. Then each minibook begins with a minitable of contents that shows you at a glance what chapters are included in that minibook. Useful running heads appear at the top of each page to point out the topic discussed on that page. And handy thumb tabs run down the side of the pages to help you find each minibook quickly. Finally, a comprehensive index lets you find information anywhere in the entire book.

This isn't the kind of book you pick up and read from start to finish, as though it were a cheap novel. (If I ever see you reading it at the beach, I'll kick sand in your face.) This book is more like a reference — the kind of book you can pick up, turn to just about any page, and start reading. You don't have to memorize anything in this book. It's a need-to-know book: You pick it up when you need to know something. Need to know how to set up a DHCP server in Windows? Pick up the book. Need to know how to create a user account in Linux? Pick up the book. Otherwise, put it down, and get on with your life.

Within this book, you may note that some web addresses break across two lines of text. If you're reading this book in print and want to visit one of these web pages, simply key in the web address exactly as it's noted in the text, pretending as though the line break doesn't exist. If you're reading this as an e-book, you've got it easy — just click the web address to be taken directly to the web page.

Foolish Assumptions

As I was writing this book, I made a few assumptions about you, the reader:

✦ **You are responsible for or would like to be responsible for a computer network.** The network we speak of may be small – just a few computers, or large – consisting of dozens or even hundreds of computers. The network may already exist, or it may be a network you would like to build. But one way or another, I assume that managing the network is, at least in part, your responsibility.

✦ **You are an experienced computer user.** You don't need to be an expert, but this book assumes a modest level of experience with computers.

✦ **You are familiar with Windows.** This book touches on Mac and Linux network, but the primary focus is on creating and managing networks of Windows computers.

Icons Used in This Book

Like any *For Dummies* book, this book is chock-full of helpful icons that draw your attention to items of particular importance. You find the following icons throughout this book:

Hold it — technical stuff is just around the corner. Read on only if you have your pocket protector.

Pay special attention to this icon; it lets you know that some particularly useful tidbit is at hand.

Did I tell you about the memory course I took?

Danger, Will Robinson! This icon highlights information that may help you avert disaster.

Beyond the Book

In addition to the material in the print or e-book you're reading right now, this product also comes with some access-anywhere goodies on the web:

✦ **Cheat Sheet:** You can find the Cheat Sheet for this book at www.dummies. com/cheatsheet/networkingaio. There you'll find tables where you can record key network and Internet connection information, the RJ-45 pin connections, private IP address ranges, and useful websites for networking information.

✦ **Web Extras:** You can find the Web Extras for this book at www.dummies. com/extras/networkingaio. Here you'll find free articles on everything from common network bottlenecks to enabling VPN on an iPhone and more!

Where to Go from Here

Yes, you can get there from here. With this book in hand, you're ready to plow right through the rugged networking terrain. Browse the table of contents, and decide where you want to start. Be bold! Be courageous! Be adventurous! And above all, have fun!

Book I
Planning a Network

Contents at a Glance

Chapter 1: Understanding Networks 7

Chapter 2: Planning a Network 23

Chapter 3: Installing Network Hardware. 41

Chapter 4: Setting Up a Server. 53

Chapter 5: Configuring Windows Clients. 63

Chapter 6: Mac Networking 73

Chapter 7: Configuring Other Network Features 81

Chapter 8: Setting Up a Wireless Network 89

Chapter 1: Understanding Networks

In This Chapter

✔ Introducing computer networks

✔ Finding out all about clients, servers, and peers

✔ Understanding the various types of networks

✔ Looking at the requirements for network servers

✔ Examining server operating systems

The first computer network was invented when ancient mathematicians connected their abacuses (or is it *abaci?*) with kite string so they could instantly share their abacus answers with each other. Over the years, computer networks have become more and more sophisticated. Now, instead of string, networks use electrical cables, fiber optic cables, or wireless radio signals to connect computers to each other. The purpose, however, has remained the same: sharing information and getting work done faster.

This chapter describes the basics of what computer networking is and how it works.

Defining a Network

A *network* is simply two or more computers, connected, so that they can exchange information (such as email messages or documents) or share resources (say, disk storage or printers). In most cases, this connection is made via electrical cables that carry the information in the form of electrical signals. Other types of connections are used, too. For example, computers can communicate via fiber optic cables at extremely high speeds by using impulses of light. And in a wireless network, computers communicate by using radio signals. Look, Ma! No hands!

In addition to the hardware that supports a network, you also need special software to enable communications. In the early days of networking, you had to add this software to each computer on the network. Nowadays, network support is built in to all major operating systems, including all current versions of Windows, Macintosh operating systems, and Linux.

Network building blocks

All networks, large or small, require specialized network hardware to make them work. For a small network, this hardware may consist of nothing more than computers equipped with network ports, a cable for each computer, and a network switch that all the computers plug in to via the cable. Larger networks probably have additional components, such as routers or repeaters.

Small or large, though, all networks are built from the following basic building blocks:

+ **Client computers:** These computers are what end users use to access the resources of the network. Client computers are typically computers located on users' desks. They usually run a desktop version of Windows. In addition, the client computers usually run some type of application software, such as Microsoft Office. Client computers are sometimes referred to as *workstations.*

+ **Server computers:** These computers provide shared resources, such as disk storage and printers, as well as network services, such as email and Internet access. Server computers typically run a specialized network operating system, such as Windows Server, NetWare, or Linux, along with special software to provide network services. For example, a server may run Microsoft Exchange to provide email services for the network, or it may run Apache Web Server so that the computer can serve web pages.

+ **Network interface:** This interface — sometimes called a *network port —* is installed on a computer to enable the computer to communicate over a network. Almost all network interfaces implement a networking standard called *Ethernet.*

A network interface is sometimes called a NIC, which is techie for *network interface card.* In the early days of networking, you actually had to install a separate circuit card on the computer to provide a network interface. Nowadays, nearly all computers come with network interfaces built in as an integral part of the computer's motherboard. Although separate network cards are rarely required these days, the term NIC is still frequently used to refer to the network interface.

You well might still have to install separate network interface cards to provide more than one network interface on a single computer, or to replace a built-in network interface that has malfunctioned without having to replace the entire motherboard.

✦ **Cable:** Computers in a network are usually physically connected to each other using cable. Although several types of cable have been popular over the years, most networks today use a twisted-pair cable, which is also known by its official designation, 10BaseT. Twisted-pair cable is also sometimes referred to as Cat-5 or Cat-6 cable. These terms refer to the standards that determine the maximum speed with which the cable can carry data: Cat-6 is rated for more speed than Cat-5.

Twisted-pair cable can also be referred to simply as "copper" to distinguish it from fiber optic cable, which is used for the highest-speed network connections. Fiber optic cable uses strands of glass to transmit light signals at very high speeds.

In many cases, connecting cables are run through the walls and converge on a central room (a wiring closet). For smaller networks, though, the cables are often just strung along the floor, hidden behind desks and other furniture whenever possible.

✦ **Switches:** You don't typically use a network cable to connect computers directly to each other. Instead, each computer is connected by cable to a central switch, which connects to the rest of the network.

For small networks, switches are simple table-top devices that contain a small number of ports, typically 8 or 16. (Do the math: You use an 8-port switch to connect up to eight computers.)

For larger networks, switches can be mounted on equipment racks and feature 24 or perhaps 48 ports.

Switches can also be connected to each other to build larger networks. Note that connecting two switches to each other requires one port on each of the switches to make the connection. Thus, two 8-port switches connected to each other can accommodate as many as 14 computers. Although the switches have 16 ports between them, one of the ports on each switch is used to connect the switches to each other.

For more information about switches, see the "Network Topology" section later in this chapter.

✦ **Wireless networks:** In a wireless network, most cables and switches are moot. Radio transmitters and receivers take the place of cables.

The main advantage of wireless networking is its flexibility: no cables to run through walls or ceilings, and client computers can be located anywhere within range of the network broadcast.

There are trade-offs, though. For example, wireless networks are inherently less secure than a cabled network because anyone within range can intercept the radio signals. In addition, cabled networks are inherently faster and more stable than wireless networks.

✦ **Network software:** What really makes a network work is software, which has to be set up just right to get a network working. Server computers typically use a special operating systems called a *server operating system* that is designed to provide services such as file sharing or email connections for the clients on the network. In addition, client computers need to have their network settings configured properly to access the network.

One of the most important networking choices to make is which server operating system to use on the network's servers. Much of the task of building a new network and managing an existing one is configuring and maintaining the server operating systems.

For most business networks, the best choice for the server operating system is the server version of Windows, called Windows Server. The most popular alternative is Linux.

Seeing the benefits of networking

Truth time: Computer networks are a pain to set up. Having said that, the benefits of using a network make the pain worthwhile. And, you don't have to be a Ph.D. to understand the benefits of networking. In fact, you learned everything you need to know about the benefits of networking in kindergarten. In a nutshell, networks are all about sharing: information, resources, and applications.

✦ **Sharing information:** Networks allow users to share information in several different ways. The most common way is sharing individual files. For example, two or more people can work together on a single spreadsheet file or word processing document. In most networks, a large hard drive on a central server computer is set up as a common storage area where users can store files to be shared with other users.

Networks allow users to communicate with each other in other ways. For example, with messaging applications, network users exchange messages using an email app, such as Microsoft Outlook. Users can also hold online meetings over a network. In fact, with inexpensive video cameras and the right software, users can hold videoconferences over the network.

✦ **Sharing resources:** Network users can share certain computer resources, such as printers, disk storage, and Internet connections, resulting in significant cost savings. For example, instead of buying separate printers for each user in the group, go for a single high-speed printer with advanced features like collating, stapling, and duplex printing that an entire workgroup can share.

Disk storage can also be shared resources. In fact, providing users with access to a shared disk storage is the most common method of sharing files on a network. A computer whose main purpose in life is to host shared disk storage is called a *file server.*

In actual practice, entire disk drives aren't usually shared. Instead, individual folders on a networked disk drive are shared. This way, the network administrator can allow different network users to have access to different shared folders. For example, a company may set up shared folders for its sales department and accounting department. Then, sales personnel can access the sales department's folder, and accounting personnel can access the accounting department's folder. And, for security reasons, the sales department can be locked out of the accounting department's folder, and vice versa.

You can share other resources on a network, too (for example, an Internet connection). In the early days of the Internet, each user accessing the Internet typically had a personal modem connection. Nowadays, networks typically provide a shared, high-speed Internet connection that everyone on the network can access.

✦ **Sharing applications:** Another common reason to network is to allow users to work together on a single business application. For example, an accounting department may have special software that can be used from several computers at the same time. Or a sales-processing department may have an order-entry application that runs on several computers to handle a large volume of orders.

Comparing Clients and Servers

A network computer that manages the disk storage, printers, and other resources shared with other network computers is a *server.* This term will come up repeatedly throughout this book, so burn it into your brain. Write it on the back of your left hand.

Any network computer that's not a server is a *client.* You have to remember this term, too. Write it on the back of your right hand.

Only two kinds of computers are on a network: servers and clients. Look at your left hand and then look at your right hand. Do not wash your hands until you have these terms memorized.

The distinction between servers and clients in a network would be some-what fun to study in a sociology class. Think of the haves and the have-nots in society:

+ **Haves:** Usually, the most powerful and expensive computers in a network are the servers. This fact makes sense because every user on the network shares the server's resources.

+ **Have-nots:** The cheaper and less-powerful computers in a network are the clients. Clients are the computers used by individual users for every-day work. Because clients' resources don't have to be shared, they don't have to be as fancy.

Most networks have more clients than servers. For example, a network with ten clients can probably get by with one server.

Understanding Dedicated Servers and Peers

In some networks, a server computer is a server computer and nothing else, dedicated solely to the task of managing shared resources such as disk storage and printers. Such a server is a "dedicated" server because it can perform no other tasks than network services. A network that relies on dedi-cated servers is sometimes called a *client/server network*.

Other networks take an alternative approach, enabling any computer on the network to function as both a client and a server. Thus, any computer can share its printers and hard drives with other computers on the network. And while a computer is working as a server, you can still use that same com-puter for other functions such as word processing. This type of network is a *peer-to-peer network* — computers are thought of as peers, or equals.

While you're walking the dog tomorrow morning, ponder these points con-cerning the difference between dedicated server networks and peer-to-peer networks:

+ Peer-to-peer networking has been built in to all versions of Windows since Windows 95. Thus, you don't have to buy any additional software to turn your computer into a server. All you have to do is enable the Windows Server features.

+ The network server features built in to desktop versions of Windows (including Windows 10, 8.1, 8, 7, Vista, and XP) aren't very efficient because these versions of Windows weren't designed primarily to be net-work servers. If you're going to dedicate a computer to the task of being a full-time server, use a full-fledged server operating system, such as Windows Server 2016 or 2012.

Seeing Networks Big and Small

Networks come in all sizes and shapes. In fact, networks are commonly based on the geographical size they cover, as described in the following list:

✦ **Local area networks (LAN):** In this type of network, computers are relatively close together, such as within the same office or building.

Don't let the descriptor "local" fool you. A LAN doesn't imply that a network is small. A LAN can contain hundreds or even thousands of computers. What makes a network a LAN is that all its connected computers are located within close proximity. Usually a LAN is contained within a single building, but a LAN can extend to several buildings on a campus, provided that the buildings are close to each other (typically within 300 feet of each other although greater distances are possible with special equipment).

✦ **Wide area networks (WAN):** These networks span a large geographic territory, such as an entire city or a region or even a country. WANs are typically used to connect two or more LANs that are relatively far apart. For example, a WAN may connect an office in San Francisco with an office in New York.

The geographic distance, not the number of computers involved, makes a network a WAN. If an office in San Francisco and an office in New York each have only one computer, the WAN will have a grand sum of two computers — but will span more than 3,000 miles.

✦ **Metropolitan area networks (MAN):** This kid of network is smaller than a typical WAN but larger than a LAN. Typically, a MAN connects two or more LANs within the same city but that are far enough apart that the networks can't be connected via a simple cable or wireless connection.

Looking Closer at Servers

Server computers are the lifeblood of any network. Servers provide the shared resources that network users crave, such as file storage, databases, email, web services, and so on. Choosing the equipment you use for your network's servers is one of the key decisions you'll make when you set up a network. In the following sections, I describe some of the various ways you can equip your network's servers.

What's important in a server

Here are some general things to keep in mind when picking a server computer for your network:

✦ **Scalability:** The ability to increase the size and capacity of the server computer without unreasonable hassle. Purchasing a server computer that just meets your current needs is a major mistake because (rest assured) your needs will double within a year. If at all possible, equip your servers with far more disk space, RAM, and processor power than you currently need.

✦ **Reliability:** The old adage "you get what you pay for" applies especially well to server computers. Why spend $5,000 on a server computer when you can buy one with seemingly similar specifications at a discount electronics store for a mere $1,000? The main reason: reliability. When a client computer fails, only the person who uses that computer is affected. When a server fails, however, everyone on the network is affected. The less-expensive computer is probably made of inferior components that are more likely to fail, and does not have redundant components built in. (For example, many server computers have two power supplies, two CPUs, two or more network interfaces, and other redundant components.)

✦ **Availability:** This concept is closely related to reliability. When a server computer fails, how long does it take to correct the problem and get the server up and running again? Server computers are designed so their components can be easily diagnosed and replaced, which minimizes the downtime that results when a component fails. In some servers, components are *hot swappable* (certain components can be replaced without shutting down the server). Some servers are fault-tolerant so that they can continue to operate even if a major component fails.

✦ **Service and support:** Service and support are often overlooked factors when picking computers. If a component in a server computer fails, do you have someone on site qualified to repair the broken computer? If not, you should get an on-site maintenance contract for the computer.

Don't settle for a maintenance contract that requires you to take the computer in to a repair shop or, worse, mail it to a repair facility. You can't afford to be without your server that long. Get a maintenance contract that provides for on-site service and repair of your server, 24 hours a day, 7 days a week.

Components of a server computer

The hardware components that make up a typical server computer are similar to the components used in less-expensive client computers. However, server computers are usually built from higher-grade components than client computers for the reasons given in the preceding section. The following paragraphs describe the typical components of a server computer:

✦ **Motherboard:** A motherboard is the computer's main electronic circuit board to which all the other components of your computer are connected. More than any other component, the motherboard *is* the computer. All other components attach to the motherboard.

The major components on the motherboard include the processor (CPU); supporting circuitry (the chipset); memory (RAM); expansion slots; a standard IDE hard drive controller; input/output (I/O) ports for devices such as keyboards, mice, and printers; a graphics adapter; and one or more network interfaces.

✦ **Processor:** The CPU is the brain of the computer. Although the processor isn't the only component that affects overall system performance, it's the one that most people think of first when deciding what type of server to purchase. At the time of this writing, Intel had two processor models specifically designed for use in server computers:

- *Itanium 9300:* 4 or 8 cores, 1.73 to 2.53 GHz

- *Xeon:* 4 to 18 cores, 1.9 to 3.2 GHz

Each motherboard is designed to support a particular type of processor. CPUs come in two basic mounting styles: slot or socket. However, you can choose from several types of slots and sockets, so you have to make sure that the motherboard supports the specific slot or socket style used by the CPU. Some server motherboards have two or more slots or sockets to hold two or more CPUs.

Clock speed refers to how fast the basic clock that drives the processor's operation ticks. In theory, the faster the clock speed, the faster the processor. However, clock speed alone is reliable only for comparing processors within the same family. In fact, Intel Itanium processors are faster than Xeon processors at the same clock speed. (Itanium processor models contain more advanced circuitry than the older model, so they can accomplish more work with each tick of the clock.)

The number of processor cores also has a dramatic effect on performance. Each processor core acts as if it's a separate processor. Most server computers use one or two processors with multiple cores.

✦ **Memory:** Don't scrimp on memory. People rarely complain about servers having too much memory. Many different types of memory are available, so you have to pick the right type of memory to match the memory supported by your motherboard. The total memory capacity of the server depends on the motherboard. It isn't unusual to see servers configured with anywhere from 32GB to 512GB of RAM.

✦ **Hard drives:** Most desktop computers use inexpensive consumer-grade SATA hard drives, which are adequate for individual users. Because of their low cost, SATA drives are sometimes also used in inexpensive servers. But because performance and reliability are important in servers, many servers rely on faster and more reliable SCSI or Serialld Attached SCSI (SAS) disk drives instead.

✦ **Network interfaces:** The network connection is one of the most important parts of any server. Ideally, your server should have at least two network interfaces. Additional network interfaces not only improve the performance of your server, but also make it more reliable: If one of the network interfaces should fail, the others can pick up the ball.

✦ **Video:** Fancy graphics aren't that important for a server computer. You don't need to equip your server with a fancy video card; the video interface that's built in to the motherboard will suffice. (This is one of the few areas where it's acceptable to cut costs on a server.)

✦ **Power supply:** Because a server usually has more devices than a typical desktop computer, it requires a larger power supply (typically 600 watts). If the server houses a large number of hard drives, it may require an even larger power supply.

Because the power supply is one of the most likely components to fail, many server computers have two built-in power supplies for redundancy. That way, if one of the power supplies should fail, the other can pick up the load and keep the server running.

Server form factors

Form factor refers to the size, shape, and packaging of a hardware device. Server computers typically come in one of three form factors:

✦ **Tower case:** Most servers are housed in a traditional tower case, similar to the tower cases used for desktop computers. A typical server tower case is 18" high, 20" deep, and 9" wide with room inside for a mother-board, five or more hard drives, and other components. Tower cases also come with built-in power supplies.

Some server cases include advanced features specially designed for serv-ers, such as redundant power supplies (so both servers can continue operating if one of the power supplies fails), hot-swappable fans, and hot-swappable disk drive bays. (*Hot-swappable* components can be replaced without powering down the server.)

✦ **Rack mount:** If you need only a few servers, tower cases are fine. You can just place the servers next to each other on a table or in a cabinet that's specially designed to hold servers. If you need more than a few servers, though, space can quickly become an issue. For example, what if your departmental network requires a bank of ten file servers? You'd need a pretty long table.

Rack-mount servers are designed to save space when you need more than a few servers in a confined area. A rack-mount server is housed in a small chassis that's designed to fit into a standard 19" equipment rack. The rack allows you to vertically stack servers to save space.

✦ **Blade servers:** Blade servers are designed to save even more space than rack-mount servers. A *blade server* is a server on a single card that can be mounted alongside other blade servers in a blade chassis, which itself fits into a standard 19" equipment rack. A typical blade chassis holds six or more servers, depending on the manufacturer.

One of the key benefits of using blade servers is that you don't need a separate power supply for each server. Instead, the blade enclosure pro-vides power for all its blade servers. Some blade server systems provide rack-mounted power supplies that can serve several blade enclosures mounted in a single rack.

In addition, the blade enclosure provides keyboard, video, and mouse (KVM) switching so that you don't have to use a separate KVM switch. You can control any of the servers in a blade server network from a single keyboard, monitor, and mouse. (For more information, see the sidebar, "Saving space with a KVM switch.")

Another big benefit of using blade servers is that they drastically cut down the amount of cable clutter. With rack-mount servers, each server requires its own power, keyboard, video, mouse, and network cables. With blade servers, a single set of cables can service all the servers in a blade enclosure.

Saving space with a KVM switch

If you have more than two or three servers in one location, consider getting a KVM switch to save space by connecting several server computers to a single keyboard, monitor, and mouse. Then, you can control any of the servers from a single keyboard, monitor, and mouse by turning a dial or by pressing a button on the KVM switch.

Simple KVM switches are mechanical affairs that let you choose from 2–16 (or more)

computers. More elaborate KVM switches can control more computers, using a pop-up menu or a special keyboard combination to switch among computers. Some advanced KVMs can even control a mix of PCs and Macintosh computers from a single keyboard, monitor, and mouse.

To find more information about KVM switches, search online for *KVM.*

Operating systems for server computers

The server operating system is what enables your server computers to do their magic. Server operating systems provide essential functions such as providing basic security services, sharing disk storage and printers, and so on. Here are some of these core server operating system features:

✦ **Network services:** Obviously, a server operating system must provide networking capabilities in order for it to function on a network. If your client computers can't connect to your servers, your network will be useless. For this reason, it's a good idea to make sure your server computers are equipped with more than one network interface. That way, if one of the interfaces fails, the other can pick up the slack and keep your server connected to your network.

In addition to basic network connectivity, one of your servers will typically be responsible for providing some essential software services that are required to keep a network operating in an efficient manner. One of these is called Dynamic Host Configuration Protocol (DHCP); it's the service that recognizes computers and other devices that want to join the network, providing each with a unique address so that all the devices on the network can identify one another. For more information about this vital service, refer to Book III, Chapter 4.

A second basic service that is provided by one of the servers on your network is called Domain Name System (DNS). This service is what enables people to use network names instead of the actual addresses that are handed out by DHCP. It's also the service that enables people to browse the World Wide Web using addresses such as `www.dummies.com` rather than cryptic addresses. For more information about this important service, please refer to Book III, Chapter 5.

✦ **File-sharing services:** One of the most important functions of a server operating system is its ability to share resources with other network users. The most common shared resource is the server's file system. A network server must be able to share some or all of its disk space with other users so that those users can treat the server's disk space as an extension of their own computers' disk spaces.

The server operating system allows the system administrator to determine which portions of the server's file system to share. Although an entire hard drive can be shared, this isn't common. Instead, individual directories or folders are shared. The administrator can control which users are allowed to access each shared folder.

Because file sharing is the reason why many network servers exist, server operating systems have more sophisticated disk management features than are found in desktop operating systems. For example, most server operating systems can manage two or more hard drives as if they were a single drive. In addition, most can create *mirrors,* which automatically keep backup copies of drives on a second drive.

✦ **Multitasking:** Only one user at a time uses a desktop computer; however, multiple users simultaneously use server computers. As a result, a server operating system must provide support for multiple users who access the server remotely via the network.

At the heart of multiuser support is *multitasking,* which is the capability of an operating system to execute more than one program (a task or a process) at a time. Multitasking operating systems are like the guy who used to spin plates balanced on sticks on the old *Ed Sullivan Show* back in the 1950s. He'd run from plate to plate, trying to keep them all spinning so they wouldn't fall off the sticks — and just for grins, he was blindfolded or rode on a unicycle.

Although multitasking creates the appearance that two or more programs are executing on the computer at one time, in reality, a computer with a single processor can execute only one program at a time. The operating system switches the CPU from one program to another to create the appearance that several programs are executing simultaneously, but at any given moment, only one of the programs is actually executing. The others are patiently waiting for their turns. (However, if the computer has more than one CPU, the CPUs *can* execute programs simultaneously, which is multiprocessing.)

For multitasking to work reliably, the server operating system must completely isolate the executing programs from each other. Otherwise, one program may perform an operation that adversely affects another program. Multitasking operating systems do this by providing each task with its own unique address space that makes it almost impossible for one task to affect memory that belongs to another task.

+ **Directory services:** Directories are everywhere. When you need to make a phone call, you look up the number in a phone directory. When you need to find the address of a client, you look up the name in your address book. And when you need to find the Sam Goody store at a shopping mall, you look for the mall directory.

   Networks have directories, too. Network directories provide information about the resources that are available on the network, such as users, computers, printers, shared folders, and files. Directories are an essential part of any server operating system.

   The most popular directory service used today is called *Active Directory* (AD). AD is a database that organizes information about a network and allows users and computers to gain permission to access network resources. AD is simple enough to use for small networks with just a few dozen computers and users, but powerful enough to work with large networks containing tens of thousands of computers.

+ **Security services:** All server operating systems must provide some measure of security to protect the network from unauthorized access. Hacking seems to be the international pastime these days. With most computer networks connected to the Internet, anyone anywhere in the world can and probably will try to break into your network.

   The most basic type of security is handled through *user accounts,* which grant individual users the right to access the network resources and also govern what resources each user can access. User accounts are secured by passwords, so a good password policy is a cornerstone of any security system. Password policies can require that passwords have a minimum length and include a mix of letters, numbers, and symbols. In addition, passwords can be set to expire after a certain number of days, so users can be forced to frequently change their passwords.

   Most server operating systems also provide for *data encryption,* which scrambles data before it's sent over the network or saved on disk, and *digital certificates,* which are used to ensure that users are who they say they are and files are what they claim to be.

The overwhelming majority of business networks rely on server versions of Windows, known as Windows Server. Microsoft periodically releases updated versions of Windows Server, so Windows Server is frequently improved, and older versions are occasionally rendered obsolete. Currently, the most commonly used versions are Windows Server 2008, Windows Server 2012, Windows Server 2012 Release 2, and the latest-and-greatest version, known as Windows Server 2016.

Most of this book assumes that you'll be using Windows Server version 2012, 2012 Release 2, or 2016 for your servers. However, Windows Server is not the only server operating system that is available. The most popular alternative is Linux, a free server operating system that is often used for Internet-based applications such as web servers. For more information about Linux, refer to Book IX.

Chapter 2: Planning a Network

In This Chapter

✔ **Making a network plan**

✔ **Taking stock of your computer stock**

✔ **Making sure that you know why you need a network**

✔ **Making the basic network decisions that you can't avoid**

✔ **Looking at additional topics your plan should address**

*O*kay, so you're convinced that you need to network your computers. What now? Do you stop by Computers-R-Us on the way to work, install the network before drinking your morning coffee, and expect the network to be fully operational by noon?

I don't think so.

Networking your computers is just like any other worthwhile endeavor: Doing it right requires a bit of planning. This chapter helps you to think through your network before you start spending money. It shows you how to come up with a networking plan that's every bit as good as the plan that a network consultant would charge thousands of dollars for. See? This book is already saving you money!

Making a Network Plan

Before you begin any networking project, whether a new network installation or an upgrade of an existing network, make a detailed plan *first*. If you make technical decisions too quickly, before studying all the issues that affect the project, you'll regret it. You'll discover too late that a key application won't run over the network, the network has unacceptably slow performance, or key components of the network don't work together.

Here are some general thoughts to keep in mind while you create your network plan:

✦ **Don't rush the plan.** The most costly networking mistakes are the ones that you make before you install the network. Think things through and consider alternatives.

✦ **Write down the network plan.** The plan doesn't have to be a fancy, 500-page document. If you want to make it look good, pick up a ½-inch three-ring binder, which is big enough to hold your network plan with plenty of room to spare.

✦ **Ask someone else to read your network plan before you buy anything.** Preferably, ask someone who knows more about computers than you do.

✦ **Keep the plan up to date.** If you add to the network, dig up the plan, dust it off, and update it.

 "The best laid schemes of mice and men gang aft agley, and leave us naught but grief and pain for promised joy." Robert Burns lived a few hundred years before computer networks, but his famous words ring true. A network plan isn't chiseled in stone. If you discover that something doesn't work the way you thought it would, that's okay. Just change your plan.

Being Purposeful

One of the first steps in planning your network is making sure that you understand why you want the network in the first place. Here are some of the more common reasons for needing a network, all of them quite valid:

✦ *My co-worker and I exchange files using flash drives just about every day.* With a network, trading files is easier.

✦ *I don't want to buy everyone a color laser printer when I know the one we have now just sits there taking up space most of the day.* So wouldn't buying a network be better than buying a color laser printer for every computer?

✦ *I want everyone to be able to access the Internet.* Many networks, especially smaller ones, exist solely for sharing an Internet connection.

✦ *Business is so good that one person typing in orders eight hours each day can't keep up.* With a network, more than one person can enter orders, which expedites orders and possibly saves on overtime expenses.

✦ *My brother-in-law just put in a network at his office.* No one wants to be behind the times.

✦ *I already have a network, but it's so old that it may as well be made of kite string and tin cans.* An improved network speeds up access to shared files, provides better security, is easier to manage, and is more reliable.

After you identify all the reasons why you think you need a network, write them down. Don't worry about winning the Pulitzer Prize for your stunning prose. Just make sure that you write down what you expect a network to do for you. If you were making a 500-page networking proposal, you'd place the description of why a network is needed in a tabbed section labeled Justification. In your ½-inch network binder, file the description under Purpose.

As you consider the reasons why you need a network, you may conclude that you don't need a network after all. That's okay. You can always use the binder for your stamp collection.

Taking Stock

One of the initial challenges of planning a network is figuring out how to work with the computers that you already have. In other words, how do you get from here to there? Before you can plan how to get "there," you have to know where "here" is. In other words, you have to take a thorough inventory of your current computers.

What you need to know

You need to know the following information about each of your computers:

✦ **The processor type and, if possible, its clock speed:** It would be nice if each of your computers had a shiny new i7 6-Core processor. In most cases, though, you find a mixture of computers: some new, some old, some borrowed, some blue. You may even find a few archaic Pentium computers.

You can't usually tell what kind of processor a computer has just by looking at the computer's case. But you can easily find out by right-clicking Computer on the Start menu and choosing Properties.

✦ **The size of the hard drive and the arrangement of its partitions:** To find the size of your computer's hard drive, open the Computer window, right-click the drive icon, and choose the Properties command from the shortcut menu that appears. Figure 2-1 shows the Properties dialog box for a 922GB hard drive that has about 867GB of free space.

Figure 2-1:
The
Properties
dialog box
for a disk
drive.

If your computer has more than one hard drive, Windows lists an icon for each drive in the Computer window. Jot down the size and amount of free space available on each drive.

✦ **The amount of memory:** To find this information in Windows, right-click Computer from the Start menu and choose the Properties command. The amount of memory on your computer is shown in the dialog box that appears. For example, Figure 2-2 shows the System Properties dialog box for a computer with 8GB of RAM.

✦ **The operating system version:** This you can also deduce from the System Properties dialog box. For example, the Properties page shown in Figure 2-2 indicates that the computer is running Windows 7 Ultimate.

✦ **What kind of printer, if any, is attached to the computer:** Usually, you can tell just by looking at the printer. You can also tell by double-clicking the Printers icon in Control Panel.

✦ **Any other devices connected to the computer:** A DVD or Blu-ray drive? Scanner? External disk? Webcam? Battle droid? Hot tub?

✦ **What software is used on the computer:** Microsoft Office? AutoCAD? QuickBooks? Make a complete list and include version numbers.

Figure 2-2:
The
Properties
page for a
computer
with 8GB
of RAM.

Programs that gather information for you

Gathering information about your computers is a lot of work if you have
more than a few computers to network. Fortunately, several software programs are available that can automatically gather the information for you.
These programs inspect various aspects of a computer, such as the CPU
type and speed, amount of RAM, and the size of the computer's hard drives.
Then they show the information on the screen and give you the option of
saving the information to a hard drive file or printing it.

Windows comes with just such a program: Microsoft System Information.
Choose Start ➪ All Programs ➪ Accessories ➪ System Tools ➪ System
Information.

When you fire up Microsoft System Information, you see a window similar to
the one shown in Figure 2-3. Initially, Microsoft System Information displays
basic information about your computer, such as your version of Microsoft
Windows, the processor type, the amount of memory on the computer,
and so on. You can obtain more detailed information by clicking Hardware
Resources, Components, or other categories in the left side of the window.

Figure 2-3:
Let the
System
Information
program
gather the
data you
need.

To Dedicate or Not to Dedicate: That Is the Question

One of the most basic questions that a network plan must answer is whether the network will have one or more dedicated servers, or rely completely on peer-to-peer networking.

A *peer-to-peer* network doesn't have a dedicated server computer. Read more about this type of network, as well as dedicated servers, in Book I, Chapter 1.

If the only reason for purchasing your network is to share a printer and an Internet connection and to exchange an occasional file, you probably don't need a dedicated server computer. In that case, you can create a peer-to-peer network by using the computers that you already have. However, all but the smallest networks will benefit from having at least one separate, dedicated server computer.

Considering Server Roles

Assuming that your network will require one or more dedicated servers, you should next consider what types of servers the network will need. In some cases, a single server computer can fill one or more of these roles. Whenever possible, limit each server computer to a single server function.

File servers

File servers provide centralized disk storage conveniently shared by client computers on the network. The most common file server task is storing shared files and programs. For example, members of a small workgroup can use a file server to store common Microsoft Office documents.

You set file servers to ensure that two users don't try to update the same file at the same time. The file servers do this by *locking* a file while a user updates the file so that other users can't access the file until the first user finishes. For document files (for example, word processing or spreadsheet files), the whole file is locked. For database files, the lock can be applied just to the portion of the file that contains the record or records being updated.

Print servers

Sharing printers is another main reason why many small networks exist. Although it isn't necessary, a server computer can be dedicated for use as a *print server,* whose sole purpose is to collect information being sent to a shared printer by client computers and print it in an orderly fashion.

✦ A single computer may double as both a file server and a print server, but performance is better if you use separate print and file server computers.

✦ With inexpensive inkjet printers running about $100, just giving each user a dedicated printer is tempting. However, you get what you pay for. Instead of buying $100 printers for 15 users, you may be better off buying one $1,500 laser printer and sharing it. The $1,500 laser printer will be much faster, will probably produce better-looking output, and will be less expensive to operate.

Web servers

A *web server* runs software that enables the computer to host a World Wide Web (via the Internet) website or a website on a private intranet. The two most popular web server programs are Microsoft IIS (Internet Information Services), which runs on Windows systems and Apache, an open source web server that runs on Linux systems.

Mail servers

A *mail server* handles the network's email needs. It is configured with email server software, such as Microsoft Exchange Server. Exchange Server is designed to work with Microsoft Outlook, the email client software that comes with Microsoft Office.

Mail servers actually do much more than just send and receive electronic mail. For example, here are some of the features that Exchange Server offers beyond simple email:

✦ Calendaring

✦ Collaboration

✦ Audio and video conferencing

✦ Chat rooms and instant messaging (IM) services

✦ Custom forms

Note that email applications can easily be hosted in the cloud — that is, on the Internet, eliminating the need for you to configure and maintain your own email server. Microsoft provides cloud hosting for Exchange as part of Office 365, and many smaller organizations use Google's Gmail service to host their email.

Database servers

A *database server* is a server computer that runs database software, such as Microsoft SQL Server 2014. Database servers are usually used along with customized business applications, such as accounting or marketing systems.

Application servers

An *application server* is a server computer that runs a specific application. For example, you might use an accounting application that requires its own server. In that case, you'll need to dedicate a server to the accounting application.

License servers

Some organizations use software that requires licenses that are distributed from a centralized license server. For example, engineering firms often use computer-aided design (CAD) software such as AutoCAD that requires a license server. In that case, you'll need to set up a server to handle the licensing function.

Choosing a Server Operating System

If you determine that your network will require one or more dedicated servers, the next step is to determine what server operating system those servers should use. If possible, all the servers should use the same server operating system so that you don't find yourself supporting different operating systems.

Although you can choose from many server operating systems, from a practical point of view, your choices are limited to the following:

✦ Windows Server 2012 R2 or 2016

✦ Linux or another version of Unix

✦ OS X, the server version of Apple's Mac operating system

For more information, read Chapter 1 of this minibook.

Considering Cable

Over the years, several different types of cables have been used for networking. But today, almost all cabled networks are built using simple copper-based Unshielded Twisted-Pair (UTP) cable. Figure 2-4 shows a twisted-pair cable.

Figure 2-4:
Twisted-
pair cable.

When you use UTP cable to construct an Ethernet network, you connect the computers in a starlike arrangement, in which each computer is connected to a central point. At the center of the star is a device called a *switch,* which you learn about in the next section. Depending on the model, a single switch can connect from 4 to 48 or more devices.

Here are a few additional details that you should know about twisted-pair cabling:

✦ UTP cable consists of four pairs of thin wire twisted around each other; several such pairs are gathered up inside an outer insulating jacket. Ethernet uses two pairs of wires, or four wires altogether.

✦ UTP cable comes in various grades known as *categories*. Don't use any-thing less than Cat5e cable for your network. Although lower category cables may be less expensive, they won't be able to support faster networks.

Although higher-category cables are more expensive than lower-category cables, the real cost of installing Ethernet cabling is the labor required to actually pull the cables through the walls. As a result, I recommend that you always invest in Cat5e cable at the minimum.

✦ UTP cable connectors look like modular phone connectors but are a bit larger. UTP connectors are officially called RJ-45 connectors.

✦ UTP cable can be purchased in prefabricated lengths, but for most jobs you'll want to purchase the cable in bulk and have a professional installer attach the connectors. Or, you can attach the connectors yourself using a simple crimping tool you can purchase for about $50.

✦ The maximum allowable cable length between the switch and the computer is 100 meters (about 328 ft.).

Surmising Switches

As I mention in the previous section, computers and other devices are con-nected to a network in a starlike configuration, and the device at the center of the star is called a *switch*. Figure 2-5 shows a switch with four computers connected to it.

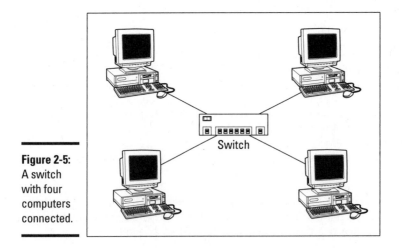

Figure 2-5:
A switch
with four
computers
connected.

Switch

A switch contains a number of *ports,* each of which is a receptacle that can accommodate an RJ-45 jack connected to a UTP cable. In Figure 2-5, there are four UTP cables. One end of each of these cables is plugged into a port on the switch, and the other end is plugged into the computer's network adapter.

Although it may not be obvious from the figure, the switch does not have to be in the same room as the computers. In fact, ideally the switch will be in a separate room from the computers. The cables run through the ceilings and the walls from the location of the switch to the location of the computers, within the 100-meter limit of UTP cable. (The switches are generally located in the same room as the servers.)

Here are some additional ins and outs for working with switches:

✦ Because you must run a cable from each computer to the switch, find a central location for the switch to which you can easily route the cables.

✦ The switch requires electrical power, so make sure that an electrical outlet is handy.

✦ Purchase a switch with at least twice as many connections as you need. Don't buy an eight-port switch if you want to network eight computers because when (not *if*) you add the ninth computer, you'll have to buy another switch.

✦ You can connect — or *daisy-chain* — switches to one another, as shown in Figure 2-6. You connect one end of a cable to a port on one switch and the other end to a port on the other switch.

Although you can daisy-chain as many as three switches together, in actual practice you should avoid daisy-chaining whenever possible. Daisy-chaining is inherently inefficient, because it sends traffic for all the devices connected to the daisy-chained switch over a single cable. In addition, daisy-chaining slows the network down because the second switch must receive and then retransmit each packet of information that is sent to it.

✦ If you need more ports than a single switch can provide, you can use *stackable switches.* Stackable switches have high-speed direct connections that enable two or more switches to be connected in such a way that they behave as if they were a single switch. (This type of connection is sometimes called a *back-plane connection.*) If a single switch will suffice for you now, but there is a reasonable chance that you might outgrow it and need a second switch, I suggest you invest in a stackable switch so that you can expand your network later without daisy-chaining.

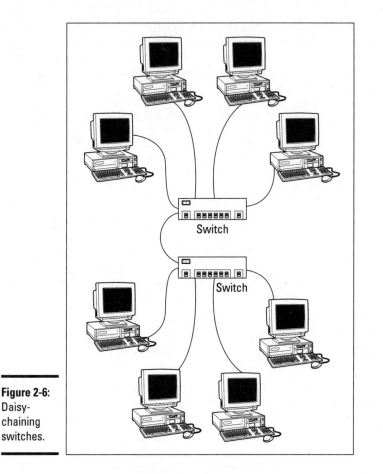

Figure 2-6:
Daisy-
chaining
switches.

✦ A common switch arrangement for larger networks is to use a high-performance switch in the same room with the servers, and then daisy-chain it to smaller switches that are closer to clients. For example, in a multistory building, there might be a central switch in the server room and a workgroup switch on each floor. All the devices on a given floor connect directly to the workgroup switch on that floor, which in turn connects to the central switch in the server room.

✦ Professional-quality network switches have network-management features that allow you to log in to the switch, usually via a web interface, to monitor and configure the switch. Such switches are called *managed switches.* Consumer-grade switches, also called *unmanaged switches,* are less expensive primarily because they do not support this feature. If you have more than a few dozen users, you'll want to invest in managed switches.

Planning the Network Topology

Topology refers to the way the devices in your network are connected to each other via network switches. You'll need to determine what kind of switches to use, how many, where to run the cable, where to locate the switches, and so on.

Here are just a few of the questions to consider:

✦ Where will the servers be located? Will there be just a single switch in the server room, or will there be a central switch with workgroup switches located closer to the computers?

✦ Where will you place workgroup switches? On a desktop somewhere within the group or in a small wiring closet?

✦ How many client computers will you place on each workgroup switch, and how many switches will you need?

✦ If you need more than one switch, how will you connect the switches to each other?

✦ If you need wireless networking, what kind of wireless networking devices will you need, where will you put them, and how will you connect them to the network?

Here are a few additional tidbits to consider when planning your network infrastructure:

✦ Unless you're installing a very small network (say, 15 or fewer devices), don't use inexpensive consumer-grade switches purchased from retail electronic stores. Instead, invest in good, professional-quality managed switches. These switches will give you better performance, better reliability, and the ability to monitor and manage your network in ways that simply are not possible with consumer-grade switches.

✦ Avoid using too many switches. Try to have no more than two switches between any of your client computers and your servers. If at all possible, use just a single switch for everything. If that means purchasing a 48-port switch for a network with 30 devices, do it. The results will be more reliable than if you use a pair of 24-port switches, or (yikes!) four 8-port switches all strung together.

✦ If you're installing new network cable, don't scrimp on the cable itself. Because installing network cable is a labor-intensive task, the cost of the cable itself is a small part of the total cable installation cost. Spend a little extra to install higher-grade cable now so you won't have to replace the cable in a few years when it's time to upgrade the network

Be sure to check out Chapter 3 of this minibook for more information about network cabling. Make sure you understand the information in that chapter before you plan your infrastructure.

Planning the TCP/IP Implementation

In addition to planning for the physical parts of your network infrastructure (cables, switches, ports, and so on), you'll also need to plan the details of how you'll implement TCP/IP for your network. TCP/IP is the basic networking protocol that your network uses to keep track of the individual computers and other devices on the network. Each computer or device will need an IP address (for example, 10.0.101.65). You'll need to devise a plan for how these addresses will be allocated.

You learn everything you need to know about TCP/IP in Book III, Chapter 3, so make sure you understand the information in that chapter before you complete this part of your plan. For now, here are some of the main points your plan should address:

✦ **The subnet structure of your network:** Will everything be on a single subnet, or will you use two or more subnets to separate different types of devices?

✦ **The DHCP structure:** What server will be responsible for DHCP? What will be the DHCP scope — that is, the range of addresses that are given out by DHCP? How will the size of your scope accommodate all the devices that will require DHCP on the subnet, with plenty of room for growth? (Be especially careful if you connect a wireless access point to the same subnet that your cabled network is on. You'll be surprised how quickly you can run out of IP addresses when every one of your users brings an iPhone and an iPad.)

✦ **The static IP addresses of devices whose IP should never change:** These devices may include servers, printers, firewalls, and other managed devices.

Drawing Diagrams

One of the most helpful techniques for creating a network plan is to draw a picture of it. The diagram can be a detailed floor plan, showing the actual location of each network component: a *physical map.* If you prefer, the diagram can be a *logical map,* which is more abstract and Picasso-like. Any time you change the network layout, update the diagram. Also include a detailed description of the change, the date that the change was made, and the reason for the change.

You can diagram very small networks on the back of a napkin, but if the network has more than a few computers, you'll want to use a drawing program to help you create the diagram. One of the best programs for this purpose is Microsoft Visio, shown in Figure 2-7.

Figure 2-7:
Using Visio
to draw a
network
diagram.

Here's a rundown of some of the features that make Visio so useful:

✦ Smart shapes and connectors maintain the connections drawn between network components, even if you rearrange the layout of the components on the page.

✦ Stencils provide dozens of useful shapes for common network components — not just for client and server computers, but for routers, hubs, switches, and just about anything else you can imagine. If you're really picky about the diagrams, you can even purchase stencil sets that have accurate drawings of specific devices, such as Cisco routers or IBM mainframe computers.

✦ You can add information to each computer or device in the diagram, such as the serial number or physical location. Then, you can quickly print an inventory that lists this information for each device in the diagram.

✦ You can easily create large diagrams that span multiple pages.

More Questions Your Network Plan Should Address

In addition to the basic questions of why you need a network, what kind of servers you need to provide, and what kind of infrastructure your network will require, your network plan should address the following questions:

✦ **Does it allow for growth?** What growth areas do you anticipate over the next few years? Does this network plan provide for such growth? For example, if you currently have 20 devices on the network, a 24-port switch may be adequate for today. But you should consider a 48-port switch instead. It will cost more now, but will simplify your expansion down the road.

   Similarly, if you anticipate that each office will have just one employee, consider what you'll have to do if you run out of offices and end up putting two employees in each office. If you run a single cable to each office now, you'll have to pay to have a second cable run later. Better to spend a little more for extra cable and have the installer pull two cables to each office. (Better yet, have the installer pull three cables to each office: When you move a second employee into the office, you may also put a printer in there.)

✦ **How will you secure it?** What kind of safety precautions will you take to keep unwanted visitors off of your network? You'll need a strong, well-configured firewall to keep intruders from breaking in to your network via your Internet connection. If you're installing wireless access points, you'll have to take precautions to secure the wireless networks. And you'll need strong password policies to prevent hackers who do manage to get on to your network from getting at any valuable data.

   For more information about network security, refer to Book II, Chapters 3 and 4.

✦ **How will you back it up?** You'll need to include a solid plan to back up your servers and the data that resides on them. That plan will probably require additional hardware, such as separate disk storage to hold the first level of backup data, as well as a means to get the backed up files off-site so they can survive a true disaster such as a fire or flood.

   You'll also need to be certain that you provide adequate network disk storage so that all users can put all their work on the network, where it can be backed up. In lieu of that, you'll need a plan that backs up not only your servers, but also the client computers.

For more information about backing up your network, refer to Book II, Chapter 8.

✦ **How will you recover from failures?** Make sure you have a plan in place that will protect you from the commonplace maladies of daily life such as occasional power failures, as well as from the unforeseen, such as vandalism, theft, or fire. Every device on your network, no matter how insignificant, should be protected by battery backup. When possible, you should have spares of critical components.

For more information about disaster recovery, see Book II, Chapter 9.

Chapter 3: Installing Network Hardware

In This Chapter

✔ **Installing network cable**

✔ **Attaching cable connectors**

✔ **Figuring out pinouts for twisted-pair cabling**

✔ **Installing switches**

After you plan your network, then comes the fun of actually putting everything together. In this chapter, I describe some of the important details for installing network hardware, including cables and switches, as well as professional touches like patch panels and cable management.

Working with Cable

Most Ethernet networks are built using twisted-pair cable (also known as UTP cable), which resembles phone cable but isn't the same. For more information about the general characteristics of twisted-pair cable, see Chapter 2 of this minibook.

In the following sections, you find out what you need to know to select and install twisted-pair cable.

Cable categories

Twisted-pair cable comes in various grades, or *Categories*.

Higher-Category cables are more expensive than lower-Category cables, but the real cost of installing Ethernet cabling is the labor required to actually pull the cables through the walls. You should never install anything less than Category 5 cable. And if at all possible, invest in Category 5e (the *e* stands for enhanced) or even Category 6 cable to allow for upgrades to your network.

Table 3-1 lists the various categories of twisted-pair cable.

Cat got your tongue?

Twisted-pair cable grades are categories specified by the ANSI/EIA standard 568. ANSI stands for American National Standards Institute; EIA stands for Electronic Industries Association. The higher the number, the faster the data transfer rate, so Cat5 is faster than Cat2. If you want to sound like you know what you're talking about, say "Cat 5e" instead of "Category 5e." Twisted pair is often referred to as UTP (unshielded twisted pair). Now you're hip.

Table 3-1	Twisted-Pair Cable Categories	
Category	*Maximum Data Rate*	*Intended Use*
1	1 Mbps	Voice only
2	4 Mbps	4 Mbps token ring
3	16 Mbps	10BaseT Ethernet
4	20 Mbps	16 Mbps token ring
5	100 Mbps (2 pair)	100BaseT Ethernet
	1,000 Mbps (4 pair)	Gigabit Ethernet
5e	1,000 Mbps (2 pair)	Gigabit Ethernet
6	1,000 Mbps (2 pair)	Gigabit Ethernet
6a	10,000 Mbps	10 gigabit (experimental)
7	10,000 Mbps	10 gigabit (experimental)

What's with the pairs?

Most twisted-pair cable has four pairs of wires, for a total of eight wires. Standard Ethernet actually uses only two of the pairs, so the other two pairs are unused. You may be tempted to save money by purchasing cable with just two pairs of wires, but that's a bad idea. If a network cable develops a problem, you can sometimes fix it by switching over to one of the extra pairs. If you try to carry a separate connection over the extra pairs, though, electrical interference will prevent the signals from getting through.

Don't give in to temptation to use the extra pairs for some other purpose, such as for a voice line. The electrical noise generated by voice signals in the extra wires can interfere with your network.

To shield or not to shield

Unshielded twisted-pair cable (UTP) is designed for normal office environments. When you use UTP cable, you must be careful not to route cable close to fluorescent light fixtures, air conditioners, or electric motors (such as automatic door motors or elevator motors). UTP is the least expensive type of cable.

In environments with a lot of electrical interference, such as factories, you may want to use shielded twisted-pair cable (STP). STP can cost up to three times more than regular UTP, so you won't want to use STP unless you have to. With a little care, UTP can withstand the amount of electrical interference found in a normal office environment.

Most STP cable is shielded by a layer of aluminum foil. For buildings with unusually high amounts of electrical interference, you can use more expensive, braided copper shielding for even more protection.

When to use plenum cable

The outer sheath of both shielded and unshielded twisted-pair cable comes in two varieties:

+ **PVC:** The most common and least expensive type.

+ **Plenum:** A special type of fire-retardant cable designed for use in the plenum space of a building (typically, in the hollows below a floor or above a ceiling).

   Plenum cable has a special Teflon coating that not only resists heat, but also gives off fewer toxic fumes if it does burn. Unfortunately, plenum cable costs more than twice as much as ordinary PVC cable.

Most local building codes require that you use plenum cable whenever the wiring is installed within the plenum space of the building.

Plenum space

Plenum space is a compartment in the building's air distribution system — typically, the space above a suspended ceiling or under a raised floor.

The area above a suspended ceiling is *not* a plenum space if both the delivery and return lines of the air conditioning and heating system are ducted. Plenum cable is required only if the air conditioning and heating system are not ducted. When in doubt, have the local inspector look at your facility before you install cable.

Sometimes solid, sometimes stranded

The actual copper wire that composes the cable comes in two varieties: solid and stranded. Your network will have some of each.

+ **Stranded cable:** Each conductor is made from a bunch of very small wires twisted together. Stranded cable is more flexible than solid cable, so it doesn't break as easily. However, stranded cable is more expensive than solid cable and isn't very good at transmitting signals over long distances. Stranded cable is best used for patch cables, such as the cable used to connect a computer to a wall jack or the cable used to connect patch panels to hubs and switches.

  Strictly speaking, the cable that connects your computer to the wall jack is a *station cable* — not a patch cable. Patch cables are used in the wiring closet, usually to connect patch panels to switches.

+ **Solid cable:** Each conductor is a single solid strand of wire. Solid cable is less expensive than stranded cable and carries signals farther, but it isn't very flexible. If you bend it too many times, it will break. Solid cable is usually used for permanent wiring within the walls and ceilings of a building.

Installation guidelines

The hardest part about installing network cable is the physical task of pulling the cable through ceilings, walls, and floors. This job is just tricky enough that I recommend that you don't attempt it yourself except for small offices. For large jobs, hire a professional cable installer. You may even want to hire a professional for small jobs if the ceiling and wall spaces are difficult to access.

Here are some general pointers to keep in mind if you decide to install cable yourself:

✦ You can purchase twisted-pair cable in prefabricated lengths, such as 50 ft., 75 ft., or 100 ft. You can also special-order prefabricated cables in any length you need. However, attaching connectors to bulk cable isn't that difficult. I recommend that you use prefabricated cables only for very small networks and only when you don't need to route the cable through walls or ceilings.

✦ Always use a bit more cable than you need, especially if you're running cable through walls. For example, when you run a cable up a wall, leave a few feet of slack in the ceiling above the wall. That way, you'll have plenty of cable if you need to make a repair later on.

✦ When running cable, avoid sources of interference, such as fluorescent lights, big motors, x-ray machines, and so on. The most common source of interference for cables that are run behind dropped ceiling panels are fluorescent lights; be sure to give light fixtures a wide berth as you run your cable. Three feet should do it.

✦ The maximum allowable cable length between a hub and the computer is 100 meters (about 328 ft.).

✦ If you must run cable across the floor where people walk, cover the cable so that no one trips over it. Inexpensive cable protectors are available at most hardware stores.

✦ When running cables through walls, label each cable at both ends. Most electrical supply stores carry pads of cable labels that are perfect for the job. These pads contain 50 sheets or so of precut labels with letters and numbers. They look much more professional than wrapping a loop of masking tape around the cable and writing on the tape with a marker.

If nothing else, use a permanent marker to write directly on the cable.

✦ When several cables come together, tie them with plastic cable ties or – better yet – strips of Velcro. Avoid using masking tape if you can; the tape doesn't last, but the sticky glue stuff does. It's a mess a year later. Cable ties are available at electrical supply stores.

✦ Cable ties have all sorts of useful purposes. Once on a backpacking trip, I used a pair of cable ties to attach an unsuspecting buddy's hat to a high tree limb. He wasn't impressed with my innovative use of the cable ties, but my other hiking companions were.

✦ When you run cable above suspended ceiling panels, use cable ties, hooks, or clamps to secure the cable to the actual ceiling or to the metal frame that supports the ceiling tiles. Don't just lay the cable on top of the tiles.

Getting the tools that you need

Of course, to do a job right, you must have the right tools.

Start with a basic set of computer tools, which you can get for about $15 from any computer store or large office-supply store. These kits include the right screwdrivers and socket wrenches to open up your computers and insert adapter cards. (If you don't have a computer toolkit, make sure that you have several flat-head and Phillips screwdrivers of various sizes.)

If all your computers are in the same room and you're going to run the cables along the floor and you're using prefabricated cables, the computer tool kit should contain everything that you need.

If you're using bulk cable and plan on attaching your own connectors, you need the following tools in addition to the tools that come with the basic computer toolkit:

✦ **Wire cutters:** You need decent wire cutters to cut UTP cable.

✦ **Crimp tool:** Use this tool to attach the connectors to the cable. Don't use a cheap $10 crimp tool. A good one will cost $100 but will save you many headaches in the long run. Remember this adage: When you crimp, you mustn't scrimp.

✦ **Wire stripper:** You need this only if the crimp tool doesn't include a wire stripper.

If you plan on running cables through walls, you need these additional tools:

✦ **A hammer**

✦ **A keyhole saw:** This is useful if you plan on cutting holes through walls to route your cable.

✦ **A flashlight**

✦ **A ladder**

✦ **Someone to hold the ladder**

✦ **Possibly a fish tape:** A *fish tape* is a coiled-up length of stiff metal tape. To use it, you feed the tape into one wall opening and fish it toward the other opening, where a partner is ready to grab it when the tape arrives. Next, your partner attaches the cable to the fish tape and yells something like, "Let 'er rip!" or "Bombs away!" Then you reel in the fish tape and the cable along with it. (You can find fish tape in the electrical section of most well-stocked hardware stores.)

If you plan on routing cable through a concrete subfloor, you need to rent a jackhammer and a backhoe and hire someone to hold a yellow flag while you work.

Pinouts for twisted-pair cables

Each pair of wires in a twisted-pair cable is one of four colors: orange, green, blue, or brown. The two wires that make up each pair are complementary: One is a solid color, and the other is white with a stripe of the corresponding color. For example, the orange pair has an orange wire and then a white wire with an orange stripe. Likewise, the blue pair has a blue wire and a white wire with a blue stripe.

When you attach a twisted-pair cable to a modular connector or jack, you must match up the right wires to the right pins. You can use several different standards to wire the connectors. To confuse matters, you can use one of the two popular standard ways of hooking up the wires. One is known as EIA/TIA 568A; the other is EIA/TIA 568B, also known as AT&T 258A. Table 3-2 shows both wiring schemes.

Table 3-2		Pin Connections for Twisted-Pair Cable	
Pin Number	*Function*	*EIA/TIA 568A*	*EIA/TIA 568B AT&T 258A*
Pin 1	Transmit +	White/green	White/orange
Pin 2	Transmit –	Green	Orange
Pin 3	Receive +	White/orange	White/green
Pin 4	Unused	Blue	Blue
Pin 5	Unused	White/blue	White/blue
Pin 6	Receive –	Orange	Green
Pin 7	Unused	White/brown	White/brown
Pin 8	Unused	Brown	Brown

It doesn't matter which of these wiring schemes you use, but pick one and stick with it. If you use one wiring standard on one end of a cable and the other standard on the other end, the cable won't work.

The only difference between the two wiring standards is which pair is used to transmit data and which pair is used to receive data. In the EIA/TIA 568A standard, the green pair is used to transmit and the orange pair is used to receive. In the EIA/TIA 568B and AT&T 258A standards, the orange pair is used to transmit and the green pair to receive.

Attaching RJ-45 connectors

RJ-45 connectors for twisted-pair cables aren't too difficult to attach if you have the right crimping tool. The trick is in both making sure that you attach each wire to the correct pin and pressing the tool hard enough to ensure a good connection.

Here's the procedure for attaching an RJ-45 connector:

1. **Cut the end of the cable to the desired length.**

   Make sure that you make a square cut — not a diagonal cut.

2. **Insert the cable into the stripper portion of the crimp tool so that the end of the cable is against the stop.**

   Squeeze the handles and slowly pull the cable out, keeping it square. This strips off the correct length of outer insulation without puncturing the insulation on the inner wires.

3. **Arrange the wires so that they lay flat and line up according to Table 3-2.**

   You'll have to play with the wires a little bit to get them to lay out in the right sequence.

4. **Slide the wires into the pinholes on the connector.**

   Double-check to make sure that all the wires slipped into the correct pinholes.

5. **Insert the plug and wire into the crimping portion of the tool and then squeeze the handles to crimp the plug.**

   Squeeze it tight!

6. **Remove the plug from the tool and double-check the connection.**

   You're done!

Here are a few other points to remember when dealing with RJ-45 connectors and twisted-pair cable:

✦ The pins on the RJ-45 connectors aren't numbered, but you can tell which is pin 1 by holding the connector so that the metal conductors are facing up, as shown in Figure 3-1. Pin 1 is on the left.

✦ Be extra careful to follow the rules of Cat5 cabling. That means, among other things, making sure that you use Cat5 components throughout. The cable and all the connectors must be up to Cat5 specs. When you attach the connectors, don't untwist more than one-half inch of cable. And don't try to stretch the cable runs beyond the 100m maximum. When in doubt, have cable for a 100 Mbps Ethernet system professionally installed.

Pin connections:
Pin 1 - White/Orange
Pin 2 - Orange
Pin 3 - White/Green
Pin 6 - Green

Figure 3-1:
Attaching
an RJ-45
connector
to twisted-
pair cable.

Wall jacks and patch panels

From the files of "Sure, You Could Do This, But Here's Why This Is a Bad Idea," you could run a single length of cable from a network switch in a wiring closet through a hole in the wall, up the wall to the space above the ceiling, through the ceiling space to the wall in an office, down the wall, through a hole, and all the way to a desktop computer. Here's the pitfall, though: Every time someone moves the computer or even cleans behind it, the cable will get moved a little bit. Eventually, the connection will fail, and the RJ-45 plug will have to be replaced. Then the cables in the wiring closet will quickly become a tangled mess.

The smarter path is to put a wall jack at the user's end of the cable and con-nect the other end of the cable to a patch panel. Then, the cable itself is com-pletely contained within the walls and ceiling spaces. To connect a computer to the network, you plug one end of a patch cable (properly called a *station cable*) into the wall jack and plug the other end into the computer's network interface. In the wiring closet, you use a patch cable to connect the wall jack to the network switch. Figure 3-2 shows how this arrangement works.

Connecting a twisted-pair cable to a wall jack or a patch panel is similar to connecting it to an RJ-45 plug. However, you don't usually need any special tools. Instead, the back of the jack has a set of slots that you lay each wire across. You then snap a removable cap over the top of the slots and press it down. This forces the wires into the slots, where little metal blades pierce the insulation and establish the electrical contact.

When you connect the wire to a jack or patch panel, be sure to carefully follow the color-code label on the jack, and to untwist as little of the wire as possible. If you untwist too much of the wire, the signals that pass through the wire may become unreliable.

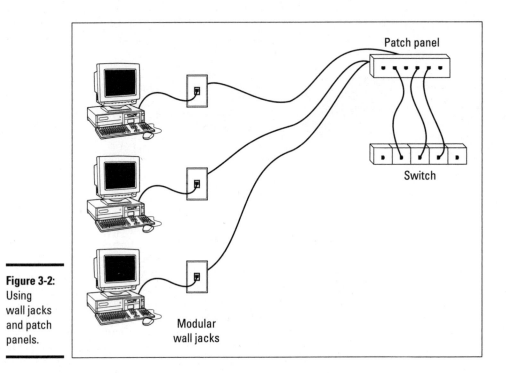

Figure 3-2:
Using
wall jacks
and patch
panels.

Patch panel

Switch

Modular
wall jacks

Installing Switches

Setting up a network switch is remarkably simple. In fact, you need to know only a few details:

✦ Installing a switch is usually very simple. Just plug in the power cord and then plug in patch cables to connect the network.

✦ Each port on the switch has an RJ-45 jack and an LED indicator that lights up when a connection has been established on the port. If you plug one end of a cable into the port and the other end into a computer or other network device, the Link light should come on. If it doesn't, something is wrong with the cable, the hub (or switch port), or the device on the other end of the cable.

✦ Each port may also have an LED indicator that flashes to indicate network activity. If you stare at a switch for awhile, you can find out who uses the network most by noting which activity indicators flash the most.

✦ The ports may also have an LED that indicates the speed of the connection that has been established. For example, the LED might light green for a 1GB connection but amber for a 100MB connection. You can use this LED to identify ports that have potential cabling problems, as computers that should connect at 1GB will often connect at 100MB instead if the cable is suspect.

Daisy-Chaining Switches

If a single switch doesn't have enough ports for your entire network, you can connect switches together by *daisy-chaining* them. On older switches, you sometimes had to use special cables (called *crossover cables*) or designated ports (called *uplink ports*) to daisy-chain switches together. Modern switches don't require this extra consideration. Instead, you can daisy-chain two switches simply by connecting any port on the first switch to any port on the second switch.

Note that you should not chain more than three switches together. As explained in Chapter 2 of this minibook, you can get around this rule by using stackable switches. Stackable switches have a special type of cable connector that connects two or more switches in a way that lets them function as if they were a single switch. Stackable switches are a must for large networks.

When you daisy-chain switches, be careful to avoid creating a loop. For example, suppose you have three switches, called SW1, SW2, and SW3. If you daisy-chain SW1 to SW2, and then daisy-chain SW2 to SW3, and then finally daisy-chain SW3 to SW1, you will have created a loop. When that happens, all insanity will break loose and your network will grind to a halt. (A good reason to use managed switches instead of inexpensive consumer-grade switches is that managed switches can detect such loops and quickly shut them down.)

Chapter 4: Setting Up a Server

In This Chapter

⌐ **Thinking about the different ways to install a server operating system**

⌐ **Getting ready for the installation**

⌐ **Installing a server operating system**

⌐ **Figuring out what to do after you install the server operating system**

A fter you've installed the network cables and other devices, such as hubs and switches, the next step in building a network is usually setting up a server. After you physically connect the server computer to the network, you can install the server operating system (NOS) on the server. Then, you can configure it to provide the network services that you expect and need from the server.

The Many Ways to Install a Server Operating System

Regardless of which server OS you choose to use for your network servers, you can use any of several common ways to actually install the server OS software on the server computer. The following sections describe these alternatives.

Full install versus upgrade

One of the basic server OS installation choices is whether you want to perform a full installation or an upgrade installation. In some cases, you may be better off performing a full installation even if you're installing the server OS on a computer that already has an earlier version of the server OS installed.

✦ **Full:** If you're installing the server OS on a brand-new server, you'll be performing a *full installation* that installs the OS and configures it with default settings.

✦ **Upgrade:** If you're installing the server OS on a server computer that already has a server operating system installed, you can perform an *upgrade installation* that replaces the existing operating system with the new one but retains as many of the settings from the existing operating system as possible.

✦ **Multiboot:** You can also perform a full installation on a computer that already has an OS installed. In that case, you have the option of deleting the existing operating system or performing a *multiboot installation* that installs the new server OS alongside the existing OS. Then, when you restart the computer, you can choose which operating system you want to run.

Although multiboot installation may sound like a good idea, it's fraught with peril. I suggest that you avoid multiboot unless you have a specific reason to use it. For more information about multiboot setups, see the sidebar, "Giving multiboot the boot."

You can't upgrade a client version of Windows to a server version. Instead, you must perform a full installation, which deletes the existing Windows OS, or a multiboot installation, which leaves the existing client Windows intact. Either way, however, you can preserve existing data on the Windows computer when you install the server version.

Giving multiboot the boot

Multiboot installations enable you to have more than one OS on a single computer. Of course, only one OS can be running at any time. When you boot the computer, a menu appears with each installed OS listed. You can choose which OS to boot from this menu.

Multiboot is most useful for software developers or network managers who want to make sure that software is compatible with a wide variety of OSs. Rather than set up a bunch of separate computers with different OS versions, you can install several OSs on a single PC and use that one PC to test the software. For production network servers, however, you probably don't need to have more than one OS installed.

If you still insist on loading two or more OSs on a network server, be sure to install each OS into its own disk partition. Although most NOSes let you install two (or more) OSs into

a single partition, doing so is not a very good idea. To support two OSs in a single partition, both systems have to play a risky shell game with key system files — moving or renaming them each time you restart the computer. Unfortunately, things can go wrong. For example, if lightning strikes and the power goes out just as the NOS is switching the startup files around, you may find yourself with a server that can't boot to any of its installed OSs.

The best way to set up a multiboot system is to install each OS into its own partition. Then, you can use a boot manager program to choose the partition you want to boot from when you start the computer.

Better yet, use a virtualization product such as VMware or Microsoft's Hyper-V. Then, you can set up virtual machines and install the server operating system. For more information, refer to Chapters 1, 2, and 3 of Book IV.

Installing over the network

Normally, you install the server operating system directly from the DVD distribution discs on the server's DVD drive. However, you can also install the OS from a shared drive located on another computer, provided that the server computer already has access to the network. You can either use a shared DVD drive or you can copy the entire contents of the distribution DVD disc onto a shared hard drive.

Obviously, the server computer must have network access in order for this technique to work. If the server already has an OS installed, it probably already has access to the network. If not, you can boot the computer from a disc that has basic network support.

If you're going to install the server operating system onto more than one server, you can save time by first copying the distribution CD onto a shared hard drive. That's because even the fastest CD-ROM drives are slower than the network. Even with a basic 100 Mbps network, access to hard drive data over the network is much faster than access to a local CD-ROM drive.

Gathering Your Stuff

Before you install a server operating system, you should gather everything you need so you don't have to look for something in the middle of the setup. The following sections describe the items you're most likely to need.

A capable server computer

Obviously, you have to have a server computer on which to install the server operating system. Each server operating system has a list of the minimum hardware requirements supported by the OS. For example, Table 4-1 summarizes the minimum requirements for the Standard Edition of Windows Server, known as Windows Server 2012. (At the time I wrote this, the minimum requirements for Windows Server 2016 had not been published.)

My suggestion is that you take these minimums with a grain of salt. Windows Server 2012 will crawl like a snail with 512MB of RAM; I wouldn't bother with less than 4GB, and 16GB is a more appropriate minimum for most purposes.

Table 4-1	Minimum Hardware Requirements for Windows Server 2012
Item	*Windows Server 2012*
CPU	1.4 GHz
RAM	512MB
Free disk space	32GB

You should also check your server hardware against the list of compatible hardware published by the maker of your server operating system. For example, Microsoft publishes a list of hardware that it has tested and certified as compatible with Windows servers. This list is the Hardware Compatibility List (HCL). You can check the HCL for your specific server by going to the Microsoft website at `www.microsoft.com/windows/ compatibility/windows-7/en-us/default.aspx`.

You can also test your computer's compatibility by running the Check System Compatibility option from the Windows distribution CD-ROM.

The server OS

You also need a server OS to install. You'll need either the distribution DVDs or access to a copy of them over the network. In addition to the discs, you need the product key to successfully install the product. If you have the actual DVDs, the product key should be on a sticker attached to the case.

Other software

In most cases, the installation program should be able to automatically configure your server's hardware devices and install appropriate drivers. Just in case, though, you should dig out the driver disks that came with your devices, such as network interface cards (NICs), SCSI devices, DVD drives, printers, scanners, and so on.

A working Internet connection

This isn't an absolute requirement, but the installation will go much smoother if you have a working Internet connection before you start. The installation process may use this Internet connection for several things:

✦ **Downloading late-breaking updates or fixes to the operating system**

This can eliminate the need to install a service pack after you finish installing the server operating system.

✦ **Locating drivers for nonstandard devices**

This can be a big plus if you can't find the driver disk for your obscure SCSI card.

✦ **Activating the product after you complete the installation (for Microsoft OSs)**

A good book

You'll spend lots of time watching progress bars during installation, so you may as well have something to do while you wait. May I recommend *War and Peace*?

Making Informed Decisions

When you install a server operating system, you have to make some decisions about how you want the OS and its servers configured. Most of these decisions aren't cast in stone, so don't worry if you're not 100 percent sure how you want everything configured. You can always go back and reconfigure things. However, you'll save yourself time if you make the right decisions up front rather than just guess when the setup program starts asking you questions.

The following list details most of the decisions that you'll need to make. (This list is for Windows Server 2012 installations. For other server operating systems, the decisions may vary slightly.)

+ **The existing OS:** If you want to retain the existing OS, the installation program can perform a multiboot setup, which allows you to choose which operating system to boot to each time you start the computer. This is rarely a good idea for server computers, so I recommend that you elect to delete the existing OS.

+ **Partition structure:** Most of the time, you'll want to treat the entire server disk as a single partition. However, if you want to divide the disk into two or more partitions, you should do so during setup. (Unlike most of the other setup decisions, this one is hard to change later.)

+ **File system:** Windows Server 2012 provides two choices for the file system to format the server's disk: NT File System (NTFS) and Resilient File System (ReFS). The NTFS file system has been around since 1993. ReFS is a brand new file system which offers several important improvements over NTFS. However, because it is so new, most network administrators are going to be reluctant to use it — at least not right away. So NTFS will still be the file system of choice for the time being.

+ **Computer name:** During the OS setup, you're asked to provide the computer name used to identify the server on the network. If your network has only a few servers, you can just pick a name such as Server01 or MyServer. If your network has more than a few servers, you'll want to follow an established guideline for creating server names.

✦ **Administrator password:** Okay, this one is tough. You don't want to pick something obvious, like Password, Administrator, or your last name. On the other hand, you don't want to type in something random that you'll later forget because you'll find yourself in a big pickle if you forget the administrator password. I suggest that you make up a complex password comprising a mix of uppercase and lowercase letters, some numerals, and a special symbol or two; then write it down and keep it in a secure location where you know it won't get lost.

✦ **Networking protocols:** You'll almost always need to install the TCP/IP protocol, the Microsoft network client protocol, and file and printer sharing. Depending on how the server will be used, you may want to install other protocols as well.

✦ **TCP/IP configuration:** You'll need to know what IP address to use for the server. Even if your network has a DHCP server to dynamically assign IP addresses to clients, most servers use static IP addresses.

✦ **Workgroup or domain:** You'll need to decide whether the server will join a domain or just be a member of a workgroup. In either case, you'll need to know the domain name or the workgroup name.

Final Preparations

Before you begin the actual installation, you should take a few more steps:

✦ Clean up the server's disk by uninstalling any software that you don't need and removing any old data that is no longer needed. This cleanup is especially important if you're converting a computer that's been in use as a client computer to a server. You probably don't need Microsoft Office or a bunch of games on the computer after it becomes a server.

✦ Do a complete backup of the computer. Operating system setup programs are almost flawless, so the chances of losing data during installation are minimal. But you still face the chance that something may go wrong.

✦ If the computer is connected to an uninterruptible power supply (UPS) that has a serial or USB connection to the computer, unplug the serial or USB connection. In some cases, this control connection can confuse the operating system's setup program when it tries to determine which devices are attached to the computer.

✦ If the computer has hard drives compressed with DriveSpace or DoubleSpace, uncompress the drives before you begin.

✦ Light some votive candles, take two Tylenol, and put on a pot of coffee.

Installing a Server Operating System

The following sections present an overview of a typical installation of Windows Server 2012 R2. Although the details vary, the overall installation process for other server operating systems is similar.

In most cases, the best way to install Windows Server 2012 R2 is to perform a new install directly from the DVD installation media. Although upgrade installs are possible, your server will be more stable if you perform a new install. (For this reason, most network administrators avoid upgrading to Windows Server 2012 R2 until it's time to replace the server hardware.)

To begin the installation, insert the DVD distribution media in the server's DVD drive and then restart the server. This causes the server to boot directly from the distribution media, which initiates the setup program.

As the setup program proceeds, it leads you through two distinct installation phases: Collecting Information and Installing Windows. The following sections describe these installation phases in greater detail.

Phase 1: Collecting information

In the first installation phase, the setup program asks for the preliminary information that it needs to begin the installation. A setup wizard prompts you for the information necessary to install Windows Server 2012 R2. Specifically:

✦ **Language:** Select your language, time zone, and keyboard type.

✦ **Product Key:** Enter the 25-character product key that came with the installation media. If setup says you entered an invalid product key, double-check it carefully. You probably just typed the key incorrectly.

✦ **Operating System Type:** The setup program lets you select Windows Server 2012 Standard Edition or Core. Choose Standard Edition to install the full server operating system; choose Core if you want to install the new text-only version.

✦ **License Agreement:** The official license agreement is displayed. You have to agree to its terms in order to proceed.

✦ **Install Type:** Choose an Upgrade or Clean Install type.

✦ **Disk Location:** Choose the partition in which you want to install Windows.

Phase 2: Installing Windows

In this phase, Windows setup begins the actual process of installing Windows. The following steps are performed in sequence:

1. **Copying Files:** Compressed versions of the installation files are copied to the server computer.

2. **Expanding Files:** The compressed installation files are expanded.

3. **Installing Features:** Windows server features are installed.

4. **Installing Updates:** The setup program checks Microsoft's website and downloads any critical updates to the operating system.

5. **Completing Installation:** When the updates are installed, the setup program reboots so it can complete the installation.

Configuring Your Server

After you've installed Windows Server 2012, the computer automatically reboots, and you're presented with the Server Manager program as shown in Figure 4-1.

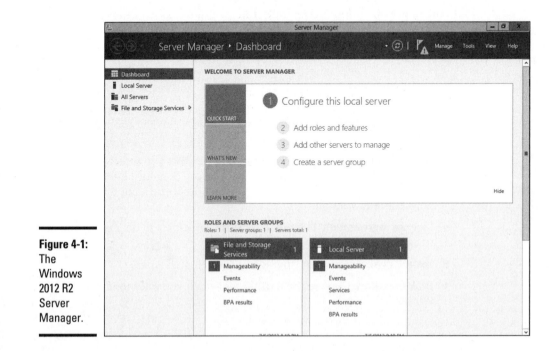

Figure 4-1:
The Windows 2012 R2 Server Manager.

From Server Manager, you can perform a number of tasks that are necessary to configure the server for production use. In particular, you'll need to:

✦ Configure network settings, especially if the server needs a static IP address.

✦ Set the computer name to something other than the default generated by the setup program.

✦ Join a domain.

✦ Add additional server roles, such as DHCP, DNS, IIS, and so on.

✦ Add more operating system features.

✦ Configure security features, such as the Windows Firewall.

For more information about completing the server configuration, refer to Book VII, Chapter 1.

Chapter 5: Configuring Windows Clients

In This Chapter

✔ Configuring network connections for Windows clients

✔ Changing the computer's name

✔ Joining a domain

*B*efore your network setup is complete, you must configure the network's client computers. In particular, you have to configure each client's network interface card so that it works properly, and you have to install the right protocols so that the clients can communicate with other computers on the network.

Fortunately, the task of configuring client computers for the network is child's play in Windows. For starters, Windows automatically recognizes your network interface card when you start up your computer. All that remains is to make sure that Windows properly installed the network protocols and client software.

With each version of Windows, Microsoft has simplified the process of configuring client network support. In this chapter, I describe the steps for configuring networking for Windows 10. The procedures for previous versions of Windows are similar.

Configuring Network Connections

Windows automatically detects and configures network adapters, so you don't have to manually install device drivers for your network adapters. When Windows detects that a network adapter is present on the system, Windows automatically creates a network connection and configures it to support basic networking protocols. You may need to change the configuration of a network connection manually, however.

The following steps show you how to configure your network adapter on a Windows 10 system:

1. **Click the Start icon (or press the Start button on the keyboard), and then tap or click Settings.**

   The Settings page appears, as shown in Figure 5-1.

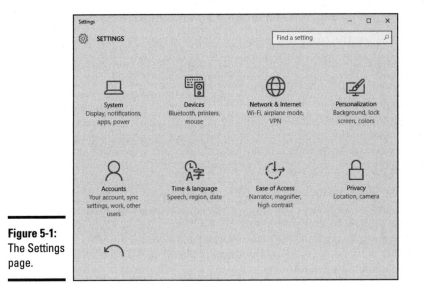

2. **Click Network & Internet.**

   The Network & Internet page appears, as shown in Figure 5-2.

3. **Click Ethernet.**

   The Ethernet settings page appears, as shown in Figure 5-3.

4. **Click Change Adapter Options.**

   The Network Connections page appears, as shown in Figure 5-4. This page lists each of your network adapters. In this case, only a single wired Ethernet adapter is shown. If the device has more than one adapter, additional adapters will appear on this page.

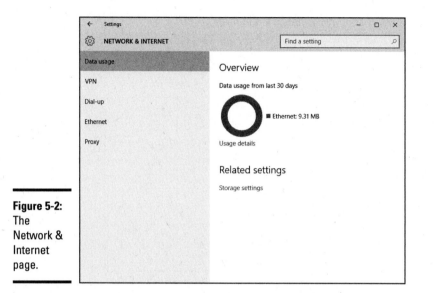

Figure 5-2:
The
Network &
Internet
page.

Figure 5-3:
The
Ethernet
settings
page.

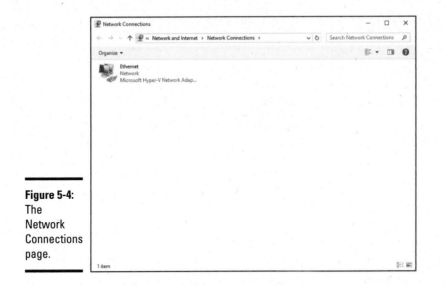

Figure 5-4:
The
Network
Connections
page.

5. **Right-click the connection that you want to configure and then choose Properties from the contextual menu that appears.**

   This action opens the Properties dialog box for the network adapter, as shown in Figure 5-5.

Figure 5-5:
The network
adapter
Properties
dialog box.

6. **To configure the network adapter card settings, click Configure.**

The Network Connection Properties dialog box appears, as shown in Figure 5-6. This dialog box has seven tabs that let you configure the adapter:

- *General:* This tab shows basic information about the adapter, such as the device type and status.

- *Advanced:* This tab lets you set a variety of device-specific parameters that affect the operation of the adapter.

- *About:* Displays information about the device's patent protection.

- *Driver:* This tab displays information about the device driver that's bound to the NIC and lets you update the driver to a newer version, roll back the driver to a previously working version, or uninstall the driver.

- *Details:* With this tab, you can inspect various properties of the adapter such as the date and version of the device driver. To view the setting of a particular property, select the property name from the drop-down list.

- *Events:* This tab lists recent events that have been logged for the device.

- *Power Management:* This tab lets you configure power management options for the device.

Figure 5-6:
The Properties dialog box for a network connection.

When you click OK to dismiss the Network Adapter Properties dialog box, the network connection's Properties dialog box closes and you are returned to the Network Connections page (refer to Figure 5-4). Right-click the network adapter and choose Properties again to continue the procedure.

7. **Review the list of connection items listed in the Properties dialog box.**

   The most important items you commonly see are:

   - *Client for Microsoft Networks:* This item is required if you want to access a Microsoft Windows network. It should always be present.

   - *File and Printer Sharing for Microsoft Networks:* This item allows your computer to share its files or printers with other computers on the network.

     This option is usually used with peer-to-peer networks, but you can use it even if your network has dedicated servers. If you don't plan to share files or printers on the client computer, however, you should disable this item.

   - *Internet Protocol Version 4 (TCP/IPv4):* This item enables the client computer to communicate by using the version 4 standard TCP/IP protocol.

   - *Internet Protocol Version 6 (TCP/IPv6):* This item enables version 6 of the standard TCP/IP protocol. Typically, both IP4 and IP6 are enabled, even though most networks rely primarily on IP4.

8. **If a protocol that you need isn't listed, click the Install button to add the needed protocol.**

   A dialog box appears, asking whether you want to add a network client, protocol, or service. Click Protocol and then click Add. A list of available protocols appears. Select the one you want to add; then click OK.

9. **To remove a network item that you don't need (such as File and Printer Sharing for Microsoft Networks), select the item, and click the Uninstall button.**

   For security reasons, you should make it a point to remove any clients, protocols, or services that you don't need.

10. **To configure TCP/IP settings, click Internet Protocol (TCP/IP); click Properties to display the TCP/IP Properties dialog box (shown in Figure 5-7); adjust the settings; and then click OK.**

    The TCP/IP Properties dialog box lets you choose among these options:

    - *Obtain an IP Address Automatically:* Choose this option if your network has a DHCP server that assigns IP addresses automatically. Choosing this option dramatically simplifies administering TCP/IP on your network. (See Book III, Chapter 4, for more information about DHCP.)

- *Use the Following IP Address:* If your computer must have a specific IP address, choose this option and then type the computer's IP address, subnet mask, and default gateway address. (For more information about these settings, see Book III, Chapter 3.)

- *Obtain DNS Server Address Automatically:* The DHCP server can also provide the address of the Domain Name System (DNS) server that the computer should use. Choose this option if your network has a DHCP server. (See Book III, Chapter 5, for more information about DNS.)

- *Use the Following DNS Server Addresses:* Choose this option if a DNS server isn't available. Then type the IP addresses of the primary and secondary DNS servers.

Figure 5-7:
Configuring
TCP/IP.

Joining a Domain

When Windows first installs, it isn't joined to a domain network. Instead, it's available as part of a workgroup, which is an unmanaged network suitable only for the smallest of networks with just a few computers and without dedicated servers. To use a computer in a domain network, you must join the computer to the domain. Here are the steps for Windows 10:

1. **Click the Start icon (or press the Start button on the keyboard), and then tap or click Settings.**

   The Settings page appears (refer to Figure 5-1).

2. **Click System.**

The System settings page appears, as shown in Figure 5-8.

Figure 5-8:
The System
settings
page.

3. **Click About.**

The PC settings appear, as shown in Figure 5-9.

Figure 5-9:
The PC
settings
page.

4. **(Optional) To change the name of the computer, click Rename PC.**

You'll be prompted to enter a new name, and then reboot the computer.

Before you join a domain, you should ensure that the computer's name won't be the same as the name of a computer that's already a member of the domain. If it is, you should first change the name.

If you do change the computer's name, repeat the procedure from Step 1 after the reboot.

5. **Click Join a Domain.**

The Join a Domain dialog box appears, as shown in Figure 5-10.

Figure 5-10:
Joining a domain.

6. **Enter the domain name and click Next.**

You're prompted for the username and password of a user who has administration privileges on the domain, as shown in Figure 5-11.

Figure 5-11:
You must provide domain administrator credentials to join a domain.

7. **Click OK.**

8. **Enter the username and password for an Administrator account when prompted.**

   You're asked to provide this information only if a computer account hasn't already been created for the client computer.

9. **When informed that you need to restart the computer, click Restart Now.**

   The computer is restarted and added to the domain.

Chapter 6: Mac Networking

In This Chapter

✔ **Hooking up a Mac network**

✔ **Using a Mac network**

✔ **Mixing Macs and PCs**

*T*his book dwells on networking Windows-based computers, as though Microsoft were the only game in town. I'm sure plenty of people in Redmond, WA (where Microsoft is headquartered) wished that it were so. But alas, there is an entirely different breed of computer: the Apple Macintosh, more commonly referred to simply as *Mac*.

Every Mac ever built, even an original 1984 model, includes networking support. Newer Mac computers have better built-in networking features than older Mac computers, of course. The newest Macs include either built-in gigabit Ethernet connections or 802.11n wireless connections, or both. Support for these network connections is pretty much automatic, so all you have to do is plug your Mac into a network or connect to a wireless network, and you're ready to go.

This chapter presents what you need to know to network Mac computers. You learn how to control basic Mac network options such as TCP/IP and file sharing. And you learn how to join a Mac to a Windows domain network.

Basic Mac Network Settings

Most network settings on an Mac are automatic. If you prefer, you can look at and change the default network settings by following these steps:

1. **Choose System Preferences, then choose Networking.**

The Network preferences page appears, as shown in Figure 6-1.

Figure 6-1:
Network
preferences.

2. **Click Advanced.**

   The advanced network settings are displayed, as shown in Figure 6-2.

Figure 6-2:
Advanced
network
settings.

3. **Click the TCP/IP tab to view or change the TCP/IP settings.**

   This brings up the TCP/IP settings, as shown in Figure 6-3. From this page, you can view the currently assigned IP address for the computer.

And, if you want, you can assign a static IP address by changing the Configure IPv4 drop-down setting from Using DHCP to Manually. Then, you can enter your own IP address, subnet mask, and router address.

Figure 6-3:
TCP/IP
settings.

4. **Click the DNS tab to view or change the DNS settings.**

This brings up the DNS settings shown in Figure 6-4. Here, you can see the DNS servers currently being used, and you can add additional DNS servers if you want.

Figure 6-4:
DNS
settings.

5. **Click the Hardware tab to view hardware information.**

   This brings up the settings shown in Figure 6-5. The most useful bit of information on this tab is the MAC address, which is sometimes needed to set up wireless network security. (For more information, refer to Chapter 2 of Book II.)

Figure 6-5: Hardware settings.

What about OS X Server?

At one time, Apple offered a dedicated network operating system known as Mac OS X Server (the *X* is pronounced *Ten,* not *Ex).* In 2011, Apple merged Mac OS X Server with its desktop operating system and made the server components of the operating system available as an inexpensive add-on you can purchase from the App Store. For the latest version of OS X (10.8, released in July 2012), the Server App enhancement can be purchased for under $20.

The Server App download adds a variety of network server features to OS X, including:

✔ **Apache web server,** which also runs on Windows and Linux systems

✔ **MySQL,** which is also available in Windows and Linux versions

✔ **Wiki Server,** which lets you set up web-based wiki, blog, and calendaring sites

✔ **NetBoot,** a feature that simplifies the task of managing network client computers

✔ **Spotlight Server,** which lets you search for content on remote file servers

✔ **Podcast Producer,** which lets you create and distribute multimedia programs

Joining a Domain

If you are using a Mac in a Windows domain environment, you can join the Mac to the domain by following these steps:

1. **Choose Settings, then choose Users & Groups.**

This brings up the Users & Groups page, as shown in Figure 6-6.

Figure 6-6:
Users &
Groups.

2. **Select the user account you want to join to the domain, then click Login Options.**

The Login Options page appears, as shown in Figure 6-7.

Figure 6-7:
Login
Options.

3. **If the lock icon at the bottom-left corner of the page is locked, click it and enter your password when prompted.**

   By default, the user login options are locked to prevent unauthorized changes. This step unlocks the settings so that you can join the domain.

4. **Click the Join button.**

   You are prompted to enter the name of the domain you want to join, as shown in Figure 6-8.

Figure 6-8:
Joining a
domain.

5. **Enter the name of the domain you want to join.**

   When you enter the domain name, the dialog box will expand to allow you to enter domain credentials to allow you to join the domain, as shown in Figure 6-9.

Figure 6-9:
Authenticat-
ing with the
domain.

6. **Enter the name and password of a domain administrator account, then click OK.**

   You are returned to the Login Options page, which shows that you have successfully joined the domain, as shown in Figure 6-10.

7. **Close the Users & Groups window.**

Figure 6-10:
Congratula-
tions! You
have now
joined the
domain.

Connecting to a Share

Once you have joined a domain, you can access its network shares via the
Finder. Just follow these steps:

1. **Click Finder.**

This opens the Finder, as shown in Figure 6-11.

Figure 6-11:
Welcome to
the Finder.

2. Choose Go ⇨ Connect to Server.

The Connect to Server dialog box appears, as shown in Figure 6-12.

Figure 6-12:
The Connect
to Server
dialog box.

3. Type the smb path that leads to the server share you want to connect to.

To type a smb path, follow this syntax:

```
smb://server-name/share-name
```

Replace the *server-name* with the name of the server that contains the share and *share-name* with the name of the share. For example, to connect to a share named `files` on a server named `lowe01`, type `smb://lowe01/files`.

4. Click Connect.

You'll be prompted for login credentials.

5. Enter a domain username and password, then click OK.

Precede the user name with the domain name, separated by a backslash. For example, if the domain name is `lowewriter.pri` and the username is `Doug`, enter `lowewriter.pri\Doug` as the username.

Once connected, the files in the share will be displayed in the Finder window. You can then open files directly from the share (provided you have the right software, such as Microsoft Office, to read the files). You can also drag and drop files between the Mac and the file shares.

Chapter 7: Configuring Other Network Features

In This Chapter

✔ Setting up network printers

✔ Using a network printer's web interface

✔ Mapping network drives

*A*fter you have your network servers and clients up and running, you still have many details to attend to before you can pronounce your network "finished." In this chapter, you discover a few more configuration chores that have to be done: configuring Internet access, setting up network printers, configuring email, and configuring mapped network drives.

Configuring Network Printers

Before network users can print on the network, the network's printers must be properly configured. For the most part, this task is a simple one. All you have to do is configure each client that needs access to the printer.

 Before you configure a network printer to work with network clients, read the client configuration section of the manual that came with the printer. Many printers come with special software that provides more advanced printing and networking features than the standard features provided by Windows. If so, you may want to install the printer manufacturer's software on your client computers rather than use the standard Windows network printer support.

Adding a network printer

The exact procedure for adding a network printer varies a bit, depending on the Windows version that the client runs. The following steps describe the procedure for Windows 10; the procedure for previous versions of Windows is similar:

1. **Click the Start icon (or press the Start button on the keyboard), and then tap or click Settings.**

The Settings page appears, as shown in Figure 7-1.

Figure 7-1:
The Settings
page.

2. **Click Devices.**

   The Devices page appears, as shown in Figure 7-2.

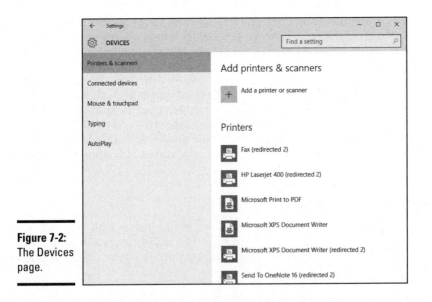

Figure 7-2:
The Devices
page.

3. **Click Add a Printer or Scanner.**

The Printers & Scanners page appears, as shown in Figure 7-3. Windows scavenges your network looking for printers that are available for your use. Any printers that it finds are listed.

Figure 7-3:
Pick a printer.

> ← Settings   — □ ×
>
> ⚙ DEVICES   [Find a setting 🔍]
>
> **Printers & scanners**
> Connected devices
> Mouse & touchpad
> Typing
> AutoPlay
>
> Add printers & scanners
>
> ↻ Refresh
>
> 🖨 NPIOFF485 (HP LaserJet 400 M401dne) Printer
>
> The printer that I want isn't listed
>
> Printers
>
> 🖨 Fax (redirected 2)
>
> 🖨 HP Laserjet 400 (redirected 2)
>
> 📄 Microsoft Print to PDF
>
> 📄 Microsoft XPS Document Writer

4. **Click the printer you want to use.**

If you can't find the printer you want to use, click The Printer That I Want Isn't Listed and enter the name of the printer or its IP address.

5. **Click Add Device.**

The wizard copies to your computer the correct printer driver for the network printer.

You're done! The network printer has been added to the client computer.

If you're experienced with the Devices and Printers page from previous editions of Windows, you'll be happy to know that you can still get to that page. Just scroll down to the bottom of the Devices settings page (refer to Figure 7-2) and click Devices and Printers in the Related Settings section. This brings up the familiar Devices and Printers page, which lists the printers available on your computer. From this page, you can right-click a printer and choose any of the following options:

+ **See What's Printing:** Displays the list of files that are currently being printed.

+ **Set as Default Printer:** Sets the selected printer as the default printer.

+ **Printing Preferences:** Sets the printing defaults for this printer.

+ **Printer Properties:** Displays and sets the basic printer properties, such as the printer's name, its port and driver, and so on.

+ **Remove Device:** Removes the printer.

Accessing a network printer using a web interface

Printers that have a direct network connection often include a built-in web server that lets you manage the printer from any browser on the network. Figure 7-4 shows the home page for an HP LaserJet 400 M401dne printer. This web interface lets you view status information about the printer and check the printer's configuration. You can even view error logs to find out how often the printer jams.

Figure 7-4:
Using a printer's web interface.

To call up a printer's web interface, enter its IP address or host name in the address bar of any web browser.

In addition to simply displaying information about the printer, you can adjust the printer's configuration from a web browser. Figure 7-5 shows the networking settings page for the HP printer. Here, you can view and change the network configuration details, such as the TCP/IP host name, IP address, subnet mask, domain name, and so on.

Figure 7-5:
Changing
network
settings via
a printer's
web
interface.

As the network administrator, you may need to visit the printer's web page frequently. I suggest that you add it to your browser's Favorites menu so that you can get to it easily. If you have several printers, add them to a folder named Network Printers.

Mapping Network Drives

One of the main reasons that users want to use a network is to access shared disk storage located on network file servers. Although you can do this in several ways, the most common method is called *mapping*. Mapping assigns a drive letter to a shared folder on a network server. Then the user can use the drive letter to access the shared folder as though that folder were a local drive.

Before you map network drives for your network's client computers, you should devise a strategy for sharing folders and mapping them to drives. Here are just two possibilities:

✦ **For private storage,** you can create a separate shared folder for each user on the file server and then map a drive letter on each user's computer to that user's shared folder. You can create shares named jBrannan, dHodgson, and mCaldwell, for example. Then you can map drive N: to jBrannan on jBrannan's computer, dHodgson on dHodgson's computer, and mCaldwell on mCaldwell's computer.

✦ **For shared storage for an entire department,** you can create a share for the entire department and then map a drive to that share on each computer in the department. You may map drive M: to a share named Marketing for the entire Marketing department to use, for example.

After you've decided how to map the file server's shared folder, the next step is creating and sharing the folders on the server. For information about how to do that, refer to the appropriate chapters on specific network operating systems later in this book.

When you're ready to map drives on the client computers, follow these steps:

1. **Open File Explorer (formerly known as Windows Explorer).**

   To do so, click the Start button, and then choose File Explorer.

2. **Select This Computer.**

3. **Click the Computer ribbon tab.**

   File Explorer displays the Computer ribbon tab, as shown in Figure 7-6.

4. **Click Map Network Drive, and then click Map Network Drive.**

   The Map Network Drive dialog box appears, as shown in Figure 7-7.

5. **Select the drive letter that you want to map from the Drive drop-down list.**

6. **Type a valid path to the server and share what you want to map in the Folder text box.**

   To map a folder named pCaldwell on a server named MKTSERVER, for example, type **\\MKTSERVER\pCaldwell**.

   If you don't know the server or share name, click the Browse button, and browse your way to the folder that you want to map.

Figure 7-6:
The
Computer
tab in File
Explorer.

Figure 7-7:
Mapping
a network
drive.

7. **To cause the network drive to be automatically mapped each time the user logs on, select the Reconnect at Sign-in check box.**

   If you leave this check box deselected, the drive is mapped only until the next time you shut down Windows or log off.

8. **Click Finish.**

   That's it! You're done.

If you're the type who prefers to do things through the command line, you can map network drives quickly by using the NET USE command at a command prompt. Here's a NET USE command that maps drive Z: to \\ MKTSERVER\pCaldwell:

```
net use z: \\MKTSERVER\pCaldwell /persistent:yes
```

Specifying /persistent:yes causes the drive to be remapped each time the user logs on. To remove a drive mapping via the command line, use a command like this:

```
net use z: /delete
```

Here, the mapping for drive Z: is removed.

Setting up drive mappings manually as described here works well enough for small networks, but not so well for large networks. If a server or share name changes, would you want to go to 200 computers to update drive mappings? How about 2,000 computers? For larger networks, you're more likely to use either logon scripts or group policies to configure network storage for end users. You can find more information about logon scripts and group policies in Book VII, Chapters 4 and 6.

Chapter 8: Setting Up a Wireless Network

In This Chapter

✔ Looking at wireless network standards

✔ Reviewing some basic radio terms

✔ Considering infrastructure and ad-hoc networks

✔ Working with a wireless access point

✔ Configuring Windows for wireless networking

Since the beginning of Ethernet networking, cable has been getting smaller and easier to work with. The original Ethernet cable was about as thick as your thumb, weighed a ton, and was difficult to bend around tight corners. Then came coaxial cable, which was lighter and easier to work with. Coaxial cable was supplanted by unshielded twisted-pair (UTP) cable, which is the cable used for most networks today.

Although cable through the years has become smaller, cheaper, and easier to work with, it is still *cable*. So you have to cut holes in walls, pull cable through ceilings, and get insulation in your hair to wire your entire home or office.

That's why wireless networking has become so popular. With wireless networking, you don't need cables to connect your computers. Instead, wireless networks use radio waves to send and receive network signals. As a result, a computer can connect to a wireless network at any location in your home or office.

Wireless networks are especially useful for mobile devices such as laptops, tablets, and smartphones. After all, the main benefit of a mobile device is that it is, um, *mobile*. A mobile device's mobility would be severely limited if you had to plug a cable into it every time you wanted to access a network. With wireless networking, your mobile device can connect to the network no matter where you take it.

This chapter introduces you to the ins and outs of setting up a wireless network. I tell you what you need to know about wireless networking standards, how to plan a wireless network, how to install and configure wireless network components, how to create a network that mixes wireless and cabled components, how to secure a wireless network, and how to troubleshoot a wireless network when devices refuse to connect.

Diving into Wireless Networking

A *wireless network* is a network that uses radio signals rather than direct cable connections to exchange information. A computer with a wireless network connection is like a cellphone. Just as you don't have to be connected to a phone line to use a cellphone, you don't have to be connected to a network cable to use a wireless networked computer.

The following paragraphs summarize some of the key concepts and terms that you need to understand to set up and use a basic wireless network:

✦ A wireless network is often referred to as a *WLAN,* for *wireless local area network.* Some people prefer to switch the acronym around to *local area wireless network,* or *LAWN.* The term *Wi-Fi* is often used to describe wireless networks, although it technically refers to just one form of wireless network: the 802.11 standard. (See the section "Eight-Oh-Two-Dot-Eleventy Something? [Or, Understanding Wireless Standards]" later in this chapter for more information.)

✦ A wireless network has a name, known as a SSID. *SSID* stands for *service set identifier.* (Wouldn't that make a great *Jeopardy!* question? I'll take obscure four-letter acronyms for $400, please!) All the computers that belong to a single wireless network must have the same SSID.

✦ Wireless networks can transmit over any of several channels. For computers to talk to one another, they must be configured to transmit on the same channel.

✦ The simplest type of wireless network consists of two or more computers with wireless network adapters. This type of network is called an *ad-hoc mode network.*

✦ A more complex type of network is an *infrastructure mode network.* All this really means is that a group of wireless computers can be connected not only to one another, but also to an existing cabled network via a device called a *wireless access point,* or *WAP.* (I tell you more about ad-hoc and infrastructure networks later in this chapter.)

A Little High School Electronics

I was a real nerd in high school: I took three years of electronics. The electronics class at my school was right next door to the auto shop. All the cool kids took auto shop, of course, and only nerds like me took electronics. We hung in there, though, and learned all about capacitors and diodes while the cool kids were learning how to raise their cars and install 2-gigawatt stereo systems.

It turns out that a little of that high school electronics information proves useful when it comes to wireless networking — not much, but a little. You'll understand wireless networking much better if you know the meanings of some basic radio terms.

Waves and frequencies

For starters, *radio* consists of electromagnetic waves that are sent through the atmosphere. You can't see or hear them, but radio receivers can pick them up and convert them to sounds, images, or — in the case of wireless networks — data. Radio waves are actually cyclical waves of electronic energy that repeat at a particular rate called the *frequency.*

Figure 8-1 shows two frequencies of radio waves. The first is one cycle per second; the second is two cycles per second. (Real radio doesn't operate at that low a frequency, but I figured that one and two cycles per second would be easier to draw than 680,000 and 2.4 million cycles per second.)

The measure of a frequency is *cycles per second,* which indicates how many complete cycles the wave makes in 1 second (duh). In honor of Heinrich Hertz — who didn't invent catsup, but was the first person to successfully send and receive radio waves (it happened in the 1880s) — *cycles per second* is usually referred to as *Hertz,* abbreviated *Hz.* Thus, 1 Hz is one cycle per second. Incidentally, when the prefix *K* (for *kilo,* or 1,000), *M* (for *mega,* 1 million), or *G* (for *giga,* 1 billion) is added to the front of Hz, the *H* is still capitalized. Thus, 2.4 MHz is correct (not 2.4 Mhz).

The beauty of radio frequencies is that transmitters can be tuned to broadcast radio waves at a precise frequency. Likewise, receivers can be tuned to receive radio waves at a precise frequency, ignoring waves at other frequencies. That's why you can tune the radio in your car to listen to dozens of radio stations: Each station broadcasts at its own frequency.

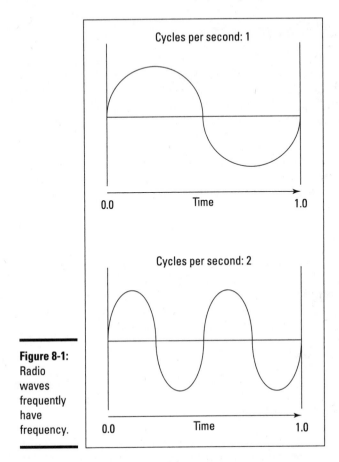

Figure 8-1:
Radio
waves
frequently
have
frequency.

Wavelength and antennas

A term related to frequency is *wavelength*. Radio waves travel at the speed of light. The term *wavelength* refers to how far the radio signal travels with each cycle. Because the speed of light is roughly 182,282 miles per second, for example, the wavelength of a 1 Hz radio wave is about 182,282 miles. The wavelength of a 2 Hz signal is about half that, a mere 91,141 miles.

As you can see, the wavelength decreases as the frequency increases. The wavelength of a typical AM radio station broadcasting at 580 KHz is about 522 yards. For a TV station broadcasting at 100 MHz, it's about 3 yards. For a wireless network broadcasting at 2.4 GHz, the wavelength is just under 5 inches.

It turns out that the shorter the wavelength, the smaller the antenna needs to be to adequately receive the signal. As a result, higher-frequency transmissions need smaller antennas. You may have noticed that AM radio stations usually have huge antennas mounted on top of tall towers, but cellphone transmitters are much smaller, and their towers aren't nearly as tall. That's because cellphones operate on a higher frequency than AM radio stations do. So who decides what type of radio gets to use specific frequencies? That's where spectrums and the FCC come in.

Spectrums and the FCC

The term *spectrum* refers to a continuous range of frequencies on which radio can operate. In the United States, the Federal Communications Commission (FCC) regulates not only how much of Janet Jackson can be shown at the Super Bowl, but also how various portions of the radio spectrum can be used. Essentially, the FCC has divided the radio spectrum into dozens of small ranges called *bands* and restricted certain uses to certain bands. AM radio, for example, operates in the band from 535 KHz to 1,700 KHz.

Table 8-1 lists some of the most popular bands. Note that some of these bands are wide — UHF television begins at 470 MHz and ends at 806 MHz — but other bands are restricted to a specific frequency. The difference between the lowest and highest frequency within a band is called the *bandwidth*.

And now, a word from the irony department

I was an English-literature major in college, so I like to use literary devices such as irony. I don't get to use it much in the computer books I write, so when I get the chance to use irony, I like to jump on it like a hog out of water.

So here's my juicy bit of irony for today: The very first Ethernet system was actually a wireless network. Ethernet traces its roots to a network called AlohaNet, developed at the University of Hawaii in 1970. This network transmitted its data by using small radios. If two computers tried to broadcast data at the same time, the computers detected the collision and tried again after a short, random delay. This technique was the inspiration for the basic technique of Ethernet, now called *carrier sense multiple access with collision detection,* or *CSMA/CD.* The wireless AlohaNet was the network that inspired Robert Metcalfe to develop his cabled network, which he called *Ethernet,* as his doctoral thesis at Harvard in 1973.

For the next 20 years or so, Ethernet was pretty much a cable-only network. It wasn't until the mid-1990s that Ethernet finally returned to its wireless roots.

Table 8-1	Popular Bands of the Radio Spectrum
Band	*Use*
535 KHz–1,700 KHz	AM radio
5.9 MHz–26.1 MHz	Shortwave radio
26.96 MHz–27.41 MHz	Citizens Band (CB) radio
54 MHz–88 MHz	Television (VHF channels 2 through 6)
88 MHz–108 MHz	FM radio
174 MHz–220 MHz	Television (VHF channels 7 through 13)
470 MHz–806 MHz	Television (UHF channels)
806 MHz–890 MHz	Cellular networks
900 MHz	Cordless phones and wireless networks
1850 MHz–1990 MHz	PCS cellular
2.4 GHz–2.4835 GHz	Cordless phones and wireless networks (802.11b and 802.11n)
4 GHz–5 GHz	Large-dish satellite TV
5 GHz	Wireless networks (802.11ac)
11.7 GHz–12.7 GHz	Small-dish satellite TV

Two of the bands in the spectrum are allocated for use by wireless networks: 2.4 GHz and 5 GHz. Note that these bands aren't devoted exclusively to wireless networks. In particular, the 2.4 GHz band shares its space with cordless phones. As a result, cordless phones sometimes interfere with wireless networks.

Eight-Oh-Two-Dot-Eleventy Something? (Or, Understanding Wireless Standards)

The most popular standards for wireless networks are the IEEE 802.11 standards. These standards are essential wireless Ethernet standards and use many of the same networking techniques that the cabled Ethernet standards (in other words, 802.3) use. Most notably, 802.11 networks use the same CSMA/CD technique as cabled Ethernet to recover from network collisions.

The 802.11 standards address the bottom two layers of the IEEE seven-layer model: the Physical layer and the Media Access Control (MAC) layer. Note that TCP/IP protocols apply to higher layers of the model. As a result, TCP/IP runs just fine on 802.11 networks.

The original 802.11 standard was adopted in 1997. Two additions to the standard, 802.11a and 802.11b, were adopted in 1999. Then came 802.11g in 2003 and 802.11n in 2009.

802.11n ruled the roost for a few years, until the latest to gain widespread acceptance came out in 2014: 802.11ac. Still more variations are in the works.

Table 8-2 summarizes the basic characteristics of the five most popular variants of 802.11.

Table 8-2	802.11 Variations		
Standard	*Speeds*	*Frequency*	*Typical Range (Indoors)*
802.11a	Up to 54 Mbps	5 GHz	150 feet
802.11b	Up to 11 Mbps	2.4 GHz	300 feet
802.11g	Up to 54 Mbps	2.4 GHz	300 feet
802.11n	Up to 450 Mbps (but most devices are in the 100 Mbps range)	2.4 GHz and 5 GHz	230 feet
801.11ac	Up to 1,300 Mbps	5 GHz	230 feet

Currently, most wireless networks are based on the 802.11n and 802.11ac standards.

Home on the Range

The maximum range of an 802.11g wireless device indoors is about 300 feet. This can have an interesting effect when you get a bunch of wireless computers together — such that some of them are in range of one another, but others are not. Suppose that Wally, Ward, and the Beaver all have wireless notebooks. Wally's computer is 200 feet away from Ward's computer, and Ward's computer is 200 feet away from Beaver's in the opposite direction (see Figure 8-2). In this case, Ward is able to access both Wally's and Beaver's computers, but Wally can access only Ward's computer, and Beaver can access only Ward's computer. In other words, Wally and Beaver won't be able to access each other's computers because they're outside the 300-feet range limit. (This is starting to sound suspiciously like an algebra problem. Now suppose that Wally starts walking toward Ward at 2 miles per hour, and Beaver starts running toward Ward at 4 miles per hour. . . .)

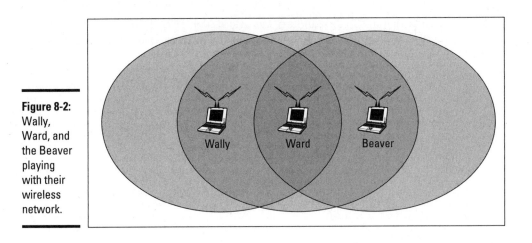

Figure 8-2:
Wally,
Ward, and
the Beaver
playing
with their
wireless
network.

Although the normal range for 802.11g is 300 feet, the range may be less in actual practice. Obstacles such as solid walls, bad weather, cordless phones, microwave ovens, backyard nuclear reactors, and so on can all conspire to reduce the effective range of a wireless adapter. If you're having trouble connecting to the network, sometimes just adjusting the antenna helps.

Also, wireless networks tend to slow down when the distance increases. 802.11g network devices claim to operate at 54 Mbps, but they usually achieve that speed only at ranges of 100 feet or less. At 300 feet, they often slow to a crawl. You should also realize that when you're at the edge of the wireless device's range, you're more likely to lose your connection suddenly due to bad weather.

Wireless Network Adapters

Each computer that will connect to your wireless network needs a *wireless network adapter,* which is similar to the network interface card (NIC) that's used for a standard Ethernet connection. Instead of having a cable connector on the back, however, a wireless network adapter has an antenna.

Just about all notebook and tablet computers come with wireless networking built in, so you don't have to add a separate wireless network adapter to a notebook computer. Many desktop computers include built-in wireless adapters as well. If yours doesn't, you can purchase one of two types of wireless adapters:

✦ **A wireless PCI card** is a wireless network adapter that you install in an available slot inside a desktop computer. To install this type of card, you need to take your computer apart, so use this type of card only if you have the expertise and the nerves to dig into your computer's guts. An 802.11ac version costs about $75.

✦ **A wireless USB adapter** is a separate device that plugs into a USB port on your computer. Because the USB adapter is a separate device, it takes up extra desk space. You can install it without taking your computer apart, however. An 802.11ac version costs about $75.

You can purchase an 802.11ac adapter for about $75.

Wireless Access Points

Unlike cabled networks, wireless networks don't need a hub or switch. If all you want to do is network a group of wireless computers, you just purchase a wireless adapter for each computer, put them all within 300 feet of one another and — voilà! — instant network.

But what if you already have an existing cabled network? Suppose that you work at an office with 15 computers all cabled up nicely, and you just want to add a couple of wireless notebook computers to the network. Or suppose that you have two computers in your den connected with network cable, but you want to link up a computer in your bedroom without pulling cable through the attic.

That's where a *wireless access point,* also known as a *WAP,* comes in. A WAP performs two functions:

✦ It acts as a central connection point for all your computers that have wireless network adapters. In effect, the WAP performs essentially the same function that a hub or switch performs for a wired network.

✦ It links your wireless network to your existing wired network so that your wired computer and your wireless computers get along like one big happy family. This sounds like the makings of a Dr. Seuss story. ("Now the wireless sneeches had hubs without wires. But the twisted-pair sneeches had cables to thires. . . .")

 Wireless access points are sometimes just called *access points,* or *APs.* An access point is a box that has an antenna (or often a pair of antennae) and an RJ-45 Ethernet port. You just plug the access point into a network cable and then plug the other end of the cable into a hub or switch, and your wireless network should be able to connect to your cabled network.

Figure 8-3 shows how an access point acts as a central connection point for wireless computers and how it bridges your wireless network to your wired network.

Figure 8-3: A wireless access point connects a wireless network to a cabled network.

Infrastructure mode

When you set up a wireless network with an access point, you're creating an *infrastructure mode* network. It's called *infrastructure mode* because the access point provides a permanent infrastructure for the network. The access points are installed at fixed physical locations, so the network has relatively stable boundaries. Whenever a mobile computer wanders into the range of one of the access points, it has come into the sphere of the network and can connect.

An access point and all the wireless computers that are connected to it are referred to as a *Basic Service Set,* or *BSS.* Each BSS is identified by a *Service Set Identifier,* or *SSID.* When you configure an access point, you specify the SSID that you want to use. The SSID is often a generic name such as *wireless,* or it can be a name that you create. Some access points use the MAC address of the WAP as the SSID.

Multifunction WAPs

Wireless access points often include other built-in features. Some access points double as Ethernet hubs or switches, and in that case, the access point will have more than one RJ-45 port. In addition, some access points include broadband cable or DSL firewall routers that enable you to connect to the Internet. Figure 8-4 shows a Linksys EA8500, an 802.11ac wireless router intended for home or small office use.

Figure 8-4:
A typical wireless router.

A multifunction access point that's designed to serve as an Internet gateway for home networks sometimes is called a *residential gateway*.

Roaming

You can use two or more wireless access points to create a large wireless network in which computer users can roam from area to area and still be connected to the wireless network. As the user moves out of the range of one access point, another access point automatically picks up the user and takes over without interrupting the user's network service.

To set up two or more access points for roaming, you must carefully place the WAPs so that all areas of the office or building that are being networked are in range of at least one of the WAPs. Then just make sure that all the computers and access points use the same SSID.

Two or more access points joined for the purposes of roaming, along with all the wireless computers connected to any of the access points, form what's called an *Extended Service Set,* or *ESS.* The access points in the ESS are usually connected to a wired network.

One of the current limitations of roaming is that each access point in an ESS must be on the same TCP/IP subnet. That way, a computer that roams from one access point to another within the ESS retains the same IP address. If the access points had a different subnet, a roaming computer would have to change IP addresses when it moved from one access point to another.

Wireless bridging

Another use for wireless access points is to bridge separate subnets that can't easily be connected by cable. Suppose that you have two office buildings that are only about 50 feet apart. To run cable from one building to the other, you'd have to bury conduit — a potentially expensive job. Because the buildings are so close, though, you can probably connect them with a pair of wireless access points that function as a *wireless bridge* between the two networks. Connect one of the access points to the first network and the other access point to the second network. Then configure both access points to use the same SSID and channel.

Ad-hoc networks

A wireless access point isn't necessary to set up a wireless network. Any time two or more wireless devices come within range of each other, they can link up to form an *ad-hoc network.* If you and a few of your friends all have notebook computers with 802.11b/g or 802.11/n wireless network adapters, for example, you can meet anywhere and form an ad-hoc network.

All the computers within range of one another in an ad-hoc network are called an *Independent Basic Service Set,* or *IBSS.*

Configuring a Wireless Access Point

The physical setup for a wireless access point is pretty simple: You take it out of the box, put it on a shelf or on top of a bookcase near a network jack and a power outlet, plug in the power cable, and plug in the network cable.

The software configuration for an access point is a little more involved but still not very complicated. It's usually done via a web interface. To get to the configuration page for the access point, you need to know the access point's IP address. Then you just type that address in the address bar of a browser on any computer on the network.

Multifunction access points usually provide DHCP and NAT services for the networks and double as the network's gateway router. As a result, they typically have a private IP address that's at the beginning of one of the Internet's private IP address ranges, such as 192.168.0.1 or 10.0.0.1. Consult the documentation that came with the access point to find out more.

If you use a multifunction access point that is both your wireless access point and your Internet router, and you can't remember the IP address, run the `IPCONFIG` command at a command prompt on any computer on the network. The Default Gateway IP address should be the IP address of the access point.

Basic configuration options

Figure 8-5 shows the main configuration screen for a typical wireless access point router. I called up this configuration page by entering **192.168.1.1** in the address bar of a web browser and then supplying the login password when prompted.

Figure 8-5:
The main configuration page for a typical wireless router.

The main setup page of this router lets you figure information such as the hostname and IP address of the router and whether the router's DHCP server should be enabled. Options that are found on additional tabs let you configure wireless settings such as the network name (also called the SSID), the type of security to enforce, and a variety of other settings

DHCP configuration

You can configure most multifunction access points to operate as a DHCP server. For small networks, it's common for the access point to also be the DHCP server for the entire network. In that case, you need to configure the access point's DHCP server. Figure 8-6 shows the DHCP configuration page for the Linksys WAP router. To enable DHCP, you select the Enable option and then specify the other configuration options to use for the DHCP server.

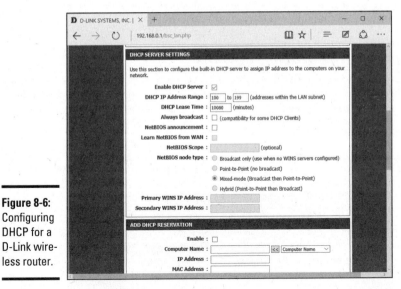

Figure 8-6:
Configuring DHCP for a D-Link wireless router.

Larger networks that have more demanding DHCP requirements are likely to have a separate DHCP server running on another computer. In that case, you can defer to the existing server by disabling the DHCP server in the access point.

For more information on configuring a DHCP server, please refer to Book III, Chapter 4.

Connecting to a Wireless Network

Connecting to a wireless network on a Windows computer is straightforward. Windows automatically detects any wireless networks that are in range and displays them in a list when you tap the Wireless icon at the bottom of the screen, as shown in Figure 8-7.

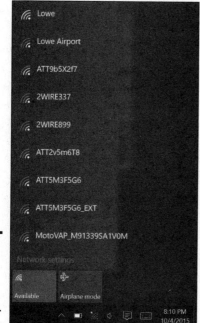

Figure 8-7:
Choosing
a wireless
network in
Windows 10.

To connect to a network, just tap it, and then enter the security key when prompted. If the key is correct, you'll be connected.

At the time you connect, you can choose to connect to the network automatically whenever it's in range. If you select this option, you won't have to select the network manually or enter the security key; you'll just be connected automatically.

Windows remembers every network you connect to, which is a plus for networks you frequently use but a drawback for networks you'll likely never use again. To tell Windows to forget a network, follow these steps:

1. **Click Start, and then tap Settings.**

   The Settings window appears.

2. **Click Network & Internet.**

   This brings up the Network & Internet page, which lists the known networks.

3. **Scroll to the bottom of the list of known networks, and then click Manage Wi-Fi Settings.**

   This brings up the Manage Wi-Fi Settings page, which includes a section titled Manage Known Networks.

4. **In the Manage Known Networks section, click the network you want to forget.**

   The network is selected, as shown in Figure 8-8.

Figure 8-8:
Forgetting a wireless network in Windows 10.

5. **Tap Forget.**

    The network will be forgotten. To log into this network again, you'll have to enter the security key.

Paying Attention to Wireless Network Security

Before you dive headfirst into the deep end of the wireless networking pool, you should consider the inherent security risks in setting up a wireless network. With a cabled network, the best security tool that you have is the lock on the front door of your office. Unless someone can physically get to one of the computers on your network, he or she can't get into your network.

If you go wireless, an intruder doesn't have to get into your office to hack into your network. He or she can do it from the office next door. Or the lobby. Or the parking garage below your office. Or the sidewalk outside. In short, when you introduce wireless devices into your network, you usher in a whole new set of security issues to deal with.

Understanding wireless security threats

Wireless networks have the same basic security considerations as wired networks. As a network administrator, you need to balance the need of legitimate users to access network resources against the risk of illegitimate users breaking into your network. That's the basic dilemma of network security. Whether the network uses cables, wireless devices, kite strings and tin cans, or smoke signals, the basic issues are the same.

At one extreme of the wireless network security spectrum is the totally open network, in which anyone within range of your wireless transmissions can log on as an administrator and gain full access to every detail of your network. At the other end is what I call the "cone-of-silence syndrome," in which the network is so secure that no one can gain access to the network — not even legitimate users.

The goal of securing a wireless network is to find the happy medium between these two extremes that meets the access and risk-management needs of your organization.

The following sections describe the types of security threats that wireless networks are most likely encounter. You should take each of these kinds of threats into consideration when you plan your network's security.

Intruders

With a wired network, an intruder usually must gain access to your facility to physically connect to your network. That's not so with a wireless network. In fact, hackers equipped with notebooks that have wireless network capability can gain access to your network if they can place themselves physically within range of your network's radio signals. Consider these possibilities:

✦ If you share a building with other tenants, the other tenants' offices may be within range.

✦ If you're in a multifloor building, the floor immediately above or below you may be in range.

✦ The lobby outside your office may be within range of your network.

✦ The parking lot outside or the parking garage in the basement may be in range.

If a would-be intruder can't get within normal broadcast range, he or she may try one of several tricks to increase the range:

✦ A would-be intruder can switch to a bigger antenna to extend the range of his or her wireless computer. Some experiments have shown that big antennas can receive signals from wireless networks miles away. In fact, I once read about someone who listened in on wireless networks based in San Francisco from the Berkeley hills, across San Francisco Bay.

✦ If a would-be intruder is serious about breaking into your network, he or she may smuggle a wireless repeater device into your facility — or near it — to extend the range of your wireless network to a location that he or she *can* get to.

A *physical* connection to your network isn't the only way an intruder can gain access, of course. You must still take steps to prevent an intruder from sneaking into your network through your Internet gateway. In most cases, this means that you need to set up a firewall to block unwanted and unauthorized traffic.

Freeloaders

Freeloaders are intruders who want to piggyback on your wireless network to get free access to the Internet. If they manage to gain access to your wireless network, they probably won't do anything malicious: They'll just fire up their web browsers and surf the Internet. These are folks who are too cheap to spend $40 per month on their own broadband connection at home, so they'd rather drive into your parking lot and steal yours.

Even though freeloaders may be relatively benign, they can be a potential source of trouble. In particular:

✦ Freeloaders use bandwidth that you're paying for. As a result, their mere presence can slow down Internet access for your legitimate users.

✦ After freeloaders gain Internet access through your network, they can potentially cause trouble for you or your organization. They may use your network to download illegal pornography, or they may try to send spam via your mail server. Most ISPs will cut you off cold if they catch you sending spam, and they won't believe you when you tell them that the spam came from a kid parked in a Pinto out in your parking lot.

✦ If you're in the business of *selling* access to your wireless network, obviously, freeloaders are a problem.

✦ Freeloaders may start out innocently looking for free Internet access. Once they get in, though, curiosity may get the better of them, leading them to snoop around your network.

✦ If freeloaders can get in, so can malicious intruders.

Eavesdroppers

Eavesdroppers just like to listen to your network traffic. They don't actually try to gain access via your wireless network — at least, not at first. They just listen.

Unfortunately, wireless networks give them plenty to listen to:

✦ Most wireless access points regularly broadcast their Service Set Identifiers (SSIDs) to anyone who's listening.

✦ When a legitimate wireless network user joins the network, an exchange of packets occurs as the network authenticates the user. An eavesdropper can capture these packets and, if security isn't set up right, determine the user's logon name and password.

✦ An eavesdropper can steal files that are opened from a network server. If a wireless user opens a confidential sales report that's saved on the network, the sales-report document is broken into packets that are sent over the wireless network to the user. A skilled eavesdropper can copy those packets and reconstruct the file.

✦ When a wireless user connects to the Internet, an eavesdropper can see any packets that the user sends to or receives from the Internet. If the user purchases something online, the transaction may include a credit card number and other personal information. (Ideally, these packets will be encrypted so that the eavesdropper won't be able to decipher the data.)

Spoilers

A *spoiler* is a hacker who gets kicks from jamming networks so that they become unusable. A spoiler usually accomplishes this act by flooding the network with meaningless traffic so that legitimate traffic gets lost in the flow. Spoilers may also try to place viruses or worm programs on your network via an unsecured wireless connection.

Rogue access points

One of the biggest problems that network administrators have to deal with is the problem of rogue access points. A *rogue access point* is an access point that suddenly appears on your network out of nowhere. What usually happens is that an employee decides to connect a notebook computer to the network via a wireless computer. So this user stops at Computers R Us on the way home from work one day, buys a Fisher-Price wireless access point for $25, and plugs it into the network without asking permission.

Now, in spite of all the elaborate security precautions you've taken to fence in your network, this well-meaning user has opened the barn door. It's *very* unlikely that the user will enable the security features of the wireless access point; in fact, he or she probably isn't even aware that wireless access devices *have* security features.

Unless you take some kind of action to find it, a rogue access point can operate undetected on your network for months or even years. You may not discover it until you report to work one day and find that your network has been trashed by an intruder who found his or her way into your network via an unprotected wireless access point that you didn't even know existed.

Here are some steps you can take to reduce the risk of rogue access points appearing on your system:

✦ Establish a policy prohibiting users from installing wireless access points on their own. Then make sure that you inform all network users of the policy, and let them know why installing an access point on their own can be such a major problem.

✦ If possible, establish a program that quickly and inexpensively grants wireless access to users who want it. Rogue access points show up in the first place for two reasons:

   • Users need the access.

   • The access is hard to get through existing channels.

If you make it easier for users to get legitimate wireless access, you're less likely to find wireless access points hidden behind file cabinets or in flower pots.

✦ Once in a while, take a walk through the premises, looking for rogue access points. Take a look at every network outlet in the building; see what's connected to it.

✦ Turn off all your wireless access points and then walk around the premises with a wireless-equipped mobile device such as a smartphone and look for wireless networks that pop up. Just because you detect a wireless network, of course, doesn't mean you've found a rogue access point; you may have stumbled onto a wireless network in a nearby office or home. But knowing what wireless networks are available from within your office will help you determine whether or not any rogue access points exist.

✦ If your network is large, consider using a software tool such as AirWave (`www.airwave.com`) to snoop for unauthorized access points.

Securing your wireless network

I hope you're convinced that wireless networks do, indeed, pose many security risks. In the following sections, I describe some steps that you can take to help secure your wireless network.

Changing the password

Probably the first thing you should do when you install a wireless access point is change its administrative password. Most access points have a built-in, web-based setup page that you can access from any web browser to configure the access point's settings. The setup page is protected by a username and password, but the username and password are initially set to default values that are easy to guess.

For Linksys access points, for example, the default username is blank, and the password is `admin`. If you leave the username and password set to their default values, anyone can access the access point and change its configuration settings, thus bypassing any other security features that you enable for the access point.

So, the first step in securing your wireless access point is changing the setup password to a value that can't be guessed. I suggest that you use a random combination of numerals and both uppercase and lowercase letters. Be sure to store the password in a secure location. (If you forget the password, you can press the Reset button on the router to restore it to its factory default. Then you can log on by using the default password, which you can find with the documentation that came with the router.)

Securing the SSID

The next step is to secure the SSID that identifies the network. A client must know the access point's SSID to join the wireless network. If you can prevent unauthorized clients from discovering the SSID, you can prevent them from accessing your network.

Securing the SSID isn't a complete security solution, so you shouldn't rely on it as your only security mechanism. SSID security can slow down casual intruders who are just looking for easy and free Internet access, but it isn't possible to prevent serious hackers from discovering your SSID.

You can do three things to secure your SSID:

✦ **Change the SSID from the default.** Most access points come preconfigured with well-known default SSIDs, such as those listed in Table 8-3. By changing your access point's SSID, you can make it more difficult for an intruder to determine your SSID and gain access.

Table 8-3	Common Default SSID Values
SSID	*Manufacturer*
3com	3Com
Compaq	Compaq
Linksys	Linksys
Tsunami	Cisco
Wireless	NetGear
WLAN	DLink
WLAN	SMC

✦ **Disable SSID broadcast.** Most access points frequently broadcast their SSIDs so that clients can discover the network when they come within range. Clients that receive this SSID broadcast can use the SSID to join the network.

You can increase network security somewhat by disabling the SSID broadcast feature. That way, clients won't automatically learn the access point's SSID. To join the network, a client computer must figure out the SSID on its own. Then you can tell your wireless network users the SSID to use when they configure their clients.

Unfortunately, when a client computer connects to a wireless network, it sends the SSID to the access point in an unencrypted packet. So a sophisticated intruder who's using a packet sniffer to eavesdrop on your wireless network can determine your SSID as soon as any legitimate computer joins the network.

✦ **Disable guest mode.** Many access points have a guest-mode feature that enables client computers to specify a blank SSID or to specify "any" as the SSID. If you want to ensure that only clients that know the SSID can join the network, you must disable this feature.

Enabling WEP

WEP stands for *wired equivalent privacy* and is designed to make wireless transmission as secure as transmission over a network cable. WEP encrypts your data by using either a 40-bit key or a 128-bit key. Keep in mind that 40-bit encryption is faster than 128-bit encryption and is adequate for most purposes. So unless you work for the Central Intelligence Agency, I suggest that you enable 40-bit encryption.

Note: WEP is less secure than other security methods such as WPA and WPA2. You should use WEP only if you need to connect to devices that do not support WPA or WPA2.

To use WEP, both the client and the server must know the encryption keys being used. A client that doesn't know the access point's encryption keys won't be able to join the network.

You can specify encryption keys for WEP in two ways. The first way is to create the ten-digit key manually by making up a random number. The second method, which I prefer, is to use a *passphrase,* which can be any word or combination of numerals and letters that you want. WEP automatically converts the passphrase to the numeric key used to encrypt data. If the client knows the passphrase used to generate the keys on the access point, the client will be able to access the network.

As it turns out, security experts have identified several flaws in WEP that compromise its effectiveness. As a result, with the right tools, a sophisticated intruder can get past WEP. So although it's a good idea to enable WEP, you shouldn't count on it for complete security.

Besides just enabling WEP, you should take two steps to increase its effectiveness:

✦ **Make WEP mandatory.** Some access points have a configuration setting that enables WEP but makes it optional. This setting may prevent eavesdroppers from viewing the data transmitted on WEP connections, but it doesn't prevent clients that don't know your WEP keys from accessing your network.

✦ **Change the encryption keys.** Most access points come preconfigured with default encryption keys that make it easy for even casual hackers to defeat your WEP security. You should change the default keys, either by using a passphrase or by specifying your own key. Figure 8-9 shows the WEP key configuration page for a typical access point (in this case, a D-Link DIR-868L).

Figure 8-9: Changing the WEP settings on a D-Link wireless router.

Using WPA and WPA2

WPA, which stands for *Wi-Fi Protected Access,* is a newer form of security for wireless networks that's designed to plug some of the holes of WEP. WPA is similar in many ways to WEP. The big difference is that when you use WPA, the encryption key is automatically changed at regular intervals, thus thwarting all but the most sophisticated efforts to break the key. Most newer wireless devices support WPA. If your equipment supports it, I suggest that you use it.

Here are a few additional things to know about WPA:

✦ A small office and home version of WPA, called WPA-PSK, bases its encryption keys on a passkey value that you supply. True WPA devices, however, rely on a special authentication server to generate the keys.

✦ All versions of Windows since Windows XP Service Pack 2 have built-in support for WPA.

✦ The official IEEE standard for WPA is 802.11i. However, WPA devices were widely available before the 802.11i standard was finalized; as a result, not all WPA devices implement every aspect of 802.11i.

✦ The original version of WPA has been superseded by a newer version, named WPA2.

Using MAC address filtering

MAC address filtering allows you to specify a list of MAC addresses for the devices that are allowed to access the network or are prohibited from accessing the network. If a computer with a different MAC address tries to join the network via the access point, the access point will deny access.

MAC address filtering is a great idea for wireless networks with a fixed number of clients. If you set up a wireless network at your office so that a few workers can connect their notebook computers, you can specify the MAC addresses of those computers in the MAC filtering table. Then other computers won't be able to access the network via the access point.

Unfortunately, it isn't difficult to configure a computer to lie about its MAC address. Thus, after a potential intruder determines that MAC filtering is being used, he or she can just sniff packets to determine an authorized MAC address and then configure his or her computer to use that address. (This practice is called *MAC spoofing*.) So you shouldn't rely on MAC address filtering as your only means of security.

Figure 8-10 shows the screen used to edit the MAC address table for a D-Link wireless access point.

Don't neglect the basics

The security techniques described in this chapter are specific to wireless networks. They should be used alongside the basic security techniques that are presented in Book III. In other words, don't forget the basics, such as these:

✔ Use strong passwords for your user accounts.

✔ Apply security patches to your servers.

✔ Change default server account information (especially the administrator password).

✔ Disable unnecessary services.

✔ Check your server logs regularly.

✔ Install virus protection.

✔ Back up!

Figure 8-10:
A MAC
address
table for
a D-Link
wireless
router.

Placing your access points outside the firewall

The most effective security technique for wireless networking is placing all your wireless access points *outside* your firewall. That way, all network traffic from wireless users will have to travel through the firewall to access the network.

As you can imagine, doing this can significantly limit network access for wireless users. To get around those limitations, you can enable a virtual private network (VPN) connection for your wireless users. The VPN will allow full network access to authorized wireless users.

Obviously, this solution requires a bit of work to set up and can be a little inconvenient for your users, but it's an excellent way to fully secure your wireless access points.

Troubleshooting a wireless network

Wireless networks are great until something goes haywire. When a regular network doesn't work, you usually know about it right away because the network simply becomes unavailable. You can't display web pages, read email, or access files on shared drives.

The troubleshooting chapters in Book II address the most common problems encountered on cabled networks. But wireless networks can cause problems of their own. And to add to the frustration, wireless networks tend to degrade rather than completely fail. Performance gets slower. Web pages that usually pop up in a second or two take 15 to 20 seconds to appear. Or sometimes they don't appear at all, but if you try again a few minutes later, they download fine.

This following sections offer some troubleshooting tips that can help you restore normalcy to a failing wireless network.

Checking for obvious problems

Before you roll up your sleeves and take drastic corrective action, you should check for a few obvious things if you're having wireless network trouble. The following list highlights some basic things you should check for:

✦ Is everything turned on? Make sure you have lights on your wireless access point/router, as well as on your cable or DSL modem.

✦ Many access point/routers use a power supply transformer that plugs into the wall. Make sure that the transformer is plugged into the wall outlet and that the small cable that comes out of the transformer is plugged into the power connector on the access point/router.

✦ Are the cables connected? Check the network cable that connects your access point/router to the cable or DSL modem.

✦ Try restarting everything. Turn off the computer, the access point/router, and your cable or DSL modem. Leave everything off for at least two minutes. Then turn everything back on. Sometimes, simply cycling the power off and back on clears up a connection problem.

Pinpointing the problem

If you can't connect to the Internet, one of the first steps (after you've made sure that everything is turned on) is finding out whether the problem is with your access point/router or with your broadband connection. Here is one way you can check to find out whether your wireless connection is working:

1. **Open a command prompt window by choosing Start**➪**Run, typing** cmd, **and pressing Enter.**

2. **At the command prompt, type** ipconfig, **and press Enter.**

   You should get a display similar to this:

   ```
   Ethernet adapter Wireless Network Connection:
           Connection-specific DNS Suffix  . : hsd1.ca.comcast.net)).
           IP Address. . . . . . . . . . . : 192.168.1.101
           Subnet Mask . . . . . . . . . . : 255.255.255.0
           Default Gateway . . . . . . . . : 192.168.1.1
   ```

If the display resembles this but with different numbers, you're connected to the wireless network, and the problem most likely lies with your broadband modem.

But if the IP Address, Subnet Mask, and Default Gateway indicate 0.0.0.0 instead of valid IP addresses, you have a problem with your wireless network.

Changing channels

One of the most common sources of wireless network trouble is interference from other wireless devices. The culprit might be a cordless phone, or it could be a neighbor who also has a wireless network.

The simplest solution to this type of interference is changing channels. 802.11b access points let you select 1 of 11 different channels to broadcast on. If you're having trouble connecting to your access point, try changing the channel. To do that, you must log on to the router with the administrator password. Then hunt around the router's administrator pages until you find the controls that let you change the channel.

You may have to try changing the channel several times before you solve the problem. Unfortunately, 802.11b channels overlap slightly, which means that broadcasts on one channel may interfere with broadcasts on adjacent channels. Thus, if you're having trouble connecting on channel 1, don't bother switching to channel 2. Instead, try switching to channel 5 or 6. If that doesn't work, switch to channel 10 or 11.

Fiddling with the antennas

Sometimes, you can fix intermittent connection problems by fiddling with the antennas on the access point and your computer's wireless adapter. This procedure is similar to playing with old-fashioned rabbit-ear antennas on a TV to get the best reception.

The angles of the antennas sometimes make a difference, so try adjusting the antenna angles. In addition, you usually have better results if you place the access point at a high location, such as on top of a bookshelf.

In some cases, you may actually need to add a high-gain antenna to the access point to increase its range. A high-gain antenna simply snaps or screws onto the access point to provide a bigger antenna. Figure 8-11 shows high-gain antennas that are designed to work with Linksys access points. Antennas such as these cost about $70 for the pair.

Figure 8-11:
High-gain
antennas
for a Linksys
wireless
router.

Photo courtesy of Linksys

A more drastic fix is to add a signal booster to your access point. A *signal booster* is a power amplifier that increases the transmission power of most wireless devices by a factor of five. A typical signal booster costs about $100.

Adding another access point

If you have a computer that's out of range of your access point, one solution is to add a second access point closer to the problematic computer. Most likely, the only difficulty will be getting an Ethernet cable to the location where you want to put your second access point.

If possible, you can simply run a length of cable through your walls or attic to the second access point. If that solution isn't feasible, you can use a HomePlug or HomePNA network connection for the second access point.

An alternative to a second access point is simply adding a range extender such as the Linksys AC1200 Amplify shown in Figure 8-12. This handy device plugs directly into any electrical outlet and provides a pass-through outlet so you can still use your vacuum cleaner. Just plug this device midway between your access point and the computer that's having trouble connecting.

Figure 8-12:
A wireless repeater such as this one from Linksys can help increase the range of your wireless network.

Photo courtesy of Linksys

Help! I forgot my router's password!

I mention many times throughout this book that you should always change the default passwords that come with computer and operating systems to more secure passwords, usually consisting of a random combination of letters, digits, and special symbols.

Ideally, you've already taken my sage advice and changed the password on your combination wireless access point/router. Good for you. But what if you forget the password later? Is there any way to get back into your access point/router then?

Fortunately, there is. Most access point/routers have a reset button. It's usually located on the back or on the bottom of the router's case. Press this button to restore the access point/router to its factory default settings. That action resets the administrator password to the factory default — and also resets any other custom settings you've applied, so you may have to reconfigure your router to get it working again.

Book II
Network Administration

Find five common network bottlenecks in a free article at `www.dummies.com/extras/networkingaio`.

Contents at a Glance

Chapter 1: Help Wanted: Job Description for a Network Administrator 121

Chapter 2: Security 101 135

Chapter 3: Managing User Accounts 145

Chapter 4: Firewalls and Virus Protection. 153

Chapter 5: Blocking Spam 165

Chapter 6: Managing Network Software. 177

Chapter 7: Solving Network Problems. 189

Chapter 8: Backing Up Your Data 205

Chapter 9: Disaster Recovery and Business Continuity Planning. . .217

Chapter 1: Help Wanted: Job Description for a Network Administrator

In This Chapter

✔ Deciphering the many jobs of the network administrator

✔ Dusting, vacuuming, and mopping

✔ Managing the network users

✔ Choosing the right tools

✔ Getting certified

*H*elp wanted. Network administrator to help small business get control of a network run amok. Must have sound organizational and management skills. Only moderate computer experience required. Part-time only.

Does this ad sound like one that your company should run? Every network needs a network administrator, whether the network has 2 computers or 200. Of course, managing a 200-computer network is a full-time job, whereas managing a 2-computer network isn't. At least, it shouldn't be.

This chapter introduces you to the boring job of network administration. Oops . . . you're probably reading this chapter because you've been elected to be the network manager, so I'd better rephrase that: This chapter introduces you to the wonderful, exciting world of network management! Oh, boy! This is going to be fun!

Knowing What Network Administrators Do

Simply put, network administrators administer networks, which means that they take care of the tasks of installing, configuring, expanding, protecting, upgrading, tuning, and repairing the network. Network administrators take care of the network hardware, such as cables, hubs, switches, routers, servers, and clients, as well as network software, such as network operating systems, email servers, backup software, database servers, and application software. Most importantly, network administrators take care of network users by answering their questions, listening to their troubles, and solving their problems.

On a big network, these responsibilities constitute a full-time job. Large networks tend to be volatile: Users come and go, equipment fails, cables break, and life in general seems to be one crisis after another.

Smaller networks are much more stable. After you get your network up and running, you probably won't have to spend much time managing its hardware and software. An occasional problem may pop up, but with only a few computers on the network, problems should be few and far between.

Regardless of the network's size, all network administrators must attend to several common chores:

✦ **Equipment upgrades:** The network administrator should be involved in every decision to purchase new computers, printers, or other equipment. In particular, the network administrator should be prepared to lobby for the most network-friendly equipment possible, such as network-ready printers, ample network disk storage, and an adequate backup system.

✦ **Configuration:** The network administrator must put on the pocket protector whenever a new computer is added to the network. The network administrator's job includes considering what changes to make to the cabling configuration, what computer name to assign to the new computer, how to integrate the new user into the security system, what rights to grant the user, and so on.

✦ **Software upgrades:** Every once in a while, your trusty OS vendor (likely, Microsoft) releases a new version of your network operating system (NOS). The network administrator must read about the new version and decide whether its new features are beneficial enough to warrant an upgrade. In most cases, the hardest part of upgrading to a new version of your network operating system is determining the *migration path* — that is, how to upgrade your entire network to the new version while disrupting the network or its users as little as possible. Upgrading to a new NOS version is a major chore, so you need to carefully consider the advantages that the new version can bring.

✦ **Patches:** Between upgrades, Microsoft releases patches and service packs that fix minor problems with its server operating systems. For more information, see the section "Patching Up Your Operating System and Software" later in this chapter. (Other software vendors also regularly release patches and service packs, so it isn't only Microsoft software that must be kept up to date.)

✦ **Performance maintenance:** One of the easiest traps that you can get sucked into is the quest for network speed. The network is never fast enough, and users always blame the hapless network manager. So the administrator spends hours and hours tuning and tweaking the network to squeeze out that last two percent of performance.

✦ **Ho-hum chores:** Network administrators perform routine chores, such as backing up the servers, archiving old data, freeing up server hard drive space, and so on. Much of network administration is making sure that things keep working and finding and correcting problems before any users notice that something is wrong. In this sense, network administration can be a thankless job.

✦ **Software inventory:** Network administrators are also responsible for gathering, organizing, and tracking the entire network's software inventory. You never know when something is going to go haywire on Joe in Marketing's ancient Windows XP computer and you're going to have to reinstall that old copy of WordPerfect. Do you have any idea where the installation discs are?

Choosing the Part-Time Administrator

The larger the network, the more technical support it needs. Most small networks — with just a dozen or so computers — can get by with a part-time network administrator. Ideally, this person should be a closet computer geek: someone who has a secret interest in computers but doesn't like to admit it. Someone who will take books home and read them over the weekend. Someone who enjoys solving computer problems just for the sake of solving them.

The job of managing a network requires some computer skills, but it isn't entirely a technical job. Much of the work that the network administrator does is routine housework. Basically, the network administrator dusts, vacuums, and mops the network periodically to keep it from becoming a mess.

Here are some additional ideas on picking a part-time network administrator:

✦ The network administrator needs to be an organized person. Conduct a surprise office inspection and place the person with the neatest desk in charge of the network. (Don't warn anyone in advance, or everyone may mess up his or her desk intentionally the night before the inspection.)

✦ Allow enough time for network administration. For a small network (say, no more than 20 or so computers), an hour or two each week is enough. More time is needed upfront as the network administrator settles into

**Book II
Chapter 1**

Help Wanted:
Job Description
for a Network
Administrator

the job and discovers the ins and outs of the network. After an initial settling-in period, though, network administration for a small office network doesn't take more than an hour or two per week. (Of course, larger networks take more time to manage.)

✦ Make sure that everyone knows who the network administrator is and that the network administrator has the authority to make decisions about the network, such as what access rights each user has, what files can and can't be stored on the server, how often backups are done, and so on.

✦ Pick someone who is assertive and willing to irritate people. A good network administrator should make sure that backups are working *before* a hard drive fails and make sure that antivirus protection is in place *before* a virus wipes out the entire network. This policing will irritate people, but it's for their own good.

✦ In most cases, the person who installs the network is also the network administrator. This is appropriate because no one understands the network better than the person who designs and installs it.

✦ The network administrator needs an understudy — someone who knows almost as much about the network, is eager to make a mark, and smiles when the worst network jobs are delegated.

✦ The network administrator has some sort of official title, such as Network Boss, Network Czar, Vice President in Charge of Network Operations, or Dr. Network. A badge, a personalized pocket protector, or a set of Spock ears helps, too.

Establishing Routine Chores

Much of the network administrator's job is routine stuff — the equivalent of vacuuming, dusting, and mopping. Or if you prefer, changing the oil and rotating the tires every 3,000 miles. Yes, it's boring, but it has to be done.

✦ **Backup:** The network administrator needs to make sure that the network is properly backed up. If something goes wrong and the network isn't backed up, guess who gets the blame? On the other hand, if disaster strikes, yet you're able to recover everything from yesterday's backup with only a small amount of work lost, guess who gets the pat on the back, the fat bonus, and the vacation in the Bahamas? Chapter 8 of this minibook describes the options for network backups. You'd better read it soon.

✦ **Protection:** Another major task for network administrators is sheltering your network from the evils of the outside world. These evils come in many forms, including hackers trying to break into your network and virus programs arriving through email. Chapter 4 of this minibook describes this task in more detail.

✦ **Clean-up:** Users think that the network server is like the attic: They want to throw files up there and leave them forever. No matter how much storage your network has, your users will fill it up sooner than you think. So the network manager gets the fun job of cleaning up the attic once in a while. Oh, joy. The best advice I can offer is to constantly complain about how messy it is up there and warn your users that spring cleaning is coming up.

Managing Network Users

Managing network technology is the easiest part of network management. Computer technology can be confusing at first, but computers aren't nearly as confusing as people. The real challenge of managing a network is managing the network's users.

The difference between managing technology and managing users is obvious: You can figure out computers, but you can never really figure out people. The people who use the network are much less predictable than the network itself. Here are some tips for dealing with users:

✦ **Training:** Training is a key part of the network manager's job. Make sure that everyone who uses the network understands it and knows how to use it. If the network users don't understand the network, they may unintentionally do all kinds of weird things to it.

✦ **Respect:** Never treat your network users like they're idiots. If they don't understand the network, it isn't their fault. Explain it to them. Offer a class. Buy them each a copy of *Networking All-in-One For Dummies* and tell them to read it during their lunch hour. Hold their hands. But don't treat them like idiots.

✦ **Aids:** Make up a network cheat sheet that contains everything that the users need to know about using the network on one page. Make sure that everyone gets a copy.

✦ **Responsive:** Be as responsive as possible when a network user complains of a network problem. If you don't fix the problem soon, the user may try to fix it. You probably don't want that.

The better you understand the psychology of network users, the more prepared you'll be for the strangeness they often serve up. Toward that end, I recommend that you read the *Diagnostic and Statistical Manual of Mental Disorders* (also known as *DSM-IV*) cover to cover.

**Book II
Chapter 1**

Help Wanted:
Job Description
for a Network
Administrator

Patching Up Your Operating System and Software

One of the annoyances that every network manager faces is applying software patches to keep your OS and other software up to date. A software *patch* is a minor update that fixes small glitches that crop up from time to time, such as minor security or performance issues. These glitches aren't significant enough to merit a new version of the software, but they're important enough to require fixing. Most patches correct security flaws that computer hackers have uncovered in their relentless attempts to prove that they're smarter than security programmers.

Periodically, all the recently released patches are combined into a *service pack*. Although the most diligent network administrators apply all patches as they're released, many administrators just wait for the service packs.

For all versions of Windows, you can use Windows Update to apply patches to keep your operating system and other Microsoft software up to date. You can find Windows Update in the Start menu. Or, you can fire up Internet Explorer and browse to `http://update.microsoft.com`. Windows Update automatically scans your computer's software and creates a list of software patches and other components that you can download and install. You can also configure Windows Update to automatically notify you of updates so that you don't have to remember to check for new patches.

For larger networks, you can set up a server that runs Microsoft's Windows Software Update Services (WSUS) to automate software updates. WSUS, which is a built-in role on Windows Server 2012 and later, essentially lets you set up your own Windows Update site on your own network. Then, you have complete control over how software updates are delivered to the computers on your network. For more information, see `www.microsoft.com/windows serversystem/updateservices`.

Discovering Software Tools for Network Administrators

Network administrators need certain tools to get their jobs done. Administrators of big, complicated, and expensive networks need big, complicated, and expensive tools. Administrators of small networks need small tools.

Some of the tools that the administrator needs are hardware tools, such as screwdrivers, cable crimpers, and hammers. The tools that I'm talking about here, however, are software tools. Here's a sampling of the tools you'll need:

✦ **A diagramming tool:** A diagramming tool lets you draw pictures of your network. Visio (from Microsoft) is great for drawing the types of diagrams you'll want to make as a network administrator.

✦ **A network discovery program:** For larger networks, you may want to invest in a network discovery program such as Spiceworks (www.spice works.com) that can automatically document your network's structure for you. These programs scan the network carefully, looking for computers, printers, routers, and other devices. They then create a database of the network components, draw diagrams for you, and chug out helpful reports.

✦ **The network's built-in tools:** Many software tools that you need to manage a network come with the network itself. As the network administrator, read through the manuals that come with your network software to see what management tools are available. For example, Windows includes a net diag command that you can use to make sure that all the computers on a network can communicate with each other. (You can run net diag from an MS-DOS prompt.) For TCP/IP networks, you can use the TCP/IP diagnostic commands summarized in Table 1-1.

Table 1-1	TCP/IP Diagnostic Commands
Command	*What It Does*
arp	Displays address resolution information used by the Address Resolution Protocol (ARP)
hostname	Displays your computer's host name
ipconfig	Displays current TCP/IP settings
nbtstat	Displays the status of NetBIOS over TCP/IP connections
netstat	Displays statistics for TCP/IP
nslookup	Displays Domain Name System (DNS) information
ping	Verifies that a specified computer can be reached
route	Displays the PC's routing tables
tracert	Displays the route from your computer to a specified host

✦ **System Information:** This program that comes with Windows is a useful utility for network managers.

✦ **Hotfix Checker:** This handy tool from Microsoft scans your computers to see what patches need to be applied. You can download the free Hotfix Checker from Microsoft online (search for "**hfnetchk.exe**").

✦ **Microsoft Baseline Security Analyzer:** If you prefer GUI-based tools, check out Microsoft Baseline Security Analyzer. You can download it from Microsoft online free of charge (search for *Microsoft Baseline Security Analyzer*).

✦ **A utility program:** I suggest that you get one of those 100-in-1 utility programs, such as Symantec's Norton Utilities. Norton Utilities includes invaluable utilities for repairing damaged hard drives, rearranging the directory structure of your hard drive, gathering information about your computer and its equipment, and so on.

Never use a hard drive repair program that wasn't designed to work with the OS or version that your computer uses or the file system you've installed. Any time that you upgrade to a newer version of your operating system, you should also upgrade your hard drive repair programs to a version that supports the new operating system version.

✦ **A protocol analyzer:** A *protocol analyzer* monitors and logs the individual packets that travel along your network. (Protocol analyzers are also called *packet sniffers.*) You can configure the protocol analyzer to filter specific types of packets, watch for specific types of problems, and provide statistical analysis of the captured packets. Most network administrators agree that Sniffer, by NetScout (`www.netscout.com`), is the best protocol analyzer available. However, it's also one of the most expensive. If you prefer a free alternative, check out Wireshark, which you can download free from `www.wireshark.org`.

✦ **Network Monitor:** All current versions of Windows include Network Monitor, which provides basic protocol analysis and can often help solve pesky network problems.

Building a Library

One of Scotty's best lines in the original *Star Trek* series was when he refused to take shore leave so he could get caught up on his technical journals. "Don't you ever relax?" asked Kirk. "I am relaxing!" Scotty replied.

To be a good network administrator, you need to read computer books. Lots of them. And you need to enjoy doing it. If you're the type who takes computer books with you to the beach, you'll make a great network administrator.

You need books on a variety of topics. I'm not going to recommend specific titles, but I do recommend that you get a good, comprehensive book on each of the following topics:

✦ Network security and hacking

✦ Wireless networking

✦ Network cabling and hardware

✦ Ethernet

✦ Windows Server 2008 or 2012

✦ Windows 7, 8, 8.1, and 10

✦ Linux

✦ TCP/IP

✦ DNS

✦ Sendmail or Microsoft Exchange Server, depending on which email server you use

In addition to books, you may also want to subscribe to some magazines to keep up with what's happening in the networking industry. Here are a few you should probably consider, along with their web addresses:

✦ *InformationWeek:* www.informationweek.com

✦ *InfoWorld:* www.infoworld.com

✦ *Network Computing:* www.networkcomputing.com

✦ *Network World:* www.networkworld.com

✦ *2600 The Hacker Quarterly* (a great magazine on computer hacking and security): www.2600.com

The Internet is one of the best sources of technical information for network administrators. You'll want to stock your browser's Favorites menu with plenty of websites that contain useful networking information. In addition, you may want to subscribe to one of the many online newsletters that deliver fresh information on a regular basis via email.

Book II
Chapter 1

Help Wanted:
Job Description
for a Network
Administrator

Getting Certified

Remember the scene near the end of *The Wizard of Oz* when the Wizard grants the Scarecrow a diploma, the Cowardly Lion a medal, and the Tin Man a testimonial?

Network certifications are kind of like that. I can picture the scene now:

The Wizard: "And as for you, my network-burdened friend, any geek with thick glasses can administer a network. Back where I come from, there are people who do nothing but configure Cisco routers all day long. And they don't have any more brains than you do. But they do have one thing you don't have: certification. And so, by the authority vested in me by the Universita Committeeatum E Pluribus Unum, I hereby confer upon you the coveted certification of CND."

You: "CND?"

The Wizard: "Yes, that's, uh, *Certified Network Dummy.*"

You: "The Seven Layers of the OSI Reference Model are equal to the Sum of the Layers on the Opposite Side. Oh, joy, rapture! I feel like a network administrator already!"

My point is that certification in and of itself doesn't guarantee that you really know how to administer a network. That ability comes from real-world experience — not exam crams.

Nevertheless, certification is becoming increasingly important in today's competitive job market. So you may want to pursue certification, not just to improve your skills, but also to improve your résumé. Certification is an expensive proposition. Each test can cost several hundred dollars, and depending on your technical skills, you may need to buy books to study or enroll in training courses before you take the tests.

You can pursue two basic types of certification: vendor-specific certification and vendor-neutral certification. The major software vendors such as Microsoft and Cisco provide certification programs for their own equipment and software. CompTIA, a nonprofit industry trade association, provides the best-known vendor-neutral certification.

The following sections describe some of the certifications offered by CompTIA, Microsoft, Novell, and Cisco.

CompTIA

www.comptia.org

✦ **A+** is a basic certification for an entry-level computer technician. To attain A+ certification, you have to pass two exams: one on computer hardware, the other on operating systems.

✦ **Linux+ Powered by LPI** covers basic Linux skills such as installation, operations, and troubleshooting. This certification is vendor neutral, so it doesn't depend on any particular version of Linux.

✦ **Network+** is a popular vendor-neutral networking certification. It covers four major topic areas: Media and Topologies, Protocols and Standards, Network Implementation, and Network Support.

✦ **Server+** covers network server hardware. It includes details such as installing and upgrading server hardware, installing and configuring an NOS, and so on.

✦ **Security+** is for security specialists. The exam topics include general security concepts, communication security, infrastructure security, basics of cryptography, and operational/organizational security.

Microsoft

www.microsoft.com/learning/mcp

✦ **MTA** (Microsoft Technology Associate) is a general certification in either IT Infrastructure, Database, or Developer technology.

✦ **MCSE** (Microsoft Certified Solutions Expert) is a prestigious certification for networking professionals who design and implement networks. To gain this certification, you have to pass several rigorous exams. Microsoft offers separate Windows Server 2008 and Windows Server 2012 certification tracks.

✦ **MCSA** (Microsoft Certified Solutions Associate) is for networking professionals who administer existing networks.

Cisco

www.cisco.com/web/learning/certifications

✦ **CCENT** (Cisco Certified Entry Network Technician) is an entry-level certification. A CCENT should be able to install, configure, and operate Cisco equipment for branch-level networks.

✦ **CCNA** (Cisco Certified Network Associate) is an entry-level apprentice certification. A CCNA should be able to install, configure, and operate Cisco equipment for small networks (under 100 nodes).

✦ **CCNP** (Cisco Certified Network Professional) is a professional-level certification for Cisco equipment. A CCNP should be able to install, configure, and troubleshoot Cisco networks of virtually any size.

✦ **CCDP** (Cisco Certified Design Professional) is for network design professionals. Both the CCDA and CCNA certifications are prerequisites for the CCDP.

✦ **CCIE** (Cisco Certified Internetwork Expert) is an expert-level certification, which can be had in several varieties, including routing, security, wireless, and service provider.

✦ **CCAr:** (Cisco Certified Architect) is the top dog of Cisco certifications.

✦ **CCT** (Cisco Certified Technician) is a certification for those who can diagnose and repair Cisco equipment.

✦ **And much more!** There are many more Cisco certifications to choose from, including certification for security, voice technology, wireless networking, and more.

**Book II
Chapter 1**

Help Wanted:
Job Description
for a Network
Administrator

Gurus Need Gurus, Too

No matter how much you know about computers, plenty of people know more than you do. This rule seems to apply at every rung of the ladder of computer experience. I'm sure that a top rung exists somewhere, occupied by the world's best computer guru. However, I'm not sitting on that rung, and neither are you. (Not even Bill Gates is sitting on that rung. In fact, Bill Gates got to where he is today by hiring people on higher rungs.)

As the local computer guru, one of your most valuable assets can be a knowledgeable friend who's a notch or two above you on the geek scale. That way, when you run into a real stumper, you have a friend to call for advice. Here are some tips for handling your own guru:

✦ In dealing with your own guru, don't forget the Computer Geek's Golden Rule: "Do unto your guru as you would have your own users do unto you." Don't pester your guru with simple stuff that you just haven't spent the time to think through. If you have thought it through and can't come up with a solution, however, give your guru a call. Most computer experts welcome the opportunity to tackle an unusual computer problem. It's a genetic defect.

✦ If you don't already know someone who knows more about computers than you do, consider joining your local PC users' group. The group may even have a subgroup that specializes in your networking software or may be devoted entirely to local folks who use the same networking software that you use. Odds are good that you're sure to make a friend or two at a users' group meeting. Also, you can probably convince your boss to pay any fees required to join the group.

✦ If you can't find a real-life guru, try to find an online guru. Check out the various computing newsgroups on the Internet. Subscribe to online newsletters that are automatically delivered to you via email.

Helpful Bluffs and Excuses

As network administrator, you just won't be able to solve a problem sometimes, at least not immediately. You can do two things in this situation. The first is to explain that the problem is particularly difficult and that you'll have a solution as soon as possible. The second solution is to look the user in the eyes and, with a straight face, try one of these phony explanations:

✦ Blame it on the version of whatever software you're using. "Oh, they fixed that with version 39."

✦ Blame it on cheap, imported memory chips.

✦ Blame it on Democrats. Or Republicans. Doesn't matter.

✦ Blame it on oil company executives.

✦ Blame it on global warming.

✦ Hope that the problem wasn't caused by stray static electricity. Those types of problems are very difficult to track down. Tell your users that not properly discharging themselves before using their computers can cause all kinds of problems.

✦ You need more memory.

✦ You need a bigger hard drive.

✦ You need a faster processor.

✦ Blame it on Jar-Jar Binks.

✦ You can't do that in Windows 10.

✦ You can only do that in Windows 10.

✦ Could be a virus.

✦ Or sunspots.

✦ No beer and no TV make Homer something something something. . . .

Book II
Chapter 1

Help Wanted:
Job Description
for a Network
Administrator

Chapter 2: Security 101

In This Chapter

✔ Assessing the risk for security

✔ Determining your basic security philosophy

✔ Physically securing your network equipment

✔ Figuring out user account security

✔ Using other network security techniques

If you're not on a network, computer security is easy. You simply lock your door when you leave work for the day and rest easy, secure in the knowledge that the bad guys have to break down the door to get to your computer.

A network changes all that. Now, anyone with access to any computer on the network can break into the network and steal *your* files. Not only do you have to lock your door, but you also have to make sure that other people lock their doors, too.

Fortunately, network operating systems (NOSs) have built-in provisions for network security, making it difficult for people to steal your files, even if they do break down the door. All modern NOSs have security features that are more than adequate for all but the most paranoid users.

And when I say *more* than adequate, I mean it. Most networks have security features that would make even Maxwell Smart happy. Using all these security features is kind of like Smart insisting that the Chief lower the "Cone of Silence" (which worked so well that Max and the Chief couldn't hear each other!).

Don't make your system so secure that even the good guys can't get their work done.

If any computer on your network is connected to the Internet, you have to contend with a whole new world of security issues. For more information about Internet security, see Chapter 4 of this minibook. Also, if your network supports wireless devices, you have to contend with wireless security issues.

Do You Need Security?

Most small networks are in small businesses or departments where every-one knows and trusts everyone else. Folks don't lock up their desks when they take a coffee break, and although everyone knows where the petty cash box is, money never disappears.

Network security isn't necessary in an idyllic setting like this one — or is it? You bet it is. Here's why any network should be set up with at least some minimal concern for security:

✦ **Mitts off:** Even in the friendliest office environment, some information is and should be confidential. If this information is stored on the network, you want to store it in a directory that's available only to authorized users.

✦ **Hmm:** Not all security breaches are malicious. A network user may be routinely scanning files and come across a filename that isn't familiar. The user may then call up the file, only to discover that it contains confiden-tial personnel information, juicy office gossip, or your résumé. Curiosity, rather than malice, is often the source of security breaches.

✦ **Trust:** Sure, everyone at the office is trustworthy now. However, what if someone becomes disgruntled, a screw pops loose, and he decides to trash the network files before jumping out the window? Or what if some-one decides to print a few $1,000 checks before packing off to Tahiti?

✦ **Temptation:** Sometimes the mere opportunity for fraud or theft can be too much for some people to resist. Give people free access to the payroll files, and they may decide to vote themselves a raise when no one is looking.

If you think that your network contains no data worth stealing, think again. For example, your personnel records probably contain more than enough information for an identity thief: names, addresses, phone num-bers, Social Security numbers, and so on. Also, your customer files may contain your customers' credit card numbers.

✦ **Malice:** Hackers who break into your network may not be interested in stealing your data. Instead, they may be looking to plant a *Trojan horse* program on your server, which enables them to use your server for their own purposes. For example, someone may use your server to send thou-sands of unsolicited spam email messages. The spam won't be traced back to the hackers; it will be traced back to you.

✦ **Whoops:** Finally, bear in mind that not everyone on the network knows enough about how your operating system and the network work to be trusted with full access to your network's data and systems. One careless mouse click can wipe out an entire directory of network files. One of the best reasons for activating your network's security features is to protect the network from mistakes made by users who don't know what they're doing.

Considering Two Approaches to Security

When you're planning how to implement security on your network, you should first consider which of two basic approaches to security you will take:

+ **Open-door:** You grant everyone access to everything by default and then place restrictions just on those resources to which you want to limit access.

+ **Closed-door:** You begin by denying access to everything and then grant specific users access to the specific resources that they need.

In most cases, an open-door policy is easier to implement. Typically, only a small portion of the data on a network really needs security, such as confidential employee records or secrets such as the Coke recipe. The rest of the information on a network can be safely made available to everyone who can access the network.

A closed-door approach results in tighter security, but can lead to the Cone of Silence Syndrome: Like Max and the Chief who can't hear each other talk while they're under the Cone of Silence, your network users will constantly complain that they can't access the information that they need. As a result, you'll find yourself frequently adjusting users' access rights. Choose the closed-door approach only if your network contains a lot of very sensitive information — and only if you're willing to invest time administrating your network's security policy.

Think of an open-door approach as an *entitlement model,* in which the basic assumption is that users are entitled to network access. In contrast, a closed-door policy is a *permissions model,* in which the basic assumption is that users aren't entitled to anything but must get permission for every network resource that they access.

Physical Security: Locking Your Doors

The first level of security in any computer network is physical security. I'm amazed when I walk into the reception area of an accounting firm and see an unattended computer sitting on the receptionist's desk. As often as not, the receptionist has logged on to the system and then walked away from the desk, leaving the computer unattended.

Physical security is important for workstations but vital for servers. Any hacker worth his salt can quickly defeat all but the most paranoid security measures if he or she can gain physical access to a server. To protect the server, follow these guidelines:

✦ Lock the computer room.

✦ Give the keys only to people you trust.

✦ Keep track of who has the keys.

✦ Mount the servers on cases or racks with locks.

✦ Disable the floppy drive on the server. (A common hacking technique is to boot the server from a floppy, thus bypassing the carefully crafted security features of the network operating system.)

✦ Keep a trained guard dog in the computer room and feed it only enough to keep it hungry and mad. (Just kidding.)

There's a big difference between a locked door and a door with a lock. Locks are worthless if you don't use them.

Client computers should be physically secure as well. Instruct users to not leave their computers unattended while they're logged on. In high-traffic areas (such as the receptionist's desk), users should secure their computers with the keylock. Additionally, users should lock their office doors when they leave.

Here are some other potential threats to physical security that you may not have considered:

✦ **Off-hours personnel:** The nightly cleaning crew probably has complete access to your facility. How do you know that the person who vacuums your office every night doesn't really work for your chief competitor or doesn't consider computer hacking to be a sideline hobby? You don't, so you'd better consider the cleaning crew a threat.

✦ **Dumpster diving:** What about your trash? Paper shredders aren't just for Enron accountants. Your trash can contain all sorts of useful information: sales reports, security logs, printed copies of the company's security policy, even handwritten passwords. For the best security, every piece of paper that leaves your building via the trash bin should first go through a shredder.

✦ **Backups:** Where do you store your backup tapes? Don't just stack them up next to the server. Not only does that make them easy to steal, it also defeats one of the main purposes of backing up your data in the first place: securing your server from physical threats, such as fires. If a fire burns down your computer room and the backup tapes are sitting unprotected next to the server, your company may go out of business — and you'll certainly be out of a job. Store the backup tapes securely in a fire-resistant safe and keep a copy off-site, too.

✦ **Hubs and servers:** I've seen some networks in which the servers are in a locked computer room, but the hubs or switches are in an unsecured closet. Remember that every unused port on a hub or a switch represents an open door to your network. The hubs and switches should be secured just like the servers.

Securing User Accounts

Next to physical security, the careful use of user accounts is the most important type of security for your network. Properly configured user accounts can prevent unauthorized users from accessing the network, even if they gain physical access to the network. The following sections describe some of the steps that you can take to strengthen your network's use of user accounts.

Obfuscating your usernames

Huh? When it comes to security, *obfuscation* simply means picking obscure usernames. For example, most network administrators assign usernames based on some combination of the user's first and last names, such as BarnyM or baMiller. However, a hacker can easily guess such a user ID if she knows the name of at least one employee. After the hacker knows a username, she can focus on breaking the password.

You can slow down a hacker by using more obscure names — and here's how:

✦ Add a random three-digit number to the end of the name. For example: BarnyM320 or baMiller977.

✦ Throw a number or two into the middle of the name. For example: Bar6nyM or ba9Miller2.

✦ Make sure that usernames are different from email addresses. For example, if a user's email address is `baMiller@Mydomain.com`, do *not* use baMiller as the user's account name. Use a more obscure name.

Do *not* rely on obfuscation to keep people out of your network! Security by obfuscation doesn't work. A resourceful hacker can discover even the most obscure names. The purpose of obfuscation is to slow down intruders — not to stop them. If you slow down an intruder, you're more likely to discover that she is trying to crack your network before she successfully gets in.

Using passwords wisely

One of the most important aspects of network security is using passwords. Usernames aren't usually considered secret. And even if you use obscure names, casual hackers will eventually figure them out.

Passwords, on the other hand, are indeed top secret. Your network password is the one thing that keeps an impostor from logging on to the network by using your username and therefore receiving the same access rights that you ordinarily have. *Guard your password with your life.*

Here are some tips for creating good passwords:

✦ Don't use obvious passwords, such as your last name, your kid's name, or your dog's name.

✦ Don't pick passwords based on your hobbies, either. A friend of mine is into boating, and his password is the name of his boat. Anyone who knows him can guess his password after a few tries. Five lashes for naming your password after your boat.

✦ Store your password in your head, not on paper. Especially bad: Writing down your password on a sticky note and sticking it on your computer's monitor. Ten lashes for that. (If you must write down your password, write it on digestible paper that you can swallow after you memorize the password.)

✦ Most NOSs enable you to set an expiration time for passwords. For example, you can specify that passwords expire after 30 days. When a user's password expires, the user must change it. Your users may consider this process a hassle, but it helps to limit the risk of someone swiping a password and then trying to break into your computer system later.

✦ You can also configure user accounts so that when they change passwords, they can't specify a password that they've used recently. For example, you can specify that the new password can't be identical to any of the user's past three passwords.

✦ You can also configure security policies so that passwords must include a mixture of uppercase letters, lowercase letters, numerals, and special symbols. Thus, passwords like DIMWIT or DUFUS are out. Passwords like 87dIM@wit or duF39&US are in.

✦ Use a biometric ID device, like a fingerprint reader, as a way to keep passwords. These devices store your passwords in a secret encoded file, then supply them automatically to whatever programs or websites require them — but only after the device has read your fingerprint. Fingerprint readers, which used to be exotic and expensive, are available for as little as $50.

A password-generator For Dummies

How do you come up with passwords that no one can guess but that you can remember? Most security experts say that the best passwords don't correspond to any words in the English language, but consist of a random sequence of letters, numbers, and special characters. Yet, how in the heck are you supposed to memorize a password like `Dks4%DJ2`, especially when you have to change it three weeks later to something like `3pQ&X(d8`?

Here's a compromise solution that enables you to create passwords that consist of two four-letter words back to back. Take your favorite book (if it's this one, you need to get a life) and turn to any page at random. Find the first four- or five-letter word on the page. Suppose that word is `When`. Then repeat the process to find another four- or five-letter word; say you pick the word `Most` the second time. Now combine the words to make your password: `WhenMost`. I think you agree that `WhenMost` is easier to remember than `3PQ&X(D8` and is probably just about as hard to guess. I probably wouldn't want the folks at the Los Alamos Nuclear Laboratory using this scheme, but it's good enough for most of us.

Book II
Chapter 2

Security 101

Here are some additional thoughts on concocting passwords from your favorite book:

✦ If the words end up being the same, pick another word. And pick different words if the combination seems too commonplace, such as `WestWind` or `FootBall`.

✦ For an interesting variation, insert the page numbers on which you found both words either before or after the words. For example: `135Into376Cat` or `87Tree288Wing`. The resulting password will be a little harder to remember, but you'll have a password worthy of a Dan Brown novel.

✦ To further confuse your friends and enemies, use archaic language: for example, medieval words from Chaucer's *Canterbury Tales.* Chaucer is a great source for passwords because he lived before the days of word processors with spell-checkers. He wrote *seyd* instead of *said, gret* instead of *great,* and *litel* instead of *little.* And he used lots of seven-letter and eight-letter words suitable for passwords, such as *glotenye* (gluttony), *benygne* (benign), and *opynyoun* (opinion). And he got an A in English.

✦ If you do decide to go with passwords such as `KdI22UR3xdkL`, you can find random password generators on the Internet. Just go to a search engine, such as Google (`www.google.com`), and search for *password generator.* You can find web pages that generate random passwords based on criteria that you specify, such as how long the password should be, whether it should include letters, numbers, punctuation, uppercase and lowercase letters, and so on.

If you use any of these password schemes and someone breaks into your network, don't blame me. You're the one who's too lazy to memorize D#Sc$h4@bb3xaz5.

Securing the Administrator account

At least one network user must have the authority to use the network without any of the restrictions imposed on other users. This user — the *administrator* — is responsible for setting up the network's security system. To do that, the administrator must be exempt from all security restrictions.

Many networks automatically create an administrator user account when you install the network software. The username and password for this initial administrator are published in the network's documentation and are the same for all networks that use the same NOS. One of the first things that you must do after getting your network up and running is to change the password for this standard administrator account. Otherwise, your elaborate security precautions will be a complete waste of time. Anyone who knows the default administrator username and password can access your system with full administrator rights and privileges, thus bypassing the security restrictions that you so carefully set up.

Don't forget the password for the administrator account! If a network user forgets his password, you can log on as the supervisor and change that user's password. If you forget the administrator's password, though, you're stuck.

Hardening Your Network

In addition to taking care of physical security and user account security, you should also take steps to protect your network from intruders by configuring the other security features of the network's servers and routers. The following sections describe the basics of hardening your network.

Using a firewall

A *firewall* is a security-conscious router that sits between your network and the outside world and prevents Internet users from wandering into your local area network (LAN) and messing around. Firewalls are the first line of defense for any network that's connected to the Internet.

You should *never* connect a network to the Internet without installing a carefully configured firewall. For more information about firewalls, read Chapter 4 of this minibook.

Disabling unnecessary services

A typical NOS can support dozens of different types of network services: file and printer sharing, web server, mail server, and many others. In many cases, these features are installed on servers that don't need or use them. When a server runs a network service that it doesn't really need, the service not only robs CPU cycles from other services that are needed, but also poses an unnecessary security threat.

When you first install an NOS on a server, you should enable only those network services that you know the server will require. You can always enable services later if the needs of the server change.

Patching your servers

Hackers regularly find security holes in network operating systems. After those holes are discovered, the OS vendors figure out how to plug the hole and then release a software patch for the security fix. The trouble is that most network administrators don't stay up to date with these software patches. As a result, many networks are vulnerable because they have well-known holes in their security armor that should have been fixed but weren't.

Even though patches are a bit of a nuisance, they're well worth the effort for the protection that they afford. Fortunately, newer versions of the popular network operating systems have features that automatically check for updates and let you know when a patch should be applied.

Securing Your Users

Security techniques — physical security, user account security, server security, and locking down your servers — are child's play compared with the most difficult job of network security: securing your network's users. All the best-laid security plans are for naught if your users write down their passwords on sticky notes and post them on their computers.

The key to securing your network users is to create a written network security policy and stick to it. Have a meeting with everyone to go over the security policy to make sure that everyone understands the rules. Also, make sure to have consequences when violations occur.

Here are some suggestions for some basic security rules you can incorporate into your security policy:

✦ Never write down your password or give it to someone else.

✦ Accounts should not be shared. Never use someone else's account to access a resource that you can't access under your own account. If you need access to some network resource that isn't available to you, you should formally request access under your own account.

✦ Likewise, never give your account information to a co-worker so that he or she can access a needed resource. Your co-worker should instead formally request access under his or her own account.

✦ Don't install any software or hardware on your computer — especially wireless access devices or modems — without first obtaining permission.

✦ Don't enable file and printer sharing on workstations without first getting permission.

✦ Never attempt to disable or bypass the network's security features.

Chapter 3: Managing User Accounts

In This Chapter

✔ Understanding user accounts

✔ Looking at the built-in accounts

✔ Using rights and permissions

✔ Working with groups and policies

✔ Running login scripts

*U*ser accounts are the backbone of network security administration. You can determine who can access your network, as well as what network resources each user can and can't access. You can restrict access to the network to just specific computers or to certain hours of the day, and you can lock out users who no longer need to access your network.

The specific details for managing user accounts are unique to each network operating system (NOS) and are covered in separate chapters later in this book. This chapter simply introduces you to the concepts of user account management so you know what you can and can't do, regardless of which NOS you use.

Exploring What User Accounts Consist Of

User accounts allow the network administrator to determine who can access the network and what network resources each user can access. Every user who accesses a network must have a user account. In addition, user accounts can be customized to provide many convenience features for users, such as a personalized Start menu or a display of recently used documents.

Every user account is associated with a username (sometimes called a *user ID*), which the user must enter when logging on to the network. Each account also has other information associated with it:

✦ **The user's password:** This also includes the password policy, such as how often the user has to change his or her password, how complicated the password must be, and so on.

+ **The user's contact information:** This includes full name, phone number, email address, mailing address, and other related information.

+ **Account restrictions:** This includes restrictions that allow the user to log on only during certain times of the day. This feature enables you to restrict your users to normal working hours so that they can't sneak in at 2 a.m. to do unauthorized work. This feature also discourages your users from working overtime because they can't access the network after hours, so use it judiciously. You can also specify that the user can log on only at certain computers.

+ **Account status:** You can temporarily disable a user account so that the user can't log on.

+ **Home directory:** This specifies a shared network folder where the user can store documents.

+ **Dial-in permissions:** These authorize the user to access the network remotely.

+ **Group memberships:** These grant the user certain rights based on groups to which they belong. For more information, see the section, "Assigning Permissions to Groups," later in this chapter.

Looking at Built-In Accounts

Most NOSs come preconfigured with two built-in accounts: Administrator and Guest. In addition, some server services, such as web or database servers, create their own user accounts under which to run. The following sections describe the characteristics of these accounts.

The Administrator account

The Administrator account is the King of the Network. This user account isn't subject to any of the account restrictions to which other, mere mortal accounts must succumb. If you log on as the administrator, you can do anything.

Because the Administrator account has unlimited access to your network, you should secure it *immediately* after you install the server. When the NOS Setup program asks for a password for the Administrator account, start off with a good random mix of uppercase and lowercase letters, numbers, and symbols. Don't pick some easy-to-remember password to get started, thinking you'll change it to something more cryptic later. You'll forget, and in the meantime, someone will break in and reformat the server's C: drive or steal your customers' credit card numbers.

Here are a few additional things worth knowing about the Administrator account:

✦ You can't delete it. The system must always have an administrator.

✦ You can grant administrator status to other user accounts. However, you should do so only for users who really need to be administrators.

✦ You should use it only when you really need to do tasks that require administrative authority. Many network administrators grant administrative authority to their own user accounts. That isn't a very good idea. If you're killing some time surfing the web or reading your email while logged on as an administrator, you're just inviting viruses or malicious scripts to take advantage of your administrator access. Instead, you should set yourself up with two accounts: a normal account that you use for day-to-day work, and an Administrator account that you use only when you need it.

Book II
Chapter 3

Managing User
Accounts

✦ The default name for the Administrator account is usually simply Administrator. You may want to consider changing this name. Better yet, change the name of the Administrator account to something more obscure and then create an ordinary user account that has few (if any) rights and give that account the name Administrator. That way, hackers who spend weeks trying to crack your Administrator account password will discover that they've been duped after they finally break the password. In the meantime, you'll have a chance to discover their attempts to breach your security and take appropriate action.

✦ Above all, don't forget the Administrator account password. Write it down in permanent ink and store it in Fort Knox, a safe deposit box, or some other secure location.

The Guest account

Another commonly created default account is the Guest account, which is set up with a blank password and few (if any) access rights. A Guest account is designed to allow people to step up to a computer and log on, but after they do, it then prevents them from doing anything. Sounds like a waste of time to me. I suggest disabling the Guest account.

Service accounts

Some network users aren't actual people. I don't mean that some of your users are subhuman. Rather, some users are actually software processors that require access to secure resources and therefore require user accounts. These user accounts are usually created automatically for you when you install or configure server software.

For example, when you install the Microsoft web server (IIS), an Internet user account called IUSR is created. The complete name for this account is `IUSR_<servername>`. So if the server is named WEB1, the account is named `IUSR_WEB1`. IIS uses this account to allow anonymous Internet users to access the files of your website.

As a general rule, don't mess with these accounts unless you know what you're doing. For example, if you delete or rename the IUSR account, you must reconfigure IIS to use the changed account. If you don't, IIS will deny access to anyone trying to reach your site. (Assuming that you *do* know what you're doing, renaming these accounts can increase your network's security. However, don't start playing with these accounts until you research the ramifications.)

Assigning User Rights

User accounts and passwords are only the front line of defense in the game of network security. After a user gains access to the network by typing a valid user ID and password, the second line of security defense — rights — comes into play.

In the harsh realities of network life, all users are created equal, but some users are more equal than others. The Preamble to the Declaration of Network Independence contains the statement, "We hold these truths to be self-evident, that *some* users are endowed by the network administrator with certain inalienable rights. . . ."

Here's a partial list of the user rights that are possible with Windows servers:

✦ **Log on locally.** The user can log on to the server computer directly from the server's keyboard.

✦ **Change system time.** The user can change the time and date registered by the server.

✦ **Shut down the system.** The user can perform an orderly shutdown of the server.

✦ **Back up files and directories.** The user can perform a backup of files and directories on the server.

✦ **Restore files and directories.** The user can restore backed-up files.

✦ **Take ownership of files and other objects.** The user can take over files and other network resources that belong to other users.

Controlling User Access with Permissions (Who Gets What)

User rights control what a user can do on a network-wide basis. *Permissions* enable you to fine-tune your network security by controlling access to specific network resources, such as files or printers, for individual users or groups. For example, you can set up permissions to allow users in the accounting department to access files in the server's \ACCTG directory. Permissions can also enable some users to read certain files but not modify or delete them.

Each NOS manages permissions in a different way. Whatever the details, the effect is that you can give permission to each user to access certain files, folders, or drives in certain ways.

Book II
Chapter 3

Managing User
Accounts

Any permissions that you specify for a folder apply automatically to any of that folder's subfolders, unless you explicitly specify a different set of permissions for the subfolder.

Windows refers to file system rights as *permissions*. Windows servers have six basic permissions, listed in Table 3-1. You can assign any combination of Windows permissions to a user or group for a given file or folder. To assign these permissions, simply right-click the file or folder you want to assign the permissions to, choose Properties, and then open the Permissions tab.

For more information about setting permissions in Windows Server, refer to Chapter 5 of Book VII.

Table 3-1	Windows Basic Permissions	
Permission	*Abbreviation*	*What the User Can Do*
Read	R	Open and read the file
Write	W	Open and write to the file
Execute	X	Run the file
Delete	D	Delete the file
Change	P	Change the permissions for the file
Take Ownership	O	Take ownership of the file

Note the last permission listed in Table 3-1. In Windows, the concept of file or folder ownership is important. Every file or folder on a Windows server system has an owner. The *owner* is usually the user who creates the file or folder. However, ownership can be transferred from one user to another. So why the Take Ownership permission? This permission prevents someone from creating a bogus file and giving ownership of it to you without your permission. Windows doesn't allow you to give ownership of a file to another user. Instead, you can give another user the right to take ownership of the file. That user must then explicitly take ownership of the file.

Assigning Permissions to Groups

A *group account* doesn't represent an individual user. Instead, it represents a group of users who use the network in a similar way. Instead of granting access rights to each user, grant the rights to the group and then assign individual users to the group. When you assign a user to a group, that user inherits the rights specified for the group.

For example, suppose you create an Accounting group and then give those group members access to the network's accounting files and applications. Then, instead of granting each Accounting user access to those files and applications, you simply make each accounting user a member of the Accounting group.

Here are a few additional details about groups:

✦ **Groups are key to network-management nirvana.** As much as possible, avoid managing network users individually. Instead, clump them into groups and manage the groups. When all 50 users in the accounting department need access to a new file share, would you rather update 50 user accounts — or just one group account?

✦ **A user can belong to more than one group.** As I mention earlier, a user in a group inherits the rights of that group — and belonging to more than one group can prove helpful. For example, suppose you have Accounting, Sales, Marketing, and Finance groups. A user who needs to access Accounting and Finance can be made a member of both groups.

✦ **You can grant or revoke specific rights to individual users to override the group settings.** For example, you may want to allow department managers only to modify files in a folder while all other users can read but not modify the files.

Understanding User Profiles

A *user profile* is a Windows feature that keeps track of an individual user's preferences for his Windows configuration. For a non-networked computer, profiles enable two or more users to use the same computer, each with its own desktop settings, such as wallpaper, colors, Start menu options, and so on.

The real benefit of user profiles becomes apparent when profiles are used on a network. A user's profile can be stored on a server computer and accessed whenever that user logs on to the network from any Windows computer on the network.

The following are some of the elements of Windows that are governed by settings in the user profile:

✦ Desktop settings from the Display Properties dialog box, including wallpaper, screen savers, and color schemes

✦ Start menu programs and Windows toolbar options

✦ Favorites, which provide easy access to the files and folders that the user accesses frequently

✦ Network settings, including drive mappings, network printers, and recently visited network locations

✦ Application settings, such as option settings for Microsoft Word

✦ The Documents/My Documents folder (OS-dependent)

Automating Tasks with Logon Scripts

A *logon script* is a batch file that runs automatically whenever a user logs on. Logon scripts can perform several important logon tasks for you, such as mapping network drives, starting applications, synchronizing the client computer's time-of-day clock, and so on. Logon scripts reside on the server, in a special folder named NETLOGON. Each user account can specify whether to use a logon script and which script to use.

Here's a sample logon script that maps a few network drives and synchronizes the time:

```
net use m: \\MYSERVER\Acct
net use n: \\MYSERVER\Admin
net use o: \\MYSERVER\Dev
net time \\MYSERVER /set /yes
```

Logon scripts are a little out of vogue because most of what a logon script does can be done via user profiles. Still, many administrators prefer the simplicity of logon scripts, so they're still used even on modern versions of Windows Server.

Chapter 4: Firewalls and Virus Protection

In This Chapter

✔ Understanding what firewalls do

✔ Examining the different types of firewalls

✔ Looking at virus protection

✔ Discovering Windows security

*I*f your network is connected to the Internet, a whole host of security issues bubble to the surface. You probably connected your network to the Internet so that your network's users could access the Internet. Unfortunately, however, your Internet connection is a two-way street. Not only does it enable your network's users to step outside the bounds of your network to access the Internet, but it also enables others to step in and access your network.

And step in they will. The world is filled with hackers looking for networks like yours to break into. They may do it just for fun, or they may do it to steal your customer's credit card numbers or to coerce your mail server into sending thousands of spam messages on their behalf. Whatever their motive, rest assured that your network will be broken into if you leave it unprotected.

This chapter presents an overview of two basic techniques for securing your network's Internet connection: firewalls and virus protection.

Firewalls

A *firewall* is a security-conscious router that sits between the Internet and your network with a single-minded task: preventing *them* from getting to *us*. The firewall acts as a security guard between the Internet and your local area network (LAN). All network traffic into and out of the LAN must pass through the firewall, which prevents unauthorized access to the network.

Some type of firewall is a must-have if your network has a connection to the Internet, whether that connection is broadband (cable modem or digital subscriber line; DSL), T1, or some other high-speed connection. Without it, sooner or later a hacker will discover your unprotected network and tell his friends about it. Within a few hours, your network will be toast.

You can set up a firewall two basic ways. The easiest way is to purchase a *firewall appliance,* which is basically a self-contained router with built-in firewall features. Most firewall appliances include a web-based interface that enables you to connect to the firewall from any computer on your network using a browser. You can then customize the firewall settings to suit your needs.

Alternatively, you can set up a server computer to function as a firewall computer. The server can run just about any network operating system (NOS), but most dedicated firewall systems run Linux.

Whether you use a firewall appliance or a firewall computer, the firewall must be located between your network and the Internet, as shown in Figure 4-1. Here, one end of the firewall is connected to a network hub, which is in turn connected to the other computers on the network. The other end of the firewall is connected to the Internet. As a result, all traffic from the LAN to the Internet and vice versa must travel through the firewall.

Figure 4-1:
Using a
firewall
appliance.

The term *perimeter* is sometimes used to describe the location of a firewall on your network. In short, a firewall is like a perimeter fence that completely surrounds your property and forces all visitors to enter through the front gate.

The Many Types of Firewalls

Firewalls employ four basic techniques to keep unwelcome visitors out of your network. The following sections describe these basic firewall techniques.

Packet filtering

A *packet-filtering* firewall examines each packet that crosses the firewall and tests the packet according to a set of rules that you set up. If the packet passes the test, it's allowed to pass. If the packet doesn't pass, it's rejected.

Packet filters are the least expensive type of firewall. As a result, packet-filtering firewalls are very common. However, packet filtering has a number of flaws that knowledgeable hackers can exploit. As a result, packet filtering by itself doesn't make for a fully effective firewall.

Packet filters work by inspecting the source and destination IP and port addresses contained in each Transmission Control Protocol/Internet Protocol (TCP/IP) packet. TCP/IP *ports* are numbers assigned to specific services that help to identify for which service each packet is intended. For example, the port number for the HTTP protocol is 80. As a result, any incoming packets headed for an HTTP server will specify port 80 as the destination port.

Port numbers are often specified with a colon following an IP address. For example, the HTTP service on a server whose IP address is 192.168.10.133 would be 192.168.10.133:80.

Literally thousands of established ports are in use. Table 4-1 lists a few of the most popular ports.

The rules that you set up for the packet filter either permit or deny packets that specify certain IP addresses or ports. For example, you may permit packets that are intended for your mail server or your web server and deny all other packets. Or, you may set up a rule that specifically denies packets that are heading for the ports used by NetBIOS. This rule keeps Internet hackers from trying to access NetBIOS server resources, such as files or printers.

One of the biggest weaknesses of packet filtering is that it pretty much trusts that the packets themselves are telling the truth when they say who they're from and who they're going to. Hackers exploit this weakness by using a hacking technique called *IP spoofing,* in which they insert fake IP addresses in packets that they send to your network.

Another weakness of packet filtering is that it examines each packet in isolation without considering what packets have gone through the firewall before and what packets may follow. In other words, packet filtering is *stateless.* Rest assured that hackers have figured out how to exploit the stateless nature of packet filtering to get through firewalls.

Book II
Chapter 4

Firewalls and
Virus Protection

Table 4-1	Some Well-Known TCP/IP Ports
Port	*Description*
20	File Transfer Protocol (FTP)
21	File Transfer Protocol (FTP)
22	Secure Shell Protocol (SSH)
23	Telnet
25	Simple Mail Transfer Protocol (SMTP)
53	Domain Name Server (DNS)
80	World Wide Web (HyperText Transport Protocol; HTTP)
110	Post Office Protocol (POP3)
119	Network News Transfer Protocol (NNTP)
137	NetBIOS Name Service
138	NetBIOS Datagram Service
139	NetBIOS Session Service
143	Internet Message Access Protocol (IMAP)
161	Simple Network Management Protocol (SNMP)
194	Internet Relay Chat (IRC)
389	Lightweight Directory Access Protocol (LDAP)
396	NetWare over IP
443	HTTP over TLS/SSL (HTTPS)

In spite of these weaknesses, packet filter firewalls have several advantages that explain why they are commonly used:

✦ **Efficient:** They hold up each inbound and outbound packet for only a few milliseconds while they look inside the packet to determine the destination and source ports and addresses. After these addresses and ports are determined, the packet filter quickly applies its rules and either sends the packet along or rejects it. In contrast, other firewall techniques have a more noticeable performance overhead.

✦ **Almost completely transparent to users:** The only time a user will be aware that a packet filter firewall is being used is when the firewall rejects packets. Other firewall techniques require that clients and/or servers be specially configured to work with the firewall.

✦ **Inexpensive:** Even consumer-grade routers include built-in packet filtering.

Stateful packet inspection (SPI)

Stateful packet inspection (SPI) is a step up in intelligence from simple packet filtering. A firewall with stateful packet inspection looks at packets in groups rather than individually. It keeps track of which packets have passed through the firewall and can detect patterns that indicate unauthorized access. In some cases, the firewall may hold on to packets as they arrive until the firewall gathers enough information to make a decision about whether the packets should be authorized or rejected.

Stateful packet inspection was once found only on expensive, enterprise-level routers. Now, however, SPI firewalls are affordable enough for small- or medium-sized networks to use.

Circuit-level gateway

A *circuit-level gateway* manages connections between clients and servers based on TCP/IP addresses and port numbers. After the connection is established, the gateway doesn't interfere with packets flowing between the systems.

For example, you could use a Telnet circuit-level gateway to allow Telnet connections (port 23) to a particular server and prohibit other types of connections to that server. After the connection is established, the circuit-level gateway allows packets to flow freely over the connection. As a result, the circuit-level gateway can't prevent a Telnet user from running specific programs or using specific commands.

Application gateway

An *application gateway* is a firewall system that is more intelligent than a packet-filtering firewall, stateful packet inspection, or circuit-level gateway firewall. Packet filters treat all TCP/IP packets the same. In contrast, application gateways know the details about the applications that generate the packets that pass through the firewall. For example, a web application gateway is aware of the details of HTTP packets. As a result, it can examine more than just the source and destination addresses and ports to determine whether the packets should be allowed to pass through the firewall.

In addition, application gateways work as proxy servers. Simply put, a *proxy server* is a server that sits between a client computer and a real server. The proxy server intercepts packets that are intended for the real server and processes them. The proxy server can examine the packet and decide to pass it on to the real server, or it can reject the packet. Or, the proxy server may be able to respond to the packet itself without involving the real server at all.

For example, web proxies often store copies of commonly used web pages in a local cache. When a user requests a web page from a remote web server, the proxy server intercepts the request and checks whether it already has a copy of the page in its cache. If so, the web proxy returns the page directly to the user. If not, the proxy passes the request on to the real server.

Application gateways are aware of the details of how various types of TCP/IP servers handle sequences of TCP/IP packets to can make more intelligent decisions about whether an incoming packet is legitimate or is part of an attack. As a result, application gateways are more secure than simple packet-filtering firewalls, which can deal with only one packet at a time.

The improved security of application gateways, however, comes at a price. Application gateways are more expensive than packet filters, both in terms of their purchase price and in the cost of configuring and maintaining them. In addition, application gateways slow network performance because they do more detailed checking of packets before allowing them to pass.

The Built-In Windows Firewall

Windows comes with a built-in packet-filtering firewall. If you don't have a separate firewall router, you can use this built-in firewall to provide a basic level of protection. Note, however, that you should rely on the Windows firewall only as a last resort. If at all possible, use a separate firewall rather than the Windows firewall to protect your network.

Here are the steps to activate the firewall in Windows:

1. **Choose Start ⇨ Control Panel.**

2. **In the Control Panel, click System and Security.**

3. **On the System and Security page, click Windows Firewall.**

4. **On the Windows Firewall page, click Turn Windows Firewall On or Off.**

The page shown in Figure 4-2 appears.

5. **Select the Turn On Windows Firewall radio button.**

Note that there are two such buttons: one for home and work (private) networks and one for public networks. If you have a separate router for your work or home network, you can leave the home and work (private) network firewall turned off. But always turn on the firewall for public networks.

6. **Click OK.**

The firewall is enabled.

Figure 4-2:
Activating
the firewall.

Do *not* enable Windows Firewall if you're using a separate firewall router to protect your network. Because the other computers on the network are connected directly to the router and not to your computer, Windows Firewall won't protect the rest of the network. Additionally, as an unwanted side effect, the rest of the network will lose the ability to access your computer.

Windows Firewall is turned on by default. If your computer is already behind a firewall, you should disable Windows Firewall. (In some cases, the network's group policy settings may prevent you from disabling Windows Firewall. In that case, you must change the group policy so that Windows Firewall can be disabled. For more information about group policy, see Book VII, Chapter 6.)

Virus Protection

Viruses are one of the most misunderstood computer phenomena around these days. What is a virus? How does it work? How does it spread from computer to computer? I'm glad you asked.

What is a virus?

Make no mistake — viruses are real. Now that most people are connected to the Internet, viruses have really taken off. Every computer user is susceptible to attacks by computer viruses, and using a network increases your vulnerability because it exposes all network users to the risk of being infected by a virus that lands on any one network user's computer.

Viruses don't just spontaneously appear out of nowhere. Viruses are computer programs that are created by malicious programmers who've lost a few screws and should be locked up.

What makes a virus a virus is its capability to make copies of itself that can be spread to other computers. These copies, in turn, make still more copies that spread to still more computers, and so on, ad nauseam.

Then, the virus patiently waits until something triggers it — perhaps when you type a particular command or press a certain key, when a certain date arrives, or when the virus creator sends the virus a message. What the virus does when it strikes also depends on what the virus creator wants the virus to do. Some viruses harmlessly display a "gotcha" message. Some send an email to everyone it finds in your address book. Some wipe out all the data on your hard drive. Ouch.

Many years ago, in the prehistoric days of computers, viruses were passed from one computer to another by latching themselves onto floppy disks. Whenever you borrowed a floppy disk from a buddy, you ran the risk of infecting your own computer with a virus that may have stowed away on the disk.

Virus programmers have discovered that email is a very efficient method to spread their viruses. Typically, a virus masquerades as a useful or interesting email attachment, such as instructions on how to make $1,000,000 in your spare time, pictures of naked celebrities, or a Valentine's Day greeting from your long-lost sweetheart. When a curious but unsuspecting user opens the attachment, the virus springs to life, copying itself onto the user's computer — sometimes sending copies of itself to all the names in the user's address book.

After the virus works its way onto a networked computer, the virus can then figure out how to spread itself to other computers on the network. It can also spread itself by burrowing into a flash drive so that when the flash drive is inserted into another computer, that computer may become infected as well.

Here are some more tidbits about protecting your network from virus attacks:

✦ The term *virus* is often used to refer not only to true virus programs (which are able to replicate themselves) but also to any other type of program that's designed to harm your computer. These programs include so-called *Trojan horse* programs that usually look like games but are, in reality, hard drive formatters.

✦ A *worm* is similar to a virus, but it doesn't actually infect other files. Instead, it just copies itself onto other computers on a network. After a worm has copied itself onto your computer, there's no telling what it may do there. For example, a worm may scan your hard drive for interesting information, such as passwords or credit card numbers, and then email them to the worm's author.

✦ Computer virus experts have identified several thousand "strains" of viruses. Many of them have colorful names, such as the I Love You virus, the Stoned virus, and the Michelangelo virus.

✦ Antivirus programs can recognize known viruses and remove them from your system, and they can spot the telltale signs of unknown viruses. Unfortunately, the idiots who write viruses aren't idiots (in the intellectual sense), so they're constantly developing new techniques to evade detection by antivirus programs. New viruses are frequently discovered, and antivirus programs are periodically updated to detect and remove them.

Antivirus programs

The best way to protect your network from virus infection is to use an antivirus program. These programs have a catalog of several thousand known viruses that they can detect and remove. In addition, they can spot the types of changes that viruses typically make to your computer's files, thus decreasing the likelihood that some previously unknown virus will go undetected.

It would be nice if Windows came with built-in antivirus software, but alas — it does not. Free options are available, such as Microsoft Security Essentials, but you're better off purchasing a high-quality antivirus program on your own. The two best-known antivirus programs for Windows are Symantec Security by Symantec and VirusScan Enterprise by McAfee.

The people who make antivirus programs have their fingers on the pulse of the virus world and frequently release updates to their software to combat the latest viruses. Because virus writers are constantly developing new viruses, your antivirus software is next to worthless unless you keep it up to date by downloading the latest updates.

Here are several approaches to deploying antivirus protection on your network:

✦ **Install antivirus software on each network user's computer.** This technique would be the most effective if you could count on all your users to keep their antivirus software up to date. Because that's an unlikely proposition, you may want to adopt a more reliable approach to virus protection.

✦ **Managed antivirus services place antivirus client software on each client computer in your network.** Then, an antivirus server automatically updates the clients on a regular basis to make sure that they're kept up to date.

✦ **Server-based antivirus software protects your network servers from viruses.** For example, you can install antivirus software on your mail server to scan all incoming mail for viruses and remove them before your network users ever see them.

✦ **Some firewall appliances include antivirus enforcement checks that don't allow your users to access the Internet unless their antivirus software is up to date.** This type of firewall provides the best antivirus protection available.

Safe computing

Besides using an antivirus program, you can take a few additional precautions to ensure virus-free computing. If you haven't talked to your kids about these safe-computing practices, you had better do so soon.

✦ **Regularly back up your data.** If a virus hits you, and your antivirus software can't repair the damage, you may need the backup to recover your data. Make sure that you restore from a backup that was created before you were infected by the virus!

✦ **If you buy software from a store and discover that the seal has been broken on the disc package, take the software back.** Don't try to install it on your computer. You don't hear about tainted software as often as you hear about tainted beef, but if you buy software that's been opened, it may well be laced with a virus infection.

✦ **Use your antivirus software to scan your disk for virus infection after your computer has been to a repair shop or worked on by a consultant.** These guys don't intend harm, but they occasionally spread viruses accidentally, simply because they work on so many strange computers.

✦ **Don't open email attachments from people you don't know or attachments you weren't expecting.**

✦ **Use your antivirus software to scan any floppy disk or CD that doesn't belong to you before you access any of its files.**

Using Windows Action Center

Windows Action Center, which comes with Windows, monitors the status of security-related issues on your computer. You can summon the Windows Action Center by opening the Control Panel, clicking System and Security, and then clicking Action Center; see Figure 4-3.

Figure 4-3: The Windows Action Center.

The Windows Action Center alerts you to issues with your computer's security status as well as reminds you of maintenance that should be done, such as installing operating system updates.

Here are additional points to ponder concerning the Windows Action Center:

✦ A flag icon (shown in the margin) appears in the notification area on the right end of the Windows taskbar to alert you to items you should attend to in the Windows Action Center.

✦ Earlier versions of Windows included a similar feature called the Windows Security Center, which you can access from the Control Panel.

Chapter 5: Blocking Spam

In This Chapter

✔ **Understanding what spam is**

✔ **Seeing how antispam filters can block spam**

✔ **Options for setting up an antispam solution**

✔ **Dealing with the spam that still gets through**

Spam, spam, spam, spam, spam, spam, and spam.

So goes the famous Monty Python sketch, in which a woman at a restaurant just wants to order something that doesn't have spam in it.

That pretty much sums up the situations with most people's inboxes these days. The legitimate email gets lost among the spam emails. Wouldn't you like to look at an inbox that wasn't filled with spam?

Nobody likes spam. You don't like it, and your users don't like it either. And believe me, they'll let you know if they're getting too much spam in their inboxes. They'll hold you personally responsible for every email with an offensive subject line, every email that tries to sell them stuff they aren't interested in, and every email that attempts to get them to provide their bank account password or credit card number.

As a network administrator, part of your job is protecting your users from spam. The holy grail of antispam is a solution that never allows a single piece of spam into anyone's inbox, but at the same time never mistakenly identifies a single legitimate piece of email as spam.

Good luck. This level of perfection doesn't exist. The best thing you can hope for is to find the right balance: a happy medium that lets only a small amount of actual spam through to users' inboxes and only occasionally misidentifies legitimate email as spam.

In this chapter, I explain what you need to know to find and deploy such a solution. I fill you in on the various kinds of spam, where spam comes from, how spammers get people's email addresses, and — most important — the many effective techniques you can employ to keep spam out of your users' inboxes.

Defining Spam

The most basic definition of *spam* is any email that arrives in your inbox that you didn't ask for. Spam is unsolicited email. It's email that isn't welcome, email that you aren't expecting. It's email from people you don't know or haven't heard of, usually trying to sell you something you aren't interested in or couldn't possibly need, and often trying to trick you into parting with either your money or your valuable personal information, or both.

One of the defining characteristics of spam is that it's sent out in bulk, often to thousands or even millions of recipients all at once. Most spam is not particularly well targeted. Instead of taking the time to figure out who might be interested in a particular product, spammers find it easier and cheaper to pitch their products to every email address they can get their hands on.

Spam is often compared to junk mail of the physical kind — the brochures, catalogs, and other solicitations that show up in your mailbox every day. In fact, spam is often called "junk email."

However, there is a crucial difference between physical junk mail and junk email. With physical junk mail, the sender must pay the cost of postage. As a result, even though junk mail can be annoying, most junk mail is carefully targeted. Junk mailers don't want to waste their money on postage to send mail to people who aren't interested in what they have to sell. They carefully measure response rates to ensure that their mailings are profitable.

In contrast, it costs very little money to send huge numbers of emails. To be sure, spam is expensive. But the bulk of the cost of spam is borne by the recipients, who must spend time and money to receive, store, and manage the unwelcome email, and by the network providers, who must build out their networks with ever greater capacity and speed to accommodate the huge volumes of spam emails that their networks must carry.

Estimates vary, but most studies indicate that as much as three-quarters of all the email sent via the Internet is spam. At the time that I wrote this, there were indications that spam was actually becoming less common, accounting for closer to half of all the emails sent. But some organizations report that 80 percent or 90 percent of the email that they receive is actually spam.

One thing is sure: Spam is not just annoying; it's dangerous. Besides filling up your users' inboxes with unwanted email, spam emails often carry attachments that harbor viruses or other malware, or entice your users into clicking links that take them to websites that can infect your network. If your network is ever taken down by a virus, there's a very good chance that the virus entered your network by way of spam.

So, understanding spam and taking precautions to block it are an important part of any network administrator's job.

Sampling the Many Flavors of Spam

Spam is unsolicited and/or unwanted email. That's a pretty broad definition, but there are several distinct categories of spam:

✦ **Advertisements:** Most spam is advertising from companies you've never heard of, trying to sell you products you aren't interested in. The most common type of product pitched by spam emails are pharmaceuticals, but spam also commonly promotes food supplements, knock-offs of expensive products such as watches or purses, weight-loss products, and so on.

✦ **Phishing emails:** Among the most annoying and dangerous types of spam are phishing emails, which try to get you to divulge private information such as credit card account numbers or passwords. Phishing email masquerades as legitimate email from a bank or other well-known institution and often includes a link to a phony website that resembles the institution's actual website. For example, you might get an email informing you that there was a suspicious charge on your credit card, with a link you can click to log in to verify that the charge is legitimate. When you click the link, you're taken to a page that looks exactly like your credit card company's actual page. However, the phony page exists solely to harvest your username and password.

Another type of phishing email includes an attachment that claims to be an unpaid invoice or a failed parcel delivery notice. The attachment contains a Trojan that attempts to infect your computer with malware.

✦ **Scams:** The most common type of email scam is called an *advance-fee scam,* in which you're promised a large reward or prize in the future for advancing a relatively small amount of money now in the form of a wire transfer or money order. You may have heard of or actually received the classic scam known as the Nigerian prince scam, in which a Nigerian needs your help to transfer a huge amount of money (for example, $40 million) but can't use an African bank account. The prince needs to use your personal bank account, and will pay you a percentage — perhaps $1 million — for your help. But you must first open a Nigerian account with a minimum balance — of perhaps $10,000 — to facilitate the transfer. All you have to do is wire the money, and they'll take care of the rest.

There are many variations of this story, but they all have one thing in common: They're too good to be true. They offer you a huge amount of money later, in exchange for a relatively small amount of money now.

✦ **Ads for pornographic websites:** Such websites are notorious for being top sources of viruses and other malware.

✦ **Get-rich-quick schemes:** Pyramid schemes, multilevel marketing schemes, phony real-estate schemes, you name it — they're all in a category of spam that promises to make you rich.

✦ **Backscatter:** Backscatter is a particularly annoying phenomenon in which your inbox becomes flooded with dozens or perhaps hundreds of non-delivery reports (NDRs), indicating that an email that you allegedly sent didn't arrive. When you examine the NDRs, you can easily determine that you never sent an email to the intended recipient. What's actually going on here is that your email address has been used as the From address in a spam campaign, and you're receiving the NDRs from the mail servers of those spam emails that were not deliverable.

Though technically not spam, many uses consider advertisements and news-letters from companies they *have* dealt with in the past to be a form of spam. An important element of the definition of spam is the word *unsolicited*. When you register at a company's website, you're effectively inviting that company to send you email.

Using Antispam Software

The most effective way to eliminate spam from your users' inboxes is to use antispam software. *Antispam software* examines all incoming email with the intent of distinguishing between spam and legitimate email. Depending on how the software is configured, email identified as spam is deleted, moved to a separate location, or simply marked as possible spam by adding a tag to the email's subject line.

Antispam software works by analyzing every piece of incoming email using sophisticated techniques that determine the likelihood that the email is, indeed, spam. When a certain threshold of probability is reached, the email is deemed to be spam and deleted, moved, or tagged. If the threshold is not reached, the email is passed on to the user as usual.

Microsoft Exchange mailboxes include a Junk folder that is often the ulti-mate destination of email identified as spam. You should always check your Junk folder whenever you can't find an email you're expecting.

Not all antispam programs use the Junk folder. Some programs store spam email outside of the user's mailbox, in a separate location on the network or perhaps on the cloud. These programs usually deliver a daily email (often called a *digest*) that lists the emails that were identified as spam. You should review this email whenever you can't find an email you're expecting.

Determining whether an email is spam is not an exact science. As a result, *false positives* (in which a legitimate piece of email is mistakenly identified as spam) and *false negatives* (in which a spam email is not detected as spam and makes it into the user's inbox) are not uncommon. False positives can result in your users not receiving emails they're expecting. False negatives can leave users scratching their heads wondering how in the world the spam filter didn't catch the spam. Sometimes email that to a human is obviously spam slips right by the antispam software.

The challenge of any antispam tool is finding the right balance of not too many false positives and not too many false negatives. Most antispam tools let you tune the filters to some degree, setting them to be more or less permissive — that is, erring on the side of more false negatives or more false positives. The stricter the filters are set, the more false positives you'll have. Loosening the filters will result in more false negatives.

The possibility of false negatives is one of the main reasons that it's rarely a good idea to configure an antispam program to simply delete spam. Most programs can be configured to delete only the most obvious spam emails — the ones that can be identified as spam with 100 percent certainty. Email that is probably spam but with less than 100 percent certainty should be marked as spam but not deleted.

Understanding Spam Filters

Antispam programs use a variety of different techniques to determine the probability of a given piece of email being spam. These techniques are employed by *filters,* which examine each piece of email; each filter uses a specific technique.

Here are some of the most commonly used filter types:

✦ **Keyword checking:** The most obvious way to identify spam is to look for certain words that appear either in the email's subject line or in the email body. For example, a keyword checking filter might look for profanity, sexual terms, and other words or phrases such as "Get rich quick!"

Although this is the most obvious way to identify spam, it's also the least reliable. Spammers learned long ago to leave common words out of their spams to avoid these types of filters. Often they intentionally misspell words or substitute numbers or symbols for letters, such as the numeral 0 for the letter *o,* or the symbol ! for the letter *l.*

The biggest problem with keyword checking is that it often leads to false positives. Friends and relatives might intentionally or inadvertently use any of the banned words in their emails. Sometimes, the banned words appear in the middle of otherwise completely innocent words. For example, if you list *Cialis* as a keyword that you want blocked, you'll also block the words *spe__cialis__t* or *so__cialis__t*.

For these reasons, keyword filters are typically used only for the most obvious and offensive words and phrases, if they're used at all.

✦ **Bayesian analysis:** One of the most trusted forms of spam filtering is *Bayesian analysis,* which works by assuming that certain words occur more often in spam email than in other email. This sounds a lot like keyword checking, but Bayesian analysis is much more sophisticated than simple keyword checking. The Bayesian filter maintains an index of words that are likely to be encountered in spam emails. Each word in this index has a probability associated with it, and each word in the email being analyzed is looked up in this index to determine the overall probability of the email being spam. If the probability calculated from this index exceeds a certain threshold, the email is marked as spam.

Here's where the magic of Bayesian analysis comes in: The index is self-learning, based on the user's actual email. Whenever the filter misidentifies an email, the user trains the filter by telling the filter that it was incorrect. The user typically does this by clicking a button labeled "This is spam" or "This is not spam." When the user clicks either of these buttons, the filter adjusts the probability associated with the words that led it to make the wrong conclusion. So, when the filter encounters a similar email in the future, it's more likely to make the correct determination.

✦ **Sender Policy Framework (SPF):** Surprisingly, SMTP (the Internet email protocol) has very poor built-in security. In particular, any email server can easily send email that claims to be from any domain. This makes it easy to forge the From address in an email. SPF lets you designate via DNS which specific email servers are allowed to send email from your domain. An antispam SPF filter works by looking up the sending email server against the SPF records in the DNS of the domain specified by the email's From address.

✦ **Blacklisting:** Another trusted form of spam filtering is a *blacklist* (also known as *blocklist*), which uses a list of known spammers to block email from sources that aren't trustworthy. There are two types of blacklists: private and public. A private blacklist is a list that you set up yourself to designate sources you don't want to accept email from. A public blacklist is a list that is maintained by a company or organization and is available for others to use.

Note that simply blacklisting a sender email address isn't much help. That's because the sender email address is easy to forge. Instead, blacklists track individual email servers that are known to be sources of spam.

Unfortunately, spammers don't usually set up their own servers to send out their spam. Instead, they hijack other servers to do their dirty work. Legitimate email servers can be hijacked by spammers and, thus, become spam sources, often without the knowledge of their owners. This raises the unfortunate possibility that your own email server might be taken over by a spammer, and you might find your email server listed on a public blacklist. If that happens, you won't be able to send email to anyone who uses that blacklist until you have corrected the problem that allowed your server to be hijacked and petitioned the blacklist owners to have your server removed.

✦ **Whitelisting:** One of the most important elements of any antispam solution is a *whitelist,* which ensures that email from known senders will never be blocked. Typically, the whitelist consists of a list of email addresses that you trust. When the antispam tool has confirmed that the From address in the email has not been forged (perhaps by use of an SPF filter), the whitelist filters looks up the address in the whitelist database. If the address is found, the email is immediately marked as legitimate email, and no other filters are applied. So, if the email is marked as legitimate by the whitelist filter, the other filters are not used.

Most whitelist filters will let you whitelist entire domains, as well as individual email addresses. You most certainly do *not* want to whitelist domains of large email providers such as `gmail.com` or `comcast.net`. But you should whitelist the domains of all your business partners and clients to ensure that emails from new employees at these key companies are never marked as spam.

Some antispam programs automatically add the recipient addresses of all outgoing emails to the whitelist. In other words, anyone that you send an email to is automatically added to the whitelist. Over time, this feature can drastically reduce the occurrence of false positives.

Use the whitelist to preemptively allow important email that you're expecting from new customers, vendors, or service providers. For example, if you switch payroll providers, find out in advance what email addresses the new provider will be using so that your payroll staff doesn't miss important emails.

✦ **Graylisting:** Graylisting is an effective antispam technique that exploits the fact that if a legitimate email server can't successfully deliver an email on its first attempt, the server will try again later, typically in 30 minutes. A graylist filter automatically rejects the first attempt to deliver a message but keeps track of the details of the message it rejected. Then, when the same message is received a second time, the graylist filter accepts the message and makes note of the sender so that future messages from the sender are accepted on the first attempt.

Graylisting works because spammers usually configure their servers to not bother with the second attempt. Thus, the graylist filter knows that if a second copy of the email arrives after the initial rejection, the mail is probably legitimate.

The drawback of graylisting is that the first time you receive an email from a new sender, the email will be delayed. Many users find that the benefit of graylisting is not worth the cost of the delayed emails, so they simply disable the graylist filter.

Looking at Three Types of Antispam Software

The many different antispam programs that are available fall into three broad categories: on-premises, appliance, and cloud based (hosted). The following sections describe the relative merits of each of these approaches to providing antispam for your organization.

On-premises antispam

An on-premises antispam program runs on a server on your network and interacts directly with your email server. Email that arrives at your server is passed over to the antispam program, which evaluates the email to determine whether it's spam or legitimate mail. The antispam software uses a variety of techniques to identify spam and can usually be configured for optimal performance. Email that is identified as legitimate is handed back to the email server for normal processing. Depending on how you configure the software, email that is identified as spam may be sent to your users' Junk folders or stored in some other location.

In smaller organizations, the antispam software can run on the same server as the email server (for example, Microsoft Exchange). In larger organizations, the antispam software can be configured to run on its own dedicated server, separate from the mail server(s).

Here are some of the advantages of using an on-premises antispam product:

✦ **You have complete control over the configuration and operation of the software.** Most on-premises antispam software is highly configurable, often providing a dozen or more distinct filtering methods, which you can customize in many different ways. (For more information, see the section "Understanding Spam Filtering," later in this chapter.)

✦ **On-premises antispam software is usually tightly integrated not only with Microsoft Exchange but also with Microsoft Outlook.** Spam email typically appears in the users' Junk folders, and the software often provides an Outlook add-in that makes it easy for users to mark incorrectly identified email.

✦ **On-premises software is relatively inexpensive.** Typically, you pay an upfront fee to purchase the license, as well as an annual maintenance fee to receive regular updates not only to the software but also to the spam filters.

Here are the main disadvantages of on-premises antispam software:

✦ **You're responsible for installing, patching, configuring, updating, and otherwise maintaining the software.**

✦ **Because the relationship between the email server and the antispam software is complicated, on-premises antispam software periodically malfunctions.** Such a malfunction usually halts mail flow throughout your organization. It then becomes your responsibility to correct the problem so that mail begins flowing again. (This usually happens just at the moment when your boss is expecting an important email, and you'll find yourself diagnosing and fixing the problem while your boss watches over your shoulder.)

✦ **On-premises antispam software increases the workload on your servers, requiring additional resources in the form of processor time, RAM, disk storage, and network bandwidth.**

Book II
Chapter 5

Blocking Spam

Antispam appliances

An *antispam appliance* is essentially an on-premises server in a dedicated box that you install at your location. The appliance is usually a self-contained Linux-based computer running antispam software that is pre-installed on the appliance. This makes the appliance essentially plug-and-play; you just set it up, connect it to your network, turn it on, and configure it using a simple web-based interface. When the appliance is up and running, it can provide many, if not all, of the features of on-premises antispam software.

Here are some of the main advantages of using an antispam appliance:

✦ Because the appliance includes its own hardware and pre-installed operating system, you don't have to worry about purchasing hardware separately, installing an operating system, installing software, or any of the other tasks associated with setting up a server.

✦ After it's set up, an appliance will pretty much take care of itself. You'll need to check on it once in a while, but appliances are designed to be self-sufficient.

✦ The appliance may provide other security features, such as antivirus and firewall protection. Thus, a single appliance can handle many of your network's security and protection needs.

Using an antispam appliance is not without its disadvantages:

✦ **Eventually, you'll outgrow the appliance.** For example, if the number of users on your network doubles, you may run out of disk space.

✦ **If the appliance fails, you may have trouble getting it back up and running.** When a normal Windows server fails, you can usually troubleshoot the problem and get the server back up and running. Because of the self-contained nature of an appliance, troubleshooting it can be difficult when it's nonresponsive.

Cloud-based antispam services

A cloud-based antispam service (also called *hosted antispam*) is an Internet-based service that filters your email before it ever arrives at your mail server. When you use hosted antispam, you reconfigure your public DNS so that your mail server (the MX record) points to the cloud-based antispam server rather that to your mail server. That way, all email sent to your organization is first processed by the servers at the antispam service before it ever arrives at your mail server. Only those emails that are deemed to be legitimate are forwarded to your mail server; spam emails are stored in the cloud, where they can be reviewed and retrieved by your users if necessary.

Typically, you pay for hosted antispam based on how many users you have. For example, you might pay a monthly fee of $2 per user. As your organization grows, you simply purchase additional subscriptions.

Here are some of the main advantages of using cloud-based antispam:

✦ **You get to skip the hassle of installing and configuring software, integrating the software with Exchange, maintaining and patching the software, and all the other chores associated with hosting your own server on your own premises.** Your monthly subscription charges cover the cost of someone else doing all that work.

✦ **Because you don't have to buy software or hardware, there is no initial investment.** You simply subscribe to the service and pay the monthly service charges. (As an added bonus, if you're dissatisfied with the service, you can easily move to a different one. Switching to a different antispam appliance or on-premises solution is a much more complicated and expensive affair.)

✦ **A cloud-based antispam solution scales easily with your organization.** If you double the number of users, you simply pay twice as much per month. You don't have to worry about running out of disk space, RAM, clock cycles, or network bandwidth.

✦ **Cloud-based antispam takes a huge load off your network and your mail server.** Because someone else filters your spam for you, spam never enters your network. In most organizations, email is one of the most taxing applications running on the network. Using cloud-based antispam can easily cut incoming network traffic in half; in some cases, it might cut traffic by as much as 90 percent.

As you would expect, there are drawbacks to using cloud-based antispam:

✦ **You give up some control.** Cloud-based services usually have fewer configuration options than on-premises software. For example, you'll probably have fewer options for customizing the spam filters.

✦ **If the service goes down, so does your incoming email.** You won't be able to do anything about it except call technical support. And you can count on getting a busy signal, because when the service goes down, it isn't just you that's affected; it's all its customers. (Of course, this gives such services plenty of motivation to ensure that they fix the problem right away.)

Minimizing Spam

No antispam program is perfect, so you need to understand and expect that a certain amount of spam will get through to your inbox. Here are some tips that you (and your users) should keep in mind to minimize the amount of spam that gets through undetected:

✦ **Never trust email that requests your password or credit card.** A bank will *never* send you an email notifying you of a potential problem and containing a link to its online portal's login page. Nor will a credit card company ever send you an email alerting you to potential fraud and containing a link to a page that requests your credit card number to verify the transaction. Such emails may look very convincing, but you can rest assured they're fraudulent.

If you're in doubt, do *not* click the link. Instead, open a browser window and navigate to the address you know for a fact to be the legitimate login page for your bank or credit card company's web portal.

✦ **Never open attachments in spam.** Attachments in a spam email almost certainly contain malware. Often, the malware in a spam email harvests all the contacts from your computer and sends them to the spammer, or hijacks your computer so the spammer can use it to send spam email.

✦ **Do not reply to spam.** If you reply to spam email, you merely confirm to the spammers that they've found a legitimate email address. You'll get even more spam.

✦ **Use your antispam program's "This is spam" feature.** If your antispam program has a "This is spam" or similar button, be sure to use it. Doing so alerts the antispam program that it has missed a spam message, which helps improve the filters the antispam program uses to detect spam.

✦ **Unsubscribe from legitimate emails.** Much of what many users consider to be spam is actually mail from legitimate organizations. If the spam is from a reputable organization, it probably isn't really spam; you probably at one time signed up to receive emails from the organization. Click the unsubscribe link on these types of emails to remove yourself from the mailing list.

Spammers often include an unsubscribe link on their spam emails. If the email is actually spam, clicking the unsubscribe link is akin to replying to the spam — it simply confirms to the spammers that they've found a legitimate email address, and you'll just get more spam. Worse yet, the link may take you to a malicious website that will attempt to install malware on your computer. So, before you click the unsubscribe link, make sure that the email is indeed from a legitimate sender.

✦ **Protect your email address.** Be careful who you give your email address to, especially when you fill out forms online. Make sure you give your email address only to trusted websites. And read the fine print when you sign up for an account — you'll often find check boxes that allow you to opt out of mailings such as newsletters or announcements about product updates and so on.

✦ **Use an alternate email address.** One useful technique to manage the amount of spam you get is to set up a free email account with a provider such as Gmail. Then use this email account for websites that require an email address for registration when you don't want to use your real email address. You can delete or change the alternate email address if it becomes the target of spam.

✦ **Don't publish your email address.** If you have a personal website or are on social media, don't publish your email address there. Spammers use scanning software that trolls the Internet looking for email addresses.

Chapter 6: Managing Network Software

In This Chapter

✔ Understanding the types of software licenses

✔ Using license servers

✔ Exploring the deployment options

✔ Keeping up to date with patches and service packs

An important task of any network administrator is managing the various bits and pieces of software that are used by your users throughout the network. Most, if not all, of your network users will have a version of Microsoft Office installed on their computers. Depending on the type of business, other software may be widely used. For example, accounting firms require accounting software; engineering firms require engineering software; and the list goes on.

Long gone are the days when you could purchase one copy of a computer program and freely install it on every computer on your network. Most software has built-in features — commonly called "copy protection" — designed to prevent such abuse. But even in the absence of copy protection, nearly all software is sold with a license agreement that dictates how many computers you can install and use the software on. As a result, managing software licenses is an important part of network management.

Some software programs have a license feature that uses a server computer to regulate the number of users who can run the software at the same time. As the network administrator, your job is to set up the license server and keep it running.

Another important aspect of managing software on the network is figuring out the most expedient way to install the software on multiple computers. The last thing you want to do is manually run the software's Setup program individually on each computer in your network. Instead, you'll want to use the network itself to aid in the deployment of the software.

Finally, you'll want to ensure that all the software programs installed throughout your network are kept up to date with the latest patches and updates from the software vendors.

This chapter elaborates on these aspects of network software management.

Understanding Software Licenses

Contrary to popular belief, you don't really buy software. Instead, you buy the right to use the software. When you purchase a computer program at a store, all you really own after you complete the purchase is the box the software comes in, the disks/discs the software is recorded on, and a license that grants you the right to use the software according to the terms offered by the software vendor. The software itself is still owned by the vendor.

That means that you're obligated to follow the terms of the license agreement that accompanies the software. Very few people actually read the complete text of a software agreement before they purchase and use software. If you do, you'll find that a typical agreement contains restrictions, such as the following:

✦ **You're allowed to install the software on one and only one computer.** Some license agreements have specific exceptions to this, allowing you to install the software on a single computer at work and a single computer at home, or on a single desktop computer and a single notebook computer, provided that both computers are used by the same person. However, most software licenses stick to the one-computer rule.

✦ **The license agreement probably allows you to make a backup copy of the disks/discs.** The number of backup copies you can make, though, is probably limited to one or two.

✦ **You aren't allowed to reverse-engineer the software.** In other words, you can't use programming tools to dissect the software in an effort to learn the secrets of how it works.

✦ **Some software restricts the kinds of applications it can be used for.** For example, you might purchase a student or home version of a program that prohibits commercial use. And some software — for example, Oracle's Java — prohibits its use for nuclear facilities.

✦ **Some software has export restrictions that prevent you from taking it out of the country.**

✦ **Nearly all software licenses limit the liability of the software vendor to replacing defective installation disks/discs.** In other words, the software vendor isn't responsible for any damage that might be caused by bugs in the software. In a few cases, these license restrictions have been set aside in court, and companies have been held liable for damage caused by defective software. For the most part, though, you use software at your own risk.

In many cases, software vendors give you a choice of several different types of licenses to choose from. When you purchase software for use on a network, you need to be aware of the differences between these license types so you can decide which type of license to get. The most common types are

✦ **Retail:** The software you buy directly from the software vendor, a local store, or an online store. A retail software license usually grants you the right for a single user to install and use the software. Depending on the agreement, the license may allow that user to install the software on two computers — one at work and one at home. The key point is that only one user may use the software. (However, it is usually acceptable to install the software on a computer that's shared by several users. In that case, more than one user can use the software, provided they use it one at a time.)

The main benefit of a retail license is that it stays with the user when the user upgrades his or her computer. In other words, if you get a new computer, you can remove the software from your old computer and install it on your new computer.

✦ **OEM:** For software that's installed by a computer manufacturer on a new computer. (OEM stands for *original equipment manufacturer.*) For example, if you purchase a computer from Dell and order Microsoft Office Professional along with the computer, you're getting an OEM license. The most important thing to know about an OEM license is that it applies only to the specific computer for which you purchased the software. You are never allowed to install the software on any computer other than the one for which you purchased the software.

Thus, if one day in a fit of rage you throw your computer out the fifth-floor window of your office and the computer smashes into little pieces in the parking lot below, your OEM version of Office is essentially lost forever. When you buy a replacement computer, you'll have to buy a new OEM license of Office for the new computer. You can't install the old software on the new computer.

If this sounds like a severe limitation, it is. However, OEM licenses are usually substantially less expensive than retail licenses. For example, a retail license of Microsoft Office 2010 Professional sells for about $500. The OEM version is less than $400.

✦ **Volume:** Allows you to install and use the software on more than one computer. The simplest type of volume license simply specifies how many computers on which you can install the software. For example, you might purchase a 20-user version of a program that allows you to install the software on 20 computers. Usually, you're on the honor system to make sure that you don't exceed the quantity. You want to set up some type of system to keep track of this type of software license. For example, you could create an Excel spreadsheet in which you record the name of each person for whom you install the software.

Volume licenses can become considerably more complicated. For example, Microsoft offers several different types of volume license programs, each with different pricing and different features and benefits. Table 6-1 summarizes the features of the more popular license programs. For more information, refer to www.microsoft.com/licensing.

Table 6-1	Microsoft Volume License Plans
Plan	**Features**
Open License	Purchase as few as five end-user licenses.
Open Value	Purchase as few as five end-user licenses and receive free upgrades during the subscription term (three years).
Select License	This is a licensing program designed for companies with 250 or more employees.
Enterprise	This is an alternative to the Select License program that's designed to cost-effectively provide Windows Vista, Office, and certain other programs throughout an organization of at least 250 employees.

✦ **Subscription:** A *subscription* isn't really a separate type of license but rather an optional add-on to a volume license. The added subscription fee entitles you to technical support and free product upgrades during the term of the subscription, which is usually annual. For some types of products, the subscription also includes periodic downloads of new data. For example, antivirus software usually includes a subscription that regularly updates your virus signature data. Without the subscription, the antivirus software would quickly become ineffective.

Using a License Server

Some programs let you purchase network licenses that enable you to install the software on as many computers as you want, but regulate the number of people who can use the software at any given time. To control how many people use the software, a special license server is set up. Whenever a user starts the program, the program checks with the license server to see whether a license is available. If so, the program is allowed to start, and the number of available licenses on the license server is reduced by one. Later, when the user quits the program, the license is returned to the server.

One of the most commonly used license server software is FlexNet Publisher, by Flexera Software. (This program used to be named FlexLM, and many programs that depend on it still distribute it as FlexLM.) It's used by AutoCAD as well as by many other network software applications. FlexNet Publisher uses special license files issued by a software vendor to indicate how many licenses of a given product you purchased. Although the license file is a simple text file, its contents are cryptic and generated by a program that only the software vendor has access to. Here's an example of a typical license file for AutoCAD:

```
SERVER server1 000ecd0fe359
USE_SERVER
VENDOR adskflex port=2080
INCREMENT 57000ARDES_2010_0F adskflex 1.000 permanent 6 \
        VENDOR_STRING=commercial:permanent BORROW=4320
SUPERSEDE \
        DUP_GROUP=UH ISSUED=07-May-2007 SN=339-71570316 SIGN="102D \
        85EC 1DFE D083 B85A 46BB AFB1 33AE 00BD 975C 8F5C 5ABC 4C2F \
        F88C 9120 0FB1 E122 BA97 BCAE CC90 899F 99BB 23C9 CAB5 613F \
        E7BB CA28 7DBF 8F51 3B21" SIGN2="033A 6451 5EEB 3CA4 98B8 F92C \
        184A D2BC BA97 BCAE CC90 899F 2EF6 0B45 A707 B897 11E3 096E 0288 \
        787C 997B 0E2E F88C 9120 0FB1 782C 00BD 975C 8F5C 74B9 8BC1"
```

(Don't get any wild ideas here. I changed the numbers in this license file so that it won't actually work. I'm not crazy enough to publish an actual valid AutoCAD license file!)

One drawback to opting for software that uses a license server is that you have to take special steps to run the software when the server isn't available. For example, what if you have AutoCAD installed on a notebook computer, but you want to use it while you're away from the office? In that case, you have two options:

✦ **Use virtual private network (VPN) software to connect to the network.** After you're connected with the VPN, the license server will be available so you can use the software. (Read about VPNs in the preceding chapter.)

✦ **Borrow a license.** When you borrow a license, you can use the software for a limited period of time while you're disconnected from the network. Of course, the borrowed license is subtracted from the number of available licenses on the server.

In most cases, the license server is a mission-critical application — as important as any other function on your network. If the license server goes down, all users who depend on it will be unable to work. Don't worry; they'll let you know. They'll be lining up outside your door demanding to know when you can get the license server up and running so they can get back to work.

Because the license server provides such an important function, treat it with special care. Make sure that the license server software runs on a stable, well-maintained server computer. Don't load up the license server computer with a bunch of other server functions.

And make sure that it's backed up. If possible, install the license server software on a second server computer as a backup. That way, if the main license server computer goes down and you can't get it back up and running, you can quickly switch over to the backup license server.

Options for Deploying Network Software

After you acquire the correct license for your software, the next task of the network administrator is to deploy the software: that is, installing the software on your users' computers and configuring the software so that it runs efficiently on your network. The following sections describe several approaches to deploying software to your network.

Deploying software manually

Most software is shipped on CD or DVD media along with a Setup program that you run to install the software. The Setup program usually asks you a series of questions, such as where you want the program installed, whether you want to install all of the program's features or just the most commonly used features, and so on. You may also be required to enter a serial number, registration number, license key, or other code that proves you purchased the software. When all these questions are answered, the Setup program then installs the program.

If only a few of your network users will be using a particular program, the Setup program may be the most convenient way to deploy the program. Just take the installation media with you to the computer you want to install the program on, insert the disc into the CD/DVD drive, and run the Setup program.

When you finish manually installing software from a CD or DVD, don't forget to remove the disc from the drive! It's easy to leave the disc in the drive, and if the user rarely or never uses the drive, it might be weeks or months before anyone discovers that the disc is missing. By that time, you'll be hard-pressed to remember where it is.

Running Setup from a network share

If you plan on installing a program on more than two or three computers on your network, you'll find it much easier to run the Setup program from a network share rather than from the original CDs or DVDs. To do so, follow these steps:

1. **Create a network share and a folder within the share where you can store the Setup program and other files required to install the program.**

   I usually set up a share named Software and then create a separate folder in this share for each program I want to make available from the network. You should enable Read access for all network users, but allow full access only for yourself and your fellow administrators. (Read more about setting permissions in Chapter 3 of this minibook.)

Read more about creating shares and setting permissions in Chapter 5 of Book VII.

2. **Copy the entire contents of the program's CD or DVD to the folder you create in Step 1.**

   To do so, insert the CD or DVD in your computer's CD/DVD drive. Then, use Windows Explorer to select the entire contents of the disc and drag it to the folder you create in Step 1.

3. **Alternatively, you can choose Start⟲Run and enter** cmd **to open a command prompt. Then, enter a command, such as this:**

   ```
   xcopy d:\*.* \\server1\software\someprogram\*.* /s
   ```

   In this example, d: is the drive letter of your CD/DVD drive, *server1* is the name of your file server, and *software* and *someprogram* are the names of the share and folder you created in Step 1.

4. **To install the program on a client computer, open a Windows Explorer window, navigate to the share and folder you create in Step 1, and double-click the** Setup.exe **file.**

   This launches the Setup program.

5. **Follow the instructions displayed by the Setup program.**

   When the Setup program is finished, the software is ready to use.

Copying the Setup program to a network share spares you the annoyance of carrying the installation discs to each computer you want to install the software on. It doesn't spare you the annoyance of purchasing a valid license for each computer, though! It's illegal to install the software on more computers than the license you acquired from the vendor allows.

Installing silently

Copying the contents of a program's installation media to a network share does spare you the annoyance of carrying the installation discs from computer to computer, but you still have to run the Setup program and answer all its annoying questions on every computer. Wouldn't it be great if there were a way to automate the Setup program so that after you run it, it runs without any further interaction from you? With many programs, you can.

In some cases, the Setup program itself has a command line switch that causes it to run silently. You can usually find out what command line switches are available by entering the following at a command prompt:

```
setup /?
```

With luck, you'll find that the Setup program itself has a switch, such as / quiet or /silent, that installs the program with no interaction, using the program's default settings.

If the Setup program doesn't offer any command line switches, don't despair. The following procedure describes a technique that often lets you silently install the software:

1. **Open an Explorer window and navigate to**

   - *Windows 8, Windows 7, and Vista:* C:\Users*name*\AppData\ Local\Temp

   - *Windows XP:* C:\Documents and Settings*name*\Local Settings\Temp

   Then, delete the entire contents of this folder.

   This is the Temporary folder where various programs deposit temporary files. Windows may not allow you to delete every file in this folder, but it's a good idea to begin this procedure by emptying the Temp folder as much as possible.

2. **Run the Setup program and follow the installation steps right up to the final step.**

   When you get to the confirmation screen that says the program is about ready to install the software, stop! *Do not* click the OK or Finish button.

3. **Return to the Temp folder you open in Step 1, and then poke around until you find the .msi file created by the Setup program you run in Step 2.**

   The .msi file is the actual Windows Installer program that Setup runs to install the program. It may have a cryptic name, such as 84993882.msi.

4. **Copy the .msi file to the network share from which you want to install the program on your client computers.**

   For example, \\\server1\\software\\someprogram.

5. **(Optional) Rename the .msi file to setup.msi.**

   This step is optional, but I prefer to run setup.msi rather than 84993882.msi.

6. **Use Notepad to create a batch file to run the .msi file with the /quiet switch.**

To create the batch file

a. *Right-click in the folder where the* `.msi` *file is stored.*

b. *Choose New ⇨ Text Document.*

c. *Change the name of the text document to* `Setup.bat`.

d. *Right-click the* `Setup.bat` *file and choose Edit.*

e. *Add the following line to the file:*

```
setup.msi /quiet
```

7. Save the file.

You can now install the software by navigating to the folder you created the `setup.bat` file in and double-clicking the `setup.bat` file.

Creating an administrative installation image

Some software, such as Microsoft Office and AutoCAD, comes with tools that let you create a fully configured silent setup program that you can then use to silently install the software. For Microsoft software, this silent setup program is called an "administrative installation image." (Note that the OEM versions of Microsoft Office don't include this feature. You need to purchase a volume license to create an administrative installation.)

To create an administrative image, you simply run the configuration tool supplied by the vendor. The configuration tool lets you choose the installation options you want to have applied when the software is installed. Then, it creates a network setup program on a network share that you specify. You can then install the software on a client computer by opening an Explorer window, navigating to the network share where you saved the network setup program, and running the network setup program.

Pushing out software with group policy

One final option you should consider for network software deployment is using Windows Group Policy to automatically install software to network users. Group Policy is a feature of recent versions of Windows Server (2003 and later) that lets you create policies that are assigned to users. You use the Windows Group Policy feature to specify that certain users should have certain software programs available to them.

Note that group policies aren't actually assigned to individual users, but to Organizational Units (OUs), which are used to categorize users in Active Directory. Thus, you might create a Group Policy to specify that everyone in the Accounting Department OU should have Microsoft Excel.

Then, whenever anyone in the Accounting department logs on to Windows, Windows checks to make sure that Excel is installed on the user's computer. If Excel is *not* installed, Windows advertises Excel on the computer. *Advertising* software on a computer means that a small portion of the software is downloaded to the computer — just enough to display an icon for the program on the Start menu and to associate Excel with the Excel file extensions (`.xls`, `.xlsx`).

If the user clicks the Start menu icon for the advertised application or attempts to open a document that's associated with the advertised application, the application is automatically installed on the user's computer. The user will have to wait a few minutes while the application is installed, but the installation is automatic.

For more information about setting up group policy software installation, search Google or any other search engine for *Group Policy Software.*

Keeping Software Up to Date

One of the annoyances that every network manager faces is applying software patches to keep the operating system and other software up to date. A software *patch* is a minor update that fixes the small glitches that crop up from time to time, such as minor security or performance issues. These glitches aren't significant enough to merit a new version of the software, but they're important enough to require fixing. Most patches correct security flaws that computer hackers have uncovered in their relentless attempts to wreak havoc on the computer world.

Periodically, all the recently released patches are combined into a service pack. Although the most diligent network administrators apply all patches when they're released, many administrators just wait for the service packs.

Windows includes the Windows Update feature that automatically installs patches and service packs when they become available. These patches apply not just to Windows but to other Microsoft software as well. To use Windows Update, open the Control Panel, click System and Security, and then click Windows Update. A window appears, such as the one shown in Figure 6-1.

From the Windows Update window, you can click the Install Updates button to download any updates that apply to your computer. You can also configure Windows Update so that it automatically checks for updates and installs them without asking. To set this option, click the Change Settings link. This displays the Windows Update Change Settings page, as shown in Figure 6-2.

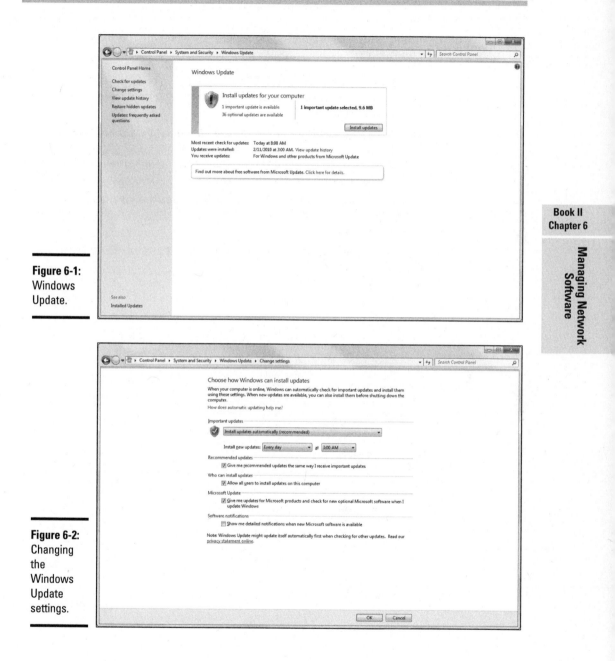

Figure 6-1:
Windows
Update.

Figure 6-2:
Changing
the
Windows
Update
settings.

The Important Updates drop-down list gives you several options for automatic operation:

+ **Install Updates Automatically:** Checks for updates on a regular basis and installs them without asking. You can specify how often to check for updates and at what time.

+ **Download Updates But Let Me Choose Whether to Install Them:** If you're a picky computer user, you should choose this option. It automatically downloads the updates but then gives you the option of whether or not to install them. This lets you opt out of updates you may not want.

+ **Check for Updates But Let Me Choose Whether to Download and Install Them:** This option lets you determine which updates should be downloaded.

+ **Never Check for Updates:** This option disables automatic updates altogether.

Chapter 7: Solving Network Problems

In This Chapter

⌐ **Checking the obvious things**

⌐ **Fixing computers that have expired**

⌐ **Pinpointing the cause of trouble**

⌐ **Restarting client and server computers**

⌐ **Reviewing network event logs**

⌐ **Keeping a record of network woes**

*F*ace it: Networks are prone to breaking.

They have too many parts. Cables. Connectors. Cards. Switches. Routers. All these parts must be held together in a delicate balance, and the network equilibrium is all too easy to disturb. Even the best-designed computer networks sometimes act as if they're held together with baling wire, chewing gum, and duct tape.

To make matters worse, networks breed suspicion. After your computer is attached to a network, users begin to blame the network every time something goes wrong, regardless of whether the problem has anything to do with the network. You can't get columns to line up in a Word document? Must be the network. Your spreadsheet doesn't add up? The @#$% network's acting up again. The stock market's down? Arghhh!!!!!!

The worst thing about network failures is that sometimes they can shut down an entire company. It's not so bad if just one user can't access a particular shared folder on a file server. If a critical server goes down, however, your network users may be locked out of their files, applications, email, and everything else they need to conduct business as usual. When that happens, they'll be beating down your doors and won't stop until you get the network back up and running.

In this chapter, I review some of the most likely causes of network trouble and suggest some basic troubleshooting techniques that you can employ when your network goes on the fritz.

When Bad Things Happen to Good Computers

Here are some basic troubleshooting steps explaining what you should examine at the first sign of network trouble. In many (if not most) of the cases, one of the following steps can get your network back up and running:

1. **Make sure that your computer and everything attached to it is plugged in.**

   Computer geeks love it when a user calls for help, and they get to tell the user that the computer isn't plugged in or that its power strip is turned off. They write it down in their geek logs so that they can tell their geek friends about it later. They may even want to take your picture so that they can show it to their geek friends. (Most "accidents" involving computer geeks are a direct result of this kind of behavior. So try to be tactful when you ask a user whether he or she is sure the computer is actually turned on.)

2. **Make sure that your computer is properly connected to the network.**

3. **Note any error messages that appear on the screen.**

4. **Try restarting the computer.**

   An amazing number of computer problems are cleared up by a simple restart of the computer. Of course, in many cases, the problem recurs, so you'll have to eventually isolate the cause and fix the problem. Some problems are only intermittent, and a simple reboot is all that's needed.

5. **Try the built-in Windows network troubleshooter.**

   For more information, see the section, "Using the Windows Networking Troubleshooter," later in this chapter.

6. **Check the free disk space on your computer and on the server.**

   When a computer runs out of disk space or comes close to it, strange things can happen. Sometimes you get a clear error message indicating such a situation, but not always. Sometimes the computer just grinds to a halt; operations that used to take a few seconds now take a few minutes.

7. **Do a little experimenting to find out whether the problem is indeed a network problem or just a problem with the computer itself.**

   See the section "Time to Experiment," later in this chapter, for some simple things that you can do to isolate a network problem.

8. **Try restarting the network server.**

   See the section "Restarting a Network Server," later in this chapter.

Fixing Dead Computers

If a computer seems totally dead, here are some things to check:

+ **Make sure that the computer is plugged in.**

+ **If the computer is plugged into a surge protector or a power strip, make sure that the surge protector or power strip is plugged in and turned on.** If the surge protector or power strip has a light, it should be glowing. Also, the surge protector may have a Reset button that needs to be pressed.

+ **Make sure that the computer's On/Off switch is turned on.** This advice sounds too basic to even include here, but many computers have two power switches: an on/off switch on the back of the computer, and a push-button on the front that actually starts the computer. If you push the front button and nothing happens, check the switch on the back to make sure it's in the ON position.

To complicate matters, newer computers have a Sleep feature, in which they appear to be turned off but really they're just sleeping. All you have to do to wake such a computer is jiggle the mouse a little. (I used to have an uncle like that.) It's easy to assume that the computer is turned off, press the power button, wonder why nothing happened, and then press the power button and hold it down, hoping it will take. If you hold down the power button long enough, the computer will actually turn itself off. Then, when you turn the computer back on, you get a message saying the computer wasn't shut down properly. Arghhh! The moral of the story is to jiggle the mouse if the computer seems to have nodded off.

+ **If you think the computer isn't plugged in but it looks like it is, listen for the fan.** If the fan is running, the computer is getting power, and the problem is more serious than an unplugged power cord. (If the fan isn't running but the computer is plugged in and the power is on, the fan may be out to lunch.)

+ **If the computer is plugged in and turned on but still not running, plug a lamp into the outlet to make sure that power is getting to the outlet.** You may need to reset a tripped circuit breaker or replace a bad surge protector. Or you may need to call the power company. (If you live in California, don't bother calling the power company. It probably won't do any good.)

+ **Check the surge protector.** Surge protectors have a limited life span. After a few years of use, many surge protectors continue to provide electrical power for your computer, but the components that protect your computer from power surges no longer work. If you're using a surge protector that is more than two or three years old, replace the old surge protector with a new one.

 ✦ **Make sure that the monitor is plugged in and turned on.** The monitor has a separate power cord and switch. (The monitor actually has two cables that must be plugged in. One runs from the back of the monitor to the back of the computer; the other is a power cord that comes from the back of the monitor and must be plugged into an electrical outlet.)

 ✦ **Make sure that all cables are plugged in securely.** Your keyboard, monitor, mouse, and printer are all connected to the back of your computer by cables.

Make sure that the other ends of the monitor and printer cables are plugged in properly, too.

 ✦ **If the computer is running but the display is dark, try adjusting the monitor's contrast and brightness.** Some monitors have knobs that you can use to adjust the contrast and brightness of the monitor's display. They may have been turned down all the way.

Ways to Check a Network Connection

The cables that connect client computers to the rest of the network are finicky beasts. They can break at a moment's notice, and by "break," I don't necessarily mean "to physically break in two." Although some broken cables look like someone got to the cable with pruning shears, most cable problems aren't visible to the naked eye.

 ✦ **Twisted-pair cable:** If your network uses twisted-pair cable, you can quickly tell whether the cable connection to the network is good by looking at the back of your computer. Look for a small light located near where the cable plugs in; if this light is glowing steadily, the cable is good. If the light is dark or it's flashing intermittently, you have a cable problem (or a problem with the network card or the hub or switch that the other end of the cable is plugged in to).

If the light isn't glowing steadily, try removing the cable from your computer and reinserting it. This action may cure the weak connection.

 ✦ **Patch cable:** Hopefully, your network is wired so that each computer is connected to the network with a short (six feet or so) patch cable. One end of the patch cable plugs into the computer, and the other end plugs into a cable connector mounted on the wall. Try quickly disconnecting and reconnecting the patch cable. If that doesn't do the trick, try to find a spare patch cable that you can use.

 ✦ **Switches:** Switches are prone to having cable problems, too — especially switches that are wired in a "professional manner," involving a rat's nest of patch cables. Be careful whenever you enter the lair of the rat's nest. If you need to replace a patch cable, be very careful when you disconnect the suspected bad cable and reconnect the good cable in its place.

A Bunch of Error Messages Just Flew By!

Error messages that display when your computer boots can provide invaluable clues to determine the source of the problem.

If you see error messages when you start up the computer, keep the following points in mind:

+ **Don't panic if you see a lot of error messages.** Sometimes, a simple problem that's easy to correct can cause a plethora of error messages when you start your computer. The messages may look as if your computer is falling to pieces, but the fix may be very simple.

+ **If the messages fly by so fast that you can't see them, press your computer's Pause key.** Your computer comes to a screeching halt, giving you a chance to catch up on your error-message reading. After you've read enough, press the Pause key again to get things moving. (On keyboards that don't have a Pause key, pressing Ctrl+Num Lock or Ctrl+S does the same thing.)

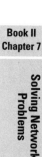

+ **If you miss the error messages the first time, restart the computer and watch them again.**

+ **Better yet, press F8 when you see the Starting Windows message.** This displays a menu that allows you to select from several startup options. (Note that this won't work on Windows 8, 8.1, or 10.)

Double-Checking Your Network Settings

I swear that there are little green men who sneak into offices at night, turn on computers, and mess up TCP/IP configuration settings just for kicks. These little green men are affectionately known as *networchons*.

Remarkably, network configuration settings sometimes get inadvertently changed so that a computer, which enjoyed the network for months or even years, one day finds itself unable to access the network. So one of the first things you do, after making sure that the computers are actually on and that the cables aren't broken, is a basic review of the computer's network settings. Check the following:

+ **At a command prompt, run `ipconfig` to make sure that TCP/IP is up and running on the computer and that the IP addresses, subnet masks, and default gateway settings look right.**

+ **Call up the network connection's Properties dialog box and make sure that the necessary protocols are installed correctly.**

✦ **Open the System Properties dialog box (double-click System in Control Panel) and check the Computer Name tab.**

Make sure that the computer name is unique and also that the domain or workgroup name is spelled properly.

✦ **Double-check the user account to make sure that the user really has permission to access the resources he needs.**

For more information about network configuration settings, see Book II, Chapters 3 and 6.

Using the Windows Networking Troubleshooter

Windows comes with a built-in troubleshooter that can often help you to pin down the cause of a network problem. Figure 7-1 shows the Windows 8 version. Answer the questions asked by the troubleshooter and click Next to move from screen to screen. The Networking Troubleshooter can't solve all networking problems, but it does point out the causes of the most common problems.

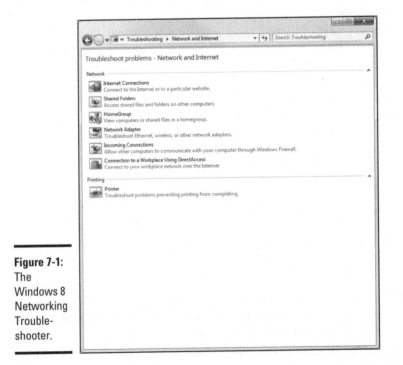

Figure 7-1:
The Windows 8 Networking Trouble-shooter.

The procedure for starting Networking Troubleshooter depends on which version of Windows you're using:

✦ **Windows 8 and Windows 7:** Open Control Panel, click View Network Status and Tasks, and then click Troubleshoot Problems. Then select the troubleshooter that seems most directly related to the problem you're experiencing. You'll find troubleshooters for wireless network problems, home networks, and local area network (LAN) and Internet connections.

✦ **Windows Vista:** Choose Start ⇨ Help and Support, click Troubleshooting, and then click the link for the network troubleshooter that seems most directly related to the problem you're experiencing. You'll find trouble-shooters for wireless network problems, home networks, and local area network (LAN) and Internet connections.

✦ **Windows XP:** Choose Start ⇨ Help and Support ⇨ Networking and the Web ⇨ Fixing Network or Web Problems. Then click Home and Small Office Networking Troubleshooter.

Time to Experiment

If you can't find some obvious explanation for your troubles — like the computer is unplugged — you need to do some experimenting to narrow down the possibilities. Design your experiments to answer one basic question: Is it a network problem or a local computer problem?

Here are some ways you can narrow down the cause of the problem:

✦ **Try performing the same operation on someone else's computer.** If no one on the network can access a network drive or printer, something is probably wrong with the network. On the other hand, if the error occurs on only one computer, the problem is likely with that computer. The way-ward computer may not be reliably communicating with the network or configured properly for the network, or the problem may have nothing to do with the network at all.

✦ **If you're able to perform the operation on another computer without problems, try logging on to the network with another computer using your own username.** Then see whether you can perform the operation without error. If you can, the problem is probably on your computer. If you can't, the problem may be with the way your user account is configured.

✦ **If you can't log on at another computer, try waiting for a bit.** Your account may be temporarily locked out. This can happen for a variety of reasons — the most common of which is trying to log on with the wrong password several times in a row. If you're still locked out an hour later, call the network administrator and offer a doughnut.

Who's on First?

When troubleshooting a networking problem, it's often useful to find out who is actually logged on to a network server. For example, if a user can't access a file on the server, you can check whether the user is logged on. If so, you know that the user's account is valid, but the user may not have permission to access the particular file or folder that he's attempting to access. On the other hand, if the user isn't logged on, the problem may lie with the account itself or how the user is attempting to connect to the server.

It's also useful to find out who's logged on in the event that you need to restart the server. For more information about restarting a server, see the section, "Restarting a Network Server," later in this chapter.

To find out who is currently logged on to a Windows server, right-click the Computer icon on the desktop and choose Manage from the menu that appears. This brings up the Computer Management window. Open System Tools in the tree list and then open Shared Folders and select Sessions. A list of users who are logged on appears.

You can immediately disconnect all users by right-clicking Sessions in the Computer Management window and choosing All Tasks ⇨ Disconnect All. Be warned, however, that this can cause users to lose data.

Restarting a Client Computer

Sometimes, trouble gets a computer so tied up in knots that the only thing you can do is reboot. In some cases, the computer just starts acting weird. Strange characters appear on the screen, or Windows goes haywire and doesn't let you exit a program. Sometimes, the computer gets so confused that it can't even move. It just sits there, like a deer staring at oncoming headlights. It won't move, no matter how hard you press Esc or Enter. You can move the mouse all over your desktop, or you can even throw it across the room, but the mouse pointer on the screen stays perfectly still.

When a computer starts acting strange, you need to reboot. If you must reboot, you should do so as cleanly as possible. I know this procedure may seem elementary, but the technique for safely restarting a client computer is worth repeating, even if it is basic:

1. **Save your work if you can.**

   Use the File ⇨ Save command to save any documents or files that you were editing when things started to go haywire. If you can't use the menus, try clicking the Save button on the toolbar. If that doesn't work, try pressing Ctrl+S (the standard keyboard shortcut for the Save command).

2. **Close any running programs if you can.**

   Use the File⇨Exit command or click the Close button in the upper-right corner of the program window. Or press Alt+F4.

3. **Restart the computer.**

   - *Windows XP:* Choose Start⇨Turn Off Computer to summon the Shut Down Windows dialog box. Select the Restart option, and then click OK.

   - *Windows 7 and Vista:* Click the Start button, click the right arrow that appears at the bottom-right corner of the Start menu, and then click Restart.

   - *Windows 8:* Oddly enough, shutting down Windows 8 is a bit challenging. You can stare at the Windows 8 desktop all day and not find an intuitive way to shut down your computer. The secret lies in the Charms Bar, which you can find by hovering the mouse over the lower right corner of the screen. Next, click the Settings icon, and then click the Shut Down icon.

   - *Windows 8.1 and 10:* Click the Start button, click the Power Options button, and then choose Restart.

If restarting your computer doesn't seem to fix the problem, you may need to turn your computer off and then turn it on again. To do so, follow the previous procedure but choose Shut Down instead of Restart.

Here are a few things to try if you have trouble restarting your computer:

1. **If your computer refuses to respond to the Start⇨Shut Down command, try pressing Ctrl+Alt+Delete.**

   This is called the "three-finger salute." It's appropriate to say, "Queueue" while you do it.

   When you press Ctrl+Alt+Delete, Windows displays a dialog box that enables you to close any running programs or shut down your computer entirely.

2. **If pressing Ctrl+Alt+Delete doesn't do anything, you've reached the last resort. The only thing left to do is turn off the computer by pressing the power On/Off button and holding it down for a few seconds.**

   Turning off your computer by pressing the power button is a drastic action that you should take only after your computer becomes completely unresponsive. Any work you haven't yet saved to disk is lost. (Sniff.) (If your computer doesn't have a Reset button, turn off the computer, wait a few moments, and then turn the computer back on again.)

If at all possible, save your work before restarting your computer. Any work you haven't saved is lost. Unfortunately, if your computer is totally tied up in knots, you probably can't save your work. In that case, you have no choice but to push your computer off the digital cliff.

Booting in Safe Mode

Windows provides a special start-up mode called *Safe Mode* that's designed to help fix misbehaving computers. When you start your computer in Safe Mode, Windows loads only the most essential parts of itself into memory — the bare minimum required for Windows to work. Safe Mode is especially useful when your computer has developed a problem that prevents you from using the computer at all.

To boot in Safe Mode on a Windows 7 or earlier computer, first restart the computer. Then, as soon as the computer begins to restart, start pressing the F8 key — just tap away at it until a menu titled Advanced Boot Options appears. One of the options on this menu is Safe Mode; use the up- or down-arrow keys to select that option and then press Enter to boot in Safe Mode.

On a Windows 8, 8.1, or 10 computer, you can reboot into Safe Mode by holding down the Shift key when you choose the Restart command.

Using System Restore

System Restore is a Windows feature that periodically saves important Windows configuration information and allows you to later return your system to a previously saved configuration. This can often fix problems by reverting your computer to a time when it was working.

By default, Windows saves restore points whenever you install new software on your computer or apply a system update. Restore points are also saved automatically every seven days.

Although System Restore is turned on by default, you should verify that System Restore is active and running to make sure that System Restore points are being created. To do that, right-click Computer in the Start menu, choose Properties, and then click the System Protection tab. The dialog box shown in Figure 7-2 is displayed. Verify that the Protection status for your computer's C: drive is On. If it isn't, select the C: drive and click the Configure button to configure System Restore for the drive.

Figure 7-2:
The System
Protection
tab of the
System
Properties
dialog box.

If your computer develops a problem, you can restore it to a previously
saved restore point by clicking System Restore on the System Protection
tab. This brings up the System Restore Wizard, as shown in Figure 7-3. This
wizard allows you to select the restore point you want to use.

Figure 7-3:
Use System
Restore to
restore your
system to an
earlier con-
figuration.

Here are a few additional thoughts to remember about System Restore:

✦ System Restore *does not* delete data files from your system. Thus, files in your Documents folder won't be lost.

✦ System Restore *does* remove any applications or system updates you've installed since the time the restore point was made. Thus, you need to reinstall those applications or system updates — unless, of course, you determine that an application or system update was the cause of your problem in the first place.

✦ System Restore automatically restarts your computer. The restart may be slow because some of the changes made by System Restore happen after the restart.

✦ Do *not* turn off or cut power to your computer during System Restore. Doing so may leave your computer in an unrecoverable state.

✦ After completing a System Restore, you may discover that the user can't log on to the computer because the computer complains about the "domain trust relationship" being lost. This happens because the internal password that Active Directory uses to verify the identity of the computer has been reset by the System Restore to a previous version. The only solution is to log in to a local account on the computer, leave the domain, reboot the computer, log in again using a local account, rejoin the domain, and reboot the computer again. Sigh.

Restarting Network Services

Once in awhile, the OS service that supports the task that's causing you trouble inexplicably stops or gets stuck. If users can't access a server, it may be because one of the key network services has stopped or is stuck.

You can review the status of services by using the Services tool, as shown in Figure 7-4. To display it, right-click Computer on the Start menu and choose Manage; then, expand the Services and Applications node and click Services. Review this list to make sure that all key services are running. If an important service is paused or stopped, restart it.

Which services qualify as "important" depends on what roles you define for the server. Table 7-1 lists a few important services that are common to most Windows network operating systems (NOS). However, many servers require additional services besides these. In fact, a typical server will have many dozens of services running simultaneously.

Key services usually stop for a reason, so simply restarting a stopped service probably won't solve your network's problem — at least, not for long. You should review the System log to look for any error messages that may explain why the service stopped in the first place.

Figure 7-4:
Looking at services (Windows 8).

Table 7-1	Key Windows Services
Service	*Description*
Computer Browser	Maintains a list of computers on the network that can be accessed. If this service is disabled, the computer won't be able to use browsing services, such as My Network Places.
DHCP Client	Enables the computer to obtain its IP address from a Dynamic Host Configuration Protocol (DHCP) server. If this service is disabled, the computer's Internet Protocol (IP) address won't be configured properly.
DNS Client	Enables the computer to access a Domain Name Server (DNS) server to resolve DNS names. If this service is disabled, the computer won't be able to handle DNS names, including Internet addresses and Active Directory names.
Server	Provides basic file- and printer-sharing services for the server. If this service is stopped, clients won't be able to connect to the server to access files or printers.
Workstation	Enables the computer to establish client connections with other servers. If this service is disabled, the computer won't be able to connect to other servers.

Restarting a Network Server

Sometimes, the only way to flush out a network problem is to restart the network server that's experiencing trouble.

Restarting a network server is something you should do only as a last resort. Windows Server is designed to run for months or even years at a time without rebooting. Restarting a server invariably results in a temporary shutdown of the network. If you must restart a server, try to do it during off hours if possible.

Before you restart a server, check whether a specific service that's required has been paused or stopped. You may be able to just restart the individual service rather than the entire server. For more information, see the section "Restarting Network Services," earlier in this chapter.

Here's the basic procedure for restarting a network server:

1. **Make sure that everyone is logged off the server.**

   The easiest way to do that is to restart the server after normal business hours, when everyone has gone home for the day. Then, you can just shut down the server and let the shutdown process forcibly log off any remaining users.

   To find out who's logged on, refer to the earlier section, "Who's on First?"

2. **After you're sure the users have logged off, shut down the network server.**

   You want to do this step behaving like a good citizen if possible — decently, and in order. Use the Start ⇨ Shut Down command to shut down the server. This summons a dialog box that requires you to indicate the reason for the shutdown. The information you supply here is entered into the server's System log, which you can review by using Event Viewer.

3. **Reboot the server computer or turn it off and then on again.**

   Watch the server start up to make sure that no error messages appear.

4. **Tell everyone to log back on and make sure that everyone can now access the network.**

Remember the following when you consider restarting the network server:

   ✦ **Restarting the network server is more drastic than restarting a client computer.** Make sure that everyone saves his or her work and logs off the network before you do it! You can cause major problems if you blindly turn off the server computer while users are logged on.

   ✦ **Obviously, restarting a network server is a major inconvenience to every network user.** Better offer treats.

Looking at Event Logs

One of the most useful troubleshooting techniques for diagnosing network problems is to review the network operating system's built-in event logs. These logs contain information about interesting and potentially troublesome events that occur during the daily operation of your network. Ordinarily, these logs run in the background, quietly gathering information about network events. When something goes wrong, you can check the logs to see whether the problem generated a noteworthy event. In many cases, the event logs contain an entry that pinpoints the exact cause of the problem and suggests a solution.

To display the event logs in a Windows server, use Event Viewer, which is available from the Administrative Tools menu. For example, Figure 7-5 shows an Event Viewer from a Windows Server 2012 system. The tree listing on the left side of Event Viewer lists five categories of events that are tracked: Application, Security, System, Directory Service, and File Replication Service. Select one of these options to see the log that you want to view. For details about a particular event, double-click the event to display a dialog box with detailed information about the event.

Figure 7-5:
Event
Viewer.

Documenting Your Trials and Tribulations

For a large network, you probably want to invest in problem-management software that tracks each problem through the entire process of trouble-shooting, from initial report to final resolution. For small- and medium-sized networks, it's probably sufficient to put together a three-ring binder with pre-printed forms. Or record your log in a Word document or an Excel spreadsheet.

Regardless of how you track your network problems, the tracking log should include the following information:

✦ **The real name and the network username of the person reporting the problem**

✦ **The date the problem was first reported**

✦ **An indication of the severity of the problem**

   Is it merely an inconvenience, or is a user unable to complete his or her work because of the problem? Does a work-around exist?

✦ **The name of the person assigned to resolve the problem**

✦ **A description of the problem**

✦ **A list of the software involved, including versions**

✦ **A description of the steps taken to solve the problem**

✦ **A description of any intermediate steps that were taken to try to solve the problem, along with an indication of whether those steps were "undone" when they didn't help solve the problem**

✦ **The date the problem was finally resolved**

Chapter 8: Backing Up Your Data

In This Chapter

✔ Understanding the need for backups

✔ Working with tape drives and other backup media

✔ Understanding the different types of backups

✔ Mastering tape rotation and other details

*I*f you're the hapless network manager, the safety of the data on your network is your responsibility. In fact, it's your primary responsibility. You get paid to lie awake at night worrying about your data. Will it be there tomorrow? If it's not, can you get it back? And — most important — if you can't get it back, will you have a job tomorrow?

This chapter covers the ins and outs of being a good, responsible, trustworthy network manager. No one gives out merit badges for this stuff, but someone should.

Backing Up Your Data

Having data backed up is the cornerstone of any disaster recovery plan. Without backups, a simple hard drive failure can set your company back days or even weeks while it tries to reconstruct lost data. In fact, without backups, your company's very existence is in jeopardy.

The main goal of a backup is simple: Keep a spare copy of your network's critical data so that no matter what happens, you never lose more than one day's work. The stock market may crash, hanging chads may factor into another presidential election, and George Lucas may decide to make a pre-prequel. When you stay on top of your backups, though, you'll never lose more than one day's work.

The way to do this, naturally, is to make sure that data is backed up on a daily basis. For many networks, you can back up all the network hard drives every night. And even if full nightly backups aren't possible, you can still use techniques that can ensure that every file on the network has a backup copy that's no more than one day old.

Where to Back Up Your Data

If you plan on backing up the data on your network server's hard drives, you obviously need some type of media on which to back up the data. You could copy the data onto CDs, but a 500GB hard drive would need more than 750 CDs for a full backup. That's a few more discs than most people want to keep in the closet. You could use DVDs, but you'll still need about a dozen of them, as well as an hour or so to fill each one. Sigh. That means devoting a Saturday to creating your backup.

Because of the limitations of CDs and DVDs, most network administrators back up network data to another type of storage device. The three most common options are described in this list:

✦ **Tape:** Magnetic tape is the oldest storage medium for backups and is still one of the most widely used. One big advantage of tape backups is that tape cartridges are small and can thus be easily transported to an offsite location.

✦ **Network Attached Storage (NAS):** A *Network Attached Storage* device connects directly to your network. NAS devices are often used as backup devices because they're inexpensive. In addition, because they're relatively small and easy to remove, like tape, they can be transported offsite.

✦ **Cloud backup:** An increasingly popular option is to use a third-party service to back up data to a remote location via the Internet. Cloud backup has the advantage of already being offsite.

Backing Up to Tape

One of the benefits of tape backup is that you can run it unattended. In fact, you can schedule a tape backup to run automatically during off hours when no one is using the network. For unattended backups to work, though, you must ensure that you have enough tape capacity to back up your entire network server's hard drive without having to manually switch tapes. If your network server has only 100GB of data, you can easily back it up onto a single tape. If you have 1,000GB of data, however, invest in a tape drive that features a magazine changer that can hold several tapes and automatically cycle them in and out of the drive. That way, you can run your backups unattended.

You can choose from several distinct types of tape backup systems:

✦ **Travan drives:** A popular style of tape backup for small servers is a Travan drive, which comes in a variety of models with tape capacities ranging from 20GB to 40GB. You can purchase a 20GB drive for less than $200.

✦ **DAT, DLT, and LTO units:** For larger networks, you can get tape backup units that offer higher capacity and faster backup speed than Travan drives — for more money, of course. Digital Audio Tape (DAT) units can back up as much as 80GB on a single tape, and DLT (Digital Linear Tape) drives can store up to 800GB on one tape. Linear Tape Open (LTO) drives can store 2.5TB on a single tape. DAT, DLT, and LTO drives can cost $1,000 or more, depending on the capacity.

✦ **Robotic units:** If you're really up the backup creek, with hundreds of gigabytes to back up, you can get robotic tape backup units that automatically fetch and load tape cartridges from a library. That way, you can do complete backups without having to load tapes manually. As you can likely guess, these units aren't inexpensive: Small ones, which have a library of about eight tapes and a total backup capacity of more than 5,000GB, start at about $4,000.

Backup Software

All versions of Windows come with a built-in backup program. In addition, most tape drives come with backup programs that are often faster or more flexible than the standard Windows backup.

You can also purchase sophisticated backup programs that are specially designed for networks that have multiple servers with data that must be backed up. For a basic Windows file server, you can use the backup program that comes with Windows Server. Server versions of Windows come with a decent backup program that can run scheduled, unattended tape backups.

Backup programs do more than just copy data from your hard drive to tape. Backup programs use special compression techniques to squeeze your data so that you can cram more data onto fewer tapes. Compression factors of 2:1 are common, so you can usually squeeze 100GB of data onto a tape that would hold only 50GB of data without compression. (Tape drive manufacturers tend to state the capacity of their drives by using compressed data, assuming a 2:1 compression ratio. Thus, a 200GB tape has an uncompressed capacity of 100GB.)

Whether you achieve a compression factor of 2:1 depends on the nature of the data you're backing up:

✦ **Documents:** If your network is used primarily for Microsoft Office applications and is filled with Word and Excel documents, you'll probably get better than 2:1 compression.

✦ **Graphics:** If your network data consists primarily of graphic image files, you probably won't get much compression. Most graphic image file formats are already compressed, so they can't be compressed much more by the backup software's compression methods.

Backup programs also help you keep track of which data has been backed up and which hasn't. They also offer options, such as incremental or differential backups that can streamline the backup process, as I describe in the next section.

If your network has more than one server, invest in good backup software. One popular is Yosemite Backup, made by BarracudaWare (www.barracudaware.com). Besides being able to handle multiple servers, one of the main advantages of backup software (such as Yosemite Backup) is that it can properly back up Microsoft Exchange server data.

Types of Backups

You can perform five different types of backups. Many backup schemes rely on full daily backups, but for some networks, using a scheme that relies on two or more of these backup types is more practical.

The differences among the five types of backups involve a little technical detail known as the archive bit. The *archive bit* indicates whether a file has been modified since it was backed up. The archive bit is a little flag that's stored along with the filename, creation date, and other directory information. Any time a program modifies a file, the archive bit is set to the On position. That way, backup programs know that the file has been modified and needs to be backed up.

The differences among the various types of backups center on whether they use the archive bit to determine which files to back up, as well as whether they flip the archive bit to the Off position after they back up a file. Table 8-1 summarizes these differences, which I explain in the following sections.

Backup programs allow you to select any combination of drives and folders to back up. As a result, you can customize the file selection for a backup operation to suit your needs. For example, you can set up one backup plan that backs up all a server's shared folders and drives, plus its mail server stores, but then leaves out folders that rarely change, such as the operating system folders or installed program folders. You can then back up those folders on a less-regular basis. The drives and folders that you select for a backup operation are collectively called the *backup selection*.

The archive bit would have made a good Abbott and Costello routine. ("All right, I wanna know who modified the archive bit." "What." "Who?" "No, What." "Wait a minute . . . just tell me what's the name of the guy who modified the archive bit!" "Right.")

Table 8-1	How Backup Types Use the Archive Bit	
Backup Type	*Selects Files Based on Archive Bit?*	*Resets Archive Bits After Backing Up?*
Normal	No	Yes
Copy	No	No
Daily	No*	No
Incremental	Yes	Yes
Differential	Yes	No

Selects files based on the Last Modified date.

Normal backups

A *normal backup* — also called a *full backup* — is the basic type of backup. In a normal backup, all files in the backup selection are backed up regardless of whether the archive bit has been set. In other words, the files are backed up even if they haven't been modified since the last time they were backed up. When each file is backed up, its archive bit is reset, so backups that select files based on the archive bit setting won't back up the files.

When a normal backup finishes, none of the files in the backup selection has its archive bit set. As a result, if you immediately follow a normal backup with an incremental backup or a differential backup, files won't be selected for backup by the incremental or differential backup because no file will have its archive bit set.

The easiest backup scheme is to simply schedule a normal backup every night. That way, all your data is backed up on a daily basis. Then, if the need arises, you can restore files from a single tape or set of tapes. Restoring files is more complicated when other types of backups are involved.

Do normal backups nightly if you have the tape capacity to do them unattended — that is, without having to swap tapes. If you can't do an unattended normal backup because the amount of data to be backed up is greater than the capacity of your tape drive(s), you have to use other types of backups in combination with normal backups.

If you can't get a normal backup on a single tape, and you can't afford a second tape drive or a tape changer, take a hard look at the data that's being included in the backup selection. I recently worked on a network that was difficult to back up onto a single tape. When I examined the data that was being backed up, I discovered a large amount of static data that was essentially an online archive of old projects. This data was necessary because network users needed it for research purposes, but the data was read-only. Even though the data never changed, it was being backed up to tape every night, and the backups required two tapes. After I removed this data from the cycle of nightly backups, the backups were able to squeeze onto a single tape again.

If you remove static data from the nightly backup, make sure that you have a secure backup of the static data on tape, CD-RW, or some other media.

Copy backups

A *copy backup* is similar to a normal backup except that the archive bit isn't reset when each file is copied. As a result, copy backups don't disrupt the cycle of normal and incremental or differential backups.

Copy backups usually aren't incorporated into regular, scheduled backups. Instead, you use a copy backup when you want to do an occasional one-shot backup. If you're about to perform an operating system upgrade, for example, you should back up the server before proceeding. If you do a full backup, the archive bits are reset, and your regular backups are disrupted. If you do a copy backup, however, the archive bits of any modified files remain unchanged. As a result, your regular normal and incremental or differential backups are unaffected.

If you don't incorporate incremental or differential backups into your backup routine, the difference between a copy backup and a normal backup is moot.

Daily backups

A *daily backup* backs up just those files that changed the same day when the backup was performed. A daily backup examines the modification date stored with each file's directory entry to determine whether a file should be backed up. Daily backups don't reset the archive bit.

I'm not a big fan of this option because of the small possibility that some files may slip through the cracks. Someone may be working late one night and modify a file after the evening's backups have completed — but before midnight — meaning that those files won't be included in the following night's backups. Incremental or differential backups, which rely on the archive bit rather than the modification date, are more reliable.

Incremental backups

An *incremental backup* backs up only those files that were modified since the last time you did a backup. Incremental backups are a lot faster than full backups because your network users probably modify only a small portion of the files on the server on any given day. As a result, if a full backup takes three tapes, you can probably fit an entire week's worth of incremental back-ups on a single tape.

When an incremental backup copies each file, it resets the file's archive bit. That way, the file will be backed up again before your next normal backup only when a user modifies the file again.

Here are some thoughts about using incremental backups:

✦ **The easiest way to use incremental backups is the following:**

  • A *normal* backup every Monday

   If your full backup takes more than 12 hours, you may want to do it on Friday so that it can run over the weekend.

  • An *incremental* backup on each remaining normal business day (for example, Tuesday, Wednesday, Thursday, and Friday)

✦ **When you use incremental backups, the complete backup consists of the full backup tapes and all the incremental backup tapes that you've made since you did the full backup.**

   If the hard drive crashes, and you have to restore the data onto a new drive, you first restore Monday's normal backup and then restore each of the subsequent incremental backups.

✦ **Incremental backups complicate restoring individual files because the most recent copy of the file may be on the full backup tape or on any of the incremental backups.**

   Backup programs keep track of the location of the most recent version of each file to simplify the process.

✦ **When you use incremental backups, you can choose whether you want to**

  • Store each incremental backup on its own tape.

  • Append each backup to the end of an existing tape.

   Often, you can use a single tape for a week of incremental backups.

Differential backups

A *differential backup* is similar to an incremental backup except that it doesn't reset the archive bit when files are backed up. As a result, each dif-ferential backup represents the difference between the last normal backup and the current state of the hard drive.

To do a full restore from a differential backup, you first restore the last normal backup and then restore the most recent differential backup.

Suppose that you do a normal backup on Monday and differential backups on Tuesday, Wednesday, and Thursday, and your hard drive crashes Friday morning. On Friday afternoon, you install a new hard drive. To restore the data, you first restore the normal backup from Monday. Then you restore the differential backup from Thursday. The Tuesday and Wednesday differential backups aren't needed.

The main difference between incremental and differential backups is that

✦ *Incremental* backups result in smaller and faster backups.

✦ *Differential* backups are easier to restore.

If your users often ask you to restore individual files, consider using differential backups.

Local versus Network Backups

When you back up network data, you have two basic approaches to running the backup software:

✦ You can perform a *local backup,* in which the backup software runs on the file server itself and backs up data to a tape drive that's installed in the server.

✦ Or you can perform a *network backup,* in which you use one network computer to back up data from another network computer. In a network backup, the data has to travel over the network to get to the computer that's running the backup.

If you run the backups from the file server, you'll tie up the server while the backup is running, and users will complain that their server access has slowed to a snail's pace. On the other hand, if you run the backup over the network from a client computer or a dedicated backup server, you'll flood the network with gigabytes of data being backed up. Then your users will complain that the entire network has slowed to a snail's pace.

Network performance is one of the main reasons why you should try to run your backups during off hours, when other users aren't accessing the network. Another reason to run backups during off hours is so that you can perform a more thorough backup. If you run your backup while other users are accessing files, the backup program is likely to skip any files that are being accessed by users at the time the backup runs. As a result, your backup won't include those files. Ironically, the files most likely to get left out of the backup are often the files that need backing up the most, because they're the files that are being used and modified.

Here are some extra thoughts on client and server backups:

✦ **Backing up directly from the server isn't necessarily more efficient than backing up from a client because data doesn't have to travel over the network.** The network may well be faster than the tape drive. The network probably won't slow down backups unless you back up during the busiest time of the day, when hordes of network users are storming the network gates.

✦ **To improve network backup speed and to minimize the effect that network backups have on the rest of the network, consider using a 1,000 Mbps switch instead of a normal 100 Mbps switch to connect the servers and the backup client.** That way, network traffic between the server and the backup client won't bog down the rest of the network.

✦ **Any files that are open while the backups are running won't get backed up.** That's usually not a problem, because backups are run at off hours when people have gone home. If someone leaves his computer on with a Word document open, however, that Word document won't be backed up. One way to solve this problem is to set up the server so that it automatically logs everyone off the network before the backups begin.

✦ **Some backup programs have special features that enable them to back up open files.** The Windows Server 2003 and 2008 backup programs do this by creating a snapshot of the volume when it begins, thus making temporary copies of any files that are modified during the backup. The backup backs up the temporary copies rather than the versions being modified. When the backup finishes, the temporary copies are deleted.

How Many Sets of Backups Should You Keep?

Don't try to cut costs by purchasing one backup tape and reusing it every day. What happens if you accidentally delete an important file on Tuesday and don't discover your mistake until Thursday? Because the file didn't exist on Wednesday, it won't be on Wednesday's backup tape. If you have only one tape that's reused every day, you're outta luck.

The safest scheme is to use a new backup tape every day and keep all your old tapes in a vault. Pretty soon, though, your tape vault can start looking like the warehouse where they stored the Ark of the Covenant at the end of *Raiders of the Lost Ark*.

As a compromise between these two extremes, most users purchase several tapes and rotate them. That way, you always have several backup tapes to fall back on, just in case the file you need isn't on the most recent backup tape. This technique is *tape rotation,* and several variations are commonly used:

+ **The simplest approach is to purchase three tapes and label them A, B, and C.** You use the tapes on a daily basis in sequence: A the first day, B the second day, and C the third day; then A the fourth day, B the fifth day, C the sixth day, and so on. On any given day, you have three generations of backups: today's, yesterday's, and the day-before-yesterday's. Computer geeks like to call these the *grandfather, father,* and *son* tapes.

+ **Purchase five tapes and use one each day of the workweek.** This is another simple approach.

+ **A variation of the A, B, and C approach is to buy eight tapes.** Take four of them, and write *Tuesday* on one label, *Wednesday* on the second, *Thursday* on the third, and *Friday* on the fourth label. On the other four tapes, write *Monday 1, Monday 2, Monday 3,* and *Monday 4.* Now tack up a calendar on the wall near the computer, and number all the Mondays in the year: 1, 2, 3, 4, 1, 2, 3, 4, and so on.

  On Tuesday through Friday, you use the appropriate daily backup tape. When you run a full backup on Monday, consult the calendar to decide which Monday tape to use. With this scheme, you always have four weeks' worth of Monday backup tapes, plus individual backup tapes for the rest of the week.

+ **If bookkeeping data lives on the network, make a backup copy of all your files (or at least all your accounting files) immediately before closing the books each month; then retain those backups for each month of the year.** This doesn't necessarily mean that you should purchase 12 additional tapes. If you back up just your accounting files, you can probably fit all 12 months on a single tape. Just make sure that you back up with the "append to tape" option rather than the "erase tape" option so that the previous contents of the tape aren't destroyed. Also, treat this accounting backup as completely separate from your normal daily backup routine.

Keep at least one recent full backup at another location. That way, if your office should fall victim to an errant Scud missile or a rogue asteroid, you can re-create your data from the backup copy that you stored offsite. Make sure that the person entrusted with the task of taking the backups to this offsite location is trustworthy.

A Word about Tape Reliability

From experience, I've found that although tape drives are very reliable, they do run amok once in a while. The problem is that they don't always tell you when they're not working. A tape drive (especially one of the less-expensive Travan drives; refer to "All about Tapes and Tape Drives," earlier in this chapter) can spin along for hours, pretending to back up your data — but in reality, your data isn't being written reliably to the tape. In other words, a tape drive can trick you into thinking that your backups are working just fine. Then, when disaster strikes and you need your backup tapes, you may just discover that the tapes are worthless.

Don't panic! Here's a simple way to assure yourself that your tape drive is working. Just activate the "compare after backup" feature of your backup software. As soon as your backup program finishes backing up your data, it rewinds the tape, reads each backed-up file, and compares it with the original version on the hard drive. If all files compare, you know that your backups are trustworthy.

Here are some additional thoughts about the reliability of tapes:

✦ The compare-after-backup feature doubles the time required to do a backup, but that doesn't matter if your entire backup fits on one tape. You can just run the backup after hours. Whether the backup and repair operation takes one hour or ten doesn't matter, as long as it's finished by the time the network users arrive at work the next morning.

✦ If your backups require more than one tape, you may not want to run the compare-after-backup feature every day. Be sure to run it periodically, however, to check that your tape drive is working.

✦ If your backup program reports errors, throw away the tape, and use a new tape.

✦ Actually, you should ignore that last comment about waiting for your backup program to report errors. You should discard tapes *before* your backup program reports errors. Most experts recommend that you should use a tape only about 20 times before discarding it. If you use the same tape every day, replace it monthly. If you have tapes for each day of the week, replace them twice yearly. If you have more tapes than that, figure out a cycle that replaces tapes after about 20 uses.

About Cleaning the Heads

An important aspect of backup reliability is proper maintenance of your tape drives. Every time you back up to tape, little bits and specks of the tape rub off onto the read and write heads inside the tape drive. Eventually, the heads become too dirty to read or write data reliably.

To counteract this problem, clean the tape heads regularly. The easiest way to clean them is to use a cleaning cartridge for the tape drive. The drive automatically recognizes when you insert a cleaning cartridge and then performs a routine that wipes the cleaning tape back and forth over the heads to clean them. When the cleaning routine is done, the tape is ejected. The whole process takes only about 30 seconds.

Because the maintenance requirements of drives differ, check each drive's user's manual to find out how and how often to clean the drive. As a general rule, clean drives once weekly.

The most annoying aspect of tape drive cleaning is that the cleaning cartridges have a limited life span, and unfortunately, if you insert a used-up cleaning cartridge, the drive accepts it and pretends to clean the drive. For this reason, keep track of how many times you use a cleaning cartridge and replace it as recommended by the manufacturer.

Backup Security

Backups create an often-overlooked security exposure for your network: No matter how carefully you set up user accounts and enforce password policies, if any user (including a guest) can perform a backup of the system, that user may make an unauthorized backup. In addition, your backup tapes themselves are vulnerable to theft. As a result, make sure that your backup policies and procedures are secure by taking the following measures:

✦ **Set up a user account for the user who does backups.** Because this user account has backup permission for the entire server, guard its password carefully. Anyone who knows the username and password of the backup account can log on and bypass any security restrictions that you place on that user's normal user ID.

✦ **Counter potential security problems by restricting the backup user ID to a certain client and a certain time of the day.** If you're really clever (and paranoid), you can probably set up the backup user's account so that the only program it can run is the backup program.

✦ **Use encryption to protect the contents of your backup tapes.**

✦ **Secure the backup tapes in a safe location, such as . . . um, a safe.**

Chapter 9: Disaster Recovery and Business Continuity Planning

In This Chapter

✔ Realizing the need for backups

✔ Making a plan

✔ Practicing disaster recovery

✔ Remembering tape rotation and other details

*O*n April Fools' Day about 20 years ago, my colleagues and I discovered that some loser had broken into the office the night before and pounded our computer equipment to death with a crowbar. (I'm not making this up.)

Sitting on a shelf right next to the mangled piles of what used to be a Wang minicomputer system was an undisturbed disk pack that contained the only complete backup of all the information that was on the destroyed computer. The vandal didn't realize that one more swing of the crowbar would have escalated this major inconvenience into a complete catastrophe. Sure, we were up a creek until we could get the computer replaced. And in those days, you couldn't just walk into your local Computer Depot and buy a new computer off the shelf — this was a Wang minicomputer system that had to be specially ordered. After we had the new computer, though, a simple restore from the backup disk brought us right back to where we were on March 31. Without that backup, getting back on track would have taken months.

I've been paranoid about disaster planning ever since. Before then, I thought that disaster planning meant doing good backups. That's a part of it, but I can never forget the day we came within one swing of the crowbar of losing everything. Vandals are probably much smarter now: They know to smash the backup disks as well as the computers themselves. Being prepared for disasters entails much more than just doing regular backups.

Nowadays, the trendy term for disaster planning is a business continuity plan (BCP). I suppose the term "disaster planning" sounded too negative, like we were planning for disasters to happen. The new term refocuses attention on the more positive aspect of preparing a plan that will enable a business to carry on with as little interruption as possible in the event of a disaster.

For more in-depth information about this topic, please refer to *IT Disaster Recovery Planning For Dummies,* by Peter Gregory (Wiley).

Assessing Different Types of Disasters

Disasters come in many shapes and sizes. Some types of disasters are more likely than others. For example, your building is more likely to be struck by lightning than to be hit by a comet. In some cases, the likelihood of a particular type of disaster depends on where you're located. For example, crippling snowstorms are more likely in New York than in Florida.

In addition, the impact of each type of disaster varies from company to company. What may be a disaster for one company may only be a mere inconvenience for another. For example, a law firm may tolerate a disruption in telephone service for a day or two. Loss of communication via phone would be a major inconvenience but not a disaster. To a telemarketing firm, however, a day or two with the phones down is a more severe problem because the company's revenue depends on the phones.

One of the first steps in developing a business continuity plan is to assess the risk of the various types of disasters that may affect your organization. Weigh the likelihood of a disaster happening with the severity of the impact that the disaster would have. For example, a meteor crashing into your building would probably be pretty severe, but the odds of that happening are miniscule. On the other hand, the odds of your building being destroyed by fire are much higher, and the consequences of a devastating fire would be about the same as those from a meteor impact.

The following sections describe the most common types of risks that most companies face. Notice throughout this discussion that although many of these risks are related to computers and network technology, some are not. The scope of business continuity planning is much larger than just computer technology.

Environmental disasters

Environmental disasters are what most people think of first when they think of disaster recovery. Some types of environmental disasters are regional. Others can happen pretty much anywhere.

✦ **Fire:** Fire is probably the first disaster that most people think of when they consider disaster planning. Fires can be caused by unsafe conditions; carelessness, such as electrical wiring that isn't up to code; natural causes, such as lightning strikes; or arson.

✦ **Earthquakes:** Not only can earthquakes cause structural damage to your building, but they can also disrupt the delivery of key services and utilities, such as water and power. Serious earthquakes are rare and unpredictable, but some areas experience them with more regularity than others. If your business is located in an area known for earthquakes, your BCP should consider how your company would deal with a devastating earthquake.

✦ **Weather:** Weather disasters can cause major disruption to your business. Moderate weather may close transportation systems so that your employees can't get to work. Severe weather may damage your building or interrupt delivery of services, such as electricity and water.

✦ **Water:** Flooding can wreak havoc with electrical equipment, such as computers. If floodwaters get into your computer room, chances are good that the computer equipment will be totally destroyed. Flooding can be caused not only by bad weather but also by burst pipes or malfunctioning sprinklers.

✦ **Lightning:** Lightning storms can cause electrical damage to your computer and other electronic equipment from lightning strikes as well as surges in the local power supply.

Book II
Chapter 9

Disaster Recovery
and Business
Continuity Planning

Deliberate disasters

Some disasters are the result of deliberate actions by others. For example:

✦ **Intentional damage:** Vandalism or arson may damage or destroy your facilities or your computer systems. The vandalism or arson may be targeted at you specifically, by a disgruntled employee or customer, or it may be random. Either way, the effect is the same.

Don't neglect the possibility of sabotage. A disgruntled employee who gets hold of an administrator's account and password can do all sorts of nasty things to your network.

✦ **Theft:** Theft is always a possibility. You may come to work someday to find that your servers or other computer equipment have been stolen.

✦ **Terrorism:** Terrorism used to be something that most Americans weren't concerned about, but September 11, 2001, changed all that. No matter where you live in the world, the possibility of a terrorist attack is real.

Disruption of services

You may not realize just how much your business depends on the delivery of services and utilities. A BCP should take into consideration how you will deal with the loss of certain services:

✦ **No juice:** Electrical power is crucial for computers and other types of equipment. During a power failure once (I live in California, so I'm used to it), I discovered that I can't even work with pencil and paper because all my pencil sharpeners are electric. Electrical outages are not uncommon, but the technology to deal with them is readily available. Uninterruptible power supply (UPS) equipment is reliable and inexpensive.

✦ **No communications:** Communication connections can be disrupted by many causes. A few years ago, a railroad overpass was constructed across the street from my office. One day, a backhoe cut through the phone lines, completely cutting off our phone service — including our Internet connection — for a day and a half.

✦ **No water:** An interruption in the water supply may not shut down your computers, but it can disrupt your business by forcing you to close your facility until the water supply is reestablished.

Equipment failure

Modern companies depend on many different types of equipment for their daily operations. The failure of any of these key systems can disrupt business until the systems are repaired:

✦ **Computer equipment failure can obviously affect business operations.**

✦ **Air-conditioning systems are crucial to regulate temperatures, especially in computer rooms.** Computer equipment can be damaged if the temperature climbs too high.

✦ **Elevators, automatic doors, and other equipment may also be necessary for your business.**

Other disasters

You should assess many other potential disasters. Here are just a few:

✦ Labor disputes

✦ Loss of key staff because of resignation, injury, sickness, or death

✦ Workplace violence

✦ Public health issues, such as epidemics, mold infestations, and so on

✦ Loss of a key supplier

✦ Nearby disaster, such as a fire or police action across the street that results in your business being temporarily blocked off

Analyzing the Impact of a Disaster

With a good understanding of the types of disasters that can affect your business, you can turn your attention to the impact that these disasters can have on your business. The first step is to identify the key business processes that can be impacted by different types of disasters. These business processes are different for each company. For example, here are a few of the key business processes for a publishing company:

+ **Editorial,** such as managing projects through the process of technical editing, copyediting, and production

+ **Acquisition,** such as determining product development strategies, recruiting authors, and signing projects

+ **Human resource,** such as payroll, hiring, employee review, and recruiting

+ **Marketing,** including sales tracking, developing marketing materials, sponsoring sales conferences, and exhibiting at trade events

+ **Sales and billing,** such as filling customer orders, maintaining the company website, managing inventory, and handling payments

+ **Executive and financial,** such as managing cash flow, securing credit, raising capital, deciding when to go public, and deciding when to buy a smaller publisher or sell out to a bigger publisher

The impact of a disruption to each of these processes will vary. One common way to assess the impact of business process loss is to rate the impact of various degrees of loss for each process. For example, you may rate the loss of each process for the following time frames:

+ 0 to 2 hours

+ 2 to 24 hours

+ 1 to 2 days

+ 2 days to 1 week

+ More than 1 week

For some business processes, an interruption of two hours or even one day may be minor. For other processes, even the loss of a few hours may be very costly.

Developing a Business Continuity Plan

A BCP is simply a plan for how you will continue operation of your key business processes should the normal operation of the process fail. For example, if your primary office location is shut down for a week because of a major fire across the street, you won't have to suspend operations if you have a business continuity plan in place.

The key to a BCP is redundancy of each component that is essential to your business processes. These components include:

✦ **Facilities:** If your company already has multiple office locations, you may be able to temporarily squeeze into one of the other locations for the duration of the disaster. If not, you should secure arrangements in advance with a real estate broker so that you can quickly arrange an alternate location. By having an arrangement made in advance, you can move into an emergency location on a moment's notice.

✦ **Computer equipment:** It doesn't hurt to have a set of spare computers in storage somewhere so that you can dig them out to use in an emergency. Preferably, these computers would already have your critical software installed. The next best thing would be to have detailed plans available so that your IT staff can quickly install key software on new equipment to get your business up and running.

Always keep a current set of backup tapes at an alternate location.

✦ **Phones:** Discuss emergency phone services in advance with your phone company. If you're forced to move to another location on 24-hour notice, how quickly can you get your phones up and running? And can you arrange to have your incoming toll-free calls forwarded to the new location?

✦ **Staff:** Unless you work for a government agency, you probably don't have redundant employees. However, you can make arrangements in advance with a temp agency to provide clerical and administrative help on short notice.

✦ **Stationery:** This sounds like a small detail, but you should store a supply of all your key stationery products (letterhead, envelopes, invoices, statements, and so on) in a safe location. That way, if your main location is suddenly unavailable, you don't have to wait a week to get new letterhead or invoices printed.

✦ **Hard copy files:** Keep a backup copy of important printed material (customer billing files, sales records, and so on) at an alternate location.

Holding a Fire Drill

Remember in grade school when the fire alarm would go off and your teacher would tell you and the other kids to calmly put down your work and walk out to the designated safe zone in an orderly fashion? Drills are important so that if a real fire occurs, you don't run and scream and climb all over each other in order to be the first one to get out.

Any disaster recovery plan is incomplete unless you test it to see whether it works. Testing doesn't mean that you should burn your building down one day to see how long it takes you to get back up and running. You should, though, periodically simulate a disaster in order to prove to yourself and your staff that you can recover.

The most basic type of disaster recovery drill is a simple test of your network backup procedures. You should periodically attempt to restore key files from your backup tapes just to make sure that you can. You achieve several benefits by restoring files on a regular basis:

+ **Tapes are unreliable.** The only way to be sure that your tapes are working is to periodically restore files from them.

+ **Backup programs are confusing to configure.** I've seen people run backup jobs for years that don't include all the data they think they're backing up. Only when disaster strikes and they need to recover a key file do they discover that the file isn't included in the backup.

+ **Restoring files can be a little confusing, especially when you use a combination of normal and incremental or differential backups.** Add to that the pressure of having the head of the company watching over your shoulder while you try to recover a lost file. If you regularly conduct file restore drills, you'll familiarize yourself with the restore features of your backup software in a low-pressure situation. Then, you can easily restore files for real when the pressure's on.

You can also conduct walk-throughs of more serious disaster scenarios. For example, you can set aside a day to walk through moving your entire staff to an alternate location. You can double-check that all the backup equipment, documents, and data are available as planned. If something is missing, it's better to find out now rather than while the fire department is still putting water on the last remaining hot spots in what used to be your office.

Book III

Protocols

Local Area Connection Properties   ⊗ ✕

Networking | Sharing

Connect using:

🖧 Realtek PCIe GBE Family Controller

Configure...

This connection uses the following items:

☑ 🖧 Client for Microsoft Networks
☑ 🖳 VMware Bridge Protocol
☑ 🖳 QoS Packet Scheduler
☑ 🖳 File and Printer Sharing for Microsoft Networks
☑ ⊥ Internet Protocol Version 6 (TCP/IPv6)
☑ ⊥ Internet Protocol Version 4 (TCP/IPv4)
☑ ⊥ Link-Layer Topology Discovery Mapper I/O Driver
☑ ⊥ Link-Layer Topology Discovery Responder

Install... | Uninstall | Properties

Description
Allows your computer to access resources on a Microsoft network.

OK | Cancel

web extras

Read about the best April Fool's Day RFCs in an article at www.dummies.com/extras/networkingaio.

Contents at a Glance

Chapter 1: Understanding Network Protocols and Standards 227

Chapter 2: Introduction to TCP/IP and the Internet 249

Chapter 3: Understanding IP Addresses 257

Chapter 4: Using DHCP 275

Chapter 5: Using DNS 291

Chapter 6: Using FTP 317

Chapter 7: TCP/IP Tools and Commands 339

Chapter 1: Understanding Network Protocols and Standards

In This Chapter

✓ Discovering protocols

✓ Deciphering the layers of the OSI reference model

✓ Understanding an Ethernet

✓ Getting the inside scoop on TCP/IP and IPX/SPX

✓ Finding out about other important protocols

*P*rotocols and standards make networks work together. Protocols make it possible for the various components of a network to communicate with each other, and standards make it possible for different manufacturers' network components to work together. This chapter introduces you to the protocols and standards that you're most likely to encounter when building and maintaining a network.

Understanding Protocols

A *protocol* is simply a set of rules that enable effective communications to occur. You encounter protocols every day and probably don't even realize it. When you pay for groceries with a debit card, the clerk tells you how much the groceries cost, and then you swipe your debit card in the card reader, punch in your security code, indicate whether you want cash back, enter the amount of the cash back if you so indicated, and verify the total amount. You then cross your fingers behind your back and say a quiet prayer while the machine authorizes the purchase. Assuming the amount is authorized, the machine prints out your receipt.

Here's another example of an everyday protocol: making a phone call. You probably take most of the details of the phone-calling protocol for granted, but it's pretty complicated if you think about it:

✦ When you pick up a phone, you listen for a dial tone before dialing the number (unless you're using a cellphone). If you don't hear a dial tone, you know that someone else in your family is talking on the phone, or something is wrong with your phone.

✦ When you hear the dial tone, you dial the number of the party you want to reach. If the person you want to call is in the same area code, you simply dial that person's seven-digit phone number. If the person is in a different area code, you dial 1, the three-digit area code, and the person's seven-digit phone number.

✦ If you hear a series of long ringing tones, you wait until the other person answers the phone. If the phone rings a certain number of times with no answer, you hang up and try again later. If you hear a voice say, "Hello," you begin a conversation with the other party. If the person on the other end of the phone has never heard of you, you say, "Sorry, wrong number," hang up, and try again.

✦ If you hear a voice that rambles on about how they're not home but they want to return your call, you wait for a beep and leave a message.

✦ If you hear a series of short tones, you know the other person is talking to someone else on the phone. So you hang up and try again later.

✦ If you hear a sequence of three tones that increase in pitch, followed by a recorded voice that says "We're sorry . . ." you know that the number you dialed is invalid. Either you dialed the number incorrectly, or the number has been disconnected.

You get the point. Exchanges — using a debit card or making a phone call — follow the same rules every time they happen.

Computer networks depend upon many different types of protocols. These protocols are very rigidly defined, and for good reason. Network cards must know how to talk to other network cards to exchange information, operating systems must know how to talk to network cards to send and receive data on the network, and application programs must know how to talk to operating systems to know how to retrieve a file from a network server.

Protocols come in many different types. At the lowest level, protocols define exactly what type of electrical signal represents a 1 and what type of signal represents a 0. At the highest level, protocols allow (say) a computer user in the United States to send an email to another computer user in New Zealand — and in between are many other levels of protocols. You find out more about these levels of protocols (often called "layers") in the upcoming section, "Seeing the Seven Layers of the OSI Reference Model."

Protocols tend to be used together in matched sets called *protocol suites.* The two most popular protocol suites for networking are TCP/IP and Ethernet. TCP/IP, originally developed for Unix networks, is the protocol of the Internet and most local area networks (LANs). Ethernet is a low-level protocol that spells out the electrical characteristics of the network hardware used by most LANs. A third important protocol is IPX/SPX, which is an alternative to TCP/IP, and originally developed for NetWare networks. In the early days of networking, IPX/SPX was widely used in LANs, but TCP/IP is now the preferred protocol.

Understanding Standards

As I mention earlier, a *standard* is an agreed-upon definition of a protocol. In the early days of computer networking, each computer manufacturer developed its own networking protocols. As a result, you couldn't easily mix equipment from different manufacturers on a single network.

Then along came standards to save the day. Hurrah! Because standards are industry-wide protocol definitions not tied to a particular manufacturer, you can mix and match equipment from different vendors. As long as the equipment implements the standard protocols, it should be able to coexist on the same network.

Many organizations are involved in setting standards for networking. The five most important organizations are

✦ **American National Standards Institute (ANSI):** The official standards organization in the United States. ANSI is pronounced *AN-see*. `www.ansi.org`

✦ **Institute of Electrical and Electronics Engineers (IEEE):** An international organization that publishes several key networking standards — in particular, the official standard for the Ethernet networking system (known officially as IEEE 802.3). IEEE is pronounced *eye-triple-E*. `www.ieee.org`

✦ **International Organization for Standardization (ISO):** A federation of more than 100 standards organizations throughout the world. If I had studied French in high school, I'd probably understand why the acronym for International Organization for Standardization is ISO, and not IOS. `www.iso.org`

✦ **Internet Engineering Task Force (IETF):** The organization responsible for the protocols that drive the Internet. `www.ietf.org`

✦ **World Wide Web Consortium (W3C):** An international organization that handles the development of standards for the World Wide Web. `www.w3.org`

**Book III
Chapter 1**

**Understanding
Network Protocols
and Standards**

Seeing the Seven Layers of the OSI Reference Model

"OSI" sounds like the name of a top-secret government agency you hear about only in Tom Clancy novels. What it really stands for in the networking world is Open Systems Interconnection, as in the Open Systems Interconnection Reference Model, affectionately known as the *OSI model.*

The OSI model breaks the various aspects of a computer network into seven distinct layers. These layers are kind of like the layers of an onion: Each successive layer envelops the layer beneath it, hiding its details from the levels above. The OSI model is also like an onion in that if you start to peel it apart to have a look inside, you're bound to shed a few tears.

The OSI model is not a networking standard in the same sense that Ethernet and TCP/IP are networking standards. Rather, the OSI model is a framework into which the various networking standards can fit. The OSI model specifies what aspects of a network's operation can be addressed by various network standards. So, in a sense, the OSI model is sort of a standard of standards.

Table 1-1 summarizes the seven layers of the OSI model.

Table 1-1		The Seven Layers of the OSI Model
Layer	*Name*	*Description*
1	Physical	Governs the layout of cables and devices, such as repeaters and hubs.
2	Data Link	Provides MAC* addresses to uniquely identify network nodes and a means for data to be sent over the Physical layer in the form of packets. Bridges and switches are Layer 2 devices.
3	Network	Handles routing of data across network segments.
4	Transport	Provides for reliable delivery of packets.
5	Session	Establishes sessions between network applications.
6	Presentation	Converts data so that systems that use different data formats can exchange information.
7	Application	Allows applications to request network services.

MAC = Media Access Control. Read more about MAC and bridges and switches in "The Data Link layer."

The first three layers are sometimes called the *lower layers*. They deal with the mechanics of how information is sent from one computer to another over a network. Layers 4–7 are sometimes called the *upper layers*. They deal with how application software can relate to the network through application programming interfaces.

The following sections describe each of these layers in greater detail.

The seven layers of the OSI model are a somewhat idealized view of how networking protocols should work. In the real world, actual networking protocols don't follow the OSI model to the letter. The real world is always messier. Still, the OSI model provides a convenient — if not completely accurate — conceptual picture of how networking works.

The Physical layer

The bottom layer of the OSI model is the *Physical layer.* It addresses the physical characteristics of the network, such as the types of cables used to connect devices, the types of connectors used, how long the cables can be, and so on. For example, the Ethernet standard for 10BaseT cable specifies the electrical characteristics of the twisted-pair cables, the size and shape of the connectors, the maximum length of the cables, and so on. The star, bus, ring, and mesh network topologies described in Chapter 1 of this minibook apply to the Physical layer.

Another aspect of the Physical layer is the electrical characteristics of the signals used to transmit data over the cables from one network node to another. The Physical layer doesn't define any meaning to those signals other than the basic binary values of 1 and 0. The higher levels of the OSI model must assign meanings to the bits that are transmitted at the Physical layer.

One type of Physical layer device commonly used in networks is a *repeater,* which is used to regenerate the signal whenever you need to exceed the cable length allowed by the Physical layer standard. 10BaseT hubs are also Physical layer devices. Technically, they're known as *multiport repeaters* because the purpose of a hub is to regenerate every packet received on any port on all the hub's other ports. Repeaters and hubs don't examine the contents of the packets that they regenerate, though. If they did, they would be working at the Data Link layer, and not at the Physical layer.

The *network adapter* (also called a network interface card; NIC) installed in each computer on the network is a Physical layer device. You can display information about the network adapter (or adapters) installed in a Windows computer by displaying the adapter's Properties dialog box, as shown in Figure 1-1. To access this dialog box in Windows, open the Control Panel, choose Network and Sharing Center, and then choose Change Adapter Settings. Then right-click the Local Area Connection icon and choose Properties from the menu that appears.

**Book III
Chapter 1**

**Understanding
Network Protocols
and Standards**

Figure 1-1:
The Proper-
ties dialog
box for a
network
adapter.

The Data Link layer

The *Data Link layer* is the lowest layer at which meaning is assigned to the bits that are transmitted over the network. Data link protocols address things, such as the size of each packet of data to be sent, a means of addressing each packet so that it's delivered to the intended recipient, and a way to ensure that two or more nodes don't try to transmit data on the network at the same time.

The Data Link layer also provides basic error detection and correction to ensure that the data sent is the same as the data received. If an uncorrectable error occurs, the data link standard must specify how the node is to be informed of the error so that it can retransmit the data.

At the Data Link layer, each device on the network has an address: the Media Access Control (MAC). This address is hard-wired into every network device by the manufacturer. MAC addresses are unique; no two network devices made by any manufacturer anywhere in the world can have the same MAC address.

You can see the MAC address for a computer's network adapter by opening a command window and running the `ipconfig /all` command, as shown in Figure 1-2. In this example, the MAC address of the network card is 00-40-F4-CD-A9-50. (The `ipconfig` command refers to the MAC address as the *physical address.*)

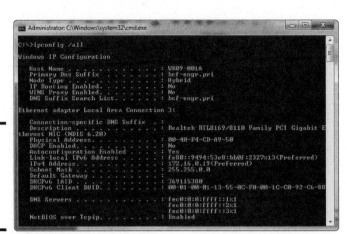

**Book III
Chapter 1**

**Understanding
Network Protocols
and Standards**

Figure 1-2:
Display
the MAC
address of
a network
adapter.

One of the most import functions of the Data Link layer is to provide a
way for packets to be sent safely over the physical media without interference from other nodes attempting to send packets at the same time. The
two most popular ways to do this are CSMA/CD and token passing. (Take a
deep breath. CSMA/CD stands for Carrier Sense Multiple Access/Collision
Detection.) Ethernet networks use CSMA/CD, and token ring networks use
token passing.

Two types of Data Link layer devices are commonly used on networks:

✦ **Bridge:** An intelligent repeater that's aware of the MAC addresses of the
nodes on either side of the bridge and can forward packets accordingly.

Switch: An intelligent hub that examines the MAC address of arriving
packets to determine which port to forward the packet to.

The Network layer

The *Network layer* handles the task of routing network messages from one
computer to another. The two most popular Layer 3 protocols are IP (which
is usually paired with TCP) and IPX (typically paired with SPX for use with
Novell and Windows networks).

Network layer protocols provide two important functions: logical addressing
and routing. The following sections describe these functions.

CSMA/CD is a mouthful!

An important function of the Data Link layer is to make sure that two computers don't try to send packets over the network at the same time. If they do, the signals will collide with each other, and the transmission will be garbled. Ethernet accomplishes this feat by using CSMA/CD. This phrase is a mouthful, but if you take it apart piece by piece, you'll get an idea of how it works.

✔ *Carrier Sense* means that whenever a device wants to send a packet over the network media, it first listens to the network media to see whether anyone else is already sending a packet. If it doesn't hear any other signals on the media, the computer assumes that the network is free, so it sends the packet.

✔ *Multiple Access* means that nothing prevents two or more devices from trying to send a message at the same time. Sure, each device listens before sending. However, suppose that two devices listen, hear nothing, and then proceed to send their packets at the same time? Picture

what happens when you and someone else arrive at a four-way stop sign at the same time. You wave the other driver on, he or she waves you on, you wave, he or she waves, you both wave, and then you both go at the same time.

✔ *Collision Detection* means that after a device sends a packet, it listens carefully to see whether the packet crashes into another packet. This is kind of like listening for the screeching of brakes at the four-way stop. If the device hears the screeching of brakes, it waits a random period of time and then tries to send the packet again. Because the delay is random, two packets that collide are sent again after different delay periods, so a second collision is unlikely.

CSMA/CD works pretty well for smaller networks. After a network hits about 30 computers, however, packets start to collide like crazy, and the network slows to a crawl. When that happens, the network should be divided into two or more separate sections that are sometimes called *collision domains*.

Logical addressing

As I mention earlier, every network device has a physical address — a MAC address — assigned to the device at the factory. When you buy a network interface card to install into a computer, the MAC address of that card is fixed and can't be changed. So what happens if you want to use some other addressing scheme to refer to the computers and other devices on your network? This is where the concept of logical addressing comes in; with a logical address, you can access a network device by using an address that you assign.

Logical addresses are created and used by Network layer protocols, such as IP or IPX. The Network layer protocol translates logical addresses to MAC addresses. For example, if you use IP as the Network layer protocol, devices on the network are assigned IP addresses, such as 207.120.67.30. Because the IP protocol must use a Data Link layer protocol to send packets to devices, IP must know how to translate the IP address of a device to the device's MAC address.

You can use the `ipconfig` command (shown earlier in Figure 1-2) to see the IP address of your computer. The IP address shown in that figure is 172.16.0.19. Another way to display this information is to use the System Information command, found on the Start menu under Start ⇨ All Programs ⇨ Accessories ⇨ System Tools ⇨ System Information. The IP address is highlighted in Figure 1-3. Notice that the System Information program displays a lot of other useful information about the network besides the IP address. For example, you can also see the MAC address and what protocols are being used.

Figure 1-3: Find network information from System Information.

Book III Chapter 1

Understanding Network Protocols and Standards

Although the exact format of logical addresses varies depending on the protocol being used, most protocols divide the logical address into two parts:

✦ **Network address:** Identifies which network the device resides on

✦ **Device address:** Identifies the device on that network

In a typical IP address — say, 192.168.1.102 — the network address is 192.168.1, and the device address (called a *host address* in IP) is 102.

Similarly, IPX addresses consist of two parts: a network address and a node address. In an IPX address, the node address is the same as the MAC address. As a result, IPX doesn't have to translate between Layer 2 and Layer 3 addresses.

Routing

Routing comes into play when a computer on one network needs to send a packet to a computer on another network. In this case, a router is used to forward the packet to the destination network. In some cases, a packet may have to travel through several intermediate networks in order to reach its final destination network. You can find out more about routers in Chapter 3 of this minibook.

An important feature of routers is that you can use them to connect networks that use different Layer 2 protocols. For example, a router can be used to send a packet from an Ethernet to a token ring network. As long as both networks support the same Layer 3 protocol, it doesn't matter whether their Layer 1 and Layer 2 protocols are different.

A protocol is considered routable if it uses addresses that include a network part and a host part. Any protocol that uses physical addresses isn't routable because physical addresses don't indicate to which network a device belongs.

The Transport layer

The *Transport layer* is where you find two of the most well-known networking protocols: TCP (typically paired with IP) and SPX (typically paired with IPX). As its name implies, the Transport layer is concerned with the transportation of information from one computer to another.

The main purpose of the Transport layer is to ensure that packets are transported reliably and without errors. The Transport layer does this task by establishing connections between network devices, acknowledging the receipt of packets, and resending packets that aren't received or are corrupted when they arrive.

In many cases, the Transport layer protocol divides large messages into smaller packets that can be sent over the network efficiently. The Transport layer protocol reassembles the message on the receiving end, making sure that all the packets that make up a single transmission are received so that no data is lost.

For some applications, speed and efficiency are more important than reliability. In such cases, a connectionless protocol can be used. As you can likely guess, a connectionless protocol doesn't go to the trouble of establishing a connection before sending a packet: It simply sends the packet. TCP is a connection-oriented Transport layer protocol. The connectionless protocol that works alongside TCP is User Datagram Protocol (UDP).

You can view information about the status of TCP and UDP connections by running the `Netstat` command from a command window, as Figure 1-4 shows. In the figure, you can see that several TCP connections are established.

Figure 1-4:
See TCP
and UDP
connections.

**Book III
Chapter 1**

Understanding
Network Protocols
and Standards

In fact, you can use the command `Netstat /N` to see the numeric network addresses instead of the names. With the `/N` switch, the output in Figure 1-4 would look like this:

```
Active Connections
    Proto  Local Address          Foreign Address        State
    TCP    127.0.0.1:2869         127.0.0.1:54170        ESTABLISHED
    TCP    127.0.0.1:5357         127.0.0.1:54172        TIME_WAIT
    TCP    127.0.0.1:27015        127.0.0.1:49301        ESTABLISHED
    TCP    127.0.0.1:49301        127.0.0.1:27015        ESTABLISHED
    TCP    127.0.0.1:54170        127.0.0.1:2869         ESTABLISHED
    TCP    192.168.1.100:49300    192.168.1.101:445      ESTABLISHED
```

TCP is a connection-oriented Transport layer protocol. *UDP* is a connectionless Transport layer protocol.

The Session layer

The *Session layer* establishes *conversations* — sessions — between networked devices. A *session* is an exchange of connection-oriented transmissions between two network devices. Each transmission is handled by the Transport layer protocol. The session itself is managed by the Session layer protocol.

A single session can include many exchanges of data between the two computers involved in the session. After a session between two computers has been established, it's maintained until the computers agree to terminate the session.

The Session layer allows three types of transmission modes:

+ **Simplex:** Data flows in only one direction.

+ **Half-duplex:** Data flows in both directions, but only in one direction at a time.

+ **Full-duplex:** Data flows in both directions at the same time.

In actual practice, the distinctions in the Session, Presentation, and Application layers are often blurred, and some commonly used protocols actually span all three layers. For example, SMB — the protocol that is the basis of file sharing in Windows networks — functions at all three layers.

The Presentation layer

The *Presentation layer* is responsible for how data is represented to applications. The most common representation for representing character data today is called UTF-8, which uses 8-bit sets to represent most characters found in Western alphabets. UTF-8 is compatible with an older standard called ASCII.

UTF-8 is sometimes called *Unicode,* which is a standard for representing the characters found in most of the world's writing systems. Technically, UTF-8 is a particular method of implementing Unicode, so although the two terms are related, they are not identical.

Some computers, in particular IBM mainframe computers, use a different code called Extended Binary Coded Decimal Interchange Code (EBCDIC). ASCII and EBCDIC aren't compatible. To exchange information between a mainframe computer and a Windows computer, the Presentation layer must convert the data from ASCII to EBCDIC, and vice versa.

Besides simply converting data from one code to another, the Presentation layer can also apply sophisticated compression techniques so that fewer bytes of data are required to represent the information when it's sent over the network. At the other end of the transmission, the Presentation layer then uncompresses the data.

The Presentation layer can also scramble the data before it's transmitted and then unscramble it at the other end by using a sophisticated encryption technique that even Sherlock Holmes would have trouble breaking.

The Application layer

The highest layer of the OSI model, the Application layer deals with the techniques that application programs use to communicate with the network. The name of this layer is a little confusing. Application programs (such as Microsoft Office or QuickBooks) aren't a part of the Application layer. Rather, the Application layer represents the programming interfaces that application programs use to request network services.

Some of the better-known Application layer protocols are

+ **Domain Name System (DNS):** For resolving Internet domain names
+ **File Transfer Protocol (FTP):** For file transfers
+ **Simple Mail Transfer Protocol (SMTP):** For email
+ **Server Message Block (SMB):** For file sharing in Windows networks
+ **Network File System (NFS):** For file sharing in Unix networks
+ **Telnet:** For terminal emulation

Following a Packet through the Layers

Figure 1-5 shows how a packet of information flows through the seven layers as it travels from one computer to another on the network. The data begins its journey when an end-user application sends data to another network computer. The data enters the network through an Application layer interface, such as SMB. The data then works its way down through the protocol stack. Along the way, the protocol at each layer manipulates the data by adding header information, converting the data into different formats, combining packets to form larger packets, and so on. When the data reaches the Physical layer protocol, it's placed on the network media (in other words, the cable) and sent to the receiving computer.

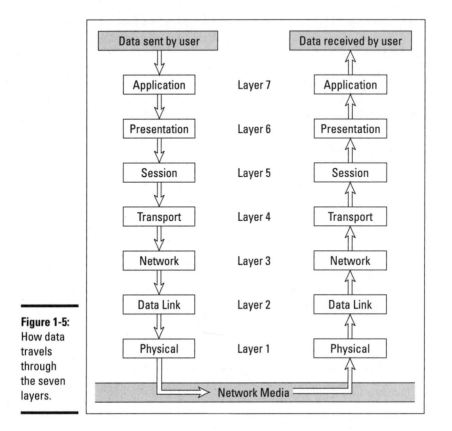

Figure 1-5:
How data travels through the seven layers.

When the receiving computer receives the data, the data works its way up through the protocol stack. Then, the protocol at each layer reverses the processing that was done by the corresponding layer on the sending computer. Headers are removed, data is converted back to its original format, packets that were split into smaller packets are recombined into larger messages, and so on. When the packet reaches the Application layer protocol, it's delivered to an application that can process the data.

The Ethernet Protocol

As I mention earlier, the first two layers of the OSI model deal with the physical structure of the network and the means by which network devices can send information from one device on a network to another. By far, Ethernet is the most popular set of protocols for the Physical and Data Link layers.

Ethernet has been around in various forms since the early 1970s. (For a brief history of Ethernet, see the sidebar, "Ethernet folklore and mythology.") The current incarnation of Ethernet is defined by the 802.3 IEEE standard. Various flavors of Ethernet operate at different speeds and use different types of media. However, all the versions of Ethernet are compatible with each other, so you can mix and match them on the same network by using devices such as bridges, hubs, and switches to link network segments that use different types of media.

The actual transmission speed of Ethernet is measured in millions of bits per second, or Mbps. Ethernet comes in three different speed versions:

+ **Standard Ethernet:** 10 Mbps

+ **Fast Ethernet:** 100 Mbps

+ **Gigabit Ethernet:** 1,000 Mbps

Network transmission speed refers to the maximum speed that can be achieved over the network under ideal conditions. In reality, the actual throughput of an Ethernet network rarely reaches this maximum speed.

Ethernet operates at the first two layers of the OSI model — the Physical and the Data Link layers. However, Ethernet divides the Data Link layer into two separate layers: the Logical Link Control (LLC) layer and the Medium Access Control (MAC) layer. Figure 1-6 shows how the various elements of Ethernet match up to the OSI model.

The following sections describe Standard Ethernet, Fast Ethernet, and Gigabit Ethernet in more detail.

**Book III
Chapter 1**

**Understanding
Network Protocols
and Standards**

OSI	Ethernet		
Data Link Layer	Logical Link Control (LLC)		
	Medium Access Control (MAC)		
Physical Layer	<u>Standard Ethernet</u> 10Base5 10Base2 10BaseT 10BaseFX	<u>Fast Ethernet</u> 100BaseTX 100BaseT4 100BaseFX	<u>Gigabit Ethernet</u> 1000BaseT 1000BaseLX

Figure 1-6:
Ethernet and the OSI model.

Standard Ethernet

Standard Ethernet is the original Ethernet. It runs at 10 Mbps, which was considered fast in the 1970s but is pretty slow by today's standards. Although plenty of existing Standard Ethernet is still in use, it's considered obsolete and should be replaced by Gigabit Ethernet as soon as possible.

Standard Ethernet comes in four incarnations, depending on the type of cable used to string the network together:

✦ **10Base5:** This original Ethernet cable was thick (about as thick as your thumb), heavy, and difficult to work with. It's seen today only in museum exhibits.

✦ **10Base2:** This thinner type of coaxial cable (it resembles television cable) became popular in the 1980s and lingered into the early 1990s. Plenty of 10Base2 cable is still in use, but it's rarely installed in new networks. 10Base2 (like 10Base5) uses a bus topology, so wiring a 10Base2 network involves running cable from one computer to the next until all the computers are connected in a segment.

✦ **10BaseT:** Unshielded twisted-pair (UTP) cable became popular in the 1990s because it's easier to install, lighter, and more reliable, and also it offers more flexibility in how networks are designed. 10BaseT networks use a star topology with hubs at the center of each star. Although the maximum length of 10BaseT cable is only 100 meters, hubs can be chained to extend networks well beyond the 100-meter limit.

10BaseT cable has four pairs of wires twisted together throughout the entire span of the cable. However, 10BaseT uses only two of these wire pairs, so the unused pairs are spares.

✦ **10BaseFL:** Fiber optic cables were originally supported at 10 Mbps by the 10BaseFL standard. However, because faster fiber optic versions of Ethernet now exist, 10BaseFL is rarely used.

Fast Ethernet

Fast Ethernet refers to Ethernet that runs at 100 Mbps, which is ten times the speed of Standard Ethernet. Here are the three varieties of Fast Ethernet:

✦ **100BaseT4:** The 100BaseT4 protocol allows transmission speeds of 100 Mbps over the same UTP cable as 10BaseT networks. To do this, it uses all four pairs of wire in the cable. 100BaseT4 simplifies the task of upgrading an existing 10BaseT network to 100 Mbps.

Ethernet folklore and mythology

Here's how Ethernet came to be so popular. The original idea for the Ethernet was hatched in the mind of Robert Metcalfe, a graduate computer science student at Harvard University. Looking for a thesis idea in 1970, he refined a networking technique used in Hawaii — the AlohaNet (actually a wireless network) — and developed a technique that would enable a network to efficiently use as much as 90 percent of its capacity. By 1973, he had his first Ethernet network up and running at the famous Xerox Palo Alto Research Center (PARC). Bob dubbed his network "Ethernet" in honor of the thick network cable, which he called "the ether." (Xerox PARC was busy in 1973. In addition to Ethernet, PARC developed the first personal computer that used a graphical user interface (GUI) complete with icons, windows, and menus, and the world's first laser printer.)

In 1979, Xerox began working with Intel and DEC (a once-popular computer company) to make Ethernet an industry standard networking product. Along the way, they enlisted the help of the IEEE, which formed committee number 802.3 and began the process of standardizing Ethernet in 1981. The 802.3 committee released the first official Ethernet standard in 1983.

Meanwhile, Bob Metcalfe left Xerox, turned down a job offer from Steve Jobs to work at Apple computers, and started a company called the Computer, Communication, and Compatibility Corporation — now known as 3Com. 3Com has since become one of the largest manufacturers of Ethernet equipment in the world.

✦ **100BaseTX:** The most commonly used standard for office networks today is 100BaseTX, which transmits at 100 Mbps over just two pairs of a higher grade of UTP cable than the cable used by 10BaseT. The higher-grade cable is Category 5. Most new networks are wired with Cat5 or better cable.

✦ **100BaseFX:** The fiber optic version of Ethernet running at 100 Mbps is 100BaseFX. Because fiber optic cable is expensive and tricky to install, it isn't used much for individual computers in a network. However, it's commonly used as a network backbone. For example, a fiber backbone is often used to connect individual workgroup hubs to routers and servers.

Gigabit Ethernet

Gigabit Ethernet is Ethernet running at a whopping 1,000 Mbps, which is 100 times faster than the original 10 Mbps Ethernet. Gigabit Ethernet was once considerably more expensive than Fast Ethernet, so it was used only when the improved performance justified the extra cost. However, today Gigabit Ethernet is the standard for nearly all desktop and laptop PCs.

Gigabit Ethernet comes in two flavors:

✦ **1000BaseT:** Gigabit Ethernet can run on Cat5 UTP cable, but higher grades such as Cat5e or Cat6 are preferred because they're more reliable.

✦ **1000BaseLX:** Several varieties of fiber cable are used with Gigabit Ethernet, but the most popular is 1000BaseLX.

The TCP/IP Protocol Suite

TCP/IP, the protocol on which the Internet is built, is not a single protocol but rather an entire suite of related protocols. TCP is even older than Ethernet. It was first conceived in 1969 by the Department of Defense. For more on the history of TCP/IP, see the sidebar, "The fascinating story of TCP/IP," later in this chapter. Currently, the Internet Engineering Task Force (IETF) manages the TCP/IP protocol suite.

The TCP/IP suite is based on a four-layer model of networking similar to the seven-layer OSI model. Figure 1-7 shows how the TCP/IP model matches up with the OSI model and where some of the key TCP/IP protocols fit into the model. As you can see, the lowest layer of the model, the Network Interface layer, corresponds to the OSI model's Physical and Data Link layers. TCP/IP can run over a wide variety of Network Interface layer protocols, including Ethernet, as well as other protocols, such as token ring and FDDI (an older standard for fiber optic networks).

Figure 1-7: TCP/IP and the OSI model.

OSI Layers	TCP/IP Layers	TCP/IP Protocols				
Application Layer	Application Layer	HTTP	FTP	Telnet	SMTP	DNS
Presentation Layer						
Session Layer						
Transport Layer	Transport Layer	TCP			UDP	
Network Layer	Network Layer	IP				
Data Link Layer	Network Interface Layer	Ethernet		Token Ring		Other Link-Layer Protocols
Physical Layer						

The Application layer of the TCP/IP model corresponds to the upper three layers of the OSI model — the Session, Presentation, and Application layers. Many protocols can be used at this level. A few of the most popular are HTTP, FTP, Telnet, SMTP, DNS, and SNMP.

In the following sections, I point out a few more details of the three most important protocols in the TCP/IP suite: IP, TCP, and UDP.

IP

Internet Protocol (IP) is a Network layer protocol responsible for delivering packets to network devices. The IP protocol uses logical IP addresses to refer to individual devices rather than physical (MAC) addresses. Address Resolution Protocol (ARP) handles the task of converting IP addresses to MAC addresses.

Because IP addresses consist of a network part and a host part, IP is a routable protocol. As a result, IP can forward a packet to another network if the host isn't on the current network. After all, the capability to route packets across networks is where IP gets its name. An *Internet* is a just a series of two or more connected TCP/IP networks that can be reached by routing.

10Base what?

The names of Ethernet cable standards resemble the audible signals a quarterback might shout at the line of scrimmage. In reality, the cable designations consist of three parts:

✔ The first number is the speed of the network in Mbps. So, 10BaseT is for 10 Mbps networks (Standard Ethernet), 100BaseTX is for 100 Mbps networks (Fast Ethernet), and 1000BaseT is for 1,000 Mbps networks (Gigabit Ethernet).

✔ "Base" (short for "baseband") indicates the type of network transmission that the cable uses. Baseband transmissions carry one signal at a time and are relatively simple to implement. The alternative to baseband is *broadband,* which can carry more than one signal at a time but is more difficult to implement. At one time, broadband incarnations of the 802.*x* networking standards existed, but they have all but fizzled due to lack of use.

✔ The tail end of the designation indicates the cable type. For coaxial cables, a number is used that roughly indicates the maximum length of the cable in hundreds of meters. 10Base5 cables can run up to 500 meters. 10Base2 cables can run up to 185 meters. (The IEEE rounded 185 up to 200 to come up with the name 10Base2.) If the designation ends with a T, twisted-pair cable is used. Other letters are used for other types of cables.

TCP

Transmission Control Protocol (TCP) is a connection-oriented Transport layer protocol. TCP lets a device reliably send a packet to another device on the same network or on a different network. TCP ensures that each packet is delivered, if at all possible, by establishing a connection with the receiving device and then sending the packets. If a packet doesn't arrive, TCP resends the packet. The connection is closed only after the packet has been successfully delivered or an unrecoverable error condition has occurred.

One key aspect of TCP is that it's always used for one-to-one communications. In other words, TCP allows a single network device to exchange data with another single network device. TCP isn't used to broadcast messages to multiple network recipients. Instead, UDP is used for that purpose.

The fascinating story of TCP/IP

Some people are fascinated by history. They subscribe to cable TV just to get the History Channel. If you're one of those history buffs, you may be interested in the following chronicle of TCP/IP's humble origins. (For maximum effect, play some melancholy violin music in the background as you read the rest of this sidebar.)

In the summer of 1969, the four mop-topped singers from Liverpool were breaking up. The war in Vietnam was escalating. Astronauts Neil Armstrong and Buzz Aldrin walked on the moon. And the Department of Defense built a computer network called ARPANET to link its defense installations with several major universities throughout the United States.

By the early 1970s, ARPANET was becoming difficult to manage. So it was split into two networks: one for military use, called MILNET; and the other for nonmilitary use. The nonmilitary network retained the name ARPANET. To link MILNET with ARPANET, a new method of connecting networks — Internet Protocol (IP) — was invented.

The whole purpose of IP was to enable these two networks to communicate with each other.

Fortunately, the designers of IP realized that it wouldn't be too long before other networks wanted to join in the fun, so they designed IP to allow for more than two networks. In fact, their ingenious design allowed for tens of thousands of networks to communicate via IP.

The decision was a fortuitous one, as the Internet quickly began to grow. By the mid-1980s, the original ARPANET reached its limits. Just in time, the National Science Foundation (NSF) decided to get into the game. NSF had built a network called NSFNET to link its huge supercomputers. NSFNET replaced ARPANET as the new background for the Internet. Around that time, such magazines as *Time* and *Newsweek* began writing articles about this new phenomenon called the Internet, and the *Net* (as it became nicknamed) began to grow like wildfire. Soon NSFNET couldn't keep up with the growth, so several private commercial networks took over management of the Internet backbone. The Internet has grown at a dizzying rate ever since, and nobody knows how long this frenetic growth rate will continue. One thing is sure: TCP/IP is now the most popular networking protocol in the world.

Many well-known Application layer protocols rely on TCP. For example, when a user running a web browser requests a page, the browser uses HTTP (HyperText Transfer Protocol) to send a request via TCP to a web server. When that web server receives the request, it uses HTTP to send the requested web page back to the browser, again via TCP. Other Application layer protocols that use TCP include Telnet (for terminal emulation), FTP (for file exchange), and SMTP (for email).

UDP

User Datagram Protocol (UDP) is a connectionless Transport layer protocol used when the overhead of a connection isn't required. After UDP has placed a packet on the network (via the IP protocol), it forgets about it. UDP doesn't guarantee that the packet arrives at its destination. Most applications that use UDP simply wait for any replies expected as a result of packets sent via UDP. If a reply doesn't arrive within a certain period of time, the application either sends the packet again or gives up.

Probably the best-known Application layer protocol that uses UDP is the Domain Name System (DNS). When an application needs to access a domain name (such as `www.wiley.com`), DNS sends a UDP packet to a DNS server to look up the domain. When the server finds the domain, it returns the domain's IP address in another UDP packet.

Other Protocols Worth Knowing About

Although the vast majority of networks now use Ethernet and TCP/IP, a few other networking protocols are still in use and are therefore worth knowing about. In particular:

✦ **Network Basic Input/Output System (NetBIOS):** The basic application programming interface for network services on Windows computers. It's installed automatically when you install TCP/IP, but doesn't show up as a separate protocol when you view the network connection properties. (Refer to Figure 1-1.) NetBIOS is a Session layer protocol that can work with Transport layer protocols, such as TCP, SPX, or NetBEUI.

✦ **Network BIOS Extended User Interface (NetBEUI):** A Transport layer protocol designed for early IBM and Microsoft networks. NetBEUI is now considered obsolete.

✦ **IPX/SPX:** A protocol suite made popular in the 1980s by Novell for use with its NetWare servers. TCP/IP has become so dominant that IPX/SPX is rarely used now.

**Book III
Chapter 1**

**Understanding
Network Protocols
and Standards**

✦ **AppleTalk:** Apple's suite of network protocols. The AppleTalk suite includes a Physical and Data Link layer protocol called LocalTalk, but can also work with standard lower-level protocols, including Ethernet and token ring.

✦ **Systems Network Architecture (SNA):** An IBM networking architecture dating back to the 1970s, when mainframe computers roamed the earth and PCs had barely emerged from the primordial computer soup. SNA was designed primarily to support huge terminals such as airline reservations and banking systems, with tens of thousands of terminals attached to central host computers. Now that IBM mainframes support TCP/IP and terminal systems have all but vanished, SNA is beginning to fade away. Still, many networks that incorporate mainframe computers have to contend with SNA.

Chapter 2: Introduction to TCP/IP and the Internet

In This Chapter

✔ Introducing the Internet

✔ Familiarizing yourself with TCP/IP standards

✔ Figuring out how TCP/IP lines up with the OSI reference model

✔ Discovering important TCP/IP applications

Many years ago, Transmission Control Protocol/Internet Protocol (TCP/IP) was known primarily as the protocol of the Internet. The biggest challenge of getting a local area network (LAN) connected to the Internet was figuring out how to mesh TCP/IP with the proprietary protocols that were the basis of the LANs — most notably Internetwork Packet Exchange/Sequenced Packet Exchange (IPX/SPX) and NetBIOS Extended User Interface (NetBEUI).

But then, some years ago, network administrators realized that they could save the trouble of combining TCP/IP with IPX/SPX and NetBEUI by eliminating IPX/SPX and NetBEUI from the equation altogether. As a result, TCP/IP is not just the protocol of the Internet now, but it's also the protocol on which most LANs are based.

This chapter is a gentle introduction to the Internet in general and the TCP/IP suite of protocols in particular. After I get the introductions out of the way, you'll be able to focus more in-depth on the detailed TCP/IP information given in the remaining chapters of Book III.

What Is the Internet?

The Goliath of all computer networks, the Internet links hundreds of millions of computer users throughout the world. Strictly speaking, the Internet is a network of networks. It consists of hundreds of thousands of separate computer networks, all interlinked, so that a user on any of those networks can reach out and potentially touch a user on any of the other networks. This network of networks connects more than a billion computers to each other. (That's right, *billion* with a *b*.)

Just how big is the Internet?

Because the Internet is not owned or controlled by any one organization, no one knows how big the Internet really is. Several organizations do attempt to periodically determine the size of the Internet, including the Internet Systems Consortium (ISC), which completed its last survey in July 2015 and found that well over a billion host computers are connected to the Internet. The first year the ISC did the survey (1993), it found only 1.3 million host computers.

Unfortunately, no one knows how many actual users are on the Internet. Each host can support a single user — or in the case of domains, hundreds of thousands or perhaps even millions of users. No one really knows. Still, the indisputable point is that the Internet is big and growing every day.

You can check the latest Internet statistics from ISC by visiting its website at www.isc.org.

One of the official documents (RFC 2026) of the Internet Engineering Task Force (IETF) defines the Internet as "a loosely organized international collaboration of autonomous, interconnected networks." Broken down piece by piece, this definition encompasses several key aspects of what the Internet is:

✦ **Loosely organized:** No single organization has authority over the Internet. As a result, the Internet is not highly organized. Online services, such as America Online or MSN, are owned and operated by individual companies that control exactly what content appears on the service and what software can be used with the service. No one exercises that kind of control over the Internet. As a result, you can find just about any kind of material imaginable on the Internet. No one guarantees the accuracy of information that you find on the Internet, so you have to be careful as you work your way through the labyrinth.

✦ **International:** Nearly 200 countries are represented on the Internet, from Afghanistan to Zimbabwe.

✦ **Collaboration:** The Internet exists only because many different organizations cooperate to provide the services and support needed to sustain it. For example, much of the software that drives the Internet is open source software that's developed collaboratively by programmers throughout the world, who constantly work to improve the code.

✦ **Autonomous:** The Internet community respects that organizations that join the Internet are free to make their own decisions about how they configure and operate their networks. Although legal issues sometimes boil up, for the most part, each player on the Internet operates independently.

✦ **Interconnected:** The whole key to the Internet is the concept of *interconnection,* which uses standard protocols that enable networks to communicate with each other. Without the interconnection provided by the TCP/IP protocol, the Internet would not exist.

✦ **Networks:** The Internet would be completely unmanageable if it consisted of half a billion individual users, all interconnected. That's why the Internet is often described as a network of networks. Most individual users on the Internet don't access the Internet directly. Instead, they access the Internet indirectly through another network, which may be a LAN in a business or academic environment, or a dialup or broadband network provided by an Internet service provider (ISP). In each case, however, the users of the local network access the Internet via a gateway IP router.

The Internet is composed of several distinct types of networks: Government agencies, such as the Library of Congress and the White House; military sites (did you ever see *War Games* or any of the *Terminator* movies?); educational institutions, such as universities and colleges (and their libraries); businesses, such as Microsoft and IBM; ISPs, which allow individuals to access the Internet; and commercial online services, such as America Online and MSN.

A Little Internet History

The Internet has a fascinating history, if such things interest you. There's no particular reason why you should be interested in such things, of course, except that a superficial understanding of how the Internet got started may help you to understand and cope with the way this massive computer network exists today. So here goes.

The Internet traces its beginnings back to a small network called ARPANET, built by the Department of Defense in 1969 to link defense installations. ARPANET soon expanded to include not only defense installations but universities as well. In the 1970s, ARPANET was split into two networks: one for military use (renamed MILNET) and the original ARPANET (for nonmilitary use). The two networks were connected by a networking link called IP — the *Internet protocol* — so called because it allowed communication between two networks.

The good folks who designed IP had the foresight to realize that soon, more than two networks would want to be connected. In fact, they left room for tens of thousands of networks to join the game, which is a good thing because it wasn't long before the Internet began to take off.

By the mid-1980s, ARPANET was beginning to reach the limits of what it could do. Enter the National Science Foundation (NSF), which set up a nationwide network designed to provide access to huge *supercomputers,* those monolithic computers used to discover new prime numbers and calculate the orbits of distant galaxies. The supercomputers were never put to much use, but the network that was put together to support the supercomputers — NSFNET — was used. In fact, NSFNET replaced ARPANET as the new backbone for the Internet.

Then, out of the blue, it seemed as if the whole world became interested in the Internet. Stories about it appeared in *Time* and *Newsweek.* Any company that had "dot com" in its name practically doubled in value every month. Al Gore claimed he invented the Internet. The Net began to grow so fast that even NSFNET couldn't keep up, so private commercial networks got into the game. The size of the Internet nearly doubled every year for most of the 1990s. Then, in the first few years of the millennium, the growth rate slowed a bit. However, the Internet still seems to be growing at the phenomenal rate of about 30 to 50 percent per year, and who knows how long this dizzying rate of growth will continue.

TCP/IP Standards and RFCs

The TCP/IP protocol standards that define how the Internet works are managed by the IETF. However, the IETF doesn't impose standards. Instead, it simply oversees the process by which ideas are developed into agreed-upon standards.

An Internet standard is published in the Request for Comments (RFC) document. When a document is accepted for publication, it is assigned an RFC number by the IETF. The RFC is then published. After it's published, an RFC is never changed. If a standard is enhanced, the enhancement is covered in a separate RFC.

At the time of this writing, more than 3,500 RFCs were available from the IETF website (www.ietf.org). The oldest RFC is RFC 0001, published in April 1969. It describes how the host computers communicated with each other in the original ARPANET. The most recent RFC (as of May 2012) is RFC 6636, a proposed standard entitled "Tuning the Behavior of the Internet Group Management Protocol (IGMP) and Multicast Listener Discovery (MLD) for Routers in Mobile and Wireless Networks."

Not all RFCs represent Internet standards. The following paragraphs summarize the various types of RFC documents:

✦ **Internet Standards Track:** This type of RFC represents an Internet standard. Standards Track RFCs have one of three maturity levels, as described in Table 2-1. An RFC enters circulation with Proposed Standard status but may be elevated to Draft Standard status — and, ultimately, to Internet Standard status.

Table 2-1   Maturity Levels for Internet Standards Track RFCs

Maturity Level	Description
Proposed Standard	Generally stable, have resolved known design choices, are believed to be well understood, have received significant community review, and appear to enjoy enough community interest to be considered valuable.
Draft Standard	Well understood and known to be quite stable. At least two interoperable implementations must exist, developed independently from separate code bases. The specification is believed to be mature and useful.
Internet Standard	Have been fully accepted by the Internet community as highly mature and useful standards.

✦ **Experimental specifications:** These are a result of research or development efforts. They're not intended to be standards, but the information they contain may be of use to the Internet community.

✦ **Informational specifications:** These simply provide general information for the Internet community.

✦ **Historic specifications:** These RFCs have been superseded by a more recent RFC and are thus considered obsolete.

✦ **Best Current Practice (BCP):** RFCs are documents that summarize the consensus of the Internet community's opinion on the best way to perform an operation or procedure. BCPs are guidelines, not standards.

Table 2-2 summarizes the RFCs that apply to the key Internet standards described in this book.

Table 2-2		RFCs for Key Internet Standards
RFC	**Date**	**Description**
768	August 1980	User Datagram Protocol (UDP)
791	September 1981	Internet Protocol (IP)
792	September 1981	Internet Control Message Protocol (ICMP)
793	September 1981	Transmission Control Protocol (TCP)
826	November 1982	Ethernet Address Resolution Protocol (ARP)
950	August 1985	Internet Standard Subnetting Procedure
959	October 1985	File Transfer Protocol (FTP)
1034	November 1987	Domain Names — Concepts and Facilities (DNS)
1035	November 1987	Domain Names — Implementation and Specification (DNS)
1939	May 1996	Post Office Protocol Version 3 (POP3)
2131	March 1997	Dynamic Host Configuration Protocol (DHCP)
3376	November 1997	Internet Group Management Protocol (IGMP) (Updates RFC 2236 and 1112)
7230 through 7235	June 2014	Hypertext Transfer Protocol – HTTP/1.1
5321	October 2008	Simple Mail Transfer Protocol (SMTP)

My favorite RFC is 1149, an experimental specification for the "Transmission of IP datagrams on avian carriers." The specification calls for IP datagrams to be written in hexadecimal on scrolls of paper and secured to "avian carriers" with duct tape. (Not surprisingly, it's dated April 1, 1990. Similar RFCs are frequently submitted on April 1.)

The TCP/IP Protocol Framework

Like the seven-layer OSI reference model, TCP/IP protocols are based on a layered framework. TCP/IP has four layers, as shown in Figure 2-1. These layers are described in the following sections.

Network Interface layer

The lowest level of the TCP/IP architecture is the Network Interface layer. It corresponds to the OSI Physical and Data Link layers. You can use many different TCP/IP protocols at the Network Interface layer, including Ethernet and token ring for LANs and protocols such as X.25, Frame Relay, and ATM for wide area networks (WANs).

The Network Interface layer is assumed to be unreliable.

Network layer

The Network layer is where data is addressed, packaged, and routed among networks. Several important Internet protocols operate at the Network layer:

✦ **Internet Protocol (IP):** A routable protocol that uses IP addresses to deliver packets to network devices. IP is an intentionally unreliable protocol, so it doesn't guarantee delivery of information.

✦ **Address Resolution Protocol (ARP):** Resolves IP addresses to hardware Media Access Control (MAC) addresses, which uniquely identify hardware devices.

✦ **Internet Control Message Protocol (ICMP):** Sends and receives diagnostic messages. ICMP is the basis of the ubiquitous `ping` command.

✦ **Internet Group Management Protocol (IGMP):** Used to multicast messages to multiple IP addresses at once.

Transport layer

The Transport layer is where sessions are established and data packets are exchanged between hosts. Two core protocols are found at this layer:

✦ **Transmission Control Protocol (TCP):** Provides reliable connection-oriented transmission between two hosts. TCP establishes a session between hosts, and then ensures delivery of packets between the hosts.

✦ **User Datagram Protocol (UDP):** Provides connectionless, unreliable, one-to-one or one-to-many delivery.

Application layer

The Application layer of the TCP/IP model corresponds to the Session, Presentation, and Application layers of the OSI reference model. A few of the most popular Application layer protocols are

✦ **HyperText Transfer Protocol (HTTP):** The core protocol of the World Wide Web.

✦ **File Transfer Protocol (FTP):** A protocol that enables a client to send and receive complete files from a server.

✦ **Telnet:** The protocol that lets you connect to another computer on the Internet in a terminal emulation mode.

✦ **Simple Mail Transfer Protocol (SMTP):** One of several key protocols that are used to provide email services.

✦ **Domain Name System (DNS):** The protocol that allows you to refer to other host computers by using names rather than numbers.

Chapter 3: Understanding IP Addresses

In This Chapter

✔ Delving into the binary system

✔ Digging into IP addresses

✔ Finding out how subnetting works

✔ Looking at network address translation

*O*ne of the most basic components of TCP/IP is IP addressing. Every device on a TCP/IP network must have a unique IP address. In this chapter, I describe the ins and outs of these IP addresses. Enjoy!

Understanding Binary

Before you can understand the details of how IP addressing works, you need to understand how the binary numbering system works because binary is the basis of IP addressing. If you already understand binary, please skip to the section "Introducing IP Addresses." I don't want to bore you with stuff that's too basic.

Counting by ones

Binary is a counting system that uses only two numerals: 0 and 1. In the decimal system (with which most people are accustomed), you use 10 numerals: 0–9. In an ordinary decimal number — such as 3,482 — the rightmost digit represents ones; the next digit to the left, tens; the next, hundreds; the next, thousands; and so on. These digits represent powers of ten: first 10^0 (which is 1); next, 10^1 (10); then 10^2 (100); then 10^3 (1,000); and so on.

In binary, you have only two numerals rather than ten, which is why binary numbers look somewhat monotonous, as in 110011, 101111, and 100001.

The positions in a binary number (called *bits* rather than *digits*) represent powers of two rather than powers of ten: 1, 2, 4, 8, 16, 32, and so on. To figure the decimal value of a binary number, you multiply each bit by its corresponding power of two and then add the results. The decimal value of binary 10111, for example, is calculated as follows:

```
  1 x 20 = 1 x  1  =  1
 +1 x 21 = 1 x  2  =  2
 +1 x 22 = 1 x  4  =  4
 +0 x 23 = 0 x  8  =  0
 +1 x 24 = 1 x 16  = 16
                    ----
                     23
```

Fortunately, converting a number between binary and decimal is something a computer is good at — so good, in fact, that you're unlikely ever to need to do any conversions yourself. The point of learning binary is not to be able to look at a number such as 1110110110110 and say instantly, "Ah! Decimal 7,606!" (If you could do that, Piers Morgan would probably interview you, and they would even make a movie about you.)

Instead, the point is to have a basic understanding of how computers store information and — most important — to understand how the binary counting system works, which I describe in the following section.

Here are some of the more interesting characteristics of binary and how the system is similar to and differs from the decimal system:

✦ **In decimal, the number of decimal places allotted for a number determines how large the number can be.** If you allot six digits, for example, the largest number possible is 999,999. Because 0 is itself a number, however, a six-digit number can have any of 1 million different values.

Similarly, the number of bits allotted for a binary number determines how large that number can be. If you allot eight bits, the largest value that number can store is 11111111, which happens to be 255 in decimal.

✦ **To quickly figure how many different values you can store in a binary number of a given length, use the number of bits as an exponent of two.** An eight-bit binary number, for example, can hold 2^8 values. Because 2^8 is 256, an eight-bit number can have any of 256 different values. This is why a *byte* — eight bits — can have 256 different values.

✦ **This "powers of two" thing is why computers don't use nice, even, round numbers in measuring such values as memory or disk space.** A value of 1K, for example, is not an even 1,000 bytes: It's actually 1,024 bytes because 1,024 is 2^{10}. Similarly, 1MB is not an even 1,000,000 bytes but instead 1,048,576 bytes, which happens to be 2^{20}.

One basic test of computer nerddom is knowing your powers of two because they play such an important role in binary numbers. Just for the fun of it, but not because you really need to know, Table 3-1 lists the powers of two up to 32.

Table 3-1			Powers of Two		
Power	*Bytes*	*Kilobytes*	*Power*	*Bytes*	*K, MB, or GB*
2^1	2		2^{17}	131,072	128K
2^2	4		2^{18}	262,144	256K
2^3	8		2^{19}	524,288	512K
2^4	16		2^{20}	1,048,576	1MB
2^5	32		2^{21}	2,097,152	2MB
2^6	64		2^{22}	4,194,304	4MB
2^7	128		2^{23}	8,388,608	8MB
2^8	256		2^{24}	16,777,216	16MB
2^9	512		2^{25}	33,554,432	32MB
2^{10}	1,024	1K	2^{26}	67,108,864	64MB
2^{11}	2,048	2K	2^{27}	134,217,728	128MB
2^{12}	4,096	4K	2^{28}	268,435,456	256MB
2^{13}	8,192	8K	2^{29}	536,870,912	512MB
2^{14}	16,384	16K	2^{30}	1,073,741,824	1GB
2^{15}	32,768	32K	2^{31}	2,147,483,648	2GB
2^{16}	65,536	64K	2^{32}	4,294,967,296	4GB

Table 3-1 also shows the common shorthand notation for various powers of two. The abbreviation *K* represents 2^{10} (1,024). The *M* in *MB* stands for 2^{20}, or 1,024K, and the *G* in *GB* represents 2^{30}, which is 1,024MB. These shorthand notations don't have anything to do with TCP/IP, but they're commonly used for measuring computer disk and memory capacities, so I thought I'd throw them in at no charge because the table had extra room.

Doing the logic thing

One of the great things about binary is that it's very efficient at handling special operations: namely, logical operations. Four basic logical operations exist although additional operations are derived from the basic four operations. Three of the operations — AND, OR, and XOR — compare two binary digits (bits). The fourth (NOT) works on just a single bit.

The following list summarizes the basic logical operations:

✦ **AND:** Compares two binary values. If both values are 1, the result of the AND operation is 1. If one or both of the values are 0, the result is 0.

✦ **OR:** Compares two binary values. If at least one value is 1, the result of the OR operation is 1. If both values are 0, the result is 0.

✦ **XOR:** Compares two binary values. If one of them is 1, the result is 1. If both values are 0 or if both values are 1, the result is 0.

✦ **NOT:** Doesn't compare two values but simply changes the value of a single binary value. If the original value is 1, NOT returns 0. If the original value is 0, NOT returns 1.

Table 3-2 summarizes how AND, OR, and XOR work.

Table 3-2	Logical Operations for Binary Values			
First Value	*Second Value*	*AND*	*OR*	*XOR*
0	0	0	0	0
0	1	0	1	1
1	0	0	1	1
1	1	1	1	0

Logical operations are applied to binary numbers that have more than one binary digit by applying the operation one bit at a time. The easiest way to do this manually is to line the two binary numbers on top of one another and then write the result of the operation beneath each binary digit. The following example shows how you would calculate 10010100 AND 11011101:

```
    10010100
AND 11011101
    10010100
```

As you can see, the result is 10010100.

Working with the binary Windows Calculator

The Calculator program that comes with all versions of Windows has a special Programmer mode that many users don't know about. When you flip the Calculator into this mode, you can do instant binary and decimal conversions, which can occasionally come in handy when you're working with IP addresses.

To use the Windows Calculator in Programmer mode, launch the Calculator by choosing Start ⇨ All Programs ⇨ Accessories ⇨ Calculator. Then, choose the View ⇨ Programmer command from the Calculator menu. The Calculator changes to a fancy programmer model in which all kinds of buttons appear, as shown in Figure 3-1.

Figure 3-1:
The free
Windows
Programmer
Calculator.

You can switch the number base by using the Hex, Dec, Oct, and Bin radio buttons to convert values between base 16 (hexadecimal), base 10 (decimal), base 8 (octal), and base 2 (binary). For example, to find the binary equivalent of decimal 155, enter **155** and then select the Bin radio button. The value in the display changes to 10011011.

Here are a few other things to note about the Programmer mode of the Calculator:

✦ Although you can convert decimal values to binary values with the programmer Calculator, the Calculator can't handle the dotted-decimal IP address format that's described later in this chapter. To convert a dotted-decimal address to binary, just convert each octet separately. For example, to convert 172.65.48.120 to binary, first convert 172; then convert 65; then convert 48; and finally, convert 120.

✦ The programmer Calculator has several features that are designed specifically for binary calculations, such as AND, OR, XOR, and so on.

✦ The Calculator program in Windows versions prior to Windows 7 does not have the programmer mode. However, those versions do offer a scientific mode that provides binary, hexadecimal, and decimal conversions.

Introducing IP Addresses

An *IP address* is a number that uniquely identifies every host on an IP network. IP addresses operate at the Network layer of the TCP/IP protocol stack, so they are independent of lower-level Data Link layer MAC addresses, such as Ethernet MAC addresses.

IP addresses are 32-bit binary numbers, which means that theoretically, a maximum of something in the neighborhood of 4 billion unique host addresses can exist throughout the Internet. You'd think that would be enough, but TCP/IP places certain restrictions on how IP addresses are allocated. These restrictions severely limit the total number of usable IP addresses. Many experts predict that we will run out of IP addresses soon. However, new techniques for working with IP addresses have helped to alleviate this problem, and a standard for 128-bit IP addresses has been adopted, though it still is not yet in widespread use.

Networks and hosts

IP stands for *Internet protocol,* and its primary purpose is to enable communications between networks. As a result, a 32-bit IP address actually consists of two parts:

✦ **The network ID (or network address):** Identifies the network on which a host computer can be found

✦ **The host ID (or host address):** Identifies a specific device on the network indicated by the network ID

Most of the complexity of working with IP addresses has to do with figuring out which part of the complete 32-bit IP address is the network ID and which part is the host ID, as described in the following sections.

As I describe the details of how host IDs are assigned, you may notice that two host addresses seem to be unaccounted for. For example, the Class C addressing scheme, which uses eight bits for the host ID, allows only 254 hosts — not the 256 hosts you'd expect. The host ID can't be 0 (the host ID is all zeros) because that address is always reserved to represent the network itself. And the host ID can't be 255 (the host ID is all ones) because that host ID is reserved for use as a broadcast request that's intended for all hosts on the network.

The dotted-decimal dance

IP addresses are usually represented in a format known as *dotted-decimal notation.* In dotted-decimal notation, each group of eight bits — an *octet* — is represented by its decimal equivalent. For example, consider the following binary IP address:

```
11000000101010001000100000011100
```

To convert this value to dotted-decimal notation, first divide it into four octets, as follows:

```
11000000 10101000 10001000 00011100
```

Then, convert each of the octets to its decimal equivalent:

```
11000000 10101000 10001000 00011100
192      168      136      28
```

Then, use periods to separate the four decimal numbers, like this:

```
192.168.136.28
```

This is the format in which you'll usually see IP addresses represented.

Figure 3-2 shows how the 32 bits of an IP address are broken down into four octets of eight bits each. As you can see, the four octets of an IP address are often referred to as *w, x, y,* and *z.*

Figure 3-2:
Octets and
dotted-
decimal
notation.

32-bit IP address

Classifying IP Addresses

When the original designers of the IP protocol created the IP addressing scheme, they could have assigned an arbitrary number of IP address bits for the network ID. The remaining bits would then be used for the host ID. For example, suppose that the designers decided that half of the address (16 bits) would be used for the network, and the remaining 16 bits would be used for the host ID. The result of that scheme would be that the Internet could have a total of 65,536 networks, and each of those networks could have 65,536 hosts.

In the early days of the Internet, this scheme probably seemed like several orders of magnitude more than would ever be needed. However, the IP designers realized from the start that few networks would actually have tens of thousands of hosts. Suppose that a network of 1,000 computers joins the Internet and is assigned one of these hypothetical network IDs. Because that network will use only 1,000 of its 65,536 host addresses, more than 64,000 IP addresses would be wasted.

What about IPv6?

Most of the current Internet is based on version 4 of the Internet Protocol, also known as IPv4. IPv4 has served the Internet well for more than 30 years. However, the growth of the Internet has put a lot of pressure on IPv4's limited 32-bit address space. This chapter describes how IPv4 has evolved to make the best possible use of 32-bit addresses. Eventually, though, all the addresses will be assigned, and the IPv4 address space will be filled to capacity. When that happens, the Internet will have to migrate to the next version of IP, known as IPv6.

IPv6 is also called *IP next generation,* or *IPng,* in honor of the favorite television show of most Internet gurus, *Star Trek: The Next Generation.*

IPv6 offers several advantages over IPv4, but the most important is that it uses 128 bits for Internet addresses instead of 32 bits. The number of host addresses possible with 128 bits is a number so large that it would have made Carl Sagan proud. It doesn't just double or triple the number of available addresses, or even a thousand-fold or even a million-fold. Just for the fun of it, here is the number of unique Internet addresses provided by IPv6:

340,282,366,920,938,463,463,374,607,431,768,211,456

This number is so large it defies understanding. If the Internet Assigned Numbers Authority (IANA) had been around at the creation of the universe and started handing out IPv6 addresses at a rate of one per millisecond — that is, 1,000 addresses every second — it would now, 15 billion years later, have not yet allocated even 1 percent of the available addresses.

The transition from IPv4 to IPv6 has been slow. IPv6 is available on all new computers and has been supported on Windows since Windows XP Service Pack 1 (released in 2002). However, most ISPs still base their service on IPv4. Thus, the Internet will continue to be driven by IPv4 for at least a few more years.

Note: This is now the sixth edition of this book. Every previous edition of this book, all the way back to the very first edition published in 2004, has had this very sidebar. In 2004, I said that the Internet would continue to be driven by IPv4 for at least a few more years. "A few more years" has morphed into 12 years, and we're still living in the world of IPv4. Make no mistake: The world will eventually run out of IPv4 addresses, and we'll have to migrate to IPv6 . . . in a few years, whatever that means.

As a solution to this problem, the idea of IP address classes was introduced. The IP protocol defines five different address classes: A, B, C, D, and E. Each of the first three classes, A–C, uses a different size for the network ID and host ID portion of the address. Class D is for a special type of address called a *multicast address.* Class E is an experimental address class that isn't used.

The first four bits of the IP address are used to determine into which class a particular address fits, as follows:

✦ **Class A:** The first bit is zero.

✦ **Class B:** The first bit is one, and the second bit is zero.

✦ **Class C:** The first two bits are both one, and the third bit is zero.

✦ **Class D:** The first three bits are all one, and the fourth bit is zero.

✦ **Class E:** The first four bits are all one.

Because Class D and E addresses are reserved for special purposes, I focus the rest of the discussion here on Class A, B, and C addresses. Table 3-3 summarizes the details of each address class.

Table 3-3		IP Address Classes			
Class	Address Number Range	Starting Bits	Length of Network ID	Number of Networks	Hosts
A	1-126.x.y.z	0	8	126	16,777,214
B	128-191.x.y.z	10	16	16,384	65,534
C	192-223.x.y.z	110	24	2,097,152	254

Class A addresses

Class A addresses are designed for very large networks. In a Class A address, the first octet of the address is the network ID, and the remaining three octets are the host ID. Because only eight bits are allocated to the network ID and the first of these bits is used to indicate that the address is a Class A address, only 126 Class A networks can exist in the entire Internet. However, each Class A network can accommodate more than 16 million hosts.

Only about 40 Class A addresses are actually assigned to companies or organizations. The rest are either reserved for use by the Internet Assigned Numbers Authority (IANA) or are assigned to organizations that manage IP assignments for geographic regions such as Europe, Asia, and Latin America.

Just for fun, Table 3-4 lists some of the better-known Class A networks. You'll probably recognize many of them. In case you're interested, you can find a complete list of all the Class A address assignments at www.iana.org/ assignments/ipv4-address-space/ipv4-address-space.xml.

Table 3-4	Some Well-Known Class A Networks		
Network	*Description*	*Network*	*Description*
3	General Electric Company		
4	Level 3 Communications	22	Defense Information Systems Agency
6	Army Information Systems Center	25	UK Ministry of Defense
8	Level-3 Communications	26	Defense Information Systems Agency
9	IBM	28	Decision Sciences Institute (North)
11	DoD Intel Information Systems	29–30	Defense Information Systems Agency
12	AT&T Bell Laboratories	33	DLA Systems Automation Center
15	Hewlett-Packard Company	44	44Amateur Radio Digital Communications
16	Digital Equipment Corporation	48	Prudential Securities, Inc.
17	Apple Computer, Inc.	53	Daimler
18	MIT	55	DoD Network Information Center
19	Ford Motor Company	56	U.S. Postal Service
20	Computer Sciences Corporation		

You may have noticed in Table 3-3 that Class A addresses end with `126.x.y.z`, and Class B addresses begin with `128.x.y.z`. What happened to `127.x.y.z`? This special range of addresses is reserved for loopback testing, so these addresses aren't assigned to public networks.

Class B addresses

In a Class B address, the first two octets of the IP address are used as the network ID, and the second two octets are used as the host ID. Thus, a Class B address comes close to my hypothetical scheme of splitting the address down the middle, using half for the network ID and half for the host ID. It isn't identical to this scheme, however, because the first two bits of the first octet are required to be 10, in order to indicate that the address is a Class B address. As a result, a total of 16,384 Class B networks can exist. All Class B addresses fall within the range `128.x.y.z` to `191.x.y.z`. Each Class B address can accommodate more than 65,000 hosts.

The problem with Class B networks is that even though they are much smaller than Class A networks, they still allocate far too many host IDs. Very few networks have tens of thousands of hosts. Thus, careless assignment of Class B addresses can lead to a large percentage of the available host addresses being wasted on organizations that don't need them.

Class C addresses

In a Class C address, the first three octets are used for the network ID, and the fourth octet is used for the host ID. With only eight bits for the host ID, each Class C network can accommodate only 254 hosts. However, with 24 network ID bits, Class C addresses allow for more than 2 million networks.

The problem with Class C networks is that they're too small. Although few organizations need the tens of thousands of host addresses provided by a Class B address, many organizations need more than a few hundred. The large discrepancy between Class B networks and Class C networks is what led to the development of *subnetting,* which I describe in the next section.

Subnetting

Subnetting is a technique that lets network administrators use the 32 bits available in an IP address more efficiently by creating networks that aren't limited to the scales provided by Class A, B, and C IP addresses. With subnetting, you can create networks with more realistic host limits.

Subnetting provides a more flexible way to designate which portion of an IP address represents the network ID and which portion represents the host ID. With standard IP address classes, only three possible network ID sizes exist: 8 bits for Class A, 16 bits for Class B, and 24 bits for Class C. Subnetting lets you select an arbitrary number of bits to use for the network ID.

Two reasons compel people to use subnetting. The first is to allocate the limited IP address space more efficiently. If the Internet were limited to Class A, B, or C addresses, every network would be allocated 254, 64 thousand, or 16 million IP addresses for host devices. Although many networks with more than 254 devices exist, few (if any) exist with 64 thousand, let alone 16 million. Unfortunately, any network with more than 254 devices would need a Class B allocation and probably waste tens of thousands of IP addresses.

The second reason for subnetting is that even if a single organization has thousands of network devices, operating all those devices with the same network ID would slow the network to a crawl. The way TCP/IP works dictates that all the computers with the same network ID must be on the same physical network. The physical network comprises a single *broadcast domain,* which means that a single network medium must carry all the traffic for the network. For performance reasons, networks are usually segmented into broadcast domains that are smaller than even Class C addresses provide.

Subnets

A *subnet* is a network that falls within a Class A, B, or C network. Subnets are created by using one or more of the Class A, B, or C host bits to extend the network ID. Thus, instead of the standard 8-, 16-, or 24-bit network ID, subnets can have network IDs of any length.

Figure 3-3 shows an example of a network before and after subnetting has been applied. In the unsubnetted network, the network has been assigned the Class B address 144.28.0.0. All the devices on this network must share the same broadcast domain.

In the second network, the first four bits of the host ID are used to divide the network into two small networks, identified as subnets 16 and 32. To the outside world (that is, on the other side of the router), these two networks still appear to be a single network identified as 144.28.0.0. For example, the outside world considers the device at 144.28.16.22 to belong to the 144.28.0.0 network. As a result, a packet sent to this device will be delivered to the router at 144.28.0.0. The router then considers the subnet portion of the host ID to decide whether to route the packet to subnet 16 or subnet 32.

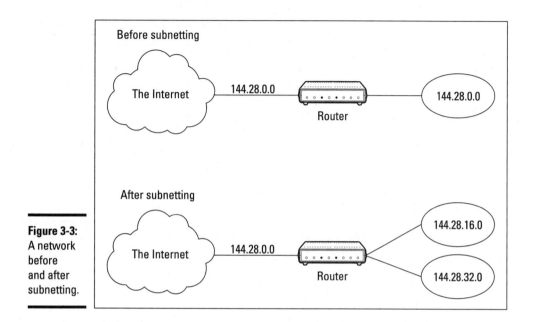

Figure 3-3:
A network
before
and after
subnetting.

Subnet masks

For subnetting to work, the router must be told which portion of the host
ID should be used for the subnet network ID. This little sleight of hand is
accomplished by using another 32-bit number, known as a *subnet mask.*
Those IP address bits that represent the network ID are represented by a 1
in the mask, and those bits that represent the host ID appear as a 0 in the
mask. As a result, a subnet mask always has a consecutive string of ones on
the left, followed by a string of zeros.

For example, the subnet mask for the subnet shown in Figure 3-3, where the
network ID consists of the 16-bit network ID plus an additional 4-bit subnet
ID, would look like this:

```
11111111 11111111 11110000 00000000
```

In other words, the first 20 bits are ones, and the remaining 12 bits are zeros.
Thus, the complete network ID is 20 bits in length, and the actual host ID
portion of the subnetted address is 12 bits in length.

To determine the network ID of an IP address, the router must have both the
IP address and the subnet mask. The router then performs a bitwise opera-
tion called a *logical AND* on the IP address in order to extract the network
ID. To perform a logical AND, each bit in the IP address is compared with the

corresponding bit in the subnet mask. If both bits are 1, the resulting bit in the network ID is set to 1. If either of the bits are 0, the resulting bit is set to 0.

For example, here's how the network address is extracted from an IP address using the 20-bit subnet mask from the previous example:

```
              144  .   28  .   16  .   17
IP address:   10010000 00011100 00010000 00010001
Subnet mask:  11111111 11111111 11110000 00000000
Network ID:   10010000 00011100 00010000 00000000
              144  .   28  .   16  .    0
```

Thus, the network ID for this subnet is 144.28.16.0.

The subnet mask itself is usually represented in dotted-decimal notation. As a result, the 20-bit subnet mask used in the previous example would be represented as 255.255.240.0:

```
Subnet mask:  11111111 11111111 11110000 00000000
              255  .   255  .   240  .    0
```

Don't confuse a subnet mask with an IP address. A subnet mask doesn't represent any device or network on the Internet. It's just a way of indicating which portion of an IP address should be used to determine the network ID. (You can spot a subnet mask right away because the first octet is always 255, and 255 is not a valid first octet for any class of IP address.)

Network prefix notation

Because a subnet mask always begins with a consecutive sequence of ones to indicate which bits to use for the network ID, you can use a shorthand notation — a *network prefix* — to indicate how many bits of an IP address represent the network ID. The network prefix is indicated with a slash immediately after the IP address, followed by the number of network ID bits to use. For example, the IP address 144.28.16.17 with the subnet mask 255.255.240.0 can be represented as 144.28.16.17/20 because the subnet mask 255.255.240.0 has 20 network ID bits.

Network prefix notation is also called *classless interdomain routing* notation (*CIDR*, for short) because it provides a way of indicating which portion of an address is the network ID and which is the host ID without relying on standard address classes.

Default subnets

The *default subnet masks* are three subnet masks that correspond to the standard Class A, B, and C address assignments. These default masks are summarized in Table 3-5.

Table 3-5		The Default Subnet Masks	
Class	*Binary*	*Dotted-Decimal*	*Network Prefix*
A	11111111 00000000 00000000 00000000	255.0.0.0	/8
B	11111111 11111111 00000000 00000000	255.255.0.0	/16
C	11111111 11111111 11111111 00000000	255.255.255.0	/24

Keep in mind that a subnet mask is not actually required to use one of these defaults because the IP address class can be determined by examining the first three bits of the IP address. If the first bit is 0, the address is Class A, and the subnet mask 255.0.0 is applied. If the first two bits are 10, the address is Class B, and 255.255.0.0 is used. If the first three bits are 110, the Class C default mask 255.255.255.0 is used.

The great subnet roundup

You should know about a few additional restrictions that are placed on subnets and subnet masks. In particular

+ **The minimum number of network ID bits is eight.** As a result, the first octet of a subnet mask is always 255.

+ **The maximum number of network ID bits is 30.** You have to leave at least two bits for the host ID portion of the address to allow for at least two hosts. If you use all 32 bits for the network ID, that leaves no bits for the host ID. Obviously, that won't work. Leaving just one bit for the host ID won't work, either, because a host ID of all ones is reserved for a broadcast address, and all zeros refers to the network itself. Thus, if you use 31 bits for the network ID and leave only 1 for the host ID, host ID 1 would be used for the broadcast address, and host ID 0 would be the network itself, leaving no room for actual hosts. That's why the maximum network ID size is 30 bits.

✦ **Because the network ID portion of a subnet mask is always composed of consecutive bits set to 1, only eight values are possible for each octet of a subnet mask:** 0, 128, 192, 224, 248, 252, 254, and 255.

✦ **A subnet address can't be all zeros or all ones.** Thus, the number of unique subnet addresses is two less than two raised to the number of subnet address bits. For example, with three subnet address bits, six unique subnet addresses are possible ($2^3 - 2 = 6$). This implies that you must have at least two subnet bits. (If a single-bit subnet mask were allowed, it would violate the "can't be all zeros or all ones" rule because the only two allowed values would be 0 or 1.)

IP block parties

A subnet can be thought of as a range or block of IP addresses that have a common network ID. For example, the CIDR 192.168.1.0/28 represents the following block of 14 IP addresses:

```
192.168.1.1    192.168.1.2    192.168.1.3    192.168.1.4
192.168.1.5    192.168.1.6    192.168.1.7    192.168.1.8
192.168.1.9    192.168.1.10   192.168.1.11   192.168.1.12
192.168.1.13   192.168.1.14
```

Given an IP address in CIDR notation, it's useful to be able to determine the range of actual IP addresses that the CIDR represents. This matter is straightforward when the octet within which the network ID mask ends happens to be 0, as in the preceding example. You just determine how many host IDs are allowed based on the size of the network ID and count them off.

However, what if the octet where the network ID mask ends is not 0? For example, what are the valid IP addresses for 192.168.1.100 when the subnet mask is 255.255.255.240? In that case, the calculation is a little harder. The first step is to determine the actual network ID. You can do that by converting both the IP address and the subnet mask to binary and then extracting the network ID as in this example:

```
              192  .   168  .  1  .   100
IP address:   11000000 10101000 00000001 01100100
Subnet mask:  11111111 11111111 11111111 11110000
Network ID:   11000000 10101000 00000001 01100000
              192  .   168  .  1  .    96
```

As a result, the network ID is 192.168.1.96.

Next, determine the number of allowable hosts in the subnet based on the network prefix. You can calculate this by subtracting the last octet of the subnet mask from 254. In this case, the number of allowable hosts is 14.

To determine the first IP address in the block, add 1 to the network ID. Thus, the first IP address in my example is `192.168.1.97`. To determine the last IP address in the block, add the number of hosts to the network ID. In my example, the last IP address is `192.168.1.110`. As a result, the `192.168.1.100` with subnet mask `255.255.255.240` designates the following block of IP addresses:

```
192.168.1.97   192.168.1.98  192.168.1.99   192.168.1.100
192.168.1.101  192.168.1.102 192.168.1.103  192.168.1.104
192.168.1.105  192.168.1.106 192.168.1.107  192.168.1.108
192.168.1.109  192.168.1.110
```

Private and public addresses

Any host with a direct connection to the Internet must have a globally unique IP address. However, not all hosts are connected directly to the Internet. Some are on networks that aren't connected to the Internet. Some hosts are hidden behind firewalls, so their Internet connection is indirect.

Several blocks of IP addresses are set aside just for this purpose, for use on private networks that are not connected to the Internet or to use on networks that are hidden behind a firewall. Three such ranges of addresses exist, summarized in Table 3-6. Whenever you create a private TCP/IP network, you should use IP addresses from one of these ranges.

Table 3-6	Private Address Spaces	
CIDR	*Subnet Mask*	*Address Range*
10.0.0.0/8	255.0.0.0	10.0.0.1–10.255.255.254
172.16.0.0/12	255.240.0.0	172.16.1.1–172.31.255.254
192.168.0.0/16	255.255.0.0	192.168.0.1– 192.168.255.254

Network Address Translation

Many firewalls use a technique called *network address translation* (NAT) to hide the actual IP address of a host from the outside world. When that's the case, the NAT device must use a globally unique IP to represent the host to the Internet. Behind the firewall, though, the host can use any IP address it wants. When packets cross the firewall, the NAT device translates the private IP address to the public IP address and vice versa.

One of the benefits of NAT is that it helps to slow down the rate at which the IP address space is assigned. That's because a NAT device can use a single public IP address for more than one host. It does so by keeping track of outgoing packets so that it can match incoming packets with the correct host. To understand how this works, consider the following sequence of steps:

1. A host whose private address is 192.168.1.100 sends a request to 216.239.57.99, which happens to be www.google.com. The NAT device changes the source IP address of the packet to 208.23.110.22, the IP address of the firewall. That way, Google will send its reply back to the firewall router. The NAT records that 192.168.1.100 sent a request to 216.239.57.99.

2. Now another host, at address 192.168.1.107, sends a request to 207.46.134.190, which happens to be www.microsoft.com. The NAT device changes the source of this request to 208.23.110.22 so that Microsoft will reply to the firewall router. The NAT records that 192.168.1.107 sent a request to 207.46.134.190.

3. A few seconds later, the firewall receives a reply from 216.239.57.99. The destination address in the reply is 208.23.110.22, the address of the firewall. To determine to whom to forward the reply, the firewall checks its records to see who is waiting for a reply from 216.239.57.99. It discovers that 192.168.1.100 is waiting for that reply, so it changes the destination address to 192.168.1.100 and sends the packet on.

Actually, the process is a little more complicated than that, because it's very likely that two or more users may have pending requests from the same public IP. In that case, the NAT device uses other techniques to figure out to which user each incoming packet should be delivered.

Chapter 4: Using DHCP

In This Chapter

✔ Discovering the basics of DHCP

✔ Exploring scopes

✔ Configuring a DHCP server

✔ Setting up a DHCP client

*E*very host on a Transmission Control Protocol/Internet Protocol (TCP/IP) network must have a unique IP address. Each host must be properly configured so that it knows its IP address. When a new host comes online, it must be assigned an IP address that's within the correct range of addresses for the subnet but not already in use. Although you can manually assign IP addresses to each computer on your network, that task quickly becomes overwhelming if the network has more than a few computers.

That's where DHCP — Dynamic Host Configuration Protocol — comes into play. *DHCP* automatically configures the IP address for every host on a network, thus assuring that each host has a valid, unique IP address. DHCP even automatically reconfigures IP addresses as hosts come and go. As you can imagine, DHCP can save a network administrator many hours of tedious configuration work.

In this chapter, you discover the ins and outs of DHCP: what it is, how it works, and how to set it up.

Understanding DHCP

DHCP allows individual computers on a TCP/IP network to obtain their configuration information — in particular, their IP address — from a server. The DHCP server keeps track of which IP addresses are already assigned so that when a computer requests an IP address, the DHCP server offers it an IP address that's not already in use.

Configuration information provided by DHCP

Although the primary job of DHCP is to dole out IP addresses and subnet masks, DHCP actually provides more configuration information than just the IP address to its clients. The additional configuration information are DHCP options. The following is a list of some common DHCP options that can be configured by the server:

+ The router address, also known as the Default Gateway address
+ The expiration time for the configuration information
+ Domain name
+ Domain Name Server (DNS) server address
+ Windows Internet Name Service (WINS) server address

DHCP servers

A DHCP server can be a server computer located on the TCP/IP network. All modern server operating systems have a built-in DHCP server. To set up DHCP on a network server, all you have to do is enable the server's DHCP function and configure its settings. In the upcoming section, "Working with a DHCP Server," I show you how to configure a DHCP server for Windows Server 2016. (The procedure for Windows Server 2012 and 2008 is similar.)

A server computer running DHCP doesn't have to be devoted entirely to DHCP unless the network is very large. For most networks, a file server can share duty as a DHCP server. This is especially true if you provide long leases for your IP addresses. (*Lease* is the term used by DHCP to indicate that an IP address has been temporarily given out to a particular computer or other device.)

Many multifunction routers also have built-in DHCP servers. If you don't want to burden one of your network servers with the DHCP function, you can enable the router's built-in DHCP server. An advantage of allowing the router to be your network's DHCP server is that you rarely need to power-down a router. In contrast, you occasionally need to restart or power-down a file server to perform system maintenance, apply upgrades, or perform troubleshooting.

Most networks require only one DHCP server. Setting up two or more servers on the same network requires that you carefully coordinate the IP address ranges (known as *scopes*) for which each server is responsible. If you accidentally set up two DHCP servers for the same scope, you may end up with duplicate address assignments if the servers attempt to assign the same IP address to two different hosts. To prevent this from happening, just set up one DHCP server unless your network is so large that one server can't handle the workload.

How DHCP actually works

You can configure and use DHCP without knowing the details of how DHCP client configuration actually works. However, a basic understanding of the process can help you to understand what DHCP is actually doing. Not only is this understanding enlightening, but it can also help when you're trouble-shooting DHCP problems.

The following paragraphs contain a blow-by-blow account of how DHCP configures TCP/IP hosts. This procedure happens every time you boot up a host computer. It also happens when you release an IP lease and request a fresh lease.

1. When a host computer starts up, the DHCP client software sends a special broadcast packet, known as a *DHCP Discover message.*

    This message uses the subnet's broadcast address (all host ID bits set to one) as the destination address and 0.0.0.0 as the source address.

    The client has to specify 0.0.0.0 as the source address because it doesn't yet have an IP address, and it specifies the broadcast address as the destination address because it doesn't know the address of any DHCP servers. In effect, the DHCP Discover message is saying, "Hey! I'm new here. Are there any DHCP servers out there?"

2. The DHCP server receives the broadcast DHCP Discover message and responds by sending a *DHCP Offer message.*

    The DHCP Offer message includes an IP address that the client can use.

    Like the DHCP Discover message, the DHCP Offer message is sent to the broadcast address. This makes sense because the client to which the message is being sent doesn't yet have an IP address and won't have one until it accepts the offer. In effect, the DHCP Offer message is saying, "Hello there, whoever you are. Here's an IP address you can use, if you want it. Let me know."

    What if the client never receives a DHCP Offer message from a DHCP server? In that case, the client waits for a few seconds and tries again. The client will try four times — at 2, 4, 8, and 16 seconds. If it still doesn't get an offer, it will try again after five minutes.

3. The client receives the DHCP Offer message and sends back a message known as a *DHCP Request message.*

    At this point, the client doesn't actually own the IP address: It's simply indicating that it's ready to accept the IP address that was offered by the server. In effect, the DHCP Request message says, "Yes, that IP address would be good for me. Can I have it, please?"

4. When the server receives the DHCP Request message, it marks the IP address as assigned to the client and broadcasts a *DHCP Ack message.*

    The DHCP Ack message says, in effect, "Okay, it's all yours. Here's the rest of the information you need to use it."

5. When the client receives the DHCP Ack message, it configures its TCP/IP stack by using the address it accepted from the server.

Book III
Chapter 4

Using DHCP

Understanding Scopes

A *scope* is simply a range of IP addresses that a DHCP server is configured to distribute. In the simplest case, where a single DHCP server oversees IP configuration for an entire subnet, the scope corresponds to the subnet. However, if you set up two DHCP servers for a subnet, you can configure each with a scope that allocates only one part of the complete subnet range. In addition, a single DHCP server can serve more than one scope.

You must create a scope before you can enable a DHCP server. When you create a scope, you can provide it with the following properties:

✦ A **scope name,** which helps you to identify the scope and its purpose

✦ A **scope description,** which lets you provide additional details about the scope and its purpose

✦ A **starting IP address** for the scope

✦ An **ending IP address** for the scope

✦ A **subnet mask** for the scope

You can specify the subnet mask with dotted-decimal notation or with network prefix notation.

✦ **One or more ranges of excluded addresses**

These addresses won't be assigned to clients. For more information, see the section "Feeling excluded?" later in this chapter.

✦ **One or more reserved addresses**

These are addresses that will always be assigned to particular host devices. For more information, see the section "Reservations suggested" later in this chapter.

✦ The **lease duration,** which indicates how long the host will be allowed to use the IP address

The client will attempt to renew the lease when half of the lease duration has elapsed. For example, if you specify a lease duration of eight days, the client will attempt to renew the lease after four days. This allows the host plenty of time to renew the lease before the address is reassigned to some other host.

✦ The **router address** for the subnet

This value is also known as the Default Gateway address.

✦ The **domain name and the IP address of the network's DNS servers and WINS servers**

Feeling excluded?

Everyone feels excluded once in awhile. With a wife, three daughters, and a female dog, I know how it feels. Sometimes, however, being excluded is a good thing. In the case of DHCP scopes, exclusions can help you to prevent IP address conflicts and can enable you to divide the DHCP workload for a single subnet among two or more DHCP servers.

An *exclusion* is a range of addresses that are not included in a scope. The exclusion range falls within the range of the scope's starting and ending addresses. In effect, an exclusion range lets you punch a hole in a scope. The IP addresses that fall within the hole won't be assigned.

Here are a few reasons for excluding IP addresses from a scope:

✦ **The computer that runs the DHCP service itself must usually have a static IP address assignment.** As a result, the address of the DHCP server should be listed as an exclusion.

✦ **Some hosts may not be able to support DHCP.** In that case, the host will require a static IP address. For example, you may have a really old MS-DOS computer that doesn't have a DHCP client. By excluding its IP address from the scope, you can prevent that address from being assigned to any other host on the network.

Reservations suggested

In some cases, you may want to assign a particular IP address to a particular host. One way to do this is to configure the host with a static IP address so that the host doesn't use DHCP to obtain its IP configuration. However, here are two major disadvantages to that approach:

✦ **TCP/IP configuration supplies more than just the IP address.** If you use static configuration, you must manually specify the subnet mask, the Default Gateway address, the DNS server address, and other configuration information required by the host. If this information changes, you have to change it not only at the DHCP server, but also at each host that you configured statically.

✦ **You must remember to exclude the static IP address from the DHCP server's scope.** Otherwise, the DHCP server won't know about the static address and may assign it to another host. Then, you'll have two hosts with the same address on your network.

A better way to assign a fixed IP address to a particular host is to create a DHCP reservation. A *reservation* simply indicates that whenever a particular host requests an IP address from the DHCP server, the server should provide it the address that you specify in the reservation. The host won't receive the IP address until the host requests it from the DHCP server, but whenever the host does request IP configuration, it will always receive the same address.

To create a reservation, you associate the IP address that you want assigned to the host with the host's Media Access Control (MAC) address. As a result, you need to get the MAC address from the host before you create the reservation. You can get the MAC address by running the command `ipconfig / all` from a command prompt.

If you set up more than one DHCP server, each should be configured to serve a different range of IP addresses. Otherwise, the servers might assign the same address to two different hosts.

How long to lease?

One of the most important decisions that you'll make when you configure a DHCP server is the length of time to specify for the lease duration. The default value is eight days, which is appropriate in many cases. However, you may encounter situations in which a longer or shorter interval may be appropriate:

✦ **The more stable your network,** the longer the lease duration can safely exist. If you only periodically add new computers to the network or replace existing computers, you can safely increase the lease duration past eight days.

What about BootP?

BootP — Bootstrap Protocol — is an Internet protocol that enables diskless workstations to boot themselves over the Internet or local network. Like DHCP, BootP allows a computer to receive an IP address assigned from a server. However, unlike DHCP, BootP also enables the computer to download a *boot image file,* which the computer can then use to boot itself from. A significant difference between BootP and DHCP is that BootP comes into play before the computer actually loads an operating system. In contrast, DHCP is used after an operating system has been loaded, during the configuration of network devices.

Most DHCP servers can also support BootP. If your network has diskless workstations, you can use the DHCP server's BootP support to boot those computers. At one time, diskless workstations were all the rage because network administrators thought they'd be easier to manage. Users hated them, however. Most diskless workstations have now been buried in landfills, and BootP isn't used much.

✦ **The more volatile the network,** the shorter the lease duration should be. For example, a wireless network in a university library is used by students who bring their laptop computers into the library to work for a few hours at a time. For this network, a duration such as one hour may be appropriate.

Don't configure your network to allow infinite duration leases. Some administrators feel that this cuts down the workload for the DHCP server on stable networks. However, no network is permanently stable. Whenever you find a DHCP server that's configured with infinite leases, look at the active leases. I guarantee you'll find IP leases assigned to computers that no longer exist.

Working with a DHCP Server

The exact steps that you should follow when configuring and managing a DHCP server depend on the network operating system that you're using. The following procedures show you how to work with a DHCP server in Windows Server 2016. The procedures for other operating systems are similar.

Installing a Windows Server 2016 DHCP server

To install the DHCP server role on Windows Server 2016, follow these steps:

1. **Click Server Manager in the taskbar.**

The Server Manager application appears.

2. **Choose Manage ⇨ Add Roles and Features.**

The Before You Begin page of the Add Roles and Features Wizard appears.

3. **Click Next.**

The Installation Type page appears.

4. **Choose Role-Based or Feature-Based Installation and then click Next.**

The wizard displays a list of available servers.

5. **Select the server on which you want to install the DHCP role on; then click Next.**

The wizard displays a list of available server roles.

6. **Select DHCP Server from the list of roles and then click Next.**

The wizard displays a list of required features that must also be installed to support DHCP.

7. Click Add Features, and then click Next.

The wizard displays a page describing what the DHCP role entails.

8. Click Next.

The wizard displays a list of available server features; the features required to support the DHCP role are already selected.

9. Click Next.

The wizard displays a summary of what the DHCP role does.

10. Click Next.

The wizard displays a confirmation page.

11. Click Install.

The wizard installs the DHCP role, which may take a few minutes. When the installation completes, a results page is displayed to summarize the results of the installation.

12. Click Close.

You're done!

Configuring a new scope

After you installed the DHCP role on Windows Server 2016, you'll need to create at least one scope so the server can start handing out IP addresses. Here are the steps:

1. In Server Manager, choose Tools ⇨ DHCP.

This brings up the DHCP management console, shown in Figure 4-1.

Figure 4-1:
The DHCP management console.

2. **Select the DHCP server you want to define the scope for, click IPv4, and then click the New Scope button on the toolbar.**

This brings up the New Scope Wizard dialog box, as shown in Figure 4-2.

Figure 4-2:
The New
Scope
Wizard
comes
to life.

3. **Click Next.**

You're prompted for the name of the scope, as shown in Figure 4-3.

Figure 4-3:
The wizard
asks for a
name for the
new scope.

4. Enter a name and optional description, and then click Next.

The wizard asks for information required to create the scope, as shown in Figure 4-4.

Figure 4-4:
The wizard asks for scope information.

5. Enter the information for the new scope.

You must enter the following information:

- *Start IP Address:* This is the lowest IP address that will be issued for this scope.

- *End IP Address:* This is the highest IP address that will be issued for this scope.

- *Subnet Mask:* This is the subnet mask issued for IP addresses in this scope.

6. Click Next.

The wizard asks whether you want to exclude any ranges from the scope range, as shown in Figure 4-5.

7. (Optional) To create an exclusion, enter the IP address range to exclude and then click Add.

You can repeat this step as many times as necessary to add any excluded addresses.

8. Click Next.

The wizard asks for the lease duration, as shown in Figure 4-6.

Figure 4-5:
Do you want
to create
exclusions?

Figure 4-6:
Set the
lease
duration.

9. **(Optional) Change the lease duration; then click Next.**

When the wizard asks whether you want to configure additional DHCP options, leave this option set to Yes to complete your DHCP configuration now.

10. **Click Next.**

The wizard asks for the default gateway information, as shown in Figure 4-7.

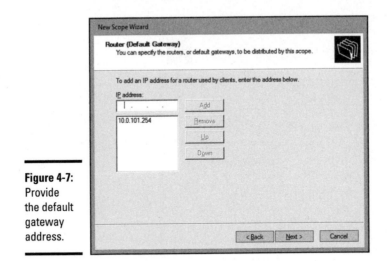

Figure 4-7:
Provide
the default
gateway
address.

11. **Enter the address of your network's router and click Add; then click Next.**

The wizard now asks for additional DNS information, as shown in Figure 4-8.

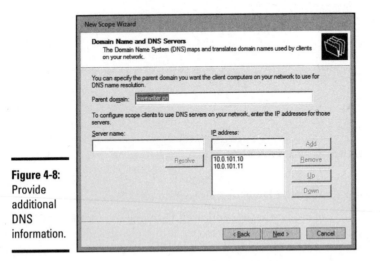

Figure 4-8:
Provide
additional
DNS
information.

12. **(Optional) If you want to add a DNS server, enter its address and then click Add.**

     Repeat this step as many times as necessary to add any additional DNS servers.

13. **Click Next.**

     The wizard next asks for WINS configuration information.

14. **(Optional) If you want to enable WINS, enter the WINS server configuration.**

     WINS isn't required for most modern networks, so you can usually just leave this page blank.

15. **Click Next.**

     The wizard now asks whether you want to activate the scope.

16. **Select Yes, I Want to Activate This Scope and then click Next.**

     A final confirmation page is displayed.

17. **Click Finish.**

     The scope is created.

How to Configure a Windows DHCP Client

Configuring a Windows client for DHCP is easy. The DHCP client is automatically included when you install the TCP/IP protocol, so all you have to do is configure TCP/IP to use DHCP. And in nearly all cases, DHCP is configured automatically when you install Windows.

If you must configure DHCP manually, bring up the Network Properties dialog box by choosing Network or Network Connections from Control Panel (depending on which version of Windows the client is running). Then, select the Internet Protocol Version 4 and click the Properties button. This brings up the dialog box shown in Figure 4-9. To configure the computer to use DHCP, select the Obtain an IP Address Automatically option and the Obtain DNS Server Address Automatically option.

Automatic private IP addressing

If a Windows computer is configured to use DHCP but the computer can't obtain an IP address from a DHCP server, the computer automatically assigns itself a private address by using a feature called Automatic Private IP

Addressing (APIPA). APIPA assigns a private address from the `169.254.x.x` range and uses a special algorithm to ensure that the address is unique on the network. As soon as the DHCP server becomes available, the computer requests a new address, so the APIPA address is used only while the DHCP server is unavailable.

Figure 4-9:
Configuring a Windows client to use DHCP.

Renewing and releasing leases

Normally, a DHCP client attempts to renew its lease when the lease is halfway to the point of being expired. For example, if a client obtains an eight-day lease, it attempts to renew the lease after four days. However, you can renew a lease sooner by issuing the `ipconfig /renew` command at a command prompt. You may want to do this if you changed the scope's configuration or if the client's IP configuration isn't working correctly.

You can also release a DHCP lease by issuing the `ipconfig /release` command at a command prompt. When you release a lease, the client computer no longer has a valid IP address. This is shown in the output from the `ipconfig /release` command:

```
C:\>ipconfig /release
Windows IP Configuration
Ethernet adapter Local Area Connection:
        Connection-specific DNS Suffix  . :
        IP Address... ... ... ... : 0.0.0.0
```

```
Subnet Mask ... ... ... . . : 0.0.0.0
Default Gateway ... ... ... :
```

Here, you can see that the IP address and subnet masks are set to `0.0.0.0` and that the Default Gateway address is blank. When you release an IP lease, you can't communicate with the network by using TCP/IP until you issue an `ipconfig /renew` command to renew the IP configuration or restart the computer.

Chapter 5: Using DNS

In This Chapter

✔ Discovering the basics of DNS

✔ Exploring zones

✔ Examining resource records

✔ Configuring a DNS server

✔ Setting up a DNS client

Domain Name Server — DNS — is the TCP/IP facility that lets you use names rather than numbers to refer to host computers. Without DNS, you'd buy books from `176.32.103.205` instead of from `www.amazon.com`, you'd sell your used furniture at `66.135.216.190` instead of on `www.ebay.com`, and you'd search the web at `173.194.43.64` instead of at `www.google.com`.

Understanding how DNS works and how to set up a DNS server is crucial to setting up and administering a Transmission Control Protocol/Internet Protocol (TCP/IP) network. (For more on that, see Chapter 1 of this mini-book.) This chapter introduces you to the basics of DNS, including how the DNS naming system works and how to set up a DNS server.

If you want to review the complete official specifications for DNS, look up RFC 1034 and 1035 at `www.ietf.org/rfc/rfc1034.txt` and `www.ietf.org/rfc/rfc1035.txt`, respectively.

Understanding DNS Names

DNS is a name service that provides a standardized system for providing names to identify TCP/IP hosts as well as a way to look up the IP address of a host, given the host's DNS name. For example, if you use DNS to look up the name `www.ebay.com`, you get the IP address of the eBay web host: `66.135.216.190`. Thus, DNS allows you to access the eBay website by using the DNS name `www.ebay.com` instead of the site's IP address.

The following sections describe the basic concepts of DNS.

Domains and domain names

To provide a unique DNS name for every host computer on the Internet, DNS uses a time-tested technique: Divide and conquer. DNS uses a hierarchical naming system that's similar to how folders are organized hierarchically on a Windows computer. Instead of folders, however, DNS organizes its names into domains. Each domain includes all the names that appear directly beneath it in the DNS hierarchy.

For example, Figure 5-1 shows a small portion of the DNS domain tree. At the very top of the tree is the *root domain,* which is the anchor point for all domains. Directly beneath the root domain are four top-level domains, named edu, com, org, and gov.

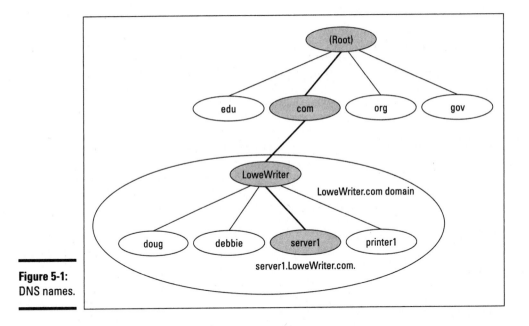

Figure 5-1:
DNS names.

In reality, many more top-level domains than this exist in the Internet's root domain. For more information, see the section "Top-Level Domains," later in this chapter.

Beneath the com domain in Figure 5-1 is another domain called LoweWriter, which happens to be my own personal domain. (Pretty clever, eh?) To completely identify this domain, you have to combine it with the name of its *parent domain* (in this case, com) to create the complete domain name:

`LoweWriter.com`. Notice that the parts of the domain name are separated from each other with periods, which are called dots. As a result, when you read this domain name, you pronounce it *LoweWriter dot com*.

Beneath the `LoweWriter` node are four host nodes, named `doug`, `debbie`, `server1`, and `printer1`. Respectively, these correspond to three computers and a printer on my home network. You can combine the host name with the domain name to get the complete DNS name for each of my network's hosts. For example, the complete DNS name for my server is `server1.LoweWriter.com`. Likewise, my printer is `printer1.LoweWriter.com`.

Here are a few additional details that you need to remember about DNS names:

✦ **DNS names are not case sensitive.** As a result, `LoweWriter` and `Lowewriter` are treated as the same name, as are `LOWEWRITER`, `LOWEwriter`, and `LoWeWrItEr`. When you use a domain name, you can use capitalization to make the name easier to read, but DNS ignores the difference between capital and lowercase letters.

✦ **The name of each DNS node can be up to 63 characters long (not including the dot) and can include letters, numbers, and hyphens.**

No other special characters are allowed.

✦ **A *subdomain* is a domain that's beneath an existing domain.** For example, the `com` domain is actually a subdomain of the root domain. Likewise, `LoweWriter` is a subdomain of the `com` domain.

✦ **DNS is a hierarchical naming system that's similar to the hierarchical folder system used by Windows.**

However, one crucial difference exists between DNS and the Windows naming convention. When you construct a complete DNS name, you start at the bottom of the tree and work your way up to the root. Thus, `doug` is the lowest node in the name `doug.LoweWriter.com`. In contrast, Windows paths are the opposite: They start at the root and work their way down. For example, in the path `\Windows\System32\dns`, `dns` is the lowest node.

✦ **The DNS tree can be up to 127 levels deep.** However, in practice, the DNS tree is pretty shallow. Most DNS names have just three levels (not counting the root). And although you'll sometimes see names with four or five levels, you'll rarely see more levels than that.

✦ **Although the DNS tree is shallow, it's very broad.** In other words, each of the top-level domains has a huge number of second-level domains immediately beneath it. For example, at the time of this writing, the `com` domain had well over 100 million second-level domains beneath it.

Fully qualified domain names

If a domain name ends with a trailing dot, that trailing dot represents the root domain, and the domain name is said to be a *fully qualified domain name* (also known as an FQDN). A fully qualified domain name is also called an *absolute name*. A fully qualified domain name is unambiguous because it identifies itself all the way back to the root domain. In contrast, if a domain name doesn't end with a trailing dot, the name may be interpreted in the context of some other domain. Thus, DNS names that don't end with a trailing dot are called *relative names*.

This is similar to how relative and absolute paths work in Windows. For example, if a path begins with a backslash, such as `\Windows\System32\dns`, the path is absolute. However, a path that doesn't begin with a backslash, such as `System32\dns`, uses the current directory as its starting point. If the current directory happens to be `\Windows`, then `\Windows\System32\dns` and `System32\dns` refer to the same location.

In many cases, relative and fully qualified domain names are interchangeable because the software that interprets them always interprets relative names in the context of the root domain. That's why, for example, you can type `www.wiley.com` (without the trailing dot) — not `www.wiley.com.` — to go to the Wiley home page in a web browser. Some applications, such as DNS servers, may interpret relative names in the context of a domain other than the root.

Top-Level Domains

A *top-level domain* appears immediately beneath the root domain. Top-level domains come in two categories: generic domains and geographic domains. These categories are described in the following sections. (Actually, a third type of top-level domain exists, which is used for reverse lookups. I describe it later in this chapter, in the section "Reverse Lookup Zones.")

Generic domains

Generic domains are the popular top-level domains that you see most often on the Internet. Originally, seven top-level organizational domains existed. In 2002, seven more were added to help ease the congestion of the original seven — in particular, the com domain.

Table 5-1 summarizes the original seven generic top-level domains. Of these, you can see that the com domain is far and away the most populated, with nearly 119 million second-level domains beneath it.

The Size column in this table indicates approximately how many second-level domains existed under each top-level domain as of October 2015, according to the website www.domaintools.com.

Table 5-1	The Original Seven Top-Level Domains	
Domain	*Description*	*Size*
com	Commercial organizations	119,940,760
edu	Educational institutions	7,466
gov	Government institutions	5,466
int	International treaty organizations	192
mil	Military institutions	2,613,099
net	Network providers	15,054,334
org	Noncommercial organizations	10,644,852

Because the com domain ballooned to an almost unmanageable size in the late 1990s, the Internet authorities approved seven new top-level domains in an effort to take some of the heat off of the com domain. Most of these domains, listed in Table 5-2, became available in 2002. As you can see, they haven't really caught on yet even though they've been around for several years.

Table 5-2	The New Seven Top-Level Domains	
Domain	*Description*	*Size*
aero	Aerospace industry	33,810
biz	Business	2,177,100
coop	Cooperatives	7,783
info	Informational sites	5,155,140
museum	Museums	1,207
name	Individual users	170,384
pro	Professional organizations	106,551

Geographic domains

Although the top-level domains are open to anyone, U.S. companies and organizations dominate them. An additional set of top-level domains corresponds to international country designations. Organizations outside the United States often use these top-level domains to avoid the congestion of the generic domains.

Table 5-3 lists those geographic top-level domains with more than 200 registered subdomains at the time of this writing, in alphabetical order. In all, about 150 geographic top-level domains exist. The exact number varies from time to time as political circumstances change.

Table 5-3	Geographic Top-Level Domains with More Than 200 Subdomains		
Domain	**Description**	**Domain**	**Description**
ac	Ascension Island	ie	Ireland
ae	United Arab Emirates	in	India
ag	Antigua and Barbuda	is	Iceland
am	Armenia	it	Italy
an	Netherlands Antilles	jp	Japan
as	American Samoa	kz	Kazakhstan
at	Austria	la	Lao People's Democratic Republic
be	Belgium	li	Liechtenstein
bg	Bulgaria	lk	Sri Lanka
br	Brazil	lt	Lithuania
by	Belarus	lu	Luxembourg
bz	Belize	lv	Latvia
ca	Canada	ma	Morocco
cc	Cocos (Keeling) Islands	md	Moldova
ch	Switzerland	nl	Netherlands
cl	Chile	no	Norway
cn	China	nu	Niue
cx	Christmas Island	pl	Poland
cz	Czech Republic	pt	Portugal
de	Germany	ro	Romania
dk	Denmark	ru	Russian Federation
ee	Estonia	se	Sweden

Domain	Description	Domain	Description
es	Spain	si	Slovenia
eu	European Union	sk	Slovakia
fi	Finland	st	São Tomé and Principe
fm	Micronesia	su	Soviet Union
fo	Faroe Islands	to	Tonga
fr	France	tv	Tuvalu
ge	Georgia	tw	Taiwan
gr	Greece	ua	Ukraine
hr	Croatia	us	United States
hu	Hungary	ws	Samoa

The Hosts File

Long ago, in a network far, far away, the entire Internet was small enough that network administrators could keep track of it all in a simple text file. This file, called the *Hosts file,* simply listed the name and IP address of every host on the network. Each computer had its own copy of the Hosts file. The trick was keeping all those Hosts files up to date. Whenever a new host was added to the Internet, each network administrator would manually update his copy of the Hosts file to add the new host's name and IP address.

As the Internet grew, so did the Hosts file. In the mid-1980s, it became obvious that a better solution was needed. Imagine trying to track the entire Internet today by using a single text file to record the name and IP address of the millions of hosts on the Internet! DNS was invented to solve this problem.

Understanding the Hosts file is important for two reasons:

✦ **The Hosts file is not dead.** For small networks, a Hosts file may still be the easiest way to provide name resolution for the network's computers. In addition, a Hosts file can coexist with DNS. The Hosts file is always checked before DNS is used, so you can even use a Hosts file to override DNS if you want.

✦ **The Hosts file is the precursor to DNS.** DNS was devised to circumvent the limitations of the Hosts file. You'll be in a better position to appreciate the benefits of DNS when you understand how the Hosts file works.

**Book III
Chapter 5**

Using DNS

The Hosts file is a simple text file that contains lines that match IP addresses with host names. You can edit the Hosts file with any text editor, including Notepad or by using the MS-DOS EDIT command. The exact location of the Hosts file depends on the client operating system, as listed in Table 5-4.

Table 5-4	Location of the Hosts File
Operating System	*Location of Hosts File*
Windows 9x/Me	`c:\windows\hosts`
Windows NT/2000	`c:\winnt\system32\drivers\etc\hosts`
Windows XP	`c:\windows\system32\drivers\etc\hosts`
Unix/Linux	`/etc/hosts`

All TCP/IP implementations are installed with a starter Hosts file. For example, Listing 5-1 shows a typical Windows TCP/IP Hosts file. As you can see, the starter file begins with some comments that explain the purpose of the file.

The Hosts file ends with comments, which show the host mapping commands used to map for the host name `localhost`, mapped to the IP address `127.0.0.1`. The IP address `127.0.0.1` is the standard loopback address. As a result, this entry allows a computer to refer to itself by using the name `localhost`.

Note that after the `127.0.0.1 localhost` entry, another `localhost` entry defines the standard IPv6 loopback address (`::1`). This is required because unlike previous versions of Windows, Vista provides built-in support for IPv6.

Prior to Windows 7, these lines were not commented out in the Hosts file. But beginning with Windows 7, the name resolution for localhost is handled by DNS itself, so its definition isn't required in the Hosts file.

Listing 5-1: A Sample Hosts File

```
# Copyright (c) 1993-2009 Microsoft Corp.
#
# This is a sample HOSTS file used by Microsoft TCP/IP for Windows.
#
# This file contains the mappings of IP addresses to host names. Each
# entry should be kept on an individual line. The IP address should
# be placed in the first column followed by the corresponding host name.
# The IP address and the host name should be separated by at least one
# space.
#
```

```
# Additionally, comments (such as these) may be inserted on individual
# lines or following the machine name denoted by a '#' symbol.
#
# For example:
#
#      102.54.94.97     rhino.acme.com          # source server
#      38.25.63.10      x.acme.com              # x client host

# localhost name resolution is handled within DNS itself.
#127.0.0.1        localhost
#::1             localhost
```

To add an entry to the Hosts file, simply edit the file in any text editor. Then, add a line at the bottom of the file, after the `localhost` entry. Each line that you add should list the IP address and the host name that you want to use for the address. For example, to associate the host name `server1.LoweWriter.com` with the IP address `192.168.168.201`, you add this line to the Hosts file:

```
192.168.168.201 server1.LoweWriter.com
```

Then, whenever an application requests the IP address of the host name `server1.LoweWriter.com`, the IP address `192.168.168.201` is returned.

You can also add an alias to a host mapping. This enables users to access a host by using the alias as an alternative name. For example, consider the following line:

```
192.168.168.201 server1.LoweWriter.com s1
```

Here, the device at address `192.168.168.201` can be accessed as `server1.LoweWriter.com` or just `s1`.

Listing 5-2 shows a Hosts file with several hosts defined.

Listing 5-2:   A Hosts File with Several Hosts Defined

```
# Copyright (c) 1993-2009 Microsoft Corp.
#
# This is a sample HOSTS file used by Microsoft TCP/IP for Windows.
#
# This file contains the mappings of IP addresses to host names. Each
# entry should be kept on an individual line. The IP address should
# be placed in the first column followed by the corresponding host name.
# The IP address and the host name should be separated by at least one
# space.
#
# Additionally, comments (such as these) may be inserted on individual
# lines or following the machine name denoted by a '#' symbol.
#
```

(continued)

**Book III
Chapter 5**

Using DNS

Listing 5-2 *(continued)*

```
# For example:
#
#     102.54.94.97     rhino.acme.com        # source server
#      38.25.63.10     x.acme.com            # x client host
# localhost name resolution is handled within DNS itself.
# 127.0.0.1       localhost
# ::1             localhost
192.168.168.200 doug.LoweWriter.com          #Doug's computer
192.168.168.201 server1.LoweWriter.com s1    #Main server
192.168.168.202 debbie.LoweWriter.com        #Debbie's computer
192.168.168.203 printer1.LoweWriter.com p1   #HP Laser Printer
```

Even if your network uses DNS, every client still has a Hosts file that defines at least `localhost`.

Understanding DNS Servers and Zones

A *DNS server* is a computer that runs DNS server software, helps to maintain the DNS database, and responds to DNS name resolution requests from other computers. Although many DNS server implementations are available, the two most popular are BIND and the Windows DNS service. BIND runs on Unix-based computers (including Linux computers), and Windows DNS (naturally) runs on Windows computers. Both provide essentially the same services and can interoperate.

The key to understanding how DNS servers work is to realize that the DNS database — that is, the list of all the domains, subdomains, and host mappings — is a massively distributed database. No single DNS server contains the entire DNS database. Instead, authority over different parts of the database is delegated to different servers throughout the Internet.

For example, suppose that I set up a DNS server to handle name resolutions for my `LoweWriter.com` domain. Then, when someone requests the IP address of `doug.LoweWriter.com`, my DNS server can provide the answer. However, my DNS server wouldn't be responsible for the rest of the Internet. Instead, if someone asks my DNS server for the IP address of some other computer, such as `coyote.acme.com`, my DNS server will have to pass the request on to another DNS server that knows the answer.

Zones

To simplify the management of the DNS database, the entire DNS namespace is divided into zones, and the responsibility for each zone is delegated to a particular DNS server. In many cases, zones correspond directly to domains. For example, if I set up a domain named `LoweWriter.com`, I can also set up a DNS zone called `LoweWriter.com` that's responsible for the entire `LoweWriter.com` domain.

However, the subdomains that make up a domain can be parceled out to separate zones, as shown in Figure 5-2. Here, a domain named `LoweWriter.com` has been divided into two zones. One zone, `us.LoweWriter.com`, is responsible for the entire `us.LoweWriter.com` subdomain. The other zone, `LoweWriter.com`, is responsible for the entire `LoweWriter.com` domain except for the `us.LoweWriter.com` subdomain.

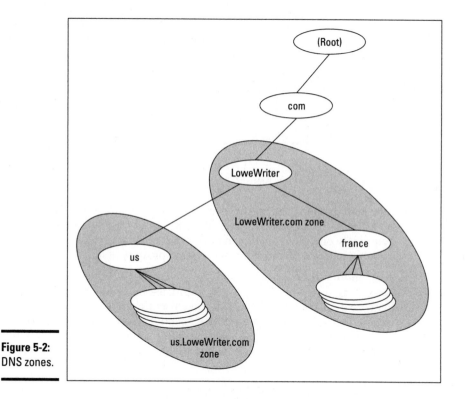

Figure 5-2:
DNS zones.

**Book III
Chapter 5**

Using DNS

Why would you do that? The main reason is to delegate authority for the zone to separate servers. For example, Figure 5-2 suggests that part of the `LoweWriter.com` domain is administered in the United States and that part of it is administered in France. The two zones in the figure allow one server to be completely responsible for the U.S. portion of the domain, and the other server handles the rest of the domain.

The old phony Hosts file trick

The Hosts file can be the basis of a fun, practical joke. Of course, neither I nor my editors or publishers recommend that you actually do this. If it gets you into trouble, don't send your lawyers to me. This sidebar is here only to let you know what to do if it happens to you.

The idea is to edit your poor victim's Hosts file so that whenever the user tries to access his favorite website, a site of your choosing comes up instead. For example, if you're trying to get your husband to take you on a cruise, add a line to his Hosts file that replaces his favorite website with the website for a cruise line. For example, this line should do the trick:

```
151.124.250.181 www.espn.com
```

Now, whenever your husband tries to call up the ESPN website, he'll get the Carnival Cruise Lines home page instead.

Of course, to actually pull a stunt like this would be completely irresponsible, especially if you didn't first make a backup copy of the Hosts file, just in case it somehow gets messed up.

Be warned: If the wrong websites suddenly start coming up, check your Hosts file to see whether it's been tampered with.

The following are the two basic types of zones:

✦ A **primary zone** is the master copy of a zone. The data for a primary zone is stored in the local database of the DNS server that hosts the primary zone. Only one DNS server can host a particular primary zone. Any updates to the zone must be made to the primary zone.

✦ A **secondary zone** is a read-only copy of a zone. When a server hosts a secondary zone, the server doesn't store a local copy of the zone data. Instead, it obtains its copy of the zone from the zone's primary server by using a process called *zone transfer*. Secondary servers must periodically check primary servers to see whether their secondary zone data is still current. If not, a zone transfer is initiated to update the secondary zone.

Primary and secondary servers

Each DNS server is responsible for one or more zones. The following are the two different roles that a DNS server can take:

✦ **Primary server for a zone,** which means that the DNS server hosts a primary zone. The data for the zone is stored in files on the DNS server. Every zone must have one primary server.

✦ **Secondary server for a zone,** which means that the DNS server obtains the data for a secondary zone from a primary server. Every zone should have at least one secondary server. That way, if the primary server goes down, the domain defined by the zone can be accessed via the secondary server or servers.

A secondary server should be on a different subnet than the zone's primary server. If the primary and secondary servers are on the same subnet, both servers will be unavailable if the router that controls the subnet goes down.

Note that a single DNS server can be the primary server for some zones and a secondary server for other zones. A server is said to be *authoritative* for the primary and secondary zones that it hosts because it can provide definitive answers for queries against those zones.

Root servers

The core of DNS comprises the *root servers,* which are authoritative for the entire Internet. The main function of the root servers is to provide the address of the DNS servers that are responsible for each of the top-level domains. These servers, in turn, can provide the DNS server address for subdomains beneath the top-level domains.

The root servers are a major part of the glue that holds the Internet together. As you can imagine, they're swamped with requests day and night. A total of 13 root servers are located throughout the world. Table 5-5 lists the IP address and the organization that oversees the operation of each of the 13 root servers.

Book III
Chapter 5

Using DNS

Table 5-5	The 13 Root Servers	
Server	IP Address	Operator
A	198.41.0.4	VeriSign Global Registry Services
B	192.228.79.201	Information Sciences Institute
C	192.33.4.12	Cogent Communications
D	128.8.10.90	University of Maryland
E	192.203.230.10	NASA Ames Research Center
F	192.5.5.241	Internet Systems Consortium
G	192.112.36.4	U.S. DOD Network Information
H	128.63.2.53	U.S. Army Research Lab
I	192.36.148.17	Autonomica
J	192.58.128.30	VeriSign Global Registry Services
K	193.0.14.129	Reseaux IP Europeens Network
L	199.7.83.42	ICANN
M	202.12.27.33	WIDE Project

DNS servers learn how to reach the root servers by consulting a *root hints* file that's located on the server. In the Unix/Linux world, this file is known as `named.root` and can be found at `/etc/named.root`. For Windows DNS servers, the file is called `cache.dns` and can be found in `\windows\system32\dns\` or `\winnt\system32\dns\`, depending on the Windows version. Listing 5-3 shows the file itself.

Listing 5-3: The `named.root` File

```
;       This file holds the information on root name servers needed to
;       initialize cache of Internet domain name servers
;       (e.g. reference this file in the "cache  .  <file>"
;       configuration file of BIND domain name servers).
;
;       This file is made available by InterNIC
;       under anonymous FTP as
;           file            /domain/named.root
;           on server       FTP.INTERNIC.NET
;       -OR-                RS.INTERNIC.NET
;
;       last update:    Dec 12, 2008
;       related version of root zone:   2008121200
;
; formerly NS.INTERNIC.NET
;
.                       3600000  IN  NS   A.ROOT-SERVERS.NET.
A.ROOT-SERVERS.NET.     3600000      A    198.41.0.4
A.ROOT-SERVERS.NET.     3600000      AAAA 2001:503:BA3E::2:30
;
; FORMERLY NS1.ISI.EDU
;
.                       3600000      NS   B.ROOT-SERVERS.NET.
B.ROOT-SERVERS.NET.     3600000      A    192.228.79.201
;
; FORMERLY C.PSI.NET
;
.                       3600000      NS   C.ROOT-SERVERS.NET.
C.ROOT-SERVERS.NET.     3600000      A    192.33.4.12
;
; FORMERLY TERP.UMD.EDU
;
.                       3600000      NS   D.ROOT-SERVERS.NET.
D.ROOT-SERVERS.NET.     3600000      A    128.8.10.90
;
; FORMERLY NS.NASA.GOV
;
.                       3600000      NS   E.ROOT-SERVERS.NET.
E.ROOT-SERVERS.NET.     3600000      A    192.203.230.10
;
; FORMERLY NS.ISC.ORG
;
.                       3600000      NS   F.ROOT-SERVERS.NET.
F.ROOT-SERVERS.NET.     3600000      A    192.5.5.241
F.ROOT-SERVERS.NET.     3600000      AAAA 2001:500:2F::F
;
```

```
; FORMERLY NS.NIC.DDN.MIL
;
.                        3600000      NS    G.ROOT-SERVERS.NET.
G.ROOT-SERVERS.NET.      3600000      A     192.112.36.4
;
; FORMERLY AOS.ARL.ARMY.MIL
;
.                        3600000      NS    H.ROOT-SERVERS.NET.
H.ROOT-SERVERS.NET.      3600000      A     128.63.2.53
H.ROOT-SERVERS.NET.      3600000      AAAA  2001:500:1::803F:235
;
; FORMERLY NIC.NORDU.NET
;
.                        3600000      NS    I.ROOT-SERVERS.NET.
I.ROOT-SERVERS.NET.      3600000      A     192.36.148.17
;
; OPERATED BY VERISIGN, INC.
;
.                        3600000      NS    J.ROOT-SERVERS.NET.
J.ROOT-SERVERS.NET.      3600000      A     192.58.128.30
J.ROOT-SERVERS.NET.      3600000      AAAA  2001:503:C27::2:30
;
; OPERATED BY RIPE NCC
;
.                        3600000      NS    K.ROOT-SERVERS.NET.
K.ROOT-SERVERS.NET.      3600000      A     193.0.14.129
K.ROOT-SERVERS.NET.      3600000      AAAA  2001:7FD::1
;
; OPERATED BY ICANN
;
.                        3600000      NS    L.ROOT-SERVERS.NET.
L.ROOT-SERVERS.NET.      3600000      A     199.7.83.42
L.ROOT-SERVERS.NET.      3600000      AAAA  2001:500:3::42
;
; OPERATED BY WIDE
;
.                        3600000      NS    M.ROOT-SERVERS.NET.
M.ROOT-SERVERS.NET.      3600000      A     202.12.27.33
M.ROOT-SERVERS.NET.      3600000      AAAA  2001:DC3::35
; End of File
```

Caching

DNS servers don't really like doing all that work to resolve DNS names, but they're not stupid. They know that if a user visits www.wiley.com today, he'll probably do it again tomorrow. As a result, name servers keep a cache of query results. The next time the user visits www.wiley.com, the name server is able to resolve this name without having to query all those other name servers.

The Internet is constantly changing, however, so cached data can quickly become obsolete. For example, suppose that John Wiley & Sons, Inc., switches its website to a different server. It can update its name servers to reflect the new IP address, but any name servers that have a cached copy of the query will be out of date.

To prevent this from being a major problem, DNS data is given a relatively short expiration time. The expiration value for DNS data is called the *TTL* (Time to Live). TTL is specified in seconds. Thus, a TTL of 60 means the data is kept for one minute.

Understanding DNS Queries

When a DNS client needs to resolve a DNS name to an IP address, it uses a library routine — a *resolver* — to handle the query. The resolver takes care of sending the query message over the network to the DNS server, receiving and interpreting the response, and informing the client of the results of the query.

A DNS client can make two basic types of queries: recursive and iterative. The following list describes the difference between these two query types. (The following discussion assumes that the client is asking the server for the IP address of a host name, which is the most common type of DNS query. You find out about other types of queries later; they, too, can be either recursive or iterative.)

✦ **Recursive queries:** When a client issues a *recursive DNS query,* the server must reply with either the IP address of the requested host name or an error message indicating that the host name doesn't exist. If the server doesn't have the information, it asks another DNS server for the IP address. When the first server finally gets the IP address, it sends it back to the client. If the server determines that the information doesn't exist, it returns an error message.

✦ **Iterative queries:** When a server receives an iterative query, it returns the IP address of the requested host name if it knows the address. If the server doesn't know the address, it returns a *referral,* which is simply the address of a DNS server that should know. The client can then issue an iterative query to the server to which it was referred.

Normally, DNS clients issue recursive queries to DNS servers. If the server knows the answer to the query, it replies directly to the client. If not, the server issues an iterative query to a DNS server that it thinks should know the answer. If the original server gets an answer from the second server, it returns the answer to the client. If the original server gets a referral to a third server, the original server issues an iterative query to the third server. The original server keeps issuing iterative queries until it either gets the answer or an error occurs. It then returns the answer or the error to the client.

A real-life DNS example

Confused? I can understand why. An example may help to clear things up. Suppose that a user wants to view the web page www.wiley.com. The following sequence of steps occurs to resolve this address:

1. The browser asks the client computer's resolver to find the IP address of www.wiley.com.

2. The resolver issues a recursive DNS query to its name server.

In this case, I'll call the name server ns1.LoweWriter.com.

3. The name server ns1LoweWriter.com checks whether it knows the IP address of www.wiley.com.

It doesn't, so the name server issues an iterative query to one of the root name servers to see whether it knows the IP address of www.wiley.com.

4. The root name server doesn't know the IP address of www.wiley.com, so it returns a list of the name servers that are authoritative for the com domain.

5. The ns1.LoweWriter.com name server picks one of the com domain name servers and sends it an iterative query for www.wiley.com.

6. The com name server doesn't know the IP address of www.wiley.com, so it returns a list of the name servers that are authoritative for the wiley.com domain.

7. The ns1.LoweWriter.com name server picks one of the name servers for the wiley.com domain and sends it an iterative query for www.wiley.com.

8. The wiley.com name server knows the IP address for www.wiley.com, so the name server returns it.

9. The ns1.LoweWriter.com name server shouts with joy for having finally found the IP address for www.wiley.com. It gleefully returns this address to the client. It also caches the answer so that the next time the user looks for www.wiley.com, the name server won't have to contact other name servers to resolve the name.

10. The client also caches the results of the query.

The next time the client needs to look for www.wiley.com, the client can resolve the name without troubling the name server.

**Book III
Chapter 5**

Using DNS

Zone Files and Resource Records

Each DNS zone is defined by a *zone file* (also known as a *DNS database* or a *master file*). For Windows DNS servers, the name of the zone file is `domain.zone`. For example, the zone file for the `LoweWriter.com` zone is named `LoweWriter.com.zone`. For Bind DNS servers, the zone files are named `db.domain`. Thus, the zone file for the `LoweWriter.com` domain would be `db.LoweWriter.com`. The format of the zone file contents is the same for both systems, however.

A zone file consists of one or more resource records. Creating and updating the resource records that comprise the zone files is one of the primary tasks of a DNS administrator. The Windows DNS server provides a friendly graphical interface to the resource records. However, you should still be familiar with how to construct resource records.

Resource records are written as simple text lines, with the following fields:

```
Owner    TTL    Class    Type    RDATA
```

These fields must be separated from each other by one or more spaces. The following list describes the five resource record fields:

+ **Owner:** The name of the DNS domain or the host that the record applies to. This is usually specified as a fully qualified domain name (with a trailing dot) or as a simple host name (without a trailing dot), which is then interpreted in the context of the current domain.

  You can also specify a single @ symbol as the owner name. In that case, the current domain is used.

+ **TTL:** Also known as *Time to Live;* the number of seconds that the record should be retained in a server's cache before it's invalidated. If you omit the TTL value for a resource record, a default TTL is obtained from the Start of Authority (SOA) record.

+ **Class:** Defines the protocol to which the record applies. You should always specify IN, for the Internet protocol. If you omit the class field, the last class field that you specified explicitly is used. As a result, you'll sometimes see zone files that specify IN only on the first resource record (which must be an SOA record) and then allow it to default to IN on all subsequent records.

+ **Type:** The resource record type. The most commonly used resource types are summarized in Table 5-6 and are described separately later in this section. Like the Class field, you can also omit the Type field and allow it to default to the last specified value.

+ **RDATA:** Resource record data that is specific to each record type.

Table 5-6		Common Resource Record Types
Type	*Name*	*Description*
SOA	Start of Authority	Identifies a zone
NS	Name Server	Identifies a name server that is authoritative for the zone
A	Address	Maps a fully qualified domain name to an IP address
CNAME	Canonical Name	Creates an alias for a fully qualified domain name
MX	Mail Exchange	Identifies the mail server for a domain
PTR	Pointer	Maps an IP address to a fully qualified domain name for reverse lookups

Most resource records fit on one line. If a record requires more than one line, you must enclose the data that spans multiple lines in parentheses.

You can include comments to clarify the details of a zone file. A comment begins with a semicolon and continues to the end of the line. If a line begins with a semicolon, the entire line is a comment. You can also add a comment to the end of a resource record. You see examples of both types of comments later in this chapter.

SOA records

Every zone must begin with an SOA record, which names the zone and provides default information for the zone. Table 5-7 lists the fields that appear in the RDATA section of an SOA record. Note that these fields are positional, so you should include a value for all of them and list them in the order specified. Because the SOA record has so many RDATA fields, you'll probably need to use parentheses to continue the SOA record onto multiple lines.

Note two things about the SOA fields:

✦ **The email address of the person responsible for the zone is given in DNS format, not in normal email format.** Thus, you separate the user from the mail domain with a dot rather than an @ symbol. For example, doug@LoweWriter.com would be listed as doug.lowewriter.com.

✦ **The serial number should be incremented every time you change the zone file.** If you edit the file via the graphic interface provided by Windows DNS, the serial number is incremented automatically. However, if you edit the zone file via a simple text editor, you have to manually increment the serial number.

Table 5-7	RDATA Fields for an SOA Record
Name	*Description*
MNAME	The domain name of the name server that is authoritative for the zone.
RNAME	An email address (specified in domain name format; not regular email format) of the person responsible for this zone.
SERIAL	The serial number of the zone. Secondary zones use this value to determine whether they need to initiate a zone transfer to update their copy of the zone.
REFRESH	A time interval that specifies how often a secondary server should check whether the zone needs to be refreshed. A typical value is 3600 (one hour).
RETRY	A time interval that specifies how long a secondary server should wait after requesting a zone transfer before trying again. A typical value is 600 (ten minutes).
EXPIRE	A time interval that specifies how long a secondary server should keep the zone data before discarding it. A typical value is 86400 (one day).
MINIMUM	A time interval that specifies the TTL value to use for zone resource records that omit the TTL field. A typical value is 3600 (one hour).

Here's a typical example of an SOA record, with judicious comments to identify each field:

```
lowewriter.com. IN  SOA (
    ns1.lowewriter.com           ; authoritative name server
    doug.lowewriter.com          ; responsible person
    148                          ; version number
    3600                         ; refresh (1 hour)
    600                          ; retry (10 minutes)
    86400                        ; expire (1 day)
    3600 )                       ; minimum TTL (1 hour)
```

NS records

Name server (NS) records identify the name servers that are authoritative for
the zone. Every zone must have at least one NS record. Using two or more
NS records is better so that if the first name server is unavailable, the zone
will still be accessible.

The owner field should either be the fully qualified domain name for the
zone, with a trailing dot, or an @ symbol. The RDATA consists of just one
field: the fully qualified domain name of the name server.

The following examples show two NS records that serve the `lowewriter.com` domain:

```
lowewriter.com.  IN  NS  ns1.lowewriter.com.
lowewriter.com.  IN  NS  ns2.lowewriter.com.
```

A records

Address (A) records are the meat of the zone file: They provide the IP addresses for each of the hosts that you want to make accessible via DNS. In an A record, you usually list just the host name in the owner field, thus allowing DNS to add the domain name to derive the fully qualified domain name for the host. The RDATA field for the A record is the IP address of the host.

The following lines define various hosts for the `LoweWriter.com` domain:

```
doug      IN  A  192.168.168.200
server1   IN  A  192.168.168.201
debbie    IN  A  192.168.168.202
printer1  IN  A  192.168.168.203
router1   IN  A  207.126.127.129
www       IN  A  64.71.129.102
```

Notice that for these lines, I don't specify the fully qualified domain names for each host. Instead, I just provide the host name. DNS will add the name of the zone's domain to these host names in order to create the fully qualified domain names.

If I wanted to be more explicit, I could list these A records like this:

```
doug.lowewriter.com.      IN  A  192.168.168.200
server1.lowewriter.com.   IN  A  192.168.168.201
debbie.lowewriter.com.    IN  A  192.168.168.202
printer1.lowewriter.com.  IN  A  192.168.168.203
router1.lowewriter.com    IN  A  207.126.127.129
www.lowewriter.com.       IN  A  64.71.129.102
```

However, all this does is increase the chance for error. Plus, it creates more work for you later if you decide to change your network's domain.

CNAME records

A *Canonical Name* (CNAME) record creates an alias for a fully qualified domain name. When a user attempts to access a domain name that is actually an alias, the DNS system substitutes the real domain name — known as the *Canonical Name* — for the alias. The owner field in the CNAME record provides the name of the alias that you want to create. Then, the RDATA field provides the Canonical Name — that is, the real name of the host.

For example, consider these resource records:

```
ftp.lowewriter.com.    IN  A      207.126.127.132
files.lowewriter.com.  IN  CNAME  www1.lowewriter.com.
```

Here, the host name of an FTP server at `207.126.127.132` is `ftp.lowewriter.com`. The CNAME record allows users to access this host as `files.lowewriter.com` if they prefer.

PTR records

A *Pointer* (PTR) record is the opposite of an address record: It provides the fully qualified domain name for a given address. The owner field should specify the reverse lookup domain name, and the RDATA field specifies the fully qualified domain name. For example, the following record maps the address `64.71.129.102` to `www.lowewriter.com`:

```
102.129.71.64.in-addr.arpa. IN  PTR  www.lowewriter.com.
```

PTR records don't usually appear in normal domain zones. Instead, they appear in special reverse lookup zones. For more information, see the section "Reverse Lookup Zones," later in this chapter.

MX records

Mail Exchange (MX) records identify the mail server for a domain. The owner field provides the domain name that users address mail to. The RDATA section of the record has two fields. The first is a priority number used to determine which mail servers to use when several are available. The second is the fully qualified domain name of the mail server itself.

For example, consider the following MX records:

```
lowewriter.com.    IN  MX  0   mail1.lowewriter.com.
lowewriter.com.    IN  MX  10  mail2.lowewriter.com.
```

In this example, the `lowewriter.com` domain has two mail servers, named `mail1.lowewriter.com` and `mail2.lowewriter.com`. The priority numbers for these servers are `0` and `10`. Because it has a lower priority number, mail will be delivered to `mail1.lowewriter.com` first. The `mail2.lowewriter.com` server will be used only if `mail1.lowewriter.com` isn't available.

The server name specified in the RDATA section should be an actual host name, not an alias created by a CNAME record. Although some mail servers can handle MX records that point to CNAMEs, not all can. As a result, you shouldn't specify an alias in an MX record.

Be sure to create a reverse lookup record (PTR, described in the next section) for your mail servers. Some mail servers won't accept mail from a server that doesn't have valid reverse lookup entries.

Reverse Lookup Zones

Normal DNS queries ask a name server to provide the IP address that corresponds to a fully qualified domain name. This kind of query is a *forward lookup*. A *reverse lookup* is the opposite of a forward lookup: It returns the fully qualified domain name of a host based on its IP address.

Reverse lookups are possible because of a special domain called the in-addr.arpa domain, which provides a separate fully qualified domain name for every possible IP address on the Internet. To enable a reverse lookup for a particular IP address, all you have to do is create a PTR record in a reverse lookup zone (a zone that is authoritative for a portion of the in-addr.arpa domain). The PTR record maps the in-addr.arpa domain name for the address to the host's actual domain name.

The technique used to create the reverse domain name for a given IP address is pretty clever. It creates subdomains beneath the in-addr.arpa domain by using the octets of the IP address, listing them in reverse order. For example, the reverse domain name for the IP address 207.126.67.129 is 129.67.126.207.in-addr.arpa.

Why list the octets in reverse order? Because that correlates the network portions of the IP address (which work from left to right) with the subdomain structure of DNS names (which works from right to left). The following description should clear this up:

✦ The 255 possible values for the first octet of an IP address each have a subdomain beneath the in-addr.arpa domain. For example, any IP address that begins with 207 can be found in the 207.in-addr.arpa domain.

✦ Within this domain, each of the possible values for the second octet can be found as a subdomain of the first octet's domain. Thus, any address that begins with 207.126 can be found in the 126.207.in-addr.arpa domain.

✦ The same holds true for the third octet, so any address that begins with `207.126.67` can be found in the `67.126.207.in-addr.arpa` domain.

✦ By the time you get to the fourth octet, you've pinpointed a specific host. The fourth octet completes the fully qualified reverse domain name. Thus, `207.126.67.129` is mapped to `129.67.126.207.in-addr.arpa`.

As a result, to determine the fully qualified domain name for the computer at `207.126.67.129`, the client queries its DNS server for the FQDN that corresponds to `129.67.126.207.in-addr.arpa`.

Working with the Windows DNS Server

Installing and managing a DNS server depends on the network operating system (NOS) that you're using. The following sections are specific to working with a DNS server in Windows Server 2012. Working with Bind in a Unix/ Linux environment is similar but without the help of a graphical user interface (GUI), and working with Windows Server 2016 is similar.

You can install the DNS server on a Windows server from the Server Manager application. Open the Server Manager and choose Manage ⇨ Add Roles and Features. Then, follow the wizard's instructions to add the DNS Role.

After you set up a DNS server, you can manage the DNS server from the DNS management console, as shown in Figure 5-3. From this management console, you can perform common administrative tasks, such as adding additional zones, changing zone settings, adding A or MX records to an existing zone, and so on. The DNS management console hides the details of the actual resource records from you, thus allowing you to work with a friendly GUI instead.

To add a new host (that is, an A record) to a zone, right-click the zone in the DNS management console and choose the Add New Host command. This brings up the New Host dialog box, as shown in Figure 5-4. From this dialog box, specify the following information.

✦ **Name:** The host name for the new host.

✦ **IP Address:** The host's IP address.

✦ **Create Associated Pointer (PTR) Record:** Automatically creates a PTR record in the reverse lookup zone file. Select this option if you want to allow reverse lookups for the host.

You can add other records, such as MX or CNAME records, in the same way.

Figure 5-3:
The DNS management console.

Figure 5-4:
The New Host dialog box.

How to Configure a Windows DNS Client

Client computers don't need much configuration in order to work properly with DNS. The client must have the address of at least one DNS server. Usually, this address is supplied by DHCP, so if the client is configured to obtain its IP address from a DHCP server, it will also obtain the DNS server address from DHCP.

To configure a client computer to obtain the DNS server location from DHCP, bring up the Network Properties dialog box by choosing Network or Network Connections in Control Panel (depending on which version of

Windows the client is running). Then, select the Internet Protocol Version 4 (TCP/IPv4) protocol and click the Properties button. This summons the dialog box shown in Figure 5-5. To configure the computer to use Dynamic Host Configuration Protocol (DHCP), select the Obtain an IP Address Automatically and the Obtain DNS Server Address Automatically options.

Figure 5-5:
Configuring a Windows client to obtain its DNS address from DHCP.

If the computer doesn't use DHCP, you can use this same dialog box to manually enter the IP address of your DNS server.

Chapter 6: Using FTP

In This Chapter

✔ Figuring out the basics of FTP

✔ Setting up an FTP server

✔ Retrieving files from an FTP server

✔ Using FTP commands

*F*ile Transfer Protocol (FTP) is the basic method for exchanging files over the Internet. If you need to access files from someone's FTP site, this chapter shows you how to do so by using a web browser or a command line FTP client. If you need to set up your own FTP server to share files with other users, this chapter shows you how to do that, too.

Discovering FTP

FTP is as old as the Internet. The first versions of FTP date to the early 1970s, and even the current FTP standard (RFC 959) dates to 1985. You can use FTP with the command line FTP client (which has a decidedly 1980s feel to it), or you can access FTP sites with most modern web browsers if you prefer a graphic interface. Old computer hounds prefer the FTP command line client, probably for nostalgic reasons.

In spite of its age, FTP is still commonly used on the Internet. For example, InterNIC (the organization that manages Internet names) maintains an FTP site at `ftp://ftp.rs.internic.net`. There, you can download important files, such as `named.root`, which provides the current location of the Internet's root name servers. Many other companies maintain FTP sites from which you can download software, device drivers, documentation, reports, and so on. FTP is also one of the most common ways to publish HTML files to a web server. Because FTP is still so widely used, it pays to know how to use it from both the command line and from a browser.

In the Windows world, an FTP server is integrated with the Microsoft web server, Internet Information Services (IIS). As a result, you can manage FTP from the IIS management console along with other IIS features. Note that the FTP component is an optional part of IIS, so you may need to install it separately if you opted to not include it when you first installed IIS.

On Unix and Linux systems, FTP isn't usually integrated with a web server. Instead, the FTP server is installed as a separate program. You're usually given the option to install FTP when you install the operating system. If you choose not to, you can always install it later.

When you run an FTP server, you expose a portion of your file system to the outside world. As a result, you need to be careful about how you set up your FTP server so that you don't accidentally allow hackers access to the bowels of your file server. Fortunately, the default configuration of FTP is pretty secure. You shouldn't tinker much with the default configuration unless you know what you're doing.

Configuring an FTP Server

In the following sections, I show you how to configure FTP services in Microsoft IIS. The examples show IIS version 10 running on Windows Server 2016, but the procedures are essentially the same for other IIS versions.

Installing FTP

Although FTP is integrated with IIS, FTP is not installed by default when you install IIS. As a result, if you didn't specifically select FTP when you installed IIS, you need to install FTP before you can set up an FTP site. Here is the procedures for Windows Server 2016:

1. **Start Server Manager and choose Manage⇨Add Roles and Features.**

2. **When you get to the page that lists the server roles, select the Web Server (IIS) role.**

3. **Continue with the wizard until you get to the Role Services page.**

4. **Select the FTP Server role service.**

5. **Finish the wizard to install the FTP service.**

Creating an FTP site

After you install FTP, you must create at least one FTP site. Here are the steps for Windows Server 2016 (the procedure for earlier versions is similar):

1. **Open Server Manager and choose Tools⇨Internet Information Services (IIS) Manager.**

   This launches the IIS Manager console, as shown in Figure 6-1.

Figure 6-1:
The IIS management console.

2. **Right-click the Sites node and choose Add FTP Site.**

   The first page of the Add FTP Site Wizard appears, as shown in Figure 6-2.

Figure 6-2:
Set the name and data folder for the FTP site.

Book III
Chapter 6

Using FTP

3. **Enter your site information.**

   a. Enter a name for your FTP site.

   b. Enter the path to the folder that will hold the FTP site's data.

   This field determines the location on the server where the data stored on the FTP site will be located. If you don't know the exact path, click the Browse button and browse to the folder location.

4. **Click Next.**

The second page of the Add FTP Site Wizard appears, as shown in Figure 6-3. On this page, you set the IP address and port number that the FTP site will use.

Figure 6-3:
Set the port and SSL security here.

a. *Leave the IP Address and Port fields unchanged unless you want to use a nonstandard port.*

By default, the FTP site will use port 21, which is the standard port for the FTP protocol.

b. *Select the SSL security option you want to use.*

If you have an SSL certificate and want to use SSL security, select either Allow SSL or Require SSL. If you select Allow SSL, users can access your site with or without SSL security. If you select Require SSL, users must always use SSL security to access the FTP site.

If you don't have a certificate available or if the site will contain data that doesn't require tight security, select No SSL.

5. **Click Next.**

The third page of the Add FTP Site Wizard appears, as shown in Figure 6-4, where you set authentication and authorization to be used for the site.

Figure 6-4:
Set basic
login
security
here.

- *Anonymous:* Select the Anonymous option if you want to allow anonymous users to access your FTP site.

  If you select this option, users can access your FTP site without providing any login information. You should specify this option only for sites that have no security requirements.

- *Basic:* Select the Basic option if you want to allow Basic authentication.

  This option allows users to log in using a Windows username and password. Note that because this option transmits the password in unencrypted form, you should use it only when you know that the connection between the user and the FTP server is secure.

- *Select the user access permissions you want to grant.*

  You can grant Read and Write permissions to All Users (as shown in the figure), to anonymous users, and to individual users or groups.

  Do not grant Write permissions to anonymous users. If you do, your FTP site will quickly become a dumping ground for all kinds of trash as word gets out about your totally unsecured FTP site.

6. **Click Finish.**

Your FTP site is created!

Changing the FTP site properties

You can change the properties for an FTP site by selecting the site in IIS Manager. This brings up a page with several icons that let you change various settings for the site, as shown in Figure 6-5.

**Book III
Chapter 6**

Using FTP

Figure 6-5:
The FTP site
page.

The following are the more important icons found on the FTP Site Properties page for configuring the properties of your FTP site:

✦ **FTP Authentication:** Enable or disable Anonymous and Basic authentication for the FTP site.

✦ **FTP Authorization:** Grant access rights to individual users, groups of users, anonymous users, or all users.

✦ **FTP Current Sessions:** Display a list of users who are currently accessing the FTP site.

✦ **FTP Directory Browsing:** Set several options that determine how users can browse the data directories in the FTP site.

✦ **FTP Firewall Support:** Set several advanced options for working with firewalls. Best leave these settings alone unless you're a firewall guru.

✦ **FTP IPv4 Address and Domain Restrictions:** Grant or deny access to users based on their IP addresses or domain names. This page is useful if you want to restrict access to a specific set of users.

✦ **FTP Logging:** Control logging for the site.

✦ **FTP Messages:** Create four customized messages that appear when users access the site, as shown in Figure 6-6.

The four messages you can configure are:

• The *Banner message* appears when a user first accesses the site, before he or she has logged on. If the site allows anonymous logons, you may mention that in the Banner message.

Figure 6-6:
Customize
the site's
messages.

- The *Welcome message* appears after the user has successfully logged on to your site.

- The *Exit message* appears when the user leaves the site.

- The *Maximum Connections message* appears when the connection limit has been exceeded.

Adding content to your FTP site

When you set up an FTP site, the data for the site is stored in a folder on one of the server's disks. To make your FTP site useful, you'll need to add files to this folder. Those files will then be available for download on the site. The easiest way to do that is to simply open Windows Explorer, browse to the folder, and copy the files you want to include. If you're not sure where the site's home folder is located, you can find it by opening the site in IIS Manager and choosing the site in the IIS Manager and clicking Basic Settings in the task pane on the right side of the screen.

The following list offers some useful tips for setting up FTP site content:

✦ **Create a `readme.txt` file in the FTP site's home directory that describes the content and rules for your site.** Hopefully, users will view this file when they visit your site. There's no guarantee that they will, but you can always hope.

✦ **If your site has a lot of files, organize them into subdirectories beneath the home directory.**

> ✦ **Stick to short filenames.** Users working with command line clients appreciate brevity because they'll have to type the filenames accurately to retrieve your files.
>
> ✦ **Don't use spaces in filenames.** Some clients balk at names that include spaces.

Accessing an FTP Site with a Browser

Modern web browsers include built-in support for FTP. Internet Explorer lets you access an FTP site almost as if it were a local disk. You can even drag and drop files to and from an FTP site.

To access an FTP site in a web browser, just type the name of the site in the address bar. If you want, you can explicitly specify the FTP protocol by typing **ftp://** before the FTP site name, but that's usually not necessary. The browser determines that the name you type is an FTP site and invokes the FTP protocol automatically.

Figure 6-7 shows you how a typical FTP site appears when accessed with Windows Explorer on a Windows 10 system. As you can see, the files and folders appear as if they were on a local disk. Double-click a folder to display the files contained in that folder; download files by dragging them from the browser window to the desktop or to another window. You can also upload files by dragging them from the desktop or another window into the FTP browser window.

Figure 6-7:
Browsing an
FTP site.

If the contents of an FTP site don't appear in the browser window, you may need to log on to the site. Choose File➪Login As to display the Log On As dialog box. If the site administrator has given you a name and password, you can enter it here to access the site. Otherwise, select the Log On Anonymously check box and then click the Log On button.

Using an FTP Command Line Client

If you're a command line junkie, you'll appreciate the FTP command that comes with Windows. It isn't pretty, but it gets the job done. At the end of this chapter, you can find a command reference that details all the subcommands you can use with the FTP command. In this section, I just show you a typical session in which I sign on to an FTP server named ftp.lowewriter. com, switch to a directory named pics, download a file, and then log off.

First, open a command window: Choose Start➪Run, type **Command** in the text box, and then click OK. Navigate to the directory to where you want to download files. This step is important because although you can change the local working directory from within the FTP command, it's much easier to just start FTP from the right directory.

To start FTP, type **ftp** with the name of the FTP server as the parameter, like this:

```
C:\>ftp ftp.lowewriter.com
```

Assuming that you typed the site name correctly, the FTP command connects to the site, displays the banner message, and prompts you to log on:

```
Connected to ftp.lowewriter.com.
220-Microsoft FTP Service
220 We have 999 spooks here, but there's always room for one more! To volunteer,
    log in as Anonymous.
User (ftp.lowewriter.com:(none)):
```

To log on anonymously, type **Anonymous** and then press Enter. The server responds by telling you that Anonymous access is allowed and asks for your email address as a password:

```
331 Anonymous access allowed, send identity (e-mail name) as password.
Password:
```

Type your email address as the password and then press Enter. The Welcome message appears, followed by the `ftp>` prompt:

```
230-Welcome to my FTP site! For spooky Halloween pictures, check out the Pics
    folder.
230 Anonymous user logged in.
ftp>
```

Whenever you see the `ftp>` prompt, the FTP command is waiting for you to enter a subcommand. Start by entering **dir** to see a directory listing:

```
200 PORT command successful.
150 Opening ASCII mode data connection for /bin/ls.
06-30-07  08:05PM       <DIR>          pics
06-30-07  07:55PM                 2365 readme.txt
06-30-07  07:55PM       <DIR>          sounds
06-30-07  07:56PM       <DIR>          videos
226 Transfer complete.
ftp: 190 bytes received in 0.00Seconds 190000.00Kbytes/sec.
ftp>
```

As you can see, the response from the `dir` command isn't quite as clean as the display from an MS-DOS command. Still, you can pick out that the directory includes three subdirectories — `pics`, `sounds`, and `videos` — and a single file, named `readme.txt`. The size of the file is 2,365 bytes.

Here's a good question: If you enter a `dir` command, why does the response read `200 PORT command successful`? The answer has to do with how the FTP protocol works. When you enter a `dir` command, the FTP client forwards a `PORT` command to the server that opens a data transfer port that is then used to return the resulting directory listing. The server replies that the `PORT` command has successfully opened a data transfer port. Then, it sends back the directory listing. Finally, it sends two more lines: one to indicate that the transfer is complete (that is, that the `dir` output has been successfully sent), and the other to summarize the number of bytes of data that were sent and the data transfer rate.

The files that I want to download are located in the `pics` subdirectory, so the next command to issue is `cd pics`. This results in the following output:

```
250 CWD command successful.
ftp>
```

Once again, the command's output isn't exactly what you'd expect. The FTP protocol doesn't actually have a CD command. Instead, it uses a command named CWD, which stands for *change working directory,* to change the directory. The Windows FTP client uses command CD instead of CWD to be more consistent with the Windows/MS-DOS user interface, which uses the command CD to change directories. When you type a CD command at the ftp> prompt, the FTP client sends a CWD command to the FTP server. The server then replies with the message CWD command successful to indicate that the directory has been changed.

Next, type **dir** again. The FTP server displays the directory listing for the pics directory:

```
200 PORT command successful.
150 Opening ASCII mode data connection for /bin/ls.
06-27-07  10:04PM              123126 door.jpg
06-27-07  10:06PM              112457 echair.jpg
06-27-07  10:06PM               81610 fence.jpg
06-27-07  10:09PM              138102 fog.jpg
06-27-07  10:09PM               83712 gallows.jpg
06-27-07  10:10PM              166741 ghost.jpg
06-27-07  09:58PM              119859 skel01.jpg
06-27-07  10:05PM               87720 wall.jpg
226 Transfer complete.
ftp: 400 bytes received in 0.00Seconds 400000.00Kbytes/sec.
ftp>
```

Here, you can see that the pics directory contains eight files. To download a file, you use the GET command, specifying the name of the file that you want to download. For example, to download the door.jpg file, type **get door.jpg**. The FTP server transfers the file to your computer and displays the following response:

```
200 PORT command successful.
150 Opening ASCII mode data connection for door.jpg(123126 bytes).
226 Transfer complete.
ftp: 123126 bytes received in 0.13Seconds 985.01Kbytes/sec.
ftp>
```

Notice again that the response indicates that the command actually processed by the server is a PORT command. The file is transferred in ASCII mode. The entire transfer takes 0.13 seconds, which works out to a transfer rate of about 985K per second.

After you download the file, you can end the session by typing **bye**. FTP responds by displaying the site's goodbye message; then it returns you to the MS-DOS command prompt:

```
221 Hurry back...
C:\>
```

Book III Chapter 6

Using FTP

Of course, FTP is a lot more involved than this simple session suggests. Still, the most common use of FTP is to download files, and most downloads are no more complicated than this example.

FTP Command and Subcommand Reference

The rest of this chapter is an FTP command reference. In the following sections, you can find complete reference information for the FTP command and all its subcommands. The first command described is the FTP command itself. After that, all the FTP command subcommands are listed in alphabetical order.

The FTP command

What it does:	Starts the FTP client so that you can transfer files to and from an FTP server
Syntax:	**ftp** [**-v**] [**-d**] [**-i**] [**-n**] [**-g**] [**-s:**filename] [**-a**]
	[**-w:**windowsize] [**-A**] [host]

Parameters:		
	-v	Turns off Verbose mode.
	-d	Turns on Debug mode.
	-i	Turns off Prompt mode.
	-n	Forces manual logon.
	-g	Turns off Glob mode.
	-s	Specifies a script file that contains FTP commands.
	-a	Specifies that any network interface can be used to bind the data connection.
	-w	Specifies the size of the transmission buffer. The default is 4K.
	-A	Automatically logs on as Anonymous.
Host:		The FTP server to which you want to connect. This can be the server's DNS name or an IP address.
Examples:		**ftp ftp.lowewriter.com**
		ftp ftp.lowewriter.com -A
More info:		Unlike most Windows commands, the switches for this command begin with a hyphen, not a slash.
		If you want to script subcommands, use the -s switch. Input redirection doesn't work with FTP.

When FTP is running, the prompt `ftp>` appears. When this prompt is displayed, you can enter any of the FTP subcommands described in the rest of this chapter.

! (Escape)

What it does:	Escapes to a command shell
Syntax:	**!**
More info:	This command brings up a temporary command prompt so that you can enter commands. To return to the `ftp>` prompt, type **exit**.

? (Help)

What it does:	Displays Help information
Syntax:	**?** [*command*]
	help [*command*]
Example:	**help mput**
More info:	? and `help` are interchangeable. If you enter **?** or **help** by itself, a list of FTP commands appears. If you enter **?** or **help** followed by a command name, a summary of that command's function appears.

append

What it does:	Uploads a file and appends it to the end of an existing file on the remote system
Syntax:	**append** *localfile* [*remotefile*]
Example:	**append extra.txt start.txt**
More info:	If you omit the *remotefile* parameter, the remote file is assumed to have the same name as the local file.

ascii

What it does:	Sets the ASCII transfer mode
Syntax:	**ascii**
More info:	This command sets the transfer type of ASCII, which is best suited for text files. ASCII is the default transfer type.

bell

What it does:	Causes the FTP client to beep when each transfer is complete
Syntax:	**bell**

More info:	This command is useful when you're downloading long files and want to take a nap during the download. Unfortunately, it doesn't beep when it sees your boss approaching your office, so you'll need some other alarm system to cover that contingency.

binary

What it does:	Sets the binary transfer type
Syntax:	**binary**
More info:	The binary file type is best for executable files and other nontext files.

bye

What it does:	Ends the FTP session and exits the FTP client
Syntax:	**bye**
More info:	This is the command to use when you're done. It's the same as the `quit` command.

cd

What it does:	Changes the working directory on the remote computer
Syntax:	**cd** *remotedirectory*
Example:	**cd pics**
More info:	Use this to change to the directory that contains the files you want to download or the directory to which you want to upload files.
	Type **cd ** to go to the root directory.

close

What it does:	Closes the session with the remote computer but doesn't leave the FTP program
Syntax:	**close**
More info:	You can use this command if you want to switch to another FTP server without leaving and restarting the FTP program. This command is the same as the `disconnect` command.

debug

What it does:	Toggles Debug mode
Syntax:	**debug**

| More info: | When Debug mode is on, the FTP client displays the actual FTP commands that are sent to the FTP server. This can be useful if you're an FTP guru trying to diagnose a problem with a server or a client, but it can also be fun if you just want to see how FTP client commands (like CD) get translated into FTP server commands (like CWD). |

delete

What it does:	Deletes the specified file on the remote computer
Syntax:	**delete** *remotefile*
Example:	**delete fright.txt**
More info:	You can delete only one file at a time with this command. To delete more than one file in a single command, use the mdelete command.

dir

What it does:	Lists contents of remote directory
Syntax:	**dir** [*remotedirectory*] [*localfile*]
Examples:	**dir**
	dir \pics
	dir \pics picdir.txt
More info:	The first parameter lets you list a directory other than the current working directory. The second parameter lets you capture the output to a file on the local computer.

disconnect

What it does:	Disconnects from the remote computer but doesn't leave the FTP program
Syntax:	**disconnect**
More info:	You can use this command if you want to switch to another FTP server without leaving and restarting the FTP program. This command is the same as the close command.

get

| *What it does:* | Downloads a file from the remote computer |
| *Syntax:* | **get** *remotefile* [*localfile*] |

Book III
Chapter 6

Using FTP

Examples:	**get boo.exe**
	get boo.exe bar.exe
More info:	This command downloads the specified file from the current working directory on the remote system to the current directory on the local system. The second parameter lets you save the file using a different name than the name used on the remote system.
	You can use this command to download only one file at a time. To download multiple files, use the `mget` command.
	This command is the same as the `recv` command.

glob

What it does:	Toggles the use of wildcards for local filenames
Syntax:	**glob**
More info:	If globbing is on, you can use * and ? characters in local filenames. Globbing is on by default.

hash

What it does:	Toggles the display of hash marks (#) to indicate transfer progress
Syntax:	**hash**
More info:	`Hash` is off by default. If you turn it on by issuing the `hash` command, a hash mark (#) appears each time a 2K data block is transferred. This helps you track the progress of transfers.

help

What it does:	Displays Help information
Syntax:	**?** [*command*]
	help [*command*]
Example:	**help mput**
More info:	**?** and `help` are interchangeable. If you enter **?** or **help** by itself, a list of FTP commands appears. If you enter **?** or **help** followed by a command name, a summary of that command's function appears.

lcd

What it does:	Changes the working directory on the local computer
Syntax:	**lcd** *localdirectory*

Example:	**lcd \ docs**
More info:	Use this to change to the directory you want to download files to or that contains files you want to upload.

literal

What it does:	Sends a native FTP command directly to the server
Syntax:	**literal** *arguments* . . .
Example:	**literal cwd pics**
More info:	Use this command if you're an FTP guru and you want to send a native FTP command to the server. It's the same as the quote command.

ls

What it does:	Lists contents of remote directory
Syntax:	**ls** [*remotedirectory*] [*localfile*]
Examples:	**ls**
	ls \pics
	ls \pics picdir.txt
More info:	The first parameter lets you list a directory other than the current working directory. The second parameter lets you capture the output to a file on the local computer.

mdelete

What it does:	Deletes multiple files
Syntax:	**mdelete** *remotefile* . . .
Examples:	**mdelete file1.txt**
	mdelete file1.txt file2.txt file3.txt
More info:	This command deletes one or more files from the current working directory on the remote system.

mdir

What it does:	Lists the contents of multiple remote directories
Syntax:	**mdir** *remotedirectory* . . . [*localfile*]
Example:	**mdir pics videos**

**Book III
Chapter 6**

Using FTP

More info:	Specify a hyphen as the last parameter to display the output on the screen. Otherwise, the last parameter will be interpreted as the name of the local file you want the directory listing captured to.

mget

What it does:	Downloads multiple files
Syntax:	**mget** *remotefile* . . .
Example:	**mget file1.txt**
	mget file1.txt file2.txt file3.txt
More info:	This command downloads one or more files from the current working directory on the remote system to the current directory on the local computer.

mkdir

What it does:	Creates a directory on the remote system
Syntax:	**mkdir** *remotedirectory*
Example:	**mdir plans**
More info:	The new subdirectory is created in the current working directory on the remote system.

mls

What it does:	Lists the contents of multiple remote directories
Syntax:	**mls** *remotedirectory* . . . [*localfile*]
Example:	**mls pics videos**
More info:	Specify a hyphen as the last parameter to display the output on the screen. Otherwise, the last parameter will be interpreted as the name of the local file you want the directory listing captured to.

mput

What it does:	Uploads multiple files
Syntax:	**mput** *localfile* . . .
Examples:	**mput file1.txt**
	mput file1.txt file2.txt file3.txt
More info:	This command uploads one or more files from the current directory on the local system to the current working directory on the remote system.

open

What it does:	Connects to an FTP server
Syntax:	**open** *remotesystem* [*port*]
Examples:	**open ftp.microsoft.com**
	open ftp.weirdport.com 1499
More info:	Specify the port number only if the remote system does not use the standard FTP ports (20 and 21).

prompt

What it does:	Toggles prompting for multiple transfers
Syntax:	**prompt**
More info:	When Prompt mode is on, you're prompted for each file before the file is transferred. Prompt mode is on by default.

put

What it does:	Uploads a file to the remote computer
Syntax:	**put** *localfile* [*remotefile*]
Examples:	**put boo.exe**
	put boo.exe bar.exe
More info:	This command uploads the specified file from the current directory on the local system to the current working directory on the remote system. The second parameter lets you save the file with a different name than the name used on the local system.

You can use this command to upload only one file at a time. To upload multiple files, use the mput command. This command is the same as the send command.

**Book III
Chapter 6**

Using FTP

pwd

What it does:	Displays the current working directory on the remote computer
Syntax:	**pwd**
More info:	If you aren't sure what the current directory is on the remote system, use this command to find out.

quit

What it does:	Ends the FTP session and quits the FTP program
Syntax:	**quit**
More info:	This is the command to use when you're done. It's the same as the bye command.

quote

What it does:	Sends a native FTP command directly to the server
Syntax:	**quote** *arguments* . . .
Example:	**quote cwd pics**
More info:	Use this command if you're an FTP guru and you want to send a native FTP command to the server. It's the same as the literal command.

recv

What it does:	Downloads a file from the remote computer
Syntax:	**recv** *remotefile* [*localfile*]
Examples:	**recv boo.exe**
	recv boo.exe bar.exe
More info:	This command downloads the specified file from the current working directory on the remote system to the current directory on the local system. The second parameter lets you save the file with a different name than the name used on the remote system.
	You can use this command to download only one file at a time. To download multiple files, use the mget command.
	This command is the same as the get command.

remotehelp

What it does:	Displays help for remote commands
Syntax:	**remotehelp** [*command*]
Example:	**remotehelp cwd**
More info:	If you enter remotehelp by itself, a list of FTP commands is displayed. If you enter remotehelp followed by a command name, a summary of that command's function appears.

rename

What it does: Renames a file on the remote system

Syntax: **rename** *filename newfilename*

Example: **rename door.jpg doorway.jpg**

More info: Use this command to change the name of a file on the remote system.

rmdir

What it does: Removes a directory on the remote system

Syntax: **rmdir** *directoryname*

Example: **rmdir oldpics**

More info: This command removes a directory and all the files in it, so use it with caution!

send

What it does: Uploads a file to the remote computer

Syntax: **send** *localfile* [*remotefile*]

Examples: **send boo.exe**

send boo.exe bar.exe

More info: This command uploads the specified file from the current directory on the local system to the current working directory on the remote system. The second parameter lets you save the file with a different name than the name used on the local system.

You can use this command to upload only one file at a time. To upload multiple files, use the `mput` command.

This command is the same as the `put` command.

status

What it does: Displays the current status of the FTP client

Syntax: **status**

More info: Use this command to display the current settings of options, such as `bell`, `prompt`, and `verbose`, as well as the current connection status.

**Book III
Chapter 6**

Using FTP

trace

What it does:	Activates Trace mode
Syntax:	**trace**
More info:	When Trace mode is on, detailed information about each packet transmission is displayed. trace is off by default and should be left off unless you're digging deep into the bowels of FTP or just want to show off.

type

What it does:	Sets the transfer type to ASCII or binary or displays the current mode
Syntax:	**type** [**ascii** or **binary**]
Examples:	**type ascii**
	type binary
	type
More info:	Use ASCII transfers for text files, and use binary transfers for nontext files.
	If you don't specify a type, the current transfer type appears.
	You can also use the ascii or binary command to switch the transfer type.

user

What it does:	Logs you on to a remote system
Syntax:	**user** *username* [*password*]
Examples:	**user doug**
	user doug notmypw
More info:	This command logs you on to the remote system by using the username and password you provide. If you omit the password, you're prompted to enter it.

verbose

What it does:	Toggles Verbose mode
Syntax:	**verbose**
More info:	When Verbose mode is on, FTP responses appear. Verbose mode is on by default.

Chapter 7: TCP/IP Tools and Commands

In This Chapter

✔ Recognizing tools and commands

✔ Making all your hosts sing with `IPConfig` and `Ping`

Most client and server operating systems that support Transmission Control Protocol/Internet Protocol (TCP/IP) come with a suite of commands and tools that are designed to let you examine TCP/IP configuration information and diagnose and correct problems. Although the exact form of these commands varies between Windows and Unix/Linux, most are surprisingly similar. This chapter is a reference to the most commonly used TCP/IP commands.

Using the arp Command

Using the `arp` command allows you to display and modify the Address Resolution Protocol (ARP) cache, which is a simple mapping of IP addresses to MAC addresses. Each time a computer's TCP/IP stack uses ARP to determine the Media Access Control (MAC) address for an IP address, it records the mapping in the ARP cache so that future ARP lookups go faster.

If you use the `arp` command without any parameters, you get a list of the command's parameters. To display the ARP cache entry for a specific IP address, use an `-a` switch followed by the IP address. For example:

```
C:\>arp -a 192.168.168.22
Interface: 192.168.168.21 --- 0x10004
  Internet Address      Physical Address      Type
  192.168.168.22        00-60-08-39-e5-a1     dynamic
C:\>
```

You can display the complete ARP cache by using `-a` without specifying an IP address, like this:

```
C:\>arp -a
Interface: 192.168.168.21 --- 0x10004
  Internet Address      Physical Address      Type
  192.168.168.9         00-02-e3-16-e4-5d      dynamic
  192.168.168.10        00-50-04-17-66-90      dynamic
  192.168.168.22        00-60-08-39-e5-a1      dynamic
  192.168.168.254       00-40-10-18-42-49      dynamic
C:\>
```

ARP is sometimes useful when diagnosing duplicate IP assignment problems. For example, suppose you can't access a computer that has an IP address of `192.168.168.100`. You try to ping the computer, expecting the ping to fail, but lo and behold — the ping succeeds. One possible cause for this may be that two computers on the network have been assigned the address `192.168.168.100`, and your ARP cache is pointing to the wrong one. The way to find out is to go to the `192.168.168.100` computer that you want to access, run `ipconfig /all`, and make a note of the physical address. Then return to the computer that's having trouble reaching the `192.168.168.100` computer, run `arp -a`, and compare the physical address with the one you noted. If they're different, that two computers are assigned the same IP address. You can then check the Dynamic Host Configuration Protocol (DHCP) or static TCP/IP configuration of the computers involved to find out why.

Using the hostname Command

The `hostname` command is the simplest of all the TCP/IP commands presented in this chapter. It simply displays the computer's host name. For example:

```
C:\>hostname
doug
C:\>
```

Here, the host name for the computer is `doug`. The Windows version of the `hostname` command has no parameters. However, the Unix/Linux versions of `hostname` let you set the computer's host name as well as display it. You do that by specifying the new host name as an argument.

Using the ipconfig Command

Using the `ipconfig` command displays information about a computer's TCP/IP configuration. It can also be used to update DHCP and Domain Name Server (DNS) settings.

Displaying basic IP configuration

To display the basic IP configuration for a computer, use the `ipconfig` command without any parameters, like this:

```
C:\>ipconfig

Windows IP Configuration


Ethernet adapter Local Area Connection:

   Connection-specific DNS Suffix  . :
   Link-local IPv6 Address . . . . . : fe80::cca:9067:9427:a911%8
   IPv4 Address. . . . . . . . . . . : 192.168.1.110
   Subnet Mask . . . . . . . . . . . : 255.255.255.0
   Default Gateway . . . . . . . . . : 192.168.1.1

Tunnel adapter Local Area Connection* 6:

   Connection-specific DNS Suffix  . :
   IPv6 Address. . . . . . . . . . . : 2001:0:4136:e38c:2c6c:670:3f57:fe91
   Link-local IPv6 Address . . . . . : fe80::2c6c:670:3f57:fe91%9
   Default Gateway . . . . . . . . . : ::

Tunnel adapter Local Area Connection* 7:

   Connection-specific DNS Suffix  . :
   Link-local IPv6 Address . . . . . : fe80::5efe:192.168.1.110%10
   Default Gateway . . . . . . . . . :
C:\>
```

When you use `ipconfig` without parameters, the command displays the name of the adapter, the domain name used for the adapter, the IP address, the subnet mask, and the default gateway configuration for the adapter. This is the easiest way to determine a computer's IP address.

If your computer indicates an IP address in the `169.254.x.x` block, odds are good that the DHCP server isn't working. `169.254.x.x` is the Class B address block that Windows uses when it resorts to IP Autoconfiguration. This usually happens only when the DHCP server can't be reached or isn't working.

Displaying detailed configuration information

You can display detailed IP configuration information by using an /all switch with the `ipconfig` command, like this:

```
C:\>ipconfig /all

Windows IP Configuration

    Host Name . . . . . . . . . . : WK07-001
    Primary Dns Suffix  . . . . . :
    Node Type . . . . . . . . . . : Hybrid
    IP Routing Enabled. . . . . . : No
    WINS Proxy Enabled. . . . . . : No

Ethernet adapter Local Area Connection:

    Connection-specific DNS Suffix  . :
    Description . . . . . . . . . . : Intel(R) PRO/100 VE Network Connection
    Physical Address. . . . . . . . : 00-12-3F-A7-17-BA
    DHCP Enabled. . . . . . . . . . : No
    Autoconfiguration Enabled . . . . : Yes
    Link-local IPv6 Address . . . . . : fe80::cca:9067:9427:a911%8(Preferred)
    IPv4 Address. . . . . . . . . . : 192.168.1.110(Preferred)
    Subnet Mask . . . . . . . . . . : 255.255.255.0
    Default Gateway . . . . . . . . : 192.168.1.1
    DNS Servers . . . . . . . . . . : 192.168.1.10
                                      68.87.76.178
    NetBIOS over Tcpip. . . . . . . : Enabled

C:\>
```

You can determine a lot of information about the computer from the `ipconfig /all` command. For example:

+ The computer's host name is WK07-001.

+ The computer's IPv4 address is 192.168.1.110, and the subnet mask is 255.255.255.0.

+ The default gateway is a router located at 192.168.1.1.

+ The DNS servers are at 192.168.1.10 and 68.87.76.178.

Renewing an IP lease

If you're having an IP configuration problem, you can often solve it by renewing the computer's IP lease. To do that, use a /renew switch, like this:

```
C:\>ipconfig /renew
Windows IP Configuration
Ethernet adapter Local Area Connection:
        Connection-specific DNS Suffix  . :
        IP Address. . . . . . . . . : 192.168.1.110
        Subnet Mask . . . . . . . . : 255.255.255.0
        Default Gateway . . . . . . : 192.168.1.1
C:\>
```

When you renew an IP lease, the `ipconfig` command displays the new lease information.

This command won't work if you configured the computer to use a static IP address.

Releasing an IP lease

You can release an IP lease by using an `ipconfig` command with the `/release` parameter, like this:

```
C:\>ipconfig /release
Windows IP Configuration
Ethernet adapter Local Area Connection:
        Connection-specific DNS Suffix  . :
        IP Address . . . . . . . . . . . : 0.0.0.0
        Subnet Mask. . . . . . . . . . . : 0.0.0.0
        Default Gateway . . . . . . . . :
C:\>
```

As you can see, the DNS suffix and default gateway for the computer are blank, and the IP address and subnet mask are set to `0.0.0.0`.

After you release the DHCP lease, you can use an `ipconfig /renew` command to obtain a new DHCP lease for the computer.

Flushing the local DNS cache

You probably won't need to do this unless you're having DNS troubles. If you've been tinkering with your network's DNS configuration, though, you may need to flush the cache on your DNS clients so that they'll be forced to reacquire information from the DNS server. You can do that by using a `/flushdns` switch:

```
C:\>ipconfig /flushdns
Windows IP Configuration
Successfully flushed the DNS Resolver Cache.
C:\>
```

Even if you don't need to do this, it's fun just to see the computer read `flushed`. If I worked at Microsoft, you'd be able to revert Windows Vista computers back to XP by using a `/flushVista` switch.

Using the nbtstat Command

nbtstat is a Windows-only command that can help solve problems with NetBIOS name resolution. (*nbt* stands for *NetBIOS over TCP/IP.*) You can use any of the switches listed in Table 7-1 to specify what nbtstat output you want to display. For example, you can use an -a switch to display the cached name table for a specified computer, like this:

```
C:\>nbtstat -a WK07-001

Local Area Connection:
Node IpAddress: [192.168.1.110] Scope Id: []

        NetBIOS Remote Machine Name Table

     Name              Type         Status
  ---------------------------------------------
     WK07-001     <00>  UNIQUE      Registered
     WORKGROUP    <00>  GROUP       Registered
     WK07-001     <20>  UNIQUE      Registered
     WORKGROUP    <1E>  GROUP       Registered
     WORKGROUP    <1D>  UNIQUE      Registered
     ..__MSBROWSE__.<01>  GROUP     Registered

     MAC Address = 00-12-3F-A7-17-BAC:\>
C:\>
```

Table 7-1	nbtstat **Command Switches**
Switch	*What It Does*
-a name	Lists the specified computer's name table given the computer's name
-A IP-address	Lists the specified computer's name table given the computer's IP address
-c	Lists the contents of the NetBIOS cache
-n	Lists locally registered NetBIOS names
-r	Displays a count of the names resolved by broadcast and via WINS
-R	Purges and reloads the cached name table from the LMHOSTS file
-RR	Releases and then reregisters all names
-S	Displays the sessions table using IP addresses
-s	Displays the sessions table and converts destination IP addresses to computer NetBIOS names

Table 7-1 lists the switches that you can use with `nbtstat` and explains the function of each switch.

Using the netstat Command

Using the `netstat` command displays a variety of statistics about a computer's active TCP/IP connections. It's a useful tool to use when you're having trouble with TCP/IP applications, such as File Transfer Protocol (FTP), HyperText Transport Protocol (HTTP), and so on.

Displaying connections

If you run `netstat` without specifying any parameters, you get a list of active connections, something like this:

```
C:\>netstat
Active Connections
   Proto  Local Address    Foreign Address           State
   TCP    Doug:1463        192.168.168.10:1053       ESTABLISHED
   TCP    Doug:1582        192.168.168.9:netbios-ssn ESTABLISHED
   TCP    Doug:3630        192.168.168.30:9100       SYN_SENT
   TCP    Doug:3716        192.168.168.10:4678       ESTABLISHED
   TCP    Doug:3940        192.168.168.10:netbios-ssn ESTABLISHED
C:\>
```

This list shows all the active connections on the computer and indicates the local port used by the connection, as well as the IP address and port number for the remote computer.

You can specify the -n switch to display both local and foreign addresses in numeric IP form:

```
C:\>netstat -n
Active Connections
   Proto  Local Address        Foreign Address        State
   TCP    192.168.168.21:1463  192.168.168.10:1053    ESTABLISHED
   TCP    192.168.168.21:1582  192.168.168.9:139      ESTABLISHED
   TCP    192.168.168.21:3658  192.168.168.30:9100    SYN_SENT
   TCP    192.168.168.21:3716  192.168.168.10:4678    ESTABLISHED
   TCP    192.168.168.21:3904  207.46.106.78:1863     ESTABLISHED
   TCP    192.168.168.21:3940  192.168.168.10:139     ESTABLISHED
C:\>
```

**Book III
Chapter 7**

**TCP/IP Tools and
Commands**

Finally, you can specify the -a switch to display all TCP/IP connections and ports that are being listened to. I won't list the output from that command here because it would run several pages, and I want to do my part for the rainforests. Suffice it to say that it looks a lot like the netstat output shown previously, but a lot longer.

Displaying interface statistics

If you use an -e switch, netstat displays various protocol statistics, like this:

```
C:\>netstat -e
Interface Statistics

                          Received             Sent
Bytes                    672932849        417963911
Unicast packets            1981755          1972374
Non-unicast packets         251869            34585
Discards                         0                0
Errors                           0                0
Unknown protocols             1829
C:\>
```

The items to pay attention to in this output are the Discards and Errors. These numbers should be zero, or at least close to it. If they're not, the network may be carrying too much traffic or the connection may have a physical problem. If no physical problem exists with the connection, try segmenting the network to see whether the error and discard rates drop.

You can display additional statistics by using an -s switch, like this:

```
C:\>netstat -s

IPv4 Statistics

    Packets Received             = 9155
    Received Header Errors       = 0
    Received Address Errors      = 0
    Datagrams Forwarded          = 0
    Unknown Protocols Received   = 0
    Received Packets Discarded   = 0
    Received Packets Delivered   = 14944
    Output Requests              = 12677
    Routing Discards             = 0
    Discarded Output Packets     = 71
    Output Packet No Route       = 0
    Reassembly Required          = 0
    Reassembly Successful        = 0
    Reassembly Failures          = 0
```

```
Datagrams Successfully Fragmented  = 0
Datagrams Failing Fragmentation    = 0
Fragments Created                  = 0
```

IPv6 Statistics

```
Packets Received                   = 3
Received Header Errors             = 0
Received Address Errors            = 0
Datagrams Forwarded                = 0
Unknown Protocols Received         = 0
Received Packets Discarded         = 0
Received Packets Delivered         = 345
Output Requests                    = 377
Routing Discards                   = 0
Discarded Output Packets           = 0
Output Packet No Route             = 0
Reassembly Required                = 0
Reassembly Successful              = 0
Reassembly Failures                = 0
Datagrams Successfully Fragmented  = 0
Datagrams Failing Fragmentation    = 0
Fragments Created                  = 0
```

ICMPv4 Statistics

	Received	Sent
Messages	6	14
Errors	0	0
Destination Unreachable	6	14
Time Exceeded	0	0
Parameter Problems	0	0
Source Quenches	0	0
Redirects	0	0
Echo Replies	0	0
Echos	0	0
Timestamps	0	0
Timestamp Replies	0	0
Address Masks	0	0
Address Mask Replies	0	0
Router Solicitations	0	0
Router Advertisements	0	0

ICMPv6 Statistics

	Received	Sent
Messages	3	7
Errors	0	0
Destination Unreachable	0	0
Packet Too Big	0	0

**Book III
Chapter 7**

**TCP/IP Tools and
Commands**

```
Time Exceeded              0            0
Parameter Problems         0            0
Echos                      0            0
Echo Replies               0            0
MLD Queries                0            0
MLD Reports                0            0
MLD Dones                  0            0
Router Solicitations       0            6
Router Advertisements      3            0
Neighbor Solicitations     0            1
Neighbor Advertisements    0            0
Redirects                  0            0
Router Renumberings        0            0

TCP Statistics for IPv4

Active Opens                        = 527
Passive Opens                       = 2
Failed Connection Attempts          = 1
Reset Connections                   = 301
Current Connections                 = 1
Segments Received                   = 8101
Segments Sent                       = 6331
Segments Retransmitted              = 301

TCP Statistics for IPv6

Active Opens                        = 1
Passive Opens                       = 1
Failed Connection Attempts          = 0
Reset Connections                   = 1
Current Connections                 = 0
Segments Received                   = 142
Segments Sent                       = 142
Segments Retransmitted              = 0

UDP Statistics for IPv4

Datagrams Received    = 6703
No Ports              = 0
Receive Errors        = 0
Datagrams Sent        = 6011

UDP Statistics for IPv6

Datagrams Received    = 32
No Ports              = 0
Receive Errors        = 0
Datagrams Sent        = 200
C:\>
```

Using the nslookup Command

The nslookup command is a powerful tool for diagnosing DNS problems. You know you're experiencing a DNS problem when you can access a resource by specifying its IP address but not its DNS name. For example, if you can get to www.ebay.com by typing **66.135.192.87** in your browser's address bar but not by typing www.ebay.com, you have a DNS problem.

Looking up an IP address

The simplest use of nslookup is to look up the IP address for a given DNS name. For example, how did I know that 66.135.192.87 was the IP address for www.ebay.com? I used nslookup to find out:

```
C:\>nslookup ebay.com
Server:  ns1.orng.twtelecom.net
Address:  168.215.210.50
Non-authoritative answer:
Name:    ebay.com
Address:  66.135.192.87
C:\>
```

As you can see, just type **nslookup** followed by the DNS name you want to look up, and nslookup issues a DNS query to find out. This DNS query was sent to the server named ns1.orng.twtelecom.net at 168.215.210.50. It then displayed the IP address that's associated with ebay.com: namely, 66.135.192.87.

**Book III
Chapter 7**

TCP/IP Tools and Commands

Get me out of here!

One of my pet peeves is that it seems as if every program that uses subcommands chooses a different command to quit the application. I can never remember whether the command to get out of nslookup is quit, bye, or exit. I usually end up trying them all. And no matter what program I'm using, I always seem to choose the one that works for some other program first. When I'm in nslookup, I use bye first. When I'm in FTP, I try exit first. Arghh! If I were King of the Computer Hill, every program that had subcommands would respond to the following commands by exiting the program and returning to a command prompt:

```
Quit            Sayonara
Exit            Ciao
Bye             Mañana
Leave           Makelikeatree
```

Of course, the final command to try would be Andgetouttahere (in honor of Biff from the *Back to the Future* movies).

In some cases, you may find that using an `nslookup` command gives you the wrong IP address for a host name. To know that for sure, of course, you have to know with certainty what the host IP address *should* be. For example, if you know that your server is `203.172.182.10` but `nslookup` returns a completely different IP address for your server when you query the server's host name, something is probably wrong with one of the DNS records.

Using nslookup subcommands

If you use `nslookup` without any arguments, the `nslookup` command enters a subcommand mode. It displays a prompt character (>) to let you know that you're in `nslookup` subcommand mode rather than at a normal Windows command prompt. In subcommand mode, you can enter various subcommands to set options or to perform queries. You can type a question mark (?) to get a list of these commands. Table 7-2 lists the subcommands you'll use most.

Table 7-2	The Most Commonly Used `nslookup` Subcommands
Subcommand	*What It Does*
`name`	Queries the current name server for the specified name.
`server name`	Sets the current name server to the server you specify.
`root`	Sets the root server as the current server.
`set type=x`	Specifies the type of records to be displayed, such as A, CNAME, MX, NS, PTR, or SOA. Specify ANY to display all records.
`set debug`	Turns on Debug mode, which displays detailed information about each query.
`set nodebug`	Turns off Debug mode.
`set recurse`	Enables recursive searches.
`set norecurse`	Disables recursive searches.
`exit`	Exits the `nslookup` program and returns you to a command prompt.

Displaying DNS records

One of the main uses of `nslookup` is to examine your DNS configuration to make sure that it's set up properly. To do that, follow these steps:

1. **At a command prompt, type** nslookup **without any parameters.**

   nslookup displays the name of the default name server and displays the > prompt.

   ```
   C:\>nslookup
   Default Server:  ns1.orng.twtelecom.net
   Address:  168.215.210.50

   >
   ```

2. **Type the subcommand** set type=any.

   nslookup silently obeys your command and displays another prompt:

   ```
   > set type=any
   >
   ```

3. **Type your domain name.**

   nslookup responds by displaying the name servers for your domain:

   ```
   > lowewriter.com
   Server:  ns1.orng.twtelecom.net
   Address:  168.215.210.50
   Non-authoritative answer:
   lowewriter.com  nameserver = NS000.NS0.com
   lowewriter.com  nameserver = NS207.PAIR.com
   lowewriter.com  nameserver = NS000.NS0.com
   lowewriter.com  nameserver = NS207.PAIR.com

   >
   ```

4. **Use a** server **command to switch to one of the domain's name servers.**

   For example, to switch to the first name server listed in Step 3, type **server NS000.NS0.com**. nslookup replies with a message that indicates the new default server:

   ```
   > server ns000.ns0.com
   Default Server:  ns000.ns0.com
   Address:  216.92.61.61

   >
   ```

5. **Type your domain name again.**

   This time, nslookup responds by displaying the DNS information for your domain:

   ```
   > lowewriter.com
   Server:  ns000.ns0.com
   Address:  216.92.61.61
   lowewriter.com
           primary name server = ns207.pair.com
           responsible mail addr = root.pair.com
           serial = 2001121009
           refresh = 3600 (1 hour)
           retry  = 300 (5 mins)
           expire = 604800 (7 days)
           default TTL = 3600 (1 hour)
   ```

**Book III
Chapter 7**

**TCP/IP Tools and
Commands**

```
lowewriter.com  nameserver = ns000.ns0.com
lowewriter.com  nameserver = ns207.pair.com
lowewriter.com  MX preference = 50, mail exchanger = sasi.pair.com
lowewriter.com  internet address = 209.68.34.15
>
```

6. **Type** exit **to leave the** **Nslookup** **program.**

   You return to a command prompt.

   ```
   > exit
   C:\>
   ```

Wasn't that fun?

Locating the mail server for an email address

If you're having trouble delivering mail to someone, you can use `nslookup` to determine the IP address of the user's mail server. Then, you can use the `ping` command to see whether you can contact the user's mail server. If not, you can use the `tracert` command to find out where the communication breaks down. (See "Using the `tracert` Command" later in this chapter for more information.)

To find a user's mail server, start `nslookup` and enter the command **set type=MX**. Then, enter the domain portion of the user's email address. For example, if the user's address is Doug@LoweWriter.com, enter **LoweWriter. com**. `nslookup` will display the MX (Mail eXchange) information for the domain, like this:

```
C:\>nslookup
Default Server:  ns7.attbi.com
Address:  204.127.198.19
> set type=mx
> lowewriter.com
Server:  ns7.attbi.com
Address:  204.127.198.19
lowewriter.com  MX preference = 50, mail exchanger = sasi.pair.com
lowewriter.com  nameserver = ns000.ns0.com
lowewriter.com  nameserver = ns207.pair.com
ns000.ns0.com   internet address = 216.92.61.61
ns207.pair.com  internet address = 209.68.2.52
>
```

Here, you can see that the name of the mail server for the `LoweWriter.com` domain is `sasi.pair.com`.

Taking a ride through DNS-Land

Ever find yourself wondering how DNS really works? I mean, how is it that you can type a DNS name like `www.disneyland.com` into a web browser and you're almost instantly transported to the Magic Kingdom? Is it really magic?

Nope. It isn't magic; it's DNS. In Book III, Chapter 5, I present a somewhat dry and theoretical overview of DNS. After you have the `nslookup` command in your trusty TCP/IP toolbox, take a little trip through the Internet's maze of DNS servers to find out how DNS gets from `www.disneyland.com` to an IP address in just a matter of milliseconds.

DNS does its whole name resolution thing so fast that it's easy to take it for granted. If you follow this little procedure, you'll gain a deeper appreciation for what DNS does literally tens of thousands of times every second of every day.

1. **At a command prompt, type** nslookup **without any parameters.**

`nslookup` displays the name of the default name server and displays the > prompt.

```
C:\>nslookup
Default Server:  ns1.orng.twtelecom.net
Address:  168.215.210.50
>
```

2. **Type** root **to switch to one of the Internet's root servers.**

`nslookup` switches to one of the Internet's 13 root servers and then displays the > prompt.

```
> root
Default Server:  A.ROOT-SERVERS.NET
Address:  198.41.0.4
```

3. **Type** www.disneyland.com.

`nslookup` sends a query to the root server to ask if it knows the IP address of `www.disneyland.com`. The root server answers with a referral, meaning that it doesn't know about `www.disneyland.com`, but you should try one of these servers because they know all about the `com` domain.

```
> www.disneyland.com
Server:  A.ROOT-SERVERS.NET
Address:  198.41.0.4
Name:    www.disneyland.com
Served by:
- A.GTLD-SERVERS.NET
         192.5.6.30
         com
- G.GTLD-SERVERS.NET
         192.42.93.30
         com
- H.GTLD-SERVERS.NET
         192.54.112.30
         com
```

```
          - C.GTLD-SERVERS.NET
                      192.26.92.30
                      com
          - I.GTLD-SERVERS.NET
                      192.43.172.30
                      com
          - B.GTLD-SERVERS.NET
                      192.33.14.30
                      com
          - D.GTLD-SERVERS.NET
                      192.31.80.30
                      com
          - L.GTLD-SERVERS.NET
                      192.41.162.30
                      com
          - F.GTLD-SERVERS.NET
                      192.35.51.30
                      com
          - J.GTLD-SERVERS.NET
                      192.48.79.30
                      Com

       >
```

4. Type server **followed by the name or IP address of one of the** com **domain name servers.**

It doesn't really matter which one you pick. `nslookup` switches to that server. (The server may spit out some other information besides what I show here; I left it out for clarity.)

```
   > server 192.48.79.30
   Default Server:  [192.5.6.30]
   Address:  192.5.6.30

   >
```

5. Type www.disneyland.com **again.**

`nslookup` sends a query to the com server to ask whether it knows where the Magic Kingdom is. The com server's reply indicates that it doesn't know where www.disneyland.com is, but it does know which server is responsible for disneyland.com.

```
   Server:  [192.5.6.30]
   Address:  192.5.6.30
   Name:    www.disney.com
   Served by:
   - huey.disney.com
               204.128.192.10
               disney.com
   - huey11.disney.com
               208.246.35.40
               disney.com

   >
```

It figures that Disney's name server is huey.disney.com. There's probably also a dewey.disney.com and a louie.disney.com.

6. Type server **followed by the name or IP address of the second-level domain name server.**

nslookup switches to that server:

```
> server huey.disney.com
Default Server:  huey.disney.com
Address:  204.128.192.10

>
```

7. Type www.disneyland.com **again.**

Once again, nslookup sends a query to the name server to find out whether it knows where the Magic Kingdom is. Of course, huey. disney.com *does* know, so it tells us the answer:

```
> www.disneyland.com
Server:   huey.disney.com
Address:  204.128.192.10
Name:     disneyland.com
Address:  199.181.132.250
Aliases:  www.disneyland.com

>
```

8. Type Exit**, and then shout like Tigger in amazement at how DNS queries work.**

And be glad that your DNS resolver and primary name server do all this querying for you automatically.

Okay, maybe that wasn't an E Ticket ride, but it never ceases to amaze me that the DNS system can look up any DNS name hosted anywhere in the world almost instantly.

Using the pathping Command

pathping is an interesting command that's unique to Windows. It's sort of a cross between the ping command and the tracert command, combining the features of both into one tool. When you run pathping, it first traces the route to the destination address much the way tracert does. Then, it launches into a 25-second test of each router along the way, gathering statistics on the rate of data loss to each hop. If the route has a lot of hops, this can take a long time. However, it can help you to spot potentially unreliable hops. If you're having intermittent trouble reaching a particular destination, using pathping may help you pinpoint the problem.

The following command output is typical of the pathping command. Using an -n switch causes the display to use numeric IP numbers only, instead of DNS host names. Although fully qualified host names are convenient, they tend to be very long for network routers, which makes the pathping output very difficult to decipher.

```
C:\>pathping -n www.lowewriter.com
Tracing route to lowewriter.com [209.68.34.15]
over a maximum of 30 hops:
  0  192.168.168.21
  1  66.193.195.81
  2  66.193.200.5
  3  168.215.55.173
  4  168.215.55.101
  5  168.215.55.77
  6  66.192.250.38
  7  66.192.252.22
  8  208.51.224.141
  9  206.132.111.118
 10  206.132.111.162
 11  64.214.174.178
 12  192.168.1.191
 13  209.68.34.15
Computing statistics for 325 seconds...
            Source to Here   This Node/Link
Hop  RTT Lost/Sent = Pct  Lost/Sent = Pct  Address
  0                                         192.168.168.21
                            0/ 100 =   0%   |
  1   1ms   0/ 100 =   0%   0/ 100 =   0%   66.193.195.81]
                            0/ 100 =   0%   |
  2  14ms   0/ 100 =   0%   0/ 100 =   0%   66.193.200.5
                            0/ 100 =   0%   |
  3  10ms   0/ 100 =   0%   0/ 100 =   0%   168.215.55.173
                            0/ 100 =   0%   |
  4  10ms   0/ 100 =   0%   0/ 100 =   0%   168.215.55.101
                            0/ 100 =   0%   |
  5  12ms   0/ 100 =   0%   0/ 100 =   0%   168.215.55.77
                            0/ 100 =   0%   |
  6  14ms   0/ 100 =   0%   0/ 100 =   0%   66.192.250.38
                            0/ 100 =   0%   |
  7  14ms   0/ 100 =   0%   0/ 100 =   0%   66.192.252.22
                            0/ 100 =   0%   |
  8  14ms   0/ 100 =   0%   0/ 100 =   0%   208.51.224.141
                            0/ 100 =   0%   |
  9  81ms   0/ 100 =   0%   0/ 100 =   0%   206.132.111.118
                            0/ 100 =   0%   |
 10  81ms   0/ 100 =   0%   0/ 100 =   0%   206.132.111.162]
                            0/ 100 =   0%   |
 11  84ms   0/ 100 =   0%   0/ 100 =   0%   64.214.174.178]
                            0/ 100 =   0%   |
 12  ---  100/ 100 =100%  100/ 100 =100%   192.168.1.191
                            0/ 100 =   0%   |
 13  85ms   0/ 100 =   0%   0/ 100 =   0%   209.68.34.15
Trace complete.
```

Using the ping Command

ping is probably the most basic TCP/IP command line tool. Its main purpose is to determine whether you can reach another computer from your computer. It uses Internet Control Message Protocol (ICMP) to send mandatory ECHO_REQUEST datagrams to the specified host computer. When the reply is received back from the host, the ping command displays how long it took to receive the response.

You can specify the host to ping by using an IP address, as in this example:

```
C:\>ping 192.168.168.10
Pinging 192.168.168.10 with 32 bytes of data:
Reply from 192.168.168.10: bytes=32 time<1ms TTL=128
Reply from 192.168.168.10: bytes=32 time<1ms TTL=128
Reply from 192.168.168.10: bytes=32 time<1ms TTL=128
Reply from 192.168.168.10: bytes=32 time<1ms TTL=128
Ping statistics for 192.168.168.10:
    Packets: Sent = 4, Received = 4, Lost = 0 (0% loss),
Approximate round trip times in milli-seconds:
    Minimum = 0ms, Maximum = 0ms, Average = 0ms
C:\>
```

By default, the ping command sends four packets to the specified host. It displays the result of each packet sent. Then it displays summary statistics: how many packets were sent, how many replies were received, the error loss rate, and the approximate round-trip time.

You can also ping by using a DNS name, as in this example:

```
C:\>ping www.lowewriter.com
Pinging lowewriter.com [209.68.34.15] with 32 bytes of data:
Reply from 209.68.34.15: bytes=32 time=84ms TTL=53
Reply from 209.68.34.15: bytes=32 time=84ms TTL=53
Reply from 209.68.34.15: bytes=32 time=84ms TTL=53
Reply from 209.68.34.15: bytes=32 time=84ms TTL=53
Ping statistics for 209.68.34.15:
    Packets: Sent = 4, Received = 4, Lost = 0 (0% loss),
Approximate round trip times in milli-seconds:
    Minimum = 84ms, Maximum = 84ms, Average = 84ms
C:\>
```

The ping command uses a DNS query to determine the IP address for the specified host, and then pings the host based on its IP address.

**Book III
Chapter 7**

**TCP/IP Tools and
Commands**

The `ping` command has a number of other switches that you'll use rarely, if ever. Some of these switches are available only for some operating systems. To find out which switches are available for your version of Ping, type **ping /?** (Windows) or **man ping** (Unix/Linux).

You can find a very interesting story about the creation of the `ping` command written by the command's author, Mike Muus, at his website at `http://ftp.arl.mil/~mike/ping.html`. (Sadly, Mr. Muus was killed in an automobile accident in November 2000.)

Using the route Command

Using the `route` command displays or modifies the computer's routing table. For a typical computer that has a single network interface and is connected to a local area network (LAN) that has a router, the routing table is pretty simple and isn't often the source of network problems. Still, if you're having trouble accessing other computers or other networks, you can use the `route` command to make sure that a bad entry in the computer's routing table isn't the culprit.

For a computer with more than one interface and that's configured to work as a router, the routing table is often a major source of trouble. Setting up the routing table properly is a key part of configuring a router to work.

Displaying the routing table

To display the routing table (both IPv4 and IPv6) in Windows, use the `route print` command. In Unix/Linux, you can just use `route` without any command line switches. The output displayed by the Windows and Unix/Linux commands are similar. Here's an example from a typical Windows client computer:

```
C:\>route print
===========================================================================
Interface List
    8 ...00 12 3f a7 17 ba ...... Intel(R) PRO/100 VE Network Connection
    1 ........................... Software Loopback Interface 1
    9 ...02 00 54 55 4e 01 ...... Teredo Tunneling Pseudo-Interface
   10 ...00 00 00 00 00 00 00 e0  isatap.{D0F85930-01E2-402F-B0FC-31DFF887F06F}
===========================================================================
IPv4 Route Table
===========================================================================
Active Routes:
Network Destination        Netmask          Gateway       Interface  Metric
          0.0.0.0          0.0.0.0      192.168.1.1   192.168.1.110    276
        127.0.0.0        255.0.0.0         On-link         127.0.0.1    306
```

```
           127.0.0.1   255.255.255.255      On-link         127.0.0.1  306
     127.255.255.255   255.255.255.255      On-link         127.0.0.1  306
         192.168.1.0     255.255.255.0      On-link     192.168.1.110  276
       192.168.1.110   255.255.255.255      On-link     192.168.1.110  276
       192.168.1.255   255.255.255.255      On-link     192.168.1.110  276
           224.0.0.0         240.0.0.0      On-link         127.0.0.1  306
           224.0.0.0         240.0.0.0      On-link     192.168.1.110  276
     255.255.255.255   255.255.255.255      On-link         127.0.0.1  306
     255.255.255.255   255.255.255.255      On-link     192.168.1.110  276
===========================================================================
Persistent Routes:
  Network Address          Netmask  Gateway Address  Metric
          0.0.0.0          0.0.0.0      192.168.1.1  Default
===========================================================================
IPv6 Route Table
===========================================================================
Active Routes:
 If Metric Network Destination      Gateway
  9     18 ::/0                      On-link
  1    306 ::1/128                   On-link
  9     18 2001::/32                 On-link
  9    266 2001:0:4136:e38c:2c6c:670:3f57:fe91/128
                                     On-link
  8    276 fe80::/64                 On-link
  9    266 fe80::/64                 On-link
 10    281 fe80::5efe:192.168.1.110/128
                                     On-link
  8    276 fe80::cca:9067:9427:a911/128
                                     On-link
  9    266 fe80::2c6c:670:3f57:fe91/128
                                     On-link
  1    306 ff00::/8                  On-link
  9    266 ff00::/8                  On-link
  8    276 ff00::/8                  On-link
===========================================================================
Persistent Routes:
  None
C:\>
```

For each entry in the routing table, five items of information are listed:

+ **The destination IP address**

  Actually, this is the address of the destination subnet, and must be interpreted in the context of the subnet mask.

+ **The subnet mask that must be applied to the destination address to determine the destination subnet**

+ **The IP address of the gateway to which traffic intended for the destination subnet will be sent**

✦ **The IP address of the interface through which the traffic will be sent to the destination subnet**

✦ **The *metric*, which indicates the number of hops required to reach destinations via the gateway**

Each packet that's processed by the computer is evaluated against the rules in the routing table. If the packet's destination address matches the destination subnet for the rule, the packet is sent to the specified gateway via the specified network interface. If not, the next rule is applied.

The computer on which I ran the route command in this example is on a private 192.168.1.0 subnet. The computer's IP address is 192.168.1.100, and the default gateway is a router at 192.168.1.1.

Here's how the rules shown in this example are used. Notice that you have to read the entries from the bottom up:

✦ **The first rule is for packets sent to 255.255.255.255, with subnet mask 255.255.255.255.** This special IP address is for broadcast packets. The rule specifies that these broadcast packets should be delivered to the local network interface (192.168.1.100).

✦ **The next rule is for packets sent to 192.168.1.255, again with subnet mask 255.255.255.255.** These are also broadcast packets and are sent to the local network interface.

✦ **The next rule is for packets sent to 192.168.1.100, again with subnet mask 255.255.255.255.** This is for packets that the computer is sending to itself via its own IP address. This rule specifies that these packets will be sent to the local loopback interface on 127.0.0.1.

✦ **The next rule is for packets sent to 192.168.1.0, with subnet mask 255.255.255.0.** These are packets intended for the local subnet. They're sent to the subnet via the local interface at 192.169.1.100.

✦ **The next rule is for packets sent to the loopback address (127.0.0.1, subnet mask 255.0.0.0).** These packets are sent straight through to the loopback interface, 127.0.0.1.

✦ **The last rule is for everything else.** All IP addresses will match the destination IP address 0.0.0.0 with subnet mask 0.0.0.0 and will be sent to the default gateway router at 192.168.1.1 via the computer's network interface at 192.168.1.100.

One major difference between the Windows version of route and the Unix/Linux version is the order in which they list the routing table. The Windows route command lists the table starting with the most general entry and works toward the most specific. The Unix/Linux version is the other way around: It starts with the most specific and works toward the more general.

The Unix/Linux order makes more sense — the Windows `route` command displays the routing list upside down.

Modifying the routing table

Besides displaying the routing table, the `route` command also lets you modify it by adding, deleting, or changing entries.

WARNING!

Don't try this unless you know what you're doing. If you mess up the routing table, your computer may not be able to communicate with anyone.

The syntax for the `route` command for adding, deleting, or changing a route entry is

```
route [-p] command dest [mask subnet] gateway [-if interface]
```

The following list describes each of the `route` command's parameters:

✦ `-p`: Makes the entry persistent. If you omit `-p`, the entry will be deleted the next time you reboot. (Use this only with `add` commands.)

✦ `command`: Add, delete, or change.

✦ `dest`: The IP address of the destination subnet.

✦ `mask subnet`: The subnet mask. If you omit the subnet mask, the default is `255.255.255.255`, meaning that the entry will apply only to a single host rather than a subnet. You usually want to include the mask.

✦ `gateway`: The IP address of the gateway to which packets will be sent.

✦ `if interface`: The IP address of the interface through which packets will be sent. If your computer has only one network interface, you can omit this.

Suppose that your network has a second router that serves as a link to another private subnet, `192.168.2.0` (subnet mask `255.255.255.0`). The interface on the local side of this router is at `192.168.1.200`. To add a static route entry that sends packets intended for the `192.168.2.0` subnet to this router, use a command like this:

```
C:\>route -p add 192.168.2.0 mask 255.255.255.0 192.168.1.200
```

Now, suppose that you later change the IP address of the router to `192.168.1.222`. You can update this route with the following command:

```
C:\>route change 192.168.2.0 mask 255.255.255.0 192.168.1.222
```

**Book III
Chapter 7**

**TCP/IP Tools and
Commands**

Notice that I specify the mask again. If you omit the mask from a route change command, the command changes the mask to 255.255.255.255!

Finally, suppose that you realize that setting up a second router on this network wasn't such a good idea after all, so you want to just delete the entry. The following command will do the trick:

```
C:\>route delete 192.168.2.0
```

Using the tracert Command

The tracert command (traceroute in Unix/Linux implementations) is one of the key diagnostic tools for TCP/IP. It displays a list of all the routers that a packet must go through to get from the computer where tracert is run to any other computer on the Internet. Each one of these routers is called a *hop*, presumably because the original designers of the IP protocol played a lot of hopscotch when they were young. If you can't connect to another computer, you can use tracert to find out exactly where the problem is occurring.

tracert makes three attempts to contact the router at each hop and displays the response time for each of these attempts. Then, it displays the DNS name of the router (if available) and the router's IP address.

To use tracert, type the tracert command followed by the host name of the computer to which you want to trace the route. For example, suppose that you're having trouble sending mail to a recipient at wiley.com. You've used nslookup to determine that the mail server for wiley.com is xmail. wiley.com, so now you can use tracert to trace the routers along the path from your computer to xmail.wiley.com:

```
C:\>tracert xmail.wiley.com
Tracing route to xmail.wiley.com [208.215.179.78]
over a maximum of 30 hops:
  1    27 ms    14 ms    10 ms  10.242.144.1
  2    11 ms    43 ms    10 ms  bar01-p5-0-0.frsnhe4.ca.attbb.net [24.130.64.125]
  3     9 ms    14 ms    12 ms  bar01-p4-0-0.frsnhe1.ca.attbb.net [24.130.0.5]
  4    25 ms    30 ms    29 ms  bic01-p6-0.elsgrdc1.ca.attbb.net [24.130.0.49]
  5    25 ms    29 ms    43 ms  bic02-d4-0.elsgrdc1.ca.attbb.net [24.130.0.162]
  6    21 ms    19 ms    20 ms  bar01-p2-0.lsanhe4.ca.attbb.net [24.130.0.197]
  7    37 ms    38 ms    19 ms  bic01-p2-0.lsanhe3.ca.attbb.net [24.130.0.193]
  8    20 ms    22 ms    21 ms  12.119.9.5
  9    21 ms    21 ms    22 ms  tbr2-p012702.la2ca.ip.att.net [12.123.199.241]
 10    71 ms   101 ms    62 ms  tbr2-p013801.sl9mo.ip.att.net [12.122.10.13]
 11    68 ms    77 ms    71 ms  tbr1-p012401.sl9mo.ip.att.net [12.122.9.141]
 12    79 ms    81 ms    83 ms  tbr1-cl4.wswdc.ip.att.net [12.122.10.29]
```

```
13    83 ms   107 ms   103 ms   tbr1-p012201.n54ny.ip.att.net [12.122.10.17]
14   106 ms    85 ms   105 ms   gbr6-p30.n54ny.ip.att.net [12.122.11.14]
15   104 ms    96 ms    88 ms   gar3-p370.n54ny.ip.att.net [12.123.1.189]
16    98 ms    86 ms    83 ms   12.125.50.162
17    85 ms    90 ms    87 ms   xmail.wiley.com [208.215.179.78]
Trace complete.
```

Wow, when I send mail to my editors at Wiley, the mail travels through 17 routers along the way. No wonder I'm always missing deadlines!

The most likely problem that you'll encounter when you use `tracert` is a timeout during one of the hops. Timeouts are indicated by asterisks where you'd expect to see a time. For example, the following `tracert` output shows the fourth hop timing out on all three attempts:

Understanding how tracert works

Understanding how `tracert` works can provide some insight that may help you to interpret the results it provides. Plus, you can use this knowledge to impress your friends, who probably don't know how it works.

The key to `tracert` is a field that's a standard part of all IP packets called TTL, which stands for *Time to Live.* In most other circumstances, a value called TTL would be a time value — not in IP packets, however. In an IP packet, the TTL value indicates how many routers a packet can travel through on its way to its destination. Every time a router forwards an IP packet, it subtracts one from the packet's TTL value. When the TTL value reaches zero, the router refuses to forward the packet.

The `tracert` command sends a series of special messages called ICMP Echo Requests to the destination computer. The first time it sends this message, it sets the TTL value of the packet to 1. When the packet arrives at the first router along the path to the destination, that router subtracts one from the TTL value, sees that the TTL value has become 0, so it sends a Time Exceeded message back to the original host. When the `tracert` command receives this Time Exceeded message, it extracts the IP address of the router from it, calculates the time it took for the message to return, and displays the first hop.

Then the `tracert` command sends another Echo Request message: this time, with the TTL value set to 2. This message goes through the first router to the second router, which sees that the TTL value has been decremented to 0 and then sends back a Time Exceeded message. When `tracert` receives the Time Exceeded message from the second router, it displays the line for the second hop. This process continues, each time with a greater TTL value, until the Echo Request finally reaches the destination.

Pretty clever, eh?

(Note that the Unix/Linux `traceroute` command uses a slightly different set of TCP/IP messages and responses to accomplish the same result.)

```
C:\>tracert xmail.wiley.com
Tracing route to xmail.wiley.com [208.215.179.78]
over a maximum of 30 hops:
  1    27 ms    14 ms    10 ms  10.242.144.1
  2    11 ms    43 ms    10 ms  bar01-p5-0-0.frsnhe4.ca.attbb.net [24.130.64.125]
  3     9 ms    14 ms    12 ms  bar01-p4-0-0.frsnhe1.ca.attbb.net [24.130.0.5]
  4     *        *        *     Request timed out.
```

Sometimes, timeouts are caused by temporary problems, so you should try
the tracert again to see if the problem persists. If you keep getting timeouts at the same router, the router could be having a genuine problem.

Book IV
Going Virtual

Windows Features — □ ×

Turn Windows features on or off

To turn a feature on, select its check box. To turn a feature off, clear its check box. A filled box means that only part of the feature is turned on.

- ☐ .NET Framework 3.5 (includes .NET 2.0 and 3.0)
- ☐ .NET Framework 4.5 Advanced Services
- ☐ Active Directory Lightweight Directory Services
- ☑ Hyper-V
  - ☑ Hyper-V Management Tools
  - ☑ Hyper-V Platform
- ☑ Internet Explorer 11
- ☐ Internet Information Services
- ☐ Internet Information Services Hostable Web Core
- ☐ Legacy Components
- ☑ Media Features
- ☐ Microsoft Message Queue (MSMQ) Server

OK   Cancel

web extras Read about virtualizing desktops in the cloud in a free article at www.dummies.com/extras/networkingaio.

Contents at a Glance

Chapter 1: Introducing Virtualization 367

Chapter 2: Working with Hyper-V 377

Chapter 3: Working with VMware 395

Chapter 4: Virtualizing Your Desktops 405

Chapter 1: Introducing Virtualization

In This Chapter

✔ Examining the basics of virtualization

✔ Looking at what a hypervisor does

✔ Considering how disks and networks are virtualized

✔ Weighing the benefits of virtualization

*V*irtualization is one of the hottest trends in networking today. According to some industry pundits, virtualization is the best thing to happen to computers since the invention of the transistor. If you haven't already begun to virtualize your network, you're standing on the platform watching as the train is pulling out.

This chapter is a brief introduction to virtualization, with an emphasis on using it to leverage your network server hardware to provide more servers using less hardware.

 Mastering a virtualization environment calls for a book of its own. I recommend two titles, both from John Wiley & Sons, Inc.: *Virtualization For Dummies,* by Bernard Golden, and *VMware Infrastructure 3 For Dummies,* by William Lowe (no relation, honest).

Understanding Virtualization

The basic idea behind virtualization is to use software to simulate the existence of hardware. This powerful idea enables you to run more than one independent computer system on a single physical computer system. Suppose that your organization requires a total of 12 servers to meet its needs. You could run each of these 12 servers on a separate computer, in which case you would have 12 computers in your server room. Or, you could use virtualization to run these 12 servers on just 2 computers. In effect, each of those computers would simulate six separate computer systems, each running one of your servers.

Each of the simulated computers is called a *virtual machine* (VM). For all intents and purposes, each VM appears to be a complete, self-contained computer system with its own processor (or, more likely, processors), memory, disk drives, CD-ROM/DVD drives, keyboard, mouse, monitor, network interfaces, USB ports, and so on.

Like a real computer, each virtual machine requires an operating system to do productive work. In a typical network server environment, each virtual machine runs its own copy of Windows Server. The operating system has no idea that it's running on a virtual machine rather than on a real machine.

Here are a few terms you need to be familiar with if you expect to discuss virtualization intelligently:

✦ **Host:** The actual physical computer on which one or more virtual machines run.

✦ **Bare metal:** Another term for the host computer that runs one or more virtual machines.

✦ **Guest:** Another term for a virtual machine running on a host.

✦ **Guest operating system:** An operating system that runs within a virtual machine. By itself, a guest is just a machine; it requires an operating system to run. The guest operating system is what brings the guest to life.

As far as licensing is concerned, Microsoft treats each virtual machine as a separate computer. Thus, if you run six guests on a single host, and each guest runs Windows Server, you need six licenses of Windows Server.

✦ **Hypervisor:** The virtualization operating system that creates and runs virtual machines. For more information about hypervisors, read the next section, "Understanding Hypervisors."

✦ **Hardware Abstraction Layer (HAL):** A layer of software that acts as a go-between to separate actual hardware from the software that interacts with it. An operating system provides a hardware abstraction layer, because it uses device drivers to communicate with actual hardware devices so that software running in the operating system doesn't have to know the details of the specific device it's interacting with. A hypervisor also provides a hardware abstraction layer that enables the guest operating systems in virtual machines to interact with virtualized hardware.

Understanding Hypervisors

At the core of virtualization is a *hypervisor,* a layer of software that manages the creation and execution of virtual machines. A hypervisor provides several core functions:

✦ It provides a HAL, which virtualizes all the hardware resources of the host computer on which it runs. This includes processor cores, RAM, and I/O devices such as disk drives, keyboards, mice, monitors, USB devices, and so on.

✦ It creates pools of these abstracted hardware resources that can be allocated to virtual machines.

✦ It creates virtual machines, which are complete implementations of an idealized computer system that has the hardware resources of the host available to it. The hardware for each virtual machine is drawn from the pools of available hardware resources managed by the hypervisor.

✦ It manages the execution of its virtual machines, allocating host hardware resources as needed to each virtual machine and starting and stopping virtual machines when requested by users.

✦ It ensures that each virtual machine is completely isolated from all other virtual machines, so that if a problem develops in one virtual machine, none of the other virtual machines is affected.

✦ It manages communication among the virtual machines over virtual networks, enabling the virtual machines to connect with each other and with a physical network that reaches beyond the host.

There are two basic types of hypervisors you should know about:

✦ **Type-1:** A type-1 hypervisor runs directly on the host computer, with no intervening operating system. This is the most efficient type of hypervisor because it has direct access to the hardware resources of the host system.

The two best-known examples of type-1 hypervisors are VMware's ESXi and Microsoft's Hyper-V. ESXi is part of a suite of popular virtualization products from VMware, and Hyper-V is the built-in virtualization platform that is included with recent versions of Windows Server.

✦ **Type-2:** A type-2 hypervisor runs as an application within an operating system that runs directly on the host computer. Type-2 hypervisors are less efficient than type-1 hypervisors because when you use a type-2 hypervisor, you add an additional layer of hardware abstraction: the first provided by the operating system that runs natively on the host, and the second by the hypervisor that runs as an application on the host operating system.

For production use, you should always use type-1 hypervisors because they're much more efficient than type-2 hypervisors. Type-1 hypervisors are considerably more expensive than type-2 hypervisors, however. As a result, many people use inexpensive or free type-2 hypervisors to experiment with virtualization before making a commitment to purchase an expensive type-1 hypervisor.

The long trek of virtualization

Kids these days think they invented everything, including virtualization.

Little do they know.

Virtualization was developed for PC-based computers in the early 1990s, around the time Captain Picard was flying the Enterprise around in *Star Trek: The Next Generation*.

But the idea is much older than that.

The first virtualized server computers predate Captain Picard by about 20 years. In 1972, IBM released an operating system called simply VM, which had nearly all the basic features found in today's virtualization products.

VM allowed the administrators of IBM's System/370 mainframe computers to create multiple independent virtual machines, each of which was called (you guessed it) a virtual machine, or VM. This terminology is still in use today.

Each VM could run one of the various guest operating systems that were compatible with the System/370 and appeared to this guest operating system to be a complete, independent System/370 computer with its own processor cores, virtual memory, disk partitions, and input/output devices.

The core of the VM system itself was called the *hypervisor* — another term that persists to this day.

The VM product that IBM released in 1972 was actually based on an experimental product that IBM released on a limited basis in 1967.

So whenever someone tells you about this new technology called *virtualization,* you can tell him or her that it was invented when *Star Trek* was on TV. When someone asks, "You mean the one with Picard?" you can say, "No, the one with Kirk."

Understanding Virtual Disks

Computers aren't the only things that are virtualized in a virtual environment. In addition to creating virtual computers, virtualization also creates virtual disk storage. Disk virtualization lets you combine a variety of physical disk storage devices to create pools of disk storage that you can then parcel out to your virtual machines as needed.

Virtualization of disk storage is nothing new. In fact, there are actually several layers of virtualization involved in an actual storage environment. At the lowest level are the actual physical disk drives. Physical disk drives are usually bundled together in arrays of individual drives. This bundling is a type of virtualization in that it creates the image of a single large disk drive that isn't really there. For example, four 2TB disk drives might be combined in an array to create a single 8TB disk drive.

Note that disk arrays are usually used to provide data protection through redundancy. This is commonly called RAID, which stands for *Redundant Array of Inexpensive Disks.*

One common form of RAID, called RAID-10, lets you create mirrored pairs of disk drives so that data is always written to both of the drives in a mirror pair. So, if one of the drives in a mirror pair fails, the other drive can carry the load. With RAID-10, the usable capacity of the complete array is equal to one-half of the total capacity of the drives in the array. For example, a RAID-10 array consisting of four 2TB drives contains two pairs of mirrored 2TB disk drives, for a total usable capacity of 4TB.

Another common form of RAID is RAID-5, in which disk drives are combined and one of the drives in the group is used for redundancy. Then, if any one of the drives in the array fails, the remaining drives can be used to re-create the data that was on the drive that failed. The total capacity of a RAID-5 array is equal to the sum of the capacities of the individual drives, minus one of the drives. For example, an array of four 2TB drives in a RAID-5 configuration has a total usable capacity of 6TB.

In a typical virtual environment, the host computers can be connected to disk storage in several distinct ways:

✦ **Local disk storage:** In local disk storage, disk drives are mounted directly into the host computer and are connected to the host computer via its internal disk drive controllers. For example, a host computer might include four 1TB disk drives mounted within the same chassis as the computer itself. These four drives might be used to form a RAID-10 array with a usable capacity of 2TB.

The main drawbacks of local disk storage is that it's limited to the physical capacity of the host computers and is available only to the host computer that it's installed in.

✦ **Storage Area Network (SAN):** In a SAN, disk drives are contained in a separate device that is connected to the host via a high-speed controller. The difference between a SAN and local storage is that the SAN is a separate device. Its high-speed connection to the host is often just as fast as the internal connection of local disk storage, but the SAN includes a separate storage controller that is responsible for managing the disk drives.

A typical SAN can hold a dozen or more disk drives and can allow high-speed connections to more than one host. A SAN can often be expanded by adding one or more expansion chassis, which can contain a dozen or more disk drives each. Thus, a single SAN can manage hundreds of terabytes of disk data.

✦ **Network Accessible Storage (NAS):** This type of storage is similar to a SAN, but instead of connecting to the hosts via a high-speed controller, a NAS connects to the host computers via standard Ethernet connections and TCP/IP. NAS is the least expensive of all forms of disk storage, but it's also the slowest.

Regardless of the way the storage is attached to the host, the hypervisor consolidates its storage and creates virtual pools of disk storage typically called *data stores.* For example, a hypervisor that has access to three 2TB RAID5 disk arrays might consolidate them to create a single 6TB data store.

From this data store, you can create *volumes,* which are essentially virtual disk drives that can be allocated to a particular virtual machine. Then, when an operating system is installed in a virtual machine, the operating system can mount the virtual machine's volumes to create drives that the operating system can access.

For example, let's consider a virtual machine that runs Windows Server. If you were to connect to the virtual machine, log in, and use Windows Explorer to look at the disk storage that's available to the machine, you might see a C: drive with a capacity of 100GB. That C: drive is actually a 100GB volume that is created by the hypervisor and attached to the virtual machine. The 100GB volume, in turn, is allocated from a data store, which might be 4TB in size. The data store is created from disk storage contained in a SAN attached to the host, which might be made up of a RAID-10 array consisting of four 2TB physical disk drives.

So, you can see that there are at least four layers of virtualization required to make the raw storage available on the physical disk drives available to the guest operating system:

✦ Physical disk drives are aggregated using RAID-10 to create a unified disk image that has built-in redundancy. RAID-10 is, in effect, the first layer of virtualization. This layer is managed entirely by the SAN.

✦ The storage available on the SAN is abstracted by the hypervisor to create data stores. This is, effectively, a second level of virtualization.

✦ Portions of a data store are used to create volumes that are then presented to virtual machines. Volumes represent a third layer of virtualization.

✦ The guest operating system sees the volumes as if they're physical devices, which can be mounted and then formatted to create usable disk storage accessible to the user. This is the fourth layer of virtualization.

Although it may seem overly complicated, these layers of virtualization give you a lot of flexibility when it comes to storage management. New disk arrays can be added to a SAN, or a new NAS can be added to the network, and then new data stores can be created from them without disrupting existing data stores. Volumes can be moved from one data store to another without disrupting the virtual machines they're attached to. In fact, you can increase the size of a volume on the fly, and the virtual machine will immediately see the increased storage capacity of its disk drives, without even requiring so much as a reboot.

Understanding Network Virtualization

When you create one or more virtual machines on a host system, you need to provide a way for those virtual machines to communicate not only with each other but also with the other physical computers on your network. To enable such connections, you must create a *virtual network* within your virtualization environment. The virtual network connects the virtual machines to each other and to the physical network.

To create a virtual network, you must create a *virtual switch,* which connects the virtual machines to each other and to a physical network via the host computer's network interfaces. Like a physical switch, a virtual switch has ports. When you create a virtual switch, you connect the virtual switch to one or more of the host computer's network interfaces. These interfaces are then connected with network cable to physical switches, which effectively connects the virtual switch to the physical network.

Then, when you create virtual machines, you connect each virtual machine to a port on the virtual switch. When all the virtual machines are connected to the switch, the VMs can communicate with each other via the switch. And they can communicate with devices on the physical network via the connections through the host computer's network interfaces.

Considering the Benefits of Virtualization

You might suspect that virtualization is inefficient because a real computer is inherently faster than a simulated computer. Although it's true that real computers are faster than simulated computers, virtualization technology has become so advanced that the performance penalty for running on a virtualized machine rather than a real machine is only a few percent.

The small amount of overhead imposed by virtualization is usually more than made up for by the simple fact that even the most heavily used servers spend most of their time twiddling their digital thumbs, waiting for something to do. In fact, many servers spend nearly *all* their time doing nothing. As computers get faster and faster, they spend even more of their time with nothing to do.

Virtualization is a great way to put all this unused processing power to good use.

Besides this basic efficiency benefit, virtualization has several compelling benefits:

✦ **Hardware cost:** You typically can save a lot of money by reducing hardware costs when you use virtualization. Suppose that you replace ten servers that cost $4,000 each with one host server. Granted, you'll probably spend more than $4,000 on that server, because it needs to be maxed out with memory, processor cores, network interfaces, and so on. So you'll probably end up spending $15,000 or $20,000 for the host server. Also, you'll end up spending something like $5,000 for the hypervisor software. But that's still a lot less than the $40,000 you would have spent on ten separate computers at $4,000 each.

✦ **Energy costs:** Many organizations have found that going virtual has reduced their overall electricity consumption for server computers by 80 percent. This savings is a direct result of using less computer hardware to do more work. One host computer running ten virtual servers uses approximately one-tenth the energy that would be used if each of the ten servers ran on separate hardware.

✦ **Reduced downtime:** Virtual environments typically have less downtime than nonvirtual environments. For example, suppose you need to upgrade the BIOS on one of your server computers. With physical servers, this type of upgrade will ordinarily require that you shut down the operating system that runs on the server, upgrade the BIOS, and then restart the server. During the upgrade, the server will be unavailable.

In a virtual environment, you don't need to shut down the servers to upgrade the BIOS on the host computer that runs the server. Instead, all you do is move the servers that run on the host that needs the upgrade to another host. When the servers are moved (an operation that can be done without shutting them down), you can shut down the host and upgrade its BIOS. Then, after you restart the host, you can move the servers back to the host — again, without shutting down the servers.

✦ **Recoverability:** One of the biggest benefits of virtualization isn't the cost savings, but the ability to recover quickly from hardware failures.

Suppose that your organization has ten servers, each running on separate hardware. If any one of those servers goes down due to a hardware failure — say, a bad motherboard — that server will remain down until you can fix the computer. On the other hand, if those ten servers are running as virtual machines on two different hosts, and one of the hosts fails, the virtual machines that were running on the failed host can be brought up on the other host in a matter of minutes.

Granted, the servers will run less efficiently on a single host than they would have on two hosts, but the point is that they'll all be running after only a short downtime.

In fact, with the most advanced hypervisors available, the transfer from a failing host to another host can be done automatically and instantaneously, so downtime is all but eliminated.

✦ **Disaster recovery:** Besides the benefit of recoverability when hardware failures occur, an even bigger benefit of virtualization comes into play in a true disaster-recovery situation. Suppose that your organization's server infrastructure consists of 20 separate servers. In the case of a devastating disaster, such as a fire in the server room that destroys all hardware, how long will it take you to get all 20 of those servers back up and running on new hardware? Quite possibly, the recovery time will be measured in weeks.

By contrast, virtual machines are actually nothing more than files that can be backed up onto tape. As a result, in a disaster-recovery situation, all you have to do is rebuild a single host computer and reinstall the hypervisor software. Then you can restore the virtual-machine backups from tape, restart the virtual machines, and get back up and running in a matter of days instead of weeks.

**Book IV
Chapter 1**

**Introducing
Virtualization**

Chapter 2: Working with Hyper-V

In This Chapter

✔ Introducing Hyper-V

✔ Working with Hyper-V Manager

✔ Creating a virtual network to support your virtual machines

✔ Creating virtual machines in Hyper-V

*H*yper-V is a virtualization platform that comes as a standard part of all versions of Windows Server since version 2008 and all versions of desktop Windows since Windows 8.

On server versions of Windows, Hyper-V provides an enterprise-grade true Type-1 hypervisor that can manage huge virtualization farms with thousands of virtual machines. The version of Hyper-V that comes with desktop Windows is called Client Hyper-V. Client Hyper-V uses the same Type-1 hypervisor as the server-grade Hyper-V. However, it doesn't have the same enterprise-level management capabilities, because it's intended for use on client computers, not for production servers.

In this chapter, I first explain some of the details of how Hyper-V works. Then I show you how to set up virtual machines using the client version of Hyper-V. That way, you can build your own virtual machines to experiment with Hyper-V without the need for expensive hardware or server software.

Understanding the Hyper-V Hypervisor

Hyper-V is a built-in component of all modern versions of Windows. So, to use Hyper-V, you don't need to purchase any additional software from Microsoft. If you own a modern Microsoft operating system, you already own Hyper-V.

Don't be confused by the fact that Hyper-V is an integral part of Windows: Although Hyper-V is built into Windows, Hyper-V is *not* a Type-2 hypervisor that runs as an application within Windows. Instead, Hyper-V is a true Type-1 hypervisor that runs directly on the host computer hardware. This is true even for the Client Hyper-V versions that are included with desktop versions of Windows.

In Hyper-V, each virtual machine runs within an isolated space called a *partition*. Each partition has access to its own processor, RAM, disk, network, and other virtual resources.

There are two types of partitions in Hyper-V: a *parent partition* and one or more *child partitions*. The parent partition is a special partition that hosts the Windows operating system that Hyper-V is associated with. Child partitions host additional virtual machines that you create as needed.

When you activate the Hyper-V feature, the hypervisor is installed and the existing Windows operating system is moved into a virtual machine that runs in the parent partition. Then, whenever you start the host computer, the hypervisor is loaded, the parent partition is created, and Windows is started in a virtual machine within the parent partition.

Although it may appear that the hypervisor is running within Windows, actually the reverse is true: Windows is running within the hypervisor.

In addition to the Windows operating system, the parent partition runs software that enables the management of virtual machines on the hypervisor. This includes creating new virtual machines, starting and stopping virtual machines, changing the resources allocated to existing virtual machines (for example, adding more processors, RAM, or disk storage), and moving virtual machines from one host to another.

Understanding Hyper-V Virtual Disks

Every Hyper-V virtual machine must have at least one virtual disk associated with it. A *virtual disk* is nothing more than a disk file that resides in the file system of the host operating system. The file has one of two file extensions, depending on which of two data formats you choose for the virtual disk:

+ **.vhd:** An older format that has a maximum virtual disk size of 2TB

+ **.vhdx:** A newer format that can support virtual disks up to 64TB

For either of these virtual disk formats, Hyper-V lets you create two different types of virtual disks:

+ **Fixed-size disk:** A virtual disk whose disk space is preallocated to the full size of the drive when you create the disk. For example, if you create a 100GB fixed-size disk using the .vhdx format, a .vhdx file of 100GB will be allocated to the drive. Even if the drive contains only 10GB of data, it will still consume 100GB of space on the host system's disk drive.

✦ **Dynamically expanding disk:** A virtual disk that has a maximum disk space, but that actually consumes only the amount of disk space that is required to hold the data on the disk. For example, if you create a dynamically expanding disk with a maximum of 100GB but only put 10GB of data on it, the .vhdx file for the disk will occupy just 10GB of the host system's disk drive.

Actually, there's a third type of disk called a *differencing disk,* which can be used to track changes made to another virtual disk. But this is an advanced topic that I don't cover in this chapter.

Don't be confused by the names *fixed size* and *dynamically expanding.* Both types of disk can be expanded later if you run out of space. The main difference is whether the maximum amount of disk space allowed for the drive is allocated when the drive is first created or as needed when data is added to the drive. Allocating the space when the drive is created results in better performance for the drive, because Hyper-V doesn't have to grab more disk space every time data is added to the drive. Both types of drives can be expanded later if necessary.

Enabling Hyper-V

Hyper-V is not automatically enabled when you install Windows; you must first enable this feature before you can use Hyper-V.

To enable Hyper-V on a server version of Windows, call up the Server Manager and open the Add Roles and Features Wizard. Then enable the Hyper-V role. When you complete the wizard, Hyper-V will install the Type-1 hypervisor and move the existing Windows Server operating system into the parent partition. You can then start building virtual machines.

To enable Hyper-V on a desktop version of Windows, follow these steps:

1. **Open the Control Panel.**

2. **Choose Programs and Features.**

   The Programs and Features window comes to life.

3. **Click Turn Windows Features On or Off.**

   The Windows Features dialog box appears, as shown in Figure 2-1.

**Book IV
Chapter 2**

**Working with
Hyper-V**

Figure 2-1:
Enabling
Hyper-V on
a desktop
version of
Windows.

4. **Select the Hyper-V feature and click OK.**

   The Client Hyper-V hypervisor is installed as an application on the existing desktop Windows operating system, and you can begin using Hyper-V.

5. **When prompted, restart the computer.**

   The reboot is required to start the Hyper-V hypervisor. When your computer restarts, it's actually the Hyper-V hypervisor that starts, not Windows. The hypervisor then loads your desktop Windows into the parent partition.

Getting Familiar with Hyper-V

To manage Hyper-V, you use the Hyper-V Manager, shown in Figure 2-2. To start this program, click the Start button, type **Hyper-V**, and then choose Hyper-V Manager.

The Hyper-V Manager window is divided into five panes:

+ **Navigation:** On the left side of the window is a navigation pane that lists the Hyper-V hosts, which Hyper-V calls *virtualization servers*. In Figure 2-2, just one host is listed: my Windows computer. In an enterprise environment where you have more than one host, each of the hosts will be listed in this pane.

+ **Virtual Machines:** This pane lists the virtual machines that are defined for the selected host. In Figure 2-2, you can see several of the Hyper-V virtual machines that I created while I wrote this book — a couple of Linux machines, a Windows 10 machine, and a couple of Windows Server 2016 machines.

Figure 2-2:
Hyper-V
Manager.

+ **Checkpoints:** In Hyper-V, a *checkpoint* is a recovery point for a virtual machine. You can create a checkpoint when you're going to make a modification to a virtual machine. Then, if something goes wrong, you can revert to the checkpoint.

+ **Virtual machine summary pane:** Below the Checkpoints pane is a pane that provides summary information for the virtual machine selected in the Virtual Machines pane. In Figure 2-2, you can see the summary information for one of the Windows Server 2016 machines. This pane has three tabs: Summary, Memory, and Networking. In the figure, the Memory tab is selected so you can see the memory that has been allocated to the machine.

+ **Actions:** The Actions tab contains buttons you can click to initiate actions for the selected host (DOUG-2014-I7) and the selected machine (WIN2016).

Creating a Virtual Switch

Before you start creating virtual machines in Hyper-V, you should create a virtual switch so that your virtual machines can communicate with each other and with the outside world. To do that, you use the Virtual Switch Manager. Here are the steps:

1. **In Hyper-V Manager, click Virtual Switch Manager.**

This brings up the Virtual Switch Manager window, as shown in Figure 2-3.

Book IV
Chapter 2

Working with
Hyper-V

Figure 2-3:
The Virtual
Switch
Manager
window.

2. **Select the type of virtual switch you want to create.**

   Hyper-V lets you create three types of switches:

   - *External:* A virtual switch that binds to a physical network adapter, which allows virtual machines to communicate with each other, as well as with other computers on your physical network. This is usually the type of switch you should create.

   - *Internal:* A virtual switch that does not bind with a physical network adapter. This type of switch lets the virtual machines on this computer communicate with each other and with the host computer, but not with other computers on your physical network.

   - *Private:* A virtual switch that lets virtual machines communicate with each other but not with the host computer or with any computers on your physical network.

3. **Click Create Virtual Switch.**

   The settings for the new virtual switch appear, as shown in Figure 2-4.

Figure 2-4:
Creating a
new virtual
switch.

4. **Type a name for the new virtual switch in the Name field.**

   Use any name you want.

5. **Select the physical network adapter you want to bind the virtual switch to.**

   If your computer has more than one network adapter, select the one you want to use. Binding the virtual switch to a physical network adapter allows the virtual machines to communicate not only with each other but also with other computers connected via the adapter you select.

6. **If your network has multiple VLANs, click the Enable Virtual LAN Identification check box and enter the VLAN ID for the VLAN you want this switch to connect to.**

   If your network does not have multiple VLANs, you can skip this step.

7. **Click OK.**

   The virtual switch is created. Your Hyper-V environment now has a virtual network in place, so you can start creating virtual machines.

Creating a Virtual Disk

Before you create a virtual machine, it's best to first create a virtual disk for the machine to use. Note that you can create a virtual disk at the same time that you create a virtual machine. However, creating the virtual disk first gives you more flexibility. So, I recommend you create virtual disks and virtual machines separately. Here are the steps to create a virtual disk:

1. **In Hyper-V Manager, click New and then choose Hard Disk.**

This brings up the New Virtual Hard Disk Wizard, as shown in Figure 2-5.

Figure 2-5:
The New
Virtual Hard
Disk Wizard.

2. **Click Next.**

You're asked which disk format to use, as shown in Figure 2-6.

3. **Select VHDX, and then click Next.**

I recommend you always use the VHDX format, which can support drives larger than 2TB.

When you click Next, the Choose Disk Type option page is displayed, as shown in Figure 2-7.

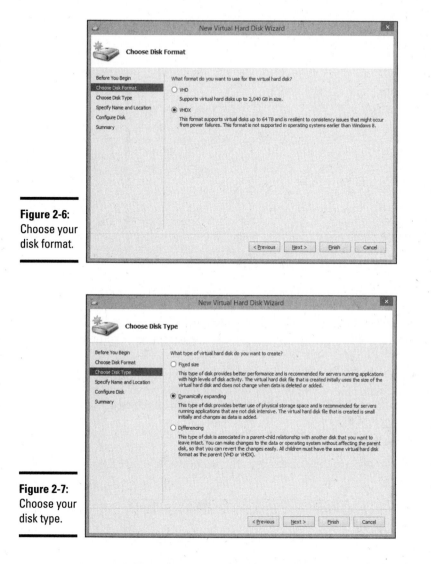

Figure 2-6:
Choose your
disk format.

Figure 2-7:
Choose your
disk type.

4. **Select the disk type you want to use.**

The options are Fixed Size, Dynamically Expanding, or Differencing.
Choose Fixed Size if you're concerned about the performance of the
disk; otherwise, choose Dynamically Expanding.

5. **Click Next.**

The page shown in Figure 2-8 appears.

Figure 2-8:
Specify the
name and
location of
the disk.

6. **Specify the name and location of the new disk.**

   Type any name you want for the virtual disk drive. Then, click the
   Browse button to browse to the disk location where you want Hyper-V
   to create the .vhdx file.

   Make sure you choose a location that has enough disk space to create
   the .vhdx file. If you're creating a dynamically expanding disk, you
   should ensure that the location has enough space to accommodate the
   drive as it grows.

7. **Click Next.**

   The Configure Disk page appears, as shown in Figure 2-9.

Figure 2-9:
Specify the
size of the
disk.

8. **Specify the maximum size for the disk drive.**

This page also allows you to copy data either from an existing physical disk drive or from an existing virtual disk drive. Copying data from an existing physical drive is a quick way to convert a physical computer to a virtual computer; just copy the physical disk to a virtual disk, and then use the new virtual disk as the basis for a new virtual machine.

9. **Click Next.**

A confirmation screen appears, summarizing the options you've selected for your new disk.

10. **Click Finish.**

The new disk is created. Note that if you selected Fixed Disk as the disk type, creating the disk can take a while because the entire amount of disk storage you specified is allocated to the disk. Be patient.

You're done! You've now created a virtual disk that can be used as the basis for a new virtual machine.

Creating a Virtual Machine

After you've created a virtual disk, creating a virtual machine to use it is a straightforward affair. Follow these steps:

1. **From Hyper-V Manager, choose New and then choose Virtual Machine.**

This brings up the New Virtual Machine Wizard, as shown in Figure 2-10.

Figure 2-10:
Say hello
to the New
Virtual
Machine
Wizard.

2. **Click Next.**

   The Specify Name and Location page appears, as shown in Figure 2-11.

Figure 2-11:
Specify the
name and
location of
the virtual
machine.

3. **Enter the name you want to use for your virtual machine.**

   You can choose any name you want here.

4. **Specify the location of the virtual machine's configuration file.**

   Every virtual machine has an XML file associated with it that defines the configuration of the virtual machine. You can allow this file to be stored in the default location, or you can override the default and specify a custom location.

5. **Click Next.**

   The Specify Generation page appears, as shown in Figure 2-12.

6. **Specify the generation you want to use for the new virtual machine.**

   In most cases, you should opt for Generation 2, which uses newer technology than Generation 1 machines. Use Generation 1 only if the guest operating system will be earlier than Windows Server 2012 or Windows 8.

Figure 2-12:
Specify the genera-tion of the new virtual machine.

7. **Click Next.**

   The Assign Memory page appears, as shown in Figure 2-13.

Figure 2-13:
Specify the memory for the new virtual machine.

8. **Indicate the amount of RAM you want to allocate for the new machine.**

   The default is 512MB, but you'll almost certainly want to increase that.

   I also recommend that you click the Use Dynamic Memory for This Virtual Machine option, which improves memory performance.

9. **Click Next.**

   The Configure Networking page appears, as shown in Figure 2-14.

Figure 2-14: Configure the networking for the new virtual machine.

10. **Select the virtual switch you want to use for the virtual machine.**

    This is the point where you realize why you needed to create a virtual switch before you start creating virtual machines. Use the Connection drop-down list to select the virtual switch you want to connect to this VM.

11. **Click Next.**

    The Connect Virtual Hard Disk page appears, as shown in Figure 2-15.

12. **Assuming you've already created a virtual disk for the virtual machine, choose the Use an Existing Virtual Hard Disk option, click Browse, and locate and select the virtual disk.**

    If you haven't already created a virtual disk, you can use the Create a Virtual Hard Disk option and create one now.

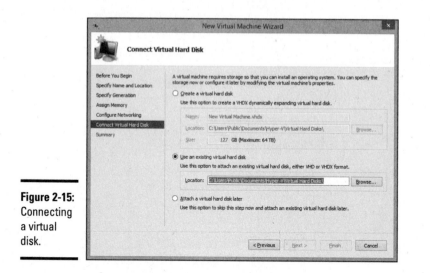

Figure 2-15:
Connecting
a virtual
disk.

13. **Click Next.**

A summary page is displayed indicating the selections you've made.

14. **Click Finish.**

The virtual machine is created.

Installing an Operating System

After you've created a virtual machine, the next step is to configure it to install an operating system. First, you'll need to get the installation media in the form of an .iso file (an .iso file is a disk image of a CD or DVD drive). After you have the .iso file in place, follow these steps:

1. **From the Hyper-V Manager, choose the new virtual machine and click Settings.**

The Settings dialog box appears, as shown in Figure 2-16.

2. **Click SCSI Controller in the Hardware list. Then select DVD Drive, and click Add.**

The configuration page shown in Figure 2-17 appears.

**Book IV
Chapter 2**

**Working with
Hyper-V**

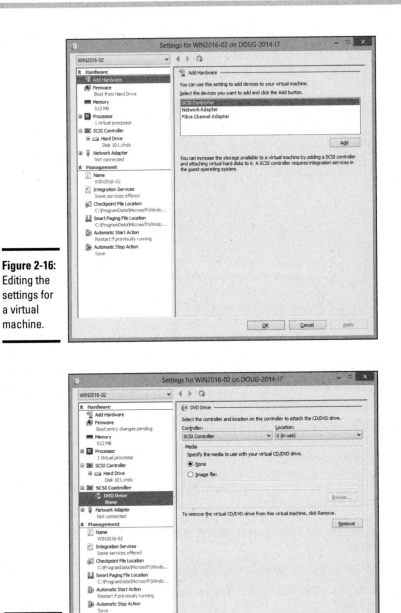

Figure 2-16:
Editing the
settings for
a virtual
machine.

Figure 2-17:
Configuring
a DVD drive.

3. **Click the Image File option, click Browse, and select the .iso file that contains the operating system's installation program.**

4. **Click OK.**

   You're returned to the Hyper-V Manager screen.

5. **With the new virtual machine still selected, click Connect.**

   A console window opens, showing that the virtual machine is currently turned off (see Figure 2-18).

Figure 2-18: Viewing a virtual machine through a console.

6. **Click Connect.**

7. **Click Start.**

   The virtual machine powers up.

8. **When prompted to press a key to boot from the CD or DVD, press any key.**

   The operating system's installation program starts.

9. **Follow the instructions of the installation program to install the operating system.**

   That's all there is to it. You've now successfully created a Hyper-V virtual machine!

Chapter 3: Working with VMware

In This Chapter

✔ Installing VMware Player

✔ Creating and using virtual machines

✔ Installing VMware Tools

*V*irtualization is a complex subject, and mastering the ins and outs of working with a full-fledged virtualization system like VMware Infrastructure is a topic that's beyond the scope of this book. You can dip your toes into the shallow end of the virtualization pond, however, by downloading and experimenting with VMware's free virtualization product, called VMware Player. You can download it from www.vmware.com.

This chapter is a brief introduction to VMware's virtualization platform and creating and using virtual machines with VMware Player.

Looking at vSphere

vSphere is an umbrella term for VMware's virtualization platform. The term *vSphere* encompasses several distinct products and technologies that work together to provide a complete infrastructure for virtualization. These products and technologies include the following:

✦ **ESXi:** ESXi is the core of vSphere; it is a Type-1 hypervisor that runs on host computers to manage the execution of virtual machines, allocating resources to the virtual machines as needed. ESXi comes in two basic flavors:

- *Installable:* The Installable version of software can be installed onto the hard drive on a host computer, much as any other operating system can be installed.

- *Embedded:* The Embedded version runs as firmware that is actually built into the host computer. It's preinstalled into read-only memory by the manufacturer of the host computer.

✦ **vCenter Server:** vCenter Server is a server application that runs on Windows Server installed in a virtual machine. vCenter is the central point for creating new virtual machines, starting and stopping virtual machines, and performing other management tasks in a vSphere environment.

✦ **vCenter Client:** vCenter Client is a Windows application that you use to access the features of a vCenter Server remotely. vCenter Client is the tool you'll work with most when you manage a vSphere environment.

✦ **VMFS:** VMFS, which stands for *Virtual Machine File System,* is the file system used by vSphere to manage disk resources that are made available to virtual machines. With VMFS, you can create *data stores* to access physical disk devices, and you can then create *volumes* on these data stores to make disk storage available to virtual machines.

Getting Started with VMware Player

VMware player is a simplified version of the vSphere environment that provides many of vSphere's features but does not utilize the Type-1 ESXi hypervisor. Instead, VMware Player is a Type-2 hypervisor that runs within a Windows environment. VMware player is useful for learning about virtualization and for simple desktop virtualization, but not for production use. I'm covering it here because experimenting with VMware Player is a great way to learn some of the basic concepts of virtualization.

Figure 3-1 shows VMware Player's main screen. From this screen, you can create a new virtual machine or run one of the virtual machines you've already created. As you can see in the figure, I've created several virtual machines: two that run various versions of Fedora (a popular Linux distribution) and one that runs Windows Server 2016.

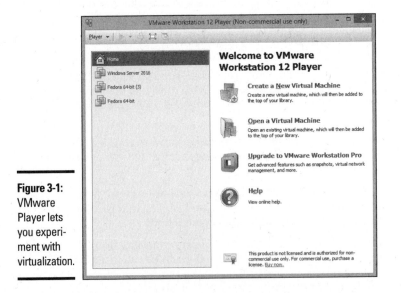

Figure 3-1:
VMware
Player lets
you experi-
ment with
virtualization.

You can run an existing virtual machine by selecting the virtual machine and clicking Play Virtual Machine. This launches the virtual machine, which opens in a new window, as shown in Figure 3-2. When you launch a virtual machine, the virtual machine behaves exactly as a real computer would when you power it up: First, it initializes its virtual hardware devices; then it loads the guest operating system that has been installed in the virtual machine.

In Figure 3-2, Windows Server 2016 has booted up and is waiting for you to press Ctrl+Alt+Del to log on.

Figure 3-2: A virtual machine running Windows Server 2016.

The prompt to press Ctrl+Alt+Del shown in Figure 3-2 illustrates one of the peculiar details of running a virtual machine within a host operating system. When you press Ctrl+Alt+Del, which operating system — the host or the guest — responds? The answer is that the host operating system responds to the Ctrl+Alt+Del before the guest operating system ever sees it.

To get around this limitation, VMware uses the special keyboard shortcut Ctrl+Alt+End to send a Ctrl+Alt+Del to the guest operating system. Alternatively, you can use the VM drop-down menu that appears in the menu bar above the virtual-machine menu. This menu lists several actions that can be applied to the virtual machine, including Send Ctrl+Alt+Del.

Another detail you should know about when working with a virtual machine is that when you click in the virtual machine's window, the VM captures your mouse and keyboard, so your input will be directed to the virtual machine rather than the host computer. If you want to break the bonds of the virtual machine and return to the host computer, press Ctrl+Alt.

Creating a Virtual Machine

Creating a new virtual machine in VMware Player is relatively easy. In fact, the most challenging part is getting hold of the installation disc for the operating system you want to install on the VM. Remember that a virtual machine is useless without a guest operating system, so you need to have the installation disc available before you create the virtual machine.

If you just want to experiment with virtualization and don't have extra licenses of a Windows Server operating system, you can always download an evaluation copy of Windows Server 2016 from www.microsoft.com. The evaluation period is six months, so you'll have plenty of time to experiment.

The downloadable trial version of Windows Server 2016 comes in the form of an .iso file, which is an image of a DVD file that you can mount within your virtual machine as though it were a real disk.

When you have your .iso file or installation disc ready to go, you can create a new virtual machine by following these steps:

1. **Click Create a New Virtual Machine on the VMware Player home screen (refer to Figure 3-1).**

    This brings up the New Virtual Machine Wizard, shown in Figure 3-3.

Figure 3-3: The first page of the New Virtual Machine Wizard.

2. **Choose the installation option you want to use.**

   You have three choices:

   - *Installer Disc:* Select this option and then choose from the drop-down list the drive you'll install from if you want to install from an actual CD or DVD.

   - *Install Disc Image File (iso):* Select this option, click the Browse button, and browse to the `.iso` file that contains the installation image.

   - *I Will Install the Operating System Later:* Select this option if you want to create the virtual machine now but install the operating system later.

   Note that the remaining steps in this procedure assume that you select a Windows Server 2016 `.iso` file as the installation option.

3. **Click Next.**

   The screen shown in Figure 3-4 appears.

Figure 3-4:
Creating a name and specifying the virtual machine disk location.

4. **Enter a name for the virtual machine.**

5. **Enter the location of the virtual machine's disk file.**

   If you want, you can click the Browse button and browse to the folder where you want to create the file.

6. **Click Next.**

   The wizard asks for the size of the disk to create for the virtual machine, as shown in Figure 3-5.

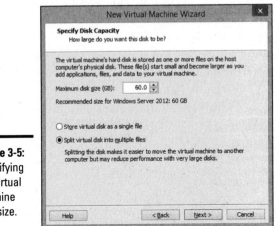

Figure 3-5:
Specifying
the virtual
machine
disk size.

7. **Set the size of the virtual machine's hard drive.**

   The default setting is 40GB, but you can change it depending on your
   needs. Note that you must have sufficient space available on the host
   computer's disk drive.

8. **Click Next.**

   The wizard displays a final confirmation page, as shown in Figure 3-6.

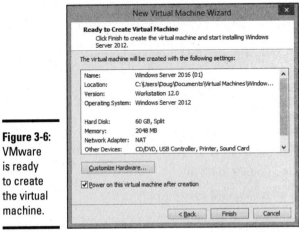

Figure 3-6:
VMware
is ready
to create
the virtual
machine.

9. **Click Finish.**

The wizard creates the virtual machine and then starts it. Because the machine doesn't have an operating system installed, it boots from the CD/DVD installation image you specified back in Step 2. In this case, I booted with the Windows Server 2016 evaluation software disk image, so the new virtual machine displays the Windows Setup screen, as shown in Figure 3-7.

Figure 3-7:
Installing
Windows
Server 2016
on a virtual
machine.

10. **Follow the steps to install the operating system.**

Installing an operating system on a virtual machine is exactly the same as installing it on a physical computer, except that the installation screens appear within a virtual machine window.

When the operating system is installed, you're done! You can start using the virtual machine.

You can adjust the hardware configuration of a virtual machine by choosing VM⇨Settings while the virtual machine is running. This command brings up the Virtual Machine Settings dialog box, shown in Figure 3-8. From this dialog box, you can adjust the virtual machine's hardware configuration, including the amount of RAM available to the virtual machine and the number of processor cores. You can also adjust the disk drive size; add CD, DVD, or floppy drives; and configure network adapters, USB connections, and sound and display settings.

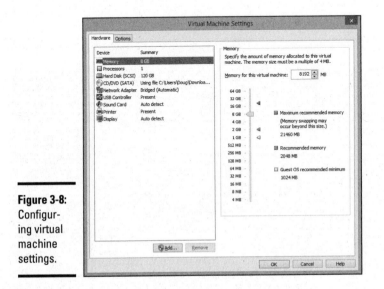

Figure 3-8:
Configuring virtual machine settings.

Installing VMware Tools

When you've installed an operating system into a VMware virtual machine, you should install an important application called *VMware Tools* before you do anything else. VMware Tools provides a variety of important functions for a VMware virtual machine:

✦ Significantly improved graphics performance

✦ Shared folders, which lets you share folders between the virtual machine and the host, making it easy to exchange files between the two

✦ A shared clipboard, which lets you copy and paste between the virtual machine and the host

✦ Synchronized time between the guest and host

✦ Better control of the mouse between guest and host

To install VMware Tools, follow this procedure:

1. Start the virtual machine.

2. On the menu of the VMware console window, choose Player ⇨ Manage ⇨ Install VMware Tools.

The dialog box shown in Figure 3-9 appears.

Figure 3-9: Installing VMware Tools.

3. Click Download and Install.

The VMware Tools are downloaded to the guest operating system. The Setup program displays the Welcome screen, shown in Figure 3-10.

Figure 3-10: Installing VMware Tools.

TIP

If the Setup program doesn't automatically start, press Windows+R, type **d:\setup.exe**, and press Enter. This will manually start the Setup program.

4. Follow the instructions in the Setup program to install the VMware tools.

When the tools are installed, you'll be prompted to restart the virtual machine.

Chapter 4: Virtualizing Your Desktops

In This Chapter

✔ Considering the possibility of virtualizing desktops instead of servers

✔ Looking at two approaches to virtualizing desktops

✔ Working with VMware's Horizon View

✔ Using Citrix XenApp

*V*irtualization is most often applied to server computers. However, more and more organizations are also applying virtualization to desktops, replacing traditional Windows desktop computers with virtual desktops that are accessed from a nontraditional type of device.

In this chapter, I present a basic overview of desktop virtualization and its benefits and introduce you to some of the technologies that can be used to implement virtual desktop infrastructure (VDI).

Introducing Desktop Virtualization

The term *desktop virtualization* refers to any software that separates an end-user's Windows desktop environment from the hardware that the environment runs on. Desktop virtualization is meant to address some of the fundamental weaknesses of the traditional practice of giving each user his or her own Windows workstation.

Here are just a few of the problems that desktop virtualization addresses:

✦ Windows workstations must be configured individually for each user. If your organization has 100 workstations and you decide to update your accounting software, you have to figure out how to deploy the update to 100 computers.

✦ Windows software frequently needs to be updated. Updates are normally delivered via Windows Update. However, deploying Windows updates separately to all your desktop computers is fraught with peril. A particular Windows update might work well on 99 percent of all computers, which means that if your organization has 100 computers, that update is likely to not work on at least one of them. That means a trip to that computer to diagnose the problem caused by the update and get the user back up and running.

✦ If a user's computer fails, that computer must be replaced. To replace the computer, you'll need to rebuild the user's profile, reinstall the user's applications, and perform other configuration work to restore the user's desktop environment.

✦ Windows computers have a dreaded thing called the C: drive. Any data stored on the C: drive belongs to that computer alone and is not easily backed up to the network. Thus, if the user's C: drive dies, its data is likely to die with it.

✦ If a user moves to another desk or office, the user must take her computer with her.

✦ If a user wants to work from home, the user can't easily access her desktop environment from her home computer. There are solutions for this problem, such as remote access software like GoToMyPC (www. gotomypc.com), but those solutions introduce problems of their own.

✦ If a user has a laptop computer in addition to a desktop computer, the user must make a special effort to ensure that the data on the desktop computer is synchronized with the data on the laptop.

✦ The user may have devices with different platforms than his or her desktop computer. For example, a user might have a Windows computer at work, a MacBook Pro at home, and an Apple iPad for the road. These platforms aren't compatible with one another, so the user can't run the same software on all three.

Desktop virtualization addresses all these problems (and more) by moving the user's desktop environment from a desktop computer to a central host computer. Then the user can access the desktop environment from any device that is compatible with the VDI technology chosen to virtualize the desktop. The advantages of this arrangement are many:

✦ If the user's computer dies, the user's desktop does not die with it. You can replace the failed computer with any other computer and simply reconnect to the virtual desktop.

✦ Operating systems and application software can be centrally managed. There is no need to visit a user's desk to install or update software.

✦ The user's desktop can be accessed from different types of devices. So, a user can access his or her desktop from a Windows computer, a MacBook, an iPad, an Android table, or even from an iPhone or Android phone.

✦ You can use thin clients at users' desks rather than full-blown Windows computers. A *thin client* is a small computer that has just enough processing power (CPU, RAM, and disk) to run the client piece of the desktop virtualization platform. Typically, the thin client runs an embedded version of Linux that is specially configured to run the client software that accesses the virtual desktop. In most cases, the end-user is not even aware that this is happening — to the user, the experience is identical to having a standard Windows computer at his or her desk.

✦ In some desktop virtualization environments, multiple users share a common Windows environment, which means that an application needs to be installed only once for it to be available for multiple users, and operating system patches need to be applied just once rather than to multiple computers.

✦ All data is kept on the host computers, which means the data can be centrally managed and backed up.

Considering Two Approaches to Desktop Virtualization

There are at least two distinct approaches to implementing desktop virtualization. The first approach is to simply create a separate virtual machine for each user and provide a way for the users to efficiently connect to their virtual machines. This approach is usually referred to as *virtual desktop infrastructure* (VDI). VDI solutions are usually built using traditional virtualization products such as Microsoft's Hyper-V or VMware's ESDi hypervisor.

The second approach is to use a single server that is designed to support multiple users and provide a way for each user to connect to his or her session on the server. This approach is often called *terminal services,* because it's based on the terminal services role that is a standard part of all versions of Windows Server.

Technically, with Windows Server 2008, Microsoft changed the name of Terminal Services to *Remote Desktop Services* to emphasize the role of Terminal Services for virtualizing desktops. The IT industry is pretty reluctant to change its phraseology, however, so most IT professionals still call it *terminal services* even though that term has been obsolete for almost a decade.

The remaining sections of this chapter describe two popular desktop virtualization products that use these two approaches. The first is VMware's Horizon View, which builds on VMware's virtualization platform. The second is Citrix XenApp, which builds on Windows Terminal Services.

Book IV Chapter 4

Virtualizing Your Desktops

Looking at VMware's Horizon View

With VMware's virtualization infrastructure, you could easily implement desktop virtualization by simply creating virtual machines for each of your users' desktops and having your users connect to their virtual machines using Remote Desktop Connection (RDC). However, you'll quickly start to realize some of the limitations of this approach.

First, you'll probably discover that the RDC client is not very efficient when it comes to intensive graphics applications. Watching YouTube videos over RDC can be frustrating, as can working with graphically oriented programs such as Adobe Photoshop.

You'll also discover that managing users' access to virtual desktop machines is difficult with vSphere. vSphere is designed to create and manage virtual servers that are typically accessed only by IT personnel. Access to those servers is controlled through Active Directory credentials; in other words, if you don't know the password, you can't log in. But vSphere isn't really designed to create hundreds of desktop VMs and make them available to hundreds of users.

To address these and other issues, VMware offers a product called VMware Horizon View that builds on the core functions of vSphere and adds features specifically designed for desktop virtualization. Here's a short list of the some of the more important features of Horizon:

+ **vSphere Desktop:** A version of vSphere specifically designed for running up to tens of thousands of desktop virtual machines

+ **vCenter Desktop:** A version of vCenter designed specifically for managing virtual resources such as hosts, RAM, processors, and disk storage in a virtual desktop environment

+ **Horizon View:** A management tool designed to provision and deploy virtual desktops

+ **Horizon View Client:** Client software for accessing virtual desktops on a variety of platforms, including Windows, Mac, iOS, and Amazon devices

+ **Horizon View Composer:** A tool for cloning desktop VMs and for managing software and operating system updates on pools of similar desktop VMs

Looking at Citrix XenApp

Citrix XenApp is a desktop virtualization environment that uses Windows Terminal Services to enable multiple users to access remote desktops from a variety of client devices, including Windows, Mac, iOS, and Amazon devices. Unlike VMware's Horizon View, XenApp does not create a separate virtual machine for each user. Instead, when users connect to XenApp, they log in to separate terminal services sessions on a common Windows server. The users then have access to all the resources and applications that are available to the Windows server.

Users connect with XenApp by using a client application called the Citrix Receiver, which can be run on Windows, Mac, iOS, or Android devices. Figure 4-1 shows Citrix Receiver running on a Windows 8.1 system.

When you configure a XenApp server, you create and publish *desktops* and *applications* that users can remotely connect to. Then, when the user connects to the XenApp server, the user is shown the applications that he or she is authorized to use. For example, Figure 4-1 shows a typical Citrix Receiver screen connected to a XenApp server. In this case, the user is authorized to open a desktop and two applications.

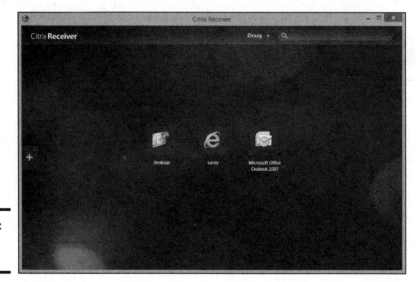

Figure 4-1:
Citrix
Receiver.

Virtualizing Your
Desktops

If the user connects to a desktop, the user sees an entire Windows desktop environment, complete with a Start menu that grants access to applications, as well as Explorer to browse disk resources. Figure 4-2 shows the Citrix Receiver connected to a desktop.

Figure 4-2:
Connecting
to a desktop.

On the other hand, a user can connect to an individual application rather than to a desktop. This feature is called *application virtualization*. When you connect to an application, that application runs on the server but only that one application's window is shown on the user's device. In other words, the user sees the individual application rather than a complete desktop. The user can then use the application as if the application were natively running on his or her device, even if the user's device is a non-Windows device.

Figure 4-3 shows an example of Microsoft Excel running on an iPhone 6 Plus via Citrix Receiver. As you can see, Citrix Receiver makes the desktop Microsoft Excel application available on my iPhone exactly as it's available on my Windows desktop. In fact, I could choose File⇨Open to summon an Open dialog box which would allow me to browse the network to open any file that would be available to me from my Windows desktop. This feature effectively extends my desktop applications to my iPhone.

Figure 4-3:
Viewing
Excel on an
iPhone.

Book V

Remote Networking

Mobile Services Properties

General | Details

Mobile Services

Exchange ActiveSync
- ☑ Enable user initiated synchronization
- ☑ Enable up-to-date notifications via SMTP and Text Messaging
  - ☑ Enable notifications to user specified SMTP addresses
- ☑ Enable Direct Push over HTTP(s)

Device Security...

Outlook Mobile Access
- ☑ Enable Outlook Mobile Access
- ☑ Enable unsupported devices

OK   Cancel   Apply   Help

Find out how to enable VPN on an iPhone in an article at www.dummies.com/
extras/networkingaio.

Contents at a Glance

Chapter 1: Managing Mobile Devices 415

Chapter 2: Working with VPN for Remote Access 429

Chapter 3: Using Remote Desktop Access 435

Chapter 4: Using Remote Assistance 447

Chapter 1: Managing Mobile Devices

In This Chapter

✔ **Looking at mobile devices**

✔ **Considering security implications**

✔ **Configuring iOS devices**

✔ **Configuring Android devices**

A computer consultant once purchased a used BlackBerry device on eBay for $15.50. When he put in a new battery and turned on the device, he discovered that it contained confidential emails and personal contact information for executives of a well-known financial institution.

Oops!

It turns out that a former executive with the company sold his old BlackBerry on eBay a few months after he left the firm. He'd assumed that because he'd removed the battery, everything on the BlackBerry had been erased.

The point of this true story is that mobile devices such as smartphones and tablet computers pose a special set of challenges for network administrators. These challenges are now being faced even by administrators of small networks. Just a few years ago, only large companies had BlackBerry or other mobile devices that integrated with Exchange email, for example. Now it isn't uncommon for companies with just a few employees to have mobile devices connected to the company network.

This chapter is a brief introduction to mobile devices and the operating systems they run, with an emphasis on iPhone and Android devices. You'll find out how these devices can interact with Exchange email and the steps you can take to ensure their security.

The Many Types of Mobile Devices

Once upon a time, there were mobile phones and PDAs. A mobile phone was just that: a handheld telephone you could take with you. The good ones had nice features such as a call log, an address book, and perhaps a crude game but not much else. PDAs — *Personal Digital Assistants* — were little handheld computers designed to replace the old-fashioned Day-Timer books people used to carry around with them to keep track of their appointment calendars and address books.

All that changed when cellular providers began adding data capabilities to their networks. Now, cellphones can have complete mobile Internet access. This fact has resulted in the addition of sophisticated PDA features to mobile phones and phone features to PDAs so that the distinctions are blurred.

The term *mobile device* is used to describe a wide assortment of devices that you can hold in one hand and that are connected through a wireless network. The term *handheld* is a similar generic name for such devices. The following list describes some of the most common specifics of mobile devices:

✦ **Mobile phone:** A *mobile phone* (or *cellphone*) is a mobile device whose primary purpose is to enable phone service. Most mobile phones include features such as text messaging, address books, appointment calendars, and games, and they may provide Internet access.

✦ **Smartphone:** A *smartphone* is a mobile phone with advanced features that aren't typically found on mobile phones. There's no clearly drawn line between mobile phones and smartphones. One distinction is whether the phone can provide integrated access to corporate email. The screen on a smartphone is typically bigger than the screen on a traditional cellphone, and the most popular models (such as the iPhone and most Android devices) do not have a keyboard at all.

✦ **Android:** Android is an open-source operating system for smartphones developed by Google. Android is far and away the most popular platform for smartphones, being used on more than 80 percent of the smartphones sold in 2015.

✦ **iOS:** iOS is the operating system used on Apple's popular iPhone and iPad mobile devices. Although outnumbered by Android devices, many people consider iOS devices to be more innovative than Android devices. The main thing that holds iOS back in market share is its cost: Apple devices are considerably more expensive than their Android equivalents.

✦ **BlackBerry:** Once upon a time, BlackBerry was the king of the smartphone game. BlackBerry had a virtual monopoly on mobile devices that synchronized well with Microsoft Exchange. Now that Android and Apple devices do that just as well as (if not better) than BlackBerry, BlackBerry has fallen out of vogue. However, BlackBerry is still around, and there are still plenty of BlackBerry users out there. (Note that newer BlackBerry phones run Android rather than the old proprietary BlackBerry operating system.)

Considering Security for Mobile Devices

As a network administrator, one of your main responsibilities regarding mobile devices is to keep them secure. Unfortunately, that's a significant challenge. Here are some of the reasons why:

✦ **Mobile devices connect to your network via other networks that are out of your control.** You can go to great lengths to set up firewalls, encryption, and a host of other security features, but mobile devices connect via public networks whose administrators may not be as conscientious as you.

✦ **Mobile devices are easy to lose.** A user might leave her smartphone at a restaurant or hotel, or it might fall out of his pocket on the subway.

✦ **Mobile devices run operating systems that aren't as security-conscious as Windows.**

✦ **Users who wouldn't dare install renegade software on their desktop computers think nothing of downloading free games or other applications to their handheld devices.** Who knows what kinds of viruses or Trojans these downloads carry?

✦ **Inevitably, someone will buy his own handheld device and connect it to your network without your knowledge or permission.**

Here are some recommendations for beefing up security for your mobile devices:

✦ Establish clear, consistent policies for mobile devices, and enforce them.

✦ Make sure employees understand that they aren't allowed to bring their own devices into your network unless you have made special provisions to allow it. In particular, I recommend you establish a separate subnet for employee-owned devices so that your employee devices don't contend for IP addresses with your main network. For more information about subnetting, refer to Book III, Chapter 3.

✦ Train your users in the security risks associated with using mobile devices.

✦ Implement antivirus protection for your mobile devices.

Managing iOS Devices

In 2007, the Apple iPhone, one of the most innovative little gadgets in many, many years, hit the technology market. As a result, in just a few short years, the iPhone captured a huge slice of a market dominated almost exclusively by RIM and its BlackBerry devices. Since then, the iPhone's share of the mobile-phone market has grown beyond that of the former king, BlackBerry.

The success of the iPhone was due in large part to the genius of its operating system, iOS. In 2010, Apple released the iPad, a tablet computer that runs the same operating system as the iPhone. And in 2012, Apple introduced a smaller version of the iPad: the iPad mini. Together, these devices are commonly known as "iOS devices."

Understanding the iPhone

The iPhone is essentially a combination of four devices:

✦ A cellphone

✦ An iPod

✦ A digital camera

✦ An Internet device with its own web browser (Safari) and applications, such as email, calendar, and contact management

The most immediately noticeable feature of the iPhone is its lack of a keyboard. Instead, nearly the entire front surface of the iPhone is a high-resolution, touch-sensitive LCD. The display is not only the main output device of the iPhone, but also its main input device. The display can become a keypad input for dialing a telephone number or a keyboard for entering text. You can also use various finger gestures, such as tapping icons to start programs or pinching to zoom in the display.

The iPhone has several other innovative features:

✦ An accelerometer tracks the motion of the iPhone in three directions. The main use of the accelerometer is to adjust the orientation of the display from landscape to portrait based on how the user is holding the phone. Some other applications — mostly games — use the accelerometer as well.

✦ A Wi-Fi interface lets the iPhone connect to local Wi-Fi networks for faster Internet access.

✦ GPS capability provides location awareness for many applications, including Google Maps.

✦ The virtual private network (VPN) client lets you connect to your internal network.

Of all the unique features of the iPhone, probably the most important is its huge collection of third-party applications that can be downloaded from a special web portal, the App Store. Many of these applications are free or cost just a few dollars. (Many are just 99 cents or $1.99.) As of this writing, more than 1.6 million apps — everything from business productivity to games — were available from the App Store.

Understanding the iPad

The iPad is essentially an iPhone without the phone but with a larger screen. Apart from these basic differences, an iPad is nearly identical to an iPhone. Any application that can run on an iPhone can also run on an iPad, and many applications are designed to take special advantage of the iPad's larger screen.

All the iOS information that follows in this chapter applies equally to iPhones and iPads.

Integrating iOS devices with Exchange

An iOS device can integrate with Microsoft Exchange email via the Exchange ActiveSync feature, which is enabled by default on Exchange 2010 and later versions.

To verify the Exchange ActiveSync feature for an individual mailbox, follow these steps:

1. **Choose Start ➪ Administrative Tools ➪ Active Directory Users and Computers.**

   The Active Directory Users and Computers console opens.

2. **Expand the domain and then locate the user you want to enable mobile access for.**

3. **Right-click the user and then choose Properties from the contextual menu.**

4. **Click the Exchange Features tab.**

   The Exchange Features options are displayed, as shown in Figure 1-1.

5. **Ensure that the Exchange ActiveSync option is enabled.**

   If the options aren't already enabled, right-click each option and choose Enable from the contextual menu.

6. **Click OK.**

7. **Repeat Steps 5 and 6 for any other users you want to enable mobile access for.**

8. **Close Active Directory Users and Computers.**

That's all there is to it. After you enable these features, any users running Windows Mobile can synchronize their handheld devices with their Exchange mailboxes.

Configuring an iOS device for Exchange email

After ActiveSync is enabled for the mailbox, you can configure an iPhone or iPad to tap into the Exchange account by following these steps:

1. **On the iPhone or iPad, tap Settings and then tap Mail, Contacts, Calendars.**

The screen shown in Figure 1-2 appears. This screen lists any existing email accounts that may already be configured on the phone and also lets you add a new account.

●●○○○ Verizon LTE   2:08 PM   ⦅ ✳ ■▯

 ‹ Settings **Mail, Contacts, Calendars**

ACCOUNTS

iCloud   ›
Contacts, Notes, Photos, Find My iPhone and 2 more...

BC&F Email   ›
Mail, Contacts, Calendars, Reminders, Notes

Add Account   ›

Fetch New Data   Push ›

MAIL

Preview   2 Lines ›

Show To/Cc Label   ⦅◯

Swipe Options   ›

Flag Style   Color ›

Ask Before Deleting   ⦅◯

Load Remote Images   ◯⦆

Organize By Thread   ◯⦆

Figure 1-2:
Adding
an email
account.

2. **Tap Add Account.**

The screen shown in Figure 1-3 appears, allowing you to choose the type of email account you want to add.

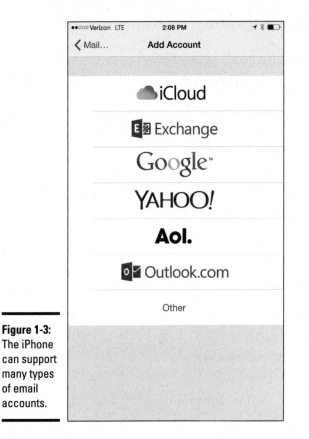

Figure 1-3:
The iPhone can support many types of email accounts.

3. **Tap Exchange.**

   The screen shown in Figure 1-4 appears, where you can enter basic information for your Exchange account.

4. **Enter your email address, password, and a description of the account.**

5. **Tap Next.**

   The screen shown in Figure 1-5 appears.

```
••○○○ Verizon  LTE        2:08 PM          ⚡ ✻ ▪▭

 Cancel           Exchange            Next


 Email        email@company.com

 Password     Required

 Description  My Exchange Account


              Exchange Device ID
          U1T2U1PE7P77H23QL5TDMMRRTK
```

Figure 1-4:
Enter your
email
address and
password.

6. **Enter either the DNS name or the IP address of your Exchange server in the Server field.**

   I entered **smtp.lowewriter.com** for my Exchange server, for example.

7. **Enter your domain name, your Windows username, and your Windows password in the appropriate fields.**

●●○○○ Verizon LTE   2:09 PM   ✈ ✳ ▪️◻️

Cancel   Next

Email   dlowe@bcf-engr.com

Server   Optional

Domain   Optional

Username   Required

Password   Required

Description Exchange

Exchange Device ID
U1T2U1PE7P77H23QL5TDMMRRTK

Figure 1-5:
Enter your
Exchange
server
information.

8. **Tap Next.**

   The screen shown in Figure 1-6 appears. Here, you select which mailbox features you want to synchronize: Mail, Contacts, Calendars, Reminders, and/or Notes.

9. **Select the features you want to synchronize and then tap Done.**

   The email account is created.

After the email account has been configured, the user can access it via the Mail icon on the iPhone's home screen.

Figure 1-6:
Select
features to
synchronize.

Managing Android Devices

This section is a brief introduction to the Android platform. You find out a bit about what Android actually is, and you discover the procedures for setting up Exchange email access on an Android phone.

Crucial differences exist between Android phones and iPhones, however. The most important difference — in many ways, the *only* important difference — is that Android phones are based on an open-source OS derived from Linux, which can be extended and adapted to work on a wide variety of hardware devices from different vendors. With the iPhone, you're locked into Apple hardware. With an Android phone, you can buy hardware from a variety of manufacturers.

Looking at the Android OS

Most people associate the Android OS with Google, and it's true that Google is the driving force behind Android. The Android OS is an open-source OS managed by the Open Handset Alliance (OHA). Google still plays a major role in the development of Android, but more than 50 companies are involved in the OHA, including hardware manufacturers (such as HTC, Intel, and Motorola), software companies (such as Google and eBay), and mobile phone operators (such as T-Mobile and Sprint-Nextel).

Technically speaking, Android is more than just an OS. It's also a complete *software stack,* which comprises several key components that work together to create the complete Android platform:

+ **The OS core,** which is based on the popular Linux OS

+ **A middleware layer,** which provides drivers and other support code to enable the OS core to work with the hardware devices that make up a complete phone, such as a touch-sensitive display, the cellphone radio, the speaker and microphone, Bluetooth or Wi-Fi networking components, and so on

+ **A set of core applications** that the user interacts with to make phone calls, read email, send text messages, take pictures, and so on

+ **A software development kit (SDK)** that lets third-party software developers create their own applications to run on an Android phone, as well as a marketplace where the applications can be marketed and sold, much as the App Store lets iPhone developers market and sell applications for the iPhone

Besides the basic features provided by all OSs, here are a few bonus features of the Android software stack:

+ An optimized graphical display engine that can produce sophisticated 2-D and 3-D graphics

+ GPS capabilities that provide location awareness that can be integrated with applications such as Google Maps

+ Compass and accelerometer capabilities that can determine whether the phone is in motion and in which direction it's pointed

+ A built-in SQL database server for data storage

+ Support for several network technologies, including Bluetooth and Wi-Fi

+ Built-in media support, including common formats for still images, audio, and video files

Perusing Android's core applications

The Android OS comes preconfigured with several standard applications, which provide the functionality that most people demand from a modern smartphone. These applications include

- ✦ **Dialer:** Provides the basic cellphone function that lets users make calls.
- ✦ **Browser:** A built-in web browser that's similar to Google's Chrome browser.
- ✦ **Messaging:** Provides text (SMS) and multimedia (MMS) messaging.
- ✦ **Email:** A basic email client that works best with Google's Gmail but that can be configured to work with other email servers, including Exchange.
- ✦ **Contacts:** Provides a contacts list that integrates with the Dialer and Email applications.
- ✦ **Camera:** Lets you use the phone's camera hardware (if any) to take pictures.
- ✦ **Calculator:** A simple calculator application.
- ✦ **Alarm Clock:** A basic alarm clock. You can set up to three different alarms.
- ✦ **Maps:** An integrated version of Google Maps.
- ✦ **YouTube:** An integrated version of YouTube.
- ✦ **Music:** An MP3 player similar to the iPod. You can purchase and download music files from Amazon.
- ✦ **Market:** Lets you purchase and download third-party applications for the Android phone.
- ✦ **Settings:** Lets you control various settings for the phone.

Integrating Android with Exchange

The Android's core Email application can integrate with Microsoft Exchange email. If you're using Exchange Server 2012, you must enable Exchange Mobile Services and then enable ActiveSync for the user's mailbox.

After you enable Exchange Mobile Services and ActiveSync on your Exchange server, you can easily configure the Android phone for email access. Just run the Email application on the Android phone, and follow the configuration steps, which ask you for basic information such as your email address, username, password, and Exchange mail server.

Chapter 2: Working with VPN for Remote Access

In This Chapter

✔ Examining VPN uses

✔ Looking at how VPN works

✔ Considering VPN clients and servers

✔ Pondering VPN hardware and software

*T*oday's network users frequently need to access their networks from remote locations: home offices, hotel rooms, beach villas, and their kid's soccer fields. In the early days of computer networking, the only real option for remotely accessing a network was to set up dialup access with telephone lines and modems, which was slow and unreliable. Today, enabling remote access to a local area network (LAN) is easily done with a virtual private network. Simply put, a virtual private network (VPN) enables remote users to access a LAN via any Internet connection.

This chapter is a short introduction to VPNs. You find out the basics of what a VPN is, how to set one up, and how to access one remotely. Enjoy!

Understanding VPN

A *virtual private network* (VPN) is a type of network connection that creates the illusion that you're directly connected to a network when in fact, you're not. For example, suppose you set up a LAN at your office, but you also occasionally work from home. But how will you access the files on your work computer from home?

✦ You could simply copy whatever files you need from your work computer onto a flash drive and take them home with you, work on the files, copy the updated files back to the flash drive, and take them back to work with you the next day.

✦ You could email the files to your personal email account, work on them at home, and then email the changed files back to your work email account.

✦ You could get a laptop and use the Windows Offline Files feature to automatically synchronize files from your work network with files on the laptop.

Or, you could set up a VPN that allows you to log on to your work network from home. The VPN uses a secured Internet connection to connect you directly to your work network, so you can access your network files as if you had a really long Ethernet cable that ran from your home computer all the way to the office and plugged directly into the work network.

There are at least three situations in which a VPN is the ideal solution:

✦ One or more workers need to occasionally work from home (as in the scenario just described). In this situation, a VPN connection establishes a connection between the home computer and the office network.

✦ Mobile users — who may not ever actually show up at the office — need to connect to the work network from mobile computers, often from locations like hotel rooms, clients' offices, airports, or coffee shops. This type of VPN configuration is similar to the home user's configuration, except that the exact location of the remote user's computer is not fixed.

✦ Your company has offices in two or more locations, each with its own LAN, and you want to connect the locations so that users on either network can access each other's network resources. In this situation, the VPN doesn't connect a single user with a remote network; instead, it connects two remote networks to each other.

Accessing your computer remotely

One of the most common reasons for setting up a VPN connection is to allow you to access a computer that is on your work network from a computer that is outside of your work network. For example, as a network administrator, you can use a VPN to connect to your work network from home. You can then use *Remote Desktop Connection* (RDC) to access your servers.

Before you can use RDC to connect remotely, you must enable remote access on you're the server computer. Right-click Computer on the Start menu and choose Properties, and then click Advanced System Settings. Click the Remote tab, and then select Allow Connections

Only from Computers Running Remote Desktop with Network Level Authentication. This option lets you grant remote access only to specific users, whom you can designate by clicking the Select Users button.

After remote access has been granted, you can access the computer remotely by connecting to the network with a VPN. Then choose Start ➪ All Programs ➪ Remote Desktop Connection. Enter the name of the computer you want to connect to, and then click Connect. You're prompted for your Windows username and password. After it's all connected, you can access the remote computer's desktop in a window.

Looking at VPN Security

The *V* in VPN stands for *virtual,* which means that a VPN creates the appearance of a local network connection when in fact the connection is made over a public network — the Internet. The term "tunnel" is sometimes used to describe a VPN because the VPN creates a tunnel between two locations, which can only be entered from either end. The data that travels through the tunnel from one end to the other is secure as long as it is within the tunnel — that is, within the protection provided by the VPN.

The *P* in VPN stands for *private,* which is the purpose of creating the tunnel. If the VPN didn't create effective security so that data can enter the tunnel only at one of the two ends, the VPN would be worthless; you may as well just open your network and your remote computer up to the Internet and let the hackers have their way.

Prior to VPN technology, the only way to provide private remote network connections was through actual private lines, which were (and still are) very expensive. For example, to set up a remote office you could lease a private T1 line from the phone company to connect the two offices. This private T1 line provided excellent security because it physically connected the two offices and could be accessed only from the two endpoints.

VPN provides the same point-to-point connection as a private leased line, but does it over the Internet instead of through expensive dedicated lines. To create the tunnel that guarantees privacy of the data as it travels from one end of the VPN to the other, the data is encrypted using special security protocols.

The most important of the VPN security protocols is *Internet Protocol Security* (IPSec), which is a collection of standards for encrypting and authenticating packets that travel on the Internet. In other words, it provides a way to encrypt the contents of a data packet so that only a person who knows the secret encryption keys can decode the data. And it provides a way to reliably identify the source of a packet so that the parties at either end of the VPN tunnel can trust that the packets are authentic.

Referring to the OSI reference model (see Book III, Chapter 1), the IPSec protocol operates at Layer 3 of the OSI model (the Network layer). What that means is that the IPSec protocol has no idea what kind of data is being carried by the packets it encrypts and authenticates. The IPSec protocol concerns itself only with the details of encrypting the contents of the packets (sometimes called the *payload*) and ensuring the identity of the sender.

Another commonly used VPN protocol is Layer 2 Tunneling Protocol (L2TP). This protocol doesn't provide data encryption. Instead, it's designed to create end-to-end connections — *tunnels* — through which data can travel. L2TP is actually a combination of two older protocols: Layer 2 Forwarding Protocol (L2FP, from Cisco) and Point-to-Point Tunneling Protocol (PPTP, from Microsoft).

Many VPNs today use a combination of L2TP and IPSec: L2TP Over IPSec. This type of VPN combines the best features of L2TP and IPSec to provide a high degree of security and reliability.

Understanding VPN Servers and Clients

A VPN connection requires a VPN server — the gatekeeper at one end of the tunnel — and a VPN client at the other end. The main difference between the server and the client is that the client initiates the connection with the server, and a VPN client can establish a connection with just one server at a time. However, a server can accept connections from many clients.

Typically, the VPN server is a separate hardware device, most often a security appliance such as a Cisco ASA security appliance. VPN servers can also be implemented in software. For example, Windows Server 2008 includes built-in VPN capabilities even though they're not easy to configure. And a VPN server can be implemented in Linux as well.

Figure 2-1 shows one of the many VPN configuration screens for a Cisco ASA appliance. This screen provides the configuration details for an IPSec VPN connection. The most important item of information on this screen is the Pre-Shared Key, which is used to encrypt the data sent over the VPN. The client will need to provide the identical key in order to participate in the VPN.

A VPN client is usually software that runs on a client computer that wants to connect to the remote network. The VPN client software must be configured with the IP address of the VPN server as well as authentication information such as a username and the Pre-Shared Key that will be used to encrypt the data. If the key used by the client doesn't match the key used by the server, the VPN server will reject the connection request from the client.

Figure 2-2 shows a typical VPN software client. When the client is configured with the correct connection information (which you can do by clicking the New button), you just click Connect. After a few moments, the VPN client will announce that the connection has been established and the VPN is connected.

Figure 2-1:
An IPSec
configura-
tion page on
a Cisco ASA
security
appliance.

Figure 2-2:
A VPN client.

A VPN client can also be a hardware device, like another security appliance. This is most common when the VPN is used to connect two networks at separate locations. For example, suppose your company has an office in Pixley and a second office in Hooterville. Each office has its own network with servers and client computers. The easiest way to connect these offices with a VPN would be to put an identical security appliance at each location. Then, you could configure the security appliances to communicate with each other over a VPN.

Chapter 3: Using Remote Desktop Access

In This Chapter

✔ Enabling the remote desktop feature

✔ Connecting to a computer remotely

✔ Using keyboard shortcuts in a Remote Desktop session

✔ Setting options for Remote Desktop

*W*indows provides two distinct built-in ways to access a computer remotely:

✦ **Remote Desktop Connection (RDC)** is designed to let you log into a Windows computer from a remote location. This is useful for managing a server without having to actually go to the computer room and accessing the server's console, or for accessing a virtual server that has not physical console.

✦ **Remote Assistance** is used to connect to an existing session of another Windows computer so that you can provide technical support for the other user.

This chapter shows you how to use the Remote Desktop Connection feature. For information about using the Remote Assistance feature, refer to the next chapter.

Enabling Remote Desktop Connection

Before you can use RDC to access a server, you must enable remote access on the server. To do that, follow these steps (on the server computer, not your desktop computer):

1. **Open the Control Panel and click System.**

   This step brings up the System settings page.

2. **Click the Remote Settings link.**

   The remote access options appear, as shown in Figure 3-1.

Figure 3-1:
Configuring
remote
access.

3. **Select the Allow Remote Connections to This Computer radio button.**

4. **Click OK.**

You're done! Repeat this procedure for each server computer you want to allow access to.

You can click the Select Users button to create a list of users who are authorized to access the computer remotely. Note that all members of the Administrators group are automatically granted access, so you don't have to add administrators to this list.

There's no question that RDC is convenient and useful. It's also inherently dangerous, however. Don't enable it unless you've taken precautions to secure your Administrator accounts by using strong passwords. Also, you should already have a firewall installed to keep unwanted visitors out of your network. For more information on account security, see Book II, Chapter 2.

Connecting Remotely

After you've enabled remote access on a server, you can connect to the server by using the remote desktop client that's automatically installed with Windows. Here's the procedure:

1. **Click the Start button and type the word** Remote. **Then click the
Remote Desktop Connection icon.**

The Remote Desktop Connection client comes to life, as shown in
Figure 3-2.

Figure 3-2:
Connecting
with Remote
Desktop
Connection.

2. **Enter the name of the computer you want to connect to.**

Alternatively, you can use the drop-down list to select the computer
from the list of available computers.

You can also enter the IP address of the computer you want to connect to.

3. **Click the Connect button.**

You're connected to the computer you selected, and then prompted for
login credentials, as shown in Figure 3-3.

Figure 3-3:
Logging in
to a remote
computer.

4. **Enter your username and password, and then click OK.**

Assuming you enter valid credentials, the desktop of the remote
computer is displayed, as shown in Figure 3-4.

Figure 3-4:
Logging in
to a remote
computer.

5. **Use the remote computer!**

You may notice in Figure 3-4 that the Remote Desktop window is not
large enough to display the entire desktop of the remote computer. As a
result, scroll bars appear to allow you to scroll the desktop horizontally
or vertically. You can always maximize the Remote Desktop window to
see the entire desktop of the remote computer.

Here are a few other tips for working with Remote Desktop Connection:

✦ **Remote Desktop allows only one user at a time to log in to the remote
computer.** If another user is remotely logged in when you try to connect,
you'll get a notice informing you that another user is already logged on.
You can either cancel or attempt to barge in on the other user's remote
session. If you choose the latter option, the other user will see a message
stating that you want to connect. If the other user accepts your request,
the other user is logged off and you're logged in. If the other user denies
your request, your attempt to log in is canceled. If the user does not
respond, eventually Windows will kick the other user off and let you in.

✦ **When you're using the Remote Desktop Connection client, you can't
just press Alt+Tab to get another program running on the client computer.** Instead, you must first minimize the RDC client's window by clicking its minimize button. Then you can access other programs running on
your computer.

✦ **If you minimize the RDC client window, you have to provide your
logon credentials again when you return.** This security feature is there
in case you forget that you have an RDC session open.

If you use RDC a lot on a particular computer (such as your own desktop computer), I suggest that you create a shortcut to RDC and place it on the desktop, at the top of the Start menu, or in the Quick Launch portion of the taskbar.

✦ **RDC has several useful configuration options that you can access by clicking the Options button.**

For more information about these options, refer to the section "Configuring Remote Desktop Options" later in this chapter.

Using Keyboard Shortcuts for Remote Desktop

When you're working in a Remote Desktop session, some of the standard Windows keyboard shortcuts don't work exactly as you expect them to. Table 3-1 lists the special keyboard shortcuts you can use in a Remote Desktop session.

Table 3-1	Keyboard Shortcuts for Remote Desktop
Shortcut	*What It Does*
Ctrl+Alt+Break	Toggles between full screen and windowed views.
Ctrl+Alt+Pause	Similar to Ctrl+Alt+Break, but instead of maximizing the remote window to full screen, it displays the remote window against a black background.
Alt+Insert	Cycles between applications running on the remote desktop, the same as Alt+Tab on your local machine.
Alt+PageUp	Same as Alt+Insert.
Alt+PageDown	Similar to Alt+Insert, but reverses the order in which applications are cycled. This is the same as Alt+Shift+Tab on your local machine.
Ctrl+Alt+End	Sends a Ctrl+Alt+Del to the remote desktop.
Alt+Home	Brings up the Start menu on the remote system.
Alt+Delete	Opens the Windows menu on a window in the remote desktop. (The Windows menu is the one at the top left of every window, with options to move, resize, minimize, maximize, and close the window.)
Ctrl+Alt+Plus Sign (+)	Captures a screen image of the entire remote desktop and saves it to the Clipboard. This is the same as pressing Print Screen on your local machine.
Ctrl+Alt+Minus Sign (–)	Captures an image of the current window and saves it to the Clipboard. This is the same as pressing Alt+Tab on your local machine.

Configuring Remote Desktop Options

Before you connect to a remote desktop session, you can set a variety of options that affect how the remote desktop session will behave. To summon these options, click the Start button, type the word **Remote**, and then click the Remote Desktop Connection icon. When the Remote Desktop Connection window appears (refer to Figure 3-2), click the Options button at the bottom left of the window. This brings up the Remote Desktop options, as shown in Figure 3-5.

Figure 3-5:
Setting the options for Remote Desktop Connection.

Figure 3-5 shows the General tab of the Remote Desktop options. On this tab, you can enter the name or IP address of the computer you want to access remotely and the username you want to connect with. You can also save the settings you've created via the other tabs or open a settings file you've previously saved.

When you click the Save or Save As buttons, your settings are saved to an .rdp file. .rdp files are associated with the Remote Desktop Connection program, so you can double-click an .rdp file to open a saved connection. In other words, an .rdp file is a handy shortcut to a remote connection.

The following sections describe the additional options that are available on the other Remote Desktop Connection tabs.

Setting the Display options

Figure 3-6 shows the Display tab of the Remote Desktop Connection dialog box. The following paragraphs describe each of the options available from this tab:

+ **Display Configuration size slider:** Use this control to set the size of your remote desktop display. If you drag the slider all the way to the right, the remote desktop will be displayed in full-screen mode. As you move the slider to the left, various display resolutions will appear. Choose the display size you want the remote computer to open up in.

+ **Use All My Monitors for the Remote Session:** If your computer has more than one monitor, select this check box to use all your monitors for the remote session. If you want to open the remote desktop in full-screen mode on just one of your monitors, leave this box deselected.

+ **Choose the Color Depth of the Remote Session drop-down list:** Use this drop-down list to choose the color quality of the remote desktop. Over slower connections, reducing the color depth will help performance.

+ **Display the Connection Bar When I Use the Full Screen:** The connection bar is a thin bar at the top of the screen that enables you to switch back to normal windowed mode. If you deselected this box, you'll have to remember that you can press Ctrl+Alt+Break to switch between full-screen and windowed mode.

Figure 3-6:
Setting the Display options for Remote Desktop Connection.

Setting the Local Resources options

The Local Resources tab, shown in Figure 3-7, lets you set the following options:

✦ **Remote Audio:** Click the Settings button to bring up a dialog box that lets you choose whether to play audio on the remote computer using the remote computer's sound card, the local computer's sound card, or not at all. This display box also lets you choose whether to allow audio recording during the remote session.

Figure 3-7:
Setting
the Local
Resources
options for
Remote
Desktop
Connection.

✦ **Apply Windows Key Combinations drop-down list:** This drop-down list lets you specify how Windows keyboard shortcuts are to be interpreted — on the remote computer, on the local computer, or on the remote computer only when it's running in full-screen mode.

✦ **Local Devices and Resources:** The Printers check box lets you access local printers from the remote session. The Clipboard check box synchronizes the local and remote clipboards, so that when you copy something to the Clipboard in the remote session, you can return to the local session and paste the Clipboard contents (or vice versa).

You can also share local drives with the remote session. To do so, click More, and then select the drives that you want to make available to the remote session, as shown in Figure 3-8.

Figure 3-8:
Sharing
drives with
the remote
computer.

Setting the Programs options

The Programs tab, shown in Figure 3-9, lets you specify a program that will automatically run when you connect to the remote computer. You can specify the path to the program's executable file, and you can also specify the working directory for the program.

For example, if you always want Active Directory Users and Computers to start when you log in to your domain controller, you could set up an .rdp file with the start program set to the path to Active Directory Users and Computers (%SystemRoot%System32\dsa.msc). Then, you won't have to manually start this program when you log in to your domain controller.

Figure 3-9:
Setting
programs
to automati-
cally run in
a remote
session.

Setting the Experience options

The options on the Experience tab, shown in Figure 3-10, control various settings that affect the responsiveness of your remote connection. The options are as follows:

✦ **Choose Your Connection Speed to Optimize Performance drop-down list:** This allows you to optimize the amount of information sent back and forth over the network based on your expected connection speed. At slower speeds, features such as the desktop background, font smoothing, window animations, and so on will be suppressed. The default setting is to let Windows choose which features to use based on the actual speed of the connection.

✦ **Persistent Bitmap Caching:** If you select this box, copies of bitmap images are stored on the local computer so they don't have to be transferred across the network every time they're needed.

✦ **Reconnect If the Connection Is Dropped:** If you select this box, the connection will be automatically reestablished if the connection is broken.

Figure 3-10:
Setting the Experience options for a Remote Desktop session.

Setting the Advanced options

The Advanced tab of the Remote Desktop Connections window, shown in Figure 3-11, lets you control two features:

✦ **Server Authentication:** Determines what to do if an authentication problem such as an unknown security certificate is encountered when connecting to the server. The default action is to warn the user, but allow the user to continue if desired. You can change this setting to always connect in spite of the authentication problem, or to never connect when a problem is encountered.

✦ **Connect from Anywhere:** These settings are used only when you use an advanced server role called Remote Desktop Gateway to manage remote access to computers on your network. For more information about this server role, search the Internet for *Remote Desktop Gateway*. (This subject is beyond the scope of this book.)

Figure 3-11: Setting the Advanced options for a Remote Desktop session.

Chapter 4: Using Remote Assistance

In This Chapter

✔ Enabling the Remote Assistance feature

✔ Helping someone remotely

✔ Working in the Remote Assistance window

*O*ne of the most annoying aspects of providing technical support for network users is that you often have to go to the user's desk to see what's going on with his or her computer. That's annoying enough if the other user's desk is across the room or down the hall, but it's almost unworkable if the user you need to support is across town or in a different city or state altogether.

Fortunately, Windows includes a handy feature called Remote Assistance, which is designed to let you provide technical support to an end-user without going to the user's location. With Remote Assistance, you can see the user's screen in a window on your own screen, so you can watch what the user is doing. You can even take control when necessary to perform troubleshooting or corrective actions to help solve the user's problems.

Note that there are commercial alternatives to Windows Remote Assistance that do a much better job at this task. This chapter shows you how to use Remote Assistance because it's free and all Windows computers since Windows XP have it.

Enabling Remote Assistance

Before you can lend assistance to a remote computer, Remote Assistance must be enabled on that computer. It is best to enable Remote Assistance before you need it, so that when the time comes, you can easily access your users' computers. But the procedure is simple enough that you can probably walk a user through the steps over the phone so that you can then gain access.

Here are the steps for Windows 7 and later:

1. **Click the Start button, type** Remote Assistance, **and click Enable Remote Assistance Invitations to Be Sent from This Computer.**

This brings up the System Properties dialog box, shown in Figure 4-1.

Figure 4-1: Enabling Remote Assistance.

2. **Select the Allow Remote Assistance Connections to This Computer option.**

3. **Click the Advanced button.**

The Remote Assistance Settings dialog box appears, as shown in Figure 4-2.

Figure 4-2: Setting the advanced Remote Assistance options.

4. **Select the Allow This Computer to Be Controlled Remotely check box.**

   This option will allow you to later take control of this computer remotely.

5. **Click OK.**

   You're returned to the System Properties dialog box.

6. **Click OK.**

   You're done. You can now initiate Remote Assistance sessions from this computer.

Inviting Someone to Help You via a Remote Assistance Session

The user requesting remote assistance must initiate the request before you can connect to the user's computer to provide help. You may need to guide your user through this procedure over the phone. Here are the steps:

1. **Click the Start button, type** Invite, **and then click Invite Someone to Connect to Your PC.**

   The Windows Remote Assistance window appears, as shown in Figure 4-3.

Figure 4-3:
The Windows Remote Assistance window.

2. **Click Invite Someone You Trust to Help You.**

   The screen shown in Figure 4-4 appears.

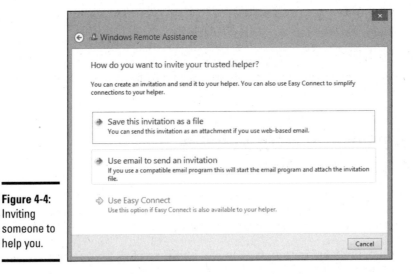

Figure 4-4:
Inviting
someone to
help you.

3. **Click Save This Invitation as a File, and save the invitation file to a convenient disk location.**

   This option creates a special file that you can save to disk. A Save As dialog box appears, allowing you to save the invitation file in any disk location you want. You can then email the invitation to your helper, who can use the invitation to connect to your PC.

   If you use Microsoft Outlook, you can alternatively choose Use Email to Send an Invitation. This option fires up Outlook and creates an email with the invitation file already attached.

   Either way, a password will be displayed, as shown in Figure 4-5. You'll need to provide this password to your helper when requested. (Typically, you'll do that over the phone.)

Figure 4-5:
You'll need
to tell your
helper the
password.

Windows Remote Assistance
Chat · Settings · Troubleshoot · Help
Give your helper the invitation file and password
W45ZF4BVPYKW
Waiting for incoming connection...

4. **Email the invitation file to the person you want to help you.**

   Use your preferred email program to send the invitation file as an attachment.

5. **Wait for your helper to request the password.**

   When your helper enters the password into his or her Remote Assistance screen, the Remote Assistance session is established. You'll be prompted for permission to allow your helper to take control of your computer, as shown in Figure 4-6.

Figure 4-6: Granting your helper permission to take control.

6. **Click Yes.**

   Your helper now has access to your computer. To facilitate the Remote Assistance session, the toolbar shown in Figure 4-7 appears. You can use this toolbar to chat with your helper or to temporarily pause the Remote Assistance session.

Figure 4-7: The Windows Remote Assistance toolbar.

Responding to a Remote Assistance Invitation

If you've received an invitation to a Remote Assistance session, you can establish the session by following these steps:

1. **Click the Start button, type** Invite, **and then click Invite Someone to Connect to Your PC.**

This brings up the Windows Remote Assistance window (refer to Figure 4-3).

2. **Click Help Someone Who Has Invited You.**

3. **Click Use an Invitation File.**

An Open dialog box appears.

4. **Locate the invitation file you were sent, select it, and click Open.**

You're prompted to enter the Remote Assistance password, as shown in Figure 4-8.

Figure 4-8:
Enter the
Remote
Assistance
password.

> Remote Assistance
>
> Enter the password to connect to the remote computer
>
> You can get this password from the person requesting assistance. A Remote Assistance session will start after you type the password and click OK.
>
> Enter password:
>
> OK   Cancel

As an alternative to Steps 1 through 3, you can simply double-click the invitation file you received. This will launch Windows Remote Assistance and prompt you for the password.

5. **Enter the password given to you by the user requesting help, and then click OK.**

The remote user is prompted to grant you permission to start the Remote Assistance session (this is where the remote user sees the screen that was shown in Figure 4-6). When the user grants permission, the Remote Assistance session is established. You can now see the user's screen in the Remote Assistance window, as shown in Figure 4-9.

Figure 4-9:
A Remote
Assistance
session in
progress.

6. **To take control of the remote user's computer, click Request Control.**

   The remote user will be prompted to allow control. Assuming that permission is granted, you can now control the other computer.

7. **Do your thing.**

   Now that you're connected to the remote computer, you can perform whatever troubleshooting or corrective actions are necessary to solve the user's problems.

8. **If necessary, use the Chat window to communicate with the user.**

   You can summon the Chat window by clicking the Chat button in the toolbar. Figure 4-10 shows a chat in progress.

9. **To conclude the Remote Assistance session, simply close the Remote Assistance window.**

   The remote user is notified that the Remote Assistance session has ended.

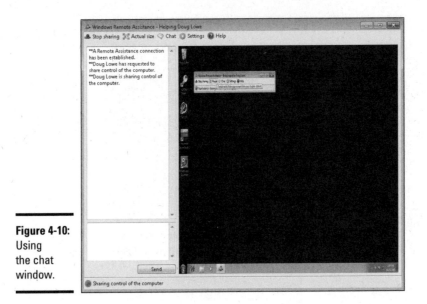

Figure 4-10:
Using
the chat
window.

Book VI
Cloud Networking

Read about five clouds and five services in a free article at www.dummies.com/extras/networkingaio.

Contents at a Glance

Chapter 1: Cloudy with a Chance of Gigabytes...................457

Chapter 2: Using Essential Cloud Services......................467

Chapter 3: Administering Office 365 477

Chapter 4: Using SharePoint Online 485

Chapter 1: Cloudy with a Chance of Gigabytes

In This Chapter

✔ Examining the basics of cloud computing

✔ Looking at three kinds of cloud computing services

✔ Understanding the pros and cons of cloud computing

✔ Perusing a few of the major cloud computing service providers

*I*n her classic children's book *Cloudy with a Chance of Meatballs*, Judi Barrett tells the story of the town of Chewandswallow, where food falls from the sky. Clouds rain down such essentials as juice and soup, and when it snows, the snow is made of ice cream.

Cloud computing is a bit like that. In a computer network, the essentials are not juice, soup, and ice cream, but CPU cycles, disk storage, and software. Traditionally, these essentials have been provided by local server computers, whether real or virtual. But in recent years, more and more companies have been obtaining these essential resources from the "cloud" — that is, from the Internet.

This chapter is a brief introduction to cloud computing. You discover what it is, the pros and cons of adopting it, and what services are provided by the major cloud computer providers.

Introducing Cloud Computing

The basic idea behind cloud computing is to outsource one or more of your networked computing resources to the Internet. The cloud represents a new way of handling common computer tasks. Following are a few examples of how the cloud way differs from the traditional way:

✦ **Email services**

- The traditional way to provide email services is to install Microsoft Exchange on a local server computer. Then your clients can connect use Microsoft Outlook to connect to the Exchange server to send and receive email.

- The cloud computing way is to contract with an Internet-based email provider such as Google Mail (Gmail). Cloud-based email services typically charge a low monthly per-user fee, so the amount you pay for your email service depends solely on the number of email users you have.

+ **Disk storage**

  - The traditional way to provide disk storage for your network applications is to set up a local file server computer with a large amount of shared disk space.

  - The cloud way is to sign up for an Internet file storage service and store your data on the Internet. Cloud-based file storage typically charges a small monthly per-gigabyte fee, so you pay only for the storage you use. The disk capacity of cloud-based storage is essentially unlimited.

+ **Accounting services**

  - The traditional way to handle accounting services for your company is to purchase expensive accounting software and install it on a local server computer.

  - The cloud way is to sign up for a web-based accounting service. Then all your accounting data is saved and managed on the provider's servers, not on yours.

Looking at the Benefits of Cloud Computing

Cloud computing is a different way of doing networking, but it isn't different just for the sake of being different: Often, it's different because it's better. Following are a few of the main benefits of moving to cloud-based networking:

+ **Cost effective:** Cloud-based computing typically is less expensive than traditional computing. Consider a typical file server application: To implement a file server, first you must purchase a file server computer with enough disk space to accommodate your users' needs, which amounts to 1TB of disk storage. You want the most reliable data storage possible, so you purchase a server-quality computer and fully redundant disk drives. For the sake of this discussion, figure that the total price of the server — including its disk drive, the operating-system license, and the labor cost of setting it up — is about $10,000. Assuming that the server will last for four years, that comes to about $2,500 per year.

If you instead acquire your disk storage from a cloud-based file sharing service, you can expect to pay about one-fourth of that amount for an equivalent amount of storage.

The same economies apply to most other cloud-based solutions. For Cloud-based email solutions, for example, typically cost around $5 per month per user — well under the cost of setting up and maintaining a Microsoft Exchange server.

✦ **Scalable:** So what happens if you guess wrong about the storage requirements of your file server, and your users end up needing 2TB instead of just 1TB? With a traditional file server, you must purchase additional disk drives to accommodate the extra space. Sooner than you want, you'll run out of capacity in the server's cabinet. Then you'll have to purchase an external storage cabinet. Eventually, you'll fill that up too.

Now suppose that after you've expanded your server capacity to 2TB, your users' needs contract to just 1TB. Unfortunately, you can't return disk drives for a refund.

With cloud computing, you pay only for the capacity you're actually using, and you can add capacity whenever you need it. In the file server example, you can write as much data as you need to the cloud storage. Each month, you're billed according to your actual usage. Thus, you don't have to purchase and install additional disk drives to add storage capacity.

✦ **Reliable:** Especially for smaller businesses, cloud services are much more reliable than in-house services. Just a week before I wrote this chapter, the tape drive that a friend uses to back up his company's data failed. As a result, he was unable to back up data for three days while the tape drive was repaired. Had he been using cloud-based backup, he could have restored his data immediately and wouldn't have been without backups for those three days.

The reason for the increased reliability of cloud services is simply a matter of scale. Most small businesses can't afford the redundancies needed to make their computer operations as reliable as possible. My friend's company can't afford to buy two tape drives so that an extra is available in case the main one fails.

By contrast, cloud services are usually provided by large companies such as Amazon, Google, Microsoft, and IBM. These companies have state-of-the-art data centers with multiple redundancies for their cloud services. Cloud storage may be kept on multiple servers so that if one server fails, others can take over the load. In some cases, these servers are in different data centers in different parts of the country. Thus, your data will still be available even in the event of a disaster that shuts down an entire data system.

✦ **Hassle-free:** Face it, IT can be a hassle. With cloud-based services, you basically outsource the job of complex system maintenance chores such as software upgrade, patches, hardware maintenance, backup, and so on. You get to consume the services while someone else takes care of making sure that the services run properly.

✦ **Globally accessible:** One of the best things about cloud services is that they're available anywhere you have an Internet connection. Suppose that you have offices in five cities. Using traditional computing, each office would require its own servers, and you'd have to carefully design systems that allowed users in each of the offices to access shared data.

With cloud computing, each office simply connects to the Internet to access the cloud applications. Cloud-based applications are also great if your users are mobile because they can access the applications anywhere they can find an Internet connection.

Detailing the Drawbacks of Cloud Computing

Although cloud computing has many advantages over traditional techniques, it isn't without its drawbacks. Here are some of the most significant roadblocks to adopting cloud computing:

✦ **Entrenched applications:** Your organization may depend on entrenched applications that don't lend themselves especially well to cloud computing — or that at least require significant conversion efforts to migrate to the cloud.

Fortunately, many cloud providers offer assistance with this migration. And in many cases, the same application that you run locally can be run in the cloud, so no conversion is necessary.

✦ **Internet connection speed:** Cloud computing shifts much of the burden of your network to your Internet connection. Your users used to access their data on local file servers over gigabit-speed connections; now they must access data over slower bandwidth Internet connections.

Although you can upgrade your connection to higher speeds, doing so will cost money — money that may offset the money you otherwise save from migrating to the cloud.

✦ **Internet connection reliability:** The cloud resources you access may feature all the redundancy in the world, but if your users access the cloud through a single Internet connection, that connection becomes a key point of vulnerability. Should it fail, any applications that depend on the cloud will be unavailable. If those applications are mission-critical, business will come to a halt until the connection is restored.

There are two ways to mitigate this risk:

- *Make sure that you're using an enterprise-class Internet connection,* not a consumer-class connection. Enterprise-class connections are more expensive but provide much better fault tolerance and repair service than consumer-class connections do.

  - *Provide redundant connections if you can.* That way, if one connection fails, traffic can be rerouted through alternative connections.

✦ **Security threats:** You can bet your life that hackers throughout the world are continually probing for ways to break through the security perimeter of all the major cloud providers. When they do, your data may be exposed.

The best way to mitigate this threat is to ensure that strong password policies are enforced.

Examining Three Basic Kinds of Cloud Services

Three distinct kinds of services can be provided via the cloud: applications, platforms, and services. The following paragraphs describe these three types of cloud services in greater detail.

Applications

Most often referred to as *Software as a Service* (SaaS), fully functional applications can be delivered via the cloud. One of the best-known examples is Google Apps, a suite of cloud-based office applications designed to compete directly with Microsoft's traditional office applications, including Word, Excel, PowerPoint, Access, and Outlook. Google Apps can also replace the back-end software often used to support Microsoft Office, including Exchange and SharePoint.

When you use a cloud-based application, you don't have to worry about any of the details that are commonly associated with running an application on your network, such as deploying the application and applying product upgrades and software patches. Cloud-based applications usually charge a small monthly fee based on the number of users running the software, so costs are low.

Also, as a cloud-based application user, you don't have to worry about providing the hardware or operating-system platform on which the application will run. The application provider takes care of that detail for you, so you can focus simply on developing the application to best serve your users' needs.

Platforms

Also referred to as *Platform as a Service* (PaaS), this class of service refers to providers that give you access to a remote virtual operating platform on which you can build your own applications.

At the simplest level, a PaaS provider gives you a complete, functional remote virtual machine that's fully configured and ready for you to deploy your applications to. If you use a web provider to host your company's website, you're already using PaaS: Most web host providers give you a functioning Linux system, fully configured with all the necessary servers, such as Apache or MySQL. All you have to do is build and deploy your web application on the provider's server.

More-complex PaaS solutions include specialized software that your custom applications can tap to provide services such as data storage, online order processing, and credit card payments. One of the best-known examples of this type of PaaS provider is Amazon.

When you use PaaS, you take on the responsibility of developing your own custom applications to run on the remote platform. But the PaaS provider takes care of the details of maintaining the platform itself, including the base operating system and the hardware on which the platform runs.

Infrastructure

If you don't want to delegate the responsibility of maintaining operating systems and other elements of the platform, you can use *Infrastructure as a Service* (IaaS). When you use IaaS, you're purchasing raw computing power that's accessible via the cloud. Typically, IaaS provides you access to a remote virtual machine. It's up to you to manage and configure the remote machine however you want.

Public Clouds versus Private Clouds

The most common form of cloud computing uses what is known as a *public cloud* — that is, cloud services that are available to anyone in the world via the Internet. Google Apps for Business is an excellent example of a public cloud service. Anyone with access to the Internet can access the public cloud services of Google Apps for Business: Just point your browser to `http://apps.google.com`.

A public cloud is like a public utility, in that anyone can subscribe to it on a pay-as-you-go basis. One of the drawbacks of public cloud services is that they're inherently insecure. When you use a public cloud service, you're entrusting your valuable data to a third party that you cannot control. Sure, you can protect your access to your public cloud services by using strong passwords, but if your account names and passwords are compromised, your public cloud services can be hacked into, and your data can be stolen. Every so often, we all hear news stories about how this company's or that company's back-door security has been compromised.

Besides security, another drawback of public cloud computing is that it is dependent on high-speed, reliable Internet connections. Your cloud service provider may have all the redundancy in the world, but if your connection to the Internet goes down, you won't be able to access your cloud services. And if your connection is slow, your cloud services will be slow.

A *private cloud* is a system that mimics many of the features of cloud computing but is implemented on a private hardware within a local network, so it isn't accessible to the general public. Private clouds are inherently more secure because the general public cannot access them. Also, they're dependent only on private network connections, so they aren't subject to the limits of a public Internet connection.

As a rule, private clouds are implemented by large organizations that have the resources available to create and maintain their own cloud servers.

A relative newcomer to the cloud computing scene is the *hybrid cloud,* which combines the features of public and private clouds. Typically, a hybrid cloud system uses a small private cloud that provides local access to some of the applications and the public cloud for others. You might maintain your most frequently used data on a private cloud for fast access via the local network and use the public cloud to store archives and other less-frequently-used data, for which performance isn't as much of an issue.

Introducing Some of the Major Cloud Providers

Hundreds, if not thousands, of companies provide cloud services. Most of the cloud computing done today, however, is provided by just a few providers, which are described in the following sections.

Amazon

By far the largest provider of cloud services in the world is Amazon. Amazon launched its cloud platform, called *Amazon Web Services* (AWS), in 2006. Since then, hundreds of thousands of customers have signed up. Some of the most notable users of AWS include Netflix, Pinterest, and Instagram.

AWS includes the following features:

✦ *Amazon CloudFront,* a PaaS content-delivery system designed to deliver web content to large numbers of users.

✦ *Amazon Elastic Compute Cloud* (also called *Amazon EC2),* an IaaS system that provides access to raw computing power.

✦ *Amazon Simple Storage Service* (also called *Amazon S3),* which provides web-based data storage for unlimited amounts of data.

✦ *Amazon Simple Queue Service* (also called *Amazon SQS),* which provides a data transfer system that lets applications send messages to other applications. SQS enables you to build applications that work together.

✦ *Amazon Virtual Private Cloud* (also called *Amazon VPC),* which uses virtual private network (VPN) connections to connect your local network to Amazon's cloud services.

Google

Google is also one of the largest providers of cloud services. Its offerings include the following:

✦ *Google Apps,* a replacement for Microsoft Office that provides basic email, word processing, spreadsheet, and database functions via the cloud. Google Apps is free to the general public and can even be used free by small businesses (up to 50 users). For larger businesses, Google offers an advanced version called *Google Apps for Business.* For $5 per month per user, you get extra features such as 25GB of email data per user, archiving, and advanced options for customizing your account policies.

✦ *Google Cloud Connect,* a cloud-based solution that lets you work with Google cloud data directly from within Microsoft Office applications.

✦ *Google App Engine,* a PaaS interface that lets you develop your own applications that work with Google's cloud services.

✦ *Google Cloud Print,* which lets you connect your printers to the cloud so that they can be accessed from anywhere.

✦ *Google Maps,* which is a Global Information System (GIS).

Microsoft

Microsoft has its own cloud strategy that is designed, in part, to protect its core business of operating systems and Office applications against competition from other cloud providers, such as Google Apps.

The following paragraphs summarize several of Microsoft's cloud offerings:

✦ *Microsoft Office 365,* a cloud-based version of Microsoft Office. According to Microsoft's website, Office 365 provides "anywhere access to cloud-based email, web conferencing, file sharing, and Office Web Apps at a low predictable monthly cost." For more information, check out www.office365.com.

✦ *SharePoint Online,* a cloud-based version of Microsoft SharePoint. For more information about SharePoint, refer to Chapter 4 of this minibook.

✦ *Windows Azure,* a PaaS offering that lets you build websites, deploy virtual machines that run Windows Server or Linux, or access cloud versions of server applications such as SQL Server.

✦ *Microsoft Business Productivity Suite,* a SaaS product that provides cloud-based access to two of Microsoft's most popular productivity servers: Microsoft Exchange and Microsoft SharePoint. The suite lets you deploy these servers without having to create and maintain your own local servers.

Getting into the Cloud

So now that you've seen how cool cloud computing can be, what should you do to take your network toward the cloud? Allow me to make a few recommendations:

✦ **Don't depend on a poor Internet connection.** First and foremost, before you take any of your network operations to the cloud, make sure that you're *not* dependent on a consumer-grade Internet connection if you decide to adopt cloud computing. Consumer-grade Internet connections can be fast, but when an outage occurs, there's no telling how long you'll wait for the connection to be repaired. You definitely don't want to wait for hours or days while the cable company thinks about sending someone out to your site. Instead, spend the money for a high-speed enterprise-class connection that can scale as your dependence on it increases.

✦ **Assess what applications you may already have running on the cloud.**
If you use Gmail rather than Exchange for your email, congratulations!
You're already a cloud user. Other examples of cloud services that you
may already be using include a remote web or FTP host, Dropbox or
another file sharing service, Carbonite or another online backup service,
a payroll service, and so on.

✦ **Don't move to the cloud all at once.** Start by identifying a single application that lends itself to the cloud. If your engineering firm archives
projects when they close and wants to get them off your primary file
server but keep them readily available, look to the cloud for a file storage
service.

✦ **Go with a reputable company.** Google, Amazon, and Microsoft are
all huge companies with proven track records in cloud computing.
Many other large and established companies also offer cloud services.
Don't stake your company's future on a company that didn't exist
six months ago.

✦ **Research, research, research.** *Hybrid Cloud For Dummies,* by Judith
Hurwitz, Marcia Kaufman, Dr. Fern Halper, and Daniel Kirsch (Wiley), is a
good place to start.

Chapter 2: Using Essential Cloud Services

In This Chapter

✔ Sharing files across the Internet

✔ Hosting online meetings

✔ Using enterprise social networks

A recent study I read concluded that most IT professionals underestimate their dependence on cloud apps by a factor of four. In other words, their companies are already using four times as many cloud-based apps as they realize. Even though you may not realize it, your company has probably already moved much of its IT infrastructure to the cloud.

In this chapter, I take a look at several of the most popular cloud-based services that you may, or may not, already be using. If you aren't already using some of these services, you should consider adopting them.

Sharing Files in the Cloud

In many cases, the easiest way to exchange files with another person is to send an email with the file attached. However, there are many situations in which that's not the best way to exchange files. For starters, many organizations limit the size of incoming or outgoing email attachments. Thus, email is not a viable option if the file you need to share is larger than the size limit.

The tried-and-true standard for sharing large files is FTP. You can either host your own FTP site or pay for FTP hosting. But FTP is not much more than an online file folder to which you can upload and download files. Compared with today's cloud-based file sharing services, FTP is archaic.

The following sections summarize a few of the best file-sharing options you can choose from.

Google Drive

Google Drive (`www.google.com/drive`) is the storage component of Google Apps. If you have a Gmail account, you already have access to 15GB of free storage on Google Drive. You can upgrade the free account to acquire additional storage:

✦ $1.99 per month for 100GB

✦ $9.99 per month for 1TB

✦ $99.99 per month for 10TB

✦ $199.99 per month for 20TB

✦ $2.99 per month for 30TB

Figure 2-1 shows a typical Google Drive page with several folders and files. You can easily upload and download files to and from Google Drive. You can share files with other Gmail users, and you can get a link to a file, which you can then email to anyone you want to have access to the file.

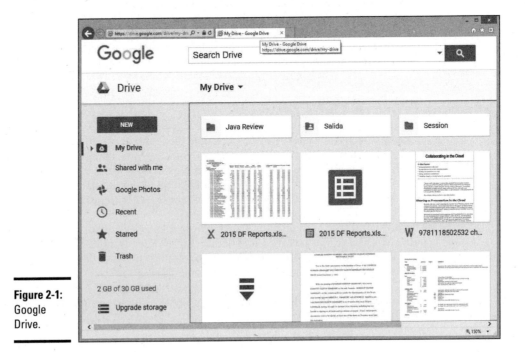

Figure 2-1:
Google
Drive.

Microsoft OneDrive

Microsoft OneDrive is the cloud storage component of Office 365. One of the best features of OneDrive is its integration with Microsoft Office applications. For example, the Save and Open commands include a link to your OneDrive account, which can be opened in a normal file browser dialog box, as shown in Figure 2-2.

Figure 2-2:
OneDrive is tightly integrated with Microsoft Office applications.

OneDrive provides 15GB of free storage. Paid plans include the following:

✦ $1.99 per month for 100GB

✦ $3.99 per month for 200GB

✦ $6.99 per month for 1TB

Dropbox

Dropbox (www.dropbox.com) is one of the oldest and best known file-sharing services. Dropbox offers everything you'd expect in a basic file-sharing service: the ability to upload and download files, share files with other Dropbox users, send file links to people who don't have a Dropbox account so they can download the file without registering, and much more.

Dropbox offers three service plans:

✦ **Dropbox Basic** is a free account that provides up to 2GB of storage.

✦ **Dropbox Pro** costs $9.99 per month and lets you store up to 1TB of data.

✦ **Dropbox for Business** costs $15 per user per month, has unlimited storage capacity, and provides advanced tools for managing teams.

Box

Box (www.box.com) is designed not just for file sharing but for business collaboration. As such, it has document collaboration tools and strong security features.

Box has a variety of personal and business plans. The free personal plan lets you store up to 10GB of data and can be upgraded to 100GB of data for $10 per month. The business plans are as follows:

✦ **Starter:** 100GB of data for $5 per user per month

✦ **Business:** Unlimited data for $15 per user per month, including custom branding (so you can add your logo and other brand information to the site), Active Directory integration, and integration with Office 365

Hosting Meetings in the Cloud

Among the most popular cloud-based services are those that provide for online meetings. These services allow multiple people to get together online for discussion, review, planning, training, and collaboration. Most online meeting sites support the following features:

✦ Virtual conference rooms where you can invite participants to join in a private meeting. Participants simply enter a meeting code to join a meeting.

✦ The ability to schedule a meeting to start at a particular time.

✦ Real-time streaming of audio and video.

✦ The audio portion of the meeting done via phone lines. With the right service plan, your participants can call into the meeting using a toll-free line.

✦ Screen sharing, so that everyone in the meeting can see your desktop.

✦ iOS and Android apps, so users of tablets and smartphones can participate.

✦ Recording.

The two most commonly used services for online meetings are GoToMeeting and WebEx.

GoToMeeting

GoToMeeting (www.gotomeeting.com), an offering of Citrix, provides all the features you'd expect in a web meeting service, including the ability to host large meetings (up to 1,000 participants).

GoToMeeting requires an app to be downloaded on the client for the user to participate in a meeting. The app is small, so it downloads and installs quickly, and it's compatible with most versions of Windows.

GoToMeeting offers three distinct types of service: GoToMeeting, designed for collaborative business meetings; GoToWebinar, designed for presentations with up to 1,000 participants; and GoToTraining, which provides interactive training for up to 2,00 participants. The plans include

✦ **GoToMeeting Starter:** $24 per month for 5 participants, $39 per month for 25 participants, and $49 per month for 100 attendees

✦ **GoToWebinar:** $89 per month for 100 attendees, $199 per month for 500 attendees, and $299 per month for 1,000 attendees

✦ **GoToTraining:** $109 per month for 25 attendees, $159 per month for 50 attendees, and $314 per month for 200 attendees

WebEx

WebEx (www.webex.com), which is owned by Cisco, provides services that are similar to GoToMeeting, but also offers additional services. The complete portfolio includes the following:

✦ **WebEx Meetings:** Lets you hold traditional online meetings. You can schedule meetings and participants can join by connecting to www.webex.com and entering the meeting number. Plans range from $24 per month for up to 8 participants to $69 per month for up to 100 participants.

+ **WebEx Meeting Center:** Lets you create virtual conference rooms that are easier to set up and use than traditional online meetings.

+ **WebEx Event Center:** Lets you hold webinars and other events. Plans range from $99 per month for up to 100 participants to $479 per month for up to 1,000 participants.

+ **WebEx Training Center:** Lets you conduct interactive training. This service includes not only standard videoconferencing tools, but also tools aimed at trainers, such as online course catalogs, enrollment forms, and grading tools.

+ **WebEx Support Center:** Lets you offer remote support and a Help desk. Unlike most help-desk tools, WebEx Support Center includes face-to-face interaction with users. The support center also includes screen-sharing tools that let the support technician take control of the user's screen.

Creating a Company Social Network

One of the latest trends in cloud computing is the adoption of Enterprise Social Networks (ESN). These networks are similar to public social networks such as Facebook and Twitter, but they're contained within an organization. Cloud-based ESNs don't require you to install any local software to manage the network; instead, the networks are supported and managed by the network provider's servers.

The main goal of an ESN is to improve communications within an organization. Toward this end, one of the primary features of any ESN is online chatting, similar to the newsfeed or chat features of public social networks. Chats can be directed at specific individuals, or they can be viewed by anyone in the organization. The use of ESN chatting can drastically reduce the amount of internal email within an organization, because employees will prefer to use the ESN chat to discuss simple matters such as meeting locations or lunch plans.

ESNs can also create groups to discuss and collaborate on specific projects or activities. Users can upload files, collaborate on documents, discuss ideas, schedule meetings, and share announcements with the group. Groups can be easily created as the need arises and disbanded when no longer necessary.

Most ESNs are cross-platform, which means they'll work not only on Windows computers but also on Macs, iOS devices, and Android devices.

So your employees can use their desktop computers, laptops, tablets, or cellphones to stay in touch via the ESN.

The following sections describe two of the most popular alternatives for building an ESN. Plenty of others are available, of course, so do a little research before you decide to adopt one for your company.

Yammer

Yammer (www.yammer.com) is a Microsoft product that is bundled with Office 365. Like most ESNs, Yammer resembles Facebook. As a result, employees who have Facebook accounts will quickly become familiar with Yammer. Figure 2-3 shows a typical Yammer screen.

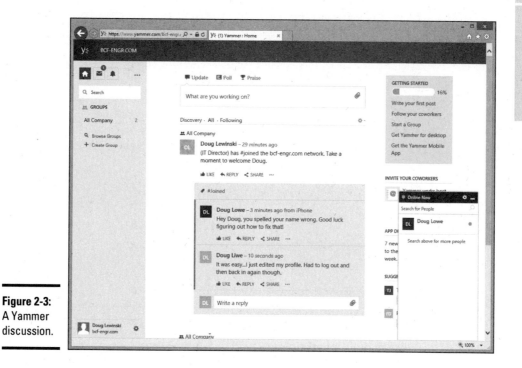

Figure 2-3:
A Yammer
discussion.

Yammer is a free service. In fact, any employee in your company can start a Yammer ESN for your company by signing up for an account using his or her company email address. Everyone who signs up using the same email domain will be part of the network.

If you want to have administrative control over the network, however, you'll need to purchase an account and pay for monthly usage fees. Because Yammer is integrated with Office 365, every Office 365 subscription includes a Yammer subscription, so you won't have to pay extra if your users already have Office 365 accounts.

Socialcast

Socialcast (`www.socialcast.com`), owned by VMware, is another popular platform for building an ESN. Figure 2-4 shows a Socialcast page.

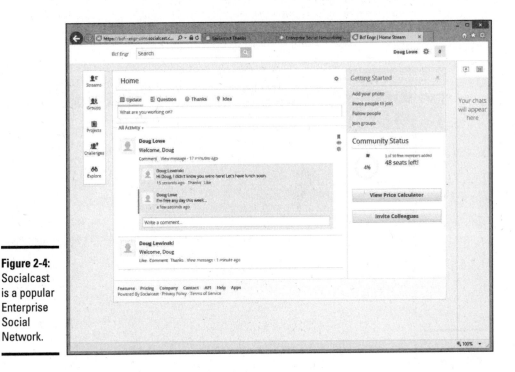

Figure 2-4: Socialcast is a popular Enterprise Social Network.

You can build a Socialcast network of up to 50 employees free of charge; just browse to `www.socialcast.com` and register using your company email address. When you have more than 50 employees in your network, you'll have to purchase additional licenses.

In addition to the standard ESN features of the basic Socialcast service, VMware offers additional features:

✦ Custom branding, which allows you to incorporate your own company logo, color schemes, and so on

✦ Single sign-on, which integrates users with their Active Directory accounts

✦ Integration with popular software applications such as SharePoint

✦ On premises hosting, if you prefer to have complete local control

Chapter 3: Administering Office 365

In This Chapter

✔ **Learning about the features of Office 365**

✔ **Exploring the Admin Center**

✔ **Managing users and licenses**

*O*ffice 365 is a collection of cloud-based services offered by Microsoft to users of its recent versions of Microsoft Office. Although you can still purchase boxed versions of Microsoft Office, many users and organizations are now opting for Microsoft' subscription-based Office 365 service. For a monthly fee, you get the privilege of using Office applications, plus additional features of the Office 365 cloud service.

In this chapter, I present the basics of how Office 365 works and how you, as a site administrator, can manage your company's Office 365 assets. These management features are not available to home users; you need a Business, Academic, Non-Profit, or Enterprise license to use the administration tools described in this chapter.

Looking at the Features Provided by Office 365

Office 365 contains a dizzying array of features. Here are the most important of these features:

✦ The core suite of Office programs, including Word, Excel, PowerPoint, Outlook, Publisher, and OneNote

✦ Tablet and online versions of the core office programs

✦ Additional Office applications, such as Access, Project, and Visio

✦ OneDrive file storage with up to 1TB of storage per user

✦ Cloud-hosted Exchange email, calendaring, and contacts

✦ Videoconferencing via Skype

✦ Corporate social networking via Yammer (for more information about Yammer, refer to Chapter 2 of this minibook)

✦ Intranet sites via SharePoint Online (for more information about SharePoint, see Chapter 4 of this minibook)

✦ Administration tools to help manage your subscription

✦ Features for developers so you can customize Office applications or create your own add-ins

If you want a complete list of all the features of Office 365 that are provided by all the different types of subscriptions, go to `https://technet.` `microsoft.com/en-us/office/dn788955.aspx`. When you see all the features that are available — nearly 500 distinct features organized into almost 50 different categories, showing which features are available for each of the 19 different license plans — your head will spin. (If you'd rather not type this long web address, or if Microsoft decides to change it, just go to your favorite search engine and search for *Office 365 Service Comparison.*)

When you log in to Office 365 (at `http://portal.office.com`), you'll see a list of your online applications, as shown in Figure 3-1. This page serves as your portal to many Office 365 features, but you can also access Office 365 features from directly within an Office application. For example, you can access your OneDrive file storage feature directly from any Office program by choosing File ➪ Open or File ➪ Save As.

Figure 3-1:
The Office
365 portal
home page.

Using the Admin Center

The Admin Center is your portal to administrative functions in Office 365. Naturally, you'll need to have administrative privileges to see the Admin Center. To open the Admin Center, log in to Office 365 and then click the Admin icon (shown in the margin). Figure 3-2 shows the opening page of the Admin Center, called the Dashboard.

On the left side of every Admin Center page is a navigation menu that lets you access the various management pages in the Admin Center. For example, to manage users, click Users; to review your billing, click Billing. To return to the Dashboard, click Dashboard at the top of the menu.

In the center section of the Dashboard, you can access the tools you need to perform the most commonly needed management tasks, such as adding new users or resetting user passwords. Note that the tasks that appear on this page will change depending on your setup. For example, the Dashboard in Figure 3-2 includes links to activate Yammer Enterprise; after you've done that, this link will disappear.

**Book VI
Chapter 3**

**Administering
Office 365**

Figure 3-2:
The Admin
Center
Dashboard.

Creating a New User

To create a new Office 365 user, follow these steps:

1. **Open the Admin Center.**

2. **Open the Active Users page by choosing Users⇨Active Users from the navigation menu.**

    The Active Users page appears, as shown in Figure 3-3.

Figure 3-3:
The Active
Users page.

3. **Click the plus sign (+) icon that appears above the list of active users (shown in the margin).**

    This brings up the dialog box shown in Figure 3-4.

4. **Enter the user's first name, last name, and display name.**

5. **Enter the user's password.**

    If you want, you can let Office 365 assign a random password for the user.

Figure 3-4:
Creating a
new user.

6. Select the licenses you want to assign to the user.

This portion of the dialog box lists the licenses that are available — that is, licenses you've purchased but haven't yet assigned to a user. If no licenses are available, you can create the user now, and then purchase a new license and edit the user account to assign the new license.

7. Click Create.

The user is created. A confirmation page such as the one shown in Figure 3-5 appears.

8. Click Close.

You're returned to the Active Users page.

Create new user account   ×

✓ User John Smith created successfully!

User name   jsmith@bcfengr.onmicrosoft.com
Password: Kobu4875
License: Office 365 Business Essentials

Close

Figure 3-5:
Congratu-
lations!
You've
created
a user.

Editing a User Account

To manage users in Admin Center, click Users in the navigation menu, and then choose Active Users. This brings up the Active Users page, which lists all the active users in your organization. To manage a particular user, select the check box next to the user's name, as shown in Figure 3-6.

From this page, you can do any of the following important management tasks for the user:

+ Reset the user's password.

+ Delete the user.

+ Edit the user's roles (for example, make the user an administrator).

+ Edit the user's profile information (such as name or job title).

+ Add the user to a group.

+ Change the user's primary email address.

Book VI
Chapter 3

Administering
Office 365

Figure 3-6:
Editing
a user.

✦ Assign an available license to a user.

✦ Manage the user's mailbox permissions.

✦ Edit the user's Exchange or Skype settings.

Considering Other Important Administrative Tasks

Besides managing users, the Admin Center has a bucketful of other management tasks you can perform. Here are some of the highlights of what you can do:

✦ **Customize your Company Profile:** Click Company Profile in the navigation pane to change your company name and contact information. You can also customize the appearance of Office 365 for your organization, setting a custom logo, site colors, and background images. And you can create custom tiles that appear in the My Apps list.

✦ **Create security groups:** Click Groups in the navigation pane to create groups, which you can use to assign permissions to Office 365 users.

✦ **Add domains:** Click Domains in the navigation pane to add your current domain name or to add new domain names to your Office 365 account.

✦ **Review billing information:** Click Billing in the navigation pane to check your billing information. Here, you can review your subscriptions, pay your bill, cancel subscriptions, change payment details, or add additional licenses to existing subscriptions.

✦ **Purchase additional services:** To purchase additional services, click Purchase Services in the navigation pane.

✦ **Access admin portals for individual Office 365 services:** Under the Admin option in the navigation pane, you'll find links to the management portals for additional Office 365 services such as Exchange and SharePoint.

Chapter 4: Using SharePoint Online

In This Chapter

✔ **Looking at SharePoint**

✔ **Creating new SharePoint pages**

✔ **Working with libraries**

This chapter covers the basics of working with SharePoint Online, which is an important component of Office 365. Note that Microsoft also offers an on-premises version of SharePoint. The current version of the on-premises version is SharePoint 2013, but a new version 2016 is expected soon.

If you're interested in adopting SharePoint for your organization, the easiest way to research SharePoint's appropriateness for your needs is to experiment with the online version.

What Is SharePoint?

SharePoint is a web application that lets you create web portals, called *sites,* which are designed to let your users work together on various types of activities. SharePoint lets you create more than one site; additional sites are known as *subsites.*

You can create several different kinds of sites in SharePoint. The most common is called a *team site.* By default, a team site puts these two features front and center on its home page:

✦ **A library for shared documents:** Users can upload and download documents from the library.

✦ **A newsfeed:** The newsfeed lets users post a continuous stream of comments and replies, similar to the newsfeed in a social network such as Facebook.

You can easily add additional components to the team site, either as elements on the home page or on separate pages. Among the things you can add are the following:

✦ Announcements

✦ Calendars

✦ Task lists

✦ Links

Connecting to SharePoint Online

You can access your SharePoint Online team site from Office 365 by logging into www.office365.com and clicking Sites in the list of applications. This takes you to a list of SharePoint sites, which should initially contain one called Team Site. Click the Team Site icon to enter your team site.

Alternatively, you can browse directly to the site's web address. (You can determine the address of the site by hovering the mouse over it; the address appears in the status bar at the bottom of the browser window.)

Figure 4-1 shows the home page of a SharePoint Online team site. Front and center on this page you'll find the newsfeed, where a few messages have been posted, and the shared documents library, where a few files have been uploaded.

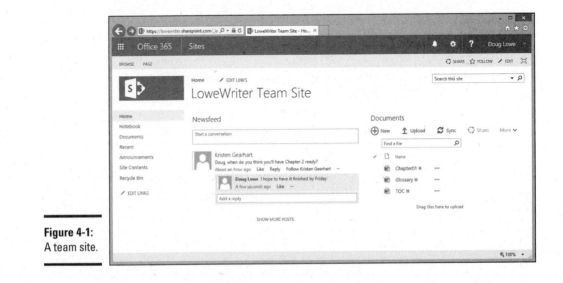

Figure 4-1:
A team site.

Besides the newsfeed and shared documents, you can see several other elements that are common to all SharePoint site pages:

✦ The banner at the top indicates that you're in the Sites section of Office 365.

✦ The gear-shaped icon in the banner lets you edit settings. If you have the correct permissions, you can edit the current site page, add a new page, or otherwise customize the team site.

✦ To the right of the settings icon is a Help button that lets you access help information to learn more about SharePoint Online.

✦ To the right of the Help button is your account name. Click your name to reveal a menu that lets you view your account profile or log off.

✦ Beneath the banner is a ribbon bar that has at least two tabs, labeled Browse and Page. The Browse tab lets you view the current page. The Page tab brings forth a ribbon of tools that apply to the current page. As you work with SharePoint, other tabs will appear in the ribbon.

✦ On the left side of the page is a navigation pane called Quick Launch, which lets you navigate the team site.

✦ The main content area, in the center of each SharePoint page, contains gadgets called *parts.* You can add parts to the page to customize its contents. The newsfeed and document library shown in Figure 4-1 are all examples of parts. You can also add text, tables, graphics, media, and other items to the page, and you can completely customize the format and layout of these items.

Adding a Part

Initially, the home page for a team site includes just a Newsfeed and a Documents part. To give you an idea of how you can customize a site page, the following procedure outlines the steps you can follow to add an Announcements part so that team announcements will appear on the home page:

1. **On the team site's home page, click Edit (found on the right side of the ribbon bar).**

The page switches to Edit mode, as shown in Figure 4-2. Notice that new tabs have appeared in the ribbon: Format Text and Insert.

Figure 4-2:
Editing a
SharePoint
page.

2. **Click Insert in the Ribbon.**

   The Insert ribbon tab appears, as shown in Figure 4-3.

Figure 4-3:
The Insert
ribbon tab.

3. **Click the Web Part button.**

   The list of available web parts appears, as shown in Figure 4-4.

4. **Select the Announcements web part.**

   You may want to peruse the list of available web parts just to see what's available. You can select a category from the Categories list on the left to see which parts are available.

5. **Click the Add button.**

   The Announcements part is added to the page, as shown in Figure 4-5.

Figure 4-4:
Choose a
web part.

Figure 4-5:
The
Announce-
ments part
is added to
the page.

6. **Click the Save button (found on the right side of the ribbon).**

The changes you've made to the page are saved, and you're returned to the page. The Announcements part now appears above the Newsfeed and Documents parts, as shown in Figure 4-6.

You're done!

Figure 4-6: The team site's home page with announcements added.

Here are a few other tips to consider when editing a page layout:

✦ You can insert as many parts on your page as you think the page can visually handle. Click anywhere on the page to control where a new part will be inserted.

✦ You can click and type text anywhere on the page. The Format Text ribbon tab provides the tools you need to change the font, size, color, and other properties of the text.

✦ You can also use the Insert ribbon tab to insert tables (which provide additional control of page layout), images, or media files.

✦ Use the Text Layout button in the Format Text ribbon tab to change the basic layout of the page. The default layout uses two columns with a header area, but other layouts are available.

Adding and Removing Announcements

Now that you've added an Announcement part to the team site home page, you might want to know how to add an announcement. It's actually easy; just follow these steps:

1. **Click the New Announcement link.**

    If you don't see a New Announcement link, you don't have adequate permissions to add new announcements. You can skip the rest of this procedure.

    Assuming that you have adequate permissions, the page shown in Figure 4-7 appears.

Book VI
Chapter 4

Using SharePoint Online

Figure 4-7:
The Announcements page.

2. **Type a subject and body for the announcement.**

3. **Set an expiration date, if you want.**

    When you set an expiration date, the message is automatically removed when it has expired.

4. **Click Save.**

   The new announcement is added to the top of the list of announcements on the home page.

   You're done! You and the site's users can now view and enjoy your latest announcement.

To edit or remove the announcement, click the announcement's title. This displays a page that lets you modify or delete the announcement.

Adding Apps

The default SharePoint site consists of several standard apps, a document library, a newsfeed, announcements, a calendar, and so on. You can add additional apps to your team site to customize it as needed. You can also add additional copies of apps that are already in the site. For example, you can add a second document library if you need to store different types of documents.

To add an app to a site, follow these steps:

1. **Click Site Contents in the Quick Launch navigation pane.**

   This brings up the Site Contents page, as shown in Figure 4-8.

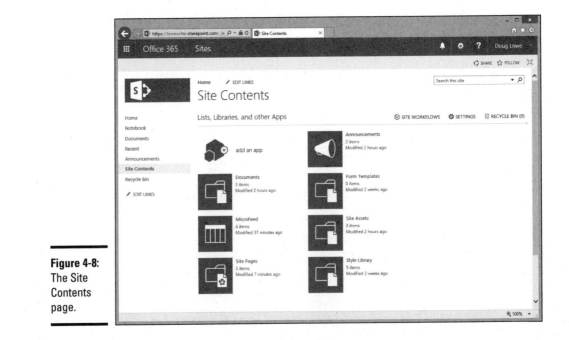

Figure 4-8: The Site Contents page.

2. **Click Add an App.**

A catalog of available apps appears, as shown in Figure 4-9. (Although it isn't apparent in this figure, there are actually dozens of apps displayed in this catalog. This figure shows just the first of 16 pages of apps that are available.)

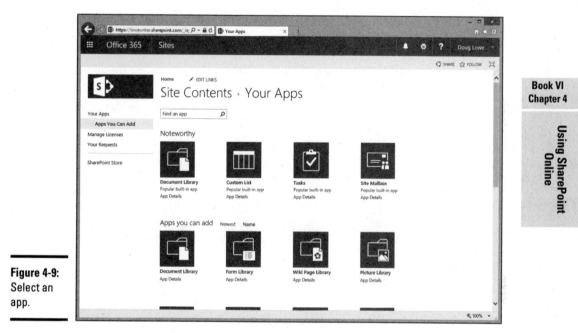

Figure 4-9: Select an app.

3. **Click the app you want to add.**

For our purposes here, I'll add another Document Library to the team site.

You can use the search box (containing the text "find an app") to help find an app. Or you can simply browse through all 16 pages of apps to get a feel for what kind of apps are available.

When you click the Document Library app, you're prompted to enter a name for your new library, as shown in Figure 4-10. Note that the information you're prompted for here may vary a bit depending on the type of app you select.

4. **Enter a name for the new Document Library, and then click Create.**

For this example, I called the new library "Research Papers." The app is added to the site and will appear in the Site Contents page.

Figure 4-10:
Entering a
name for
the new
Document
Library.

Adding Document Library   ✕

Pick a name   Name:
You can add this app multiple times to your site. Give it a
unique name.   [   ]

Advanced Options   [Create] [Cancel]

5. **In the Site Contents page, hover the mouse over the new app you added and then click the ellipses that appear in the top-right corner of the app's icon.**

   A pop-up menu appears with the choices Settings, About, and Remove.

6. **Click Settings.**

   The Settings page appears, as shown in Figure 4-11. As you can see, there are myriad settings that are available for a new document library.

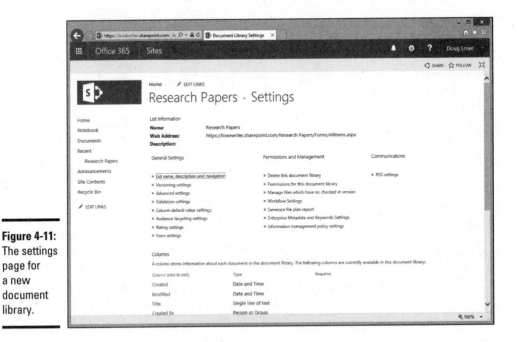

Figure 4-11:
The settings
page for
a new
document
library.

7. Click List Name, Description, and Navigation.

The General Settings page appears, as shown in Figure 4-12.

Book VI
Chapter 4

Using SharePoint Online

Figure 4-12:
The General
Settings
page.

8. Choose Yes for the Display This Document Library on the Quick Launch option, and then click Save.

The setting is saved and you're returned to the Settings page.

9. Click Home to return to the home page.

You're done! The new document library ("Research Papers") appears in the Quick Launch navigation pane, as shown in Figure 4-13.

You've successfully customized your SharePoint site by adding an app.

There are, of course, many other ways you can (and should) customize your SharePoint sites. In addition to apps, you can add additional content pages. You can customize the links that appear in the Quick Launch navigation bar. And you can thoroughly customize the look and feel of your SharePoint site. Most of these additional customization options are available from the Settings icon on the banner at the top of the page. Have fun!

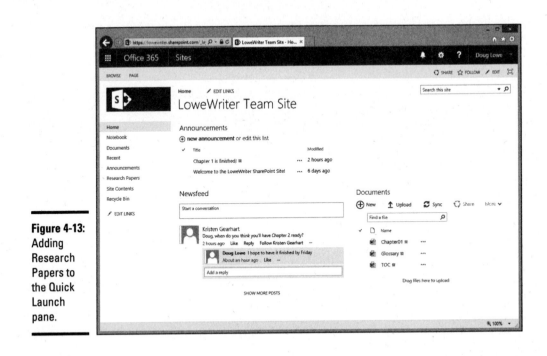

Figure 4-13:
Adding
Research
Papers to
the Quick
Launch
pane.

Book VII

Windows Server 2016 Reference

Read about data deduplication in Windows Server in an article at www.dummies.com/extras/networkingaio.

Contents at a Glance

Chapter 1: Installing and Configuring Windows Server 2016 499

Chapter 2: Managing Windows Server 2016 513

Chapter 3: Dealing with Active Directory 529

Chapter 4: Managing Windows User Accounts 541

Chapter 5: Managing a File Server 563

Chapter 6: Using Group Policy 577

Chapter 7: Troubleshooting 589

Chapter 8: Windows Commands 601

Chapter 1: Installing and Configuring Windows Server 2016

In This Chapter

✔ Making sure you have everything you need

✔ Planning how to install Windows Server 2016

✔ Installing Windows Server 2016

This chapter presents the procedures that you need to follow to install Windows Server — specifically, Windows Server 2016. Note that although the specific details provided are for Windows Server 2016, installing the previous version (just plain Windows Server 2008) is very similar, as is installing the older Windows Server 2003. So you won't have any trouble adapting these procedures if you're installing an older version.

Planning a Windows Server Installation

Before you begin the Setup program to actually install a Windows Server operating system, you need to make several preliminary decisions, as the following sections describe.

Checking system requirements

Before you install a Windows Server operating system, you should make sure that the computer meets the minimum requirements. Table 1-1 lists the official minimum requirements for Windows Server 2016. (The minimums for Windows Server 2012 are the same.) Table 1-1 also lists what I consider to be more realistic minimums if you expect satisfactory performance from the server as a moderately used file server.

Note that there is no 32-bit version of Windows Server 2016. A 64-bit processor is required, but that shouldn't be a problem, as nearly all computers manufactured since around 2007 have 64-bit processors.

Table 1-1	Minimum Hardware Requirements for Windows Server 2016 (Standard Edition)	
Item	*Official Minimum*	*A More Realistic Minimum*
CPU	1.4 GHz	3 GHz
RAM	512MB	4GB
Free disk space	32GB	100GB

Reading the release notes

Like all versions of Windows Server, Windows Server 2016 provides a set of release notes that you should read before you start Setup, just to check whether any of the specific procedures or warnings it contains applies to your situation.

At the time I wrote this, those notes weren't available yet. But you can find them online by searching for *Windows Server 2016 Release Notes* to find the link.

Deciding whether to upgrade or install

Windows offers two installation modes: full installation or upgrade installation.

A *full installation* deletes any existing operating system(s) it finds on the computer and configures the new operating system from scratch. If you do a full installation onto a disk that already has an operating system installed, the full installation offers to keep any existing data files that it finds on the disk.

An *upgrade installation* assumes that you already have a previous Windows Server (Windows Server 2012 or Windows Server 2008) installation in place. The operating system is upgraded to Windows Server 2016, preserving as many settings from the previous installation as possible.

Here are some points to ponder before you perform an upgrade installation:

+ You can't upgrade a client version of Windows to a server version.

+ With an upgrade installation, you don't have to reinstall any applications that were previously installed on the disk.

+ Always perform a full backup before doing an upgrade installation!

Considering your licensing options

Two types of licenses are required to run a Windows Server operating system: a *server license,* which grants you permission to run a single instance of the server, and *Client Access Licenses* (CALs), which grant users or devices permission to connect to the server. When you purchase Windows Server, you ordinarily purchase a server license plus some number of CALs.

To complicate matters, there are two distinct types of CALs: per-user and per-device. *Per-user* CALs limit the number of users who can access a server simultaneously, regardless of the number of devices (such as client computers) in your organization. By contrast, *per-device* CALs limit the number of unique devices that can access the server, regardless of the number of users in your organization.

Thinking about multiboot

Windows includes a *multiboot* feature that lets you set up the computer so that it has more than one operating system. When you boot up the computer, you can select the operating system you want to boot up from a menu.

Although you may be tempted to use the multiboot features to maintain previous operating system installations, I recommend against it. A much better alternative is to install Windows Server into a virtual machine using virtualization technology such as Microsoft's Hyper-V or VMware. Virtualization allows you to install a complete operating system such as Windows Server 2016 within an already-installed operating system. (Note that the Windows Server 2016 installation illustrated in this chapter and throughout this book is installed on a Hyper-V virtual machine running within Windows 8.1.)

**Book VII
Chapter 1**

Installing and Configuring Windows Server 2016

Planning your partitions

Partitioning enables you to divide a physical disk into one or more separate units called *partitions.* Each disk can have up to four partitions. All four of the partitions can be primary partitions. A *primary partition* contains one — and only one — file system. Alternatively, you can create up to three primary partitions and one extended partition, which can be subdivided into one or more logical drives. Then each logical drive can be formatted with a file system.

Windows Server 2016 offers you two file systems: NTFS and ReFS. NTFS is the tried-and-true file system that has been the standard file system for going on 20 years. The partition that Windows Server 2016 boots from must be NTFS. However, other partitions can be either NTFS or ReFS.

Although you can set up partitions for a Windows server in many ways, the following two approaches are the most common:

- ✦ **Allocate the entire disk as a single partition that will be formatted with NTFS.** The operating system is installed into this partition, and disk space that isn't needed by the operating system or other network applications can be shared.

- ✦ **Divide the disk into two partitions.** Install the operating system and any other related software (such as Exchange Server or a backup utility) on the first partition. If the first partition will contain just the operating system, 100GB is a reasonable size, although you can get by with as little as 32GB if space is at a premium. Then use the second partition for application data or network file shares.

Note that the disk partitioning scheme is independent of any hardware-based RAID configuration your server may employ. Your server may actually include five physical hard drives that are combined by the hardware disk controller to form a single logical drive, for example. Within this logical drive, you can create one or more operating-system partitions.

Deciding your TCP/IP configuration

Before you install the operating system, you should have a plan for implementing TCP/IP on the network. Here are some of the things you need to decide or find out:

- ✦ What are the IP subnet address and mask for your network?
- ✦ What is the domain name for the network?
- ✦ What is the host name for the server?
- ✦ Will the server obtain its address from DHCP?
- ✦ Will the server have a static IP address? If so, what?
- ✦ Will the server be a DHCP server?
- ✦ What is the Default Gateway for the server (that is, what is the IP address of the network's Internet router)?

- ✦ Will the server be a DNS server?

In almost all cases, you should assign the server a static IP address.

For more information about planning your TCP/IP configuration, see Book III.

Choosing workgroups or domains

A *domain* is a method of placing user accounts and various network resources under the control of a single directory database. Domains ensure that security policies are applied consistently throughout a network and greatly simplify the task of managing user accounts on large networks.

A *workgroup* is a simple association of computers on a network that makes it easy to locate shared files and printers. Workgroups don't have sophisticated directory databases, so they can't enforce strict security.

Microsoft says that workgroups should be used only for very small networks with just a few users. In fact, any network that is large enough to have a dedicated server running Windows Server 2016 is too large to use workgroups. As a result, if you're installing a Windows server, you should always opt for domains.

After you decide to use domains, you have to make two basic decisions:

✦ **What will the domain name be?** If you have a registered Internet domain name, such as mydomain.com, you may want to use it for your network's domain name. Otherwise, you can make up any name you want.

✦ **What computer or computers will be the domain controllers for the domain?** If this server is the first server in a domain, you must designate it as a domain controller. If you already have a server acting as a domain controller, you can either add this computer as an additional domain controller or designate it a member server.

You can always change the role of a server from a domain controller to a member server, and vice versa, if the needs of your network change. If your network has more than one server, it's always a good idea to create at least two domain controllers. That way, if one fails, the other one can take over.

Book VII Chapter 1

Installing and Configuring Windows Server 2016

Before You Install . . .

After you've made the key planning decisions for your Windows server installation, but before you actually start the Setup program, you should take a few precautionary steps. The following sections describe what you should do before you perform an upgrade installation.

Note: All these steps except the last one apply only to upgrades. If you're installing a Windows server on a new system, you can skip the first steps.

Backing up

Do a complete backup of the server before you begin. Although Windows Setup is reliable, sometimes, something serious goes wrong, and data is lost.

You don't have to back up the drive to external media, such as tape. If you can find a network disk share with enough free space, back up to it.

Checking the event logs

Look at the event logs of the existing server computer to check for recurring errors. You may discover that you have a problem with a SCSI device or your current TCP/IP configuration. It's better to find out now rather than in the middle of setup.

Disconnecting UPS devices

If you've installed an uninterruptible power supply (UPS) device on the server and connected it to your computer via a USB cable, you should temporarily disconnect the serial cable before you run Setup. When Setup is complete, you can reconnect the UPS device.

Running Setup

Now that you've planned your installation and prepared the computer, you're ready to run the Setup program. The following procedure describes the steps that you must follow to install Windows Server 2016 on a virtual machine using an ISO image of the installation DVD. Before you begin this procedure, you'll need to download the ISO file from Microsoft's website. Search for *Windows Server 2016 Download* to find the download site.

1. **Configure the new virtual machine with the specifications you want to use, mount the installation ISO file on the virtual DVD drive, and start the VM.**

   After a few moments, the Windows Setup Wizard fires up and asks for your language, time and currency format, and keyboard layout.

2. **Click Next.**

   The Welcome screen appears, as shown in Figure 1-1.

3. **Click Install Now.**

   Windows asks which edition of the operating system you want to install, as shown in Figure 1-2.

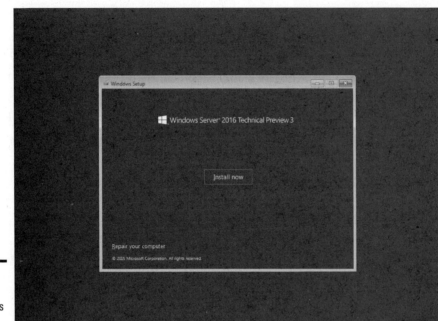

Figure 1-1:
Welcome
to Windows
Setup!

Installing and
Configuring
Windows
Server 2016

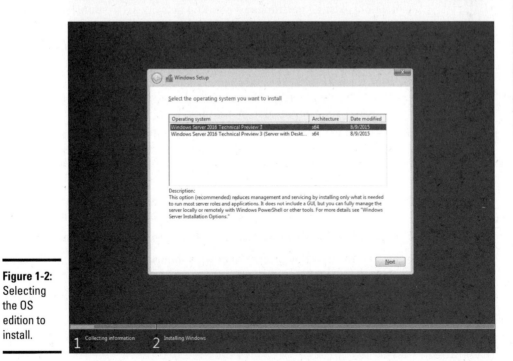

Figure 1-2:
Selecting
the OS
edition to
install.

Two editions are available:

- Windows Server 2016 (also known as Server Core), a streamlined version of the operating system that does not have a graphical user interface (GUI). You must manage this edition of the server remotely using PowerShell or Windows Management Console.

- Windows Server 2016 with Desktop Experience, a more user-friendly version of the server with a GUI modeled after Windows 10.

For this book, I use the Desktop Experience version to demonstrate how to manage various aspects of Windows Server 2016.

4. **Select the edition you want to install and then click Next.**

The Setup Wizard displays the License Agreement information. Read it if you enjoy legalese.

5. **Click I Accept the License Terms and then click Next.**

The Setup Wizard asks whether you want to perform an upgrade installation or a full installation.

6. **Click the installation option you want to use.**

Setup continues by displaying the computer's current partition information. You can select the partition that you want to use for the installation. If necessary, you can reconfigure your partitions from this screen by deleting existing partitions or creating new ones. I assume here that you want to create a single partition that uses all available space on the drive.

7. **Select the partition on which you want to install Windows and then click Next.**

Setup formats the drive and then copies files to the newly formatted drive. This step usually takes a while. I suggest you bring along your favorite book. Start reading at Chapter 1.

After all the files have been copied, Setup reboots your computer. Then Setup examines all the devices on the computer and installs any necessary device drivers. You can read Chapter 2 of your book during this time.

When Setup finishes installing drivers, it asks for the password you want to use for the computer's Administrator account, as shown in Figure 1-3.

8. **Enter the Administrator password twice and then click Finish.**

Be sure to write this password down somewhere and keep it in a secure place. If you lose this password, you won't be able to access your server.

After you've set the Administrator password, Windows displays the login screen shown in Figure 1-4.

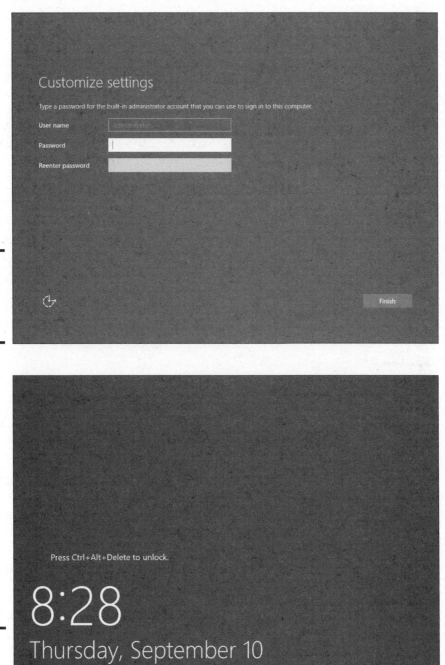

Figure 1-3:
Setting
the Admin-
istrator
password.

Figure 1-4:
Press
Ctrl+Alt+Del
to log in.

**Book VII
Chapter 1**

Installing and
Configuring
Windows
Server 2016

9. **Press Ctrl+Alt+Del, and log in using the Administrator account.**

You have to enter the password you created in Step 7 to gain access.

When you're logged in, Windows displays the Server Manager Dashboard, as shown in Figure 1-5.

Figure 1-5:
The Server
Manager
Dashboard.

The Server Manager Dashboard provides links that let you complete the configuration of your server. Specifically, you can

- Click Configure This Local Server to configure server settings such as the computer's name and the domain it belongs to, network settings such as the static IP address, and so on.

- Click Add Roles and Features to add server roles and features. (For more information, see "Adding Server Roles and Features," later in this chapter.)

- Click Add Other Servers to Manage to manage other servers in your network.

- Click Create a Server Group to create a customized group of servers.

- Click Connect This Server to Cloud Services if you integrate cloud services with your server.

Adding Server Roles and Features

Server roles are the roles that your server can play on your network — roles such as file server, web server, or DHCP or DNS server. *Features* are additional capabilities of the Windows operating system itself, such as the .NET Framework or Windows Backup. Truthfully, the distinctions between roles and features are a bit arbitrary. The web server is considered to be a role, for example, but the Telnet server is a feature. Go figure.

The following procedure describes how to install server roles. The procedure for installing server features is similar.

1. **Click Add Roles and Features on the Server Manager Dashboard.**

The Add Roles and Features Wizard appears, as shown in Figure 1-6.

Book VII
Chapter 1

Installing and
Configuring
Windows
Server 2016

Figure 1-6:
The Add
Roles and
Features
Wizard.

2. **Click Next.**

The wizard asks which of two installation types you want to perform. In most cases, you want to leave the default choice (Role-Based or Feature-Based Installation) selected. Select the alternative (Remote Desktop Services Installation) only if you're configuring a remote virtual server.

3. **Click Next.**

   The wizard lets you select the server you want to install roles or features for, as shown in Figure 1-7. In this example, only one server is listed. If you'd chosen Add Other Servers to Manage in the Server Manager Dashboard to add other servers, those servers would appear on this page as well.

Figure 1-7:
Selecting
the server to
manage.

4. **Select the server you want to manage and then click Next.**

   The Select Server Roles page, shown in Figure 1-8, appears. This page lets you select one or more roles to add to your server.

5. **Select one or more roles to install.**

   You can click each role to display a brief description of it. If you click DHCP Server, for example, the following text is displayed:

   ```
   Dynamic Host Configuration Protocol (DHCP) Server enables you to
         centrally configure, manage, and provide temporary IP addresses
         and related information for client computers.
   ```

6. **Click Next.**

   The Select Features page appears, as shown in Figure 1-9. This page lists additional server features that you can install.

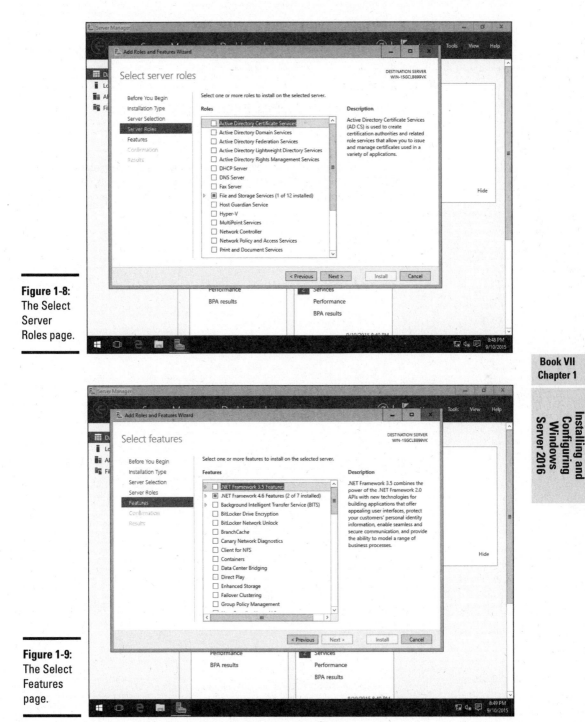

Figure 1-8:
The Select
Server
Roles page.

Book VII
Chapter 1

Installing and
Configuring
Windows
Server 2016

Figure 1-9:
The Select
Features
page.

7. **Select the features you want to install.**

   Again, you can select each feature to see a brief text description of the service.

8. **Click Next.**

   A confirmation page appears, listing the roles and features you've selected.

9. **Click Install.**

   Windows installs the server role and its features. A progress screen is displayed during the installation so that you can gauge the installation's progress. When the installation finishes, a final results page is displayed.

10. **Click OK.**

    You're done!

Chapter 2: Managing Windows Server 2016

In This Chapter

✔ Working with the trusty Administrator account

✔ Using Remote Desktop Connection to administer a server from the comfort of your desktop

✔ Perusing the list of Microsoft Management Consoles

✔ Customizing your own management console

This chapter provides an introduction to the most important tools that you'll use to administer Windows Server 2016.

Using the Administrator Account

Windows comes with a built-in account named *Administrator* that has complete access to all the features of the server. As a network administrator, you frequently log on using the Administrator account to perform maintenance chores.

Because the Administrator account is so powerful, you should always enforce good password practices for it. In other words, don't use your dog's name as the Administrator account password. Instead, pick a random combination of letters and numbers. Then change the password periodically.

Write down the Administrator account password, and keep it in a secure location. Note that by *secure location,* I don't mean taped to the front of the monitor. Keep it in a safe place where you can retrieve it if you forget it, but where it won't easily fall into the hands of someone who's looking to break into your network.

Note that you cannot delete or disable the Administrator account. If Windows allowed you to do that, you could potentially find yourself locked out of your own system.

As much as possible, you should avoid using the Administrator account. Instead, you should create accounts for each of your system administrators and grant them administrator privileges by assigning their accounts to the Administrators group.

Although you can't delete or disable the Administrator account, you can rename it. Some network managers use this ability to hide the true Administrator account. To do this, just follow these steps:

1. **Rename the Administrator account.**

   Write down the new name you use for the Administrator account, along with the password, and store it in a top-secret secure location.

2. **Create a new account named Administrator, and assign it a strong password, but don't give this account any significant privileges.**

   This new account will become a "decoy" Administrator account. The idea is to get hackers to waste time trying to crack this account's password. Even if a hacker does manage to compromise this account, he won't be able to do anything when he gets in.

Using Remote Desktop Connection

One of the most useful tools available to system administrators is a program called *Remote Desktop Connection,* or *RDC* for short. RDC lets you connect to a server computer from your own computer and use it as though you were actually sitting at the server. In short, RDC lets you administer your server computers from your own office.

Enabling remote access

Before you can use Remote Desktop Connection to access a server, you must enable remote access on the server. To do that, follow these steps (on the server computer, not your desktop computer):

1. **Open the Control Panel and then click System.**

   This step brings up the System settings page.

2. **Click the Remote Settings link.**

   This step brings up the remote access options, as shown in Figure 2-1.

3. **Select the Allow Remote Connections to This Computer radio button.**

4. **Click OK.**

You're done! Repeat this procedure for each server computer you want to allow access to.

Figure 2-1:
Configuring
remote
access.

Here are a few other points to ponder concerning remote access:

✦ You can click the Select Users button to create a list of users who are authorized to access the computer remotely. Note that all members of the Administrators group are automatically granted access, so you don't have to add administrators to this list.

✦ There's no question that RDC is convenient and useful. It's also inherently dangerous, however. Don't enable it unless you've taken precautions to secure your Administrator accounts by using strong passwords; also, you should already have a firewall installed to keep unwanted visitors out of your network. For more information on account security, see Book II, Chapter 2.

**Book VII
Chapter 2**

Managing Windows
Server 2016

Connecting remotely

After you've enabled remote access on a server, you can connect to the server by using the Remote Desktop Client that's automatically installed with Windows. Here's the procedure:

1. **Choose Start ⇨ All Programs ⇨ Accessories ⇨ Remote Desktop Connection.**

The Remote Desktop Connection client comes to life, as shown in Figure 2-2.

Figure 2-2:
Connecting
with Remote
Desktop
Connection.

2. **Enter the name of the computer you want to connect to.**

   Alternatively, you can use the drop-down list to select the computer from the list of available computers.

3. **Click the Connect button.**

   You're connected to the computer you selected, and the computer's logon screen is displayed.

4. **Log on, and use the computer.**

   After you log on, you can use the computer as though you were sitting right in front of it.

Here are a few other tips for working with the Remote Desktop Connection client:

✦ When you're using the Remote Desktop Connection client, you can't just Alt+Tab to another program running on the client computer. Instead, you must first minimize the RDC client's window by clicking its minimize button. Then you can access other programs running on your computer.

✦ If you minimize the RDC client window, you have to provide your logon credentials again when you return. This security feature is there in case you forget that you have an RDC session open.

✦ If you use RDC a lot on a particular computer (such as your own desktop computer), I suggest that you create a shortcut to RDC and place it on the desktop, at the top of the Start menu, or in the Quick Launch portion of the taskbar.

✦ RDC has several useful configuration options that you can access by clicking the Options button.

Using Microsoft Management Console

Microsoft Management Console, also known as *MMC,* is a general-purpose management tool that's used to administer many different types of objects on a Windows system. Throughout this minibook, you see many examples of MMC for working with objects such as user accounts, disk drives, event logs, and so on. This section provides a general overview of how to use MMC.

By itself, MMC doesn't actually manage anything. Instead, it's a framework that accepts management snap-ins, which do the actual managing. The main point of MMC is that it provides a consistent framework for building management snap-ins so that all the snap-ins behave in similar ways. As a result, you don't have to struggle to learn completely different tools to manage various aspects of Windows Server 2016.

Another advantage of MMC is that you can create your own custom management consoles with just the right combination of snap-ins. Suppose that you spend most of your time managing user accounts, disk devices, and IIS (Internet Information Services, the web server that comes with Windows Server 2016), and studying event logs. You can easily craft a management console with just these four snap-ins. For more information, see the section "Customizing MMC," later in this chapter.

Working with MMC

There are several ways to open a Microsoft Management Console window. The easiest is to open one of the predefined consoles that come with Windows Server 2016. To access these consoles, press the Windows key and then select Administrative Tools.

You can also start MMC from a command prompt. To start MMC without opening a snap-in, just type **mmc** at a command prompt. To open a specific console, type the path to the console file after mmc. The following command, for example, opens the Computer Management console:

```
mmc \Windows\System32\compmgmt.msc
```

Figure 2-3 shows a typical Microsoft Management Console window, displaying the Active Directory Users and Computers snap-in. As you can see, the MMC window consists of two panes. The pane on the left is a tree pane that displays a hierarchical tree of the objects that you can manage. The pane on the right is a Details pane that shows detailed information about the object that's selected in the tree pane.

Figure 2-3:
A typical
MMC
window.

The procedures for working with the information in the Details pane vary depending on the console you're viewing. Most of the consoles, however, display lists of some kind, such as settings or user accounts. Double-clicking an item usually brings up a Properties dialog box that lets you view or set properties for the object. In most cases, you can click the column headings at the top of the list to change the order in which the list items are displayed.

MMC also includes a menu and toolbar with commands and buttons that vary depending on the item selected in the tree. In particular, the Action menu contains commands that apply to the current item. The Action menu includes a New User command when you're working with the Active Directory Users and Computers console, for example, and a Defragment command when you view the Disk Defragmenter item in the Computer Management Console. As you work with different items within the different consoles, be sure to check the Action menu frequently to find out what commands are available.

Taking an overview of the MMC consoles

The Tools menu in Server Manager Dashboard gives you direct access to many useful management consoles. You find detailed descriptions of several of these tools later in this minibook. The following paragraphs give you a brief overview of the most important of these consoles:

✦ **Active Directory Domains and Trusts:** Manages the domain and trust relationships for the server.

✦ **Active Directory Sites and Services:** Manages Active Directory services.

✦ **Active Directory Users and Computers:** Lets you create and modify user accounts.

✦ **Component Services:** Lets you manage how COM+ (Component Object Model) services work on the server. You mess with this console only if you're involved in developing applications that use COM+ services.

✦ **Computer Management:** Provides access to several useful tools for managing a server. In particular, the Computer Management console provides the following management tools:

- *Event Viewer:* Lets you view event logs.

- *Shared Folders:* Lets you manage shared folders for a file server. In addition to finding out what shares are available, you can use this tool to find out which users are connected to the server and which files are open.

- *Local Users and Groups* (available only on servers that aren't domain controllers): Lets you manage local user and group accounts. For a domain controller, you use the Active Directory Users and Computers console to manage user accounts.

- *Performance:* Lets you monitor system performance counters.

- *Device Manager:* Lets you manage the hardware devices connected to a server. You'll probably use it only if you're having a problem with the server that you suspect may be hardware-related.

- *Disk Management:* Lets you view the physical disks and volumes that are available to the system. You can also use this tool to create and delete partitions, set up RAID volumes, format disks, and so on.

- *Services:* Lets you manage system services. You can use this tool to start or stop services such as Exchange email services, TCP/IP services such as DNS and DHCP, and so on.

- *WMI Control:* Lets you configure *Windows Management Instrumentation services,* which track management data about computers, users, applications, and other objects in large Enterprise networks.

✦ **DHCP:** Manages the DHCP server.

✦ **DNS:** Manages the DNS server.

✦ **Domain Controller Security Policy:** Lets you set security policy for a domain controller.

✦ **Event Viewer:** Lets you view event logs.

✦ **Group Policy Management:** Lets you set system policies that can be applied to objects such as users and groups.

✦ **Internet Information Services (IIS) Manager:** Lets you manage the services provided by IIS (Microsoft's web server) if IIS is installed on the server.

✦ **ODBC Data Sources:** Manages database connections that use ODBC. You'll probably use this console only if you're a developer or database administrator.

✦ **Performance Monitor:** Lets you monitor a server's performance and twiddle with various settings that can have positive or negative effects on performance.

✦ **Services:** Lets you start and stop Windows services. (It's also available via the Computer Management console.)

Customizing MMC

One of the best things about Microsoft Management Console is that you can customize it so that the tools you use most often are grouped together in whatever combination you choose. To create a custom console, first start Microsoft Management Console without loading a console by pressing the Windows key, typing **cmd** and pressing Enter to open a command prompt, and then entering the command **mmc**. This action creates an empty console, as shown in Figure 2-4.

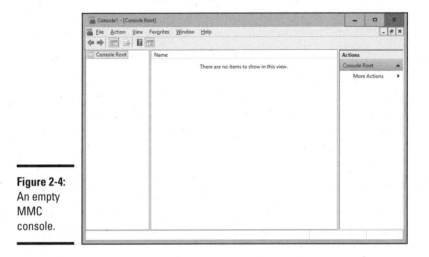

Figure 2-4:
An empty
MMC
console.

Adding snap-ins

After you've created an empty console, you can customize it by adding whatever snap-ins you want to make use of in the console. To add a snap-in, follow these steps:

1. **Choose File ⇨ Add/Remove Snap-In.**

   This command brings up the Add or Remove Snap-Ins dialog box, shown in Figure 2-5.

Figure 2-5: The Add or Remove Snap-Ins dialog box.

2. **Select the snap-in you want to add and then click the Add button.**

   Depending on which snap-in you select, a dialog box appears, asking whether you want to use the add-in to manage settings on your own computer or on a local computer.

3. **Repeat Step 2 if you want to add other snap-ins to the console.**

4. **Click OK.**

   The console is equipped with the snap-ins you've selected.

Adding taskpads

A *taskpad* is a customized page that's displayed within a console. Taskpads are designed to provide quick access to the most common chores for a particular snap-in. A taskpad can display shortcuts that run programs, execute menu commands, open web pages, or open folders. Figure 2-6 shows a simple taskpad that I created for managing local user accounts. As you can see, it includes icons that let you quickly add an account, delete an account, and change an account's password.

To add a taskpad, follow these steps:

1. **Select the tree node where you want the taskpad to appear.**

   Each taskpad you create is specific to a tree node. The taskpad shown in Figure 2-6, for example, is displayed only when you select a user account. To create this taskpad, I opened the Local Users and Groups node and selected the Users node.

2. **Choose Action ➪ New Taskpad View.**

   This step brings up the New Taskpad View Wizard, as shown in Figure 2-7.

3. **Click Next.**

   The Taskpad Style page appears, as shown in Figure 2-8.

   This page provides the following options for formatting the taskpad display:

   • *Vertical List:* If you want to include the list from the details page, you can select this option to place taskpad icons to the left of the list. I selected this option for the taskpad shown in Figure 2-6.

   • *Horizontal List:* This option places the taskpad icons below the details-page list.

Figure 2-7:
The New
Taskpad
View
Wizard.

Figure 2-8:
Setting the
style options
for a new
taskpad
page.

- *No List:* This option creates a taskpad with no list, just taskpad icons.

- *Hide Standard Tab:* Each taskpad can have a standard view, which simply lists all the items in the taskpad without showing custom tasks. The Hide Standard Tab check box, which is selected by default, hides this tab. Most of the time, you'll want to leave this check box selected.

- *Text:* This option displays descriptive information below each taskpad icon.

- *InfoTip:* This option displays descriptive information as a pop-up tip that appears when you hover the mouse over the icon.

- *List Size:* This drop-down list lets you select how much of the taskpad area should be devoted to the list. The options are Small, Medium, and Large.

It's a good thing that this wizard wasn't designed by a fast-food company. If it had been, the options for List Size would be Large, Extra Large, and MegaSuperKing.

4. **Select the taskpad options you want and then click Next.**

The next page of the wizard presents two options that let you control when the taskpad should be displayed:

- *Selected Tree Item:* The taskpad is displayed only for the specific tree item that you selected in Step 1.

- *All Tree Items That Are the Same Type As the Selected Item:* The taskpad is displayed not only for the selected tree item, but also for other items of the same type. This option is the more common choice.

5. **Select the taskpad display option and then click Next.**

The next page of the wizard asks for a name and description for the taskpad.

6. **Type a name and description for the taskpad, and then click Next.**

The final page of the New Taskpad View Wizard is displayed, as shown in Figure 2-9.

Figure 2-9:
The final
page of the
New Task-
pad View
Wizard.

7. **Select the Add New Tasks to This Taskpad After the Wizard Closes check box and then click Finish.**

This step completes the New Taskpad View Wizard but automatically launches the New Task Wizard so that you can begin adding tasks to the taskpad. The New Task Wizard begins by displaying a typical greeting page.

8. **Click Next.**

   The page shown in Figure 2-10 is displayed. This page lets you select one of three types of shortcuts to create on the taskpad:

Figure 2-10:
The New
Task Wizard
gives you
several
choices for
adding new
tasks to a
taskpad.

Figure 2-10: The New Task Wizard gives you several choices for adding new tasks to a taskpad.

- *Menu Command:* Lets you choose one of the console's menu commands. All three of the shortcuts shown in the taskpad in Figure 2-6 are menu commands.

- *Shell Command:* Lets you run another program, start a batch file, or open a web page.

- *Navigation:* Lets you go to one of the views you've added to the Favorites menu. (If you want to add shortcuts that navigate to different taskpads in a console, first add each taskpad view to your Favorites menu by navigating to the taskpad and choosing Favorites ⇨ Add to Favorites.)

9. **Choose the type of shortcut command you want to create and then click Next.**

   The page that's displayed next depends on which option you selected in Step 8. The rest of this procedure assumes that you selected the Menu Command option, which displays the page shown in Figure 2-11.

10. **Choose the command you want to use and then click Next.**

    The available commands are listed in the Available Commands list box. Note that you can bring up several different lists of available commands by choosing an option from the Command Source drop-down list.

    When you click Next, the wizard asks for a name and description for the command you've selected.

Figure 2-11:
Choosing a
menu com-
mand for
a taskpad
shortcut.

11. **Enter a name and description for the command and then click Next.**

This step brings up the page shown in Figure 2-12.

Figure 2-12:
Selecting
an icon.

12. **Choose the icon you want to use and then click Next.**

Note that in many cases, the New Task Wizard suggests an appropriate
icon. If you select a Delete command, for example, the standard Delete
icon will be selected.

When you click Next, the final page of the wizard is displayed, as shown
in Figure 2-13.

Figure 2-13:
The final
page of the
New Task
Wizard.

13. **If you want to create additional tasks, select the When I Click Finish, Run This Wizard Again check box; click Finish; and repeat Steps 8–13.**

You can run the wizard as many times as necessary to add tasks to your taskpad.

14. **When you're finished adding tasks, deselect the When I Click Finish, Run This Wizard Again check box, and click Finish.**

You're done!

Here are a few other pointers for working with taskpads:

✦ You can edit an existing taskpad by selecting the tree node that displays the taskpad and choosing Action➪Edit Taskpad View. This command brings up a Properties dialog box that lets you change the taskpad layout options and add or remove tasks.

✦ To delete a taskpad, select the tree node that displays the taskpad, and choose Action➪Delete Taskpad View.

✦ Don't forget to save (File➪Save) often while you're creating custom taskpads.

Chapter 3: Dealing with Active Directory

In This Chapter

✔ Discovering directories

✔ Examining how Active Directory is structured

✔ Setting up a domain controller

✔ Creating organizational units

*A*ctive Directory is among the most important features of Windows Server, and much of your time as a network administrator will be spent keeping Active Directory neat and tidy. This chapter lays some foundation by explaining what Active Directory is and how it works.

What Directories Do

Everyone uses directory services of one type or another every day. When you look up someone's name in a phone book, you're using a directory service. But you're also using a directory service when you make a call: When you enter someone's phone number into your touch-tone phone, the phone system looks up that number in its directory to locate that person's phone.

Almost from the very beginning, computers have had directory services. When I got started in the computer business back in the 1970s, I used IBM mainframe computers and a transaction-processing system called CICS that's still in widespread use today. CICS relied on many different directories to track such things as files available to the system, users that were authorized to access the system, and application programs that could be run.

But the problem with this directory system, and with most other directory systems that were popular in those days, is that it was made up of many small directory systems that didn't know how to talk to one another. I have the very same problem at home. I have my own little personal address book that has phone numbers and addresses for my friends and family members. I have a Day-Timer book with a bunch of other phone numbers and addresses. Then I have a church directory that lists everyone who goes to my church. Oh, and there's the list of players on the softball team I coach, and of course, my cellphone has a directory.

All counted, I probably have a dozen sources for phone numbers that I routinely call. So when I need to look up someone's phone number, I first have to decide which directory to look in. Some of my friends are listed in two or three of these sources, which raises the possibility that their listings are out of sync.

That's exactly the type of problem that Active Directory is designed to address. Before I get into the specifics of Active Directory, however, I show you the directory system that Microsoft used on Windows networks before Active Directory became available.

Remembering the Good Ol' Days of NT Domains

Active Directory was introduced with Windows 2000 Server. Before then, the directory management system in a Windows network was managed by Windows NT domains, which stored directory information in a database called the Security Account Manager (SAM) database.

PDCs and BDCs

The most important thing to know about NT domains is that they are *servercentric* — that is, every Windows NT domain is under the control of a Windows NT server computer that hosts the primary copy of the SAM database. This server is called the *Primary Domain Controller (PDC)*.

Large networks couldn't work efficiently if all directory access had to be channeled through a single computer, of course. To solve that bottleneck problem, Windows NT domains can also be serviced by one or more *Backup Domain Controllers (BDCs)*. Each BDC stores a read-only copy of the SAM database, and any changes made to the SAM database on the PDC must be propagated down to the BDC copies of the database.

Note that although any of the BDC servers can service access requests such as user logons, all changes to the SAM database must be made via the PDC. Then those changes are copied to the BDC servers. Naturally, this arrangement raises the possibility that the PDC and BDC database are out of sync.

If the PDC should fail for some reason, one of the BDCs can be promoted so that it becomes the PDC for the domain. This promotion allows the domain to continue to function while the original PDC is repaired. Because the BDC is an important backup for the PDC, it's important that all NT networks have at least one BDC.

Trusts

Many organizations have directory needs that are too complicated to store on just one NT domain PDC. In that case, the organization can create two or more separate domains for its network, each with its own PDC and BDCs. Then the organization can set up trusts among its domains.

Simply put, a *trust* is a relationship in which one domain trusts the directory information stored in another domain. The domain that does the trusting is called — you guessed it — the *trusting domain,* and the domain that contains the information being trusted is called the *trusted domain.*

Trust relationships work in one direction. Suppose that you have two domains, named DomainA and DomainB, and a trust relationship is set up so that DomainA trusts DomainB. That means that users whose accounts are defined in DomainB can log on to DomainA and access resources. The trust relationship doesn't work in the other direction, however: Users in DomainA can't log on and access resources defined in DomainB.

Also, trust relationships aren't *transitive.* (There's a word that takes you back to high-school algebra.) That means that even if DomainA trusts DomainB and DomainB trusts DomainC, DomainA doesn't automatically trust DomainC. For DomainA to trust DomainC, you'd have to create a separate trust relationship between DomainA and DomainC.

NetBIOS names

One other important characteristic of Windows NT domains is that they use NetBIOS names. Thus, NT names such as computer names and domain names are limited to 15 characters.

Actually, NetBIOS names are 16 characters long. But NT uses the last character of the 16-character NetBIOS name for its own purposes, so that character isn't available for use. As a result, NT names can be only 15 characters long.

Active Directory to the Rescue

Active Directory solves many of the inherent limitations of Windows NT domains by creating a distributed directory database that keeps track of every conceivable type of network object.

Active Directory is a comprehensive directory management system that tracks just about everything worth tracking in a Windows network, including users, computers, files, folders, applications, and much more. Much of your job as a network administrator involves working with Active Directory, so it's vital that you have a basic understanding of how it works.

One of the most important differences between Active Directory and NT domains is that Active Directory isn't servercentric. In other words, Active Directory isn't tied to a specific server computer, the way a Windows NT domain is. Although Active Directory still uses domains and domain controllers, these concepts are much more flexible in Active Directory than they are in Windows NT.

Another important difference between Active Directory and NT domains is that Active Directory uses the same naming scheme that's used on the Internet: Domain Name System (DNS). Thus, an Active Directory domain might have a name like `sales.mycompany.com`.

Understanding How Active Directory Is Structured

Like all directories, Active Directory is essentially a database management system. The Active Directory database is where the individual objects tracked by the directory are stored. Active Directory uses a *hierarchical* database model, which groups items in a treelike structure.

The terms *object, organizational unit, domain, tree,* and *forest* are used to describe the way Active Directory organizes its data. The following sections explain the meaning of these important Active Directory terms.

Objects

The basic unit of data in Active Directory is called an *object.* Active Directory can store information about many kinds of objects. The objects you work with most are users, groups, computers, and printers.

Figure 3-1 shows the Active Directory Manager displaying a list of built-in objects that come preconfigured with Windows Server 2016. To get to this management tool, choose Start ⇨ Administrative Tools ⇨ Active Directory Users and Computers. Then click the Builtin node to show the built-in objects.

Figure 3-1:
Objects
displayed by
the Active
Directory
Manager
console.

Objects have descriptive characteristics called *properties* or *attributes*. You can call up the properties of an object by double-clicking the object in the management console.

Domains

A *domain* is the basic unit for grouping related objects in Active Directory. Typically, domains correspond to departments in a company. A company with separate Accounting, Manufacturing, and Sales departments might have domains named (you guessed it) `Accounting`, `Manufacturing`, and `Sales`. Or the domains may correspond to geographical locations. A company with offices in Detroit, Dallas, and Denver might have domains named `det`, `dal`, and `den`.

Note that because Active Directory domains use DNS naming conventions, you can create subdomains that are considered to be child domains. You should always create the top-level domain for your entire network before you create any other domain. If your company is named Nimbus Brooms, and you've registered `NimbusBroom.com` as your domain name, you should create a top-level domain named `NimbusBroom.com` before you create any other domains. Then you can create subdomains such as `Accounting.NimbusBroom.com`, `Manufacturing.NimbusBroom.com`, and `Sales.NimbusBroom.com`.

If you have Microsoft Visio, you can use it to draw diagrams for your Active Directory domain structure. Visio includes several templates that provide cool icons for various types of Active Directory objects. Figure 3-2 shows a diagram that shows an Active Directory with four domains created with Visio.

Figure 3-2:
Domains
for a com-
pany with
three
departments.

NimbusBroom.com

Accounting. NimbusBroom.com   Sales. NimbusBroom.com   Manufacturing. NimbusBroom.com

Note that these domains have little to do with the physical structure of your network. In Windows NT, domains usually are related to the network's physical structure.

Every domain must have at least one *domain controller,* which is a server that's responsible for the domain. Unlike a Windows NT PDC, however, an Active Directory domain controller doesn't have unique authority over its domain. In fact, a domain can have two or more domain controllers that share administrative duties. A feature called *replication* works hard at keeping all the domain controllers in sync.

Organizational units

Many domains have too many objects to manage together in a single group. Fortunately, Active Directory lets you create one or more *organizational units,* also known as OUs. OUs let you organize objects within a domain, without the extra work and inefficiency of creating additional domains.

One reason to create OUs within a domain is to assign administrative rights to each OU of different users. Then these users can perform routine administrative tasks such as creating new user accounts or resetting passwords.

Suppose that the domain for the Denver office, named `den`, houses the Accounting and Legal departments. Rather than create separate domains for these departments, you could create organizational units for the departments.

Trees

A *tree* is a set of Active Directory names that share a namespace. The domains `NimbusBroom.com`, `Accounting.NimbusBroom.com`, `Manufacturing.NimbusBroom.com`, and `Sales.NimbusBroom.com` make up a tree that's derived from a common root domain, `NimbusBroom.com`.

The domains that make up a tree are related to one another through *transitive trusts.* In a transitive trust, if DomainA trusts DomainB and DomainB trusts DomainC, DomainA automatically trusts DomainC.

Note that a single domain all by itself is still considered to be a tree.

Forests

As its name suggests, a *forest* is a collection of trees. In other words, a forest is a collection of one or more domain trees that do *not* share a common parent domain.

Suppose that Nimbus Brooms acquires Tracorum Technical Enterprises, which already has its own root domain named `TracorumTech.com`, with several subdomains of its own. You can create a forest from these two domain trees so that the domains can trust each other. Figure 3-3 shows this forest.

The key to Active Directory forests is a database called the global catalog. The *global catalog* is sort of a superdirectory that contains information about all the objects in a forest, regardless of the domain. If a user account can't be found in the current domain, the global catalog is searched for the account. The global catalog provides a reference to the domain in which the account is defined.

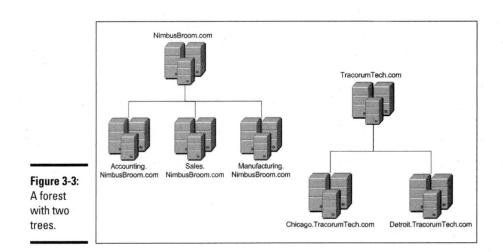

Figure 3-3:
A forest
with two
trees.

Creating a New Domain

To create a domain, you start by designating a Windows Server 2016 system to be the new domain's controller. You can do that by using the Server Manager to install Active Directory services as described in Book VII, Chapter 1. After you've installed Active Directory services, click the Notifications icon near the top-right corner of the Server Manager, and choose Promote This Server to a Domain Controller. This command launches the wizard shown in Figure 3-4.

Figure 3-4:
Creating
a domain
controller.

This wizard lets you designate the server as a domain controller. As you can see, the wizard gives you three options:

✦ **Add a Domain Controller to an Existing Domain:** Choose this option if you've already created the domain and want to add this server as a domain controller.

✦ **Add a New Domain to an Existing Forest:** If you've already created a forest but want to create a new domain within the existing forest, choose this option.

✦ **Add a New Forest:** This option is the one to choose if you're setting up a new domain in a brand-new forest.

When you create a new domain, the configuration wizard asks you for a name for the new domain. If you're creating the first domain for your network, use your company's domain name, such as `NimbusBroom.com`. If you're creating a subdomain, use a name such as `Sales.NimbusBroom.com`.

Creating an Organizational Unit

Organizational units can simplify the task of managing large domains by dividing users, groups, and other objects into manageable collections. By default, Active Directory domains include several useful OUs. The Domain Controllers OU, for example, contains all the domain controllers for the domain.

If you want to create additional organizational units to help manage a domain, follow these steps:

1. **In Server Manager, choose Tools ⇨ Active Directory Users and Computers.**

The Active Directory Users and Computers console appears, as shown in Figure 3-5.

2. **Right-click the domain you want to add the OU to, and choose New ⇨ Organizational Unit from the contextual menu.**

The New Object – Organizational Unit dialog box appears, as shown in Figure 3-6.

3. **Type a name for the new organization unit.**

4. **Click OK.**

You're done!

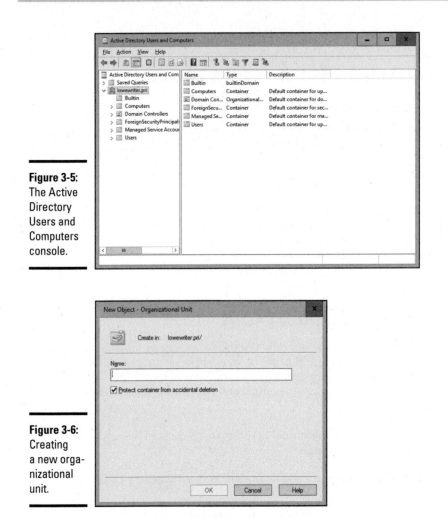

Figure 3-5:
The Active
Directory
Users and
Computers
console.

Figure 3-6:
Creating
a new orga-
nizational
unit.

Here are just a few more thoughts about OUs to ponder as you drift off to sleep:

✦ You can delegate administrative authority for an OU to another user by right-clicking the OU and choosing Select Delegate Control from the contextual menu. Then you can select the user or group that will have administrative authority over the OU. You can also choose which admin-istrative tasks will be assigned to the selected user or group.

✦ Remember that OUs aren't the same as groups. *Groups* are security principals, which means that you can assign them rights. Thereafter, when you assign a user to a group, the user is given the rights of the group. By contrast, an OU is merely an administrative tool that lets you control how user and group accounts are managed.

✦ For more information about how to create user and group accounts as well as other Active Directory objects, turn to Book VII, Chapter 4.

**Book VII
Chapter 3**

**Dealing with
Active Directory**

Chapter 4: Managing Windows User Accounts

In This Chapter

✔ Understanding user accounts

✔ Creating user accounts

✔ Setting account options

✔ Working with groups

✔ Creating a roaming profile

*E*very user who accesses a network must have a *user account*. User accounts let you control who can access the network and who can't. In addition, user accounts let you specify what network resources each user can use. Without user accounts, all your resources would be open to anyone who casually dropped by your network.

Understanding Windows User Accounts

User accounts are among the basic tools for managing a Windows server. As a network administrator, you'll spend a large percentage of your time dealing with user accounts — creating new ones, deleting expired ones, resetting passwords for forgetful users, granting new access rights, and so on. Before I get into the specific procedures of creating and managing user accounts, this section presents an overview of user accounts and how they work.

Local accounts versus domain accounts

A *local account* is a user account that's stored on a particular computer and applies only to that computer. Typically, each computer on your network will have a local account for each person who uses that computer.

By contrast, a *domain account* is a user account that's stored by Active Directory and can be accessed from any computer that's a part of the domain. Domain accounts are centrally managed. This chapter deals primarily with setting up and maintaining domain accounts.

User account properties

Every user account has several important account properties that specify the characteristics of the account. The three most important account properties are

+ **Username:** A unique name that identifies the account. The user must enter the username when logging on to the network. The username is public information. In other words, other network users can (and often should) find out your username.

+ **Password:** A secret word that must be entered to gain access to the account. You can set up Windows so that it enforces password policies, such as the minimum length of the password, whether the password must contain a mixture of letters and numerals, and how long the password remains current before the user must change it.

+ **Group membership:** The group or groups to which the user account belongs. Group memberships are the key to granting access rights to users so that they can access various network resources, such as file shares or printers, or perform certain network tasks, such as creating new user accounts or backing up the server.

Many other account properties record information about the user, such as the user's contact information, whether the user is allowed to access the system only at certain times or from certain computers, and so on. I describe some of these features in later sections of this chapter, and some are described in more detail in Book VII, Chapter 6.

Creating a New User

To create a new domain user account in Windows Server 2016, follow these steps:

1. **Choose Start ⇨ Administrative Tools ⇨ Active Directory Users and Computers.**

   This command fires up the Active Directory Users and Computers management console, as shown in Figure 4-1.

2. **Right-click the organizational unit that you want to add the user to and then choose New ⇨ User from the contextual menu.**

   This command summons the New Object – User Wizard, as shown in Figure 4-2.

Active Directory Users and Computers

File   Action   View   Help

Active Directory Users and Com	Name	Type	Description
Saved Queries	Administrator	User	Built-in account for ad...
lowewriter.pri	Allowed RO...	Security Group...	Members in this group c...
Builtin	Cert Publish...	Security Group...	Members of this group ...
Computers	Cloneable D...	Security Group...	Members of this group t...
Domain Controllers	DefaultAcco...	User	A user account manage...
ForeignSecurityPrincipal:	Denied ROD...	Security Group...	Members in this group c...
Managed Service Accoun	DnsAdmins	Security Group...	DNS Administrators Gro...
Users	DnsUpdateP...	Security Group...	DNS clients who are per...
	Domain Ad...	Security Group...	Designated administrato...
	Domain Co...	Security Group...	All workstations and ser...
	Domain Con...	Security Group...	All domain controllers i...
	Domain Gue...	Security Group...	All domain guests
	Domain Users	Security Group...	All domain users
	Enterprise A...	Security Group...	Designated administrato...
	Enterprise K...	Security Group...	Members of this group ...
	Enterprise R...	Security Group...	Members of this group ...
	Group Polic...	Security Group...	Members in this group c...
	Guest	User	Built-in account for gue...
	Key Admins	Security Group...	Members of this group ...
	Protected Us...	Security Group...	Members of this group ...
	RAS and IAS ...	Security Group...	Servers in this group can...

Figure 4-1:
The Active
Directory
Users and
Computers
management
console.

New Object - User

Create in: lowewriter.pri/Users

First name: [   ]   Initials: [   ]

Last name: [   ]

Full name: [   ]

User logon name:

[   ]   [@lowewriter.pri   ▾]

User logon name (pre-Windows 2000):

[LOWEWRITER\   ]   [   ]

[< Back]   [Next >]   [Cancel]

Figure 4-2:
Creating a
new user.

**Book VII
Chapter 4**

**Managing Windows
User Accounts**

3. **Type the user's first name, middle initial, and last name.**

   As you type the name, the New Object Wizard automatically fills in the
   Full Name field.

4. **Change the Full Name field if you want it to appear different from
   what the wizard proposes.**

   You may want to reverse the first and last names so the last name
   appears first, for example.

5. **Type the user logon name.**

   This name must be unique within the domain.

   Pick a naming scheme to follow when creating user logon names. You can use the first letter of the first name followed by the complete last name, the complete first name followed by the first letter of the last name, or any other scheme that suits your fancy.

6. **Click Next.**

   The second page of the New Object – User Wizard appears, as shown in Figure 4-3.

Figure 4-3:
Setting
the user's
password.

7. **Type the password twice.**

   You're asked to type the password twice, so type it correctly. If you don't type it identically in both boxes, you're asked to correct your mistake.

8. **Specify the password options that you want to apply.**

   The following password options are available:

   - User Must Change Password at Next Logon.
   - User Cannot Change Password.
   - Password Never Expires.
   - Account Is Disabled.

   For more information about these options, see the section "Setting account options," later in this chapter.

9. **Click Next.**

You're taken to the final page of the New Object – User Wizard, as shown in Figure 4-4.

Figure 4-4:
Verifying
the user
account
information.

> New Object - User
>
> Create in: lowewriter.pri/Users
>
> When you click Finish, the following object will be created:
>
> Full name: John Falstaff
> User logon name: jfalstaff@lowewriter.pri
> The user must change the password at next logon.
>
> < Back   Finish   Cancel

10. **Verify that the information is correct and then click Finish to create the account.**

If the account information isn't correct, click the Back button, and correct the error.

You're done! Now you can customize the user's account settings. At minimum, you'll probably want to add the user to one or more groups. You may also want to add contact information for the user or set up other account options.

An alternate way to create a new user is to simply copy an existing user. When you copy an existing user, you provide a new username and password and Windows copies all of the other property settings from the existing user to the new user.

Setting User Properties

After you've created a user account, you can set additional properties for the user by right-clicking the new user and choosing Properties from the contextual menu. This command brings up the User Properties dialog box, which has about a million tabs that you can use to set various properties for the user. Figure 4-5 shows the General tab, which lists basic information about the user, such as the user's name, office location, and phone number.

Figure 4-5:
The General tab.

The following sections describe some of the administrative tasks that you can perform via the various tabs of the User Properties dialog box.

Changing the user's contact information

Several tabs of the User Properties dialog box contain contact information for the user:

✦ **Address:** Lets you change the user's street address, post office box, city, state, zip code, and so on

✦ **Telephones:** Lets you specify the user's phone numbers

✦ **Organization:** Lets you record the user's job title and the name of his or her boss

Setting account options

The Account tab of the User Properties dialog box, shown in Figure 4-6, features a variety of interesting options that you can set for the user. From this dialog box, you can change the user's logon name. In addition, you can change the password options that you set when you created the account, and you can set an expiration date for the account.

Figure 4-6:
The
Account
tab.

The following account options are available in the Account Options list box:

✦ **User Must Change Password at Next Logon:** This option, which is selected by default, allows you to create a one-time-only password that can get the user started with the network. The first time the user logs on to the network, he or she is asked to change the password.

✦ **User Cannot Change Password:** Use this option if you don't want to allow users to change their passwords. (Obviously, you can't use this option and the preceding one at the same time.)

✦ **Password Never Expires:** Use this option if you want to bypass the password-expiration policy for this user so that the user will never have to change his or her password.

✦ **Store Password Using Reversible Encryption:** This option stores passwords by using an encryption scheme that hackers can easily break, so you should avoid it like the plague.

✦ **Account Is Disabled:** This option allows you to create an account that you don't yet need. As long as the account remains disabled, the user won't be able to log on. See the section "Disabling and Enabling User

Accounts," later in this chapter, to find out how to enable a disabled account.

✦ **Smart Card Is Required for Interactive Logon:** If the user's computer has a smart card reader to read security cards automatically, check this option to require the user to use it.

✦ **Account Is Trusted for Delegation:** This option indicates that the account is trustworthy and can set up delegations. This advanced feature usually is reserved for Administrator accounts.

✦ **Account Is Sensitive and Cannot Be Delegated:** This option prevents other users from impersonating this account.

✦ **Use DES Encryption Types for This Account:** This option beefs up the encryption for applications that require extra security.

✦ **Do Not Require Kerberos Preauthentication:** Select this option if you use a different implementation of the Kerberos protocol.

Specifying logon hours

You can restrict the hours during which the user is allowed to log on to the system by clicking the Logon Hours button on the Account tab of the User Properties dialog box. This button brings up the Logon Hours for [User] dialog box, shown in Figure 4-7.

Figure 4-7:
Restricting the user's logon hours.

Initially, the Logon Hours dialog box is set to allow the user to log on at any time of day or night. To change the hours that you want the user to have access, click a day and time or a range of days and times; choose either Logon Permitted or Logon Denied; and click OK.

Restricting access to certain computers

Normally, a user can use his or her user account to log on to any computer that's part of the user's domain. You can restrict a user to certain computers, however, by clicking the Log On To button on the Account tab of the User Properties dialog box. This button brings up the Logon Workstations dialog box, as shown in Figure 4-8.

Figure 4-8:
Restricting
the user
to certain
computers.

To restrict the user to certain computers, select the radio button labeled The Following Computers. Then, for each computer you want to allow the user to log on from, type the computer's name in the text box, and click Add.

If you make a mistake, you can select the incorrect computer name and then click Edit to change the name or Remove to delete the name.

Setting the user's profile information

The Profile tab, shown in Figure 4-9, lets you configure the user's profile information. This dialog box lets you configure three bits of information related to the user's profile:

✦ **Profile Path:** This field specifies the location of the user's roaming profile. For more information, see the section "Working with User Profiles,"
later in this chapter.

Figure 4-9:
The Profile
tab.

+ **Logon Script:** This field is the name of the user's logon script. A *logon script* is a batch file that's run whenever the user logs on. The main purpose of the logon script is to map the network shares that the user requires access to. Logon scripts are carryovers from early versions of Windows NT Server. In Windows Server 2016, profiles are the preferred way to configure the user's computer when the user logs on, including setting up network shares. Many administrators still like the simplicity of logon scripts, however. For more information, see the section "Creating a Logon Script," later in this chapter.

+ **Home Folder:** This section is where you specify the default storage location for the user.

The Profile tab lets you specify the location of an existing profile for the user, but it doesn't actually let you set up the profile. For more information about setting up a profile, see the section "Working with User Profiles," later in this chapter.

Resetting User Passwords

By some estimates, the single most time-consuming task of most network administrators is resetting user passwords. It's easy to think that users are forgetful idiots, but put yourself in their shoes. Administrators insist that they set their passwords to something incomprehensible, such as 94kD82leL384K; that they change it a week later to something more unmemorable, such as dJUQ63DWd8331; and that they don't write it down. Then administrators get mad when they forget their passwords.

So when a user calls and says that he or she forgot his or her password, the least the administrator can do is be cheerful when resetting it. After all, the user probably spent 15 minutes trying to remember it before finally giving up and admitting failure.

Here's the procedure to reset the password for a user domain account:

1. **Log on as an administrator.**

You must have administrator privileges to perform this procedure.

2. **In Server Manager, choose Tools⇨Active Directory Users and Computers.**

The Active Directory Users and Computers management console appears.

3. **Click Users in the console tree.**

4. **In the Details pane, right-click the user who forgot his or her password, and choose Reset Password from the contextual menu.**

5. **Type the new password in both password boxes.**

You have to type the password twice to ensure that you type it correctly.

6. **If desired, select the User Must Change Password at Next Logon option.**

If you select this option, the password that you assign will work for only one logon. As soon as the user logs on, he or she will be required to change the password.

7. **Click OK.**

That's all there is to it! The user's password is reset.

Disabling and Enabling User Accounts

If you want to temporarily prevent a user from accessing the network, you can disable his or her account. Then you can enable the account later, when you're ready to restore the user to full access. Here's the procedure:

1. **Log on as an administrator.**

You must have administrator privileges to perform this procedure.

Book VII Chapter 4

Managing Windows User Accounts

2. **From Server Manager, choose Tools ⇨ Active Directory Users and Computers.**

   The Active Directory Users and Computers management console appears.

3. **Click Users in the console tree.**

4. **In the Details pane, right-click the user that you want to enable or disable; then choose either Enable Account or Disable Account from the contextual menu to enable or disable the user.**

Deleting a User

Deleting a user account is surprisingly easy. Just follow these steps:

1. **Log on as an administrator.**

   You must have administrator privileges to perform this procedure.

2. **Choose Start ⇨ Administrative Tools ⇨ Active Directory Users and Computers.**

   The Active Directory Users and Computers management console appears.

3. **Click Users in the console tree.**

4. **In the Details pane, right-click the user that you want to delete and then choose Delete from the contextual menu.**

   Windows asks whether you really want to delete the user, just in case you're kidding.

5. **Click Yes.**

   Poof! The user account is deleted.

Deleting a user account is a permanent, nonreversible action. Do it only if you're absolutely sure that you'll never want to restore the user's account. If there's any possibility of restoring the account later, you should disable the account instead of delete it.

Working with Groups

A *group* is a special type of account that represents a set of users who have common network access needs. Groups can dramatically simplify the task of assigning network access rights to users. Rather than assign access rights to each user individually, you can assign rights to the group itself. Then those rights automatically extend to any user you add to the group.

The following sections describe some of the key concepts that you need to understand to use groups, along with some of the most common procedures you'll employ when setting up groups for your server.

Group types

Two distinct types of groups exist:

✦ **Security groups:** Most groups are security groups, which extend access rights to members of the group. If you want to allow a group of users to access your high-speed color laser printer, for example, you can create a group called ColorPrintUsers. Then you can grant permission to use the printer to the ColorPrintUsers group. Finally, you can add individual users to the ColorPrintUsers group.

✦ **Distribution groups:** Distribution groups aren't used as much as security groups are. They're designed as a way to send email to a group of users by specifying the group as the recipient.

Group scope

A group can have any of three distinct *scopes,* which determine what domains the group's members can belong to:

✦ **Domain local:** A group with *domain local scope* can have members from any domain. The group can be granted permissions only from the domain in which the group is defined, however.

✦ **Global:** A group with *global scope* can have members only from the domain in which the group is defined. The group can be granted permissions in any domain in the forest, however. (For more information about forests, refer to Book VII, Chapter 3.)

✦ **Universal scope:** Groups with *universal scope* are available in all domains that belong to the same forest.

As you can probably guess, universal scope groups are usually used only on very large networks.

One common way you can use domain local and global groups is as follows:

1. **Use domain local groups to assign access rights for network resources.**

To control access to a high-speed color printer, for example, create a domain local group for the printer. Grant the group access to the printer, but don't add any users to the group.

2. **Use global groups to associate users with common network access needs.**

   Create a global group for users who need to access color printers, for example. Then add each user who needs access to a color printer membership to the group.

3. **Finally, add the global group to the domain local group.**

   That way, access to the printer is extended to all members of the global group.

This technique gives you the most flexibility when your network grows.

Default groups

Windows Server 2016 comes with several predefined groups that you can use. Although you shouldn't be afraid to create your own groups when you need them, there's no reason to create your own group if you find a default group that meets your needs.

Some of these groups are listed in the Builtin container in the Active Directory Users and Computers management console. Others are listed in the Users container. Table 4-1 lists the most useful default groups in Builtin, and Table 4-2 lists the default groups in the Users container.

Table 4-1	Default Groups Located in the Builtin Container
Group	*Description*
Account Operators	This group is for users who should be allowed to create, edit, or delete user accounts but shouldn't be granted full administrator status.
Administrators	This group is for the system administrators who have full control of the domain. The Administrator account is a default member of this group. You should create only a limited number of accounts that belong to this group.
Backup Operators	This group is for users who need to perform backup operations. Because this group must have access to the files that are backed up, it presents a security risk, so you should limit the number of users that you add to this group.
Guests	This group allows members to log on but little else. The default Guest account is a member of this group.
Network Configuration	This group is allowed to twiddle with network configuration settings, including releasing and renewing DHCP leases.

Group	Description
Print Operators	This group grants users access to printers, including the ability to create and share new printers and to manage print queues.
Remote Desktop Users	This group can remotely log on to domain controllers in the domain.
Replicator	This group is required to support directory replication. Don't add users to this group.
Server Operators	These users can log on locally to a domain controller.
Users	These users can perform common tasks, such as running applications and using local and network printers.

Table 4-2   Default Groups Located in the Users Container

Group	Description
Cert Publishers	These users can publish security certificates for users and computers.
DnsAdmins	This group is installed if you install DNS. It grants administrative access to the DNS Server service.
DnsUpdateProxy	This group is installed if you install DNS. It allows DNS clients to perform dynamic updates on behalf of other clients, such as DHCP servers.
Domain Admins	These users have complete control of the domain. By default, this group is a member of the Administrators group on all domain controllers, and the Administrator account is a member of this group.
Domain Computers	This group contains all computers that belong to the domain. Any computer account created becomes a member of this group automatically.
Domain Controllers	This group contains all domain controllers in the domain.
Domain Guests	This group contains all domain guests.
Domain Users	This group contains all domain users. Any user account created in the domain is added to this group automatically.
Group Policy	These users can modify group policy for the domain.
IIS_WPG	This group is created if you install IIS. It's required for IIS to operate properly.
RAS and IAS Servers	This group is required for RAS and IAS servers to work properly.

Creating a group

If none of the built-in groups meets your needs, you can create your own
group by following these steps:

1. **Log on as an administrator.**

   You must have administrator privileges to perform this procedure.

2. **From Server Manager, choose Tools ⇨ Active Directory Users and Computers.**

   The Active Directory Users and Computers management console
   appears.

3. **Right-click the domain to which you want to add the group and then choose New ⇨ Group from the contextual menu.**

   The New Object – Group dialog box appears, as shown in Figure 4-10.

New Object - Group

    Create in: lowewriter.pri/Users

Group name:

Group name (pre-Windows 2000):

Group scope
- ○ Domain local
- ◉ Global
- ○ Universal

Group type
- ◉ Security
- ○ Distribution

OK   Cancel

Figure 4-10:
Creating a
new group.

4. **Type the name for the new group.**

   Enter the name in both text boxes.

5. **Choose the group scope.**

   The choices are Domain Local, Global, and Universal. For groups that
   will be granted access rights to network resources, choose Domain
   Local. Use Global for groups to which you'll add users and Domain Local
   groups. Use Universal groups only if you have a large network with multiple domains.

6. **Choose the group type.**

   The choices are Security and Distribution. In most cases, choose Security.

7. **Click OK.**

   The group is created.

Adding a member to a group

Groups are collections of objects, called *members*. The members of a group can be user accounts or other groups. When you create a group, it has no members. As a result, the group isn't useful until you add at least one member.

Follow these steps to add a member to a group:

1. **Log on as an administrator.**

   You must have administrator privileges to perform this procedure.

2. **Choose Start ⇨ Administrative Tools ⇨ Active Directory Users and Computers.**

   The Active Directory Users and Computers management console appears.

3. **Open the folder that contains the group to which you want to add members and then double-click the group.**

   The Group Properties dialog box appears.

4. **Click the Members tab.**

   The members of the group are displayed, as shown in Figure 4-11.

5. **Click Add, type the name of a user or another group that you want to add to this group, and click OK.**

   The member is added to the list.

6. **Repeat Step 5 for each user or group that you want to add.**

   Keep going until you've added everyone!

7. **Click OK.**

That's all there is to it.

The Group Properties dialog box also has a Member Of tab that lists each group that the current group is a member of.

Figure 4-11:
Adding
members to
a group.

Adding members to a group is only half the process of making a group useful. The other half is adding access rights to the group so that the members of the group can actually *do* something. The procedures for doing that are covered in Book VII, Chapter 5.

Working with User Profiles

User profiles automatically maintain desktop settings for Windows users. By default, a user profile is stored on the user's local computer. The following items are just some of the settings that are stored as part of the user profile:

✦ **Desktop settings** in the Display Properties dialog box, including wallpaper, screen savers, and color schemes

✦ **Start-menu programs** and Windows toolbar options

✦ **Favorites,** which provide easy access to the files and folders that the user accesses frequently

✦ **Application Data,** such as option settings, custom dictionaries, and so on

✦ **Cookies,** used for Internet browsing

✦ **Recent Documents,** which keeps shortcuts to the documents most recently accessed by the user

✦ **Templates,** which stores user templates

✦ **Network,** which keeps shortcuts to the user's network locations

✦ **Send To,** which keeps shortcuts to document-handling utilities

✦ **Local Settings,** such as history and temporary files

✦ **Printers,** which keeps shortcuts to the user's printers

✦ **Documents,** which stores the user's local documents

Types of user profiles

Four types of user profiles exist:

✦ **Local user profile:** A local user profile is stored on the user's local computer and is applied only when the user logs on to that computer. A local user profile is created automatically when a new user logs on.

✦ **Roaming user profile:** A roaming user profile is created on a network share. That way, the user can access the roaming profile when he or she logs on to any computer on the network.

✦ **Mandatory user profile:** A mandatory user profile is a roaming user profile that the user is not allowed to change. One benefit of mandatory user profiles is that users can't mess up their desktop settings. Another benefit is that you can create a single mandatory profile that can be used by multiple users.

✦ **Temporary user profile:** If a roaming or mandatory profile isn't available for some reason, a temporary user profile is automatically created for the user. The temporary profile is deleted when the user logs off, so any changes that the user makes while using a temporary profile are lost at the end of the session.

Roaming profiles

A *roaming user profile* is simply a user profile that has been copied to a network share so that it can be accessed from any computer on the network.

Before you can create roaming user profiles, you should create a shared folder on the server to hold the profiles. You can name the shared folder anything you like, but most administrators call it Users. For information on the procedure to create a shared folder, see Book VII, Chapter 5.

After you've created the shared Users folder, you can copy the profile to the server by following these steps at the user's local computer:

1. **Log on to the computer by using an account other than the one you want to make a user account.**

Windows won't let you copy the profile that you're logged on with.

2. **Click the Start button, type the word** Profile, **and choose the Configure Advanced User Profile Properties option from the menu that appears.**

   This step brings up the User Profiles dialog box, shown in Figure 4-12.

3. **Select the profile that you want to copy and then click Copy To.**

   A Copy To dialog box appears.

4. **Type the path and name for the roaming profile in the Copy Profile To box.**

   To copy a profile named Doug to the Users share on a server named Server01, for example, type **\\Server01\Users\Doug**.

5. **Click OK.**

   The profile is copied.

Now you can go back to the server, log on as an administrator, and follow these steps to designate a roaming profile for the user's domain account:

1. **From the Server Manager, choose Tools ⇨ Active Directory Users and Computers.**

   The Active Directory Users and Computers management console appears.

2. **Right-click the user account, and choose Properties from the contextual menu.**

   The User Properties dialog box appears.

3. **Click the Profile tab.**

   The Profile tab appears. (This tab is shown in Figure 4-9, earlier in this chapter, so I won't repeat it here.)

4. **Type the path and name of the profile in the Profile Path text box.**

   The path and name that you type here should be the same path and name that you used to copy the profile to the server.

5. **Click OK.**

Creating a Logon Script

A *logon script* is a batch file that's run automatically whenever a user logs on. The most common reason for using a logon script is to map the network shares that the user needs access to. Here's a simple logon script that maps three network shares:

```
echo off
net use m: \\server1\shares\admin
net use n: \\server1\shares\mktg
net use o: \\server2\archives
```

Here, two shares on server1 are mapped to drives M and N, and a share on server2 is mapped as drive O.

Book VII
Chapter 4

Managing Windows
User Accounts

If you want, you can use the special variable %username% to get the user's username. This variable is useful if you've created a folder for each user, and you want to map a drive to each user's folder, as follows:

```
net use u: \\server1\users\%username%
```

If a user logs on with the username dlowe, for example, drive U is mapped to \\server1\users\dlowe.

Scripts should be saved in the Scripts folder, which is buried deep in the bowels of the SYSVOL folder — typically, c:\Windows\SYSVOL\ Sysvol*domainname*\Scripts, where *domainname* is your domain name. Because you need to access this folder frequently, I suggest creating a short-cut to it on your desktop.

After you've created a logon script, you can assign it to a user by using the Profile tab of the User Properties dialog box. For more information, see the section "Setting the user's profile information," earlier in this chapter.

Chapter 5: Managing a File Server

In This Chapter

✔ **Configuring a file server**

✔ **Sharing folders**

✔ **Setting permissions**

*I*n this chapter, you discover how to set up and manage file and print servers for Windows Server 2016. Because the features for file and print servers are essentially the same for previous versions of Windows Server, the techniques presented in this chapter should work for older versions as well.

Understanding Permissions

Before I get into the details of setting up a file server, you need to have a solid understanding of the concept of permissions. *Permissions* allow users to access shared resources on a network. Simply sharing a resource such as a disk folder or a printer doesn't guarantee that a given user is able to access that resource. Windows makes this decision based on the permissions that have been assigned to various groups for the resource and group memberships of the user. If the user belongs to a group that has been granted permission to access the resource, the access is allowed. If not, access is denied.

In theory, permissions sound pretty simple. In practice, however, they can get pretty complicated. The following paragraphs explain some of the nuances of how access control and permissions work:

✦ Every object — that is, every file and folder — on an NTFS volume has a set of permissions called the *Access Control List (ACL)* associated with it.

✦ The ACL identifies the users and groups who can access the object and specifies what level of access each user or group has. A folder's ACL may specify that one group of users can read files in the folder, whereas another group can read and write files in the folder, and a third group is denied access to the folder.

✦ Container objects — files and volumes — allow their ACLs to be inherited by the objects that they contain. As a result, if you specify permissions for a folder, those permissions extend to the files and child folders that appear within it.

✦ Table 5-1 describes the six permissions that can be applied to files and folders on an NTFS volume.

Table 5-1	File and Folder Permissions
Permission	*Description*
Full Control	The user has unrestricted access to the file or folder.
Modify	The user can change the file or folder's contents, delete the file or folder, read the file or folder, or change the attributes of the file or folder. For a folder, this permission allows you to create new files or subfolders within the folder.
Read & Execute	For a file, this permission grants the right to read or execute the file. For a folder, this permission grants the right to list the contents of the folder or to read or execute any of the files in the folder.
List Folder Contents	This permission applies only to folders; it grants the right to list the contents of the folder.
Read	This permission grants the right to read the contents of a file or folder.
Write	This permission grants the right to change the contents of a file or its attributes. For a folder, this permission grants the right to create new files and subfolders within the folder.

✦ Actually, the six file and folder permissions comprise various combinations of *special permissions* that grant more detailed access to files or folders. Table 5-2 lists the special permissions that apply to each of the six file and folder permissions.

✦ It's best to assign permissions to groups rather than to individual users. Then if a particular user needs access to a particular resource, add that user to a group that has permission to use the resource.

Table 5-2	Special Permissions					
Special Permission	*Full Control*	*Modify*	*Read & Execute*	*List Folder Contents*	*Read*	*Write*
Traverse Folder/ Execute File	*	*	*	*		
List Folder/ Read Data	*	*	*	*	*	
Read Extended Attributes	*	*	*	*	*	

Special Permission	Full Control	Modify	Read & Execute	List Folder Contents	Read	Write
Create Files/Write Data	*	*				*
Create Folders/ Append Data	*	*				*
Write Attributes	*	*				*
Write Extended Attributes	*	*				*
Delete Subfolders and Files	*					
Delete	*	*				
Read Permissions	*	*	*	*	*	*
Change Permissions	*					
Take Ownership	*					
Synchronize	*	*	*	*	*	*

Understanding Shares

A *share* is simply a folder that is made available to other users via the network. Each share has the following elements:

+ **Share name:** The name by which the share is known over the network. To make the share name compatible with older computers, you should stick to eight-character share names whenever possible.

+ **Path:** The path to the folder on the local computer that's being shared, such as C:\Accounting.

+ **Description:** An optional one-line description of the share.

+ **Permissions:** A list of users or groups who have been granted access to the share.

When you install Windows and configure various server roles, special shared resources are created to support those roles. You shouldn't disturb these special shares unless you know what you're doing. Table 5-3 describes some of the most common special shares.

Book VII Chapter 5

Managing a File Server

Table 5-3	Special Shares
Share Name	*Description*
`drive$`	The root directory of a drive; for example, `C$` is the root share for the `C:` drive.
`ADMIN$`	Used for remote administration of a computer. This share points to the operating system folder (usually, `C: \Windows`).
`IPC$`	Used by named pipes, a programming feature that lets processes communicate with one another.
`NETLOGON`	Required for domain controllers to function.
`SYSVOL`	Another required domain controller share.
`PRINT$`	Used for remote administration of printers.
`FAX$`	Used by fax clients.

Notice that some of the special shares end with a dollar sign ($). These shares are *hidden shares* that aren't visible to users. You can still access them, however, by typing the complete share name (including the dollar sign) when the share is needed. The special share C$, for example, is created to allow you to connect to the root directory of the C: drive from a network client. You wouldn't want your users to see this share, would you? (Shares such as C$ are also protected by privileges, of course, so if an ordinary user finds out that C$ is the root directory of the server's C: drive, he or she still can't access it.)

Managing Your File Server

To manage shares on a Windows Server 2016 system, open the Server Manager, and select File and Storage Services in the task pane on the left side of the window. Then click Shares to reveal the management console shown in Figure 5-1.

The following sections describe some of the most common procedures that you'll use when managing your file server.

Using the New Share Wizard

To be useful, a file server should offer one or more *shares* — folders that have been designated as publicly accessible via the network. To create a new share, use the New Share Wizard, as described in the following procedure:

Figure 5-1:
Managing
shares in
Windows
Server 2016.

1. **In Server Manager, click File and Storage Services, click Shares, and then choose New Share from the Tasks drop-down menu.**

The opening screen of the New Share Wizard appears, as shown in Figure 5-2. Here, the wizard asks you what folder you want to share.

**Book VII
Chapter 5**

Managing a
File Server

Figure 5-2:
The New
Share
Wizard
comes
to life.

2. **Select SMB Share – Quick in the list of profiles and then click Next.**

   Next, the New Share Wizard asks for the location of the share, as shown in Figure 5-3.

Figure 5-3:
The wizard asks where you'd like to locate the share.

3. **Select the server you want the share to reside on.**

   For this example, I chose the server named `win1601`.

4. **Select the location of the share by choosing one of these two options:**

   - *Select by Volume:* This option selects the volume on which the shared folder will reside while letting the New Share Wizard create a folder for you. If you select this option, the wizard will create the shared folder on the designated volume. Use this option if the folder doesn't yet exist and you don't mind Windows placing it in the default location, which is inside a folder called Shares on the volume you specify.

   - *Type a Custom Path:* Use this option if the folder exists or if you want to create one in a location other than the Shares folder.

   For this example, I chose the Select by Volume example to allow the wizard to create the share in the `Shares` folder on the `C:` drive.

5. **Click Next.**

   The dialog box shown in Figure 5-4 appears.

Figure 5-4:
The wizard
asks for
the share
name and
description.

6. **Type the name that you want to use for the share in the Share Name box.**

   The default name is the name of the folder being shared. If the folder name is long, you can use a more succinct name here.

   For this example, I entered the share name `Data`.

7. **Enter a description for the share.**

   For this example, I left the description blank.

8. **Click Next.**

   The dialog box shown in Figure 5-5 appears.

9. **Select the share settings you'd like to use:**

   - *Enable Access-Based Enumeration:* Hides files that the user does not have permission to access

   - *Allow Caching of Share:* Makes the files available to offline users

   - *Encrypt Data Access:* Encrypts files accessed via the share

10. **Click Next.**

    The wizard displays the default permissions that will be used for the new share, as shown in Figure 5-6.

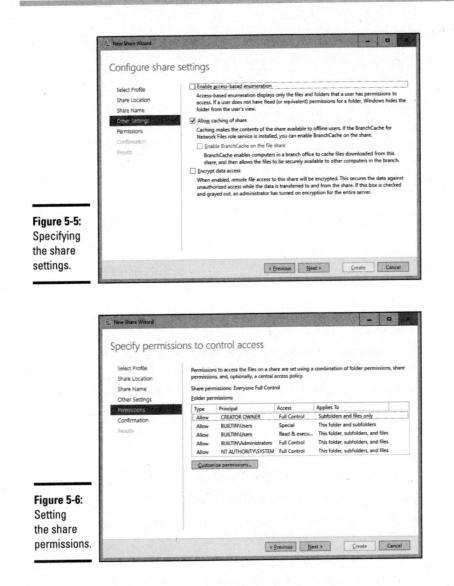

Figure 5-5:
Specifying
the share
settings.

Figure 5-6:
Setting
the share
permissions.

11. If you want to customize the permissions, click Customize Permissions.

This button summons the Advanced Security Settings for Data dialog box, which lets you customize both the NTFS and the share permissions.

12. Click Next.

The confirmation page appears, as shown in Figure 5-7.

Figure 5-7:
Confirming
your share
settings.

13. Verify that all the settings are correct and then click Create.

The share is created, and a results dialog box is displayed, as shown in
Figure 5-8.

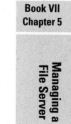

Figure 5-8:
You're
done!

Sharing a folder without the wizard

If you think wizards should be confined to *Harry Potter* movies, you can set up a share without bothering with the wizard. Just follow these steps:

1. **Press the Windows key, click Computer, and navigate to the folder that you want to share.**

2. **Right-click the folder, and choose Properties from the contextual menu.**

   This action brings up the Properties dialog box for the folder.

3. **Click the Sharing tab.**

   The Sharing tab comes to the front, as shown in Figure 5-9.

Figure 5-9:
Manually
sharing a
folder.

4. **Click the Advanced Sharing button.**

   The dialog box shown in Figure 5-10 appears.

5. **Select the Share This Folder check box to designate the folder as shared.**

   The rest of the controls in this dialog box will be unavailable until you select this check box.

Figure 5-10:
Setting the
share name.

6. **Type the name that you want to use for the share in the Share Name box, and type a description of the share in the Comments box.**

   The default name is the name of the folder being shared. If the folder name is long, you can use a more succinct name here.

   The description is strictly optional but sometimes helps users determine the intended contents of the folder.

7. **If you want to specify permissions now, click Permissions.**

   This button brings up a dialog box that lets you create permissions for the share. For more information, see the next section, "Granting permissions."

8. **Click OK.**

   The folder is now shared.

Granting permissions

When you first create a file share, all users are granted read-only access to the share. If you want to allow users to modify files in the share or allow them to create new files, you need to add permissions. Here's how to do this via Windows Explorer:

1. **Open Windows Explorer by pressing the Windows key and clicking Computer; then browse to the folder whose permissions you want to manage.**

2. **Right-click the folder you want to manage, and choose Properties from the contextual menu.**

   The Properties dialog box for the folder appears.

3. **Click the Sharing tab; then click Advanced Sharing.**

   The Advanced Sharing dialog box appears.

4. **Click Permissions.**

   The dialog box shown in Figure 5-11 appears. This dialog box lists all the users and groups to whom you've granted permission for the folder. When you select a user or group from the list, the check boxes at the bottom of the list change to indicate which specific permissions you've assigned to each user or group.

Figure 5-11:
Setting the share permissions.

5. **Click Add.**

   The dialog box shown in Figure 5-12 appears.

Figure 5-12:
The Select Users, Computers, Service Accounts, or Groups dialog box.

6. **Type the name of the user or group to whom you want to grant permission and then click OK.**

   If you're not sure of the name, click Advanced. This action brings up a dialog box that lets you search for existing users. You can click the Find Now button to display a list of all users and groups in the domain. Alternatively, you can enter the first part of the name that you're looking for before you click Find Now to search more specifically.

   When you click OK, you return to the Share Permissions tab, with the new user or group added.

7. **Select the appropriate Allow and Deny check boxes to specify which permissions to allow for the user or group.**

8. **Repeat Steps 5 through 7 for any other permissions that you want to add.**

9. **When you're done, click OK.**

Here are a few other thoughts to ponder concerning adding permissions:

✦ If you want to grant full access to everyone for this folder, don't bother adding another permission. Instead, select the Everyone group and then select the Allow check box for each permission type.

✦ You can remove a permission by selecting the permission and then clicking Remove.

✦ The permissions assigned in this procedure apply only to the share itself. The underlying folder can also have permissions assigned to it. If that's the case, whichever of the restrictions is most restrictive always applies. If the share permissions grant a user Full Control permission but the folder permission grants the user only Read permission, for example, the user has only Read permission for the folder.

Book VII
Chapter 5

Managing a
File Server

Chapter 6: Using Group Policy

In This Chapter

✔ Looking at group policy concepts

✔ Enabling group policy on a Windows Server

✔ Editing group policy objects

*G*roup policy refers to a feature of Windows operating systems that lets you control how certain aspects of Windows and other Microsoft software work throughout your network. Many features that you might expect to find in a management console, such as Active Directory Users and Computers, are controlled by group policy instead. You must use group policy to control how often users must change their passwords, for example, and how complicated their passwords must be. As a result, group policy is an important tool for any Windows network administrator.

Unfortunately, group policy can be a confusing beast. In fact, it's one of the most confusing aspects of Windows network administration. So don't be put off if you find this chapter more confusing than other chapters in this minibook. Group policy becomes clear after you spend some time actually working with it.

Understanding Group Policy

Here it is in a nutshell: Group policy consists of a collection of *group policy objects* (also called *GPOs*) that define individual policies. These policy objects are selectively applied to both users and computers. Each policy object specifies how some aspect of Windows or some other Microsoft software should be configured. A group policy object might specify the home page that's initially displayed when any user launches Internet Explorer, for example. When a user logs on to the domain, that policy object is retrieved and applied to the user's Internet Explorer configuration.

Group policy objects can apply to either computers or users. A policy that applies to a computer will be enforced for any user of the computer, and a policy that applies to a user will be enforced for that user no matter what computer he or she logs on to. As a network administrator, you'll be concerned mostly with policies that apply to users. But computer policies are useful from time to time as well.

To use group policy, you have to know how to do two things: (1) create individual group policy objects, and (2) apply — or *link* — those objects to user and computer objects. Both tasks can be a little tricky.

The trick to creating group policy objects is finding the particular setting you want to employ. Trying to find a specific group policy among the thousands of available policies can be frustrating. Suppose that you want to force all network users to change their passwords every 30 days. You know that a group policy controls the password-expiration date. But where is it? You'll find help with this aspect of working with group policy in the section titled "Creating Group Policy Objects," later in this chapter.

After you've created a group policy object, you then are faced with the task of linking it to the users or computers you want it to apply to. Creating a policy that applies to all users or computers is simple enough. But things get more complicated if you want to be more selective — for example, if you want the policy to apply only to users in a particular organizational unit (OU) or to users that belong to a particular group. You'll find help for this aspect of working with group policy in the section "Filtering Group Policy Objects," later in this chapter.

Enabling Group Policy Management on Windows Server 2016

Before you can work with group policy on a Windows Server 2016, you must enable group policy on the server. The procedure is simple enough and needs to be done only once for each server. Here are the steps:

1. **In the Server Manager, click Add Roles and Features.**

2. **Follow the wizard until you get to the Select Features page, which is shown in Figure 6-1.**

3. **If the Group Policy Management check box is not already checked, select it.**

4. **Click Next.**

5. **When the confirmation page appears, click Install.**

    Be patient; installation may take a few minutes.

6. **Click Close.**

    You're done!

After you've completed this procedure, a new command titled Group Policy Management appears on the Tools menu in the Server Manager.

Figure 6-1:
Enabling group policy management on Windows Server 2016.

Creating Group Policy Objects

The easiest way to create group policy objects is to use the Group Policy Management Console, which you can run from the Server Manager by choosing Tools➪Group Policy Management.

A single group policy object can consist of one setting or many individual group policy settings. The Group Policy Management Console presents the thousands of group policy settings that are available for your use in several categories. The more you work with group policy, the more these categories will begin to make sense. When you get started, you can expect to spend a lot of time hunting through the lists of policies to find the specific one you're looking for.

The easiest way to learn how to use the Group Policy Management Console is to use it to create a simple group policy object. In the following procedure, I show you how to create a GPO that defines a group policy enabling Windows Update for all computers in a domain so that users can't disable Windows Update.

1. **In the Server Manager, choose Tools➪Group Policy Management.**

   The Group Policy Management console appears, as shown in Figure 6-2.

Figure 6-2:
The Group Policy Management console.

2. **In the Navigation pane, drill down through the Domains node to the node for your domain, then select the Group Policy Objects node for your domain.**

3. **Right-click the Group Policy Objects node and then choose New from the contextual menu that appears.**

   This command brings up the dialog box shown in Figure 6-3.

Figure 6-3:
Creating a new group policy object.

4. **Type a name for the group policy object and then click OK.**

   For this example, type something like **Windows Update** for a policy that will manage the Windows Update feature.

   When you click OK, the group policy object is created and appears in the Group Policy Objects section of the Group Policy Management window.

5. Double-click the new group policy.

The group policy opens, as shown in Figure 6-4. Note that at this stage, the Location section of the group policy doesn't list any objects. As a result, this policy is not yet linked to any Active Directory domains or groups. I get to that topic in a moment. First, I create the policy settings.

Figure 6-4:
A new group policy object.

**Book VII
Chapter 6**

Using Group Policy

6. Click the Settings tab.

The message "Generating Report" appears for a moment, and then the group policy settings are displayed, as shown in Figure 6-5.

Figure 6-5:
Group policy settings.

7. Right-click Computer Configuration and then choose Edit from the contextual menu.

This command opens the Group Policy Management Editor, as shown in Figure 6-6, where you can edit the Computer Configuration policies.

Figure 6-6:
Editing group policy.

8. In the Navigation pane, navigate to Computer Configuration ⇨ Policies ⇨ Administrative Templates ⇨ Windows Components ⇨ Windows Update.

This step brings up the Windows Update policy settings, as shown in Figure 6-7.

Figure 6-7:
The Windows Update policy settings.

9. **Double-click Configure Automatic Updates.**

This step brings up the Configure Automatic Updates dialog box, as shown in Figure 6-8.

10. **Select Enabled to enable the policy.**

11. **Configure the Windows Update settings however you want.**

For this example, I configure Windows Update so that updates are auto-matically downloaded every day at 3 a.m.

12. **Click OK.**

You return to the Group Policy Management Editor.

13. **Close the Group Policy Management Editor window.**

This step returns you to the Group Policy Management settings window.

14. **Right-click Computer Configuration, and choose Refresh from the contextual menu.**

The Windows Update policy is visible, as shown in Figure 6-9. (To show the full details of the policy, I expanded the Administrative Templates and Windows Components/Windows Update sections of the policy report.)

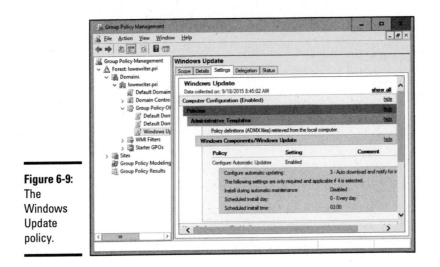

Figure 6-9:
The
Windows
Update
policy.

15. **In the Navigation pane of the Group Policy Management window, drag the new Windows Update policy object to the top-level domain (in this case, `lowewriter.pri`).**

    When you release the mouse button, the dialog box shown in Figure 6-10 appears.

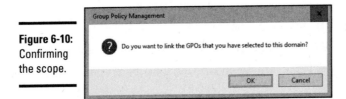

Figure 6-10:
Confirming
the scope.

16. **Click OK.**

    The domain is added to the scope, as shown in Figure 6-11.

17. **Close the Group Policy Management window.**

    The new group policy is now active.

Figure 6-11:
The policy is
finished.

Filtering Group Policy Objects

One of the most confusing aspects of group policy is that even though it applies to users and computers, you don't associate group policy objects with users or computers. Instead, you link GPOs to sites, domains, or organizational units (OUs). At first glance, this aspect may seem to limit the usefulness of group policy. For most simple networks, you'll work with group policy mostly at the domain level and occasionally at the OU level. Site-level group policy objects are used only for very large or complex networks.

Group policy wouldn't be very useful if you had to assign exactly the same policy to every user or computer within a domain. And although OUs can help break down group policy assignments, even that capability is limiting, because a particular user or computer can be a member of only one OU. Fortunately, group policy objects can have *filters* that further refine which users or computers the policy applies to. Although you can filter policy objects so that they apply only to individual users or computers, you're more likely to use groups to apply your group policy objects.

Suppose that you want to use group policy to assign two different default home pages for Internet Explorer. For the Marketing department, you want the default home page to be www.dummies.com, but for the Accounting department, you'd like the default home page to be www.beancounters.com. You can easily accomplish this task by creating two groups named Marketing and Accounting in Active Directory Users and Computers, and assigning the marketing and accounting users to the appropriate groups. Next, you can create two group policy objects: one for the Marketing department's home page and the other to assign the Accounting department's home page. Then you can link both of these policy objects to the domain and use filters to specify which group each policy applies to.

For the following procedure, I've created two group policies, named IE Home Page Dummies and IE Home Page Beancounter, as well as two Active Directory groups, named Marketing and Accounting. Here are the steps for filtering these policies to link correctly to the groups:

1. **Choose Start ⇨ Administrative Tools ⇨ Group Policy Management.**

   The Group Policy Management console appears. (Refer to Figure 6-2 for a refresher on what it looks like.)

2. **In the Navigation pane, navigate to the group policy object you want to apply the filter to.**

   For this example, I navigated to the IE Home Page Dummies policy, as shown in Figure 6-12.

Figure 6-12: The IE Home Page Dummies policy.

3. **In the Security Filtering section, click Authenticated Users and then click Remove.**

   This step removes Authenticated Users so that the policy won't be applied to all users.

4. **Click Add.**

   This step brings up the Select User, Computer, or Group dialog box, as shown in Figure 6-13.

Figure 6-13:
The Select User, Computer, or Group dialog box.

5. **Type** Marketing **in the text box and then click OK.**

   The policy is updated to indicate that it applies to members of the Marketing group, as shown in Figure 6-14.

Figure 6-14:
A policy that uses a filter.

6. **Repeat Steps 2 through 5 for the IE Home Page Beancounter policy, applying it to the Accounting group.**

   You're done!

Chapter 7: Troubleshooting

In This Chapter

✓ Examining the Event Viewer

✓ Perusing the Performance console

✓ Checking out the Computer Management console

✓ Surveying the Services console

*W*indows Server is extremely reliable. Get it configured right in the first place, and it will chug along without incident — that is, at least until something goes wrong, which is inevitable.

In this chapter, I review some of the tools that Windows provides to help you diagnose trouble. Before I start, however, I want to point you to a few other chapters that also contain troubleshooting information. This chapter deals only with those tools that apply specifically to Windows servers. You can find other information in these chapters:

✦ Book II, Chapter 7 gives you some basic network troubleshooting tips.

✦ Book III, Chapter 7 explains how to use the TCP/IP troubleshooting tools, such as `ping` and `ipconfig`.

✦ Book VII, Chapter 8 shows you some Windows commands that are often useful for troubleshooting.

Working with the Event Viewer

Windows has a built-in event-tracking feature that automatically logs a variety of interesting system events. Usually, when something goes wrong with your server, you can find at least one and maybe dozens of events in one of the logs. All you have to do is open the Event Viewer and check the logs for suspicious-looking entries.

Using the Event Viewer

To display the event logs, open the Server Manager, and choose Tools ➪ Event Viewer. This command brings up the Event Viewer, as shown in Figure 7-1. The tree on the left side of the Event Viewer lists the various categories of events that are tracked:

✦ **Application:** Lists events that were generated by application programs. In most cases, the application's developers purposely wrote these events to the event log to inform you of error conditions or developing trouble.

✦ **Security:** Lists security-related events, such as unsuccessful logon attempts, changes to security policy, and so on.

✦ **Setup:** Lists events generated during operating-system setup.

✦ **System:** Lists events related to hardware or operating-system failures. If you're having trouble with a hard drive, for example, you should check here for events related to the hard drive.

✦ **Forwarded Events:** Lists other events that were forwarded to this server.

Note that you may find other categories in this list, depending on the roles you've configured for the server.

Select one of these options to see the log that you want to view. In Figure 7-1, I clicked the System events log.

Notice the cute little icons next to the items in the log. Table 7-1 summarizes the meanings of these icons.

To see the details for a particular event, double-click the event to bring up the Event Properties dialog box, shown in Figure 7-2. Here, you can see the details of the event. In some cases, you may be able to diagnose a problem just by reading the error message displayed in this dialog box. In other cases, this information just points you in the right direction; it tells you *what* went wrong, but you still have to figure out *why*.

Table 7-1		Icons Used in the Event Log
Icon	*Name*	*Description*
	Information	A noteworthy operation completed successfully.
	Warning	An event developed a problem that wasn't fatal, though a problem may be looming on the horizon.
	Error	Something has gone wrong.

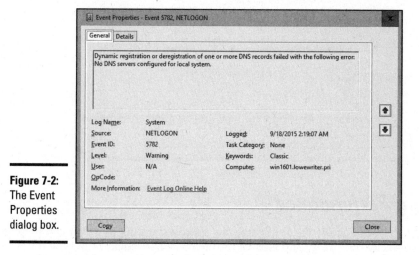

Figure 7-2: The Event Properties dialog box.

Book VII Chapter 7

Troubleshooting

Setting event log policies

To set default policies that affect how application, security, and system event logs are kept, open the Group Policy Management Editor by choosing Tools ➪ Group Policy Management from Server Manager (see Figure 7-3). You can find the event log policies in the Navigation pane by navigating to Computer Configuration ➪ Policies ➪ Windows Settings ➪ Security Settings.

You can use these policies to specify the following options for the Application, Security, and System logs:

✦ **Maximum Log Size:** This policy lets you specify the maximum size of the log in kilobytes (KB).

✦ **Prevent Local Guests Group from Accessing Log:** This policy prevents users who are logged on via a guest account from viewing the logs. Enabling this policy is a good security precaution.

✦ **Retain Log:** This policy looks as though it might let you disable the log, but it doesn't. Instead, it specifies the number of days that log data should be kept if you specify By Days as the Retention Method policy.

✦ **Retention Method for Log:** This policy specifies how log events should be overwritten when the log becomes full. Options are By Days, As Needed, and Do Not Overwrite.

Figure 7-3:
Setting the event log policies.

Monitoring Performance

The Performance Monitor console is a troubleshooting tool that can help you track down nasty and elusive problems — particularly the type that don't cause the server to crash but just cause it to run slowly. With the Performance Monitor console, you can look at many aspects of system performance to figure out why your system is dragging.

Using the Reliability and Performance Monitor

To run the Performance Monitor console, choose Tools ➪ Performance Monitor from the System Manager. The Performance Monitor comes to life, as shown in Figure 7-4.

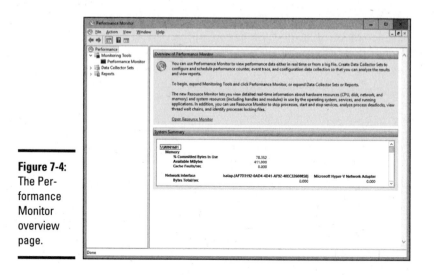

Figure 7-4:
The Per-
formance
Monitor
overview
page.

The display in Figure 7-4 shows essential performance data for the server, including memory and network interface utilization, disk access, and so on.

If you want, you can click the Open Resource Monitor link to display the Resource Monitor, which graphically displays utilization information, as shown in Figure 7-5. This display resembles something that you'd expect to see in a hospital.

Figure 7-5:
The
Resource
Monitor.

You can summon more-specific performance information by clicking Performance Monitor in the console tree of the Performance Monitor console. This action brings up the Performance Monitor, as shown in Figure 7-6.

Figure 7-6:
The Performance
Monitor.

The Performance Monitor lets you keep track of several aspects of system performance at the same time. You track each performance aspect by setting up a counter. You can choose among hundreds of counters. Table 7-2 describes some of the most commonly used counters. Notice that each counter refers to a server object, such as physical disk, memory, or the processor.

Table 7-2	**Commonly Used Performance Counters**	
Object	*Counter*	*Description*
Physical Disk	% Free Space	The percentage of free space on the server's physical disks. It should be at least 15.
Physical Disk	Average Queue Length	The number of disk operations that are waiting while the disk is busy servicing other disk operations. It should be 2 or less.
Memory	Pages/second	The number of pages retrieved per second from the virtual-memory page files. A typical value is about 2,500.
Processor	% Processor Time	The percentage of the processor's time that it's busy doing work rather than sitting idle. It should be 85 or less.

To add a counter, click the Add button (the one with the green plus sign) to bring up the Add Counters dialog box, as shown in Figure 7-7. Then select the object that you want to track from the drop-down list, choose the counter that you want to add from the list, and click Add. You can add more than one counter from this dialog box; when you're finished adding counters, click OK to dismiss the Add Counters dialog box.

Figure 7-7:
The Add
Counters
dialog box.

The act of gathering performance data slows your server, so don't leave performance logging turned on all the time. Use it only occasionally when you want to gather baseline data or when you're experiencing a performance problem.

Creating performance logs

Instead of staring at the Performance Monitor for hours on end, waiting for a performance glitch to occur, you can create a performance log — which in Windows Server 2016 is called a *Data Collector Set.* (In Windows Server 2003, it was called a *Performance Log.* I guess the intellectuals at Microsoft think the term *Data Collector Set* is more meaningful than *Performance Log.* I disagree, but they didn't ask for my opinion.)

When the network is running well, you can collect data to act as a baseline so you'll know whether performance has slipped. When the network isn't acting well, you can collect data to help isolate the problem.

To set up a performance log, follow these steps:

1. **Open the Data Collector Sets node in the Performance Monitor's console tree.**

2. **Right-click the User Defined node, and choose New ⇨ Data Collector Set from the contextual menu.**

This action brings up a wizard that steps you through the process of creating a new log, as shown in Figure 7-8.

Figure 7-8: Creating a new Data Collector Set (er, Performance Log).

4. Create new Data Collector Set.

How would you like to create this new data collector set?

Name:

New Data Collector Set

⦿ Create from a template (Recommended)

○ Create manually (Advanced)

Next   Finish   Cancel

3. **Type a name for your log, choose whether you want to use a predefined template or create your own custom log, and then click Next.**

For this example, I use one of the templates. The dialog box shown in Figure 7-9 lists the available templates.

4. **Select System Performance and then click Finish.**

Note that creating the log doesn't actually start the logging activity. To start the log, right-click it, and choose Start from the contextual menu. Alternatively, you can click the big green Start button on the toolbar. When you want to stop the log, select the log and click the Stop button, or right-click the log and choose Stop from the contextual menu.

Figure 7-9:
Data
Collector
Set
templates.

To display the data accumulated by a performance log, right-click the log, and choose Latest Report from the contextual menu. A summary of the logged data is displayed, as shown in Figure 7-10.

Figure 7-10:
Data
collected
by a perfor-
mance log.

Using the Computer Management Console

The Server Manager's Tools ⇨ Computer Management command leads you to the Computer Management console, a tool that's often useful for tracking down problems in a Windows Server 2016 system. Poke around the console tree in Computer Management, and you'll find the following:

✦ **Event Viewer:** Refer to the section "Using the Event Viewer," earlier in this chapter, for more information.

✦ **Shared Folders:** Here, you can manage your shared folders, current sessions, and open files. For more information, see Book VII, Chapter 4.

✦ **Performance Logs and Alerts:** Refer to the section "Using the Reliability and Performance Monitor," earlier in this chapter, for more information.

✦ **Device Manager:** This tool is handy for diagnosing problems with hardware devices. Device Manager lists all the hardware devices currently installed on the computer, as shown in Figure 7-11. You can double-click a device to bring up a Properties dialog box that displays information about the status of the device and lets you change drivers or configuration settings.

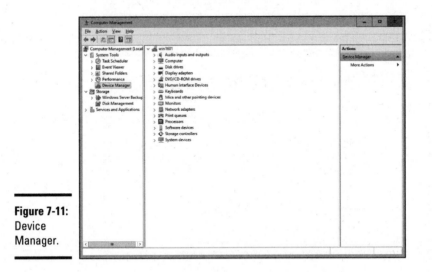

Figure 7-11:
Device
Manager.

✦ **Removable Storage:** This tool lets you track removable storage media, such as tapes and CDs, as well as manage tape and CD libraries.

+ **Disk Defragmenter:** This tool lets you optimize the way data is stored on your disks.

+ **Disk Management:** This tool lets you work with disk partitions, format disks, create mirror sets, and perform other disk operations.

+ **Services and Applications:** Here, you can manage services and applications that you've installed on the computer, such as DHCP, DNS, IIS, and so on.

Working with Services

The last troubleshooting tool I want to describe in this chapter is the Services console, which you can access by choosing Start ➪ Administrative Tools ➪ Services. As Figure 7-12 shows, the Services console displays a list of all the services that are currently running on your system.

Figure 7-12: The Services console.

Book VII Chapter 7

Troubleshooting

If a Windows server feature isn't working properly, the problem often is that something caused one of the services associated with the feature to stop. You may be able to correct the problem by calling up the Services console and restarting the service. To do that, just select the service and then click the Start the Service link.

This action doesn't correct the underlying cause of the problem, of course. If the service stopped because of a one-time error, simply restarting the service may be all that you need to do. In many cases, though, the problem that caused the service to start will resurface and cause the service to stop again.

So if you fix a problem by restarting a service, you must keep an eye out for the problem's resurgence. Usually, if the problem doesn't recur within a few days, you can safely assume that you encountered a one-time glitch and fixed it by restarting the service. But if the problem happens again, you'll need to investigate more to get to the bottom of the problem.

Chapter 8: Windows Commands

In This Chapter

✔ Getting started with a command window

✔ Taking advantage of command tricks and techniques

✔ Looking at batch files

✔ Using the amazing Net commands

*A*lthough Windows sports a fancy graphical interface that makes it possible to perform most network management tasks by pointing and clicking, you can also do almost any network management task from a command prompt. Whether you choose to do so is largely a matter of personal style. Some network administrators pride themselves on being able to type Windows commands blindfolded and with two fingers on each hand tied behind their backs. Others have fully embraced the graphical user interface and think the command line is for administrators with Unix envy.

So the choice is yours. Skip this chapter if the thought of typing commands causes you to lose sleep. If you're willing to venture forth, this chapter begins with an overview of working from the command prompt. Then it describes some of the more useful Windows commands. Finally, this chapter introduces the fine (and almost lost) art of writing batch files.

Windows Server 2016 also includes an alternative command environment known as PowerShell. *PowerShell* is an advanced command processor that has many sophisticated features that are designed especially for creating powerful scripts. For more information, see Microsoft's PowerShell site at www.microsoft.com/powershell.

Using a Command Window

Command prompts are even older than video monitors. The first computer I worked on used a teletype machine as its terminal, so the command prompt was printed on paper rather than displayed onscreen. Surprisingly, though, the concept of the command prompt hasn't changed much since those days. The system displays a prompt to let you know it's waiting for a command. When you type the command and press the Enter key, the system reads your command, interprets it, executes it, displays the results, and then displays the prompt again so that you can enter another command.

Opening and closing a command window

To get to a command prompt on a Windows server, follow these steps:

1. **Press the Windows key on your keyboard, and then type** cmd.

2. **Press the Enter key.**

The command prompt window appears, as shown in Figure 8-1.

Figure 8-1:
The
command
prompt.

You can type any commands you want in the window.

To exit the command prompt, type **Exit**, and press Enter. This action properly terminates cmd.exe and closes the command prompt window. If you try to close the command prompt window by clicking its Close button, Windows is forced to shut down cmd.exe. The process works, but you have to click your way through an intervening dialog box and wait a few seconds while Windows terminates cmd.exe. Entering the Exit command is a much faster method.

Editing commands

Most of the time, you just type commands by using the keyboard. If you make a mistake, you just retype the command, being careful not to repeat the mistake. cmd.exe, however, has several built-in editing features that can simplify the task of correcting a mistaken command or entering a sequence of similar commands:

✦ Press the right-arrow key to recall the text of the last command that you entered, one letter at a time. When you get to the spot where the new command should differ from the previous command, start typing.

✦ Press F3 to recall all the previous commands from the current cursor position to the end of the line.

✦ If you want to repeat a command that you've used recently, press the up-arrow key. This action recalls up to 50 of the most recently executed commands. You can press Enter to execute a command as is, or you can edit the command before you execute it.

Using the Control menu

Although the command window has no menu bar, it does have a menu that you can access via the control box in the top-left corner of the window. Besides the commands found on this menu for all windows (such as Move, Size, and Minimize), this menu includes three additional commands:

✦ **Edit:** The Edit command leads to a submenu with several choices. Several of these commands work together so that you can copy information from the command window to the Clipboard, and vice versa. If you choose Edit⇨Mark, you're placed in a special editing mode that lets you highlight text in the command window with the mouse. (Normally, the mouse doesn't do anything in the command window.) Then you can choose Edit⇨Copy or just press Enter to copy the text that you selected to the Clipboard.

You can also use the Edit menu to paste text from the Clipboard, to scroll the window, and to search the window for text.

✦ **Default:** This command lets you set default properties for the command window.

✦ **Properties:** This command displays a Properties dialog box that you can use to change the appearance of the window. You can change the font size, choose background colors, and make other adjustments to make the command window look good on your computer.

Special Command Tricks

Before I get into the details of using specific commands, I want to describe some techniques you should familiarize yourself with. In many cases, these techniques can let you accomplish in a single command what would otherwise take dozens of separate commands.

Wildcards

Wildcards are among the most compelling reasons to use the command prompt. With wildcards, you can process all the files that match a particular naming pattern with a single command. Suppose that you have a folder containing 500 files, and you want to delete all the files that contain the letters

Y2K and end with the extension .doc, which happens to be 50 files. If you open a Documents window, you'll spend ten minutes picking these files out from the list. From a command window, you can delete them all with the single command del *Y2K*.doc.

You can use two wildcard characters. An asterisk stands for any number of characters, including zero, and an exclamation point stands for just one character. Thus, !Text.doc would match files with names like aText.doc, xText.doc, and 4Text.doc, but not abcText.doc or just Text.doc. *Text.doc, however, would match any of the names mentioned in the previous sentence.

Wildcards work differently in Windows than they did in MS-DOS. In MS-DOS, anything you typed after an asterisk was ignored. Thus, ab*cd.doc was the same as ab*.doc. In Windows, the asterisk wildcard can come before static text, so ab*cd.doc and ab*.doc are *not* the same.

Chaining commands

You can enter two or more commands on the same line by separating the commands with an ampersand (&), like this:

```
C:\>copy *.doc a: & del *.doc
```

Here, the copy command copies all the .doc files to the A: drive. Then, the del command deletes the .doc files.

Although that technique may be convenient, it's also dangerous. What if the A: drive fills up so that all the files can't be copied? In that case, the del command executes anyway, deleting the files that didn't get copied.

A safer alternative is to use two ampersands, telling Windows to execute the second command only if the first command finishes successfully:

```
C:\>copy *.doc a: && del *.doc
```

Now the del command will be executed only if the copy command succeeds.

You can also use two pipe characters (the *pipe* is the vertical bar character that's above the backslash on the keyboard) to execute the second command only if the first command fails. Thus,

```
C:\>copy *.doc a: || echo Oops!
```

displays the message Oops! if the copy command fails.

Finally, you can use parentheses to group commands. Then you can use the other symbols in combination:

```
C:\>(copy *.doc a: && del *.doc) || echo Oops!
```

Here, the files are copied and then deleted if the copy was successful. If either command fails, the message is displayed.

Redirection and piping

Redirection and piping are related techniques. *Redirection* lets you specify an alternative destination for output that will be displayed by a command or an alternative source for input that should be fed into a command. You can save the results of an ipconfig /all command to a file named mycon-fig.txt like this:

```
C:\>ipconfig /all > myconfig.txt
```

Here, the greater-than sign (>) is used to redirect the command's console output.

If a command accepts input from the keyboard, you can use input redirection to specify a file that contains the input you want to feed to the command. You can create a text file named lookup.txt with subcommands for a command such as nslookup. Then you can feed those scripted subcommands to the nslookup command, like this:

```
C:\>nslookup < lookup.txt
```

Piping is a similar technique. It takes the console output from one command and feeds it into the next command as input. Piping is often used with special commands called *filters,* which are designed to read input from the console, modify the data in some way, and then write it to the console.

Suppose that you want to display the contents of a file named users.txt sorted into alphabetical order. You can use the Type command, which displays a file on the console, and then pipe the output into the Sort command, a filter that sorts its input and displays the sorted output on the console. The resulting command looks like this:

```
C:\>type users.txt | sort
```

The vertical bar is often called the *pipe character* because it's the symbol used to indicate piping.

Environment variables

The command shell makes several *environment variables* available to commands. Environment variables all begin and end with percent signs. You can use an environment variable anywhere in a command. The command

```
C:\>echo %OS% running on a %PROCESSOR_IDENTIFIER%
```

displays a line such as this:

```
Windows_NT running on an x86 Family 15 Model 2 Stepping 8, GenuineIntel
```

Interestingly, later versions of Windows Server all display `Windows_NT` for the operating-system name.

If the environment variable represents a path, you may need to enclose it in quotation marks, like this:

```
C:\>dir "%HOMEPATH%"
```

This command displays the contents of the user's home directory. The quotation marks are required here because the environment variable expands to a pathname that may include spaces, and the command shell requires that long filenames that include spaces be enclosed in quotation marks.

Table 8-1 lists the environment variables that are available to you and your commands.

Table 8-1	Environment Variables
Variable	*Description*
`%ALLUSERSPROFILE%`	The location of the All Users profile
`%APPDATA%`	The path where applications store data by default
`%CD%`	The path to the current directory
`%CMDCMDLINE%`	The command line that was used to start the command shell
`%CMDEXTVERSION%`	The version number of the command shell
`%COMPUTERNAME%`	The computer's name
`%COMSPEC%`	The path to the command shell executable (`cmd.exe`)
`%DATE%`	The current date in the format generated by the `date /t` command

Variable	Description
%ERRORLEVEL%	The error returned by the most recent command
%HOMEDRIVE%	The drive letter of the user's home directory
%HOMEPATH%	The path to the user's home directory
%HOMESHARE%	The network path to the user's shared home directory
%LOGONSERVER%	The name of the domain controller the user logged on to
%NUMBER_OF_PROCESSORS%	The number of processors on the computer
%OS%	The name of the operating system
%PATH%	The current search path
"%PATHEXT%"	A list of the extensions the operating system treats as executable files
%PROCESSOR_ARCHITECTURE%	The chip architecture of the processor
%PROCESSOR_IDENTIFIER%	A description of the processor
%PROCESSOR_REVISION%	The revision level of the processor
%PROMPT%	The current prompt string
%RANDOM%	A random number between 1 and 32,767
%SYSTEMDRIVE%	The drive containing the operating system
%SYSTEMROOT%	The path to the operating system
%TEMP%	The path to a temporary folder for temporary files
%TMP%	Same as %TEMP%
%TIME%	The time in the format produced by the time /t command
%USERDOMAIN%	The name of the user's domain
%USERNAME%	The user's account name
%USERPROFILE%	The path to the user's profile
%WINDIR%	The path to the operating-system directory

Batch files

A *batch file* is simply a text file that contains one or more commands. Batch files are given the extension .bat and can be run from a command prompt as though they were commands or programs. You can also run a batch file from the Start menu by choosing Start ⇨ Run, typing the name of the batch file, and clicking OK.

As a network administrator, you'll find plenty of uses for batch files. Most of them won't be very complicated. Here are some examples of very simple batch files I've used:

✦ I once used a one-line file to copy the entire contents of an important shared network drive to a user's computer every night at 10 p.m. The user had just purchased a new Dell computer with a 100GB drive, and the server had only a 20GB drive. The user wanted a quick-and-dirty backup solution that would complement the regular tape backups that ran every night.

✦ I've also used a pair of short batch files to stop and then restart an Exchange server before and after nightly backups.

✦ If I frequently need to work with several related folders at the same time, I create a short batch file that opens Explorer windows for each of the folders. (You can open an Explorer window from a batch file simply by typing the path to the folder that you want to open as a command.) Then I place the batch file on my desktop so that I can get to it quickly.

You can also use batch files to create logon scripts that are executed whenever a user logs on. Microsoft keeps trying to get users to use profiles instead of logon scripts, but many networks still use logon scripts.

The EventCreate Command

The `EventCreate` command lets you create an event that's added to one of the Windows event logs. This command can be useful if you want to make a note of something unusual that's happened. It's often used in batch files to mark the start or completion of a task such as a nightly backup.

Here's the basic syntax:

```
eventcreate [options]
eventcreate /T type /D "description" /ID eventide
   [/L logname] [/SO sourcename]
   [/S system [/U username [/P password]]]
```

Here's a description of the options:

✦ **/T:** Specifies the type. The options are `Information`, `Warning`, and `Error`.

✦ **/D:** Provides a descriptive message that's saved in the log. Use quotes if the message contains more than one word.

✦ **/ID:** A number from 1 to 1,000.

✦ **/L:** The name of the log to write the event to. The default is `Application`.

✦ **/SO:** A string that represents the source of the event. The default is `EventCreate`. If you specify this option, you must also specify the `/L` option.

✦ **/S:** The name of the system on which the event should be recorded.

✦ **/U:** The user account to use when logging the event. You can specify this option only if you also specify `/S`.

✦ **/P:** The password. You can specify this option only if you also specify `/U`.

Here's an example that writes an informational message to the Application log:

```
eventcreate /t information /id 100 /d "Nightly processing completed" /L Application /
    SO Nightly
```

Figure 8-2 shows an event created by the preceding command.

Figure 8-2: An event generated by the Event-Create command.

Net Commands

Among the most useful commands for network administrators are the Net Services commands. All these commands are two-word commands beginning with `Net` — such as `Net Use` and `Net Start`. In the following sections,

I present the Net commands in alphabetical order for handy reference. First, though, I want to point out a few details about the Net commands:

✦ You can get a quick list of the available Net commands by typing **net /?** at a command prompt.

✦ You can get brief help for any Net command by typing **net help *command***. To display help for the Net Use command, for example, type **net help use**. (Yes, we all could use some help.)

✦ Many of the Net commands prompt you for confirmation before completing an operation. For these commands, you can specify /Y or /N to bypass the confirmation prompt. You'll want to do that if you include these commands in a batch file that runs unattended. Note that you can use /Y or /N on any Net command, even if it doesn't prompt you for confirmation. So I suggest that you place /Y on every Net command in a batch file that you intend to run unattended.

The Net Accounts command

This command updates user account policies for password requirements. Here's the command syntax:

```
net accounts [/forcelogoff:{minutes | no}]
   [/minpwlen:length] [/maxpwage:{days | unlimited}]
   [/minpwage:days] [/uniquepw:number]
   [/domain]
```

The following paragraphs describe the parameters for the Net Accounts command:

✦ **forcelogoff:** Specifies how long to wait before forcing a user off the system when the user's logon time expires. The default value, no, prevents users from being forced to log off. If you specify a number, the user will be warned a few minutes before being forcibly logged off.

✦ **minpwlen:** Specifies the minimum length for the user's password. *Length* can be 0 through 127. The default is 6.

✦ **maxpwage:** Specifies the number of days a user's password is considered to be valid. Unlimited means that the password will never expire. *Days* can be from 1 through 49,710, which is about 135 years. The default is 90.

✦ **minpwage:** Specifies the minimum number of days after a user changes a password before the user can change it again. The default value is 0. You usually should set this value to 1 day to prevent users from bypassing the Uniquepw policy.

✦ **uniquepw:** Indicates how many different passwords the user must use before he or she is allowed to reuse the same password. The default setting is 5. The range is 0 through 24.

✦ **domain:** Specifies that the operation should be performed on the primary domain controller rather than on the local computer.

If you enter `Net Accounts` without any parameters, the command simply displays the current policy settings.

Here's an example that sets the minimum and maximum password ages:

```
C:\>net accounts /minpwage:7 /maxpwage:30
```

The Net Computer command

This command creates or deletes a computer account. Here's the syntax:

```
net computer \\computername {/add | /del}
```

The following paragraphs describe the parameters for the `Net Computer` command:

✦ *Computername:* Specifies the computer to add or delete

✦ **add:** Creates a computer account for the specified computer

✦ **del:** Deletes the specified computer account

Here's an example that adds a computer named Theodore:

```
C:\>net computer \\theodore /add
```

The Net Config command

This command lets you view or configure various network services. Here's the syntax:

```
net config [{server|workstation}] [options]
```

To configure server settings, use this syntax:

```
net config server [/autodisconnect:time] [/srvcomment:"text"] [/hidden:{yes | no}]
```

The following paragraphs describe the parameters for the `Net Config` command:

✦ **server:** Lets you display and configure the Server service while it's running.

✦ **workstation:** Lets you display and configure the workstation service while it's running.

✦ **autodisconnect:** Specifies how long a user's session can be inactive before it's disconnected. Specify –1 to never disconnect. The range is –1 to 65,535 minutes, which is about 45 days. The default is 15 minutes.

✦ **srvcomment:** Specifies a description of the server. The comment can be up to 48 characters long and should be enclosed in quotation marks.

✦ **hidden:** Specifies whether the server appears in screens that display available servers. Hiding a server doesn't make the server unavailable; it just means that the user will have to know the name of the server to access it. The default is No.

Here's an example that sets a server's descriptive comment:

```
C:\>net config server /srvcomment:"DHCP Server"
```

The Net Continue command

This command continues a service you've suspended with the net pause command. Here's the syntax:

```
net continue service
```

Here are some typical services that you can pause and continue:

✦ **netlogon:** The Net Logon service.

✦ **schedule:** The Task Scheduler service.

✦ **server:** The Server service.

✦ **workstation:** The Workstation service.

Here's an example that continues the Workstation service:

```
C:>net continue workstation
```

If the service name has embedded spaces, enclose the service name in quotation marks. This command continues the NT LM Security Support Provider service:

```
C:\>net continue "nt lm security support provider"
```

The Net File command

This command lists all open shared files and the number of file locks placed on each file. You can also use this command to close files and remove locks, which is a useful procedure when a user manages to accidentally leave a file open or locked. Here's the syntax:

```
C:\>net file [id [/close]]
```

The following paragraphs describe the Net File command's parameters:

+ **id:** The file's identification number.

+ **close:** Closes an open file and releases any locks that were placed on the file.

To close a file, you must issue the command from the server where the file is shared.

net files works, too.

To close an open file, first run net file without any parameters to list the open files. Here's a sample of the output that you can expect from net file:

```
File     Path           Username   #locks
----------------------------------------------
0        C:\BUDGET.DOC  WARD       0
1        C:\RECIPE.MDF  JUNE       4
```

Next, run net file again, specifying the file number displayed for the file that you want to close. To close the RECIPE.MDF file, for example, use this command:

```
C:\>net file 1 /close
```

The Net Group command

This command lets you add, display, or change global groups. This command has several different syntaxes, depending on how you intend to use it.

To display information about a group or to change a group's comment, use this syntax:

```
net group groupname [/comment:"text"] [/domain]
```

To create a new group, use this syntax:

```
net group groupname /add [/comment:"text"] [/domain]
```

To delete a group, use this syntax:

```
net group groupname /delete [/domain]
```

Finally, to add or remove users from a group, use this syntax:

```
net group groupname username[ ...] {/add | /delete} [/domain]
```

The following paragraphs describe the parameters that you can use with the net group command:

✦ **groupname:** Specifies the name of the group to add, change, or delete. If you specify this parameter and no others, a list of users in the group appears.

✦ **comment:** Specifies a comment for the group. The comment can be up to 48 characters in length and should be enclosed in quotation marks.

✦ **domain:** Specifies that the operation should be performed on the primary domain controller rather than on the local computer.

✦ **add:** Creates a new group or adds users to an existing group. Before you add a user to a group, you must create a user account for the user.

✦ **delete:** Removes a group or removes users from the group.

✦ **username:** Specifies one or more usernames to be added to or removed from the group. If you list more than one name, separate the names with spaces.

Windows isn't picky: You can specify net groups rather than net group if you want.

This example lists all the groups on a server:

```
C:\>net group
```

This example adds a group named Admin:

```
C:\>net group Admin /add
```

This example adds three users to the Admin group:

```
C:\>net group Admin Ward Wally June /add
```

This example lists the users in the Admin group:

```
C:\>net group Admin
```

The Net Help command

This command displays help for the `net` command or for a specific `net` subcommand. Here's the basic syntax:

```
net help [command]
```

The *command* parameter can be any of the following commands:

accounts	help	share
computer	helpmsg	start
config	localgroup	statistics
config server	name	stop
config workstation	pause	time
continue	print	use
file	send	user
group	session	view

You can type **net help services** to display a list of services that you can start via the `Net Start` command.

The Net Helpmsg command

This command displays an explanation of network error codes. Here's the syntax:

```
net helpmsg message#
```

The *message#* parameter should be the four-digit number displayed when the error occurred. If you get an error with message 2180, for example, use this command to see an explanation of the error:

```
C:\>net helpmsg 2180
The service database is locked.
EXPLANATION
Another program is holding the service database lock.
ACTION
Wait for the lock to be released and try again later. If it is possible to determine
    which program is holding the lock, then end that program.
```

The Net Localgroup command

This command lets you add, display, or change local groups. This command has several different syntaxes, depending on how you intend to use it.

Book VII
Chapter 8

Windows
Commands

To display information about a local group or to change a local group's comment, use this syntax:

```
net localgroup groupname [/comment:"text"] [/domain]
```

To create a new group, use this syntax:

```
net localgroup groupname /add [/comment:"text"] [/domain]
```

To delete a group, use this syntax:

```
net localgroup groupname /delete [/domain]
```

Finally, to add users to or remove users from a group, use this syntax:

```
net localgroup groupname username[ ...] {/add | /delete} [/domain]
```

The following paragraphs describe the parameters that you can use with the `net localgroup` command:

✦ **groupname:** Specifies the name of the group to add, change, or delete. If you specify this parameter and no others, a list of users in the group appears.

✦ **comment:** Specifies a comment for the group. The comment can be up to 48 characters in length and should be enclosed in quotation marks.

✦ **domain:** Specifies that the operation should be performed on the primary domain controller rather than on the local computer.

✦ **add:** Creates a new group or adds users to an existing group. Before you add a user to a group, you must create a user account for the user.

✦ **delete:** Removes a group or removes users from the group.

✦ **username:** Specifies one or more usernames to be added to or removed from the group. If you list more than one name, separate the names with spaces.

This example lists all the local groups:

```
C:\>net localgroup
```

This example adds a local group named Admin:

```
C:\>net localgroup Admin /add
```

This example adds three users to the Admin local group:

```
C:\>net localgroup Admin Ward Wally June /add
```

This example lists the users in the Admin group:

```
C:\>net localgroup Admin
```

The Net Name command

This command creates or removes an alias that can be used to send messages to the computer, or it lists any existing aliases. Here's the syntax:

```
net name [name {/add|/delete}]
```

You can use the following parameters with the net name command:

+ **name:** The name of the alias to create or remove
+ **add:** Creates the alias
+ **delete:** Removes the alias

Use net name to specify a name for receiving messages. You must start the Messenger service before you can use net name. Each messaging name must be unique on the network. Names created with net name are strictly for messaging — not for group names.

To list the current names for a computer, use the net name command like this:

```
C:\>net name
Name
------------------------------------------------------------
DOUG
DOUG LOWE
The command completed successfully.
```

To add the name T1000 to your computer, use this command:

```
C:\>net name T1000 /add
```

To delete the name, use this command:

```
C:\>net name T1000 /delete
```

The Net Pause command

This command temporarily pauses a service. It's a good idea to pause a service for a while before you stop the service altogether. That gives users who are currently using the service a chance to finish any pending tasks, while at the same time preventing other users from beginning new sessions with the service. To reactivate the service later, use the net continue command.

The syntax to pause a service is

```
net pause service
```

Here are some typical services that you can pause:

+ **netlogon:** The Net Logon service
+ **schedule:** The Task Scheduler service
+ **server:** The Server service
+ **workstation:** The Workstation service

Here's an example that pauses the Workstation service:

```
CL>net pause workstation
```

If the service name has embedded spaces, enclose the service name in quotation marks. This command pauses the NT LM Security Support Provider service, for example:

```
C:\>net pause "nt lm security support provider"
```

The Net Print command

This command displays information about print jobs and shared print queues. To display information about a print queue, use this syntax:

```
net print \\computername\sharename
```

To display information about a specific print job or to change the status of a print job, use this syntax:

```
net print [\\computername] job# [/hold | /release | /delete]
```

The following paragraphs describe the parameters of the Net Print command:

+ **\\computername:** Specifies the name of the computer sharing the printer.
+ **sharename:** Lists the name of the shared printer.
+ **job#:** Lists the identification number for the print job.
+ **hold:** Prevents a job in a queue from printing. The job remains in the queue but isn't printed until it's released from the queue.
+ **release:** Releases a job that was held.
+ **delete:** Removes a job from the print queue.

To display the status of the print queue for a printer named LASER1 on a computer named PSERVER, use this command:

```
C:\>net print \\PSERVER\LASER1
Printers at \\PSERVER
Name              Job #    Size      Status
-----------------------------------------------------------
LASER1Queue     3 jobs               *Printer Active*
    Ward          54       43546     Printing
    Wally         55       13565     Waiting
    Beaver        56       18321     Waiting
```

Now suppose that you happen to be user Beaver, and you want to crowd ahead of Wally's print job. All you have to do is issue this command:

```
C:\>net print \\PSERVER 55 /hold
```

The Net Send command

This command lets you send messages to other users on the network. The message pops up, interrupting whatever the user is doing. Use this command sparingly, or you'll lose friends quickly. Here's the syntax:

```
net send {name | * | /domain[:name] | /users} message
```

Here's what the parameters do:

+ **name:** Provides the name of the user or computer to whom you want to send the message. (This parameter can also be an alias created by the Net Name command.) If the name includes spaces, enclose it in quotes.

+ ***:** Sends the message to all computers in the domain or workgroup.

+ **domain:** Sends the message to everyone in the computer's domain or workgroup. If you specify a domain name, the message is sent to all users in the specified domain or workgroup.

+ **users:** Sends the message to all users who are currently connected to the server.

+ **message:** Provides the message to be sent. Interestingly, you don't have to enclose the message in quotes, even if it contains spaces.

To send the message I'm shutting down the server in 10 minutes to everyone on the network, use this command:

```
C:\>net send * I'm shutting down the server in 10 minutes
```

To send the message How about lunch? to a user named Pooh, use this command:

```
C:\>net send pooh How about lunch?
```

The Net Session command

This command lets you view current server connections and kick users off, if you feel inclined. Here's the syntax:

```
net session [\\ComputerName] [/delete]
```

Here's what the parameters do:

+ **computerName:** Indicates which computer's session you want to view or disconnect. If you omit this parameter, all sessions are listed.

+ **delete:** Disconnects the computer's session. Any open files are immediately closed. If you use this parameter without specifying a computer name, all computers currently connected to the server are disconnected.

This command is an obviously dangerous one. If you disconnect users while they're updating files or before they have a chance to save their work, they'll be hopping mad.

To find out who is connected to a computer, use this command:

```
C:\>net session
Computer   User name      Client type    Opens  Idle time
----------------------------------------------------------
\\DEN      Ward           Windows XP     1      00:00:4
\\BEDROOM  Administrator  Windows 2008   0      02:15:17
```

The Net Share command

This command lets you manage shared resources. To display information about all shares or a specific share, use this syntax:

```
net share [ShareName]
```

To create a new share, use this syntax:

```
net share ShareName=path [{/users:number|/unlimited}] [/remark:"text"]
    [/cache: {manual|automatic|no}]
```

To change the properties of an existing share, use this syntax:

```
net share ShareName [{/users:number|unlimited}] [/remark:"text"]
    [/cache: {manual|automatic|no}]
```

To delete an existing share, use this syntax:

```
net share {ShareName|drive:path} /delete
```

Here's what the parameters do:

✦ *ShareName:* Specifies the share name. Use this parameter by itself to display information about the share.

✦ *path:* Specifies the path to the folder to be shared. The path should include a drive letter. If the path includes spaces, enclose it in quotation marks.

✦ `users:` Specifies how many users can access the share concurrently.

✦ `unlimited:` Specifies that an unlimited number of users can access the share concurrently.

✦ `remark:` Creates a descriptive comment for the share. The comment should be enclosed in quotation marks.

✦ `cache:` Specifies the caching option for the share.

✦ `delete:` Stops sharing the folder.

If you use `net share` without any parameters, all the current shares are listed, as shown in this example:

```
C:\>net share
Sharename   Resource                     Remark
-------------------------------------------------------
ADMIN$      C:\WINNT                     Remote Admin
C$          C:\                          Default Share
print$      C:\WINNT\SYSTEM\SPOOL
IPC$                                     Remote IPC
LASER       LPT1                         Spooled Laser printer
```

The following example creates a share named Docs:

```
C:\>net share Docs=C:\SharedDocs /remark:"Shared documents"
```

The Net Start command

This command lets you start a networking service or display a list of all the services that are currently running. The syntax is

```
net start [service]
```

In most cases, you'll use this command to start a service that you've previously stopped with the `net stop` command. In that case, you should first

**Book VII
Chapter 8**

**Windows
Commands**

run the `net start` command without any parameters to find the name of the service that you want to stop. Make a note of the exact spelling of the service that you want to stop. Then use the `net stop` command to stop the service. When you want to restart the service, use the `net start` command again — this time specifying the service to start.

Suppose that you need to stop your DNS server. Using `net start`, you discover that the name of the service is DNS Server, so you use the following command to stop it:

```
C:\>net stop "DNS Server"
```

Later, you can use this command to restart the service:

```
C:\>net start "DNS Server"
```

The Net Statistics command

This command lists the statistics log for the local Workstation or Server service. The syntax is

```
net statistics [{workstation | server}]
```

You can specify `workstation` or `server` to indicate the service for which you'd like to view statistics.

If you use `net statistics workstation`, the following information appears:

✦ The computer name

✦ The date and time when the statistics were last updated

✦ The number of bytes and server message blocks (SMB) received and transmitted

✦ The number of read and write operations that succeeded or failed

✦ The number of network errors

✦ The number of sessions that failed, disconnected, or were reconnected

✦ The number of connections to shared resources that succeeded or failed

If you use `Net Statistics Server`, the following information is listed:

✦ The computer name

✦ The date and time when the statistics were last updated

✦ The number of sessions that have been started, disconnected automatically, and disconnected because of errors

✦ The number of kilobytes sent and received, and the average response time

✦ The number of password and permission errors and violations

✦ The number of times the shared files, printers, and communication devices were used

✦ The number of times the size of the memory buffer was exceeded

The Net Stop command

This command lets you stop a networking service. The syntax is

```
net stop service
```

To use this command, first run the net start command to determine the exact spelling of the service that you want to stop. If the service name includes spaces, enclose it in quotation marks.

You can restart the service later by using the net start command.

The following example stops the DNS service:

```
C:\>net stop "DNS Server"
```

**Book VII
Chapter 8**

The Net Time command

This command synchronizes the computer's clock with the clock on another computer. To access a clock on another computer in the same domain or workgroup, use this form:

```
net time \\ComputerName [/set]
```

To synchronize time with a domain, use this form:

```
net time /domain[:DomainName] [/set]
```

To use an RTS time server, use this syntax:

```
net time /rtsdomain[:DomainName] [/set]
```

To specify the computer to use for Network Time Protocol, use this syntax:

```
net time [\\ComputerName] [/querysntp] [/setsntp[:NTPServerList]]
```

**Windows
Commands**

To set the computer's clock to match the Server01 clock, use this command:

```
C:\>net time \\Server01 /set
```

The Net Use command

This command connects to or disconnects from a shared resource on another computer and maps the resource to a drive letter. Here's the complete syntax:

```
net use [{drive | *}]
        [{\\computername\sharename]
        [{password | *}]]
        [/user:[domainname\]username]
        [/savecred]
        [/smartcard]
        [{/delete | /persistent:{yes | no}}]
```

To set up a home directory, use this syntax:

```
net use [drive [/home[{password | *}]
        [/delete:{yes | no}]]]
```

And to control whether connections should be persistent, use this:

```
net use [/persistent:{yes | no}]
```

Here's what the parameters do:

+ *drive:* Specifies the drive letter. (Note that for a printer, you should specify a printer device such as LPT1: here instead of a drive letter.) If you specify an asterisk, Windows will determine what drive letter to use.

+ *\\computername\sharename:* Specifies the server and share name to connect to.

+ *password:* Provides the password needed to access the shared resource. If you use an asterisk, you're prompted for the password.

+ **user:** Specifies the username to use for the connection.

+ **savecred:** Saves the credentials for reuse later if the user is prompted for a password.

+ **smartcard:** Specifies that the connection should use a smart card for authorization.

+ **delete:** Deletes the specified connection. If you specify an asterisk (*), all network connections are canceled.

✦ `persistent:` Specifies whether connections should be persistent.

✦ **home:** Connects to the home directory.

To display all current connections, type **net use** with no parameters.

The following example shows how to create a persistent connection to a drive named Acct on a server named Server01, using drive K:

```
C:\>net use k: \\Server01\Acct /persistent: yes
```

The following example drops the connection:

```
C:\>net use k: /delete
```

The Net User command

This command creates or changes user accounts. To display a user's information, use this form:

```
net user username
```

To update user information, use this form:

```
net user [username [password | *] [options]] [/domain]
```

To add a new user, use this form:

```
net user username [password | *] /add [options] [/domain]
```

To delete a user, use this form:

```
net user username /delete [/domain]
```

Most of the parameters for this command are straightforward. The `options` parameters, however, can have a variety of settings. Table 8-2 lists the descriptions of these options as presented by the `Net Help Users` command.

To display information for a particular user, use the command like this:

```
C:\>net user Doug
```

To add a user account for Theodore Cleaver with the username Beaver, use this command:

```
C:\>net user Beaver /add /fullname:"Theodore Cleaver"
```

Table 8-2	The Options Parameters
Options	*Description*
/ACTIVE:{YES | NO}	Activates or deactivates the account. If the account isn't active, the user can't access the server. The default is YES.
/COMMENT:"text"	Provides a descriptive comment about the user's account (maximum of 48 characters). Enclose the text in quotation marks.
/COUNTRYCODE:nnn	Uses the operating-system country code to implement the specified language files for a user's help and error messages. A value of 0 signifies the default country code.
/EXPIRES:{date | NEVER}	Causes the account to expire if date is set. NEVER sets no time limit on the account. An expiration date is in the form *mm/dd/yy* or *dd/mm/yy*, depending on the country code. The month can be a number, spelled out, or abbreviated with three letters. The year can be two or four numbers. Use slashes (/), not spaces, to separate parts of the date.
/FULLNAME:"name"	Is a user's full name (rather than a username). Enclose the name in quotation marks.
/HOMEDIR:pathname	Sets the path for the user's home directory. The path must exist.
/PASSWORDCHG:{YES | NO}	Specifies whether users can change their own passwords. The default is YES.
/PASSWORDREQ:{YES | NO}	Specifies whether a user account must have a password. The default is YES.
/PROFILEPATH[:path]	Sets a path for the user's logon profile.
/SCRIPTPATH:pathname	Is the location of the user's logon script.
/TIMES:{times | ALL}	Is the logon hours. TIMES is expressed as *day*[-*day*][,*day*[-*day*]],*time*[-*time*][,*time*[-*time*]], limited to 1-hour increments. Days can be spelled out or abbreviated. Hours can be 12- or 24-hour notation. For 12-hour notation, use am or pm (without periods) or a.m. or p.m. ALL means that a user can always log on, and a blank value means that a user can never log on. Separate day and time entries with a comma, and separate multiple day and time entries with a semicolon.

Options	Description
`/USERCOMMENT:"text"`	Lets an administrator add or change the User Comment for the account.
`/WORKSTATIONS:`	Lists as many as eight computers from which a user {*ComputerName*[,. . .] | *} can log on to the network. If `/WORKSTATIONS` has no list or if the list is *, the user can log on from any computer.

The Net View command

This command displays information about your network. If you use it without parameters, it displays a list of the computers in your domain. You can use parameters to display resources that are being shared by a particular computer. Here's the syntax:

```
net view [\\computername] [/domain[:domainname]]
net view /network:nw [\\computername]
```

Here's what the parameters do:

✦ **computername:** Specifies the computer whose shared resources you want to view.

✦ **domainname:** Specifies the domain you want to view, if it's other than the current domain.

Here's typical output from a `net view` command:

```
C:\>net view
Server Name            Remark
-------------------------------------------------
\\Server01             Main file server
\\Print01              Main print server
```

The RunAs Command

The `runas` command lets you run a program from a command prompt by using the credentials of another user account. Here's the basic syntax:

```
runas /user:username [other parameters] program
```

To run the Microsoft Management Console with the dom1 domain's administrator account, for example, you can use this command:

```
runas /user:dom1\administrator mmc
```

Assuming that the username is valid, you'll be prompted for the user's password. Then the program will be run using the specified user's account.

Here are some of the parameters you can use with the RunAs command:

+ **/user:** Specifies the domain and username. You can use either of two forms to specify the domain and username: *domain\username* or *username@domain*.

+ **/profile:** Specifies that the user's profile should be loaded. (This option is on by default, so you don't have to specify it explicitly.)

+ **/noprofile:** Doesn't load the user's profile. Although this parameter can cause the application to load faster, it can also prevent some applications from functioning properly.

+ **/env:** Uses the current environment instead of the user's.

+ **/netonly:** Indicates that the user account isn't valid in the current domain. (If you use /netonly, the username must be specified in the form *domain\username*; the *username@domain* form won't work.)

+ **/savecred:** Saves the password so that it has to be entered only the first time the RunAs command is used.

Using the /savecred parameter is an extremely bad idea, as it creates a gaping security hole. In short, after you've used /savecred, any user at the computer can use the RunAs command to run any program with administrator privileges.

+ **/smartcard:** Specifies that the user's credentials will be supplied by a smart card device.

Book VIII

Using Other Windows Servers

Add Roles and Features Wizard

Select server roles

DESTINATION SERVER
win1601.lowewriter.pri

Before You Begin
Installation Type
Server Selection
Server Roles
Features
Confirmation
Results

Select one or more roles to install on the selected server.

Roles

- [ ] Active Directory Certificate Services
- [x] Active Directory Domain Services (Installed)
- [ ] Active Directory Federation Services
- [ ] Active Directory Lightweight Directory Services
- [ ] Active Directory Rights Management Services
- [x] DHCP Server (Installed)
- [x] DNS Server (Installed)
- [ ] Fax Server
- [▪] File and Storage Services (2 of 12 installed)
- [ ] Host Guardian Service
- [ ] Hyper-V
- [ ] MultiPoint Services
- [ ] Network Controller
- [ ] Network Policy and Access Services
- [ ] Print and Document Services

Description

Web Server (IIS) provides a reliable, manageable, and scalable Web application infrastructure.

< Previous   Next >   Install   Cancel

web extras

Find out how to get rid of auto-mapped mailboxes in a free article at `www.dummies.com/extras/networkingaio`.

Contents at a Glance

Chapter 1: Using Internet Information Services 631

Chapter 2: Managing Exchange Server 2016. 641

Chapter 3: Using SQL Server 2014 659

Chapter 1: Using Internet Information Services

In This Chapter

✔ Configuring a server to use IIS

✔ Working with the default website

✔ Creating your own websites

Internet Information Services (IIS) is the web server that comes with Windows Server. It's an essential piece of software for hosting public websites, and it's also a must for any network that includes an intranet with web pages designed to be used by your network users.

In this chapter, you find out how to set up IIS and perform the most common types of maintenance chores, such as creating new websites.

Installing IIS

IIS is a free component of Windows Server, but it's not installed by default. After you've completed the installation of Windows Server, you must add the Web Server role to enable IIS. The following procedure is for Windows Server 2016, but the procedure for Windows Server 2012 (or 2008, for that matter) is similar:

1. **Open the Server Manager; then choose Add Roles and Features.**

   The Add Roles and Features Wizard comes to life.

2. **Follow the steps of the Add Roles and Features Wizard up to the Select Server Roles step.**

   The Select Server Roles page is shown in Figure 1-1.

3. **Select the Web Server (IIS) check box and then click Next.**

   The Add Roles and Features Wizard asks whether you want to install the related IIS Management Console, as shown in Figure 1-2.

Figure 1-1:
The Select Server Roles page of the Add Roles and Features Wizard.

Figure 1-2:
Installing the IIS Management Console.

4. **Click Add Features; then click Next.**

The Select Features page appears.

5. **Click Next.**

The Features page appears.

6. **Click Next.**

The Web Server Role (IIS) page appears, as shown in Figure 1-3.

Figure 1-3:
The Web Server Role (IIS) page of the Add Roles and Features Wizard.

7. **Click Next.**

   The Select Role Services page appears, as shown in Figure 1-4. This page lists a variety of optional services that can be configured for IIS.

Figure 1-4:
The Select Role Services page of the Add Roles and Features Wizard.

8. **Select the services you want to configure for IIS.**

   If you want, you can study this list and try to anticipate which features you think you'll need. Or you can just leave the default options selected.

TIP

You can always return to the Add Roles and Features Wizard to add features you leave out here.

9. **Click Next.**

A confirmation page appears.

10. **Click Install.**

The features you selected are installed. This may take a few minutes, so now would be a good time to take a walk.

When the installation finishes, an Installation Results page is displayed to verify that IIS was properly installed.

11. **Click Close.**

IIS is now installed and ready to use!

Understanding the Default Website

Initially, IIS is configured with a single website, called the *default website*. You can test that IIS is up and running by logging in as a standard user (not an administrator), opening a browser window on the server and typing **http://localhost** in the address bar. You can also reach this page by entering your local domain name in the address bar, such as **lowewriter.pri**. Figure 1-5 shows the standard welcome page that appears when you browse to the default site.

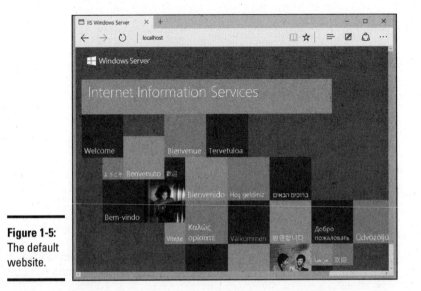

Figure 1-5:
The default
website.

The actual files that make up the default website are stored on the server's `C:` drive in a folder named `\inetpub\wwwroot`. When you browse to the default website without requesting a specific file (simply by **localhost** in the address bar, for example), IIS looks for the following files, in this order:

✦ `default.htm`

✦ `default.asp`

✦ `index.htm`

✦ `index.html`

✦ `iisstart.htm`

✦ `default.aspx`

Initially, `c:\inetpub\wwwroot` contains just two files: `iisstart.htm` and `welcome.png`. The `iisstart.htm` file is the file that's displayed when you browse to the website; it contains the HTML necessary to display the image contained in the `welcome.png` file, which is the image you actually see on the page.

You can preempt the standard page for the default website by providing your own file one of the preceding names. You can follow these steps, for example, to create a simple `default.htm` file that displays the words *Hello World!* as the start page for the default website:

1. **Log in as an administrator, open an Explorer window, and browse to `c:\inetpub\wwwroot`.**

2. **Choose File ➪ New ➪ Text Document, type** default.htm **for the filename, and press Enter.**

3. **Right-click the `default.htm` file you just created, and choose Open With ➪ Notepad from the contextual menu.**

4. **Enter the following text in the Notepad window:**

   ```
   <HTML>
   <BODY>
   <H1>Hello World!</H1>
   </BODY>
   </HTML>
   ```

5. **Choose File ➪ Save to save the file and then choose File ➪ Exit to quit Notepad.**

6. **Log out, log in as a standard user, and open a browser window.**

7. **Type** http://localhost **in the address bar, and press Enter.**

   The page shown in Figure 1-6 appears.

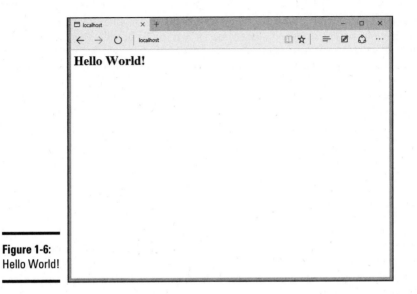

Figure 1-6:
Hello World!

Creating Websites

IIS has the ability to host multiple websites. This is an extremely useful feature not only for web servers that host public sites, but also for web servers that host internal (intranet) sites. You might create a separate intranet website for Human Resources and assign it the website name hr. Then, assuming that the domain name is lowewriter.pri, users can browse to the website by using the address hr.lowewriter.pri.

Here are the steps:

1. **Using Windows Explorer, create a folder in which you will save the files for the new website.**

   For this example, I created a folder named c:\HR-Web-Site.

2. **In Server Manager, choose Tools⇨Internet Information Services (IIS) Manager.**

   The IIS Manager springs to life, as shown in Figure 1-7.

3. **In the navigation pane, open the primary domain and Sites node. Then right-click Sites and choose Add Website from the contextual menu.**

   The Add Website dialog box appears, as shown in Figure 1-8.

Figure 1-7:
The IIS
Manager.

Figure 1-8:
The Add
Website
dialog box.

**Book VIII
Chapter 1**

**Using Internet
Information
Services**

4. **Enter a name for the website in the Site Name text box.**

For this example, I used HR.

5. **Click the Browse button (the one with the ellipsis), browse to the folder you created in Step 1, and then click OK.**

For this example, I browsed to `C:\HR-Web-Site`.

6. **In the Host Name text box, enter the exact DNS name you want to use for the site.**

For this example, I entered `hr.lowewriter.pri`.

7. **Click OK.**

The newly created website appears below the Sites node in the IIS Manager, as shown in Figure 1-9.

Figure 1-9: The HR website appears in the IIS Manager.

8. **Close the IIS Manager.**

9. **Create a web page to display in the folder you created in Step 1.**

For this example, I used Notepad to create a text file named `default.htm`, with the following text:

```
<HTML>
<BODY>
<H1>Welcome to the HR Website!</H1>
</BODY>
</HTML>
```

10. **In Server Manager, choose Tools ⇨ DNS.**

This brings up the DNS Manager console, as shown in Figure 1-10.

11. **In the navigation pane, navigate to the node for your domain.**

In this example, I navigated to `lowewriter.pri`.

12. **Choose Action ⇨ New Alias (CNAME).**

The New Resource Record dialog box appears, as shown in Figure 1-11.

Figure 1-10:
The DNS
Manager
console.

Figure 1-11:
Creating
a CNAME
record.

13. **Enter the alias name you want to use in the Alias Name text box.**

For this example, I entered simply `hr`.

14. **Enter the computer name of your web server in the text box labeled Fully Qualified Domain Name (FQDN) for Target Host.**

For this example, I entered `lserver01`.

15. **Click OK.**

    The DNS alias is created.

16. **Close the DNS Manager console.**

17. **Open a browser window.**

18. **Browse to the alias address you just created.**

    For this example, I browsed to `hr.lowewriter.pri`. Figure 1-12 shows the resulting page.

Figure 1-12:
Viewing a website.

Chapter 2: Managing Exchange Server 2016

In This Chapter

✔ Working with the Exchange Server consoles

✔ Managing mailboxes

✔ Granting mailbox access

Although not strictly a part of Windows Server, Exchange Server is the mail server software that's used on most Windows networks. Yes, I know Microsoft doesn't call Exchange Server a *mail server*. It's a *messaging and collaboration server*. But the basic reason for Exchange Server's existence is email. The other messaging and collaboration features are just icing on the cake.

In this chapter, you discover how to perform the most commonly requested maintenance chores for Exchange Server, such as how to create a new mailbox, grant a user access to an additional mailbox, and deal with mailbox size limits. The examples shown in this chapter are for Exchange Server 2016, but the procedures are similar for previous versions.

Creating a Mailbox

In previous versions of Exchange, you managed mailboxes using the Exchange Management Console. In the 2013 and 2016 versions of Exchange, you use the web-based Exchange Administrative Center (EAC) instead. To start EAC, choose Start ➪ All Apps ➪ Microsoft Exchange 2016 ➪ Exchange Administrative Center.

When you create a new mailbox, you can either specify either an existing Active Directory user or use EAC to create a new Active Directory user and mailbox at the same time. The following procedure describes the steps you should follow to create a new Active Directory user with a mailbox:

1. **Open the Exchange Administrative Center by choosing Start ➪ All Apps ➪ Microsoft Exchange Server 2016 ➪ Exchange Administrative Center.**

2. **When prompted, enter your username and password.**

   The EAC comes to life, as shown in Figure 2-1.

3. **Click the plus sign (+) icon above the list of mailboxes, and then choose User Mailbox.**

   The User Mailbox page appears, as shown in Figure 2-2.

4. **Enter the alias for the new mailbox.**

   The alias is the portion of the email address that appears before the at (@) sign. For example, in the email address mitchell@lowewriter.com, the alias is `mitchell`.

5. **Choose New User.**

6. **Type the user's first name, middle initial, and last name.**

   As you type the name, the Display Name field is automatically filled in.

7. **Change the Display Name field if you want it to appear different from what was proposed.**

   You may want to reverse the first and last names so the last name appears first, for example.

Figure 2-2:
Creating
a user
mailbox.

8. **Enter the user logon name.**

   This name must be unique within the domain and will be used to form the user's email address.

9. **Enter the password twice.**

   You're asked to type the password twice, so type it correctly. If you don't type it identically in both boxes, you're asked to correct your mistake.

10. **If the password is temporary, select the User Must Change Password at Next Logon check box.**

    This setting requires the user to change the temporary password the first time he or she logs on.

11. **Click Save.**

    The user's mailbox is created and appears in the EAC Recipients page, as shown in Figure 2-3.

12. **Pat yourself on the back; then click Finish.**

    You're done!

Book VIII
Chapter 2

Managing
Exchange Server
2016

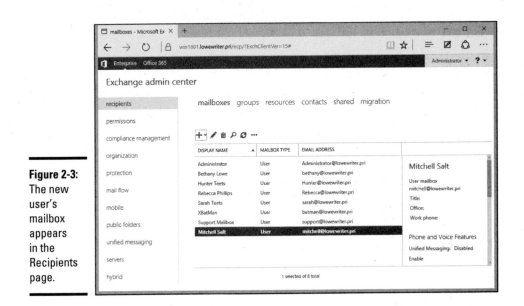

Figure 2-3:
The new
user's
mailbox
appears
in the
Recipients
page.

Managing Mailboxes

After you've set up a mailbox, you can use the Exchange Administrative Center to manage the settings of the mailbox. To do that, just select the mailbox you want to manage, and click the Edit icon (shown in the margin). This action brings up the User Mailbox page, which is the portal to many of the most frequently used features of Exchange.

The following sections describe several commonly used features you can enable when you edit a mailbox.

Enabling mailbox features

Exchange Mailbox Features refers to several features of Exchange mailboxes that are controlled via the Mailbox Features tab of the User Mailbox page. This tab is shown in Figure 2-4.

The following paragraphs describe some of the features that are controlled from this tab:

✦ **Outlook on the Web:** Lets the user access his or her Exchange mailbox from a web browser rather than from an Outlook client. With this feature enabled, the user can read email from any computer that has an Internet connection.

Figure 2-4:
The Mailbox
Features tab.

✦ **Exchange ActiveSync:** Activates the ActiveSync feature, which allows Exchange data to synchronize with mobile devices such as iPhones or Windows Mobile phones.

✦ **MAPI:** Enables email using the MAPI protocol.

✦ **POP3:** Enables email using the POP3 protocol.

✦ **IMAP4:** Enables email using the IMAP4 protocol.

✦ **Archiving:** Enables the Exchange Archive feature, which is available only with the Enterprise edition of Exchange.

✦ **Mail Flow:** Lets you set delivery options such as creating an automatic forwarder, as described in the next section.

✦ **Message Size Restrictions:** Lets you set the maximum size of incoming or outgoing messages.

Creating a forwarder

A *forwarder* is a feature that automatically forwards any incoming email to another email address. This feature is most often used when an employee is on vacation or leave and the employee's manager has requested that someone else temporarily handle the absent employee's email.

**Book VIII
Chapter 2**

Managing
Exchange Server
2016

To configure a forwarder, follow these steps:

1. **In Exchange Administrative Center, open the User Mailbox page for the user.**

2. **Select the Mailbox Features tab, and then click View Details in the Mail Flow section.**

   The delivery options are displayed, as shown in Figure 2-5.

Figure 2-5:
Setting the delivery options.

3. **Select the Enable Forwarding check box.**

4. **Click the Browse button.**

   The Select Recipient window appears, as shown in Figure 2-6.

5. **Select the recipient you want to forward the email to and then click OK.**

   The name you selected is displayed in the text box next to the Browse button in the Delivery Options page (refer to Figure 2-5).

6. **If you want the email to be delivered to this user's mailbox in addition to the forwarding address, select the Deliver Message to Both Forwarding Address and Mailbox check box.**

   If you leave this option deselected, only the forwarding address will receive the email; the mail won't be delivered to this user's mailbox.

Figure 2-6:
Select the
recipient
for the
forwarder.

7. **Click OK to close the Delivery Options page.**

   You return to the User Mailbox page.

8. **Click Save to save your changes.**

Setting mailbox storage limits

Exchange lets you set a limit on the size of each user's mailbox. In a very small organization, you can probably get away without imposing strict mailbox size limits. But if your organization has 20 or more users, you need to limit the size of each user's mailbox to prevent the Exchange private mail store from getting out of hand.

Exchange provides five kinds of storage limits for user mailboxes:

✦ **Issue Warning At:** When this limit is exceeded, an email warning is sent to the user to let him know that his mailbox is getting large.

✦ **Prohibit Send At:** When this limit is reached, the user can't send email, but the mailbox continues to receive email. The user won't be able to send emails again until she deletes enough emails to reduce the mailbox size below the limit.

+ **Prohibit Send and Receive At:** When this limit is reached, the mailbox shuts down and can neither send nor receive emails.

+ **Keep Deleted Items for (Days):** Most users don't realize it, but when they permanently delete an item from their mailbox, the item isn't really permanently deleted. Instead, Exchange retains the item for the period specified by this limit. The default is 14 days.

+ **Keep Deleted Mailboxes for (Days):** This limit specifies how long Exchange should retain mailboxes that you delete.

You can (and should) set a default storage limit that applies to all mailboxes in your organization. You can also override these limits for specific users.

To configure the default storage limits for all mailboxes, follow these steps:

1. **In Exchange Administrative Center, select Databases.**

A list of databases for your Exchange environment appears, as shown in Figure 2-7. In this example, there is just one database. For larger Exchange environments, you may see several databases.

Figure 2-7:
The
Exchange
Admin
Center
Databases
page.

2. **Double-click the database whose limits you want to change.**

The Mailbox Database page appears, as shown in Figure 2-8.

Figure 2-8:
The Mailbox
Database
page.

3. **Select Limits.**

   The Mailbox Database Limits page is displayed, as shown in Figure 2-9.

Figure 2-9:
The Mailbox
Database
Limits page.

4. **Change the Storage Limits settings to meet your needs.**

By default, the storage limits are set quite high: Warnings are issued at about 1.9GB, send permission is revoked at 2GB, and both send and receive permissions are revoked at 2.3GB. These limits are generous, but bear in mind that if you have 100 users, your mailbox database may grow to 200GB. You may want to set lower limits.

5. **Click Save.**

The limits you set take effect immediately.

If you impose restrictive default storage limits for your users, you may want to relax the limits on a case-by-case basis. Some users may require a larger mailbox because of the type of work they do, and you probably don't want to impose a tight limit on your boss.

Fortunately, it's easy to override the default limits for a specific user. Here are the steps:

1. **In Exchange Administrative Center, choose Recipients, then double-click the mailbox you want to edit.**

The user's mailbox page appears.

2. **Select Mailbox Usage.**

The Mailbox Usage page is displayed, as shown in Figure 2-10.

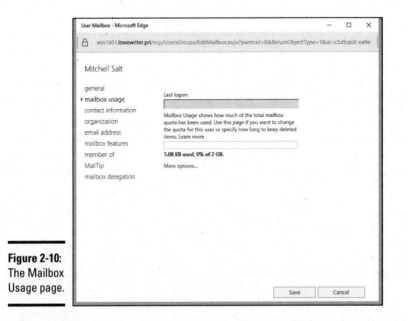

Figure 2-10:
The Mailbox
Usage page.

3. Click More Options.

The mailbox limits options are displayed, as shown in Figure 2-11.

> User Mailbox - Microsoft Edge — □ ×
>
> 🔒 win1601.**lowewriter.pri**/ecp/UsersGroups/EditMailbox.aspx?pwmcid=8&ReturnObjectType=1&id=c5dfcac8-ea9e-
>
> Mitchell Salt
>
> general
> ▸ mailbox usage
> contact information
> organization
> email address
> mailbox features
> member of
> MailTip
> mailbox delegation
>
> Mailbox Usage shows how much of the total mailbox quota has been used. Use this page if you want to change the quota for this user or specify how long to keep deleted items. Learn more
>
> 5.08 KB used, 0% of 2 GB.
>
> ● Use the default quota settings from the mailbox database
> ○ Customize the quota settings for this mailbox
>
> *Issue a warning at (GB):
> 1.9
>
> *Prohibit send at (GB):
> 2
>
> *Prohibit send and receive at (GB):
> 2.3
>
> ● Use the default retention settings from the mailbox database
> ○ Customize the retention settings for this mailbox
>
> *Keep deleted items for (days):
>
> Save   Cancel

4. Change the Storage Limits settings to meet your needs.

You can adjust any of the mailbox limits up or down to create limits for the user that are either more or less restrictive than the defaults for the database.

5. Click Save.

The limits you set take effect immediately.

You can configure many other features of Exchange via the Exchange Management Console. You should take some time to explore all the nodes in the navigation pane and to examine the Properties dialog boxes for the various types of Exchange objects that appear when you select each node.

Configuring Outlook for Exchange

After you've created an Exchange mailbox for a user, you can configure that user's Outlook client software to connect to the user's account. Although you can do this configuration directly within Outlook, it's better to do it outside Outlook, using the Control Main Mail applet. Here are the steps:

1. **Open Control Panel, and open the Mail applet.**

The dialog box shown in Figure 2-12 appears.

Figure 2-12:
The Mail
Setup dialog
box.

2. **Click the Show Profiles button.**

The dialog box shown in Figure 2-13 appears, listing the mail profiles that already exist on the computer.

Figure 2-13:
The mail
profiles.

3. **Double-click the user's profile.**

The Mail Setup dialog box shown in Figure 2-14 appears.

Figure 2-14:
The Mail
Setup dialog
box.

4. **Click the E-mail Accounts button.**

The Account Settings dialog box appears, as shown in Figure 2-15.

Figure 2-15:
The
Account
Settings
dialog box.

**Book VIII
Chapter 2**

**Managing
Exchange Server
2016**

5. **Click the New icon.**

An Add E-mail Account dialog box appears. Don't enter your email address as prompted in this dialog box; instead, proceed to Step 6.

6. **Click the Manually Configure Server Settings or Additional Server Types option and then click Next.**

A dialog box asks you what type of email account you want to create. The choices are (a) Outlook.com or Exchange ActiveSync Compatible Service or (b) POP 3 or IMAP.

7. **Select the Outlook.com or Exchange ActiveSync Compatible Service option and then click Next.**

   The Server Settings dialog box shown in Figure 2-16 appears.

8. **Enter the name of the Exchange server and the username in the appropriate text boxes; then click Next.**

   After your account information is verified, a confirmation message is displayed.

9. **Click OK.**

   The confirmation message disappears, and the last page of the E-Mail Accounts Wizard appears.

10. **Click the Finish button.**

    The wizard is dismissed.

11. **Choose File ⇨ Exit to close Outlook.**

12. **Restart Outlook.**

    The mailbox should be configured.

Viewing Another Mailbox

Sometimes, you want to set up Outlook so that in addition to the user's main mailbox, he or she has access to another user's mailbox. Suppose that you create a user named Support so that your customers can send email to Support@YourCompany.com to ask technical support questions. If you don't set up at least one of your users so that he or she can read the Support mailbox, any mail sent to Support@YourCompany.com will languish unanswered. Assuming that this situation isn't what you want, you can set up one or more of your users to access the Support mailbox so that those users can read and respond to the mail.

First, you must configure the Support user account's mailbox so that it grants access rights to each user whom you want to access the account. To do that, follow these steps:

1. **In Exchange Administrative Center, open the User Mailbox page for the user.**

2. **Select Mailbox Delegation.**

The Mailbox Usage page is displayed, as shown in Figure 2-17. (For this figure, I scrolled to the bottom of the page to show the Full Access settings.)

Figure 2-17: The Mailbox Delegation page.

3. **Click the Add icon.**

The Select Full Access page opens, as shown in Figure 2-18.

Figure 2-18:
The Select
Full Access
page.

4. **Select the user you want to grant access to; then click OK.**

   You're returned to the wizard. The user you added is selected in the list of users who have access to the mailbox.

5. **Click the Save button.**

   The mailbox rights are updated.

After you've granted access to the account, you can configure the user's Outlook to read the Support account. Follow these steps:

1. **On the user's computer, start Outlook, and choose Tools⇨Account.**

   The Account Settings dialog box is displayed.

2. **Select your main email account and then click Change.**

   The Server Settings dialog box appears, as shown in Figure 2-19.

3. **Click the More Settings button to open the Microsoft Exchange dialog box and then click the Advanced tab.**

   The Advanced tab is shown in Figure 2-20.

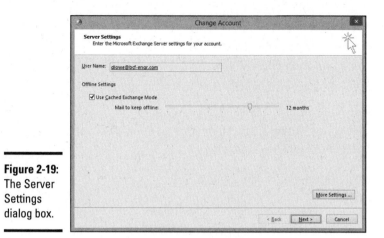

Figure 2-19:
The Server Settings dialog box.

Figure 2-20:
The Advanced tab.

4. **Click the Add button.**

   A dialog box appears, prompting you for the name of the mailbox you want to add.

5. **Type the name of the mailbox you want to add and then click OK.**

   The mailbox is added to the list box in the Microsoft Exchange dialog box (refer to Figure 2-19).

6. **Click OK.**

   You're returned to the Server Settings dialog box.

7. **Click Next and then click Finish.**

   You're done! Now you can view the Support mailbox.

To view the mailbox, you need to open the Folder List window in Outlook (by choosing View⇨Folder List). Then you can double-click the Support mailbox in the list to open it.

Chapter 3: Using SQL Server 2014

In This Chapter

✔ Looking at relational databases and SQL

✔ Installing SQL Server 2014

SQL Server 2014 is the latest and greatest version of the most common database server used on Microsoft networks.

This chapter introduces you to the basics of installing and running SQL Server 2014. It begins with a basic introduction to relational databases and SQL. Then it shows you how to manage a SQL Server database by using SQL Server 2014 Management Studio.

Note: The information in this chapter applies to previous versions of SQL Server as well.

What Is a Database?

A *database* is simply an organized collection of information. Here are some examples of databases from everyday life:

✦ Your personal address book

✦ The shoebox that contains your tax records for the year

✦ Your baseball card collection

✦ All those parking tickets conveniently stuffed into your car's glove compartment

✦ The phone book (well, from everyday life in the good ol' days anyway)

✦ That pile of score cards that has been accumulating in the bottom of your golf bag for 15 years

You can think of each of these databases as a collection of records. In database lingo, a *record* consists of all the useful information that you can gather about a particular thing. In your address book, each record represents one of your friends (or enemies). For your tax records database, each receipt in the shoebox is a record.

Each snippet of information that makes up a record is called a *field*. Using the address book as an example once again, each person's record (that is, each entry in your address book) consists of several fields: name; street address; city; state; zip code; phone number; email address; and other information that may be optional, such as the person's birthday, whether you sent a Christmas card to the person last year, or how much money the person owes you.

SQL Server is designed to create and manage computerized databases that are similar to these noncomputerized databases. Like your address book or shoebox full of tax records, a SQL Server database is a collection of records, and each record is a collection of fields. The biggest difference is that in a SQL Server database, the information is stored on a server computer's hard drive rather than in a shoebox.

What Is a Relational Database?

SQL Server is a database management server that creates and maintains relational databases. Unfortunately, the term *relational database* is one of the most used and abused buzzwords in the computer business. The term has at least three meanings. A *relational database* can be

+ **A database in which data is stored in tables:** In a relational database, groups of similar records are called *tables*. A database usually consists of more than one table; in fact, it isn't uncommon for a single database to have dozens of tables. You can establish relationships between and among these tables based on common information. A sales database, for example, might contain a table of customer information and a table of invoices, with both tables containing a customer-number column that establishes a relationship between the tables.

+ **A database model based on a Coneheads branch of mathematics called Set Theory:** This is actually the most technically precise definition of a relational database, but only computer geeks know or care. Contrary to popular belief, the term *relational database* is derived not from the ability to create relationships among tables, but from the term *relation,* a mathematical term that refers to the way data is arranged into tables of rows and columns.

    (It's a little-known fact that relational-database theory was developed at around the same time that the Coneheads from the planet Remulak first visited Earth, back in the 1970s. I've always suspected that these two developments are — dare I say it? — related.)

+ **A database that's accessed via SQL:** *SQL,* which stands for *Structured Query Language,* provides a practical way to access data stored in relational tables. A database that's based on SQL is inherently relational because SQL stores its data in tables and is based on Set Theory. SQL Server, as its name implies, is based on SQL.

From a practical point of view, the third definition is the most important: A relational database is a database that you can access via SQL. Thus, SQL Server is used for relational databases. The next section dives a little more deeply into what SQL is.

What Is SQL?

SQL, which stands for *Structured Query Language,* is a language designed to extract, organize, and update information in relational databases. Originally, SQL was envisioned as an English-like query language that untrained end users could use to access and update relational database data. In reality, SQL is nothing like English, and it's far too complicated and esoteric for untrained users, but it has become the overwhelming favorite among programmers who develop applications that access relational databases.

SQL dialects

Like most computer languages, SQL has several dialects. In fact, each major brand of SQL database server has its own dialect of SQL. These dialects are 95 percent the same, so a basic SQL statement is likely to work the same way regardless of the database server you use it with. But the ways that the more advanced features of SQL work have many variations.

The version of SQL used by Microsoft's SQL Server is known as *T-SQL.*

How do you pronounce SQL?

Here's something you've probably wondered ever since you first saw the letters *SQL:* How do you pronounce it? Two schools of thought exist on the subject:

✔ Spell out the letters: *S-Q-L.*

✔ Pronounce it like the word *sequel.*

Either way is acceptable, but *sequel* is hipper.

You can always tell how a writer pronounces *SQL* by checking to see whether the author writes "a SQL query" or "an SQL query."

You can impress even the staunchest SQL expert by pointing out that originally, the language was called SEQUEL by the IBM engineers who created the first version way back in the 1970s. SEQUEL stood for *Structured English Query Language.* Someone must have correctly pointed out that aside from borrowing a few words from English, such as `select` and `create`, SEQUEL actually bore no resemblance whatsoever to English. So *English* was dropped from the name, and the acronym was shortened from SEQUEL to SQL.

SQL statements

Like other programming languages, SQL uses statements to get its work done. Table 3-1 lists the most commonly used statements.

Table 3-1	Common SQL Statements
SQL Statement	*What It Does*
Use	Identifies the name of the database that subsequent SQL statements apply to.
select	Retrieves data from one or more tables. This is the SQL statement that's used the most.
Insert	Inserts one or more rows into a table.
delete	Deletes one or more rows from a table.
update	Updates existing rows in a table.
create	Creates tables and other database objects.
alter	Alters the definition of a table or other database object.
drop	Deletes a table or other database object.

Using the select statement

As the name *Structured Query Language* suggests, queries are what SQL is all about. Thus, the select statement is the most important of the SQL statements. A select statement extracts data from one or more tables in a database and creates a *result set* containing the selected rows and columns.

In a select statement, you list the table or tables from which you want to retrieve the data; the specific columns you want to retrieve (you may not be interested in everything that's in the table); and other clauses that indicate which specific rows should be retrieved, what order the rows should be presented in, and so on.

Here's a simple select statement that retrieves data from a table named movie, which contains information about your favorite movies:

```
select title, year
    from movie
    order by year
```

Now take this statement apart piece by piece:

✦ `select title, year` names the columns you want included in the query result (`title` and `year`).

✦ `from movie` names the table you want the rows retrieved from (`movie`).

✦ `order by year` indicates that the result should be sorted in sequence by the `year` column so that the oldest movie appears first.

In other words, this `select` statement retrieves the title and date for all the rows in the `movie` table and sorts them into `year` sequence.

If you want the query to retrieve all the columns in each row, you can use an asterisk instead of naming the individual columns:

```
select * from movie order by year;
```

Both examples so far include an `order by` clause. In a SQL database, the rows stored in a table are not assumed to be in any particular sequence. As a result, if you want to display the results of a query in sequence, you must include an `order by` clause in the `select` statement.

Suppose that you want to find information about one particular video title. To select certain rows from a table, use the `where` clause in a `select` statement:

```
select title, year from movie
    where year <= 1980
    order by year
```

Here, the `select` statement selects all rows in which the `year` column is less than or equal to 1980. The results are ordered by the `year` column.

Perhaps you want to retrieve all rows except those that match certain criteria. Here's a query that ignores movies made in the 1970s (which is probably a good idea, with exceptions like *The Godfather* and *Young Frankenstein*):

```
select title, year from movie
    where year < 1970 or year > 1979
    order by year;
```

You can do much more with `select` statements, of course. But this chapter isn't about SQL itself; it's about installing and using SQL Server. So get ready to move on to the good stuff.

Using SQL Server 2014 Management Studio

SQL Server Management Studio is a component of SQL Server 2014 that runs on workstation computers and lets you manage any or all of the SQL Server instances on your network. You run it by choosing Start ⇨ SQL Server Management Studio on any computer on which you have installed the Management Studio. SQL Server Management Studio begins by displaying a Connect to Server dialog box, as shown in Figure 3-1. You can use this dialog box to connect to any SQL Server instance on your network.

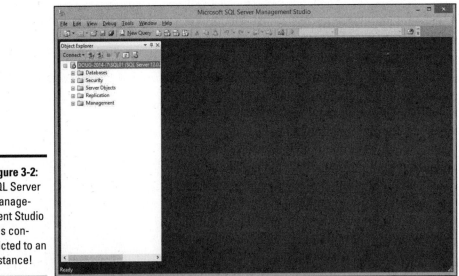

Figure 3-1: Connecting to a SQL Server instance.

To connect to a SQL Server instance, specify the instance name and your logon credentials, and then click Connect. After you've connected, SQL Server Management Studio displays the screen shown in Figure 3-2.

Figure 3-2: SQL Server Management Studio has connected to an instance!

The following sections explain how to perform some of the most common SQL Server chores: creating databases and tables, viewing database data, and so on.

Creating a New Database

To create a new database, follow these steps:

1. **Right-click the Databases node in the Navigation pane (on the left side of SQL Server Management Studio window), and choose New Database from the contextual menu that appears.**

   This brings up the New Database dialog box, shown in Figure 3-3.

**Book VIII
Chapter 3**

Using SQL Server 2014

Figure 3-3:
Creating a new database.

2. **Type a name for the new database in the Database Name field.**

3. **In the Owner field, enter the domain username of the user who is responsible for the database.**

   You can leave this field set to the default if you want to be listed as the owner.

4. **If you want, change the settings for the database and log files.**

   You can change the following settings:

   - *Initial Size:* This setting refers to the amount of disk space initially allocated to the files. The defaults are a ridiculously small 3MB for the database and 1MB for the log files. Unless your databases are going to be extremely small, you probably should increase these defaults.

   - *Autogrowth:* This setting sets the incremental amount by which the database grows when it exceeds the allocated capacity. Again, you'll probably want to change these amounts for any but the smallest databases.

   - *Path:* This setting points the way to the folder where the files are stored. By default, the files are created under the Program Files folder on the server's C: drive. You may want to change this setting to a more appropriate location. (You'll have to scroll the database files section of the NewDatabase dialog to the right to see this setting.)

   - *File Name:* You can change this setting if you want to use a filename that's different from the database name. (You'll have to scroll the database files section of the NewDatabase dialog to the right to see this setting.)

   Note that you can change additional options by clicking Options or Filegroups in the top-left corner of the New Database dialog box. These pages link to additional pages of options you can set to tweak the behavior of the database.

5. **Click OK.**

   SQL Server grinds and whirs for a few moments while it creates the new database. When it's finished, the database appears below the Databases node, as shown in Figure 3-4.

   That's all!

The new database is ready to use. It won't be very useful until you define some tables, of course, so read on.

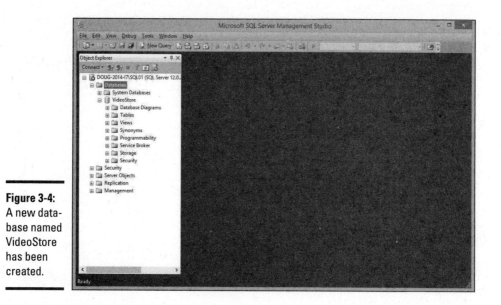

Figure 3-4:
A new database named VideoStore has been created.

Creating Tables

A database is nothing more than a container for various types of database objects. The most important of these objects are *tables,* which hold the actual data that makes up the database. A database isn't very useful without at least one table. Most real-world databases have more than one table; in fact, many databases have dozens of tables.

To create a table, follow these steps:

1. **Right-click the Tables node for the database, and choose Table from the contextual menu.**

    The window shown in Figure 3-5 appears.

2. **Type the name of the first column of the table and then press the Tab key.**

3. **Choose the data type for the column and then press the Tab key.**

    SQL Server has several data types to choose among for each column. Use the drop-down list to choose the appropriate type.

Figure 3-5:
Creating a
new table.

4. **Use the Allow Nulls check box to indicate whether the column should allow null values; then press the Tab key.**

   Nulls are among the most confusing aspects of database design and programming. In a SQL database, *null* means that the item doesn't have a value. It's different from zero (for numbers) or an empty string (for text). Allowing a column to have null values introduces programming complexities, because when you retrieve the value of a column, the program has to anticipate that the value may be missing. But prohibiting nulls (by deselecting the check box) also introduces complexities, because you have to make sure that you provide an explicit value for every column.

   The phrase *null value* is actually an oxymoron. Because *null* means the absence of a value, it doesn't make sense to say that a column can have a null value or that the value of a column is null.

5. **Repeat Steps 2 through 4 to create additional columns.**

   Figure 3-6 shows how the table looks after several columns have been defined.

Figure 3-6:
A table with several columns.

6. **When all the columns have been created, select the column you want to use as a key field for the table, right-click the column, and choose Set Primary Key from the contextual menu.**

   A little key icon appears next to that column to indicate that it's the primary key.

   (The *primary key* provides a unique value that can be used to identify each row in the table. Most tables use a single column, such as Customer Number or Invoice Number, as the primary key. But some tables create the primary key by combining two or more columns. This type of key is called a *composite key.*)

7. **Right-click the table-name tab that appears above the list of columns, and choose Save from the contextual menu.**

   A Save dialog box appears, prompting you to enter a name for the table.

8. **Type a name for the table and then click OK.**

   The table is created.

Note that each column has a properties page that appears when you select the column. You can set a variety of properties for each column, including the following:

✦ **Default Value:** A value that's supplied for the column if no value is provided when a row is created. This property is especially useful for columns that don't allow null values.

✦ **Description:** A text description that you can use to explain the purpose of the column.

✦ **Identity Specification:** Used to create an *identity field,* which is a field whose value is generated automatically when rows are created. Often, an identity field is used as the primary key field for a table when it's desirable for the table to have a primary key, but no other column in the table provides a unique value for each row.

When you create an identity field, you can specify two settings that affect how the values are generated: the seed and the increment. The *seed* is the value used for the first row in the table. The *increment* is a value that's added to the seed for each subsequent row. If you specify 1000 for the seed and 1 for the increment, the rows in the table will be numbered 1001, 1002, 1003, and so on.

Editing Tables

SQL Management Studio includes a spreadsheetlike feature that lets you edit the contents of database tables directly. To use it, right-click the table you want to edit, and choose Open Table from the contextual menu. The table opens in a spreadsheetlike window. Then you can add data to the table by entering table values for each row. Figure 3-7 shows a table after some data has been added via the Open Table command.

Note that in addition to inserting new rows, you can edit existing rows. You can also delete one or more rows by selecting the rows you want to delete and pressing the Delete key.

Figure 3-7:
A table with several rows added via the Open Table command.

Working with Queries

SQL Management Studio includes a query tool that lets you type SQL commands and execute them. You can type any SQL statement you want in a query window and then click the Execute button to execute the query.

There are two important rules to follow when you work with queries:

✦ Each SQL statement in the query should end with a semicolon.

✦ You must begin the query with a `use` statement that provides the name of the database.

Here's an example of a query that follows these two rules:

```
use VideoStore;
select * from movies;
```

The `use` statement indicates that the query applies to the `VideoStore` database, and the `select` statement retrieves all the data from the `movies` table.

To use the query tool, click the New Query button on the toolbar. Then enter the statements for your query in the window, and click the Execute button on the toolbar. The results of the query are displayed in the window, as shown in Figure 3-8.

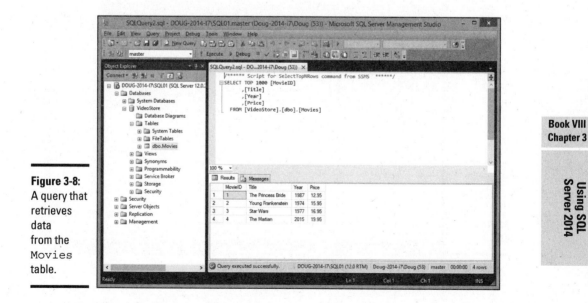

Figure 3-8:
A query that retrieves data from the Movies table.

Working with Scripts

One final feature of SQL Management Studio I want to cover in this chapter is the use of scripts. Although you can create databases by using the graphical features presented earlier in this chapter (in the sections "Creating a New Database" and "Creating Tables"), it's actually much better practice to write SQL scripts that contain the CREATE commands necessary to create the database, as well as its tables and other objects. That's because during the development and operation of any database application, you often need to delete the database and re-create it from scratch. By scripting these actions, you can delete the database and re-create it simply by running a script.

Fortunately, SQL Management Studio can generate scripts from existing databases and tables. Thus, you can use the visual design features of SQL Management Studio to create your databases initially; then you can generate scripts that let you delete and re-re-create the database easily.

To create a script for a database or table, just right-click the database or table and choose one of the Script As commands from the contextual menu. Figure 3-9 shows the script that results when I right-click the movies table and choose Script Table As ➪ CREATE To ➪ New Query Window. As you can see, this command generated a CREATE TABLE statement along with other advanced SQL statements to create the Movies table automatically.

Figure 3-9:
A script that creates the Movies table.

After you've created the script, you can save it to a text file by clicking the Save button. Then you can run the script at any time by following these steps:

1. **Choose File ⇨ Open ⇨ File.**

2. **Select the file you saved the script to.**

3. **Click Open.**

4. **Click the Execute button to run the script.**

The only limitation of this technique is that although you can generate scripts to define your databases and tables, you can't automatically generate scripts to insert data into your tables. If you want scripts that insert data, you have to manually create the INSERT statements to insert the data.

Book IX
Managing Linux Systems

web extras Find five additional useful Linux commands in an article at www.dummies.com/extras/networkingaio.

Contents at a Glance

Chapter 1: Installing a Linux Server 677

Chapter 2: Getting Used to Linux 689

Chapter 3: Basic Linux Network Configuration 701

Chapter 4: Running DHCP and DNS 713

Chapter 5: Doing the Samba Dance 723

Chapter 6: Running Apache 737

Chapter 7: Running Sendmail 749

Chapter 8: Running FTP 759

Chapter 9: Linux Commands 765

Chapter 1: Installing a Linux Server

In This Chapter

✔ Getting ready to install Linux

✔ Installing Linux

✔ Completing the setup

This chapter presents the procedures that you need to follow to install Linux on a server computer. The details provided are specifically for Fedora 22, a free Linux distribution sponsored by Red Hat. However, the procedures for installing other distributions of Linux are similar, so you won't have any trouble adapting these procedures if you're using a different distribution.

Planning a Linux Server Installation

Before you begin the installation program, you need to make a number of preliminary decisions. The following sections describe the decisions that you need to make before you install Linux.

Checking system requirements

Before you install Linux, make sure that the computer meets the minimum requirements. Although the minimum requirements for Linux are considerably less than those for the latest version of Windows Server, you can't run Linux on an abacus. The following paragraphs summarize the minimum capabilities you need:

✦ **A Pentium-based computer:** Even an ancient and slow Pentium 3 system will run some builds of Linux although performance will be slow. The minimum recommended for Fedora 22 is a Pentium 4.

✦ **768MB of RAM or more:** Of course, the more the better, but Linux can make do with much less RAM than Windows.

✦ **A hard drive with enough free space to hold the packages that you need to install:** A suitable minimum is 10GB.

✦ **A DVD-ROM drive from which to install the operating system**

✦ **Just about any video card and monitor combination:** You don't need anything fancy for a server. In fact, fancy video cards often lead to hardware compatibility issues. Stick to a basic video card.

✦ **An extra mouse:** If you're converting an old junker computer to a Linux server and you've lost the mouse (that seems to happen a lot), pick one up at your local office supply store. A cheap one costs only about $15.

✦ **A network interface card (NIC)**

For the purposes of this chapter, I'll be installing Fedora into a VMware virtual machine configured with 4GB of RAM, two processor cores, and 150GB of disk space.

Choosing a distribution

Because the *kernel* (that is, the core operating functions) of the Linux operating system is free, several companies have created their own *distributions* of Linux, which include the Linux OS along with a bundle of packages, such as administration tools, web servers, and other useful utilities, as well as printed documentation.

The following are some of the more popular Linux distributions:

✦ **Fedora:** One of the popular Linux distributions. You can download Fedora free from `http://fedoraproject.org`. You can also obtain it by purchasing any of several books on Fedora that include the Fedora distribution on DVD or CD-ROM.

All the examples in this book are based on Fedora 22.

✦ **Mandriva Linux:** Another popular Linux distribution, one that is often recommended as the easiest for first-time Linux users to install. This distribution was formerly known as *Mandrake Linux.* Go to `www.mandriva.com` for more information.

✦ **Ubuntu:** A Linux distribution that has gained popularity in recent years. It focuses on ease of use. For more information, go to `www.ubuntu.com`.

✦ **SUSE:** Pronounced *SOO-zuh,* like the name of the famous composer of marches; a popular Linux distribution sponsored by Novell. You can find more information at `www.suse.com`.

✦ **Slackware:** One of the oldest Linux distributions and still popular, especially among Linux old-timers. A full installation of Slackware gives you all the tools that you need to set up a network or Internet server. See `www.slackware.com` for more information.

All distributions of Linux include the same core components: the Linux kernel, an X Server, popular windows managers such as GNOME and KDE, compilers, Internet programs such as Apache, Sendmail, and so on.

However, not all Linux distributions are created equal. In particular, the manufacturer of each distribution creates its own installation and configuration programs to install and configure Linux.

The installation program is what makes or breaks a Linux distribution. All the distributions I list in this section have easy-to-use installation programs that automatically detect the hardware that's present on your computer and configure Linux to work with that hardware, thus eliminating most — if not all — manual configuration chores. The installation programs also let you select the Linux packages that you want to install and let you set up one or more user accounts besides the root account.

I can't see my C: drive!

Linux and Windows have a completely different method of referring to your computer's hard drives and partitions. The differences can take some getting used to for experienced Windows users.

Windows uses a separate letter for each drive and partition on your system. For example, if you have a single drive formatted into three partitions, Windows identifies the partitions as drives `C:`, `D:`, and `E:`. Each of these drives has its own root directory, which can, in turn, contain additional directories used to organize your files. As far as Windows is concerned, drives `C:`, `D:`, and `E:` are completely separate drives even though the drives are actually just partitions on a single drive.

Linux doesn't use drive letters. Instead, Linux combines all the drives and partitions into a single directory hierarchy. In Linux, one of the partitions is designated as the *root* partition. The root partition is roughly analogous to the root directory of the `C:` drive on a Windows system. Then, the other partitions can be *mounted* on the root partition and treated as if they were directories on the root partition. For example, you may designate the first partition as the root partition and then mount the second partition as `/user` and the third

partition as `/var`. Then, any files stored in the `/user` directory would actually be stored in the second partition, and files stored in the `/var` directory would be stored in the third partition.

The directory to which a drive mounts is called the drive's *mount point*.

Notice that Linux uses regular forward slash characters (`/`) to separate directory names rather than the backward slash characters (`\`) used by Windows. Typing backslashes instead of regular slashes is one of the most common mistakes made by new Linux users.

While I'm on the subject, Linux uses a different convention for naming files, too. In Windows, filenames end in a three- or four-letter extension that's separated from the rest of the filename by a period. The extension is used to indicate the file type. For example, files that end in `.exe` are program files, but files that end in `.doc` are word-processing documents.

Linux doesn't use file extensions, but periods are often used in Linux filenames to separate different parts of the name — and the last part often indicates the file type. For example, `ldap.conf` and `pine.conf` are both configuration files.

Going virtual

Another common way to install Linux is in a virtual machine running within the Windows operating system. In fact, all the examples in this minibook were tested using VMware Workstation Player, a free virtualization platform you can download from www.vmware.com. You can also use Microsoft's Hyper-V or any of several other virtualization products, many of which are free. For more information, see Book IV.

Deciding on your TCP/IP configuration

Before you install the OS, you should have a plan for how you will implement TCP/IP on the network. Here are some of the things you need to decide or find out:

✦ The public IP subnet address and mask for your network

✦ The domain name for the network

✦ The host name for the server

✦ Whether the server obtain its address from DHCP

✦ Whether the server have a static IP address — and if so, what

✦ Whether the server be a DHCP server

✦ The default gateway for the server — that the IP address of the network's Internet router

✦ Whether the server be a DNS server

If the server will host TCP/IP servers (such as DHCP or DNS), you'll probably want to assign the server a static IP address.

For more information about planning your TCP/IP configuration, see Book III.

Installing Fedora 22

After you plan your installation and prepare the computer, you're ready to actually install Linux. The following procedure describes the steps you must follow to install Fedora 22 on a virtual machine using a downloaded .iso file containing the Fedora installation media.

Note that, for this example, I chose to install the workstation version of Fedora. You can also install the server version of Fedora, but the server version does not configure a graphical user interface (GUI) by default. The workstation version works well as a server and provides GUI tools to simplify basic configuration tasks.

1. **Download the Fedora 22 `.iso` file from the Fedora project's download page, connect it to the virtual machine's optical drive, and start the virtual machine.**

The download is located at `https://getfedora.org`.

When you start the VM, a bunch of text messages fly across the screen. Eventually, the first page of the setup program is displayed, as shown in Figure 1-1.

Figure 1-1:
Choose a
language
to begin
the Fedora
installation.

2. **Choose your language, and then click Continue.**

The Installation Summary page is displayed, as shown in Figure 1-2.

3. **Click Installation Destination.**

The installation program displays the Installation Destination screen, shown in Figure 1-3.

4. **If necessary, adjust the installation destination settings.**

The Installation Destination screen indicates the disk volume on which Fedora will be installed. The default setting is to automatically create a partition on the empty primary drive and then install Fedora into the new partition. You should adjust these settings only if you want to install Fedora into a different location.

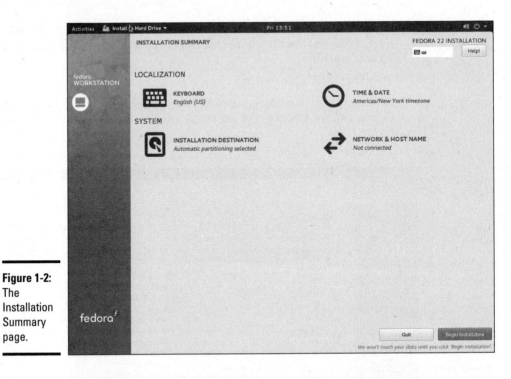

Figure 1-2:
The
Installation
Summary
page.

Figure 1-3:
The
Installation
Destination
screen.

Virtual consoles and the installation program

Linux is inherently a command line–oriented OS. Graphical user interfaces — including the installation program's GUI — are provided by an optional component called *X Window System*. However, while you're working with the GUI of the installation program, Linux keeps several additional command line consoles open. Normally, you don't need to use every one of these consoles during installation. However, if something goes wrong during installation, these consoles may be useful:

✔ **Console 1: The Installation dialog box.** This is the main installation console. You see it when Setup first starts. After the GUI takes over, it's hidden in the background. You can call it up by pressing Ctrl+Alt+F1.

✔ **Console 2: Shell prompt.** This console provides you with a shell prompt, from which you can enter Linux commands. If you need to do something manually during installation, you can do it from this console. The keyboard shortcut is Ctrl+Alt+F2.

✔ **Console 3: Install log.** This console lists messages generated by the installation program. You can get to it by pressing Ctrl+Alt+F3.

✔ **Console 4: System log.** This console displays system-related messages. You can get to it by pressing Ctrl+Alt+F4.

✔ **Console 5: Other messages.** Still more messages may appear in this console, which you can open by pressing Ctrl+Alt+F5.

✔ **Console 6: X graphical display.** This is the console where the GUI of the installation program is displayed. If you use a Ctrl+Alt keyboard combination to view any of the other logs, press Ctrl+Alt+F7 to return to the installation GUI.

5. **Click Done.**

   You're returned to the Installation Summary screen.

6. **Click Time & Date.**

   The Time & Date screen appears, as shown in Figure 1-4.

7. **Select the correct time zone and location, and then click Done.**

   You're returned to the Installation Summary page.

8. **Click Network & Host Name.**

   The Network & Host Name screen is displayed, as shown in Figure 1-5.

9. **Enter the name you want to assign this computer and then click Done.**

   You're returned to the Installation Summary screen.

10. **Click Begin Installation.**

    The Configuration screen is displayed, as shown in Figure 1-6.

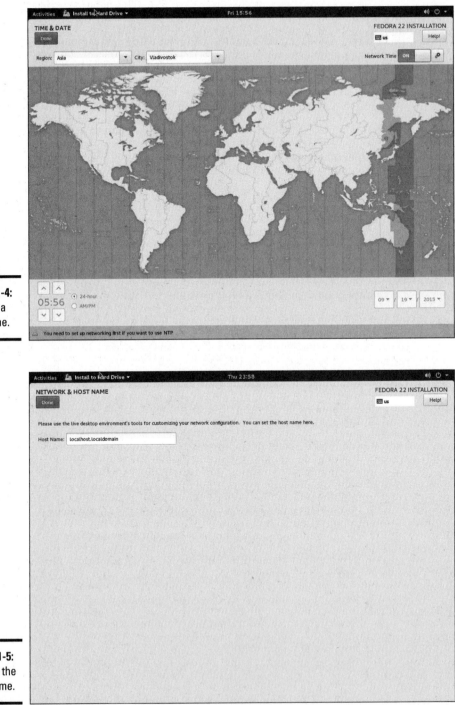

Figure 1-4:
Choose a
time zone.

Figure 1-5:
Choose the
host name.

Figure 1-6:
The Con-
figuration
screen.

11. **Click Root Password.**

The Root Password screen is displayed, as shown in Figure 1-7.

12. **Enter a password for the root account.**

It's vital that the root account be protected by a strong password, so choose a good one. Write down the password somewhere and store it in a secure location away from the computer.

13. **Click Done.**

You're returned to the Configuration screen.

14. **Click User Creation.**

The Create User screen appears, as shown in Figure 1-8. This screen lets you create a user account so you'll have at least one user other than the root.

15. **Enter a name and password for the user account, and then click Done.**

You're returned to the Configuration screen.

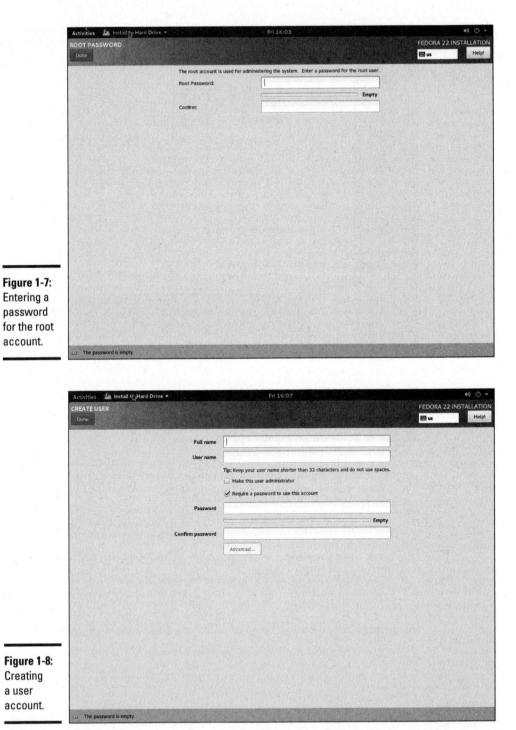

Figure 1-7:
Entering a
password
for the root
account.

Figure 1-8:
Creating
a user
account.

16. **Click Finish Configuration.**

    Fedora fiddles for a bit with the configuration details and then displays the screen shown in Figure 1-9.

Figure 1-9:
Fedora
announces
that it is
done!

17. **Remove the installation disk from the drive, and then click Reboot.**

    The system is rebooted. Installation is done!

Chapter 2: Getting Used to Linux

In This Chapter

✔ **Getting used to the Linux way of thinking**

✔ **Logging on and off Linux**

✔ **Using a GUI**

✔ **Working with commands**

✔ **Setting up user accounts**

*B*efore you can set up Linux to do serious networking, you need to discover the basics of getting around Linux. In this chapter, you find out those basics. You see how to log on and off Linux, how the Linux file system works, and how to use commands. I also introduce you to GNOME, the graphical user interface (GUI) that's used most with Fedora and many other Linux distributions. Finally, I show you the basics of setting up a Linux user account.

In this chapter, I assume that you have plenty of experience with Windows, so I focus mostly on the differences between Linux and Windows — which, unfortunately, are myriad.

Linux: It Isn't Windows

Before I get into the details of actually using a Linux system, you need to understand some basic differences between Linux and Windows that will puzzle you at first. Linux looks a lot like Windows, but underneath, it's very different. You won't have any trouble finding out how to point and click your way through the GNOME user interface, but before long, you'll run into Linux file-naming conventions, terminal windows, configuration files, and a host of other significant differences.

The following sections describe some of the more important differences between Linux and Windows.

X Window

Linux doesn't have a built-in graphical user interface (GUI) as Windows does. Instead, the GUI in Linux is provided by an optional component called *X Window System.* You can run Linux without X Window, in which case you interact with Linux by typing commands. If you prefer to use a GUI, you must install and run X Window.

X Window is split into two parts:

✦ A server component, called an **X Server,** handles the basic chores of managing multiple windows and providing graphics services for application programs.

✦ A user interface (UI) component, called a **window manager,** provides UI features such as menus, buttons, toolbars, a taskbar, and so on. Several different window managers are available, each with a different look and feel. The most popular is GNOME. I describe it in more detail later in this chapter, in the section "Using GNOME."

Virtual consoles

Linux is a true multiuser OS. This means that you can log on to Linux by using one user account and then log on by using a different account, so that you're logged on twice at the same time. You switch back and forth between the different user sessions, and actions that you take in one session don't affect any of your other sessions.

In addition to an X Window client such as GNOME, Linux provides a traditional text-based environment — a *console* — through which you can enter Linux commands to perform any function available in Linux. The more you work with Linux, the more you'll discover the limitations of even a sophisticated GUI such as GNOME. When that happens, you'll turn to a console where you can enter brute-force commands.

Because Linux is a multiuser system, it lets you work with more than one console. In fact, you actually have six virtual consoles at your disposal. You can switch to a particular virtual console by pressing Ctrl+Alt+F1 through F6. For example, to switch to virtual console 3, press Ctrl+Alt+F3.

When a GUI such as GNOME is running, you can switch to it by pressing Ctrl+Alt+F7.

Understanding the file system

The Linux file system is a bit different from the Windows file system. Two of the most obvious differences are actually superficial:

✦ Linux uses forward slashes rather than backward slashes to separate directories. Thus, /home/doug is a valid path in Linux; \Windows\System32 is a valid path in Windows.

✦ Linux filenames don't use extensions. You can use periods within a filename, but unlike Windows, the final period doesn't identify a file extension.

The fundamental difference between the Linux and Windows file system is that Linux treats everything in the entire system as a file, and it organizes everything into one gigantic tree that begins at a single root. When I say, "Everything is treated as a file," I mean that hardware devices such as floppy drives, serial ports, and Ethernet adapters are treated as files.

The root of the Linux file system is the root partition from which the OS boots. Additional partitions, including other devices that support file systems such as CD-ROM drives, floppy drives, or drives accessed over the network, can be grafted into the tree as directories called *mount points.* Thus, a directory in the Linux file system may actually be a separate hard drive.

Another important aspect of the Linux file system is that the directories that compose a Linux system are governed by a standard called the Filesystem Hierarchy Standard (FHS). This standard spells out which directories a Linux file system should have. Because most Linux systems conform to this standard, you can trust that key files will always be found in the same place.

Table 2-1 lists the top-level directories that are described in the FHS.

Table 2-1	Top-Level Directories in a Linux File System
Directory	*Description*
/bin	Essential command binaries
/boot	Static files of the boot loader
/dev	Devices
/etc	Configuration files for the local computer
/home	Home directories for users
/lib	Shared libraries and kernel modules
/mnt	Mount point for file systems mounted temporarily
/opt	Add-on applications and packages
/root	Home directory for the root user
/sbin	Essential system binaries
/tmp	Temporary files
/usr	Read-only, shared files such as binaries for user commands and libraries
/var	Variable data files

On Again, Off Again

Any user who accesses a Linux system, whether locally or over a network, must be authenticated by a valid user account on the system. In the following sections, you find out how to log on and off of a Linux system and how to shut down the system.

Logging on

When Linux boots up, it displays a series of startup messages as it starts the various services that compose a working Linux system. Assuming that you selected X Window when you installed Linux, you're eventually greeted by the screen shown in Figure 2-1. To log on to Linux, click your username, then type your password and press Enter. (Note that this logon procedure is for Fedora. Other distributions have similar logon procedures.)

Figure 2-1:
Begin by
logging on.

  As a part of the installation process (described in Chapter 1 of this mini-book), you created a user account other than the root account. You should use this user account rather than the root user account whenever possible. Use the root account only when you are making major changes to the system's configuration. When you're doing routine work, log on as an ordinary user in order to avoid accidentally corrupting your system.

When you log on, Linux grinds its gears for a moment and then displays the GNOME desktop, which I describe later in this chapter.

Logging off

After you've logged on, you'll probably want to know how to log off. To do so, click the power icon in the upper-right corner of the screen, click your account name, and then choose Log Out. A dialog box asks whether you're sure that you want to log out. Click Log Out.

Shutting down

As with any OS, you should never turn off the power to a Linux server without first properly shutting down the system. You can shut down a Linux system by using one of these two techniques:

✦ Press Ctrl+Alt+Delete.

✦ Click the power icon in the upper-right corner of the screen, click the power icon in the menu that appears, and then choose Power Off.

Using GNOME

Figure 2-2 shows a typical GNOME desktop. Although the GNOME desktop looks a lot different from the Windows desktop, many of the basic skills used for working with Microsoft Windows — such as moving or resizing windows, minimizing or maximizing windows, and using drag-and-drop to move items between windows — are almost exactly the same in GNOME.

The following paragraphs describe some of the key features of the GNOME desktop:

✦ The Activities Overview provides a single access point for all GNOME applications. It provides fast access to common functions, such as Internet browsing, email, or file management, as well as desktop access to other applications. You can access Activities Overview by pressing the Windows key on the keyboard or clicking Activities in the top-left corner. (The screen in Figure 2-2 shows the Activities Overview open.)

✦ The search box in the top-middle portion of the desktop is the easiest way to find things in GNOME. For example, if you want to run the gedit program to edit a text file, search for *gedit*. Or if you want to fiddle with network settings, search for *Network*.

✦ To manage your system or user settings, click your name at the top right of the screen. This reveals a menu with options for various settings.

Figure 2-2:
The
desktop.

Getting to a Command Shell

You can get to a command shell in one of two basic ways when you need
to run Linux commands directly. The first is to press Ctrl+Alt+F*x* to switch
to one of the virtual consoles, where F*x* is one of the function keys, from F1
through F12. (If you aren't sure which function key to use to open a virtual
console, refer to the "Virtual consoles" section in this chapter.) Then, you
can log on and run commands to your heart's content. When you're done,
press Ctrl+Alt+F7 to return to GNOME.

Alternatively, you can open a command shell directly in GNOME by opening
the Activities Overview, clicking Applications, and then clicking the Terminal
icon. This opens a command shell in a window right on the GNOME desktop,
as shown in Figure 2-3. Because this shell runs within the user account that
GNOME is logged on as, you don't have to log on. You can just start typing
commands. When you're done, type **Exit** to close the window.

Figure 2-3:
A terminal
window.

Enabling the SUDO Command

Throughout the remaining chapters of this minibook, you'll see many examples of commands entered in a terminal window that begin with the word `sudo`. This command is an essential part of Linux administration. It lets you execute Linux commands with permissions of the root user account.

The `sudo` command is required because many Linux administrative commands can only be run under by the root user. You could simply log in as the root user to run such commands, but that's considered a risky practice because the root user can do virtually anything in a Linux environment. It's safer to log in with an ordinary user account and use `sudo` to enable access to administrative functions.

For example, you'll often use the `dnf` command to install new software on a Linux system. The `dnf` command is one of those commands that can only be run by the root user. So you'll need to use `sudo` to run the `dnf` command. To use `sudo`, you simply prefix the command you want to run with the word `sudo`, as in the following example:

```
sudo dnf install dhcp
```

Here, the command `dnf install dhcp` will be run as the root user. Note that for security purposes, the `sudo` command prompts you for your own password before it runs the `dnf` command.

To enable your user account for `sudo`, the root user must add your account name to a group called `wheel`, because by default the `sudo` program is configured to allow all users in this group to run commands as the root user.

To add yourself to the `wheel` group, you must edit a configuration file called `group`, which is found in the `etc/` folder. Here are the steps to edit this file:

1. **Log in as the root user.**

   The Gnome desktop appears.

2. **Click Activities at the top left of the Gnome desktop, and then choose Files.**

   The File Manager appears, as shown in Figure 2-4.

Figure 2-4: The File Manager window.

3. **Click Computer in the navigation pane on the left side of the File Manager window.**

   The folders at the computer's root level appear, as shown in Figure 2-5.

Figure 2-5: The root-level folders.

4. **Double-click the etc folder.**

   The files in the etc folder appear.

5. **Locate and double-click the file named group.**

   The group file is opened in the gedit text editor, as shown in Figure 2-6.

| Open ▼ | ⌂ | *group /etc | Save | ≡ | × |

```
root:x:0:
bin:x:1:
daemon:x:2:
sys:x:3:
adm:x:4:
tty:x:5:
disk:x:6:
lp:x:7:
mem:x:8:
kmem:x:9:
wheel:x:10:
cdrom:x:11:
mail:x:12:
man:x:15:
dialout:x:18:
floppy:x:19:
games:x:20:
tape:x:33:
video:x:39:
ftp:x:50:
lock:x:54:
audio:x:63:
nobody:x:99:
users:x:100:
apache:x:48:
utmp:x:22:|
utempter:x:35:
avahi-autoipd:x:170:
ssh_keys:x:999:
input:x:998:
systemd-journal:x:190:
systemd-timesync:x:997:
```

Plain Text ▼   Tab Width: 8 ▼   Ln 26, Col 11   ▼   INS

Figure 2-6:
Editing the
group file.

6. **Locate the line that starts with wheel:x:10:**

7. **Add your username to the end of this line.**

   For example, since my username is dlowe, I edited the line to read as follows:

   ```
   wheel:x:10:dlowe
   ```

8. **Click the Save button.**

   The group file is saved with your changes.

9. **Close the gedit and File Manager windows.**

   You're done! You can now use the sudo command.

Managing User Accounts

One of the most common network administration tasks is adding a user account. The Setup Agent prompts you to create a user account the first time you start Linux after installing it. However, you'll probably need to create additional accounts.

Each Linux user account has the following information associated with it:

+ **Username:** The name the user types to log on to the Linux system.
+ **Full name:** The user's full name.
+ **Home directory:** The directory that the user is placed in when he or she logs on. In Fedora, the default home directory is `/home/username`. For example, if the username is `blowe`, the home directory will be `/home/blowe`.
+ **Shell:** The program used to process Linux commands. Several shell programs are available. In most distributions, the default shell is `/bin/bash`.
+ **Group:** You can create group accounts, which make it easy to apply identical access rights to groups of users.
+ **User ID:** The internal identifier for the user.

You can add a new user by using the `useradd` command. For example, to create a user account named `kgearhart`, using default values for the other account information, open a Terminal window or switch to a virtual console and type this command:

```
sudo useradd kgearhart
```

The `useradd` command has many optional parameters that you can use to set account information, such as the user's home directory and shell.

Fortunately, most Linux distributions come with special programs that simplify routine system management tasks. Fedora is no exception. It comes with a program called User Manager, shown in Figure 2-7. To start this program, click Activities, click Applications, and then double-click Users and Groups (scroll down to find it).

To create a user with User Manager, click the Add User button. This brings up a dialog box that asks for the user's name, password, and other information. Fill out this dialog box and then click OK.

The User Manager also lets you create groups. You can simplify the task of administering users by applying access rights to groups rather than individual users. Then, when a user needs access to a resource, you can add the user to the group that has the needed access.

Figure 2-7:
Managing
users and
groups.

To create a group, click the Add Group button. A dialog box appears, asking for the name of the new group. Type the name you want and then click OK.

To add a user to a group, click the Groups tab in the User Manager. Then, double-click the group to which you want to add users. This brings up the Group Properties dialog box. Click the Group Users tab and then select the users that you want to belong to the group.

Chapter 3: Basic Linux Network Configuration

In This Chapter

✔ Configuring network interfaces

✔ Looking directly at network configuration files

✔ Using the ifconfig command to display network status

*I*n many cases, configuring a Linux server for networking is a snap. When you install Linux, the installation program automatically detects your network adapters and installs the appropriate drivers. Then, you're prompted for basic network configuration information, such as the computer's IP address, host name, and so on.

However, you may need to manually change your network settings after installation. You may also need to configure advanced networking features that aren't configured during installation. In this chapter, you discover the basic procedures for configuring Linux networking services.

Using the Network Configuration Program

Before you can use a network interface to access a network, you have to configure the interface's basic TCP/IP options, such as its IP address, host name, Domain Name System (DNS) servers, and so on. This configuration is automatically set up when you install Linux, but you may need to change it later on. In this section, I show you how to do that by using Fedora's Network settings program. You can access this program by clicking your name in the top-right corner of the screen, choosing Settings, and then choosing Network.

If you prefer a more masochistic approach to configuring your network, see the section "Working with Network Configuration Files," later in this chapter.

The Network Configuration program lets you configure the basic TCP/IP settings for a network interface by pointing and clicking your way through tabbed windows. Here are the steps:

1. **Click Activities and type** Network. **Then click the Network icon (shown in the margin).**

   The Network application appears, as shown in Figure 3-1.

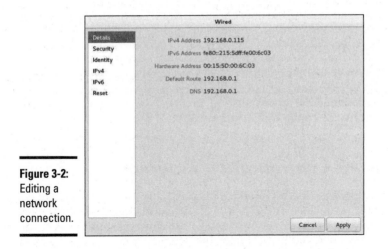

Figure 3-1:
The
Network
application.

2. Select the network interface that you want to configure and then click the Options button (shown in the margin).

This summons the Editing window, as shown in Figure 3-2.

Figure 3-2:
Editing a
network
connection.

3. Click the IPv4 Settings tab.

The screen shown in Figure 3-3 is displayed.

4. To configure the device to use DHCP, select Automatic (DHCP) in the Addresses drop-down.

If you plan on setting up this computer to be your network's DHCP or DNS server, you shouldn't select this check box. Instead, you should assign a static IP address as described in Step 5.

Figure 3-3:
Configuring
IPv4
settings.

5. **To configure the device with a static IP address, select Manual in the Method drop-down.**

This enables the controls shown in Figure 3-4.

Figure 3-4:
Manual IP
configuration.

6. **Enter the address, netmask, and gateway addresses.**

The IP address should be located on your network's private subnet. Typically, you'll use an address in the form 192.168.*x.x*.

If you're setting up this computer to be the gateway router that will manage traffic between your local network and the Internet, use a static address that's easy to remember, such as 192.168.1.1.

The subnet mask should be the mask that's appropriate for the IP address you choose. For a 192.168.*x.x* address, use 255.255.255.0.

The default gateway address should be the address of the gateway router that links your network to the Internet. If this computer *is* the gateway router, specify the gateway address provided to you by your Internet service provider (ISP).

7. **Enter the IP addresses for the DNS servers that you want to use in the DNS Servers text box.**

   If your network runs its own DNS server, you can specify its address here. Otherwise, you have to get the DNS server addresses from your ISP.

   To enter more than one DNS server address, enter the first DNS address, then click the plus sign (+) button located beneath and to the right of the DNS server address to display a text box for the second DNS server address.

8. **Click Apply.**

   Any changes you made to the network configuration are saved, and you return to the Network application.

9. **Restart the network services.**

   For the gory details on how to do that, see the next section.

Restarting Your Network

Whenever you make a configuration change to your network, you must restart Linux networking services for the change to take effect. If you find that annoying, just be thankful that you don't have to restart the entire computer. Simply restarting the network services is sufficient.

Open a console by pressing Ctrl+Alt+*n*, where *n* is a number from 2–7. Log in using the root account and then enter the following command:

```
service network restart
```

To confirm that the service was properly restarted, you'll see a message similar to this:

```
Restarting network (via systemctl):                    [ OK ]
```

Working with Network Configuration Files

Like other OS services, the Linux network is configured by settings that are specified in configuration files that you can find in the /etc directory or in one of its subdirectories. Graphical configuration programs, such as Fedora

Network Configuration, are actually little more than glorified text editors that enable you to select network configuration options from user-friendly screens and then save your configuration changes to the standard configuration files. If you prefer to do the grunt work yourself, you can open the configuration files in a text editor and make changes to them directly.

Any time you open a configuration file in a text editor, you run the risk of messing up your system's configuration. So be careful!

Table 3-1 lists the main Linux network configuration files and describes what each file does. The details of these files are described in the sections that follow.

Table 3-1	Linux Network Configuration Files	
File	*Location*	*Description*
network	/etc/sysconfig	Basic network configuration
hostname	/etc	Specifies the host name (obsolete, but should still be present)
ifcfg-xxxx	-/etc/sysconfig/network-scripts	IP settings for the network adapter named xxxx
hosts	/etc	Lists host address mappings
resolv.conf	/etc	Lists DNS nameservers
nsswitch.conf	/etc	Specifies the name search order
xinetd.conf	/etc	Specifies which network services are started automatically

The Network file

The Network file, which lives in /etc/sysconfig, specifies basic configuration settings for your network. Here's a typical Network file:

```
NETWORKING=yes
HOSTNAME=LSERVER
GATEWAY=192.168.1.1
```

This file specifies that networking is enabled, the computer's host name is LSERVER, and the default gateway address is 192.168.1.1.

The following paragraphs describe all the settings that are valid for this file:

✦ NETWORKING: Specifies YES or NO to enable or disable networking for the computer.

✦ HOSTNAME: Specifies the host name for this computer. You should also specify this name in /etc/hostname although that file is considered obsolete and is used only by some old programs. Note that this can be a simple host name (like LSERVER) or a fully qualified domain name (like Lserver.LoweWriter.com).

✦ FORWARD_IPV4: Specifies YES or NO to enable or disable IP forwarding. Specify FORWARD_IPV4=YES to set up a router.

✦ GATEWAY: Specifies the IP address of the computer's Default Gateway. If the network has a gateway router, specify its address here. If this computer is the network's gateway router, specify the gateway IP address provided by your ISP.

✦ GATEWAYDEV: Specifies the interface (such as eth0) that should be used to reach the gateway.

The ifcfg files

Each network interface has an ifcfg configuration file located in /etc/sysconfig/network-scripts. The device name is added to the end of the filename. So, for example, the configuration file for an interface named p2p1 is called ifcfg-p2p1.

This file is created and updated by the Network Configuration program, so you don't have to edit it directly (if you don't want to).

Here's a typical ifcfg file for an interface that has a static IP address:

```
DEVICE=p2p1
BOOTPROTO=none
ONBOOT=yes
USERCTL=no
IPADDR=192.168.1.200
NETMASK=255.255.255.0
BROADCAST=192.168.1.255
NETWORK=192.168.1.0
```

Here's an example for an interface that uses DHCP:

```
DEVICE=p2p1
BOOTPROTO=dhcp
ONBOOT=yes
USERCTL=no
```

Here, the `ifcfg` file doesn't have to specify the IP address information because the interface gets that information from a DHCP server.

The following paragraphs describe the settings that you're most likely to see in this file:

✦ DEVICE: The name of the device, such as `eth0` or `eth1`.

✦ USERCTL: Specifies `YES` or `NO` to indicate whether local users are allowed to start or stop the network.

✦ ONBOOT: Specifies `YES` or `NO` to indicate whether the device should be enabled when Linux boots up.

✦ BOOTPROTO: Specifies how the device gets its IP address. Possible values are `NONE` for static assignment, `DHCP`, or `BOOTP`.

✦ BROADCAST: The broadcast address used to send packets to everyone on the subnet: for example, 192.168.1.255.

✦ NETWORK: The network address: for example, 192.168.1.0.

✦ NETMASK: The subnet mask: for example, 255.255.255.0.

✦ IPADDR: The IP address for the adapter.

The Hosts file

The Hosts file is a simple list of IP addresses and the host names associated with each address. You can think of the Hosts file as a local DNS database of sorts. Whenever Linux needs to resolve a DNS name, it first looks for the name in the Hosts file. If Linux finds the name there, it doesn't have to do a DNS lookup; it simply uses the IP address found in the Hosts file.

For small networks, common practice is to list the host name for each computer on the network in the Hosts file on each computer. Then, whenever you add a new computer to the network, you just update each computer's Hosts file to include the new computer. That's not so bad if the network has just a few computers, but you wouldn't want to do it that way for a network with 1,000 hosts. That's why other name resolution systems are more popular for larger networks.

The default Linux Hosts file looks something like this:

```
# Do not remove the following line, or various programs that require
# network functionality will fail.
127.0.0.1  localhost.localdomain  localhost
```

Here, the names `localhost.localdomain` and `localhost` both resolve to 127.0.0.1, which is the standard local loopback address.

Here's an example of a Hosts file that has some additional entries:

```
# Do not remove the following line, or various programs that require
# network functionality will fail.
127.0.0.1  LServer localhost.localdomain  localhost
192.168.1.1     linksys
192.168.1.100   ward.cleaver.com ward
192.168.1.101   june.cleaver.com june
192.168.1.102   wally.cleaver.com wally
192.168.1.103   theodore.cleaver.com theodore beaver
```

Here, I defined host names for each of the Cleaver family's four computers and their Linksys router. Each computer can be accessed by using one of two names (for example, `ward.cleaver.com` or just `ward`), except the last one, which has three names.

The resolv.conf file

The `resolv.conf` file lists the DNS nameservers that can be consulted to perform DNS lookups. A typical `resolv.conf` file looks like this:

```
nameserver 192.168.1.110
nameserver 204.127.198.19
nameserver 63.249.76.19
```

If you have set up a nameserver on your own network, its IP address should be the first one listed.

The nsswitch.conf file

This configuration file controls how name resolution works when looking up various types of objects, such as host addresses and passwords. Listing 3-1 shows the sample `nsswitch.conf` file that comes with Fedora Linux. As you can see, this file is loaded with comments that explain what the various settings do.

You can use the `files`, `db`, and `dns` keywords to specify how objects should be retrieved. `files` specifies that the local file should be used, `db` specifies a database lookup, and `dns` specifies that a DNS server should be consulted.

The order in which you list these keywords determines the order in which the data sources are searched. Thus, if you want host names to be resolved first by the local Hosts file and then by DNS, you should include the following line in `nsswitch`:

```
hosts:  files dns
```

Listing 3-1:   A Sample `/etc/nsswitch.conf` **File**

```
#
# /etc/nsswitch.conf
#
# An example Name Service Switch config file. This file should be
# sorted with the most-used services at the beginning.
#
# The entry '[NOTFOUND=return]' means that the search for an
# entry should stop if the search in the previous entry turned
# up nothing. Note that if the search failed due to some other reason
# (like no NIS server responding) then the search continues with the
# next entry.
#
# Legal entries are:
#
#      nisplus or nis+    Use NIS+ (NIS version 3)
#      nis or yp          Use NIS (NIS version 2), also called YP
#      dns                Use DNS (Domain Name Service)
#      files              Use the local files
#      db                 Use the local database (.db) files
#      compat             Use NIS on compat mode
#      hesiod             Use Hesiod for user lookups
#      [NOTFOUND=return]  Stop searching if not found so far
#
# To use db, put the "db" in front of "files" for entries you want to be
# looked up first in the databases
#
# Example:
#passwd:    db files nisplus nis
#shadow:    db files nisplus nis
#group:     db files nisplus nis

passwd:     files
shadow:     files
group:      files
initgroups: files

#hosts:     db files nisplus nis dns
hosts:      files dns

# Example - obey only what nisplus tells us...
#services:  nisplus [NOTFOUND=return] files
#networks:  nisplus [NOTFOUND=return] files
#protocols: nisplus [NOTFOUND=return] files
#rpc:       nisplus [NOTFOUND=return] files
#ethers:    nisplus [NOTFOUND=return] files
#netmasks:  nisplus [NOTFOUND=return] files

bootparams: nisplus [NOTFOUND=return] files
```

(continued)

Listing 3-1 *(continued)*

```
ethers:      files
netmasks:    files
networks:    files
protocols:   files
rpc:         files
services:    files

netgroup:    files

publickey:   nisplus

automount:   files
aliases:     files nisplus
```

The xinetd.conf file

Xinetd is a service that oversees a variety of networking services, such as
Telnet or Finger. Xinetd listens for requests on the ports on which these services talk and automatically starts the service when a connection is made.
Xinetd is controlled by the configuration file xinetd.conf, which is found
in the /etc directory, and each of the services controlled by Xinetd is in
turn controlled by a configuration file found in the /etc/xinet.d directory.

You should leave most of the settings in these configuration files alone
unless you've studied up on Xinetd. (You can find out more about it at www.
xinetd.org.) However, you may want to modify the configuration files in
order to enable or disable specific services.

Each service controlled by Xinetd has a configuration file in the /etc/
xinet.d directory. Each configuration file ends with a line that enables or
disables the service. For example, here's the configuration file for Telnet, /
etc/xinet.d/telnet:

```
# default: on
# description: The telnet server serves telnet sessions; it uses \
#       unencrypted username/password pairs for authentication.
service telnet
{
    Flags             = REUSE
    socket_type       = stream
    wait              = no
    user              = root
    server            = /usr/sbin/in.telnetd
    log_on_failure   += USERID
    disable           = yes
}
```

Here, the last line disables Telnet. You can enable the Telnet service by
changing the last line to disable = no.

Displaying Your Network Configuration with the ifconfig Command

Linux doesn't have an `ipconfig` command like Windows. Instead, the command that you use to display information about your network configuration is `ifconfig`. You can also use this command to set network configuration options, but in most cases, using the Network Configuration program or directly editing the network configuration files is easier.

If you enter `ifconfig` without any parameters, you get output similar to the following:

```
lo: flags=73<UP,LOOPBACK,RUNNING> mtu 16436
        inet addr:127.0.0.1  netmask:255.0.0.0
        inet6 ::1 prefixlen 128 scopeid 0x10<host>
        loop txqueuelen 0 (local loopback)
        RX packets 12  bytes 720 (720.0 B)
        RX errors 0  dropped 0  overruns 0  frame 0
        TX packets 12  bytes 720 (720.0 B)
        TX errors 0  dropped 0  overruns 0  frame 0
p2p1: flags=4163<UP,BROADCAST,RUNNING,MULTICAST> mtu 1500
        inet addr:10.0.2.15  netmask:255.255.255.0 broadcast 10.0.2.255
        inet6 fe00::a00:27ff:fe08::3f5a prefixlen 64 scopeid 0x20<link>
        ether 08:00:27:08:3f:5a txqueuelen 1000 (Ethernet)
        RX packets 273  bytes 208816 (203.9 KiB)
        RX errors 0  dropped 0  overruns 0  frame 0
        TX packets 278  bytes 27696 (27KiB)
        TX errors 0  dropped 0  overruns 0  frame 0
```

From this output, you can tell that the IP address of the Ethernet adapter (p2p1) is 10.0.2.15, the broadcast address is 10.0.2.255, and the netmask is 255.255.255.0. You can also see transmit and receive statistics as well as information about the hardware configuration, such as the MAC address and the adapter's interrupt and memory base address assignments.

Linux offers many other commands that can help you configure and troubleshoot a network. Many of these commands are described in detail in Chapter 9 of this minibook.

Chapter 4: Running DHCP and DNS

In This Chapter

✔ Dealing with DHCP

✔ Running a DNS server

✔ Understanding BIND configuration files

*O*ne of the main reasons why many network administrators add Linux servers to their networks is to run Internet services, such as DHCP and DNS. These services were originally developed for the Unix environment, so they tend to run better under Linux than they do under Windows.

Well, that's the theory, at least. The most recent versions of Windows are probably just as good at running these services as Linux. Still, if you prefer to set up these services on a Linux server, this chapter is for you.

Running a DHCP Server

DHCP is the TCP/IP protocol that automatically assigns IP addresses to hosts as they come on the network. (DHCP stands for Dynamic Host Control Protocol, but that won't be on the test.) For a very small network (say, fewer than ten hosts), you don't really need DHCP: You can just configure each computer to have a static IP address. For larger networks, however, DHCP is almost a must. Without DHCP, you have to manually plan your entire IP address scheme and manually configure every computer with its IP information. Then, if a critical address — such as your Internet gateway router or your DNS server address — changes, you have to manually update each computer on the network. As you can imagine, DHCP can save you a lot of time.

Even for small networks, however, DHCP can be a timesaver. For example, suppose that you have a notebook computer that you take back and forth between your home and office. If you don't set up a DHCP server at home, you have to change the computer's static IP address each time you move the computer. With DHCP, the computer can change IP addresses automatically.

For the complete lowdown on DHCP, please read to Book III, Chapter 4. In the following sections, I show you how to install and configure a DHCP server on the Fedora 12 Linux distribution.

Installing DHCP

You can quickly find out whether DHCP is installed on your system by entering the following command from a shell prompt:

```
sudo dnf install dhcp
```

If DHCP has already been installed, the `dnf` command will let you know that the package is already installed and that it has nothing to do. Otherwise, the `dnf` command will ask your permission to install the package:

```
Total download size: 801 k
Installed size: 1.5 M
Is this ok [y/N]:
```

Enter **y** to proceed with the installation. After a few moments, `dnf` will announce that the installation is complete.

Configuring DHCP

You configure DHCP settings through a file called `dhcpd.conf` that lives in the `/etc` directory. Fedora provides you with a sample configuration file located in the directory

```
/usr/share/doc/dhcp-version/dhcpd.conf.sample
```

Open this file in the text editor and then save it to the `/etc` directory, changing its name from `dhcpd.conf.sample` to just `dhcpd.conf`. Then, edit the file to reflect the settings that you want to use.

Listing 4-1 shows the sample configuration file that comes with Fedora. (The exact contents of this file vary from release to release and include additional comments that I've removed for the sake of brevity.)

Listing 4-1:   A Sample `dhcpd.conf` File

```
ddns-update-style interim;
ignore client-updates;
subnet 192.168.0.0 netmask 255.255.255.0 {
# --- default gateway
        option routers                  192.168.0.1;
        option subnet-mask              255.255.255.0;
        option nis-domain               "domain.org";
```

```
        option domain-name              "domain.org";
        option domain-name-servers      192.168.0.1;
        option time-offset              -18000;   # Eastern Standard Time
#       option ntp-servers              192.168.0.1;
#       option netbios-name-servers     192.168.0.1;
# --- Selects point-to-point node (default is hybrid). Don't change this
# -- unless you understand Netbios very well
#       option netbios-node-type 2;
        range dynamic-bootp 192.168.0.128 192.168.0.255;
        default-lease-time 21600;
        max-lease-time 43200;
        # we want the nameserver to appear at a fixed address
        host ns {
                next-server marvin.redhat.com;
                hardware ethernet 12:34:56:78:AB:CD;
                fixed-address 207.175.42.254;
                }
}
```

The following paragraphs describe some of the key points of this file:

✦ ddns-update-style: The DHCP standards group is in the midst of deciding exactly how DHCP will handle changes to DNS data. This option specifies that the interim method should be used. This line is required — so don't mess with it.

✦ subnet: This line specifies a subnet that's managed by this DHCP server. Following the subnet ID and netmask is an opening bracket; all the options that appear between this bracket and the closing bracket in the last line of the file belong to this subnet. In some cases, your DHCP server may dole out IP configuration information for two or more subnet groups. In that case, you need additional subnet groups in the configuration file.

✦ option routers: This line provides the IP address of the Default Gateway.

✦ option subnet mask: This line provides the subnet mask for the subnet.

✦ option nis-domain: This line provides the NIS domain name. This line is important only if you've set up one or more NIS servers.

✦ option domain-name: This line provides the domain name for the network.

✦ option domain-name-servers: This line provides the IP addresses of your DNS servers.

✦ range: This line specifies the range of addresses that the DHCP server will assign for this subnet.

♦ `default-lease-time`: This line determines the default lease time in seconds.

♦ `max-lease-time`: This line determines the maximum life of a lease.

♦ `host`: This line specifies a reservation. The host group specifies the MAC address for the host and the fixed IP address to be assigned.

Starting DHCP

After you set up the configuration file, you can start DHCP by opening a terminal window or virtual console and entering the following command:

```
dhcpd start
```

If an error exists in the configuration file, a message to that effect is displayed. You have to edit the file in order to correct the error and then start the DHCP service again.

You should also restart the service whenever you make a change to the configuration file. To restart DHCP, enter this command:

```
dhcpd restart
```

To automatically start DHCP whenever you start the computer, run this command:

```
chkconfig -level 35 dhcpd on
```

Running a DNS Server

Linux comes with BIND, the best DNS server that money can buy. BIND is an extremely powerful program. Some people make entire careers of setting up and configuring BIND. In these few short pages, I just touch on the very basics of setting up a DNS server on your network.

You can find plenty of details about DNS in Book III, Chapter 5. Please review that chapter before playing with BIND on your Linux system.

Installing BIND

You can quickly find out whether BIND is installed on your system by entering the following command from a shell prompt:

```
sudo dnf install bind
```

If BIND has already been installed, the `dnf` command will let you know that the package is already installed and that it has nothing to do. Otherwise, the `dnf` command will ask your permission to install the package. Enter **y** to install the package.

Looking at BIND configuration files

Although Fedora Linux includes a handy BIND configuration tool, you still need to know the location and purpose of each of BIND's basic configuration files. These files are described in the following sections.

named.conf

This file, found in the `/etc` directory, is the basic BIND configuration file. This file contains global properties and links to the other configuration files.

Because the Fedora BIND configuration tool edits this file, you shouldn't edit this file directly. If you need to set your own configuration options, use `named.custom` instead.

Here's a typical `named.conf` file:

```
## named.conf - configuration for bind
#
# Generated automatically by redhat-config-bind, alchemist et al.
# Any changes not supported by redhat-config-bind should be put
# in /etc/named.custom
#
controls {
        inet 127.0.0.1 allow { localhost; } keys { rndckey; };
};
include "/etc/named.custom";
include "/etc/rndc.key";
zone  "0.0.127.in-addr.arpa" {
                type master;
                file  "0.0.127.in-addr.arpa.zone";
};
zone  "localhost" {
                type master;
                file "localhost.zone";
};
zone  "lowewriter.com" {
                type master;
                file  "lowewriter.com.zone";
};
```

The line `include "/etc/named.custom";` is what causes the `named.custom` file to be read in. The `zone` lines name the zone files for each domain for which the server is responsible.

By default, this file always includes two zones:

✦ `0.0.127.in-addr.arpa`: The reverse-lookup zone for `localhost`

✦ `localhost`: The zone file for the local computer

Any other zones that you added through the Fedora BIND configuration tool appear in this file as well.

named.custom

This file, also found in `/etc`, lets you add information to the `named.conf` file. Here's a typical `named.custom` file:

```
## named.custom - custom configuration for bind
#
# Any changes not currently supported by redhat-config-bind should be put
# in this file.
#
zone  "." {
    type hint;
    file  "named.ca";
};
options {
        directory "/var/named/";
};
```

One reason to use this file is if you want to include zone files that you create yourself without the aid of the Fedora BIND configuration program. If you want to include your own zone file, just add a zone statement that names the zone file. For example, suppose that you want to add a zone named `cleaver.com`, and you manually created the `cleaver.com.zone`. To include this zone, add these lines to the `named.custom` file:

```
zone  "cleaver.com" {
    type master;
    file  "cleaver.com.zone";
};
```

named.ca

This file, located in the `/var/named` directory, lists the names and addresses of the Internet's root servers. It's a fascinating file to look at because it helps to unveil the mystery of how the Internet really works. You shouldn't change it, however, unless, of course, you happen to be the administrator of one of the Internet's root servers — in which case, I hope you're not reading this book to learn how BIND works.

Listing 4-2 shows a typical `named.ca` file. The exact contents of this file varies from release to release.

Listing 4-2: A Sample dhcpd.conf File

```
; <<>> DiG 9.9.2-P1-RedHat-9.9.2-6.P1.fc18 <<>> +bufsize=1200
+norec @a.root-servers.net
; (2 servers found)
;; global options: +cmd
;; Got answer:
;; ->>HEADER<<- opcode: QUERY, status: NOERROR, id: 25828
;; flags: qr aa; QUERY: 1, ANSWER: 13, AUTHORITY: 0, ADDITIONAL: 23

;; OPT PSEUDOSECTION:
; EDNS: version: 0, flags:; udp: 512
;; QUESTION SECTION:
;.                      IN      NS

;; ANSWER SECTION:
.                       518400  IN      NS      a.root-servers.net.
.                       518400  IN      NS      b.root-servers.net.
.                       518400  IN      NS      c.root-servers.net.
.                       518400  IN      NS      d.root-servers.net.
.                       518400  IN      NS      e.root-servers.net.
.                       518400  IN      NS      f.root-servers.net.
.                       518400  IN      NS      g.root-servers.net.
.                       518400  IN      NS      h.root-servers.net.
.                       518400  IN      NS      i.root-servers.net.
.                       518400  IN      NS      j.root-servers.net.
.                       518400  IN      NS      k.root-servers.net.
.                       518400  IN      NS      l.root-servers.net.
.                       518400  IN      NS      m.root-servers.net.

;; ADDITIONAL SECTION:
a.root-servers.net.     3600000 IN      A       198.41.0.4
a.root-servers.net.     3600000 IN      AAAA    2001:503:ba3e::2:30
b.root-servers.net.     3600000 IN      A       192.228.79.201
c.root-servers.net.     3600000 IN      A       192.33.4.12
d.root-servers.net.     3600000 IN      A       199.7.91.13
d.root-servers.net.     3600000 IN      AAAA    2001:500:2d::d
e.root-servers.net.     3600000 IN      A       192.203.230.10
f.root-servers.net.     3600000 IN      A       192.5.5.241
f.root-servers.net.     3600000 IN      AAAA    2001:500:2f::f
g.root-servers.net.     3600000 IN      A       192.112.36.4
h.root-servers.net.     3600000 IN      A       128.63.2.53
h.root-servers.net.     3600000 IN      AAAA    2001:500:1::803f:235
i.root-servers.net.     3600000 IN      A       192.36.148.17
i.root-servers.net.     3600000 IN      AAAA    2001:7fe::53
j.root-servers.net.     3600000 IN      A       192.58.128.30
j.root-servers.net.     3600000 IN      AAAA    2001:503:c27::2:30
k.root-servers.net.     3600000 IN      A       193.0.14.129
k.root-servers.net.     3600000 IN      AAAA    2001:7fd::1
l.root-servers.net.     3600000 IN      A       199.7.83.42
l.root-servers.net.     3600000 IN      AAAA    2001:500:3::42
m.root-servers.net.     3600000 IN      A       202.12.27.33
m.root-servers.net.     3600000 IN      AAAA    2001:dc3::35

;; Query time: 78 msec
;; SERVER: 198.41.0.4#53(198.41.0.4)
;; WHEN: Mon Jan 28 15:33:31 2013
;; MSG SIZE  rcvd: 699
```

An organization named InterNIC keeps the `named.ca` file up to date. You can download the most current version of `named.ca` from the InterNIC FTP site at `ftp.internic.net`. Every once in awhile, InterNIC publishes a new version of this file, so you should check now and then to make sure that your file is current.

named.local

This file, located in `/var/named`, is a zone file for your local computer — that is, for the `localhost` domain. Rarely (if ever) do you need to modify it. It typically looks like this:

```
$TTL 86400
@     IN    SOA   localhost. root.localhost. (
                  1997022700 ; Serial
                  28800      ; Refresh
                  14400      ; Retry
                  3600000    ; Expire
                  86400 )    ; Minimum
      IN    NS    localhost.
1     IN    PTR   localhost.
```

Zone files

Each zone for which your DNS server is authoritative should have a zone file, named *domain*`.zone` and located in the `/var/named` directory. If you like to edit DNS records directly, you can create this file yourself. Or you can use the point-and-click interface of the Fedora BIND configuration tool to automatically create the file.

Here's a typical zone file, named `lowewriter.com.zone`:

```
$TTL 86400
@     IN    SOA   ns207.pair.com.  root.localhost (
                  2 ; serial
                  28800 ; refresh
                  7200 ; retry
                  604800 ; expire
                  86400 ; ttl
                  )
      IN    NS    ns000.ns0.com.
      IN    NS    ns207.pair.com.
@     IN    MX    1    sasi.pair.com.
www   IN    A     209.68.34.15
```

Table 4-1 lists the most common types of records that appear in zone files. For a complete description of each of these record types, see Book III, Chapter 5.

Table 4-1		**Common Resource Record Types**
Type	*Name*	*Description*
SOA	Start Of Authority	Identifies a zone
NS	Name Server	Identifies a name server that is authoritative for the zone
A	Address	Maps a fully qualified domain name to an IP address
CNAME	Canonical Name	Creates an alias for a fully qualified domain name
MX	Mail Exchange	Identifies the mail server for a domain
PTR	Pointer	Maps an IP address to a fully qualified domain name for reverse lookups

Restarting BIND

BIND runs as a service called named. As a result, when you make changes to your DNS configuration, you have to restart the named service to apply the changes. To do that, use this command:

```
service named restart
```

You can also restart the named service from the Service Configuration tool. Choose Main Menu ⇨ System Settings ⇨ Server Settings ⇨ Services. This brings up a dialog box that lists all the running services. Scroll down the list to find named, select it, and then click the Restart button.

Chapter 5: Doing the Samba Dance

In This Chapter

- ✔ Finding out what Samba does
- ✔ Installing Samba on your Linux computer
- ✔ Configuring Samba the easy way
- ✔ Tweaking the smb.conf file
- ✔ Using the Samba client

*U*ntil now, you probably thought of Samba as a Brazilian dance with intricate steps and fun rhythms. In the Linux world, however, *Samba* refers to a file- and printer-sharing program that allows Linux to mimic a Windows file and print server so that Windows computers can use shared Linux directories and printers. If you want to use Linux as a file or print server in a Windows network, you need to know how to dance the Samba.

Understanding Samba

Because Linux and Windows have such different file systems, you can't create a Linux file server simply by granting Windows users access to Linux directories. Windows client computers wouldn't be able to access files in the Linux directories. Too many differences exist between the file systems. For example:

- ✦ Linux filenames are case sensitive, whereas Windows filenames are not. For example, in Windows, `File1.txt` and `file1.txt` are the same file. In Linux, they're different files.

- ✦ In Linux, periods aren't used to denote file extensions. Linux filenames don't use extensions.

- ✦ Windows has file attributes like *read-only* and *archive*. Linux doesn't have these.

More fundamentally, Windows networking uses the Server Message Block (SMB) protocol to manage the exchange of file data among file servers and clients. Linux doesn't have SMB support built in.

That's why Samba is required. Samba is a program that mimics the behavior of a Windows-based file server by implementing the SMB protocol. So when you run Samba on a Linux server, the Windows computers on your network see the Linux server as if it were a Windows server.

Like a Windows server, Samba works by designating certain directories as shares. A *share* is simply a directory that's made available to other users via the network. Each share has the following elements:

+ **Name:** The name by which the share is known over the network. Share names should be eight characters whenever possible.

+ **Path:** The path to the directory on the Linux computer that's being shared, such as `\Users\Doug`.

+ **Description:** A one-line description of the share.

+ **Access:** A list of users or groups who have been granted access to the share.

Samba also includes a client program that lets a Linux computer access Windows file servers.

Why did Samba's developers choose to call their program Samba? Simply because the protocol that Windows file and print servers use to communicate with each other is SMB. Add a couple of vowels to *SMB,* and you get *Samba.*

Installing Samba

To install Samba, open a console or terminal window and enter the following command:

```
sudo dnf install samba.x86_64
```

Assuming that Samba is not already installed, `dnf` will ask for your permission to install Samba. Enter **y** to proceed. Be patient while the package downloads and installs.

After you've installed the basic Samba package, you should also install the GNOME-based Samba configuration tool:

```
Sudo dnf install system-config-samba
```

This tool allows you to configure Samba from your GNOME desktop instead of by directly editing the configuration file.

One sure way to render a Samba installation useless is to enable the default Linux firewall settings on the computer that runs Samba. The Linux firewall is designed to prevent users from accessing network services, such as Samba. It's designed to be used between the Internet and your local network — not between Samba and your local network. Although you can configure the firewall to allow access to Samba only to your internal network, a much better option is to run the firewall on a separate computer. That way, the firewall computer can concentrate on being a firewall, and the file server computer can concentrate on being a file server.

Starting and Stopping Samba

Before you can use Samba, you must start its two daemons, smbd and nmbd. (*Daemon* is the Linux term for *service* – a program that runs as a background task.) Both daemons can be started at once by starting the SMB service. From a command shell, use this command:

```
sudo service smb start
```

Whenever you make a configuration change, such as adding a new share or creating a new Samba user, you should stop and restart the service with this command:

```
sudo service smb restart
```

If you prefer, you can stop and start the service with separate commands:

```
sudo service smb stop
sudo service smb start
```

If you're not sure whether Samba is running, enter this command:

```
sudo service smb status
```

You get a message indicating whether the smbd and nmbd daemons are running.

To configure Samba to start automatically when you start Linux, use this command:

```
sudo chkconfig -level 35 smb on
```

See the upcoming Tip for an explanation of level 35.

To make sure that the chkconfig command worked right, enter this command:

```
chkconfig -list smb
```

You should see output similar to the following:

```
Smb     0:off 1:off 2:off 3:on  4:off 5:on  6:off
```

You can independently configure services to start automatically for each of the six *boot levels* of Linux. Boot level 3 is normal operation without an X Server; level 5 is normal operation with an X Server. So setting SMB to start for levels 3 and 5 makes SMB available — regardless of whether you're using a graphical user interface (GUI). (Read more about X Server in Chapter 1 of this minibook.)

Using the Samba Server Configuration Tool

If you've installed the system-config-samba package, you can configure Samba using a handy GNOME-based configuration tool. To start it, click Activities, click Applications, and then click Samba. When you do so, the Samba Server Configuration tool appears, as shown in Figure 5-1. This tool lets you configure basic server settings and manage shares.

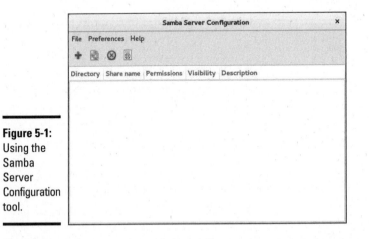

Figure 5-1:
Using the
Samba
Server
Configuration
tool.

Not all Samba configuration options are available from the Samba Server Configuration tool. For advanced Samba server configuration, you need to edit the smb.conf file directly, as described in the upcoming section, "Editing the smb.conf File."

Also, if you don't like the GNOME-based configuration tool, you can use a new web-based configuration tool called *SWAT*. For more information, use Google or another web search service to search for the package `samba-swat`.

Configuring server settings

To make your Samba server visible on the network, you need to configure its server settings. Follow these steps:

1. Choose Preferences➪Server Settings.

The Server Settings dialog box springs to life, as shown in Figure 5-2.

Figure 5-2:
Configure
server
preferences.

2. Enter the workgroup name and a description for your server.

The workgroup name must match the workgroup or domain name used by the computers that will be accessing the server.

3. Click the Security tab.

The security settings appear, as shown in Figure 5-3.

4. Set the authentication mode the way you want.

The Authentication Mode drop-down list offers five basic types of security:

- *ADS (Active Directory Security):* This mode configures the Samba server to use a Windows domain controller to verify the user. If you specify this option, you must provide the name of the domain controller in the Authentication Server text box. Also, you must set the Encrypt Passwords drop-down list to Yes if you use Domain mode.

- *Domain:* This mode configures the Samba server to use an old-style Windows NT domain. You should use this option only if your network hasn't been upgraded since Bill Clinton was president.

Figure 5-3:
Configure
security
options.

- *Server:* This mode configures Samba to use another Samba server to authenticate users. If you have more than one Samba server, this feature lets you set up user accounts on just one of the servers. Specify the name of the Samba server in which you want to perform the authentication in the Authentication Server text box.

- *Share:* This mode authorizes users separately for each share that they attempt to access.

- *User:* This is the default mode. It requires that users provide a valid username and password when they first connect to a Samba server. That authentication then grants them access to all shares on the server, subject to the restrictions of the account under which they are authorized.

5. **Set the Encrypt Passwords drop-down list to Yes.**

   This option is required to allow users of Windows 98 or later versions to connect.

6. **Set the Guest Account drop-down list to the account that you want anonymous users to access.**

   Normally, this account is set to No Guest Account, which means that guest account access is disabled.

   If you want to enable guest account access, open the Guest Account drop-down list to reveal a list of all your Linux users. Then, choose the Linux user you want to be used by guest users. Usually, you set the guest account to the predefined Linux account named Nobody.

7. **Click OK.**

   The Server Settings dialog box is dismissed.

Configuring Samba users

You must create a separate Samba user account for each network user who needs to access the Samba server. In addition, you must first create a Linux user account for each user. The Samba user account maps to an existing Linux user account, so you must create the Linux user account first.

To create a Samba user account, follow these steps:

1. **From the Samba Server Configuration window, choose Preferences⇨ Samba Users.**

   The Samba Users dialog box appears, as shown in Figure 5-4.

Figure 5-4:
The Samba Users dialog box lists your Samba users.

2. **Click the Add User button.**

   The Create New Samba User dialog box in Figure 5-5 appears.

Figure 5-5:
Add a Samba user here.

3. **From the Unix Username drop-down list, select the Linux user that you want this user to log on as.**

   If you forgot to create the Linux user account for this user, open System Settings, choose Users and Groups, and create the account now.

4. **Enter the Windows username for the user.**

   This is the name of the user's Windows user account.

5. **Type the user's password into the password fields.**

6. **Click OK.**

   You're returned to the Samba Users dialog box, which should now list the user that you just created.

7. **Repeat Steps 2–6 for any other users you want to create.**

8. **After you're done, click OK.**

   The Samba Users dialog box is dismissed.

Creating a share

To be useful, a file server should offer one or more *shares* — directories that have been designated as publicly accessible via the network. You can see a list of the current shares available from a file server by firing up the Samba Server Configuration program.

To create a new share, follow these steps:

1. **Click the Add button.**

   Refer to Figure 5-1. The Add button carries a plus sign.

   The Basic tab of the Create Samba Share dialog box shown in Figure 5-6 appears.

Figure 5-6:
Create a
share.

2. **Type the path for the directory that you want to share in the Folder text box and a name that will be used to remotely access the share in the Share Name text box.**

   If you aren't sure of the path, you can click the Choose button. This action calls up a dialog box that lets you search the server's file system for a directory folder to share. You can also create a new directory from this dialog box if the directory that you want to share doesn't yet exist. After you select or create the directory to share, click OK to return to the Create Samba Share dialog box.

3. **(Optional) Type a description of the share in the Description text box.**

   The description is strictly optional but can sometimes help users to determine the intended contents of the folder.

4. **Specify whether you want the share to be read-only or read/write.**

   The default is read-only. If you want to let users save their files on your Samba server, you need to change this setting to read/write.

5. **Click the Access tab.**

   The Access tab of the Create Samba Share dialog box appears, as shown in Figure 5-7.

Figure 5-7:
Allowing
access to
a Samba
share.

6. **If you want to limit access to the share, select the Give Access to These Users check box and then select the users to whom you want to grant access.**

   Note that users' names will appear in this box only if you create Samba users. See the earlier section, "Configuring Samba Users."

7. Click OK.

You're returned to the Samba Server Configuration window, where the share that you just added appears in the list of shares.

When you create a new share by using the Samba Server Configuration program, the share should be immediately visible to other network users. If it isn't, try restarting the Samba server as described in the earlier section, "Starting and Stopping Samba."

Editing the smb.conf File

If you like the feeling of raw power that comes from editing configuration files, fire up your favorite text editor and play with the Samba configuration file. It's called `smb.conf` and is usually located in the `/etc/samba` directory although some distributions may place this file in another location.

Figure 5-8 shows you the `smb.conf` file being edited in the standard Text Editor program, which you can access by double-clicking the configuration file.

```
Open ▼  ⊞                        smb.conf                    Save  ☰  ✕
                                /etc/samba
# This is the main Samba configuration file. For detailed information about the
# options listed here, refer to the smb.conf(5) manual page. Samba has a huge
# number of configurable options, most of which are not shown in this example.
#
# The Official Samba 3.2.x HOWTO and Reference Guide contains step-by-step
# guides for installing, configuring, and using Samba:
# http://www.samba.org/samba/docs/Samba-HOWTO-Collection.pdf
#
# The Samba-3 by Example guide has working examples for smb.conf. This guide is
# generated daily: http://www.samba.org/samba/docs/Samba-Guide.pdf
#
# In this file, lines starting with a semicolon (;) or a hash (#) are
# comments and are ignored. This file uses hashes to denote commentary and
# semicolons for parts of the file you may wish to configure.
#
# Note: Run the "testparm" command after modifying this file to check for basic
# syntax errors.
#
#---------------
# Security-Enhanced Linux (SELinux) Notes:
#
# Turn the samba_domain_controller Boolean on to allow Samba to use the useradd
# and groupadd family of binaries. Run the following command as the root user to
# turn this Boolean on:
# setsebool -P samba_domain_controller on
#
# Turn the samba_enable_home_dirs Boolean on if you want to share home
# directories via Samba. Run the following command as the root user to turn this
# Boolean on:
# setsebool -P samba_enable_home_dirs on
#
# If you create a new directory, such as a new top-level directory, label it
                    Plain Text ▼   Tab Width: 8 ▼        Ln 1, Col 1      ▼    INS
```

Figure 5-8: Editing the smb.conf file.

Any line in the `smb.conf` file that begins with a hash mark (#) or semicolon (;) is a comment. The default `smb.conf` file is loaded with comments that describe what each configuration line does. Plus, you can find many sample configuration entries that are commented out. The sample configuration lines are marked with a semicolon to distinguish them from explanatory text lines, which begin with a hash mark.

The overall structure of the smb.conf file is something like this:

```
[global]
    workgroup = workgroup
    server string = samba server
    security = USER
    encrypt passwords = yes
    smb passwd file = /etc/samba/smbpasswd
    guest ok = yes
    other global settings...
[sharename]
    comment = comment
    path = path
    writeable = yes
```

The first section of the file, marked by the [global] line, contains options that apply to the entire server. These are the options that are set by the Preferences⇨Server Settings command in the GNOME Samba Server Configuration program. Table 5-1 lists a few of the more common settings that you can use in the global section.

Table 5-1	Common Global Settings for the smb.conf File
Setting	**Description**
workgroup	The name of the workgroup or domain.
server string	The comment that describes the server.
hosts allow	Lets you limit access to the Samba server to the IP addresses listed. If a partial IP address is listed (for example, 192.168.1), it is treated as a subnet.
guest ok	Specify Yes to allow guest access.
guest account	Specifies the Linux account to be used.
security	Specifies the security mode: ADS, Domain, Server, Share, or User.

Located after the global section is a section for each share that begins with the [sharename] line. The settings in these groups specify the details of a share, such as the comment and path. Table 5-2 lists the settings that you can specify for a share.

Table 5-2	Share Settings for the smb.conf File
Setting	*Description*
`[sharename]`	The name used by the share.
`path=path`	The path to the directory to be shared.
`comment=comment`	A description of the shared resource.
`guest ok`	Specify Yes to allow guest access.
`writeonly`	Specify Yes for read/write, No for read-only.
`browseable`	Specify Yes to make the share visible in My Network Places.
`valid users`	A list of users who can access the share.
`hosts allow`	Lets you limit access to the Samba server to the IP addresses listed. If a partial IP address is listed (for example, 192.168.1), it's treated as a subnet.

After you modify the `smb.conf` file and save your changes, you need to restart the SMB service for the changes to take effect. See the earlier section "Starting and Stopping Samba."

Using the Samba Client

Earlier in this chapter, I show you how to set up Samba's server program so that you can enable a Linux computer to operate as a file server in a Windows network, thus allowing Windows clients to access files in shared directories on the Linux computer. That's the most common reason for using Samba.

But Samba can also work the other way around: It includes a program called `smbclient` that lets you access Windows file servers from a Linux computer. The `smbclient` program works much like an FTP client, so if you've used FTP before, you'll have no trouble understanding how it works.

`smbclient` is a command line tool, so you need to log on to a virtual console or open a terminal window. Then, enter the `smbclient` command, followed by the server and share name, like this:

```
smbclient //server01/share01
```

When the client successfully accesses the share, you are greeted by the friendly SMB prompt:

```
smb:\>
```

Then, you can enter smbclient commands to access the data in the shared directory. Table 5-3 summarizes the more common commands that are available at the smb:\> prompt.

Table 5-3	Commonly Used smbclient Commands
Command	*Description*
cd *directory*	Changes to the specified directory on the remote system
del *filename*	Deletes the specified file or files on the remote system
dir	Lists files in the current directory on the remote system
exit	Terminates the session
get *remote-file local-file*	Copies the specified remote file to the specified local file
lcd *directory*	Changes the local current directory to the specified directory
md *directory*	Creates a directory on the remote system
mget *wildcard-mask*	Copies all files that match the wildcard mask from the remote system to the local system
mput *wildcard-mask*	Copies all files that match the wildcard mask from the local system to the remote system
put *local-file remote-file*	Copies the specified file from the local system to the remote system
rd *directory*	Deletes the specified directory on the remote system

Chapter 6: Running Apache

In This Chapter

✔ **Getting Apache up and running**

✔ **Using the HTTP configuration tool**

✔ **Restricting access**

✔ **Creating virtual hosts**

✔ **Creating web pages**

All the popular Linux distributions come with Apache, the most popular web server on the Internet today. In most cases, Apache is installed and configured automatically when you install Linux. Then setting up a web server for the Internet or an intranet is simply a matter of tweaking a few Apache configuration settings and copying your HTML document files to Apache's home directory.

Installing Apache

To install Apache, open a console or terminal window and enter the following command:

```
sudo dnf install httpd
```

Assuming that Apache is not already installed, dnf will ask for your permission to install Apache. Enter **y** to proceed. Be patient while the package downloads and installs.

You'll also want to install the graphical configuration program by running the following command:

```
sudo dnf install system-config-httpd
```

Starting and Stopping Apache

Before you can use Apache, you must start the httpd daemon. From a command shell, use this command:

```
sudo service httpd start
```

Whenever you make a configuration change, you should stop and restart the service with this command:

```
sudo service httpd restart
```

If you prefer, you can stop and start the service with separate commands:

```
sudo service httpd stop
sudo service httpd start
```

If you're not sure whether Apache is running, enter this command:

```
sudo service httpd status
```

You get a message indicating whether the httpd daemon is running.

To configure Apache to start automatically when you start Linux, use this command:

```
sudo chkconfig --level 35 httpd on
```

To make sure that the chkconfig command worked right, enter this command:

```
sudo chkconfig --list httpd
```

You should see output similar to the following:

```
sudo httpd    0:off  1:off  2:off  3:on   4:off  5:on   6:off
```

Confirming That Apache Is Running

You can test to see whether Apache is up and running by opening the Firefox browser (choose Applications ⇨ Internet ⇨ Firefox Web Browser) and typing **localhost** in the address bar. If Apache is running on the server, a page such as the one shown in Figure 6-1 appears.

If this doesn't work, first make sure that you can ping your Linux server from the remote system. To do that, type **ping** followed by the IP address of the Linux server. If the ping command times out, you have a connectivity problem that you need to correct.

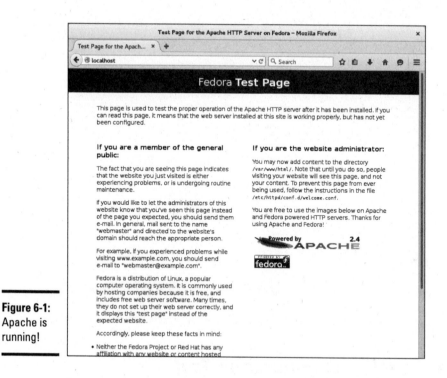

Figure 6-1:
Apache is
running!

If you can ping the Linux server but still can't reach the Apache server home
page, here are a few things to check:

✦ Make sure that the `httpd` service is running as described in the "Starting
and Stopping Apache" section, earlier in this chapter.

✦ Make sure that the Linux firewall is turned off or configured to allow
HTTP traffic. In Fedora, you can manage the firewall settings from
the GNOME-based Security Level Configuration tool. To run it, click
Activities, type **Firewall**, and then click the Firewall icon. Then select
WWW (HTTP) in the list of trusted services. Figure 6-2 shows the System
Settings Configuration tool with the firewall enabled and the HTTP
service trusted.

If you don't have the Security Level Configuration tool, you can install it
using the following command:

```
sudo dnf install system-config-securitylevel
```

Do *not* disable the firewall altogether unless you have another firewall,
such as a firewall router, between your Linux server and your Internet
connection.

Figure 6-2:
Trusting
the HTTP
service.

Using the HTTP Configuration Tool

Apache should run fine using the default configuration settings made when you install it. You can change various configuration settings, however, either by editing the Apache configuration files or by using the HTTP configuration tool, as shown in Figure 6-3. To start this tool, choose Activities ⇨ Applications ⇨ Http.

The Main tab of the HTTP configuration tool provides the basic configuration settings for Apache. Here, you can set the following options:

✦ **Server Name:** This option sets the name that the Apache server will return. If you leave this name blank, Apache will figure out the actual name of the Linux server and return it, so you need to set this option only if you want to use a different name for your Apache server.

✦ **Webmaster Email Address:** This is the email address of the webmaster for this web server.

✦ **Available Addresses:** This list box shows the addresses that Apache will service HTTP requests for. By default, Apache will reply to HTTP requests from any computer that makes the request on port 80, the standard HTTP port. You can change the port or restrict access, however, as described in the following section.

HTTP Server Configuration   ✕

| Main | Virtual Hosts | Performance Tuning |

Basic Setup

Server Name: [   ]

Webmaster email address: [root@localhost]

Available Addresses

[   ]   ➕ Add...

🖊 Edit...

❌ Delete

Set addresses for Apache to listen for requests on.

| Help | | Cancel | OK |

Figure 6-3:
Configuring
Apache's
HTTP
settings.

Whenever you use the HTTP configuration tool to change Apache's configuration, you need to restart Apache. You can do so by entering this command
from a console prompt:

```
service httpd restart
```

Allowing or Restricting Access to an Apache Server

To allow or restrict access to your Apache server, you can alter the Available
Addresses list in the Main tab of the HTTP configuration tool by using the
Add, Edit, and Delete buttons. To allow access to the HTTP standard port 80
for your server, follow these steps:

1. **Open the HTTP Configuration Tool.**

2. **Click the Add button.**

   The Add Address dialog box, shown in Figure 6-4, appears.

Add new address...

🖾 ○ Listen to all addresses

   ⦿ Address: [   ]

   Port: [80   ]

| Cancel | OK |

Figure 6-4:
Adding an
address.

3. **Select the Listen to All Addresses option.**

4. **Click OK.**

You are returned to the HTTP Configuration Tool; an entry entitled "All available addresses on port 80" now appears in the Available Addresses list.

To change the port that the Apache server uses, select All Available Addresses on Port 80 in the Available Addresses list and click Edit. This brings up the dialog box shown in Figure 6-4. Then specify the port you want to use, and click OK.

If you want to restrict access to certain IP addresses, select the All Available Addresses line, click the Edit button, select the Address radio button, and then enter the address you want to allow access to. You can enter a single IP address, but you're more likely to enter a partial IP address or an IP/netmask combination. For example, to allow access to all addresses from 212.66.5.0 to 212.66.5.255, you could enter either of the following:

```
212.66.5
212.66.5.0/255.255.255.0
```

If you want to allow access to a list of specific IP addresses, you can add lines to the Available Addresses list box. First, though, you should remove the All Available Addresses line or edit it to allow just a single address. Then click the Add button to add addresses you want to allow.

Configuring Virtual Hosts

A *virtual host* is simply a website with its own domain name hosted by an Apache server. By default, Apache is set up to serve just one virtual host, but you can add more virtual hosts. As a result, a single Apache server is able to host more than one website.

If I were so inclined, I might set up an Apache server to host my own personal website (www.lowewriter.com) that has information about my books and a second website (www.hauntedlowes.com) that has information about my favorite hobby: decorating my house for Halloween. Both of these websites could be implemented as virtual hosts on a single Apache server.

To configure a virtual host (including the default virtual host, if you have only one), you use the Virtual Hosts tab of the HTTP configuration tool, as shown in Figure 6-5.

Figure 6-5:
The Virtual
Hosts tab.

Configuring the default host

Even if you don't plan on creating additional virtual hosts, you can still use
the Virtual Hosts tab to configure the default virtual host for your website.
To do so, select the virtual host in the Virtual Hosts list, and click the Edit
button. This brings up the dialog box shown in Figure 6-6.

Figure 6-6:
Editing the
virtual host's
properties.

From this dialog box, you can configure a variety of important settings for the virtual host:

✦ **Virtual Host Name:** You use this name to refer to the virtual host.

✦ **Document Root Directory:** This is the file system location that contains the HTML documents for the website. The default is `/var/www/html`, but you can specify a different location if you want to store your HTML files somewhere else.

✦ **Webmaster Email Address:** Each virtual host can have its own webmaster email address. If you leave this option blank, the address specified for the main HTTP configuration (refer to Figure 6-3) is used.

✦ **Host Information:** This section of the dialog box lets you specify what HTTP requests should be serviced by this virtual host.

You can use the other tabs of the Virtual Host Properties dialog box to configure additional options. Figure 6-7 shows the Page Options tab, where you can set the following options:

Figure 6-7: The Page Options tab lets you set the directory search list and custom error pages.

✦ **Directory Page Search List:** This list specifies the default page for the website. The default page is displayed if the user doesn't indicate a specific page to retrieve. Then Apache looks for each of the pages listed in the Directory Page Search list and displays the first one it finds. You can use the Add, Edit, and Delete buttons to modify this list.

✦ **Error Pages:** This list lets you change the default error pages that are displayed when an HTTP error occurs. The most common HTTP error, Not Found, happens when the user requests a page that doesn't exist. If you want to create a custom error page to let the user know that the page doesn't exist or that some other error has occurred, this list is the place to do it.

Creating a virtual host

If you want to host more than one website on an Apache server, you can create additional virtual hosts. Just follow these steps:

1. **Click the Add button on the Virtual Hosts tab of the HTTP configuration tool (refer to Figure 6-5).**

   This brings up the virtual host properties, which you've already seen in Figure 6-6.

2. **In the Host Information section, choose Name Based Virtual Host from the drop-down list.**

   The Virtual Host Properties dialog box morphs into the dialog box shown in Figure 6-8.

3. **Enter the IP address and the host name for the virtual host.**

   The IP address is usually the IP address assigned to the Apache server, and the host name is the DNS name used to access the virtual host.

4. **If you want to provide an alias for the virtual host, click the Add button, enter the alias name, and click OK.**

   An alias is often used for websites that are used on an intranet rather than on public websites. If you're setting up an intranet website for your company suggestion box, for example, the full DNS name for the virtual host might be `suggestionbox.mycompany.com`. But if you provide just `suggestionbox` as an alias, users can access the suggestion-box website by using `suggestionbox` rather than `suggestionbox.mycompany.com` as the website address.

5. **Use the other tabs of the Virtual Host Properties dialog box to configure additional options.**

   You might want to use the Page Options tab (refer to Figure 6-7) to change the directory-page search list or designate custom error pages, for example.

Virtual Host Properties

| General Options | Page Options | SSL | Logging | Environment | Performance |

Basic Setup

Virtual Host Name: [Virtual Host 0]

Document Root Directory: [/var/www/html/]

Webmaster email address: [root@localhost]

Host Information

[Name based Virtual Host ⌄]

IP Address: [   ]

Host Name: [   ]

Aliases

[   ] ＋ Add...

ⓠ Edit...

⊗ Delete

Help   Cancel   OK

Figure 6-8:
Creating a
new virtual
host.

6. **Click OK.**

The virtual host is created. You're returned to the HTTP configuration tool, where the new virtual host appears in the Virtual Hosts list.

Manually Editing Apache's Configuration Files

If you're allergic to GUI configuration tools, you can configure your Apache server by editing the configuration files directly. Apache's configuration settings are located in three separate configuration files, named `httpd.conf`, `srm.conf`, and `access.conf`. These files are located in `/etc/httpd/conf` in Fedora Core Linux, but they may be in a different location in other Linux distributions. Be sure to study the Apache documentation before you start messing with these files!

Whenever you make a configuration change to Apache, you should restart Apache by using the `service httpd restart` command.

Creating Web Pages

This section is about how to create and edit HTML content for your website. Plenty of good books on how to do that are available, including my own *Creating Web Pages For Dummies Quick Reference* (Wiley). Rather, I just want to point out a few key things that you need to know to set up a website with Apache:

✦ The default location for web documents is `/var/www/html`. When you create web pages for your site, save them in that directory.

✦ When a user visits your website by typing just the domain name without a filename (`www.mydomain.com` instead of `www.mydomain.com/file1.html`), Apache displays the file named `index.html` or `index.htm`. You should give the home page for your website one of these two names.

✦ If you're a programmer, you can build complicated web-based applications with PHP, which is installed along with Apache.

Chapter 7: Running Sendmail

In This Chapter

✔ **Looking at how email works**

✔ **Installing and starting Sendmail**

✔ **Understanding basic Sendmail configuration**

✔ **Blocking spam with SpamAssassin**

✔ **Reading email with mail and Evolution**

Sendmail, which is a standard part of most Linux distributions, is one of the most popular mail server programs on the Internet. You can use Sendmail as an alternative to expensive mail server programs, such as Microsoft Exchange Server, to provide email services for your LAN. This chapter shows you how to set up and use Sendmail on a Linux server.

Spam artists — unscrupulous marketers who clutter the Internet with millions of unsolicited emails — are constantly on the prowl for unprotected Sendmail servers, which they can use to launch their spam campaigns. If you don't protect your server, sooner or later, a spammer will coax your computer into spending almost all its time sending out the spammer's email. To protect your server from becoming an indentured spam servant, you can configure it to refuse any mail that merely wants to use your computer to relay messages to other computers. See the sidebar "Don't be an open relay!" later in this chapter.

Understanding Email

Before I get into the details of installing and configuring Sendmail, I want to review some basics of how Internet email works. First, you need to understand that email consists of messages that are delivered according to an Internet protocol commonly referred to as SMTP. Simple Mail Transfer Protocol was first codified in 1983, long before Al Gore invented the Internet. Several enhancements have been made along the way, but most email on the Internet today is delivered using this nearly ancient protocol.

Interestingly, the software that delivers 70 percent of all the email on the Internet — Sendmail — also originated in the same year. In 1983, Eric Allman developed the first version of the Sendmail program as part of the Berkeley Software Distribution (BSD) of Unix, one of the earliest versions of Unix made publicly available.

The following paragraphs describe some of the key features of email that you should know about if you plan on setting up a Linux server running Sendmail:

- ✦ **Mailbox:** A *mailbox* is a simple text file that holds incoming email messages until they are processed by a mail user agent. In Fedora Linux, each user has a mailbox file in /var/mail.

- ✦ **Mail User Agent (MUA):** A program that end users can use to send and receive mail. The most widely used MUA is Microsoft Outlook. Linux comes with several MUAs. The most basic is Mail, a text-based MUA that lets you read and compose email messages from a console prompt. Fedora also includes a sophisticated graphical MUA called *Evolution,* which is similar in many ways to Microsoft Outlook. Both are described later in this chapter.

- ✦ **Mail Transfer Agent (MTA):** A program that transfers email messages between computers. Sendmail, which most of this chapter is devoted to, is an MTA. When a user uses an MUA to send an email message, the MUA delivers the message to an MTA, which then transfers the message to the intended recipient.

- ✦ **Mail Delivery Agent (MDA):** A program that accepts incoming mail from an MTA and places it in the intended recipient's mailbox. A basic MDA simply copies each message to the mailbox, but more advanced MDAs can be used to filter the incoming mail to eliminate spam or check for viruses. The default MDA for Fedora Linux is Procmail. Fedora also includes SpamAssassin, which you can use to filter spam from your incoming mail.

Installing Sendmail

To install Sendmail, open a console or terminal window and enter the following commands:

```
sudo dnf install sendmail
sudo dnf install sendmail-cf
sudo dnf install m4
```

Assuming that the Sendmail packages are not already installed, dnf will ask for your permission to install the required packages. Enter **y** to proceed. Be patient while the package downloads and installs.

Modifying sendmail.mc

Sendmail is probably one of the most difficult programs to configure that you'll ever encounter. In fact, the basic configuration file, sendmail.cf, is well more than 1,000 lines long. You don't want to mess with this file if you can possibly avoid it.

Fortunately, you don't have to. The sendmail.cf configuration file is generated automatically from a much shorter file called sendmail.mc. This file contains special macros that are processed by a program called m4. The m4 program reads the macros in the sendmail.mc file and expands them to create the actual sendmail.cf file.

Even so, the sendmail.mc file is a few hundred lines long. Configuring Sendmail isn't for the faint of heart.

You can find the sendmail.mc and sendmail.cf files in the /etc/mail directory. Before you edit these files, you should make backup copies of the current files. That way, if you mess up your mail configuration, you can quickly return to a working configuration by reinstating your backup copies.

After you make backup copies, you can safely edit sendmail.mc. When you're finished, you can regenerate the sendmail.cf file by entering these commands:

```
cd /etc/mail
m4 sendmail.mc > sendmail.cf
service sendmail restart
```

The first command changes the current working directory to /etc/mail. Then, the second command compiles the sendmail.mc command into the sendmail.cf command. Finally, the third command restarts the Sendmail service so that the changes will take effect.

You need to be aware of two strange conventions used in the sendmail.mc file:

✦ **Comments:** Unlike most configuration files, comments don't begin with a hash mark (#). Instead, they begin with the letters dnl.

✦ **Strings:** Strings are quoted in an unusual way. Instead of regular quotation marks or apostrophes, strings must begin with a backquote (`), which is located to the left of the numeral 1 on the keyboard and ends with an apostrophe ('), located to the right of the semicolon. So a properly quoted string looks like this:

```
MASQUERADE_AS(`mydomain.com')
```

Pretty strange, eh?

The following sections describe the common configuration changes that you may need to make to `sendmail.mc`.

Enabling connections

The default configuration allows connections only from localhost. If you want Sendmail to work as a server for other computers on your network, look for the following line in the `sendmail.mc` file:

```
DAEMON_OPTIONS(`Port=smtp,Addr=127.0.0.1, Name=MTA')dnl
```

Add dnl to the beginning of this line to make it a comment.

Enabling masquerading

Masquerading allows all the mail being sent from your domain to appear as if it came from the domain (for example, `wally@cleaver.net`) rather than from the individual hosts (like `wally@wally.cleaver.net`). To enable masquerading, add lines similar to these:

```
MASQUERADE_AS(`cleaver.net')dnl
FEATURE(masquerade_envelope)dnl
FEATURE(masquerade_entire_domain)dnl
MASQUERADE_DOMAIN(`cleaver.net')dnl
```

Don't be an open relay!

An *open relay* is a mail server that's configured to allow anyone to use it as a relay for sending mail. In short, an open relay sends mail when neither the sender nor the recipient is a local user. Spammers love open relays because they can use them to obscure the true origin of their junk email. As a result, open relays are a major contributor to the Internet spam problem.

Fortunately, the default configuration for the current version of Sendmail (8.14) is to not allow open relaying. As a result, you have to go out of your way to become an open relay with Sendmail. In fact, you'll have to look up the lines you'd need to add to `sendmail.mc` to enable open relaying. I'm certainly not going to list them here.

If you do need to allow relaying for specific hosts, create a file named `relay-domains` in `/etc/mail`. Then, add a line for each domain you want to allow relaying for. This line should contain nothing but the domain name. Then restart Sendmail.

Setting up aliases

An *alias* — also known as a *virtual user* — is an incoming email address that is automatically routed to local users. For example, you may want to create a generic account such as sales@*mydomain.com* and have all mail sent to that account delivered to a user named *willie*. To do that, you edit the file /etc/mail/virtusers. This file starts out empty. To create a virtual user, just list the incoming email address followed by the actual recipient.

For example, here's a `virtusers` file that defines several aliases:

```
sales@mydomain.com       willie
bob@mydomain.com         robert
marketing@mydomain.com   robert
```

After you make your changes, you should restart the Sendmail service.

Using SpamAssassin

SpamAssassin is a spam-blocking tool that uses a variety of techniques to weed the spam out of your users' mailboxes. SpamAssassin uses a combination of rule filters that scan for suspicious message content and other telltale signs of spam, as well as blacklists from known spammers. The following sections explain how to install and use it.

Installing SpamAssassin

To configure SpamAssassin for basic spam filtering, follow these steps:

1. **Ensure that Procmail is installed as your MDA.**

In Fedora, Procmail is installed by default. To make sure it's enabled, open the file /etc/mail/sendmail.mc and make sure it includes the following line:

```
FEATURE(local_procmail,`',`procmail -t -Y -a $h -d $u')dnl
```

If this line is missing, add it and then restart Sendmail.

2. **Ensure that the `spamassassin` daemon is running.**

You can do that by entering this command at a console prompt:

```
sudo service spamassassin status
```

If SpamAssassin isn't running, enter this command:

```
sudo chkconfig --level 35 spamassassin on
```

Whenever you make a configuration change, you should stop and restart the service with this command:

```
sudo service spamassassin restart
```

3. **Create a file named** `procmailrc` **in the** `/etc` **directory.**

   Use `gedit` or your favorite text editor. The file should contain these two lines:

   ```
   :0fw
   | /usr/bin/spamc
   ```

   These lines cause Procmail to run all incoming mail through the SpamAssassin client program.

4. **Restart Sendmail and SpamAssassin.**

   You can do this from Applications ⇨ System Settings ⇨ Server Settings ⇨ Services, or you can enter these commands at a console prompt:

   ```
   sudo service sendmail restart
   sudo service spamassassin restart
   ```

SpamAssassin should now be checking for spam. To make sure it's working, send some email to one of the mailboxes on your system and then open the mailbox file for that user in `\var\mail` and examine the message that was sent. If the message headers include several lines that begin with *X-Spam,* SpamAssassin is doing its job.

Customizing SpamAssassin

You can configure SpamAssassin by editing the configuration file `/etc/mail/spamassassin/local.cf`. This file contains SpamAssassin rules that are applied system wide although you can override these rules for individual users by creating a `user_prefs` file in each user's `$HOME/.spamassassin` directory.

In Fedora, the default `local.cf` file contains the following lines:

```
required_hits 5
report_safe 0
rewrite_header Subject [SPAM]
```

These lines cause SpamAssassin to add the word `[SPAM]` to the start of the subject line for any message that scores 5 or higher on SpamAssassin's spam scoring algorithm.

Although you can configure SpamAssassin to automatically delete messages that score above a specified value, most antispam experts recommend against it. Instead, adding a word such as `[SPAM]` to the header lets each user decide how he wants to handle spam by using a message filter on his email client that either deletes the marked messages or moves them to a Spam folder.

No matter how you configure SpamAssassin, you will inevitably get some false positives. For example, a long-lost friend who moved to Nigeria will email you a joke about Viagra using a Hotmail account. Odds are good that SpamAssassin will mark this message as spam. That's why arbitrarily deleting messages marked as spam isn't such a great idea, especially on a system-wide basis. Better to simply mark the messages and then let your users decide how to deal with the spam.

Blacklisting and whitelisting email addresses

SpamAssassin lets you blacklist or whitelist a specific email address or an entire domain. When you *blacklist* an address, any mail from the address will automatically be blocked, regardless of the message contents. Conversely, when you *whitelist* an address, all mail from the address will be allowed through, even if the message would otherwise be blocked as spam.

Whitelisting is a powerful tool for making sure that the people you correspond with on a regular basis don't get their email accidentally blocked by SpamAssassin. As a result, it's a good idea to add your friends, relatives, and especially your customers to a whitelist.

Likewise, blacklisting lets you mark spammers who have managed to get their spam into your system in spite of SpamAssassin's best efforts to detect their true intent.

To whitelist an address, add a line such as the following to `/etc/mail/spamassassin/local.rc`:

```
whitelist_from wally@cleaver.com
```

This allows all mail from `wally@cleaver.com` to be delivered, even if the mail might otherwise look like spam.

To blacklist an address, add a line like this:

```
blacklist_from auntida@myrelatives.com
```

This blocks all mail from your Aunt Ida.

Using the Mail Console Client

The most basic client for creating and reading email is the `mail` command. Although it doesn't have many advanced features, it is fast, so some Linux users like to use it for sending simple messages. (It is also sometimes used in scripts.) To install the `mail` command, open a terminal window and enter the following command:

```
sudo dnf install mailx
```

To read mail, open a command console, log on using the account whose mail you want to read, and enter the command `mail`. A list of all messages in your mailbox will be displayed. You can then use any of the commands listed in Table 7-1 to work with the messages in the mailbox or compose new mail messages.

Table 7-1	**Mail Commands**
Command	*Explanation*
?	Display a list of available commands.
q	Quit.
h	List the headers for all messages in the mailbox.
n	Type the next message.
t *list*	Type the specified messages. For example, t 3 types message 3, and t 4 5 types messages 4 and 5.
d *list*	Deletes one or more messages. For example, d 4 deletes message 4.
R *list*	Reply to message sender.
r *list*	Reply to message sender and all recipients.
m *user*	Compose a new message addressed to the specified user.

To compose a new message from a command prompt, follow these steps:

1. **Type** mail **followed by the email address of the recipient.**

   For example:

   ```
   mail wally@cleaver.com
   ```

   Mail responds by prompting you for the subject.

2. **Type the subject line and press Enter.**

   Mail then waits for you to enter the text of the message.

3. **Type the message text. Use the Enter key to start new lines.**

   You can enter as many lines as you want for the message.

You're done! The message is on its way.

Using Evolution

Evolution is a graphical email client that's similar in many ways to Microsoft Outlook, as Figure 7-1 shows. It includes not only email features, but also a contact list, a calendar, a task manager, and other Outlook-like features.

Figure 7-1:
Evolution
looks a lot
like Outlook.

Evolution is installed automatically as part of a Fedora Workstation install. You can install it manually with the following command:

```
sudo dnf install evolution.x86_64
```

To start Evolution, click the E-mail icon that's located in the panel at the top of the GNOME screen. The first time you run Evolution, a configuration wizard will guide you through the necessary configuration. You need to supply basic information about your email account, such as your email address and the name of your mail server.

Chapter 8: Running FTP

In This Chapter

✓ **Installing and starting the** `vsftpd` **server**

✓ **Configuring** `vsftpd`

FTP is one of the oldest and still most common methods for sending files over the Internet. This chapter shows you how to install and configure the basic FTP server that comes with most Linux distributions, Very Secure FTP Daemon (`vsftpd`). For complete information about this server, visit the official website at `www.vsftpd.beasts.org`.

If you need to access files from someone's FTP site or need instructions on setting up an FTP server on a Windows machine, please see Book III, Chapter 6.

Installing vsftpd

To install `vsftpd`, open a console or terminal window and enter the following commands:

```
sudo dnf install vsftpd
```

Assuming that `vsftpd` is not already installed, `dnf` will ask for your permission to install it. Enter **y** to proceed. Be patient while the package downloads and installs.

Starting the vsftpd Service

After you install the `vsftpd` package, you can start the FTP service by entering the following command at a console prompt:

```
/etc/init.d/vsftpd start
```

To restart the service, use this command:

```
/etc/init.d/vsftpd restart
```

Configuring FTP

You configure `vsftpd` via a configuration file named `vsftpd.conf`, located in `/etc`. The default `vsftpd.conf` file is shown in Listing 8-1. You can learn a lot about how `vsftpd` works simply by reading through this configuration file.

Listing 8-1: The `vsftpd.conf` File

```
# Example config file /etc/vsftpd/vsftpd.conf
#
# The default compiled in settings are fairly paranoid. This sample file
# loosens things up a bit, to make the ftp daemon more usable.
# Please see vsftpd.conf.5 for all compiled in defaults.
#
# READ THIS: This example file is NOT an exhaustive list of vsftpd options.
# Please read the vsftpd.conf.5 manual page to get a full idea of vsftpd's
# capabilities.
#
# Allow anonymous FTP? (Beware - allowed by default if you comment this out).
anonymous_enable=YES
#
# Uncomment this to allow local users to log in.
# When SELinux is enforcing check for SE bool ftp_home_dir
local_enable=YES
#
# Uncomment this to enable any form of FTP write command.
write_enable=YES
#
# Default umask for local users is 077. You may wish to change this to 022,
# if your users expect that (022 is used by most other ftpd's)
local_umask=022
#
# Uncomment this to allow the anonymous FTP user to upload files. This only
# has an effect if the above global write enable is activated. Also, you will
# obviously need to create a directory writable by the FTP user.
# When SELinux is enforcing check for SE bool allow_ftpd_anon_write,
#     allow_ftpd_full_access
#anon_upload_enable=YES
#
# Uncomment this if you want the anonymous FTP user to be able to create
# new directories.
#anon_mkdir_write_enable=YES
#
# Activate directory messages - messages given to remote users when they
# go into a certain directory.
dirmessage_enable=YES
#
# Activate logging of uploads/downloads.
xferlog_enable=YES
#
# Make sure PORT transfer connections originate from port 20 (ftp-data).
connect_from_port_20=YES
#
```

```
# If you want, you can arrange for uploaded anonymous files to be owned by
# a different user. Note! Using "root" for uploaded files is not
# recommended!
#chown_uploads=YES
#chown_username=whoever
#
# You may override where the log file goes if you like. The default is shown
# below.
#xferlog_file=/var/log/xferlog
#
# If you want, you can have your log file in standard ftpd xferlog format.
# Note that the default log file location is /var/log/xferlog in this case.
xferlog_std_format=YES
#
# You may change the default value for timing out an idle session.
#idle_session_timeout=600
#
# You may change the default value for timing out a data connection.
#data_connection_timeout=120
#
# It is recommended that you define on your system a unique user which the
# ftp server can use as a totally isolated and unprivileged user.
#nopriv_user=ftpsecure
#
# Enable this and the server will recognise asynchronous ABOR requests. Not
# recommended for security (the code is non-trivial). Not enabling it,
# however, may confuse older FTP clients.
#async_abor_enable=YES
#
# By default the server will pretend to allow ASCII mode but in fact ignore
# the request. Turn on the below options to have the server actually do ASCII
# mangling on files when in ASCII mode.
# Beware that on some FTP servers, ASCII support allows a denial of service
# attack (DoS) via the command "SIZE /big/file" in ASCII mode. vsftpd
# predicted this attack and has always been safe, reporting the size of the
# raw file.
# ASCII mangling is a horrible feature of the protocol.
#ascii_upload_enable=YES
#ascii_download_enable=YES
#
# You may fully customise the login banner string:
#ftpd_banner=Welcome to blah FTP service.
#
# You may specify a file of disallowed anonymous e-mail addresses. Apparently
# useful for combatting certain DoS attacks.
#deny_email_enable=YES
# (default follows)
#banned_email_file=/etc/vsftpd/banned_emails
#
# You may specify an explicit list of local users to chroot() to their home
# directory. If chroot_local_user is YES, then this list becomes a list of
# users to NOT chroot().
# (Warning! chroot'ing can be very dangerous. If using chroot, make sure that
# the user does not have write access to the top level directory within the
# chroot)
#chroot_local_user=YES
#chroot_list_enable=YES
# (default follows)
#chroot_list_file=/etc/vsftpd/chroot_list
#
```

(continued)

Listing 8-1 *(continued)*

```
# You may activate the "-R" option to the builtin ls. This is disabled by
# default to avoid remote users being able to cause excessive I/O on large
# sites. However, some broken FTP clients such as "ncftp" and "mirror" assume
# the presence of the "-R" option, so there is a strong case for enabling it.
#ls_recurse_enable=YES
#
# When "listen" directive is enabled, vsftpd runs in standalone mode and
# listens on IPv4 sockets. This directive cannot be used in conjunction
# with the listen_ipv6 directive.
listen=NO
#
# This directive enables listening on IPv6 sockets. By default, listening
# on the IPv6 "any" address (::) will accept connections from both IPv6
# and IPv4 clients. It is not necessary to listen on *both* IPv4 and IPv6
# sockets. If you want that (perhaps because you want to listen on specific
# addresses) then you must run two copies of vsftpd with two configuration
# files.
# Make sure, that one of the listen options is commented !!
listen_ipv6=YES

pam_service_name=vsftpd
userlist_enable=YES
tcp_wrappers=YES
```

You can edit this file via the Text Editor. (Choose Activities ⇨ Show Applications ⇨ gedit.) After you save your changes, you'll need to restart the vsftpd service for the changes to take effect, as described in the previous section.

The following paragraphs describe some of the more common modifications to the vsftpd.conf file:

✦ **Anonymous access:** By default, anonymous access is allowed. To prevent users from accessing the FTP site anonymously, change the anonymous_ enable line to

    anonymous_enable=NO

If you disable anonymous access, your users will have to have a Linux account on the server to access the FTP site. By default, each user will be directed to his or her home directory.

✦ **Allowing local users:** By default, local users are allowed to access the FTP site. To prevent local users from accessing the FTP site, change the local_enable line to

    local_enable=NO

You can disable either anonymous users or local users, but do *not* disable both!

✦ **Creating a read-only FTP site:** If you want to make your FTP site read-only so that users can download files but not upload, change the `write_enable` line to

```
write_enable=NO
```

✦ **Customizing the welcome banner:** You can customize the welcome banner by uncommenting the `ftpd_banner` line and adding your banner. For example

```
Ftpd_banner=Welcome to my FTP site!
```

Chapter 9: Linux Commands

In This Chapter

✔ Discovering the basics of command shells

✔ Identifying file and directory commands

✔ Discovering commands that help with packages and services

✔ Figuring out commands for managing users and groups

✔ Becoming familiar with networking commands

*L*inux has several nice graphical user interfaces (GUI) to choose from, and many of the more common Linux networking functions have graphical configuration utilities. Still, many Linux configuration tasks can be done only from a command shell. In many cases, though, the configuration utility provides access only to the most basic configuration parameters, so if you want to configure advanced features, you have to use commands. In fact, some network features don't even have a graphical configuration utility, so you have no choice but to use commands.

Even when GNOME-based alternatives are available, you'll often resort to using commands because frankly, that's what Linux was built to do. Unlike Windows, Linux relies on commands as its primary means of getting things done. If you're going to work with Linux, knowing the basic commands presented in this chapter is a must.

Command Shell Basics

A *shell* is a program that accepts commands from a command prompt and executes them. The shell displays a prompt to let you know it's waiting for a command. When you type the command and press Enter, the system reads your command, interprets it, executes it, displays the results, and then displays the prompt again so that you can enter another command.

Linux commands are case-sensitive, so be careful about capitalization when you type Linux commands.

Getting to a shell

You can work with Linux commands directly from one of the six virtual consoles. If you like the responsiveness of text mode, virtual consoles are for you. To switch to a virtual console, press Ctrl+Alt+F*x*. For example, press Ctrl+Alt+F1 to switch to virtual console 1. When you're in a virtual console, you have to answer the logon prompt with a valid username and password. To return to GNOME, press Ctrl+Alt+F7.

The alternative is to work in a terminal window within the GNOME environment. If you have an older computer, you may find that the terminal window is a little unresponsive. If your computer is relatively new, however, the terminal window will be just as responsive as the text-mode virtual console. Plus, you'll have the benefit of a scroll bar that lets you scroll to see text that otherwise would have flown off the screen.

To open a terminal window, click Activities, click Show Applications, click Utilities, then click the Terminal icon. This opens a command shell in a window right on the GNOME desktop, as shown in Figure 9-1. Because this shell runs within the user account GNOME is logged on as, you don't have to log on. You can just start typing commands. When you're done, type **Exit** to close the window.

Since you'll use Terminal often to enter commands, I suggest you make it a favorite so it always appears when you click Activities. To make Terminal a favorite, click Activities, then click Show Applications, then click Utilities. Finally, right-click Terminal and choose Add to Favorites.

Figure 9-1:
A terminal
window.

For normal Linux users, the command shell prompt character is a dollar sign ($). If you see a hash mark (#) as the prompt character, it means you're logged on as `root`. Whenever you see a hash prompt, you should be extra careful about what you do because you can easily get yourself into trouble by deleting important files or otherwise corrupting the system.

Editing commands

Most of the time, you just type commands using the keyboard. If you make a mistake, you just type the command again, being careful not to repeat the mistake. However, Linux shells have several built-in editing features that can simplify the task of correcting a mistaken command or entering a sequence of similar commands:

✦ **Repeat:** If you want to repeat a command that you've used recently, press the up-arrow key. This action recalls your most recently executed commands. You can press Enter to execute a command as is, or you can edit the command before you execute it.

✦ **Autocomplete:** The shell has a handy autocomplete feature that can finish partially spelled directory, file, or command names. Just type part of the name and then press Tab. If you've typed enough for the shell to figure out what you mean, the shell finishes the name for you. Otherwise, it just beeps, in which case you can type a few more letters and try again. In some cases, the shell displays a list of items that match what you've typed so far to help you know what to type next.

Wildcards

Wildcards are one of the most powerful features of command shells. With wildcards, you can process all the files that match a particular naming pattern with a single command. For example, suppose that you have a folder with 500 files in it, and you want to delete all the files that contain the letters Y2K and end with `.doc`, which happens to be 50 files. If you try to do this in GNOME, you'll spend ten minutes picking these files out from the list. From a shell, you can delete them all with the single command `rm *Y2K*.doc`.

You can use two basic wildcard characters. An asterisk (*) stands for any number of characters, including zero, and an exclamation mark (!) stands for just one character. Thus, `!Text.doc` matches files with names like `aText.doc`, `xText.doc`, and `4Text.doc`, but not `abcText.doc` or just `Text.doc`. However, `*Text.doc` would match any of those filenames.

You can also use brackets to indicate a range of characters to choose from. For example, `report[123]` matches the files `report1`, `report2`, or `report3`. You can also specify `report[1-5]` to match `report1`, `report2`, report3, report4, or report5. The wildcard r[aeiou]port matches files named raport, report, riport, roport, or ruport. As you can see, the possibilities are almost endless.

Redirection and piping

Redirection and piping are related techniques. *Redirection* lets you specify an alternative destination for output that will be displayed by a command or specify an alternative source for input that should be fed into a command. For example, you can save the results of an ifconfig command to /home/doug/myconfig like this:

```
$ ifconfig > /home/doug/myconfig
```

Here, the greater-than sign (>) is used to redirect the command's console output.

If a command accepts input from the keyboard, you can use input redirection to specify a file that contains the input that you want to feed to the command. For example, you can create a text file named lookup.commands with subcommands for a command such as nslookup. Then, you can feed those scripted subcommands to the nslookup command, like this:

```
$ nslookup < /home/doug/lookup.commands
```

Piping is a similar technique. It takes the console output from one command and feeds it into the next command as input. One of the most common uses of piping is to send the output of a command that displays a lot of information to the more program, which displays the output one page at a time. For example:

```
$ ifconfig | more
```

The vertical bar (|) is often called the *pipe character* because it's the symbol used to indicate piping.

Environment variables

The shell makes several environment variables available to commands. An *environment variable* is a predefined value you can use in your commands to provide commonly used information, such as the name of the current user or the operating system version. You can use an environment variable anywhere in a command by typing $ (dollar sign) followed by the environment variable name. For example, this command

```
$ echo This is $HOSTNAME running on an $HOSTTYPE
```

displays a line such as

```
This is LSERVER running on an i386
```

Table 9-1 lists some of the more useful environment variables that are available to you and your commands.

Table 9-1	Environment Variables
Variable	*Description*
HOME	The current user's home directory
HOSTNAME	The computer's host name
HOSTTYPE	The host computer type
OSTYPE	The operating system
PATH	The search order for executable programs
PROMPT_COMMAND	The command used to generate the prompt
PWD	The present working directory
SHELL	The shell being used
USERNAME	The current username

Shell scripts

A *shell script* is simply a text file that contains one or more commands which you can execute in sequence by running the script. The simplest shell scripts are just lists of commands, but advanced shell scripts can include complicated scripting statements that border on a full-featured programming language.

You can create shell scripts by using any text editor. The easiest text editor to use is gedit, which you can access from the GNOME desktop by choosing Activities ⇨ Applications ⇨ gedit. If you want your friends to think you're a Linux guru, however, take a few moments to learn how to use vi, a powerful text mode editor. To create or edit a file in vi, type the command **vi** followed by a filename. Then, type away. To use a vi command, press Esc(ape) and then type one of the commands listed in Table 9-2.

After you create a shell script, you have to grant yourself execute permission to run the script. For example, to grant yourself permission to run a script named myscript, use this command:

```
$ chmod 755 myscript
```

Table 9-2	Common vi Commands
Command	*Explanation*
i	Enters insert mode so that you can enter text at the cursor location. Move the cursor to the point where you want to enter the text first. When you're finished inserting text, press Esc to return to command mode.
:w	Saves the file. (w stands for write.)
:q	Quit.
:wq	Write and then quit.
:q!	Quit without saving.
/string	Search forward for string.
?string	Search backward for string.
n	Repeat the last search.
u	Undo the previous command.

To run a shell script, you use the sh command and provide the name of the script file. For example:

```
$ sh myscript
```

Running a command with root-level privileges

Many Linux commands perform actions that can only be done by the root user. To avoid the need to switch back and forth between your normal user account and the root user account, you can use the sudo command to perform any command using root-level permissions. To do so, just prefix the command you want to execute with the word sudo. For example:

```
sudo dnf install httpd
```

Here, the command dnf install httpd is executed using root-level permissions.

To use sudo, your Linux account must be configured by the root user to allow root-level access. For more information about how to do that, refer to Chapter 2 of this minibook.

Directory- and File-Handling Commands

Because much of Linux administration involves working with configuration files, you frequently need to use the basic directory- and file-handling commands presented in this section.

The pwd command

This command displays the current directory, which is called the *present working directory* — hence the command name pwd. Here's the syntax:

```
pwd
```

Enter this command, and you get output similar to the following:

```
$ pwd
/home/doug
```

The cd command

The cd command changes the current working directory. The syntax is as follows:

```
cd directory
```

You may want to follow the cd command with a pwd command to make sure that you changed to the right directory. For example:

```
$ cd /etc/mail
$ pwd
/etc/mail
```

To change to a subdirectory of the current directory, omit the leading slash from the directory name. For example:

```
$ pwd
/home
$ cd doug
$ pwd
/home/doug
```

You can also use the double-dot (. .) to represent the parent of the current directory. Thus, to move up one level, use the command cd . ., as follows:

```
$ pwd
/home/doug
$ cd ..
$ pwd
/home
```

The mkdir command

To create a new directory, use the mkdir command. It has the following syntax:

```
mkdir directory
```

Here's an example that creates a subdirectory named `images` in the current directory:

```
$ mkdir images
```

This example creates a directory named `/home/doug/images`:

```
$ mkdir /home/doug/images
```

The rmdir command

The `rmdir` command removes a directory. It has the following syntax:

```
rmdir directory
```

Here's an example:

```
$ rmdir /home/doug/images
```

Here, the `/home/doug/images` directory is deleted. Note that the directory must be empty to be removed, so you have to first delete any files in the directory.

The ls command

The `ls` command lists the contents of the current directory. Here's the syntax:

```
ls [options] directory
```

The following paragraphs describe the more important options for the `ls` command:

- ✦ `-a`: Lists all the files in the directory, including files that start with a period
- ✦ `-c`: Sorts entries by the time the files were last modified
- ✦ `-d`: Lists only directory names
- ✦ `-l`: Displays in long format
- ✦ `-r`: Displays files in reverse order
- ✦ `-R`: Lists the contents of all subdirectories, and subdirectories of subdirectories, and subdirectories of subdirectories of subdirectories; in other words, lists subdirectories recursively
- ✦ `-s`: Displays file sizes

✦ -S: Sorts files by size

✦ -t: Sorts files by timestamp.

✦ -u: Sorts files by the time the files were last accessed.

✦ -X: Sorts files by their extensions.

Without arguments, the ls command lists all the files in the current directory, like this:

```
$ pwd
/etc/mail
$ ls
access          helpfile          Makefile       submit.cf       virtusertable
access.db       local-host-names  sendmail.cf    submit.cf.bak   virtusertable.db
domaintable     mailertable       sendmail.mc    submit.mc
domaintable.db  mailertable.db    statistics     trusted-users
```

You can limit the display to certain files by typing a filename, which can include wildcards. For example:

```
$ ls a*
access          access.db
```

You can also specify the directory that you want to display, like this:

```
$ ls /etc/httpd
conf  conf.d  logs  modules  run
```

To display detailed information about the files in the directory, use the -l switch, as in this example:

```
$ ls /etc/mail/s* -l
-rw-r--r--    1 root     root         57427 Jul 19 16:35 sendmail.cf
-rw-r--r--    1 root     root          5798 Feb 24 16:15 sendmail.mc
-rw-------    1 root     root           628 Jul 24 17:21 statistics
-rw-r--r--    1 root     root         39028 Jul 19 17:28 submit.cf
-r--r--r--    1 root     root         39077 Feb 24 16:15 submit.cf.bak
-rw-r--r--    1 root     root           953 Feb 24 16:15 submit.mc
```

The cp command

The cp command copies files. Here's the basic syntax:

```
cp [options] source-file destination-file
```

The following list describes the more important options for the ls command:

✦ -a: The same as -dpR.

✦ -b: Makes backup copies of existing files before they're overwritten. Sounds like a good plan to me.

- ✦ `-d`: Copies links rather than the files the links point to.
- ✦ `-f`: Removes files that will be overwritten.
- ✦ `-i`: Interactively prompts for each file to be overwritten.
- ✦ `-l`: Creates links to files rather than actually copying file contents.
- ✦ `-p`: Preserves ownership and permissions.
- ✦ `-R`: Copies the contents of subdirectories recursively.
- ✦ `-s`: Creates symbolic links to files rather than actually copying file contents.
- ✦ `-u`: Replaces destination files only if the source file is newer.

To make a copy of a file within the same directory, use `cp` like this:

```
$ cp sendmail.cf sendmail.cf.backup
```

If you want to copy a file to another directory without changing the filename, use `cp` like this:

```
$ cp sendmail.cf /home/doug
```

You can use wildcards to copy multiple files:

```
$ cp send* /home/doug
```

To include files in subdirectories of the source file, use the `-R` switch, like this:

```
$ cp -R /etc/*.cf /home/doug
```

In this example, all files in the `/etc` directory or any of its subdirectories that end with `.cf` are copied to `/home/doug`.

The rm command

The `rm` command deletes files. The syntax is as follows:

```
rm [options] file
```

The options are described in the following paragraphs:

- ✦ `-f`: Removes files that will be overwritten
- ✦ `-i`: Interactively prompts for each file to be overwritten
- ✦ `-R`: Copies the contents of subdirectories recursively

To delete a single file, use it like this:

```
$ rm any.old.file
```

To delete multiple files, use a wildcard:

```
$ rm any.*
```

To delete an entire directory, use the -r switch:

```
$ rm -r /doug/old.files
```

The mv command

The mv command moves files or renames them. In Linux, moving and renaming a file is essentially the same thing. Moving a file changes the file's directory location but leaves its name the same. Renaming a file leaves the file in the same directory but changes the file's name.

The syntax of the mv command is

```
mvp [options] source-file destination
```

The following paragraphs describe the options:

✦ -b: Makes backup copies of existing files before they're overwritten. Still sounds like a good plan to me.

✦ -f: Removes files that will be overwritten.

✦ -i: Interactively prompts for each file to be overwritten.

✦ -u: Replaces destination files only if the source file is newer.

To move a file to another directory, provide a filename for the first argument and a directory for the second, like this:

```
$ mv monthly.report /home/Debbie/
```

To rename a file, provide filenames for both arguments:

```
$ mv monthly.report august.monthly.report
```

The touch command

The touch command is one of the more interesting Linux file management commands. Here's the syntax:

```
touch [options] file
```

Here are some of the options that you can use:

✦ -a: Changes the access time only

✦ -c: Doesn't create files that don't exist

✦ -m: Changes the modification time only

The basic form of the touch command looks like this:

```
$ touch monthly.report
```

If you use touch on an existing file, the touch command changes the modification date of the file. If you use it on a command that doesn't exist, the touch command creates a new, empty file.

The cat command

The cat command displays the contents of a file. It has the following syntax:

```
cat [options] [filename...]
```

The filename is optional. If you omit the filename, the cat command obtains its input from the console, which you can redirect if you want.

And, you can specify more than one filename. If you do, the files are combined to create a single output stream.

Here are some of the options you can use:

✦ -A: Displays new line characters as $, tab characters as ^I, and control characters with a caret (^)

✦ -b: Numbers all nonblank lines as they're displayed

✦ -e: Displays new line characters as $ and control characters with a caret (^)

✦ -E: Displays new line characters as $

✦ -n: Numbers lines as they are displayed

✦ -s: Squeezes multiple spaces down to a single space

✦ -t: Displays tab characters as ^I and control characters with a caret (^)

✦ -T: Displays tab characters as ^I

✦ -v: Shows nonprinting control characters with a caret (^)

Here's a basic example:

```
$ cat /etc/hosts
# Do not remove the following line, or various programs
# that require network functionality will fail.
127.0.0.1       LSERVER localhost.localdomain    localhost
$
```

If you don't provide any filename arguments, the cat command copies text from the keyboard and displays it on the console. You can use the cat command along with output redirection to quickly create a short text file, like this:

```
$ cat >mytext
This is line one.
This is line two.
This is line three.
<ctrl+D>
```

For the last line, press Ctrl+D. This signals the end of the input to the cat command.

Commands for Working with Packages and Services

As a Linux administrator, you frequently need to start and stop services and check the status of installed packages or install new packages. The following sections describe the Linux commands that help you to perform these tasks.

The service command

You use the service command to check the status of services and to start, stop, or restart services. You need to restart a service whenever you make a configuration change in order for your changes to take effect. Here's the basic syntax:

```
service [service] [ start | stop | restart ]
```

The following paragraphs describe some typical uses of the service command:

✦ To check the status of the httpd service (Apache), use this command:

```
$ service httpd status
```

✦ To stop the httpd service:

```
$ service httpd stop
```

✦ To start the `httpd` service:

    $ service httpd start

✦ To restart the `httpd` service:

    $ service httpd restart

The only trick to using the `service` command is that you have to know the name of the service. If you're not sure of the name, you can run the `service` command to display the status of all services, like this:

    $ service --status-all

It will take a few moments to list all the services, but after the command is done, you can scroll through the list to find the service that you're looking for.

Table 9-3 lists some of the more common services.

Table 9-3	Common Linux Services
Service	*Description*
atd	Runs commands scheduled by the `at` command
autof	Automatically mounts file systems
crond	Runs programs at specified times
dhcpd	The DHCP server
finger	The Internet finger service
httpd	The Apache web server
imap	The IMAP mail protocol
imaps	Secure IMAP service (SSL)
ipop3	The POP3 mail protocol
iptables	Automatic packet filtering for firewalls
isdn	ISDN services
named	The BIND DNS server
netf	The network file system
network	Activates and deactivates all network interfaces
nfs	Native Unix/Linux network file sharing
pop3s	Secure POP3 service (SSL)
sendmail	The Sendmail service
smb	The Samba file- and printer-sharing service
snmpd	SNMP
telnet	The Telnet server

The yum and dnf commands

yum, which stands for *Yellowdog Updater Modified*, is a tool for installing and updating packages on a Linux system. Until recently, yum was the preferred way to install packages on a Linux system. One of the chief advantages of yum over earlier package managers is that yum not only installs packages you tell it to install, but also automatically installs any packages that are prerequisites to the packages you ask yum to install.

yum has recently been superseded by a faster package manager called dnf. dnf and yum share pretty much the same command line options, so yum and dnf commands are mostly interchangeable.

Although dnf has many command line options, the most common way to use it is as follows:

```
dnf install package-name
```

For example, to install a package named sendmail, you would use this command:

```
dnf install sendmail
```

Note that installing a package is an action that requires root-level permissions to perform, so you'll usually use dnf or yum along with the sudo command, like this:

```
sudo dnf install sendmail
```

Commands for Administering Users

The following sections describe the Linux commands that you can use to create and manage user accounts from a command shell.

You should log on as root to perform these tasks.

The useradd command

The useradd command creates a user account. Here's the basic syntax for adding a new user:

```
useradd [options] username
```

You can also use this command to change the default options for new users. In that case, the syntax is more like this:

```
useradd -D [options]
```

If you use −D with no options, a list of the current default settings will be shown.

The options are as follows:

✦ -c *comment*: Typically the user's full name

✦ -d *home-dir*: The home directory of the new user

✦ -e *date*: The expiration date for the user

✦ -f *time*: The number of days between logons before the user is considered expired

✦ -g *group*: The initial logon group for the user

✦ -G *groups*: Additional groups the user should belong to

✦ -m: Creates the new user's home directory if it doesn't exist already

✦ -s *shell-path*: Specifies the user's logon shell

The following option is valid only with −D (which sets a default option):

✦ -b *base-dir*: Provides the default base directory if a home directory is not specified

Its most basic form, the useradd command creates a user with default option settings:

```
$ useradd theodore
```

This command creates a user named theodore.

Here's a command that specifies the user's full name in the comment option:

```
$ useradd -c 'Theodore Cleaver' theodore
```

The following command creates a temporary account named ghost that expires on Halloween 2016:

```
$ useradd -e 2016-10-31 ghost
```

If you want to see what the default values are for account options, use the -D option without any other parameters:

```
$ useradd -D
GROUP=100
HOME=/home
INACTIVE=-1
EXPIRE=
SHELL=/bin/bash
SKEL=/etc/skel
```

The usermod command

The `usermod` command modifies an existing user. It has the following syntax:

```
usermod [options] username
```

The options are as follows:

+ `c comment`: Typically the user's full name
+ `-d home-dir`: The home directory of the new user
+ `-e date`: The expiration date for a logon
+ `-f time`: The number of days between logons before the user is considered expired
+ `-g group`: The initial logon group for the user
+ `-G groups`: Additional groups the user should belong to
+ `-m`: Creates the new user's home directory if it doesn't exist already
+ `-s shell-path`: Specifies the user's logon shell
+ `-l`: Locks an account
+ `-u`: Unlocks an account

Here's an example that changes a user's full name:

```
$ usermod -c 'The Beave' theodore
```

The userdel command

The `userdel` command deletes a user. It has a simple syntax:

```
userdel [-r] username
```

If you specify `-r`, the user's home directory is deleted along with the account.

The chage command

The `chage` command modifies date policies for a user's passwords. It has the following syntax:

```
chage [options] username
```

The following paragraphs describe the options you can use:

+ `-m days`: Specifies the minimum number of days allowed between password changes.
+ `-M days`: Specifies the maximum number of days allowed between password changes.

✦ -d *date*: The date of the last password change.

✦ -E *date*: The date on which the account will expire.

✦ -W *days*: The number of days prior to the password expiring that the user will be warned the password is about to expire.

✦ -I *days*: The number of days of inactivity after the password has expired that the account is locked out. Specify 0 to disable this feature.

Here's an example that sets an account to expire on Halloween 2016:

```
$ chage -E 2016-10-31 ghost
```

If you specify a username but no other options, you're prompted to enter each option. This is a lot easier than trying to remember all the switches!

The passwd command

The passwd command changes the password for a user account. Its syntax is

```
passwd [user]
```

If you don't supply a user, the password for the current user is changed.

The passwd command prompts you to enter the new password twice to prevent the possibility of mistyping the password.

The newusers command

The newusers command provides an easy way to create a group of new user accounts. It reads a text file that contains one line for each new user, listing the user's name and password.

Here's the syntax of the newusers command:

```
newusers [filename]
```

If you omit the filename, newusers accepts input from the console.

Suppose that you have a file named /root/island.users that contains these lines:

```
gilligan    ml9jiedr
skipper     1hiecr8u
professor   dr0uxiaf
maryann     choe7rlu
ginger      jiuqled5
mrhowell    j1emoaf1
lovie       zo2priak
```

You can then create these seven stranded user accounts by issuing this command:

```
$ newusers /root/island.users
```

Because the `newusers` file contains unencrypted passwords, you shouldn't leave it lying around. Require these new users to change their passwords immediately and delete the file you used to create the users.

The groupadd command

The `groupadd` command creates a new group. It has the following syntax:

```
groupadd [options] group
```

Although you have several possible options to use, the only one you're likely to need is `-r`, which creates a system group that has special privileges.

Here's an example that creates a group named castaways:

```
$ groupadd castaways
```

That's all you have to do to create a new group. To administer the group, you use the `gpasswd` command.

The groupdel command

The `groupdel` command deletes a group. It has the following syntax:

```
groupdel group
```

Here's an example that deletes a group named castaways:

```
$ groupdel castaways
```

Poof! The group is gone.

The gpasswd command

You use the `gpasswd` command to administer a group. This command has several different syntax options.

To change the group password:

```
gpasswd [ -r | -R ] group
```

To add a user:

```
gpasswd -a user group
```

To remove a user:

```
gpasswd -d user group
```

To create group administrators and/or members:

```
gpasswd [-A administrators...] [-M members... ] group
```

The options are as follows:

- ✦ -r: Removes the password from the group.
- ✦ -R: Disables access to the group via the newgrp command.
- ✦ -a: Adds the specified user to the group.
- ✦ -d: Deletes the specified user from the group.
- ✦ -A: Specifies one or more group administrators. Use commas with no intervening spaces to separate the administrators from each other. Each administrator must be an existing user.
- ✦ -M: Specifies one or more group members. Use commas with no intervening spaces to separate the members from each other. Each member must be an existing user.

The following example adds seven group members and one administrator to a group called castaways:

```
$ gpasswd -A skipper -M skipper,gilligan,professor,maryann,
ginger,mrhowell,lovie castaways
```

If the rest of the group finally decides to throw Gilligan off the island, they can remove him from the group with this command:

```
$ gpasswd -d gilligan castaways
```

Commands for Managing Ownership and Permissions

This section presents the details of the chown and chmod commands, which are the essential tools for assigning file system rights in the Linux environment.

The chown command

The chown command changes the owner of a file. Typically, the user who creates a file is the owner of the file. However, the owner can transfer the file to someone else via this command. The basic syntax of this command is

```
chown user file
```

For example, to change the owner of a file named `rescue.plans` to user professor, use this command:

```
$ chown professor rescue.plans
```

To change ownership of all the files in the directory named `/home/island` to `professor`, use this command:

```
$ chown professor /home/island
```

Issuing the following command would be a really bad idea:

```
$ chown gilligan rescue.plans
```

The chgrp command

Every file has not only an individual owner, but also a group owner. You can change the group ownership by using the `chgrp` command, which has the following basic syntax:

```
chgrp group file
```

For example, to grant the castaways group ownership of the file `rescue.plans`, use this command:

```
$ chgrp castaways rescue.plans
```

To change group ownership of all the files in the directory named `/home/island` to castaways, use this command:

```
$ chgrp castaways /home/island
```

The chmod command

The `chmod` command lets you change the permissions for a Linux file. Before explaining the syntax of the `chmod` command, you need to look at the cryptic way that Linux reports file permissions. Linux grants three different types of permissions — read, write, and execute — for three different scopes: owner, group, and everyone. That's a total of nine permissions.

When you use the `ls` command with the `-l` option, the permissions are shown as a ten-character string that begins with a hyphen if the entry is for a file or a d if the entry is for a directory. Then, the next nine letters are the nine permissions, in this order:

- ✦ Read, write, execute for the owner
- ✦ Read, write, execute for the group
- ✦ Read, write, execute for everyone

The letters r, w, or x appear if the permission has been granted. If the permission is denied, a hyphen appears.

For example, suppose the `ls -l` command lists these permissions:

```
-rw-r--r--
```

You interpret this permission string like this:

+ The first hyphen indicates that this is a file, not a directory.
+ The next three positions are `rw-`. Therefore, the owner has read and write permission on this file, but not execute permission.
+ The next three positions are `r--`. That means the group owner has read permissions but not write or execute permission.
+ The last three positions are also `r--`. That means that everyone else has read permission but not write or execute permission.

The full syntax of the `chmod` command is pretty complex. However, you can do most of what you need to do with this form:

```
chmod specification file
```

Here, `specification` is in the form `u=rwx`, `g=rwx`, or `o=rwx` to set the permissions for the user (owner), group, and others (everyone). You don't have to specify r, w, and x; you just list the permissions that you want to grant. For example, to grant read and write permission for the user to a file named `rescue.plans`, use this command:

```
$ chmod u=rw rescue.plans
```

You can also combine specifications, like this:

```
$ chmod u=rw,g=rw,o=r rescue.plans
```

To revoke all rights for the user, group, or others, don't type anything after the equal sign. For example, this command revokes all rights for others:

```
$ chmod o= rescue.plans
```

Networking Commands

The following sections present Linux commands that are used to display information about the network or configure its settings.

The hostname command

The hostname command simply displays the computer's host name. It has the following syntax:

```
hostname [name]
```

If you use this command without any parameters, the computer's host name is displayed. If you specify a name, the computer's host name is changed to the name you specify.

The ifconfig command

ifconfig displays and sets configuration options for network interfaces. Although you can configure an Ethernet adapter using this command, you'll rarely have to. Linux does a pretty good job of automatically configuring network adapters, and the GNOME-based Network Configuration tool supplied with the Red Hat distribution should be able to handle most network configuration chores. So you'll use ifconfig mostly to display network configuration settings.

The basic syntax for ifconfig is

```
ifconfig interface [address] [netmask mask]
        [broadcast broadcast]
```

Here are the options that you can use on the ifconfig command:

✦ *interface*: The symbolic name for your network adapter. It's typically eth0 for the first Ethernet adapter or eth1 for the second adapter.

✦ *address*: The IP address you want to assign to the interface, such as 192.168.1.100.

✦ *netmask*: The subnet mask to use, such as 255.255.255.0.

✦ *broadcast*: The broadcast, which should be the highest address on the subnet. For example: 192.168.1.255.

If you enter ifconfig without any parameters, the ifconfig command displays the current status of your network adapters, like this:

```
eth0      Link encap:Ethernet  HWaddr 00:20:78:16:E0:6A
          UP BROADCAST RUNNING MULTICAST  MTU:1500  Metric:1
          RX packets:0 errors:0 dropped:0 overruns:0 frame:0
          TX packets:11 errors:0 dropped:0 overruns:0 carrier:0
          collisions:0 txqueuelen:100
          RX bytes:0 (0.0 b)  TX bytes:2916 (2.8 Kb)
          Interrupt:11 Base address:0xd000
```

```
eth1      Link encap:Ethernet  HWaddr 00:40:05:80:51:F3
          inet addr:192.168.3.100  Bcast:192.168.3.255  Mask:255.255.255.0
          UP BROADCAST RUNNING MULTICAST  MTU:1500  Metric:1
          RX packets:2358 errors:0 dropped:0 overruns:0 frame:0
          TX packets:1921 errors:0 dropped:0 overruns:0 carrier:0
          collisions:0 txqueuelen:100
          RX bytes:265194 (258.9 Kb)  TX bytes:424467 (414.5 Kb)
          Interrupt:3 Base address:0xc000
lo        Link encap:Local Loopback
          inet addr:127.0.0.1  Mask:255.0.0.0
          UP LOOPBACK RUNNING  MTU:16436  Metric:1
          RX packets:93707 errors:0 dropped:0 overruns:0 frame:0
          TX packets:93707 errors:0 dropped:0 overruns:0 carrier:0
          collisions:0 txqueuelen:0
          RX bytes:6393713 (6.0 Mb)  TX bytes:6393713 (6.0 Mb)
```

To change the IP address of an adapter, use `ifconfig` like this:

```
$ ifconfig eth0 192.168.1.200
```

The netstat command

The `netstat` command lets you monitor just about every aspect of a Linux server's network functions. This command can generate page after page of interesting information — if you know what it all means.

The two most common reasons to use `netstat` are to display the routing table and to display open TCP/IP connections. The syntax for displaying the routing table is

```
netstat -r
```

This results in a display similar to this:

```
Kernel IP routing table
Destination     Gateway        Genmask          Flags  MSS Window  irtt Iface
192.168.1.0     *              255.255.255.0    U        0 0          0 eth1
192.168.1.0     *              255.255.255.0    U        0 0          0 eth0
127.0.0.0       *              255.0.0.0        U        0 0          0 lo
```

To display TCP/IP connections, use this syntax:

```
netstat -l
```

This results in a display similar to the following:

```
Active Internet connections (only servers)
Proto Recv-Q Send-Q Local Address          Foreign Address    State
tcp       0      0 *:1024                  *:*                LISTEN
tcp       0      0 LSERVER:1025            *:*                LISTEN
tcp       0      0 *:netbios-ssn           *:*                LISTEN
tcp       0      0 *:sunrpc                *:*                LISTEN
tcp       0      0 *:http                  *:*                LISTEN
tcp       0      0 *:x11                   *:*                LISTEN
tcp       0      0 *:ssh                   *:*                LISTEN
tcp       0      0 LSERVER:ipp             *:*                LISTEN
tcp       0      0 LSERVER:smtp            *:*                LISTEN
tcp       0      0 *:https                 *:*                LISTEN
udp       0      0 *:1024                  *:*
udp       0      0 LSERVER:1026            *:*
udp       0      0 192.168.1.20:netbios-ns *:*
udp       0      0 192.168.1.20:netbios-ns *:*
udp       0      0 *:netbios-ns            *:*
udp       0      0 192.168.1.2:netbios-dgm *:*
udp       0      0 192.168.1.2:netbios-dgm *:*
udp       0      0 *:netbios-dgm           *:*
udp       0      0 *:940                   *:*
udp       0      0 *:sunrpc                *:*
udp       0      0 *:631                   *:*
  .
  .
  .
```

From this display, you can tell which Linux services are actively listening on TCP/IP ports.

The ping command

The ping command is the basic troubleshooting tool for TCP/IP. You use it to determine whether basic TCP/IP connectivity has been established between two computers. If you're having any kind of network trouble between two computers, the first troubleshooting step is almost always to see whether the computers can ping each other.

The basic syntax of ping is straightforward:

```
ping [options] address
```

The options can be

+ -c: The number of packets to send. If you omit this, ping continues to send packets until you interrupt it.

+ -d: Floods the network with packets, as many as 100 per second. Use with care!

+ -i: Specifies how many seconds to wait between sending packets. The default is one second. If you're having intermittent connection problems, you may try letting ping run for a while with this option set to a higher value, such as 60, to send a packet every minute.

+ -R: Displays the route the packets take to get to the destination computer.

ping will continue to ping the destination computer until you interrupt it by pressing Ctrl+Z.

You can specify the host to ping by using an IP address, as in this example:

```
$ ping 192.168.1.100
PING 192.168.1.100 (192.168.1.100) 56(84) bytes of data.
64 bytes from 192.168.1.100: icmp_seq=1 ttl=128 time=0.382 ms
64 bytes from 192.168.1.100: icmp_seq=2 ttl=128 time=0.345 ms
64 bytes from 192.168.1.100: icmp_seq=3 ttl=128 time=0.320 ms
64 bytes from 192.168.1.100: icmp_seq=4 ttl=128 time=0.328 ms
```

You can also ping by using a DNS name, as in this example:

```
$ ping www.lowewriter.com
PING www.lowewriter.com (209.68.34.15) 56(84) bytes of data.
64 bytes from www.lowewriter.com (209.68.34.15): icmp_seq=1 ttl=47 time=88.9 ms
64 bytes from www.lowewriter.com (209.68.34.15): icmp_seq=2 ttl=47 time=87.9 ms
64 bytes from www.lowewriter.com (209.68.34.15): icmp_seq=3 ttl=47 time=88.3 ms
64 bytes from www.lowewriter.com (209.68.34.15): icmp_seq=4 ttl=47 time=87.2 ms
```

The route command

The route command displays or modifies the computer's routing table. To display the routing table, use route without any parameters. To add an entry to the routing table, use this syntax:

```
route add [ -net | -host ] address [options]
```

To delete an entry, use this syntax:

```
route del [ -net | -host ] address [options]
```

The available options are as follows:

✦ `netmask` *mask*: Specifies the subnet mask for this entry

✦ `gw` *address*: Specifies the gateway address for this entry

✦ `dev` *if*: Specifies an interface (such as `eth0` or `eth1`) for this entry

If you enter `route` by itself, with no parameters, you'll see the routing table, as in this example:

```
$ route
Kernel IP routing table
Destination     Gateway         Genmask         Flags Metric Ref    Use Iface
192.168.1.0     *               255.255.255.0   U     0      0        0 eth1
192.168.1.0     *               255.255.255.0   U     0      0        0 eth1
169.254.0.0     *               255.255.0.0     U     0      0        0 eth1
127.0.0.0       *               255.0.0.0       U     0      0        0 lo
default         192.168.1.1     0.0.0.0         UG    0      0        0 eth1
```

Suppose that your network has a second router that serves as a link to another private subnet, 192.168.2.0 (subnet mask 255.255.255.0). The interface on the local side of this router is at 192.168.1.200. To add a static route entry that sends packets intended for the 192.168.2.0 subnet to this router, use a command like this:

```
$ route add 192.168.2.0 netmask 255.255.255.0 gw 192.168.1.200
```

The traceroute command

The `traceroute` command displays a list of all the routers that a packet must go through to get from the local computer to a destination on the Internet. Each one of these routers is a *hop*. If you're unable to connect to another computer, you can use `traceroute` to find out exactly where the problem is occurring.

Here's the syntax:

```
traceroute [-i interface] host
```

Although several options are available for the `traceroute` command, the one you're most likely to use is `-i`, which lets you specify an interface. This is useful if your computer has more than one network adapter.

Appendix A: Directory of Useful Websites

Throughout this book, I mention many websites that you can visit to glean more information about various networking topics. This appendix gathers those sites into one convenient location and adds a bunch more that are also worth visiting from time to time. Happy surfing!

Certification

Here are the sites to check out for official certification information:

✦ www.microsoft.com/learning/mcp: Microsoft's certification headquarters

✦ www.comptia.org: Independent certification, including A+, Network+, and Security+

✦ www.ibm.com/certify: IBM's certification home page

✦ www.cisco.com/certification: Cisco's certification home page

✦ www.vmware.com/certification: The place to go for information about certification in VMware tools

✦ www.redhat.com/training/certification: Red Hat's Linux certification home page

Hardware

The following websites are general resources for researching computer hardware:

✦ http://reviews.cnet.com: CNET's reviews section offers reviews on all types of computer hardware, with a special section devoted to networking.

✦ www.hardwarecentral.com: HardwareCentral is another good source for general computer hardware information, reviews, and advice.

✦ www.tomshardware.com: Tom's Hardware Guide is the place to go if you want detailed information about the latest in computer components.

The following manufacturers offer high-end networking products, including servers, routers, switches, and so on:

+ `www.hp.com/servers`: This page is the home page for Hewlett-Packard's server products.

+ `www.dell.com/servers`: This page is the home page for Dell server products.

+ `www.oracle.com/servers`: This page is the home page for Sun servers.

Home and Small-Business Networking

The following websites have general information about home and small-business networking:

+ `www.home-network-help.com`: This excellent website is devoted to helping people get their home networks up and running. The site is loaded with step-by-step procedures and flowcharts.

+ `www.practicallynetworked.com`: This site is a great source of information for home networking, with general networking information, technology backgrounders, product reviews, troubleshooting advice, and more.

+ `www.hometoys.com`: This site provides information on all sorts of gadgets for the home, including networks.

+ `www.ehpub.com`: This page is the home page of EH Publishing, which publishes several magazines about home technology.

+ `www.homepna.org`: This page is the home page of the HomePNA Alliance.

+ `www.linksys.com`: This page is the home page of Linksys, one of the most popular manufacturers of networking devices for homes and small offices, including 10/100BaseT, wireless, and even phone and Powerline devices.

+ `www.netgear.com`: This page is the home page of NETGEAR, which makes home and small-office networking devices, including 10/100BaseT adapters and switches, wireless devices, and phone-line systems.

Linux

The following website has general information about Linux:

+ `www.linux.org`: One of the best overall websites for everything Linux. It's a central source of Linux information and news, and includes many links to Linux distributions and downloadable applications.

Here are the home pages for some of the most popular distributions:

- ✦ `www.redhat.com`: The website of the most popular Linux distribution
- ✦ `www.getfedora.org`: The home page of the Fedora project
- ✦ `www.ubuntu.com`: The website of the popular Ubuntu Linux distribution
- ✦ `www.suse.com`: The SUSE distribution
- ✦ `www.caldera.com`: The Caldera distribution from SCO
- ✦ `www.slackware.com`: Slackware, one of the oldest Linux distributions

Here are the home pages for some popular Linux networking software:

- ✦ `www.isc.org/software/BIND`: The official page for BIND, the most popular DNS name server on the Internet
- ✦ `www.sendmail.org`: Official site for Sendmail, the SMTP mail exchange server
- ✦ `www.apache.org`: Official site for the Apache HTTP server
- ✦ `www.samba.org`: Official site for the Samba file and print server

Magazines

Here are some links to various magazines on networking topics:

- ✦ `www.informationweek.com`: *InformationWeek*
- ✦ `www.infoworld.com`: *InfoWorld*
- ✦ `www.networkcomputing.com`: *Network Computing*
- ✦ `www.windowsitpro.com`: *Windows IT Pro Magazine*
- ✦ `www.2600.com`: *2600 Magazine*
- ✦ `www.linuxjournal.com`: *Linux Journal*
- ✦ `www.linux-mag.com`: *Linux Magazine*

Microsoft

Microsoft's website is vast. Here are some links to a few useful areas within this huge website:

- ✦ `www.microsoft.com`: The entry point for Microsoft's website
- ✦ `www.microsoft.com/windows`: The home page for the Windows family of products

✦ `www.microsoft.com/servers`: The home page for Microsoft server products

✦ `www.microsoft.com/exchange`: The home page for Exchange

✦ `www.microsoft.com/sqlserver`: The home page for SQL Server

✦ `www.microsoft.com/sharepoint`: The home page for SharePoint

✦ `http://technet.microsoft.com`: TechNet, a great source for technical information on Microsoft technologies

✦ `http://support.microsoft.com`: Microsoft's general support site

✦ `www.office365.com`: The home page for Office 365.

Network Standards Organizations

The following websites are useful when you're researching network standards:

✦ `www.ansi.org`: The American National Standards Institute (ANSI), the official standards organization in the United States

✦ `www.ieee.org`: The Institute of Electrical and Electronics Engineers (IEEE), an international organization that publishes several key networking standards, including the official Ethernet standards (known as *IEEE 802.3)*

✦ `www.iso.org`: The International Organization for Standardization (ISO), a federation of more than 100 standards organizations throughout the world

✦ `www.internetsociety.org`: The Internet Society, an international organization for global coordination and cooperation on the Internet

✦ `www.ietf.org`: The Internet Engineering Task Force (IETF), responsible for the protocols that drive the Internet

✦ `www.iana.org`: The Internet Assigned Numbers Authority, which has responsibility for the IP address space

✦ `www.w3c.org`: The World Wide Web Consortium (W3C), an international organization that handles the development of standards for the World Wide Web

✦ `www.rfc-editor.org`: The official repository of RFCs (requests to create new standards), which includes a search facility that lets you look up RFCs by name or keyword

Reference

Several general-purpose and computer-specific reference sites provide encyclopedia-style articles or simple definitions of computer and networking terms. If you aren't sure what some new technology is, start at one of these sites:

✦ `www.webopedia.com`: Webopedia is a great online dictionary of computer and Internet terms. Not sure what *direct sequence spread spectrum* means? Look it up at Webopedia!

✦ `www.wikipedia.org`: Wikipedia is a huge, user-written online encyclopedia.

✦ `www.whatis.com`: Whatis.com is another great dictionary of computer and networking terms.

✦ `www.howstuffworks.com`: This site has general information about many types of technology: computers, automobiles, electronics, science, and more. The computer section provides good low-level introductions to various computer topics, including computer hardware, the Internet, and security.

Search

Search engines are often the first places you turn when you're trying to solve a network problem and need information fast:

✦ `www.google.com`: Google is the most popular search site on the Internet today, with a huge database of websites and newsgroup articles that's constantly updated. Google has a powerful keyword search feature that lets you refine your search as you go.

✦ `www.bing.com`: Microsoft's own search engine is designed to compete with Google.

✦ `www.yahoo.com`: Yahoo!, one of the original website catalogs, is still the best place to go if you want to browse categories rather than search for keywords.

✦ `www.zoo.com`: Zoo is a meta-search tool that searches multiple search engines at the same time.

✦ `www.dogpile.com`: Dogpile is another search-engine aggregator that searches multiple search engines at the same time.

TCP/IP and the Internet

The following sites have interesting information about the Internet:

✦ `www.internic.net`: The InterNIC website is a central point of information for domain registration. Check here for a list of accredited domain registrars.

✦ `www.networksolutions.com`: This site is the home of Network Solutions, the most popular site for registering domain names.

✦ `www.register.com`: Register.com is another domain registration site.

✦ `www.isc.org`: Members of the Internet Systems Consortium are the folks who do the twice-a-year domain survey to try to estimate how big the Internet really is.

For DNS information, try `www.dnsstuff.com`, which lets you perform a variety of DNS lookups to make sure that your DNS zones are set up correctly.

Check these sites to find information about web browsers:

✦ `www.microsoft.com/ie`: The official home page for Internet Explorer.

✦ `www.mozilla.org`: The home of Firefox, a popular alternative web browser. Many users consider Firefox to be the best web browser around.

✦ `www.opera.com`: The home of Opera, another alternative to Internet Explorer.

✦ `http://chrome.google.com`: The home of Google Chrome, Google's popular web browser.

Here are some sites that can do speed tests to let you know how fast your Internet connection is:

✦ `www.speakeasy.net`: An independently operated speed test site

✦ `www.speedtest.net`: Another independently operated speed test site

✦ `speedtest.comcast.net`: A speed test site run by Comcast

✦ `www.att.com/speedtest`: A speed test site run by AT&T

✦ `www.timewarnercable.com/speedtest`: A speed test site run by Time Warner Cable

Wireless Networking

Here are some websites with general information about wireless networking:

✦ `www.wi-fiplanet.com`: Wi-Fi Planet is a large site devoted to news, information, and product reviews for wireless networking.

Here are the websites for the most popular brands of wireless networking products:

✦ `www.linksys.com`: Linksys is a manufacturer of wireless network cards and access points.

✦ `www.netgear.com`: NETGEAR is another manufacturer of wireless components.

✦ `www.dlink.com`: D-Link is yet another manufacturer of inexpensive wireless products.

✦ `www.smc.com`: The home page for SMC, another manufacturer of wireless network products.

✦ `www.meraki.com`: Meraki, owned by Cisco, makes excellent cloud-managed wireless devices.

✦ `www.cisco.com`: Cisco is the place to go for high-end wireless networking.

Smartphones

The following websites contain useful information about various smartphone platforms:

✦ `www.blackberry.com`: The main website for BlackBerry

✦ `www.blackberryforums.com`: A popular discussion-forum website for the BlackBerry platform

✦ `www.microsoft.com/windowsphone`: The home page for the Windows Phone platform

✦ `www.android.com`: The home page for Google's Android platform

✦ `www.apple.com/iphone`: The home page for Apple's iPhone

Appendix B: Glossary

10Base2: A now obsolete type of coax cable that was once the most often used cable for Ethernet networks; also known as *thinnet* or *cheapernet.* The maximum length of a single segment is 185 meters (600 feet). 10base2 is now all but obsolete.

10Base5: The original Ethernet coax cable, now pretty much obsolete; also known as *yellow cable* or *thick cable.* The maximum length of a single segment is 500 meters (1,640 feet).

10BaseT: Twisted-pair cable, commonly used for Ethernet networks; also known as *UTP, twisted pair,* or *twisted sister* (just kidding!). The maximum length of a single segment is 100 meters (330 feet). Of the three Ethernet cable types, this one is the easiest to work with.

100BaseFX: The Ethernet standard for high-speed fiber-optic connections.

100BaseT4: An alternative standard for 100 Mbps Ethernet using four-pair Category-3 cable.

100BaseTX: The leading standard for 100 Mbps Ethernet, which uses two-pair, Category-5 twisted-pair cable.

100VG AnyLAN: A standard for 100 Mbps Ethernet that isn't as popular as 100BaseT. Like 100BaseT, 100VG AnyLAN uses twisted-pair cable.

1000BaseT: A new standard for 1,000 Mbps Ethernet using four-pair, Category-5, unshielded twisted-pair cable. 1000BaseT is also known as *Gigabit Ethernet.*

1 Trillion BaseT: Well, not really. But if current trends continue, we'll get there soon.

802.2: The forgotten IEEE standard. The more glamorous 802.3 standard relies on 802.2 for moral support.

802.3: The IEEE standard known in the vernacular as *Ethernet.*

802.11: The IEEE standard for wireless networking. Popular variants include 802.11a, 802.11ab, 802.11g, 802.11n, and 802.11ac.

8088 processor: The microprocessor chip around which IBM designed its original PC, marking the transition from the Bronze Age to the Iron Age.

80286 processor: *Computo-habilis,* an ancient ancestor of today's modern computers.

80386 processor: The first 32-bit microprocessor chip used in personal computers, long since replaced by newer, faster, 64-bit designs.

80486 processor: The last of Intel's CPU chips to have a number instead of a name. It was replaced years ago by the Pentium processor, which was eventually replaced by the *i* series (i3, i5, i7), marking the return of numbers to Intel's CPUs.

access rights: A list of rights that tells you what you can and can't do with network files or directories.

account: The way by which the network knows who you are and what rights you have on the network. You can't get into the network without one.

acronym: An abbreviation made up of the first letters of a series of words.

Active Directory: The directory service in Windows networks.

Active Server Pages: An Internet feature from Microsoft that enables you to create web pages with scripts that run on the server rather than on the client; also known as *ASP.* The newest version is called *ASP.NET.*

ActiveSync: A Windows component used to synchronize data between computers.

adapter card: An electronic card that you can plug into one of your computer's adapter slots to give it some new and fabulous capability, such as displaying 16 billion colors.

address book: In an email system, a list of users with whom you regularly correspond.

administrator: The big network cheese who's responsible for setting things up and keeping them running. Pray that it's not you. The administrator is also known as the *network manager.*

allocation unit: Windows allocates space to files one allocation unit at a time; the allocation unit typically is 2,048 or 4,096 bytes, depending on the size of the disk. An allocation unit is also known as a *cluster.* Windows Server uses allocation schemes that are more efficient than those in standard Windows.

Android: A popular open-source mobile phone and tablet platform developed by Google.

antispam program: A program that prevents spam email from reaching your inbox.

antivirus program: A program that sniffs out viruses on your network and sends them into exile.

Apache: The most popular web server on the Internet. It comes free with most versions of Linux and is available free for Windows.

appliance: A self-contained computer system that comes preloaded with software to provide a commonly required function on a network. For example, security appliances are often used to provide firewall, antivirus, and antispam protection.

Application layer: The highest layer of the OSI reference model, which governs how software communicates with the network.

archive bit: A flag that's kept for each file to indicate whether the file has been modified since it was last backed up.

ARCnet: An ancient network topology developed by Datapoint and now found only in history books. When my grandchildren are old enough, I'm going to tell them about the first computer network that I was responsible for, which actually used ARCnet and Datapoint minicomputers.

attributes: Characteristics that are assigned to files. DOS alone provides four attributes: system, hidden, read-only, and archive. Network operating systems generally expand the list of file attributes.

auto attendant: A feature of PBX systems that eliminates or reduces the need for human operators.

backbone: A trunk cable used to tie sections of a network together.

backup: A copy of your important files made for safekeeping in case something happens to the original files — something you should make every day.

banner: A fancy page that's printed between print jobs so that you can easily separate jobs from one another.

batch file: A file that contains one or more commands that are executed together as a set. You create the batch file by using a text editor and run the file by typing its name at the command prompt.

Bayesian filter: A type of spam filter that can be trained to identify spam emails.

benchmark: A repeatable test you use to judge the performance of your network. The best benchmarks are the ones that closely duplicate the type of work you routinely do on your network.

BES: See *BlackBerry Enterprise Server (BES)*.

BlackBerry: A popular smartphone made by BlackBerry.

BlackBerry Enterprise Server (BES): Software that runs on a Windows server to enable BlackBerry devices to synchronize with Microsoft Exchange.

Bluetooth: (1) A Viking king who united Denmark and Norway in the tenth century. (2) A wireless networking protocol for short-range networks, used mostly for devices such as wireless keyboards, mice, and cellphones.

bot: A program that runs automated tasks over the Internet. Many bots are malicious in nature, prowling the web looking for information they can steal.

bottleneck: The slowest link in your network, which causes work to get jammed up. The first step in improving network performance is identifying the bottlenecks.

bridge: Not the popular card game, but a device that enables you to link two networks together. Bridges are smart enough to know which computers are on which side of the bridge, so they allow only those messages that need to get to the other side to cross the bridge. This device improves performance on both sides of the bridge.

broadband: A high-speed connection used for wide-area networking.

broadcast domain: In a network, a collection of nodes that can broadcast packets to one another via the data link layer.

buffer: An area of memory that holds data en route to somewhere else. A hard drive buffer, for example, holds data as it travels between your computer and the hard drive.

bus: A type of network topology in which network nodes are strung out along a single run of cable called a *segment.* 10Base2 networks used a bus topology. *Bus* also refers to the row of expansion slots within your computer.

cable tie: Little strips of plastic that are especially handy for securing cables or bundling them together.

cache: A sophisticated form of buffering in which a large amount of memory is set aside to hold data so that it can be accessed quickly.

Category 3: An inexpensive form of unshielded twisted-pair (UTP) cable that is suitable only for 10 Mbps networks (10BaseT). Avoid using Category 3 cable for new networks.

Category 5: The higher grade of UTP cable that is suitable for 100 Mbps networks (100BaseTX) and Gigabit Ethernet (1000BaseT).

Category 5e: An enhanced version of Cat 5e that is suitable for Power over Ethernet (PoE). Cat-5e is the lowest grade Ethernet cable you should install.

Category 6: An even higher grade of UTP cable that's more reliable than Category 5 cable for Gigabit Ethernet.

CD-ROM: A high-capacity disc that uses optical technology to store data in a form that can be read but not written over.

Centrex: A type of phone system similar to a PBX, except that the system is located on the phone company's premises, not on a customer's premises.

Certified Network Dummy: Someone who knows nothing about networks but nevertheless gets the honor of installing one; also known as *CND*.

chat: What you do on the network when you talk live with another network user.

Chaucer: A dead English dude.

CHKDSK: A DOS command that checks the recordkeeping structures of a DOS hard drive for errors.

circuit: An end-to-end connection between transmitters and receivers, typically in phone systems.

click: What you do in Windows to get things done.

client: A computer that has access to the network but doesn't share any of its own resources with the network. See also ***server.***

client/server: A vague term meaning roughly that the workload is split between a client computer and a server computer.

cloud: A popular term for the Internet, with the added connotation of being able to solve all your problems, prevent world hunger, and cure cancer.

cloud computing: An approach to networking in which certain elements of a network that were traditionally implemented within a LAN (such as file storage, backup, or email services) are instead implemented remotely via the Internet.

Clouseau: The most dangerous man in all of France. Some people say he only plays the fool.

cluster: See *allocation unit.*

coaxial cable: A type of cable that contains two conductors. The center conductor is surrounded by a layer of insulation, which is then wrapped by a braided-metal conductor and an outer layer of insulation.

computer name: A unique name assigned to each computer on a network.

Cone of Silence: A running gag on the old TV series *Get Smart* in which a security device would be lowered over two people who needed to have a secure conversation. Unfortunately, the Cone of Silence worked so well that the people in it couldn't hear each other. (Anyone outside the Cone of Silence, however, could easily hear what the people in the cone were saying.)

console: In Windows, Linux, and many other operating systems, a text-mode command prompt.

Control Panel: In Windows, an application that enables you to configure various aspects of the Windows operating system.

CPU: *Central processing unit,* the brains of the computer.

crimp tool: A special tool used to attach connectors to cables. No network manager should be without one. Try not to get your fingers caught in it.

crossover cable: A cable used to connect two Ethernet devices together.

CSMA/CD: *Carrier Sense Multiple Access with Collision Detection,* the traffic-management technique used by Ethernet.

daisy-chain: A way of connecting computer components in which the first component is connected to the second, which is connected to the third, and so on. In Ethernet, you can daisy-chain hubs together.

DAT: *Digital audiotape,* a type of tape often used for network backups.

Data Link layer: The second layer of the OSI model, responsible for transmitting bits of data over the network cable.

dedicated server: A computer used exclusively as a network server.

delayed write: A hard-drive-caching technique in which data written to the hard drive is placed in cache memory and actually written to the hard drive later.

dial tone: The distinctive tone produced on a phone system to indicate that the system is ready to accept a call.

DID: *Direct Inward Dialing,* a feature of PBX systems that lets you associate an external phone number with an extension on the PBX system.

differential backup: A type of backup in which only the files that have changed since the last full backup are backed up.

DIP switch: A bank of switches used to configure an old-fashioned adapter card. Modern cards configure themselves automatically, so DIP switches aren't required. See also *jumper block.*

Direct Inward Dialing: See *DID.*

directory hash: A popular breakfast food enjoyed by Linux administrators.

disk: A device (also known as a *hard drive)* that stores information magnetically. A hard drive is permanently sealed in an enclosure and has a capacity usually measured in thousands of megabytes, also known as *gigabytes.*

distribution: A publicly available version of the Linux operating system. There are many distributions. One of the most popular is Fedora.

DNS: See *Domain Name System (DNS).*

domain: (1) In a Windows network, one or more network servers that are managed by a single network directory. (2) In the Internet, a name assigned to a network.

Domain Name System (DNS): The naming system used on the Internet, in which a network is given a domain name and individual computers are given host names.

DOS: *Disk Operating System,* the original operating system for IBM and IBM-compatible computers.

dot-matrix printer: A prehistoric type of printer that works by applying various-colored pigments to the walls of caves. Once the mainstay printer for PCs, dot-matrix printers have given way to laser printers and inkjet printers. High-speed matrix printers still have their place on the network, though, and matrix printers have the advantage of being able to print multipart forms.

dumb terminal: Back in the heyday of mainframe computers, a monitor and keyboard attached to the central mainframe. All the computing work occurred at the mainframe; the terminal only displayed the results and sent input typed at the keyboard back to the mainframe.

DVD drive: A type of optical drive similar to a CD-ROM drive but with much higher storage capacity.

Eddie Haskell: The kid who's always sneaking around, poking his nose into other people's business, and generally causing trouble. Every network has one.

editor: (1) A program for creating and changing text files. (2) A person who translates poorly written technical prose into understandable English.

email: Messages that are exchanged with other network users.

emoticon: A shorthand way of expressing emotions in email and chats by combining symbols to create smiles, frowns, and so on.

encryption: A security technique in which data is stored in an encoded (encrypted) form that can be decoded (or decrypted) only if the key used to encrypt the data is known.

enterprise computing: A trendy term that refers to a view of an organization's complete computing needs rather than just a single department's or group's needs.

Ethernet: The World's Most Popular Network Standard.

ETLA: *Extended Three-Letter Acronym,* an acronym with four letters. See also *TLA.*

Exchange Server: The software that handles email services on a Windows server.

false negative: With regards to spam, email that is mistakenly identified as legitimate when it's actually spam.

false positive: With regards to spam, email that is mistakenly identified as spam when it's actually legitimate.

Fast Ethernet: 100 Mbps Ethernet; also known as *100BaseT* or *100BaseTX.* This used to be considered fast; today, Fast Ethernet is actually incredibly slow.

FAT: *File Allocation Table,* a recordkeeping structure once used on DOS and Windows computers to keep track of the location of every file on a hard drive.

FAT32: An improved way of keeping track of hard drive files that can be used with Windows 98 and later.

FDDI: *Fiber Distributed Data Interface,* a 100 Mbps network standard used with fiber-optic backbone. When FDDI is used, FDDI/Ethernet bridges connect Ethernet segments to the backbone.

Fedora: A popular distribution of Linux.

fiber-optic cable: A blazingly fast network cable that transmits data using light rather than electricity. Fiber-optic cable is often used as the backbone in large networks, especially where great distances are involved.

file rights: The capability of a particular network user to access specific files on a network server.

file server: A network computer containing hard drives that are available to network users.

filter: A software component that analyzes email to determine if the email is spam.

firewall: A special type of router that connects a LAN to the Internet while preventing unauthorized Internet users from accessing the LAN.

fish tape: A gadget that helps you pull cable through walls.

forest: A group of Active Directory domains.

FTP: *File Transfer Protocol,* a method for retrieving files from the Internet.

full backup: A backup of all the files on a hard drive, whether or not the files have been modified since the last backup. See also *differential backup.*

gateway: A device that connects dissimilar networks. Gateways often connect Ethernet networks to mainframe computers or to the Internet.

GB: Gigabyte, roughly a billion bytes of hard drive storage (1,024MB, to be precise). See also *K, MB,* and *TB.*

generation backup: A backup strategy in which several sets of backup disks or tapes are retained; sometimes called *grandfather-father-son.*

generation gap: What happens when you skip one of your backups.

glass house: The room where the mainframe computer is kept. It's symbolic of the mainframe mentality, which stresses bureaucracy, inflexibility, and heavy iron.

GNOME: A graphical user interface that's popular on Linux systems.

group account: A type of security account that lets you group user accounts that have similar access rights.

guest: A user account that has no privileges. The guest account is designed to provide minimal network access to users who don't have a regular network account.

guru: Anyone who knows more about computers than you do.

HAL: (1) The evil computer in the classic science-fiction movie *2001: A Space Odyssey.* (2) See *Hardware Abstraction Layer.*

Hardware Abstraction Layer: A layer of software that isolates physical devices from software that uses those devices.

hotspot: An area that has access to a public wireless network. Hotspots are commonly found in airports, hotels, and trendy coffee shops.

HTML: *HyperText Markup Language,* the language used to compose pages that can be displayed via the World Wide Web.

HTTP: *HyperText Transfer Protocol,* the protocol used by the World Wide Web for sending HTML pages from a server computer to a client computer.

HTTPS: A secure form of HTTP used to transmit sensitive data such as credit-card numbers.

hub: In Ethernet, a now obsolete device that is used with 10BaseT and 100BaseT cabling to connect computers to the network. Hubs have been replaced by switches. See also *switch.*

hypervisor: Software that manages the execution of virtual machines in a virtualization environment.

I/O port address: Every I/O device in a computer — including network interface cards — must be assigned a unique address. In the old days, you had to configure the port address by using DIP switches or jumpers. Newer network cards automatically configure their own port addresses so that you don't have to mess with switches or jumper blocks.

i7 processor: A popular multicore processor made by Intel. (Variants include i3 and i5.)

IACI: Acronym for *International Association of the Computer Impaired.*

IEEE: *Institute of Electrical and Electronics Engineers,* where they send computer geeks who've had a few too many parity errors.

IIS: *Internet Information Services*, Microsoft's web server. IIS is included with all versions of Windows Server.

incremental backup: A type of backup in which only the files that have changed since the last backup are backed up. Unlike a differential backup, an incremental backup resets each file's archive bit as it backs it up. See also *archive bit, differential backup,* and *full backup.*

inkjet printer: A type of printer that creates full-color pages by spraying tiny jets of ink onto paper.

Internet: A humongous network of networks that spans the globe and gives you access to just about anything you could ever hope for, provided that you can figure out how to work it.

Internet Explorer: Microsoft's popular web browser.

interoperability: Providing a level playing field for incompatible networks to work together, kind of like NAFTA.

intranet: A network that resembles the Internet but is accessible only within a company or organization. Most intranets use the familiar World Wide Web interface to distribute information to company employees.

IP address: A string of numbers used to address computers on the Internet. If you enable TCP/IP on your network, you must provide an IP address for each computer on the network.

iPhone: A popular smartphone developed by Apple, best known for popularizing the trendy business of capitalizing the sEcond letter of words instead of the first.

ISA bus: *Industry Standard Architecture,* a once-popular type of expansion bus for accommodating adapter cards, now replaced by PCI.

ISDN: A digital telephone connection that lets you connect to the Internet at about twice the speed of a regular phone connection. It was once popular, but now, more cost-effective forms of high-speed Internet connections are available.

ISO: Acronym for *International Organization for Standardization.* Don't ask why the abbreviation is *ISO* instead of *IOS.*

ISP: *Internet service provider,* a company that provides access to the Internet for a fee.

Java: A programming language popular on the Internet.

JavaScript: A popular scripting language that can be used on web pages.

jumper block: A device used to configure an old-fashioned adapter card. To change the setting of a jumper block, you remove the jumper from one set of pins and place it on another.

K: Kilobytes, roughly one thousand bytes (1,024, to be precise). See also *GB, MB,* and *TB.*

Kerberos: (1) The mythical three-headed dog that guards the gates of Hades. (2) A network security protocol that authenticates users when they log on and grants the user a ticket that allows him or her to access resources throughout the network.

LAN: *Local area network* — what this book is all about.

LAN Manager: An obsolete network operating system that Microsoft used to sell. Microsoft long ago put all its networking eggs in the Windows basket, so LAN Manager exists only on isolated islands along with soldiers who are still fighting World War II.

laser printer: A high-quality printer that uses lasers and photon torpedoes to produce beautiful output.

Lemon-Pudding layer: A layer near the middle of the OSI reference model that provides flavor and moistness.

Linux: An open-source version of the Unix operating system that's popular as a network server.

LLC sublayer: The *logical link control sublayer* of layer 2 of the OSI model. The LLC is addressed by the IEEE 802.2 standard.

local area network: See *LAN*.

local resources: Disk drives, printers, and other devices that are attached directly to a workstation rather than accessed via the network.

log in: Same as *log on*.

log on: The process of identifying oneself to the network (or a specific network server) and gaining access to network resources.

log out: The process of leaving the network. When you log out, any network drives or printers you were connected to become unavailable to you.

logon name: In a Windows network, the name that identifies a user uniquely to the network; same as *username* or *user ID*.

logon script: A batch file that is executed when a user logs on to a Windows domain.

Mac: A popular alternative to Windows, made by Apple.

MAC Address: A unique network address given to every device ever manufactured.

MAC sublayer: The *media access control* sublayer of layer 2 of the OSI model. The MAC is addressed by the IEEE 802.3 standard.

mail server: The server computer on which email messages are stored. This same computer also may be used as a file and print server, or it may be dedicated as a mail server.

mainframe: A huge computer kept in a glass house on raised floors and cooled with liquid nitrogen. The cable that connects the hard drives to the CPU weighs more than most PCs.

mapping: Assigning unused drive letters to network drives or unused printer ports to network printers. See also *redirection.*

MB: Megabytes, roughly one million bytes (1,024K, to be precise). See also *K, GB,* and *TB.*

memory: The electronic storage where your computer stores data that's being manipulated and programs that are running. See also *RAM.*

metaphor: A literary construction suitable for Shakespeare and Steinbeck but a bit overused by writers of computer books.

Metro: The original name for Windows 8 UI, a new graphical user interface introduced with Windows 8, optimized for use on touchscreen devices.

MMC: *Microsoft Management Console,* the primary management tool used to configure Windows features.

modem: A device that converts signals the computer understands to signals that can be accurately transmitted over the phone to another modem, which converts the signals back to their original form. Computers use modems to talk to each other. *Modem* is an abbreviation of *modulator–demodulator.*

mouse: The device used to move a pointer around on a screen. *Hint:* Don't pick it up and talk into it like Scotty did in *Star Trek IV.* That's very embarrassing, especially if you've traveled millions of miles to get here.

Mr. McFeeley: The nerdy-looking mailman on *Mister Rogers' Neighborhood.* He'd make a great computer geek. Speedy delivery!

multiboot: A technique that lets you install two or more operating systems on a single computer. When you power up a computer that uses multiboot, you must select which of the installed operating systems you want to boot.

MySQL: An open-source SQL database server for Linux systems.

NAS: *Network Accessible Storage,* a popular form of data storage in which a single storage appliance operates as an independent file server attached to a network.

.NET: A Windows application environment that promises to simplify the task of creating and using applications for Windows and for the web.

NetBIOS: *Network Basic Input/Output System,* a high-level networking standard developed by IBM and used by most peer-to-peer networks. It can be used with NetWare as well.

NetWare: A popular network operating system, the proud child of Novell, Inc.

NetWare Directory Services: A feature of NetWare first introduced with Version 4, in which the resources of the servers are pooled together to form a single entity.

network: What this book is about. For more information, see Books I through IX.

network drive: A drive that resides somewhere out in the network rather than on your own computer.

network interface card: An adapter card that lets the computer attach to a network cable; also known as *NIC.*

Network layer: One of the layers somewhere near the middle of the OSI reference model. It addresses the interconnection of networks.

network manager: Hope that it's someone other than you.

Network Neighborhood: An icon used in older versions of Windows that enables you to access network servers and resources. In newer Windows versions, this icon is known as *My Network Places, Network Places,* or just *Network.*

network operating system: An operating system for networks, such as Linux or Windows Server 2003; also known as *NOS.*

Network Places: An icon on the Windows Vista desktop that enables you to access network servers and resources. (In older versions of Windows, this icon is known as *Network Neighborhood* or *My Network Places.*)

network resource: A disk drive, printer, or other device that's located in a server computer and shared with other users. By contrast, a *local resource* is located in a user's computer.

newsgroup: Internet discussion groups in which people leave messages that can be read and responded to by other Internet users.

NIC: See *network interface card.*

node: A device on the network, typically a computer or printer. A router is also a node.

NOS: See *network operating system.*

NTFS: A special type of disk format that you can use on Windows Server and Windows XP hard drives for improved performance and security.

obfuscation: A security technique that relies on using obscure names for security objects or particular user accounts. Avoiding obvious user account names can slow would-be intruders.

octet: A group of eight bits. In an IP address, each octet of the address is represented by a decimal number from 0 to 255.

offline: Not available on the network.

online: Available on the network.

operator: A user who has control of operational aspects of the network but doesn't necessarily have the power to grant or revoke access rights, create user accounts, and so on.

organizational unit: A grouping of objects in an Active Directory domain.

OSI: The agency Lee Majors worked for in *The Six Million Dollar Man;* also the *Open System Interconnection* reference model, a seven-layer fruitcake framework upon which networking standards are hung.

Outlook: A mail client from Microsoft, part of the Microsoft Office suite.

package: In Linux, a software component that can be separately installed and configured.

packet filter: A security technique used by firewalls. The firewall examines each packet that passes through it and blocks certain types of packets while allowing others to pass.

packet sniffer: See *protocol analyzer.*

packet: A manageable chunk of data sent over the network. The size and makeup of a packet (also known as a frame) are determined by the protocol being used.

parallel port: An all but obsolete type of data port that was used to connect printers. Parallel ports send data over eight "parallel" wires, one byte at a time. See also *serial port* and *USB.*

partition: (1) In disk management, a division of a single hard drive into several smaller units that are treated by the operating system as though they were separate drives. (2) In Hyper-V, the isolated space in which a virtual machine runs.

password: The only thing protecting your files from an impostor masquerading as you. Keep your password secret, and you'll have a long and happy life.

patch cable: A short cable used to connect a computer to a wall outlet, or one running from a patch panel to a hub.

PBX: *Private Branch Exchange,* a phone system that manages shared access to one or more phones (called *extensions* or *stations)* to a limited number of external phone lines.

PCI: *Peripheral Component Interconnect,* the high-speed bus design found in modern Pentium computers.

peer-to-peer network: A network in which any computer can be a server if it wants to be, kind of like the network version of the Great American Dream. You can easily construct peer-to-peer networks by using Windows.

permissions: Rights that have been granted to a particular user or group of users enabling them to access specific files.

Physical layer: The lowest layer of the OSI reference model (whatever that is). It refers to the parts of the network you can touch: cables, connectors, and so on.

ping: A program that determines whether another computer is reachable. The ping program sends a message to the other computer and waits for a reply. If the reply is received, the other computer is reachable.

plenum cable: Fire-retardant cable that has a special Teflon coating.

pocket protector: A status symbol among computer geeks.

port: A connector on the back of your computer that you can use to connect a device such as a printer, modem, mouse, and so on.

PowerShell: A powerful command-line environment for managing Windows computers.

PPP: *Point-to-Point Protocol,* the most common way of connecting to the Internet for World Wide Web access.

Presentation layer: The sixth layer of the OSI reference model, which handles data conversions, compression, decompression, and other menial tasks.

print job: A report, letter, memo, or other document that has been sent to a network printer but hasn't printed yet. Print jobs wait patiently in the queue until a printer agrees to print them.

Print Manager: In old-style Windows (Windows 3.1 and Windows for Workgroups), the program that handles print spooling.

print queue: The line that print jobs wait in until a printer becomes available.

print server: A computer that handles network printing or a device such as a JetDirect, which enables the printer to attach directly to the network.

protocol: (1) The droid C-3PO's specialty. (2) The rules of the network game. Protocols define standardized formats for data packets, techniques for detecting and correcting errors, and so on.

protocol analyzer: A program that monitors packets on a network; also called a *packet sniffer.*

punch-down block: A gadget for quickly connecting a bunch of wires, used in telephone and network wiring closets.

queue: A list of items waiting to be processed. The term usually refers to the list of print jobs waiting to be printed, but networks have lots of other types of queues as well.

RAID: *Redundant Array of Independent Disks,* a bunch of hard drives strung together and treated as though they were one drive. The data is spread out over several drives, and one of the drives keeps checking information so that if any one of the other drives fails, the data can be reconstructed.

RAM: *Random access memory,* your computer's memory chips.

RDC: See *Remote Desktop Connection.*

RDP: See *Remote Desktop Protocol.*

redirection: One of the basic concepts of networking, in which a device, such as a disk drive or printer, appears to be a local device but actually resides on the network. The networking software on your computer intercepts I/O requests for the device and redirects them to the network.

Registry: The file where Windows keeps its configuration information.

Remote Desktop Connection: A Windows feature that lets you log on to a Windows server from a remote computer so that you can manage it without physically going to the server.

Remote Desktop Protocol: The protocol used to enable Remote Desktop Connection.

Remote Installation Service: See *RIS.*

repeater: A device that strengthens a signal so that it can travel on. Repeaters are used to lengthen the cable distance between two nodes. A *multiport repeater* is the same as a *hub.*

Resilient File System (ReFS): A new file system, introduced in Windows Server 2012, that improves on the older NTFS file system.

resource: A hard drive, hard drive directory, printer, modem, CD-ROM, or other device that can be shared on the network.

ring: A type of network topology in which computers are connected to one another in a way that forms a complete circle. Imagine the Waltons standing around the Thanksgiving table holding hands, and you have the idea of a ring topology.

RIS: *Remote Installation Service,* a feature of Windows Server operating systems that lets you install from a remote location without actually being present at the server.

RJ-11: The kind of plug used by phone-system cabling.

RJ-45: The kind of plug used by 10BaseT and 100BaseT networks. It looks kind of like a modular phone plug, but it's bigger.

root: (1) The highest-level directory in a file system. (2) The administrator account in Linux.

root server: One of 13 powerful DNS servers located throughout the world that provide the core of the Internet's DNS service.

router: A device that interfaces two networks and controls how packets are exchanged between them. Routers are typically used to link a local Ethernet network to a broadband Internet connection.

Samba: A program that runs on a Linux server, allowing the Linux computer to work as a file and print server in a Windows network.

SAN: *Storage Area Network,* a type of data storage in which storage devices are networked together, usually with high-speed fiber connections.

SATA: *Serial AT Attachment,* the most common type of hard drive interface in use today, popular because of its low cost and flexibility. For server computers, SCSI is the preferred drive interface. See also *SCSI.*

ScanDisk: A Windows command that examines your hard drive for physical defects.

scheduling software: Software that schedules meetings of network users, which works only if all network users keep their calendars up to date.

scope: In DHCP, a range of IP addresses that a DCHP server manages.

SCSI: *Small Computer System Interface,* a connection used mostly for hard drives but also suitable for CD-ROM drives, tape drives, and just about anything else. SCSI is also the winner of the Acronym Computer Geeks Love to Pronounce Most Award.

segment: A single-run cable, which may connect more than two computers, with a terminator on each end.

Sendmail: An email server used on Unix and Linux systems. By some estimates, 70 percent or more of all mail on the Internet is handled by a version of Sendmail.

serial port: A port normally used to connect a modem or mouse to a DOS-based computer, sometimes called a *communications port.* See also *parallel port.*

server: A computer that's on the network and shares resources with other network users. The server may be *dedicated,* which means that its sole purpose in life is to provide service for network users, or it may be used as a client as well. See also *client.*

Service Pack: A collection of patches that are bundled together to bring an operating system up to a particular service level.

Session layer: A layer somewhere near the middle of the beloved OSI reference model that deals with sessions between network nodes.

SFT: *System Fault Tolerance,* a set of networking features designed to protect the network from faults, such as stepping on the line (known as a *foot fault).*

share name: A name that you assign to a network resource when you share it. Other network users use the share name to access the shared resource.

shared folder: A network server hard drive or a folder on a server hard drive that has been shared so that other computers on the network can access it.

shared resource: A resource, such as a hard drive or printer, that is made available to other network users.

SharePoint: A Microsoft software system that allows users to collaborate via the web.

shielded twisted pair: Twisted-pair cable with shielding, used mostly for Token Ring networks. Also known as *STP*. See also ***twisted pair.***

SMB: *Server Message Block,* the protocol that enables file sharing on Windows networks.

smiley: A face made from various keyboard characters; often used in email messages to convey emotion. : -)

SNA: *Systems Network Architecture,* a networking standard developed by IBM that dates from the mid-Mainframerasic Period, approximately 65 million years ago. SNA is used by fine IBM mainframe and AS/400 minicomputers everywhere.

sneakernet: The cheapest form of network, in which users exchange files by copying them to discs and walking them between computers.

SNMP: *Simple Network Management Protocol,* a standard for exchanging network management information between network devices that is anything but simple.

spam: Unsolicited and unwanted email.

spooling: A printing trick in which data that is intended for a printer is actually written to a temporary hard drive file and later sent to the printer.

SQL: *Structured Query Language,* a popular method of organizing and accessing information in a database.

SQL Server: Microsoft's database manager, which implements SQL databases.

SSID: A name that identifies a wireless network.

star: A type of network topology in which each node is connected to a central wiring hub. This topology gives the network a starlike appearance.

stateful packet inspection: An intelligent type of packet filtering that examines packets in groups rather than individually.

station: In a PBX system, a telephone that can be used for internal or external calls; also known as an *extension*.

subnet mask: A bit pattern used to determine which bits of an IP address represent the subnet.

subnetting: An IP addressing technique that designates the first *n* bits of an IP address as the subnet address and the remaining bits as the host address.

switch: An efficient type of hub that sends packets only to the port that's connected to the packet's recipient rather than sending packets to all the ports, as a simple hub does.

System Fault Tolerance: See *SFT*.

tape drive: The best way to back up a network server. Tape drives have become so inexpensive that even small networks should have one.

task: For a technically accurate description, enroll in a computer science graduate course. For a layperson's understanding of what a task is, picture the guy who used to spin plates on *The Ed Sullivan Show*. Each plate is a task. The poor guy had to move frantically from plate to plate to keep them all spinning. Computers work the same way. Each program task is like one of those spinning plates; the computer must service each one periodically to keep it going.

TB: Terrazzo bytes, imported from Italy; approximately one trillion bytes (1,024GB, to be precise). (Just kidding about terrazzo bytes. Actually, TB stands for terabytes.) See also *GB, K,* and *MB.*

TCP/IP: *Transmission Control Protocol/Internet Protocol,* the protocol used by the Internet.

terminator: (1) The little plug you have to use at each end of a segment of thin coax cable (10BaseT). (2) The former governor of California.

thinnet: See *10Base2.*

three-letter acronym: See *TLA*.

time sharing: A technique used on mainframe computers to enable several users to access the computer at the same time.

time-out: How long the print server waits while receiving print output before deciding that the print job has finished.

TLA: Three-letter acronym, such as FAT (File Allocation Table), DUM (Dirty Upper Memory), and HPY (Heuristic Private Yodel).

token: The thing that gets passed around the network in a Token Ring topology. See also *Token Ring*.

Token Ring: A network that's cabled in a ring topology in which a special packet called a *token* is passed from computer to computer. A computer must wait until it receives the token before sending data over the network. (*Note:* Do not confuse it with the Tolkien ring, which could mean the ruin of Middle Earth.)

top-level domain: In DNS, a domain that appears immediately beneath the root domain. The common top-level domains include com, net, org, edu, gov, mil, and int.

topology: The shape of the network; how its computers and cables are arranged. See also *bus, star,* and *ring.*

touchscreen: A monitor that responds to a user's touch.

transceiver: A doohickey that connects a network interface card (NIC) to a network cable. A transceiver is always required to connect a computer to the network, but 10Base2 and 10BaseT NICs have built-in transceivers. Transceivers were originally used with yellow cable. You can also get transceivers that convert an AUI port to 10BaseT.

Transport layer: One of those layers somewhere near the middle of the OSI reference model that addresses the way data is escorted around the network.

Trojan horse: A program that looks interesting but turns out to be something nasty, like a hard-drive reformatter.

trust: A relationship between domains in which one domain (the *trusting domain)* honors the information in the other domain (the *trusted domain).*

trustee rights: In NetWare, rights that have been granted to a particular user or group of users enabling them to access specific files.

twisted pair: A type of cable consisting of one or more pairs of wires that are twisted in a certain way to improve the cable's electrical characteristics. See also *unshielded twisted pair* and *shielded twisted pair.*

uninterruptible power supply: See *UPS.*

unshielded twisted pair: Twisted-pair cable that doesn't have a heavy metal shield around it. This type of cable (also known as *UTP)* is used for 10BaseT networks. See also *twisted pair.*

UPS: *Uninterruptible power supply,* a gizmo that switches to battery power whenever the power cuts out. The *Enterprise* didn't have one of these, which is why the lights always went out until Spock could switch to auxiliary power.

URL: *Uniform Resource Locator,* a fancy term for an Internet address. URLs are those familiar "dot" addresses, such as www-dot-microsoft-dot-com or www-dot-dummies-dot-com.

USB: A high-speed serial interface that is found on most new computers. USB can be used to connect printers, scanners, mice, keyboards, network adapters, and other devices.

user ID: The name by which you're known to the network.

user profile: The way Windows keeps track of each user's desktop settings, such as window colors, wallpaper, screen savers, Start-menu options, favorites, and so on.

user rights: Network actions that a particular network user is allowed to perform after he or she has logged on to the network. See also *file rights.*

users' group: A local association of computer users, sometimes with a particular interest, such as networking.

UTP: See *unshielded twisted pair.* See also *10BaseT.*

VBScript: A scripting language that can be used to add fancy features to web pages or create macros for Microsoft Office programs.

VGA: *Video Graphics Array,* an old but still used standard in video monitors.

virtual disk: A virtualized disk resource that can be allocated to a virtual machine.

virtual machine: A simulated computer system running on a host computer, which may support multiple virtual machines.

virtual memory: An operating-system technique in which the system simulates more memory than is physically present in the computer by swapping portions of memory out to disk.

virtual network: A simulated network created so that virtual machines can communicate with one another.

virus: An evil computer program that slips into your computer undetected, tries to spread itself to other computers, and may eventually do something bad like trash your hard drive.

Visio: A program from Microsoft that draws diagrams. It's especially good at drawing network diagrams.

VLAN: A Virtual Local Area Network, which enables you to create two or more broadcast domains on a single physical network.

VMware: The most popular software for implementing virtual machines.

voicemail: A feature of PBX and other types of phone systems in which a caller can record a message for the intended recipient of his or her call.

VoIP: *Voice over IP,* a technique for routing telephone calls over the Internet instead of over traditional phone carriers.

VPN: *Virtual Private Network*, a secure connection between a computer and a remote network or between two remote networks.

web browser: A program that enables you to display information retrieved from the Internet's World Wide Web.

WEP: *Wired Equivalent Privacy,* a security standard for wireless networks that makes wireless networking almost (but not quite) as secure as cabled networks.

Wi-Fi: The common name for wireless networking using the 802.11 protocols.

Windows: The world's most popular operating system.

Windows 7: A popular and successful version of Windows that replaced Windows Vista in 2009.

Windows 8: The version of Windows that replaced Windows 7 in late 2012.

Windows 8.1: An updated version of Windows 8.

Windows 10: The replacement for Windows 8.1.

Windows 95: A version of Windows that became available in — you guessed it — 1995. Windows 95 was the first version of Windows that didn't require DOS.

Windows 98: The successor to Windows 95, introduced in 1998. Windows 98 included a new user interface that made the Windows desktop resemble the World Wide Web.

Windows CE: A version of Windows for very small computers, such as those found in phones and other handheld devices. Windows Mobile is based on Windows CE.

Windows for Workgroups: Microsoft's first network-aware version of Windows, now obsolete.

Windows Millennium Edition: The successor to Windows 98, designed especially for home users and featuring a Home Networking Wizard that simplifies the task of setting up a home network.

Windows Mobile: A version of the Windows operating system based on Windows CE and designed for handheld mobile devices, pocket computers, and smartphones.

Windows NT: The predecessor to Windows 2000. Windows NT is available in two versions: Windows NT Client for desktop computers and Windows NT Server for server computers.

Windows Server: The server version of Windows.

Windows Vista: The Windows version that replaced Windows XP in early 2007.

Windows XP: A popular and successful version of Windows, designed for home or professional users. It was replaced by Windows Vista in 2007.

wireless: A method of networking that uses radio signals instead of cables to transmit data.

wireless access point: A device that connects wireless devices to a cabled network.

wiring closet: Large networks need a place where cables can congregate. A closet is ideal.

workstation: See *client.*

World Wide Web: A graphical method of accessing information on the Internet.

WPA: *Wi-Fi Protected Access,* a new and improved security standard for wireless networks.

WWW: See *World Wide Web.*

X10: A low-bandwidth protocol for home automation that runs over your home's power lines.

yellow cable: See *10Base5.*

zone: A portion of the DNS namespace that a particular DNS server is responsible for.

Index

Symbols and Numerics

& (ampersand), 604
' (apostrophe), 751
* (asterisk), 604, 767
$ (dollar sign), 767
! (Escape) subcommand, 329
! (exclamation point), 604, 767
> (greater-than sign), 605, 768
(hash mark), 732, 751, 767
? (Help) subcommand, 329
* parameter, 619
| (pipe character), 604, 605, 768
; (semicolon), 732
1 Trillion BaseT, 801
10Base, 245
10Base2, 801
10Base5, 801
10BaseT, 801
100BaseFX, 801
100BaseT4, 801
100BaseTX, 801
100VG AnyLAN, 801
802.2, 801
802.3, 801
802.11, 801
1000BaseT, 801
8088 processor, 801
80286 processor, 802
80386 processor, 802
80486 processor, 802

A

A+, 130
A (Address) records, 309, 311, 721
absolute name, 294
access
  restricting to computers, 549
  as a share element, 724
Access Control List (ACL), 563

access points (APs). *See* wireless access
    point (WAP)
access rights, 802
accessing
  cloud, 465–466
  command shells, 694–695, 766–767
  computers remotely, 430
  FTP sites with browser, 324–325
  network printers using web interfaces,
    84–85
Account Operators group, 554
accounting services, cloud computing and,
    458
accounts
  built-in
    about, 146
    Administrator account, 142, 146–147,
      513–514
    Guest account, 147
    Service accounts, 147–148
  defined, 802
  setting options, 546–548
  user
    about, 139, 541
    Administrator account, 142
    creating, 779
    creating logon scripts, 561
    creating users, 542–545
    deleting users, 552
    disabling, 551–552
    editing in Office 365, 482–483
    enabling, 551–552
    groups, 552–558
    local accounts compared with domain
      accounts, 541
    managing, 145–151, 541–561
    managing in Linux, 697–699
    obfuscating usernames, 139
    password-generator, 141–142
    passwords, 140
    properties, 542
    resetting passwords, 550–551

accounts *(continued)*
   setting properties, 545–550
   user profiles, 558–561
ACI (International Association of the
   Computer Impaired), 811
ACL (Access Control List), 563
acronym, 802
Actions pane (Hyper-V), 381
Active Directory (AD)
  about, 20, 529
  creating domains, 536–537
  creating organizational units, 537–539
  defined, 802
  directories, 529–530
  NT domains
    Backup Domain Controllers (BDCs),
     530–531
    NetBIOS names, 531
    Primary Domain Controllers (PDCs),
     530–531
    trusts, 531
  as a problem solver, 532
  structure of
    about, 532
    domains, 533–534
    forests, 535–536, 537
    objects, 532–533
    organizational units, 185–186, 534–535,
     537–539
    trees, 535
Active Directory Domains and Trusts
   console, 518
Active Directory Security (ADS), 727
Active Directory Sites and Services
   console, 519
Active Directory Users and Computers
   console, 519
Active Server Pages, 802
ActiveSync, 802
/ACTIVE: parameter, 626
AD. *See* Active Directory (AD)
adapter card, 802
add parameter, 611, 614, 616, 617
adding
  access points, 117–118

announcements in SharePoint Online,
   491–492
apps in SharePoint Online, 492–496
content to FTP site, 323–324
counters, 595
domain controllers to existing domains,
   537
domains in Office 365, 483
domains to existing forests, 537
features in Windows Server 2016, 509–512
forests, 537
members to groups, 557–558
network printers, 81–84
parts in SharePoint Online, 487–490
server roles in Windows Server 2016,
   509–512
snap-ins, 521
taskpads, 521–527
address book, 802
Address (A) records, 309, 311, 721
Address Resolution Protocol (ARP), 245,
   255, 339
ad-hoc networks, 90, 100
Admin Center (Office 365), 479
admin portals, for Office 365, 484
ADMIN$ share, 566
administering groups, 783–784
administering users, Linux commands for
  chage, 781–782
  gpasswd, 783–784
  groupadd, 783
  groupdel, 783
  newusers, 782–783
  passwd, 782
  useradd, 779–780
  userdel, 781
  usermod, 781
administrative installation images,
   creating, 185
administrator, 802
Administrator account
  about, 142, 146–147
  managing Windows Server 2016 with,
   513–514
Administrator password, 58

Administrators group, 554
ADS (Active Directory Security), 727
Advanced options, setting, 444–445
advance-fee scam, 167
advertisements, as spam, 167, 168
advertising software, 186
AirWave (website), 109
Alarm Clock app, 427
aliases, setting up, 753
allocation unit, 802
allowing access to Apache servers, 741–742
%ALLUSERSPROFILE% variable, 606
alter statement, 662
alternate email addresses, 176
Amazon, 463–464
Amazon CloudFront, 464
Amazon Elastic Compute Cloud (Amazon EC2), 464
Amazon Simple Queue Service (Amazon SQS), 464
Amazon Simple Storage Service (Amazon S3), 464
Amazon Virtual Private Cloud (Amazon VPC), 464
Amazon Web Services (AWS), 463–464
American National Standards Institute (ANSI), 229, 796
ampersand (&), 604
analyzing impact of disasters, 220–221
AND operator, 259–260
Android
  defined, 416, 803
  managing devices
    about, 425
    core applications, 427
    integrating with Exchange, 427
    operating system, 426
  website, 799
announcements, adding and removing in SharePoint Online, 491–492
ANSI (American National Standards Institute), 229, 796
antennas, 92–93, 116–117
antispam appliances, 173–174
antispam program, 803

antispam software
  types of, 172–175
  using, 168–169
antivirus program, 161–162, 803
Apache
  defined, 803
  running
    allowing access to Apache servers, 741–742
    configuring virtual hosts, 742–746
    confirming it's running, 738–740
    creating web pages, 747
    HTTP configuration tool, 740–741
    installing, 737
    manually editing configuration files, 746
    restricting access to Apache severs, 741–742
    starting, 737–738
    stopping, 737–738
Apache HTTP server (website), 795
Apache servers, allowing/restricting access to, 741–742
Apache web server, 76
APIPA (Automatic Private IP Addressing), 287–288
apostrophe ('), 751
%APPDATA% variable, 606
append subcommand, 329
Apple, 799. *See also* iOS
AppleTalk, 248
appliance, 803
application gateway, 157–158
Application layer, 230, 239, 256, 803
application servers, 30
application virtualization, 410
applications (apps)
  adding in SharePoint Online, 492–496
  cloud computing and, 461
  sharing, 11
APs (access points). *See* wireless access point (WAP)
archive bit, 208, 803
ARCnet, 803
ARP (Address Resolution Protocol), 245, 255, 339
arp command, 127, 339–340

ARPANET, 246, 251–252
`ascii` subcommand, 329
assigning
  IP addresses, 279
  permissions to groups, 150
  user rights, 148
asterisk (*), 604, 767
`atd` service, 778
AT&T 258A, 47
attaching RJ-45 connectors, 48–49
attachments, 175
attributes, 803
auto attendant, 803
autocompleting commands, 767
`autodisconnect` parameter, 612
`autof` service, 778
Automatic Private IP Addressing (APIPA),
    287–288
automating tasks with logon scripts, 151
autonomy, of Internet, 250–251
availability, as server consideration, 14
Average Queue Length counter, 594
AWS (Amazon Web Services), 463–464

B

backbone, 803
backing up
  data
    about, 205
    cleaning heads, 216
    local *versus* network, 212–213
    locations for, 206
    number of, 213–214
    reliability of tape, 215
    security of backups, 216
    software for, 207–208
    to tape, 206–207
    types of backup, 208–212
  defined, 803
  before installing Windows Server 2016,
    504
  network plans, 38–39
  as potential threat to physical security,
    138–139

as routine chore for network
    administrators, 124
  selecting, 208
back-plane connection, 33
backquote, 751
backscatter, 168
backslash, 294
Backup Domain Controllers (BDCs),
    530–531
Backup Operators group, 554
bands, 93
bandwidth, 93
banner, 803
bare metal, 368
BarracudaWare (website), 208
basic IP configuration, displaying, 341
Basic Service Set (BSS), 98
`.bat` extension, 607–608
batch files, 607–608, 803
Bayesian analysis, 170
Bayesian filter, 804
BCP. *See* business continuity planning
    (BCP)
BCP (Best Current Practice), 253
BDCs (Backup Domain Controllers),
    530–531
`bell` subcommand, 329–330
benchmark, 804
benefits
  of cloud computing, 458–460
  of virtualization, 373–375
Berkeley Software Distribution (BSD),
    749–750
BES (BlackBerry Enterprise Server), 804
Best Current Practice (BCP), 253
billing information, reviewing in office 365,
    483
`/bin` directory, 691
binary
  counting by ones, 257–259
  logical operations, 259–260
  Windows Calculator, 260–261
`binary` subcommand, 330
BIND
  configuration files, 717–721

installing, 716–717
restarting, 721
website, 795
Bing (website), 797
biometric ID device, 140
BISS (Independent Basic Service Set), 100
BlackBerry
  defined, 416–417, 804
  website, 799
BlackBerry Enterprise Server (BES), 804
blacklisting, 170–171, 755
blade servers, 17
blocking
  IP addresses, 272–273
  spam
    about, 165–167
    antispam software, 168–169, 172–175
    categories of spam, 167–168
    filters, 169–172
    minimizing, 175–176
Bluetooth, 804
/boot directory, 691
boot image file, 280
boot levels, 726
booting, in Safe Mode, 198
BOOTPROTO setting, 707
Bootstrap Protocol (BootP), 280
bot, 804
bottleneck, 804
Box, 470
bridges
  as Data Link layer devices, 233
  defined, 804
broadband, 804
broadcast domain, 804
BROADCAST setting, 707
broadness, of DNS trees, 293
browseable setting, 734
Browser app, 427
browsers, accessing FTP sites with, 324–325
BSD (Berkeley Software Distribution), 749–750
BSS (Basic Service Set), 98
buffer, 804

built-in accounts
  about, 146
  Administrator account, 142, 146–147, 513–514
  Guest account, 147
  Service accounts, 147–148
Builtin Container, 554–555
built-in firewall, 158–159
built-in tools, 127
business continuity planning (BCP). *See also* disaster recovery
  about, 217
  defined, 804
  developing, 221–222
bye subcommand, 330
byte, 258

C

C: drive, 679
cable
  about, 9, 41
  attaching RJ-45 connectors, 48–49
  categories of, 41–42
  considerations about, 31–32
  installing, 44–45
  patch panels, 49–50
  pinouts, 47
  plenum cable, 43–44
  shielded twisted-pair cable (STP), 43
  solid, 44
  stranded, 44
  tools for, 46–47
  unshielded twisted-pair cable (UTP), 43
  wall jacks, 49–50
cable tie, 805
cache, 305–306, 805
cache parameter, 621
CAD (computer-aided design) software, 30
Calculator app, 427
Caldera (website), 795
CALs (Client Access Licenses), 501
Camera app, 427
Canonical Name (CNAME) records, 309, 311–312, 721

carrier sense multiple access with collision detection (CSMA/CD), 93, 233, 234, 806
case sensitivity, of domain names, 293
cat command, 776–777
Cat5 cabling, 48
Category 3, 805
Category 5, 805
Category 5e, 805
Category 6, 805
CCAr (Cisco Certified Architect), 131
CCDP (Cisco Certified Design Professional), 131
CCENT (Cisco Certified Entry Network Network Technician), 131
CCIE (Cisco Certified Internetwork Expert), 131
CCNA (Cisco Certified Network Associate), 131
CCNP (Cisco Certified Network Professional), 131
CCT (Cisco Certified Technician), 131
cd command, 327, 330, 735, 771
%CD% variable, 606
CD-ROM, 805
cell phone, 416
Central Processing Unit (CPU), 806
Centrex, 805
Cert Publishers group, 555
certifications
  about, 129–131
  Microsoft, 793
  websites for, 793
Certified Network Dummy, 805
chage command, 781–782
chaining commands, 604–605
Change Permissions permission, 565
changing
  channels, 116
  default options for users, 779–780
  directories, 771
  encryption keys, 112
  FTP site properties, 321–323
  group ownership, 785
  passwords, 109
  permissions for Linux files, 785–786
  ports for Apache server, 742

user contact information, 546
user passwords, 782
channels, changing, 116
chat, 805
Chaucer, 805
Cheat Sheet (website), 4
checking
  Apache is running, 738–740
  event logs, 504
  Exchange ActiveSync feature, 419–420
  network connections, 192
  network settings, 193–194
  system requirements, 499–500, 677–678
Checkpoints pane (Hyper-V), 381
chgrp command, 785
child partition, 378
chkconfig command, 726
CHKDSK, 805
chmod command, 785–786
choosing
  distributions, 678–679
  domains, 503
  part-time network administrators, 123–124
  server operating systems, 30–31
  workgroups, 503
chores, as responsibility of network administrators, 123
chown command, 784–785
circuit, 805
circuit-level gateway, 157
Cisco, 131, 793, 799
Cisco Certified Architect (CCAr), 131
Cisco Certified Design Professional (CCDP), 131
Cisco Certified Entry Network Network Technician (CCENT), 131
Cisco Certified Internetwork Expert (CCIE), 131
Cisco Certified Network Associate (CCNA), 131
Cisco Certified Network Professional (CCNP), 131
Cisco Certified Technician (CCT), 131
Citrix Xen App, 409–411
Class A addresses, 265–267, 308

Class B addresses, 267
Class C address, 267
classifying IP addresses, 263–265
classless interdomain routing, 270
cleaning heads, 216
clean-up, as routine chore for network
    administrators, 125
click, 805
Client Access Licenses (CALs), 501
client computers
  about, 8
  restarting, 196–198
clients. *See also* servers
  about, 201
  compared with servers, 11–12
  defined, 805
  Mail Console, 755–756
  Samba, 734–735
  VPN, 432–433
Clipboard, 603
clock speed, 15
close parameter, 613
close subcommand, 330
closed-door approach, to security, 137
closing command windows, 602
cloud computing
  about, 457–458
  accessing the cloud, 465–466
  backup
    about, 206
    defined, 806
  benefits of, 458–460
  creating company social networks
    about, 472–473
    Socialcast, 474–475
    Yammer, 473–474
  defined, 806
  drawbacks of, 460–461
  hosting meetings
    about, 470–471
    GoToMeeting, 471
    WebEx, 471–472
  major providers, 463–465
  public clouds compared with private
    clouds, 462–463

sharing files
  about, 467
  Box, 470
  Dropbox, 469–470
  Google Drive, 468
  Microsoft OneDrive, 469
  types of, 461–462
cloud-based antispam services, 174–175
Clouseau, 806
cluster, 802
%CMDCMDLINE% variable, 606
%CMDEXTVERSION% variable, 606
CNAME (Canonical Name) records, 309,
    311–312, 721
CNET reviews, 793
coaxial cable, 806
collaborativeness, of Internet, 250
command prompt, exiting, 602
command shells
  about, 765
  accessing, 694–695, 766–767
  editing commands, 767
  environment variables, 768–769
  piping, 768
  redirection, 768
  running commands with root-level
    privileges, 770
  shell scripts, 769–770
  wildcards, 767–768
command windows
  about, 601
  closing, 602
  Control area, 603
  editing commands, 602–603
  opening, 602
commands. *See also* Linux commands;
    Windows commands
  autocompleting, 767
  chaining, 604–605
  editing, 602–603, 767
  repeating, 767
  running with root-level privileges, 770
comment parameter, 614, 616
comment=comment setting, 734
comments, in sendmail.mc file, 751

/COMMENT: "text" parameter, 626

communications, disruption of, 220

company profiles, customizing in Office 365, 483

compression, 207–208

CompTIA, 130

Computer Browser, 201

Computer Management console, 519, 598–599

computer name, 57, 806

computer-aided design (CAD) software, 30

computername parameter, 611, 618, 620, 627

%COMPUTERNAME% variable, 606

computernamesharename parameter, 624

computers
  accessing remotely, 430
  client
    about, 8
    restarting, 196–198
  equipment, as component of BCP, 222
  restricting access to, 549

%COMSPEC% variable, 606

Cone of Silence, 806

configuring
  decisions about, 57–58
  DHCP, 714–716
  displaying options for, 787–788
  files
    BIND, 717–721
    editing manually in Apache, 746
  FTP, 760–763
  FTP server
    adding content to FTP site, 323–324
    changing FTP site properties, 321–323
    creating FTP site, 318–321
    installing FTP, 318
  iOS devices for Exchange email, 420–425
  network connections, 63–69
  network features
    mapping network drives, 85–88
    printers, 81–85
  network printers, 81–85
  Outlook for Exchange Server 2016, 651–654

Remote Desktop options
  about, 440
  setting Advanced options, 444–445
  setting Display options, 441
  setting Experience options, 444
  setting Local Resources options, 442–443
  setting Programs options, 443
  as responsibility of network administrators, 122
  Samba server settings, 727–728
  Samba users, 729–730
  scopes, 282–287
  server, 60–61
  virtual hosts
    about, 742–743
    creating virtual hosts, 745–746
    default host, 743–745
  Windows clients
    about, 63
    configuring network connections, 63–69
    joining domains, 69–72
  Windows DHCP client, 287–289
  Windows DNS client, 315–316
  wireless access points, 100–102

Connect to Server dialog box, 80

connecting
  enabling, 752
  remotely, 436–439
  remotely with Remote Desktop Connection, 515–516
  to SharePoint Online, 486–487
  shares, 79–80
  to wireless networks, 103–105

consoles
  about, 690
  defined, 806
  Microsoft Management Console, 518–520

contact information, changing for users, 546

Contacts app, 427

container objects, 563

content, adding to FTP site, 323–324

Control area, 603

Control Panel, 806

conversations, 238

copy backups, 210
copy command, 604
"copy protection," 177
copying files in directories, 773–774
core applications, Android, 426, 427
cost, as benefit of cloud computing, 458–459
counters, 594–595
counting by ones, 257–259
/COUNTRYCODE:nnn parameter, 626
cp command, 773–774
CPU (Central Processing Unit), 806
CREATE commands, 672
Create Files/Write Data permission, 565
Create Folders/Append Data permission, 565
create statement, 662
creating
  administrative installation images, 185
  company social networks
    about, 472–473
    Socialcast, 474–475
    Yammer, 473–474
  databases, 665–667
  directories, 771–772
  domains, 536–537
  forwarders, 645–647
  FTP site, 318–321
  group policy objects (GPOs), 579–585
  groups, 556–557, 783
  libraries, 128–129
  logon scripts, 561
  mailboxes, 641–644
  organizational units, 537–539
  performance logs, 595–597
  security groups in Office 365, 483
  shares in Samba, 730–732
  tables, 667–670
  user accounts, 779
  user groups, 782–783
  users, 542–545
  users in Office 365, 480–482
  virtual disks, 384–387
  virtual hosts, 745–746
  virtual machines, 387–391, 398–402
  virtual switches, 381–383
  web pages, 747
  websites, 636–640
crimp tool, 46, 806
crond service, 778
crossover cables, 51, 806
CSMA/CD (carrier sense multiple access with collision detection), 93, 233, 234, 806
current working directory, 771
customizing
  company profiles in Office 365, 483
  Microsoft Management Console
    about, 520
    adding snap-ins, 521
    adding taskpads, 521–527
  SpamAssassin, 754–755
CWD command, 326–327
cycles per second, 91

D

daily backups, 210
daisy-chaining
  about, 33
  defined, 806
  switches, 51
DAT (digital audiotape), 807
DAT units, 207
data, backing up
  about, 205
  cleaning heads, 216
  local *versus* network, 212–213
  locations for, 206
  number of, 213–214
  reliability of tape, 215
  security of backups, 216
  software for, 207–208
  to tape, 206–207
  types of backup, 208–212
Data Collector Set, 595
data encryption, 20
Data Link layer, 230, 232–233, 807
data stores, 372
database servers, 30

databases
  about, 659–660
  creating new, 665–667
  relational, 660–661
%DATE% variable, 606
ddns-update-style, 715
dead computers, fixing, 191–192
debug subcommand, 330–331
decision-making, about configuring, 57–58
dedicated servers, 12–13, 28
Default command (Control area), 603
default groups, 554–555
default subnets, 271
default websites, 634–636
default-lease-time, 716
del command, 604, 735
del parameter, 611
delayed write, 807
delete parameter, 614, 616, 617, 618, 620,
  621, 624
Delete permission, 565
delete statement, 662
delete subcommand, 331
Delete Subfolders and Files permission,
  565
deleting
  files in directories, 774–775
  groups, 783
  users, 552, 781
deliberate disasters, 219
Dell (website), 794
deploying network software, 182–186
description
  as a share element, 724
  of shares, 565
desktop virtualization
  about, 405–407
  approaches to, 407
  Citrix XenApp, 409–411
  VMware's Horizon View, 408
detailed configuration information,
  displaying, 342
/dev directory, 691
device address, 235
Device Manager (Computer Management
  console), 598

DEVICE setting, 707
devices, 26. *See also specific devices*
DHCP. *See* Dynamic Host Configuration
  Protocol (DHCP)
DHCP Ack message, 277
DHCP Client, 201
DHCP configuration, 102
DHCP console, 519
DHCP Discover message, 277
DHCP Offer message, 277
DHCP Request message, 277
DHCP servers, running
  about, 713–714
  configuring DHCP, 714–716
  installing DHCP, 714
  starting DHCP, 716
dhcpd service, 778
*Diagnostic and Statistical Manual of Mental
  Disorders (DSM-IV),* 125
diagramming tool, 126
diagrams, drawing, 36–38
dial tone, 807
dialects, SQL, 661
Dialer app, 427
DID (Direct Inward Dialing), 807
differential backups, 211–212, 807. *See also*
  full backups
digest, 168
digital audiotape (DAT), 807
digits, 257
DIP switch, 807. *See also* jumper block
dir command, 331, 735
Direct Inward Dialing (DID), 807
directory hash, 807
directory services, 20
directory-handling, Linux commands for
  cat, 776–777
  cd, 771
  cp, 773–774
  ls, 772–773
  mkdir, 771–772
  mv, 775
  pwd, 771
  rm, 774–775
  rmdir, 772
  touch, 775–776

disabling
  guest mode, 111
  SSID broadcast, 110–111
  unnecessary services, 143
  user accounts, 551–552
disaster recovery. *See also* business
    continuity planning (BCP)
  about, 217
  analyzing impact of disasters, 220–221
  as benefit of virtualization, 375
  drills, 222–223
  types of disasters, 218–220
disconnect subcommand, 331
disconnecting UPS devices, 504
disk, 807
Disk Defragmenter (Computer Management
    console), 599
Disk Management (Computer Management
    console), 599
Disk Operating System (DOS), 808
disk storage, cloud computing and, 458
Display options, 441
displaying
  basic IP configuration, 341
  configuration options, 787–788
  contents of files, 776–777
  detailed configuration information, 342
  directories, 771
  DNS records, 350–352
  event logs, 203, 589–590
  help for Net commands, 610
  host name, 787
  interface statistics, 346–348
  list if routers, 791
  network configuration with ipconfig
    command, 711
  routing tables, 358–361, 790–791
disruption of services, 219–220
distribution groups, 553
distributions
  choosing, 678–679
  defined, 807
D-Link (website), 799
DLT units, 207
dnf command, 695, 714, 779

DNS. *See* Domain Name Server (DNS)
DNS (Domain Name System), 18–19, 807
DNS Client, 201
DNS console, 519
DNS database. *See* zone files
DNS queries, 306, 307
DNS records, displaying, 350–352
DNS servers
  about, 300
  running
    about, 716
    BIND configuration files, 717–721
    installing BIND, 716–717
DnsAdmins group, 555
DnsUpdateProxy group, 555
.doc extension, 604
documenting troubleshooting, 204
documents, backing up, 207
Dogpile (website), 797
dollar sign ($), 767
domain accounts, compared with local
    accounts, 541
Domain Admins group, 555
Domain Computers group, 555
domain controller, 534, 537
Domain Controller Security Policy console,
    519
Domain Controllers group, 555
Domain Guests group, 555
domain local scope, 553–554
Domain Name Server (DNS)
  about, 156, 239, 256, 291, 352–355
  caching, 305–306
  configuring Windows DNS client, 315–316
  DNS queries, 306, 307
  DNS servers, 300
  domain names, 292–293
  domains, 292–293
  fully qualified domain names (FQDN),
    294
  Hosts file, 297–300
  names, 291–294
  primary servers, 302–303
  reverse lookup zones, 313–314
  root servers, 303–305

Domain Name Server (DNS) *(continued)*
  running
    about, 716
    BIND configuration files, 717–721
    installing BIND, 716–717
  secondary servers, 302–303
  top-level domains
    about, 294
    generic domains, 294–295
    geographic domains, 295–297
  Windows DNS Server, 314–315
  zone files and resource records
    about, 308–309
    CNAME records, 311–312
    MX records, 312–313
    NS records, 310–311
    PTR records, 312
    A records, 311
    SOA records, 309–310
  zones, 300–302
Domain Name System (DNS), 18–19, 807
domain parameter, 611, 614, 616, 619
Domain Users group, 555
domainname parameter, 627
domains
  about, 58, 533–534
  adding
    domain controllers to existing, 537
    to existing forests, 537
    in Office 365, 483
  choosing, 503
  creating, 536–537
  defined, 807
  fully qualified domain names (FQDN), 294
  joining, 69–72, 77–79
  as security type in Samba, 727
  top-level
    about, 294
    defined, 823
    generic domains, 294–295
    geographic domains, 295–297
dot-matrix printer, 808
dotted-decimals, 262–263
drawbacks, of cloud computing, 460–461
drills, holding, 222–223
drive parameter, 624

drive share, 566
drop statement, 662
Dropbox, 469–470
DSM-IV (Diagnostic and Statistical Manual of Mental Disorders), 125
dumb terminal, 808
dumpster diving, as potential threat to physical security, 138
DVD drive, 808
Dynamic Host Configuration Protocol (DHCP)
  about, 18, 275
  configuration information provided by, 275–276
  how it works, 276–277
  scopes
    about, 278
    exclusions, 279
    lease duration, 280–281
    reservations, 279–280
  servers, 276
  structure of, 36
  working with servers, 281–287
dynamically expanding disk, 379

E

EAC (Exchange Administrative Center), 641
earthquakes, 218–219
eavesdroppers, 107
EBCDIC (Extended Binary Coded Decimal Interchange Code), 238
"Eddie Haskell," 808
EDIT command, 298
Edit command (Control area), 603
editing
  Apache configuration files manually, 746
  commands, 602–603, 767
  smb.conf file, 732–734
  tables, 670
  user accounts in Office 365, 482–483
editor, 808
EH Publishing (website), 794
EIA/TIA 568A, 47
EIA/TIA 568B, 47

802.2, 801
802.3, 801
802.11, 801
8088 processor, 801
80286 processor, 802
80386 processor, 802
80486 processor, 802
electrical power, 219–220
electronics
about, 91
antennas, 92–93
FCC (Federal Communications Commission), 93–94
frequencies, 91–92
spectrums, 93–94
wavelength, 92–93
waves, 91–92
email
about, 749–750
defined, 808
email addresses
alternate, 176
blacklisting, 755
locating mail server for, 352
protecting, 176
publishing, 176
whitelisting, 755
Email app, 427
email services, cloud computing and, 457–458
emoticon, 808
enabling
connections, 752
Hyper-V, 379–380
mailbox features, 644–645
masquerading, 752
remote access with Remote Desktop Connection, 514–515
Remote Assistance, 447–449
Remote Desktop Connection (RDC), 435–436
sudo command, 695–697
user accounts, 551–552
WEP, 111–112
encryption keys
changing, 112
defined, 808

energy cost, as benefit of virtualization, 374
Enter key, 603
enterprise computing, 808
entitlement model, 137
entrenched applications, as drawback of cloud computing, 460
/env: parameter, 628
environment variables, 606–607, 768–769
environmental disasters, 218–219
equipment failure, 220
equipment upgrades, as responsibility of network administrators, 122
Error icon, 591
error messages, 193
%ERRORLEVEL% variable, 607
ESS (Extended Service Set), 100
establishing routine chores, 124–125
ESXi, 395
/etc directory, 691, 714–716, 717–718
Ethernet
about, 8, 93, 228, 240–241
defined, 808
Fast, 241, 242–243
Gigabit, 241, 243–244
Standard, 241–242
event logs
about, 203
checking, 504
icons, 591
setting policies, 591–592
Event Properties dialog box, 590
Event Viewer
about, 203, 598
console, 519
working with
about, 589
setting event log policies, 591–592
using, 589–591
EventCreate command, 608–609
Evolution, 757
Exchange
integrating Android with, 427
integrating iOS devices with, 419–425
website, 796
Exchange ActiveSync feature, 419–420
Exchange Administrative Center (EAC), 641

Exchange Mailbox Features, 644–645
Exchange Server, 808
Exchange Server 2016, managing
  about, 641
  configuring Outlook for, 651–654
  creating mailboxes, 641–644
  managing mailboxes, 644–651
  viewing other mailboxes, 654–658
exclamation point (!), 604, 767
exclusions, 279
exit command, 350, 735
exiting command prompt, 602
Experience options, setting, 444
experimental specifications, 253
experimenting, 195
EXPIRE field, 310
/EXPIRES: parameter, 626
Extended Binary Coded Decimal
    Interchange Code (EBCDIC), 238
Extended Service Set (ESS), 100
Extended Three-Letter Acronym (ETLA), 808.
    See also Three-letter acronym (TLA)

F

F3, 603
facilities, as component of BCP, 222
failure recovery, 39
false negatives, 169, 809
false positives, 169, 809
Fast Ethernet, 242–243, 809
FAT (File Allocation Table), 809
FAT32, 809
FAX$ share, 566
FCC (Federal Communications
    Commission), 93–94
FDDI (Fiber Distributed Data Interface), 809
features, adding in Windows Server 2016,
    509–512
Federal Communications Commission
    (FCC), 93–94
Fedora
  about, 678
  defined, 809
  installing, 680–687
  website, 795

FHS (Filesystem Hierarchy Standard), 691
Fiber Distributed Data Interface (FDDI), 809
fiber-optic cable, 809
field, 660
File Allocation Table (FAT), 809
file rights, 809
file servers
  about, 29
  defined, 809
  managing
    granting permissions, 573–575
    New Share Wizard, 566–571
    permissions, 563–565
    shares, 565–566
    sharing folders without the wizard,
      572–573
file system, 57, 690–691
File Transfer Protocol (FTP)
  about, 156, 239, 256, 317–318
  accessing FTP sites with browser,
    324–325
  configuring FTP server
    adding content to FTP site, 323–324
    changing FTP site properties, 321–323
    creating FTP site, 318–321
    installing FTP, 318
  defined, 809
  FTP command and subcommands,
    328–338
  running
    about, 759
    configuring, 760–763
    installing vsftpd, 759
    starting vsftpd service, 759
  using FTP command line client, 325–328
file-handling, Linux commands for
  cat, 776–777
  cd, 771
  cp, 773–774
  ls, 772–773
  mkdir, 771–772
  mv, 775
  pwd, 771
  rm, 774–775
  rmdir, 772
  touch, 775–776

files. *See also* folders
  batch, 607–608, 803
  copying in directories, 773–774
  deleting in directories, 774–775
  displaying contents of, 776–777
  locking, 29
  moving in directories, 775
  permissions for, 564
  renaming in directories, 775
  sharing in the cloud
    about, 467
    Box, 470
    Dropbox, 469–470
    Google Drive, 468
    Microsoft OneDrive, 469
  zone
    about, 308–309, 720–721
    A records, 309, 311, 721
    CNAME records, 309, 311–312, 721
    defined, 827
    MX records, 309, 312–313, 721
    NS records, 309, 310–311, 721
    PTR records, 309, 312, 721
    SOA records, 309–310, 721
file-sharing services, 19
Filesystem Hierarchy Standard (FHS), 691
filtering
  defined, 809
  group policy objects (GPOs), 585–587
filters, 169–172, 605
`finger` service, 778
fire, 218
Firefox (website), 798
firewall appliance, 154
Firewall icon, 739
firewalls
  about, 142, 153–154
  built-in, 158–159
  defined, 809
  placing access points outside, 114
  types of, 155–158
fish tape, 46, 809
fixed-size disk, 378
flag icon, 163
FlexNet Publisher (Flexera Software),
    180–181

flushing local DNS cache, 343
folders. *See also* files
  permissions for, 564
  sharing without a wizard, 572–573
`forcelogoff` parameter, 610
forests
  about, 535–536
  adding, 537
  adding domains to existing, 537
  defined, 809
form factors, 16–17
forward lookup, 313
forwarders, creating, 645–647
`FORWARD_IPV4` setting, 706
FQDN (fully qualified domain names), 294
freeloaders, 106–107
frequencies, 91–92
FTP. *See* File Transfer Protocol (FTP)
FTP Authentication, 322
FTP Authorization, 322
`FTP` command and subcommands, 328–338
FTP command line client, 325–328
FTP Current Sessions, 322
FTP Directory Browsing, 322
FTP Firewall Support, 322
FTP IPv4 Address and Domain Restrictions,
    322
FTP Logging, 322
FTP Messages, 322
full backups, 209–210, 810. *See also*
    differential backups
Full Control permission, 564
full install, compared with upgrade install,
    53–54
Full-Duplex transmission mode, 238
`/FULLNAME:"name"` parameter, 626
fully qualified domain names (FQDN), 294

G

gateway, 810
`GATEWAY` setting, 706
`GATEWAYDEV` setting, 706
GB (Gigabyte), 810
General tab (Remote Desktop), 440
generation backup, 810

generation gap, 810

generic domains, 294–295

geographic domains, 295–297

GET command, 327, 331–332, 735

get-rich-quick schemes, 168

Gigabit Ethernet, 241, 243–244

Gigabyte (GB), 810

glass house, 810

glob subcommand, 332

global accessibility, as benefit of cloud computing, 460

global catalog, 535

global scope, 553–554

GNOME, 693–694, 810

Golden, Bernard (author)
Virtualization For Dummies, 367

Google, 141, 464, 797

Google App Engine, 464

Google Apps, 464

Google Apps for Business, 462, 464

Google Chrome (website), 798

Google Cloud Connect, 464

Google Cloud Print, 464

Google Drive, 468

Google Maps, 464

GoToMeeting, 471

GoToMyPC (website), 406

gpasswd command, 783–784

GPOs. *See* group policy objects (GPOs)

granting permissions, 573–575

graphics, backing up, 207

graylisting, 171–172

greater-than sign (>), 605, 768

Gregory, Peter (author)
IT Disaster Recovery Planning For Dummies, 217

group account, 810

group membership, 542

group policy
about, 577–578
creating group policy objects (GPOs), 579–585
enabling Group Policy Management on Windows Server 2016, 578–579

filtering group policy objects (GPOs), 585–587
pushing out software with, 185–186

Group Policy, 555

Group Policy Management
console, 519
enabling on Windows Server 2016, 578–579

group policy objects (GPOs)
about, 577
creating, 579–585
filtering, 585–587

Group Properties dialog box, 557–558, 699

groupadd command, 783

groupdel command, 783

groupname parameter, 614, 616

groups
about, 552–553
adding members, 557–558
administering, 783–784
assigning permissions to, 150
changing ownership, 785
creating, 556–557, 783
default, 554–555
deleting, 783
scope of, 553–554
types of, 553

growth, with network plan, 38

Guest account, 147

guest account setting, 733

guest ok setting, 733, 734

guest operating system, 368

guests, 368, 810

Guests group, 554

gurus, 132, 810

H

HAL (Hardware Abstraction Layer), 368, 810

Half-Duplex transmission mode, 238

Halper, Fern (author)
Hybrid Cloud For Dummies, 466

handheld, 416

hard copy files, as component of BCP, 222
hard drives
  for server computers, 16
  size of, 25–26
hardening networks, 142–143
hardware
  cost of, as benefit of virtualization, 374
  installing
    cable, 41–50
    switches, 50–52
  websites for, 793–794
Hardware Abstraction Layer (HAL), 368, 810
Hardware Compatibility List (HCL), 56
HardwareCentral (website), 793
hash mark (#), 732, 751, 767
hash subcommand, 332
hassle-free nature, as benefit of cloud
    computing, 460
HCL (Hardware Compatibility List), 56
heads, cleaning, 216
help subcommand, 332
Hertz, 91
Hewlett-Packard (website), 794
hidden parameter, 612
hidden shares, 566
hierarchical nature, of DNA, 293
historic specifications, 253
hold parameter, 618
holding drills, 222–223
/home directory, 691
Home folder, 550
home networking, websites for, 794
home parameter, 625
HOME variable, 769
/HOMEDIR:pathname parameter, 626
%HOMEDRIVE% variable, 607
%HOMEPATH% variable, 607
HomePNA Alliance (website), 794
%HOMESHARE% variable, 607
Horizon View (VMware), 408
Horizon View Chart, 408
Horizon View Composer, 408
host, 716
host ID, 262
host name, displaying, 787
hosted antispam, 174–175

hosting meetings
  about, 470–471
  GoToMeeting, 471
  WebEx, 471–472
hostname command, 127, 340, 787
hostname file, 705
HOSTNAME variable, 706, 769
hosts
  defined, 368
  IP addresses and, 262
hosts allow setting, 733, 734
hosts file, 297–300, 302, 705, 707–708
HOSTTYPE variable, 769
hot swappable, 14
Hotfix Checker, 127
hotspot, 810
hot-swappable, 17
HowStuffWorks (website), 797
HTML (HyperText Markup Language), 810
HTTP (HyperText Transfer Protocol), 256,
    810
HTTP configuration tool, 740–741
HTTP over TLS/SSL (HTTPS), 156, 810
httpd service, 778
HTTPS (HTTP over TLS/SSL), 156, 810
hubs. *See also* switches
  defined, 811
  as potential threat to physical security, 139
Hurwitz, Judith (author)
  Hybrid Cloud For Dummies, 466
  Hybrid Cloud For Dummies (Hurwitz,
    Kaufman, Halper and Kirsch), 466
HyperText Markup Language (HTML), 810
HyperText Transfer Protocol (HTTP), 256,
    810
HyperText Transport Protocol; HTTP
    (World Wide Web), 156
Hyper-V (Microsoft)
  about, 54, 378
  creating virtual disks, 384–387
  creating virtual machines, 387–391
  creating virtual switches, 381–383
  enabling, 379–380
  installing operating systems, 391–393
  panes, 380–381
  virtual disks, 378–379

hypervisors
  about, 368–369
  defined, 368, 811

I

i command, 770
i7 processor, 811
IaaS (Infrastructure as a Service), 462
IAS Server group, 555
IBM (website), 793
ICMP (Internet Control Message Protocol), 255, 357
icons
  Error, 591
  event log, 591
  explained, 3
  Firewall, 739
  flag, 163
  Information, 591
  Warning, 591
id parameter, 613
identity field, 670
IEEE (Institute of Electrical and Electronics Engineers), 229, 796, 811
IEEE 802.11 standards, 94–95
IETF (Internet Engineering Task Force), 229, 250, 252, 796
ifcfg file, 705, 706–707
ifconfig command, 787–788
IGMP (Internet Group Management Protocol), 252, 255
IIS. See Internet Information Services (IIS)
IIS_WPG group, 555
IMAP (Internet Message Access Protocol), 156
imap service, 778
imaps service, 778
increment, 670
incremental backups, 210–211, 811. See also archive bit; differential backups; full backups
Independent Basic Service Set (BISS), 100
Industry Standard Architecture (ISA) bus, 812

information, sharing, 10
Information icon, 591
informational specifications, 253
InformationWeek (website), 129, 795
InfoWorld (website), 129, 795
infrastructure, cloud computing and, 462
Infrastructure as a Service (IaaS), 462
infrastructure mode network, 90, 98–99
inkjet printer, 811
Insert statement, 662, 673
installing
  Apache, 737
  BIND, 716–717
  cable, 44–45
  compared with upgrading, 500
  DHCP, 714
  Fedora 22, 680–687
  FTP, 318
  hardware
    cable, 41–50
    switches, 50–52
  Internet Information Services (IIS), 631–634
  Linux servers
    checking system requirements, 677–678
    choosing distributions, 678–679
    installing Fedora 22, 680–687
    TCP/IP configuration, 680
    virtual machines, 680
  mail command, 756
  operating systems, 391–393
  over networks, 55
  Samba, 724–725
  Sendmail, 750
  server operating systems, 53–55, 59–60
  silently, 183–185
  SpamAssassin, 753–754
  switches, 50–51
  VMware tools, 402–403
  vsftpd, 759
  Windows Server 2016
    checking system requirements, 499–500
    choosing workgroups or domains, 503
    licensing options, 501
    multiboot, 501

planning partitions, 501–502
preparing for, 503–504
reading release notes, 500
TCP/IP configurations, 502
upgrading compared with installing, 500
Windows Server 2016 DHCP server, 281–282
Institute of Electrical and Electronics Engineers (IEEE), 229, 796, 811
integrating
Android with Exchange, 427
iOS devices with Exchange, 419–425
intentional damage, 219
interconnectedness, of Internet, 251
interface statistics, displaying, 346–348
International Association of the Computer Impaired (ACI), 811
international nature, of Internet, 250
International Organization for Standardization (ISO), 229, 796, 812
Internet
about, 249–251
defined, 811
history of, 251–252
RFCs, 252–254
size of, 250
TCP/IP protocol framework, 254–256
TCP/IP standards, 252–254
websites for, 798
Internet Assigned Numbers Authority (website), 796
Internet connection
about, 56
reliability of, as drawback of cloud computing, 460–461
speed of, as drawback of cloud computing, 460
Internet Control Message Protocol (ICMP), 255, 357
Internet Engineering Task Force (IETF), 229, 250, 252, 796
Internet Explorer
defined, 811
website, 798
Internet Group Management Protocol (IGMP), 252, 255

Internet Information Services (IIS)
about, 317
creating websites, 636–640
default website, 634–636
installing, 631–634
Manager console, 520
Internet Message Access Protocol (IMAP), 156
Internet Protocol (IP), 245, 251, 255
Internet Protocol Security (IPSec), 431
Internet Relay Chat (IRC), 156
Internet resources
AirWave, 109
American National Standards Institute (ANSI), 796
Android, 799
Apache HTTP server, 795
Apple, 799
BarracudaWare, 208
BIND, 795
Bing, 797
BlackBerry, 799
Box, 470
Caldera, 795
certifications, 793
Cheat Sheet, 4
Cisco, 131, 793, 799
Class A address assignments, 266
CNET reviews, 793
CompTIA, 130
creating, 636–640
default, 634–636
Dell, 794
D-Link, 799
DNS lookups, 798
Dogpile, 797
Dropbox, 469
EH Publishing, 794
Exchange, 796
Fedora, 678, 681, 795
Firefox, 798
Google, 141, 797
Google Apps for Business, 462
Google Chrome, 798
Google Drive, 468
GoToMeeting, 471

Internet resources *(continued)*
  GoToMyPC, 406
  hardware, 793–794
  HardwareCentral, 793
  home networking, 794
  HomePNA Alliance, 794
  HowStuffWorks, 797
  IBM, 793
  InformationWeek, 129, 795
  InfoWorld, 129, 795
  Institute of Electrical and Electronics
    Engineers (IEEE), 796
  International Organization for
    Standardization (ISO), 796
  Internet Assigned Numbers Authority, 796
  Internet Engineering Task Force (IETF),
    252, 796
  Internet Explorer, 798
  Internet Society, 796
  Internet Systems Consortium (ISC), 250,
    798
  InterNIC, 798
  iPhone, 799
  Linksys, 794, 799
  for Linux, 794–795
  Linux Journal, 795
  Linux Magazine, 795
  for magazines, 795
  Mandriva Linux, 678
  Meraki, 799
  Microsoft, 131, 795–796
  Microsoft licensing, 180
  Microsoft Office 365, 465
  Microsoft server, 796
  NETGEAR, 794, 799
  NetScout, 128
  Network Computing, 129, 795
  Network Solutions, 798
  for Network Standards Organizations, 796
  Network World, 129
  Office 365, 478, 486, 796
  Opera, 798
  Oracle, 794
  PowerShell, 601
  Red Hat, 793, 795

  for reference, 797
  Register.com, 798
  RFC repository, 796
  Samba, 795
  for search, 797
  SharePoint, 796
  Slackware, 678, 795
  small-business networking, 794
  for smartphones, 798
  SMC, 799
  Socialcast, 474
  speed tests, 798
  Spiceworks, 127
  SQL Server, 796
  SUSE, 678, 795
  for TCP/IP and Internet, 798
  TechNet, 796
  Tom's Hardware Guide, 793
  2600 Magazine, 795
  2600 The Hacker Quarterly, 129
  Ubuntu, 678, 795
  VMware, 793
  Web Extras, 4
  WebEx, 471
  Webopedia, 797
  Whatis.com, 797
  Wi-Fi Planet, 799
  Wikipedia, 797
  Windows, 795
  Windows IT Pro Magazine, 795
  Windows Phone, 799
  Windows Software Update Services
    (WSUS), 126
  Windows Update, 126
  for wireless networking, 798
  Wireshark, 128
  World Wide Web Consortium (W3C), 796
  Yahoo!, 797
  Yammer, 473
  Zoo, 797
Internet service provider (ISP), 812
Internet Society (website), 796
Internet Standards Track, 253
Internet Systems Consortium (ISC), 250,
    798

Internetwork Packet Exchange/Sequenced Packet Exchange (IPX/SPX), 228–229, 248, 249

InterNIC, 317, 798

interoperability, 811

intranet, 811

intruders, 106

inviting someone to help via Remote Assistance, 449–451

I/O port address, 811

iOS
  defined, 416
  managing devices
    about, 418
    integrating with Exchange, 419–425
    iPad, 419
    iPhone, 418–419

IP (Internet Protocol), 245, 251, 255

IP addresses
  about, 262
  assigning, 279
  binary
    about, 257
    counting by ones, 257–259
    logical operations, 259–260
    Windows Calculator, 260–261
  Class A, 265–267
  Class B, 267
  Class C, 267
  classifying, 263–265
  defined, 812
  dotted-decimals, 262–263
  hosts, 262
  looking up, 349–350
  network address translation (NAT), 273–274
  networks, 262
  static, 36
  subnetting
    about, 267–268
    blocking, 272–273
    default subnets, 271
    network prefix notation, 270
    private addresses, 273
    public addresses, 273
    rounding, 271–272

subnet masks, 269–270
subnets, 268–269

IP leases, 342–343

IP spoofing, 155

iPad, 419

IPADDR setting, 707

IPC$ share, 566

ipconfig command
  about, 101, 127, 232–233, 235, 280, 288–289, 340
  displaying
    basic IP configuration, 341
    detailed configuration information, 342
    network configuration with, 711
  flushing local DNS cache, 343
  releasing IP leases, 343
  renewing IP leases, 342–343

iPhone, 418–419, 799, 812

ipop3 service, 778

IPSec (Internet Protocol Security), 431

iptables service, 778

IPv6, 264

IPX/SPX (Internetwork Packet Exchange/ Sequenced Packet Exchange), 228–229, 248, 249

IRAS Server group, 555

IRC (Internet Relay Chat), 156

ISA (Industry Standard Architecture) bus, 812

ISC (Internet Systems Consortium), 250, 798

ISDN, 812

isdn service, 778

ISO (International Organization for Standardization), 229, 796, 812

.iso file, 391–393

ISP (Internet service provider), 812

IT Disaster Recovery Planning For Dummies (Gregory), 217

Itanium 9300, 15

iterative queries, 306

J

Java, 812

JavaScript, 812

job# parameter, 618

Join a Domain dialog box, 71
joining domains, 69–72, 77–79
jumper block, 812. *See also* DIP switch

K

K (Kilobytes), 812
Kaufman, Marcia (author)
  Hybrid Cloud For Dummies, 466
Kerberos, 812
keyboard, video, and mouse (KVM)
    switching, 17–18
keyboard shortcuts, for Remote Desktop,
    439
keyword checking, 169–170
Kilobytes (K), 812
Kirsch, Daniel (author)
  Hybrid Cloud For Dummies, 466
KVM switch, 18
KVM (keyboard, video, and mouse)
    switching, 17–18

L

L2TP (Layer 2 Tunneling Protocol), 432
LAN. *See* local area network (LAN)
LAN Manager, 812
laser printer, 813
Layer 2 Tunneling Protocol (L2TP), 432
layers. *See also* protocols
  following packets through, 239–240
  of the OSI model, 230
lcd *directory* command, 735
lcd subcommand, 332–333
LDAP (Lightweight Directory Access
    Protocol), 156
leases
  about, 276
  duration of, 280–281
  releasing, 288–289
  renewing, 288–289
Lemon-Pudding layer, 813
levels, of DNS trees, 293
/lib directory, 691

libraries
  building, 128–129
  as a feature of team sites, 485
license servers, 30, 180–182
licenses, software, 178–180
licensing options, for Windows Server
    2016, 501
lightning, 219
Lightweight Directory Access Protocol
    (LDAP), 156
link, 578
Linksys (website), 794, 799
Linksys AC1200 Amplify, 117–118
Linux
  about, 689
  basic network configuration
    displaying with ipconfig command,
      710
    files, 704–710
    Network Configuration program,
      701–704
    restarting network, 704
  command shell, 694–695
  defined, 813
  file system, 690–691
  GNOME, 693–694
  location of Hosts file in, 298
  logging off, 693
  logging on, 692
  managing user accounts, 697–699
  shutting down, 693
  sudo command, 695–697
  virtual consoles, 690
  websites for, 794–795
  X Window System, 689–690
Linux commands
  about, 765
  for administering users
    chage, 781–782
    gpasswd, 783–784
    groupadd, 783
    groupdel, 783
    newusers, 782–783
    passwd, 782
    useradd, 779–780

userdel, 781
usermod, 781
command shell basics
about, 765
accessing command shells, 766–767
editing commands, 767
environment variables, 768–769
piping, 768
redirection, 768
running commands with root-level
privileges, 770
shell scripts, 769–770
wildcards, 767–768
directory-handling
cat, 776–777
cd, 771
cp, 773–774
ls, 772–773
mkdir, 771–772
mv, 775
pwd, 771
rm, 774–775
rmdir, 772
touch, 775–776
file-handling
cat, 776–777
cd, 771
cp, 773–774
ls, 772–773
mkdir, 771–772
mv, 775
pwd, 771
rm, 774–775
rmdir, 772
touch, 775–776
for managing ownership and permissions
chgrp, 785
chmod, 785–786
chown, 784–785
networking
hostname, 787
ifconfig, 787–788
netstat, 788–789
ping, 789–790
route, 790–791
traceroute, 791

for working with packages and services
dnf, 779
service, 777–778
yum, 779
Linux Journal (website), 795
Linux Magazine (website), 795
Linux+ Powered by LPI, 130
Linux servers, installing
checking system requirements,
677–678
choosing distributions, 678–679
installing Fedora 22, 680–687
TCP/IP configuration, 680
virtual machines, 680
List Folder Contents permission, 564
List Folder/Read Data permission, 564
listing contents of directories, 772–773
literal subcommand, 333
LLC sublayer, 813
local accounts, compared with domain
accounts, 541
local area network (LAN)
about, 13, 90
defined, 812
local backups, compared with network
backups, 212–213
local disk storage, 371
local DNS cache, flushing, 343
local resources, 813
Local Resources options, setting,
442–443
local user profile, 559
locating mail server for email addresses,
352
locking files, 29
log in, 813
log out, 813
logging off, from Linux, 693
logging on
defined, 813
to Linux, 692
logical addressing, 234–235
logical AND, 269–270
logical operations, 259–260
logon hours, specifying, 548
logon name, 813

logon scripts
  about, 550
  automating tasks with, 151
  creating, 561
  defined, 813
%LOGONSERVER% variable, 607
looking up IP addresses, 349–350
Lowe, William (author)
  VMware Infrastructure 3 For Dummies, 367
ls command, 333, 772–773
LTO units, 207

M

MAC (Media Access Control) address, 94,
    232, 280, 339, 813
Mac address filtering, 113–114
MAC spoofing, 113
Mac sublayer, 813
Macs
  about, 73
  basic network settings, 73–76
  connecting to shares, 79–80
  defined, 813
  joining domains, 77–79
magazines, websites for, 795
mail command, 755–756
Mail Console client, 755–756
Mail Delivery Agent (MDA), 750
Mail Exchange (MX) records, 309, 312–313,
    721
mail servers, 29–30, 352, 813
Mail Transfer Agent (MTA), 750
Mail User Agent (MUA), 750
mailboxes
  creating, 641–644
  defined, 750
  managing
    about, 644
    creating forwarders, 645–647
    enabling mailbox features, 644–645
    setting mailbox storage limits, 647–651
  viewing, 654–658
mainframe, 813
MAN (metropolitan area network), 13

managed switches, 34
managing
  Exchange Server 2016
    about, 641
    configuring Outlook for, 651–654
    creating mailboxes, 641–644
    managing mailboxes, 644–651
    viewing other mailboxes, 654–658
  file servers
    granting permissions, 573–575
    New Share Wizard, 566–571
    permissions, 563–565
    shares, 565–566
    sharing folders without the wizard,
      572–573
  mailboxes
    about, 644
    creating forwarders, 645–647
    enabling mailbox features, 644–645
    setting mailbox storage limits, 647–651
  mobile devices
    about, 415
    Android, 425–427
    iOD, 418–425
    security, 417
    types, 416–417
  network software
    about, 177
    deploying, 182–186
    license server, 180–182
    licenses, 178–180
    updating, 186–188
  network users, 125
  user access with permissions, 149–150
  user accounts
    about, 145
    assigning permissions to groups, 150
    assigning user rights, 148
    automating tasks with logon scripts, 151
    built-in accounts, 146–148
    components of user accounts, 145–146
    controlling user access with
      permissions, 149–150
    user profiles, 150–151
  user accounts in Linux, 697–699

Windows Server 2016
  customizing Microsoft Management
    Console, 520–527
  using Administrator account, 513–514
  using Microsoft Management Console,
    517–520
  using Remote Desktop Connection,
    514–516
Windows user accounts
  about, 541
  creating logon scripts, 561
  creating users, 542–545
  deleting users, 552
  disabling, 551–552
  enabling, 551–552
  groups, 552–558
  local accounts compared with domain
    accounts, 541
  properties, 542
  resetting passwords, 550–551
  setting properties, 545–550
  user profiles, 558–561
mandatory user profile, 559
Mandriva Linux, 678
manual deployment, of network software,
  182
mapping. *See also* redirection
  defined, 814
  network drives, 85–88
Maps app, 427
Market app, 427
masquerading, enabling, 752
master file. *See* zone files
Maximum Log Size policy, 591
max-lease-time, 716
maxpwage parameter, 610
MB (Megabytes), 814
McAfee's VirusScan Enterprise, 161
MCSA (Microsoft Certified Solutions
  Associate), 131
MCSE (Microsoft Certified Solutions
  Expert), 131
md *directory* command, 735
MDA (Mail Delivery Agent), 750
mdelete subcommand, 333
mdir subcommand, 333–334

Media Access Control (MAC) address, 94,
  232, 280, 339, 813
meetings, hosting
  about, 470–471
  GoToMeeting, 471
  WebEx, 471–472
Megabytes (MB), 814
members, adding to groups, 557–558
memory. *See also* random access memory
    (RAM)
  amount of, 26
  defined, 814
  for server computers, 16
Meraki (website), 799
message parameter, 619
Messaging app, 427
metaphor, 814
Metcalfe, Robert (graduate student), 243
metric, 360
Metro, 814
metropolitan area network (MAN), 13
mget subcommand, 334, 735
Microsoft
  about, 131, 465
  certifications, 793
  licensing, 180
  website, 795–796
Microsoft Baseline Security Analyzer, 127
Microsoft Business Productivity Suite, 465
Microsoft Certified Solutions Associate
    (MCSA), 131
Microsoft Certified Solutions Expert
    (MCSE), 131
Microsoft Exchange Server, 29–30, 168
Microsoft Management Console (MMC)
  customizing
    about, 520
    adding snap-ins, 521
    adding taskpads, 521–527
  defined, 814
  managing Windows Server 2016 with
    about, 517
    consoles, 518–520
    working with, 517–518
Microsoft Office 365, 465
Microsoft OneDrive, 469

Microsoft PowerShell, 601
Microsoft Security Essentials, 161
Microsoft System Information, 27
Microsoft Technology Associate (MTA),
    131
Microsoft Visio, 37
Microsoft Windows
  defined, 825
  website, 795
Microsoft Windows 7
  activating firewall in, 158–159
  booting in Safe Mode, 198
  connecting remotely with Remote
      Desktop Connection, 515–516
  defined, 826
  enabling Remote Assistance, 448–449
  starting Networking Troubleshooter in,
      195
Microsoft Windows 8/8.1
  activating firewall in, 158–159
  booting in Safe Mode, 198
  defined, 826
  enabling Remote Assistance, 448–449
  location of Hosts file in, 298
  starting Networking Troubleshooter in,
      195
Microsoft Windows 9x/Me, location of
    Hosts file in, 298
Microsoft Windows 10
  booting in Safe Mode, 198
  defined, 826
  enabling Remote Assistance, 448–449
  location of Hosts file in, 298
Microsoft Windows 95, 826
Microsoft Windows 98, 826
Microsoft Windows 2000, location of Hosts
    file in, 298
Microsoft Windows Action Center, 162–163
Microsoft Windows Azure, 465
Microsoft Windows Calculator, 260–261
Microsoft Windows CE, 826
Microsoft Windows clients, configuring
  about, 63
  configuring network connections, 63–69
  joining domains, 69–72
Microsoft Windows commands

  about, 601
  command windows
    about, 601
    closing, 602
    Control area, 603
    editing commands, 602–603
    opening, 602
  EventCreate command, 608–609
  Net commands
    about, 609–610
    Net Accounts command, 610–611
    Net Computer command, 611
    Net Config command, 611–612
    Net Continue command, 612
    Net File command, 612–613
    Net Group command, 613–614
    Net Help command, 615
    Net Helpmsg command, 615
    Net Localgroup command, 615–617
    Net Name command, 617
    Net Pause command, 617–618
    Net Print command, 618–619
    Net Send command, 619–620
    Net Session command, 620
    Net Share command, 620–621
    Net Start command, 621–622
    Net Statistics command, 622–623
    Net Stop command, 623
    Net Time command, 623–624
    Net Use command, 624–625
    Net User command, 625–627
    Net View command, 627
  RunAs command, 627–628
  special commands
    about, 603
    batch files, 607–608
    chaining commands, 604–605
    environment variables, 606–607
    piping, 605
    redirection, 605
    wildcards, 603–604
Microsoft Windows DHCP client,
    configuring, 287–289
Microsoft Windows DNS client, configuring,
    315–316
Microsoft Windows DNS Server, 314–315

Microsoft Windows for Workgroups, 826
Microsoft Windows Group Policy, 185–186
Microsoft Windows Millennium Edition, 826
Microsoft Windows Mobile, 826
Microsoft Windows Networking
    Troubleshooter, 194–195
Microsoft Windows NT
  defined, 826
  location of Hosts file in, 298
Microsoft Windows Security Center, 163
Microsoft Windows Server, 21, 826
Microsoft Windows Server 2012, 55
Microsoft Windows Server 2016
  adding server roles and features, 509–512
  enabling Group Policy Management on,
    578–579
  installing, 281–282
    checking system requirements, 499–500
    choosing workgroups or domains, 503
    licensing options, 501
    multiboot, 501
    planning partitions, 501–502
    preparing for, 503–504
    reading release notes, 500
    TCP/IP configurations, 502
    upgrading compared with installing, 500
  managing
    customizing Microsoft Management
      Console, 520–527
    using Administrator account, 513–514
    using Microsoft Management Console,
      517–520
    using Remote Desktop Connection,
      514–516
  running setup, 504–508
Microsoft Windows Update, 126, 186–188
Microsoft Windows user accounts,
    managing
  about, 541
  creating logon scripts, 561
  creating users, 542–545
  deleting users, 552
  disabling, 551–552
  enabling, 551–552
  groups, 552–558

  local accounts compared with domain
    accounts, 541
  properties, 542
  resetting passwords, 550–551
  setting properties, 545–550
  user profiles, 558–561
Microsoft Windows Vista
  booting in Safe Mode, 198
  defined, 826
  location of Hosts file in, 298
  starting Networking Troubleshooter in,
    195
Microsoft Windows XP
  booting in Safe Mode, 198
  defined, 826
  location of Hosts file in, 298
  starting Networking Troubleshooter in,
    195
Microsoft's Hyper-V, 54
middleware layer, 426
minimizing spam, 175–176
MINIMUM field, 310
`minpwage` parameter, 610
`minpwlen` parameter, 610
`mkdir` command, 334, 771–772
MLD (Multicast Listener Discovery), 252
`mls` subcommand, 334
MMC. *See* Microsoft Management Console
  (MMC)
`mmc` command, 517
MNAME field, 310
`/mnt` directory, 691
mobile devices, managing
  about, 415
  Android, 425–427
  iOD, 418–425
  security, 417
  types, 416–417
mobile phone, 416
modem, 814
Modify permission, 564
modifying
  routing tables, 361–362, 790–791
  `sendmail.mc`, 751–753
  users, 781

monitoring performance
  about, 592
  creating performance logs, 595–597
  Reliability and Performance Monitor,
    592–595
motherboard, for server computers, 15
mouse, 814
moving files in directories, 775
mput subcommand, 334, 735
MTA (Mail Transfer Agent), 750
MTA (Microsoft Technology Associate),
  131
MUA (Mail User Agent), 750
multiboot, 54, 501, 814
multicast address, 265
Multicast Listener Discovery (MLD), 252
multifunction WAPs, 99
multitasking, 19–20
Music app, 427
Muus, Mike (author), 358
mv command, 775
MX (Mail Exchange) records, 309, 312–313,
  721
MySQL, 76, 814

N

n command, 770
name parameter, 617, 619
Name server (NS) records, 309, 310–311,
  721
name subcommand, 350
named service, 778
named.ca file, 718–720
named.conf file, 717–718
named.custom file, 718
named.local file, 720
names
  Domain Name Server (DNS), 291–294
  as share elements, 724
NAS (Network Accessible Storage), 372,
  814
NAS (Network Attached Storage), 206
NAT (network address translation),
  273–274
Navigation pane (Hyper-V), 380–381

nbstat command, 127, 344–345
NDRs (nondelivery reports), 168
.NET, 814
Net Accounts command, 610–611
Net commands
  about, 609–610
  Net Accounts command, 610–611
  Net Computer command, 611
  Net Config command, 611–612
  Net Continue command, 612
  Net File command, 612–613
  Net Group command, 613–614
  Net Help command, 615
  Net Helpmsg command, 615
  Net Localgroup command, 615–617
  Net Name command, 617
  Net Pause command, 617–618
  Net Print command, 618–619
  Net Send command, 619–620
  Net Session command, 620
  Net Share command, 620–621
  Net Start command, 621–622
  Net Statistics command, 622–623
  Net Stop command, 623
  Net Time command, 623–624
  Net Use command, 624–625
  Net User command, 625–627
  Net View command, 627
Net Computer command, 611
Net Config command, 611–612
Net Continue command, 612
net diag command, 127
Net File command, 612–613
Net Group command, 613–614
Net Help command, 615
Net Helpmsg command, 615
Net Localgroup command, 615–617
Net Name command, 617
Net Pause command, 617–618
Net Print command, 618–619
Net Send command, 619–620
Net Session command, 620
Net Share command, 620–621
Net Start command, 621–622
Net Statistics command, 622–623
Net Stop command, 623

Net Time command, 623–624
Net Use command, 88, 624–625
Net User command, 625–627
Net View command, 627
NetBEUI (Network BIOS Extended User Interface), 247
NetBIOS (Network Basic Input/Output System), 155, 247, 814
NetBIOS Datagram Service, 156
NetBIOS Name Service, 156
NetBIOS names, 531
NetBIOS Session Service, 156
NetBoot, 76
netf service, 778
NETGEAR (website), 794, 799
netlogon parameter, 612, 618
NETLOGON share, 566
NETMASK setting, 707
/netonly: parameter, 628
NetScout (website), 128
netstat command
  about, 127, 237, 345, 788–789
  displaying
    connections, 345–346
    interface statistics, 346–348
NetWare Directory Services, 815
NetWare over IP, 156, 815
Network+, 130
Network Accessible Storage (NAS), 372, 814
network address, 235
network address translation (NAT), 273–274
network administrator
  about, 121
  building libraries, 128–129
  certifications for, 129–131
  choosing part-time, 123–124
  establishing routine chores, 124–125
  excuses for, 132–133
  gurus, 132
  managing network users, 125
  patching operating system and software, 126
  roles and responsibilities of, 121–123
  software tools for, 126–128

Network Attached Storage (NAS), 206
network backups, compared with local backups, 212–213
Network Basic Input/Output System (NetBIOS), 155, 247, 814
Network BIOS Extended User Interface (NetBEUI), 247
Network Computing (website), 129, 795
network configuration files (Linux)
  about, 704–705
  hostname, 705
  hosts, 705, 707–708
  ifcfg-xxxx, 705, 706–707
  network, 705–706
  nsswitch.conf, 705, 708–710
  resolv.conf, 705, 708
  xinetd.conf, 705, 710
Network Configuration group, 554
Network Configuration program, 701–704
Network Connection Properties dialog box, 67
network connections
  checking, 192
  configuring, 63–69
network discovery program, 127
network drives
  defined, 815
  mapping, 85–88
network file, 705–706
Network File System (NFS), 239
network ID, 262
network interface card (NIC), 8, 96, 815
Network Interface layer, 254–255
network interfaces, for server computers, 16
Network layer, 230, 233–236, 255, 815
network manager, 815
Network Monitor, 128
Network Neighborhood, 815
Network News Transfer Protocol (NNTP), 156
network operating systems (NOSes), 135, 815
Network Places, 815
network port. *See* network interface card (NIC)

network prefix notation, 270
network printers, configuring, 81–85
Network Properties dialog box, 315–316
network resource, 815
network servers, restarting, 202
network services, 18–19, 200–201, 778
NETWORK setting, 707
network settings, checking, 193–194
network software
  about, 10
  managing
    about, 177
    deploying, 182–186
    license server, 180–182
    licenses, 178–180
    updating, 186–188
Network Solutions (website), 798
Network Standards Organization, websites
    for, 796
network users, managing, 125
network virtualization, 373
Network World (website), 129
networking. *See also specific topics*
  benefits of, 10–11
  Linux commands for
    hostname, 787
    ifconfig, 787–788
    netstat, 788–789
    ping, 789–790
    route, 790–791
    traceroute, 791
networking protocols, 58
NETWORKING setting, 706
networks
  about, 7–8, 251
  ad-hoc, 90, 100
  clients compared with servers, 11–12
  components of, 8–10
  configuring features
    mapping network drives, 85–88
    printers, 81–85
  dedicated servers, 12–13
  defined, 815
  hardening, 142–143
  installing over, 55
  IP addresses and, 262

peers, 12–13
planning
  about, 23–24
  being purposeful, 24–25
  cable, 31–32
  considerations, 38–39
  dedicated servers, 28
  diagrams, 36–38
  server operating systems, 30–31
  server roles, 28–30
  switches, 32–34
  taking stock, 25–28
  TCP/IP implementation, 36
  topology, 35–36
  restarting in Linux, 704
  servers, 13–21
  size of, 13
New Host dialog box, 314–315
New Share Wizard, 566–571
newsfeed, as a feature of team sites, 485
newsgroup, 815
newusers command, 782–783
NFS (Network File System), 239
nfs service, 778
NIC (network interface card), 8, 96, 815
NNTP (Network News Transfer Protocol),
    156
node, 815
nondelivery reports (NDRs), 168
/noprofile: parameter, 628
normal backups, 209–210
Norton Utilities, 128
NOSes (network operating systems), 135,
    815
NOT operator, 259–260
NS (Name server) records, 309, 310–311,
    721
NSFNET, 246, 252
nslookup command
  about, 127, 349
  displaying DNS records, 350–352
  DNS, 352–355
  locating mail server for email address,
    352
  looking up IP addresses, 349–350
  using subcommands, 350

`nsswitch.conf` file, 705, 708–710
NT domains
  Backup Domain Controllers (BDCs), 530–531
  NetBIOS names, 531
  Primary Domain Controllers (PDCs), 530–531
  trusts, 531
NTFS file system, 57, 501, 816
null value, 668
nulls, 668
`%NUMBER_OF_PROCESSORS%` variable, 607

O

objects
  about, 532–533
  container, 563
obfuscating
  defined, 816
  usernames, 139
octet, 816
ODBC Data Sources console, 520
OEM (original equipment manufacturer) license, 179
off-hours personnel, as potential threat to physical security, 138
Office 365
  about, 477
  Admin Center, 479
  creating new users, 480–482
  editing user accounts, 482–483
  features provided by, 477–478
  other administrative tasks, 483–484
  website, 796
offline, 816
`ONBOOT` setting, 707
1 Trillion BaseT, 801
100BaseFX, 801
100BaseT4, 801
100BaseTX, 801
100VG AnyLAN, 801
1000BaseT, 801
ones, counting by, 257–259
online, 816

on-premises antispam, 172–173
open relay, 752
`open` subcommand, 335
Open Systems Interconnection Reference Model. *See* OSI model
open-door approach, to security, 137
opening command windows, 602
Opera (website), 798
operating systems
  Android, 426
  installing, 391–393
  patching, 126
  for server computers, 18–21
  versions of, 26
operator, 816
`/opt` directory, 691
`option domain-name`, 715
`option domain-name-servers`, 715
`option nis-domain`, 715
`option routers`, 715
`option subnet mask`, 715
options parameters, 626–627
OR operator, 259–260
Oracle (website), 794
`order by` clause, 663
organization, of Internet, 250
Organizational Units (OUs)
  about, 185–186, 534–535
  creating, 537–539
  defined, 816
original equipment manufacturer (OEM) license, 179
OS core, 426
`%OS%` variable, 607
OS X Server, 76
OSI model
  about, 229–231
  Application layer, 239
  Data Link layer, 232–233
  defined, 816
  Network layer, 233–236
  Physical layer, 231–232
  Presentation layer, 238–239
  Session layer, 238
  Transport layer, 236–237

OSTYPE variable, 769
OUs. *See* Organizational Units (OUs)
Outlook
  configuring for Exchange Server 2016, 651–654
  defined, 816
Owner, as resource record field, 308
ownership, Linux commands for managing
  chgrp, 785
  chmod, 785–786
  chown, 784–785

p

PaaS (Platform as a Service), 462
packages
  defined, 816
  Linux commands for
    dnf, 779
    service, 777–778
    yum, 779
packet filtering, 155–156, 816
packet sniffers, 128, 818
packets
  defined, 816
  following through layers, 239–240
Pages/second counter, 594
panes (Hyper-V), 380–381
parallel port, 816. *See also* serial port
parent domain, 292
parent partition, 378
partition structure, 57
partitions, 25–26, 501–502, 679, 816
parts
  adding in SharePoint Online, 487–490
  SharePoint Online, 487
part-time network administrators, choosing, 123–124
passphrase, 111
passwd command, 782
password parameter, 624
/PASSWORDCHG: parameter, 626
password-generator, 141–142
/PASSWORDREQ: parameter, 626
passwords

about, 542
  changing, 109
  changing for users, 782
  defined, 817
  resetting for users, 550–551
  for routers, 118
  using, 140
patch cable, 192, 817
patch panels, 49–50
patching
  operating systems, 126
  as responsibility of network administrators, 122
  servers, 143
  software, 126
path
  as a share element, 724
  for shares, 565
path parameter, 621
PATH variable, 769
%PATH% variable, 607
"%PATHEXT%" variable, 607
path=path setting, 734
pathping command, 355–356
payload, 431
PBX (Private Branch Exchange), 817
PCI (Peripheral Component Interconnect), 817
PDAs (Personal Digital Assistants), 416
PDCs (Primary Domain Controllers), 530–531
peers, 12–13
peer-to-peer network, 28, 817
% Free Space counter, 594
% Processor Time counter, 594
performance, monitoring
  about, 592
  creating performance logs, 595–597
  Reliability and Performance Monitor, 592–595
performance logs, creating, 595–597
Performance Logs and Alerts (Computer Management console), 598
performance maintenance, as responsibility of network administrators, 122–123

Performance Monitor console, 520, 592–593
perimeter, 154
Peripheral Component Interconnect (PCI),
    817
permissions
  about, 563–565
  assigning to groups, 150
  changing for Linux files, 785–786
  controlling user access with, 149–150
  defined, 817
  granting, 573–575
  Linux commands for managing
    chgrp, 785
    chmod, 785–786
    chown, 784–785
  of shares, 565
permissions model, 137
persistent parameter, 625
Personal Digital Assistants (PDAs), 416
per-user CALs, 501
phishing emails, 167
phones, as component of BCP, 222
physical connection, 106
Physical layer, 230, 231–232, 817
physical security, 137–139
ping, 817
ping command, 127, 357–358, 789–790
pinouts, for twisted-pair cables, 47
pipe character (|), 604, 605, 768
piping, 605, 768
planning
  networks
    about, 23–24
    being purposeful, 24–25
    cable, 31–32
    considerations, 38–39
    dedicated servers, 28
    diagrams, 36–38
    server operating systems, 30–31
    server roles, 28–30
    switches, 32–34
    taking stock, 25–28
    TCP/IP implementation, 36
    topology, 35–36
  partitions, 501–502

Platform as a Service (PaaS), 462
platforms, cloud computing and, 462
plenum cable, 43–44, 817
plenum space, 44
pocket protector, 817
Podcast Producer, 76
Pointer (PTR) records, 309, 312, 721
Point-to-Point Protocol (PPP), 817
POP3 (Post Office Protocol), 156
pop3s service, 778
pornographic websites, ads for, 168
ports
  changing for Apache server, 742
  defined, 33, 817
  TCP/IP (Transmission Control Protocol/
    Internet Protocol), 156
Post Office Protocol (POP3), 156
power supply, for server computers, 16
PowerShell, 601, 817
PPP (Point-to-Point Protocol), 817
present working directory, 771
Presentation layer, 230, 238–239, 817
Prevent Local Guests Group from
    Accessing Log policy, 592
Primary Domain Controllers (PDCs),
    530–531
primary key, 669
primary partition, 501
primary servers, 302–303
primary zone, 302
print job, 818
Print Manager, 818
Print Operators group, 555
print queue, 818
print servers, 29, 818
PRINT$ share, 566
printers
  about, 26
  network, 81–85
private addresses, 273
Private Branch Exchange (PBX), 817
private cloud, 462–463
%PROCESSOR_ARCHITECTURE% variable,
    607
%PROCESSOR_IDENTIFIER% variable, 607

%PROCESSOR_REVISION% variable, 607
processors
  for server computers, 15–16
  types of, 25
profile information, setting for users,
    549–550
/profile: parameter, 628
profile path, 549
/PROFILEPATH[:path] parameter, 626
programs, for gathering information, 27–28
Programs options, setting, 443
prompt subcommand, 335
%PROMPT% variable, 607
PROMPT_COMMAND variable, 769
properties
  FTP site, 321–323
  user account, 542
Properties command (Control area), 603
Properties dialog box, 66, 603
protecting
  email addresses, 176
  as routine chore for network
    administrators, 124
protocol analyzer, 128, 818
protocol suites, 228
protocols. *See also* standards
  about, 227–229, 247–248
  defined, 818
  Ethernet, 240–244
  OSI model, 229–231
  packets, 239–240
  TCP/IP protocol suite, 244–247
proxy server, 157
PTR (Pointer) records, 309, 312, 721
public addresses, 273
public cloud, 462–463
publishing email addresses, 176
punch-down block, 818
pushing out software with group policy,
    185–186
put command, 335, 735
PVC, 43
pwd command, 335, 771
PWD variable, 769

Q

:q command, 770
:q! command, 770
queries, working with, 671
queue, 818
quit subcommand, 336
quote subcommand, 336

R

rack mount, 17
RAID (Redundant Array of Independent
    Disks), 317, 818
random access memory (RAM), 818. *See
    also* memory
%RANDOM% variable, 607
range, 715
range, of wireless devices, 95–96
rd directory command, 735
RDATA, as resource record field, 308, 310
RDC. *See* Remote Desktop Connection
    (RDC)
RDP (Remote Desktop Protocol), 819
Read & Execute permission, 564
Read Extended Attributes permission, 564
Read permission, 564
Read Permissions permission, 565
reading
  mail, 756
  release notes, 500
records, 659. *See also specific types*
recoverability, as benefit of virtualization,
    374–375
recursive DNS query, 306
recv subcommand, 336
Red Hat (website), 793, 795
redirection, 605, 768, 818. *See also*
    mapping
reduced downtime, as benefit of
    virtualization, 374
Redundant Array of Independent Disks
    (RAID), 317, 818

reference, websites for, 797
referral, 306
REFRESH field, 310
ReFS (Resilient File System), 57, 501, 819
Register.com (website), 798
Registry, 818
relational databases, 660–661
release command, 288
release notes, reading, 500
release parameter, 618
releasing leases, 288–289, 343
reliability
  as benefit of cloud computing, 459
  as server consideration, 14
Reliability and Performance Monitor,
    592–595
remark parameter, 621
Remember icon, 3
Remote Assistance
  about, 435, 447
  enabling, 447–449
  inviting someone to help via Remote
    Assistance session, 449–451
  responding to a Remote Assistance
    invitation, 452–454
remote desktop access
  about, 435
  configuring options, 440–445
  connecting remotely, 436–439
  enabling
    Remote Desktop Connection (RDC),
      435–436
    with Remote Desktop Connection,
      514–515
  using keyboard shortcuts, 439
Remote Desktop Connection (RDC)
  about, 408, 430
  defined, 819
  enabling, 435–436
  managing Windows Server 2016 with
    about, 514
    connecting remotely, 515–516
    enabling remote access, 514–515
Remote Desktop Protocol, 819
Remote Desktop Services, 407
Remote Desktop Users group, 555

Remote Installation Service (RIS), 819
remotehelp subcommand, 336
Removable Storage (Computer
    Management console), 598
removing
  announcements in SharePoint Online,
    491–492
  directories, 772
rename subcommand, 337
renaming files in directories, 775
renewing
  IP leases, 342–343
  leases, 288–289
repeater, 819
repeating commands, 767
Replicator group, 555
replying, to spam, 175
Request for Comments (RFCs), 252–254
reservations, 279–280
resetting user passwords, 550–551
residential gateway, 99
Resilient File System (ReFS), 57, 501, 819
resolv.conf file, 705, 708
resolver, 306
resource records
  about, 308–309, 720–721
  A records, 309, 311, 721
  CNAME records, 309, 311–312, 721
  MX records, 309, 312–313, 721
  NS records, 309, 310–311, 721
  PTR records, 309, 312, 721
  SOA records, 309–310, 721
resources
  defined, 819
  sharing, 10–11
responding, to a Remote Assistance
    invitation, 452–454
responsibilities and roles
  of network administrators, 121–123
  of servers, 28–30
restarting
  BIND, 721
  client computers, 196–198
  network servers, 202
  network services, 200–201
  networks in Linux, 704

restricting
  access to Apache severs, 741–742
  access to computers, 549
retail software license, 179
Retain Log policy, 592
Retention Method for Log policy, 592
RETRY field, 310
reverse lookup zones, 313–314
reviewing billing information in Office 365,
    483
RFC repository (website), 796
RFCs (Request for Comments), 252–254
right-arrow key, 602
ring, 819
RIS (Remote Installation Service), 819
RJ-11, 819
RJ-45, 48–49, 819
rm command, 774–775
rmdir command, 337, 772
RNAME field, 310
roaming, 99–100
roaming user profile, 559–561
robotic units, 207
rogue access points, 108–109
roles and responsibilities
  of network administrators, 121–123
  of servers, 28–30
root, 819
/root directory, 691
root domain, 292
root servers, 303–305, 819
root subcommand, 350
rounding subnets, 271–272
route command
  about, 127, 358, 790–791
  displaying routing table, 358–361
  modifying routing table, 361–362
route print command, 358
routers
  defined, 819
  displaying lists of, 791
  passwords for, 118
routine chores, establishing, 124–125
routing, 236

routing tables
  displaying, 358–361, 790–791
  modifying, 361–362, 790–791
RunAs command, 627–628
running
  Apache
    allowing access to Apache servers,
      741–742
    configuring virtual hosts, 742–746
    confirming it's running, 738–740
    creating web pages, 747
    HTTP configuration tool, 740–741
    installing, 737
    manually editing configuration files, 746
    restricting access to Apache severs,
      741–742
    starting, 737–738
    stopping, 737–738
  commands with root-level privileges, 770
  DHCP servers
    about, 713–714
    configuring DHCP, 714–716
    installing DHCP, 714
    starting DHCP, 716
  DNS servers
    about, 716
    BIND configuration files, 717–721
    installing BIND, 716–717
  FTP
    about, 759
    configuring, 760–763
    installing vsftpd, 759
    starting vsftpd service, 759
  Performance Monitor console, 592–593
  Sendmail
    about, 749
    email, 749–750
    Evolution, 757
    installing, 750
    Mail Console Client, 755–756
    modifying sendmail.mc, 751–753
    SpamAssassin, 753–755
  setup from network shares, 182–183
  setup of Windows Server 2016, 504–508

S

SaaS (Software as a Service), 461
safe computing, 162
Safe Mode, booting in, 198
Samba
  about, 723–724
  client, 734–735
  defined, 819
  editing `smb.conf` file, 732–734
  installing, 724–725
  Samba Server Configuration Tool
    about, 726–727
    configuring Samba users, 729–730
    configuring server settings, 727–728
    creating shares, 730–732
    starting, 725–726
    stopping, 725–726
    website, 795
Samba Server Configuration Tool
  about, 726–727
  configuring Samba users, 729–730
  configuring server settings, 727–728
  creating shares, 730–732
SAN (Storage Area Network), 371, 820
SATA (Serial AT Attachment), 820. *See also* Small Computer System Interface (SCSI)
`savecred` parameter, 624, 628
Save/Save As buttons, 440
`/sbin` directory, 691
scalability
  as benefit of cloud computing, 459
  as server consideration, 14
scams, 167
ScanDisk, 820
`schedule` parameter, 612, 618
scheduling software, 820
scopes
  about, 276, 278
  configuring, 282–287
  defined, 820
  exclusions, 279
  of groups, 553–554
  lease duration, 280–281
  reservations, 279–280

`Script As` commands, 672
`/SCRIPTPATH:`*`pathname`* parameter, 626
scripts, working with, 672–673
SCSI (Small Computer System Interface), 820. *See also* Serial AT Attachment (SATA)
SDK (software development kit), 426
search, websites for, 797
secondary servers, 302–303
secondary zone, 302
secure location, 513
Secure Shell Protocol (SSH), 156
securing SSID, 110–111
security
  about, 135
  approaches to, 137
  of backups, 216
  creating groups in Office 365, 483
  as drawback of cloud computing, 461
  firewalls
    about, 153–154
    types of, 155–158
  hardening networks, 142–143
  importance of, 136–137
  for mobile devices, 417
  of network plan, 38
  physical, 137–139
  user accounts, 139–142
  users, 143–144
  for virtual private network (VPN), 431–432
  virus protection
    about, 159–161
    antivirus program, 161–162
    safe computing, 162
  for wireless networks
    about, 105
    enabling WEP, 111–112
    MAC address filtering, 113–114
    passwords, 109
    SSID, 110–111
    threats to, 105–109
    WPA/WPA2, 112–113
Security+, 130
security groups, 553
`security` setting, 733

seed, 670
segment, 820
`select` statement, 662–663, 671
semicolon (;), 732
`send` subcommand, 337
Sender Policy Framework (SPF), 170
Sendmail
  defined, 820
  running
    about, 749
    email, 749–750
    Evolution, 757
    installing, 750
    Mail Console Client, 755–756
    modifying `sendmail.mc`, 751–753
    SpamAssassin, 753–755
`sendmail` service, 778
`sendmail.mc`, modifying, 751–753
Serial AT Attachment (SATA), 820. *See*
    also Small Computer System Interface
    (SCSI)
SERIAL field, 310
serial port. *See also* parallel port; USB
  defined, 820
Server+, 130
server computers
  about, 8, 55–56
  components of, 15–16
  operating systems for, 18–21
server license, 501
Server Message Block (SMB), 239, 723, 821
`server name` subcommand, 350
server operating systems
  about, 10
  choosing, 30–31
  installing, 53–55, 59–60
Server Operators group, 555
server OS, 56
`server` parameter, 611, 612, 618
server roles, adding in Windows Server
    2016, 509–512
`server string` setting, 733
servercentric, 530
servers. *See also* clients
  about, 13, 201
    as security type in Samba, 728

application, 30
choosing server operating systems,
    30–31
compared with clients, 11–12
components of server computers, 15–16
configuring, 60–61
considerations for, 14
database, 30
dedicated, 28
defined, 805, 820
Dynamic Host Configuration Protocol
    (DHCP), 276, 281–287
file
  about, 29
  defined, 809
  managing, 563–575
form factors, 16–17
license, 30, 180–182
Linux, installing
  checking system requirements, 677–678
  choosing distributions, 678–679
  installing Fedora 22, 680–687
  TCP/IP configuration, 680
  virtual machines, 680
mail, 29–30, 352, 813
operating systems for server computers,
    18–21
patching, 143
as potential threat to physical security,
    139
primary, 302–303
print, 29
roles of, 28–30
root, 303–305, 819
secondary, 302–303
setting up
  about, 53, 58
  configuring servers, 60–61
  decision-making, 57–58
  gathering components, 55–57
  installing server operating systems,
    53–55, 59–60
VPN, 432–433
web, 29
service, 725
Service accounts, 147–148

service and support, as server
  consideration, 14
`service` command, 777–778
Service Pack, 820
Service Set Identifier (SSID), 90, 98,
  110–111, 822
services, Linux commands for
  `dnf`, 779
  `service`, 777–778
  `yum`, 779
Services and Applications (Computer
  Management console), 599
Services console, 520, 599–600
Session layer, 230, 238, 820
`set debug` subcommand, 350
`set nodebug` subcommand, 350
`set norecurse` subcommand, 350
`set recurse` subcommand, 350
`set type=x` subcommand, 350
setting(s)
  account options, 546–548
  Advanced options, 444–445
  basic Mac, 73–76
  Display options, 441
  event log policies, 591–592
  Experience options, 444
  Local Resources options, 442–443
  mailbox storage limits, 647–651
  Programs options, 443
  user profile information, 549–550
  user properties
    about, 545–546
    changing contact information, 546
    restricting access to certain computers,
      549
    setting account options, 546–548
    setting user's profile information,
      549–550
    specifying logon hours, 548
Settings app, 427
setup
  aliases, 753
  running for Windows Server 2016,
    504–508
  running from network shares, 182–183

servers
  about, 53, 58
  configuring servers, 60–61
  decision-making, 57–58
  gathering components, 55–57
  installing server operating systems,
    53–55, 59–60
  wireless networks
    about, 89–90
    connecting to wireless networks,
      103–105
    electronics, 91–94
    range, 95–96
    roaming, 99–100
    wireless access points, 97–99,
      100–102
    wireless network adapters, 96–97
    wireless network security, 105–118
    wireless networking, 90
    wireless standards, 94–95
SFT (System Fault Tolerance), 820
Share, as security type in Samba, 728
share name, 821
shared folder, 821
Shared Folders (Computer Management
  console), 598
shared resource, 821
sharename parameter, 618, 621
[sharename] setting, 734
SharePoint
  defined, 821
  website, 796
SharePoint Online
  about, 465, 485–486
  adding
    announcements, 491–492
    apps, 492–496
    parts, 487–490
  connecting to, 486–487
  removing announcements, 491–492
shares
  about, 565–566
  connecting, 79–80
  creating in Samba, 730–732
  defined, 724

sharing
  applications, 11
  files in the cloud
    about, 467
    Box, 470
    Dropbox, 469–470
    Google Drive, 468
    Microsoft OneDrive, 469
  folders without a wizard, 572–573
  information, 10
  resources, 10–11
shell, 765
shell scripts, 769–770
SHELL variable, 769
shielded twisted-pair (STP) cable, 43, 821
shutting down Linux, 693
signal booster, 117
silent installs, 183–185
Simple Mail Transfer Protocol (SMTP), 156,
    239, 256
Simple Network Management Protocol
    (SNMP), 156, 821
Simplex transmission mode, 238
size
  of hard drive, 25–26
  of networks, 13
Slackware, 678, 795
Small Computer System Interface (SCSI),
    820. *See also* Serial AT Attachment
    (SATA)
small-business networking, websites for,
    794
smartcard parameter, 624, 628
smartphones, 416, 798
SMB (Server Message Block), 239, 723, 821
smb service, 778
smbclient command, 734–735
smb.conf file, editing, 732–734
SMC (website), 799
smiley, 821
SMTP (Simple Mail Transfer Protocol), 156,
    239, 256
SNA (Systems Network Architecture), 248,
    821
snap-ins, adding, 521

sneakernet, 821
SNMP (Simple Network Management
    Protocol), 156, 821
snmpd service, 778
SOA (Start of Authority) records, 309–310,
    721
social networks, company
  about, 472–473
  Socialcast, 474–475
  Yammer, 473–474
Socialcast, 474–475
software
  about, 26, 56
  backup, 207–208
  computer-aided design (CAD), 30
  network
    about, 10
    managing, 177–188
  patching, 126
Software as a Service (SaaS), 461
software development kit (SDK), 426
software inventory, as responsibility of
    network administrators, 123
software licenses, 178–180
software tools, for network administrators,
    126–128
software upgrades, as responsibility of
    network administrators, 122
solid cable, 44
solving network problems. *See*
    troubleshooting
spam
  blocking
    about, 165–167
    antispam software, 168–169, 172–175
    categories of spam, 167–168
    filters, 169–172
    minimizing, 175–176
  defined, 821
SpamAssassin
  about, 753
  blacklisting email addresses, 755
  customizing, 754–755
  installing, 753–754
  whitelisting email addresses, 755

special commands
  about, 603
  batch files, 607–608
  chaining commands, 604–605
  environment variables, 606–607
  piping, 605
  redirection, 605
  wildcards, 603–604
special permissions, 564–565
specifying logon hours, 548
spectrums, 93–94
speed tests, 798
SPF (Sender Policy Framework), 170
SPI (stateful packet inspection), 157, 822
Spiceworks (website), 127
spoilers, 108
spooling, 821
Spotlight Server, 76
SQL. *See* Structured Query Language (SQL)
SQL dialects, 661
SQL Server
  defined, 821
  website, 796
SQL Server 2014
  about, 659
  creating tables, 667–670
  databases
    about, 659–660
    creating new, 665–667
    relational databases, 660–661
  editing tables, 670
  queries, 671
  scripts, 672–673
  SQL
    about, 661
    dialects, 661
    `select` statement, 662–663
    statements, 662
SQL Server 2014 Management Studio,
  664–665
SQL Server 2014 Management Studio,
  664–665
SQL statements, 662
`srvcomment` parameter, 612
SSH (Secure Shell Protocol), 156

SSID (service set identifier), 90, 98,
  110–111, 822
stackable switches, 33
staff, as component of BCP, 222
Standard Ethernet, 241–242
standards. *See also* protocols
  about, 229
  following packets through layers, 239–240
  OSI model, 229–231
  wireless, 94–95
star, 822
Start of Authority (SOA) records, 309–310,
  721
starting
  Apache, 737–738
  DHCP, 716
  Evolution, 757
  firewall in Windows 7/8, 158–159
  Samba, 725–726
  `vsftpd` service, 759
  Windows Calculator, 261
stateful packet inspection (SPI), 157, 822
static IP addresses, 36
station, 822
station cable, 44, 49
stationery, as component of BCP, 222
`status` subcommand, 337
stopping
  Apache, 737–738
  Samba, 725–726
Storage Area Network (SAN), 371, 820
storage limits, for mailboxes, 647–651
STP (shielded twisted-pair cable), 43, 821
stranded cable, 44
`/string` command, 770
`?string` command, 770
strings, in `sendmail.mc` file, 751
structure (Active Directory)
  about, 532
  domains, 533–534
  forests, 535–536, 537
  objects, 532–533
  organizational units, 185–186, 534–535,
    537–539
  trees, 535

Structured Query Language (SQL)
  about, 661
  defined, 821
  dialects, 661
  select statement, 662–663
  statements, 662
subcommands, 350
subdomains, 293
subnet, 715
subnet masks, 269–270, 822
subnets
  about, 268–269
  default, 271
  rounding, 271–272
  structure of, 36
subnetting
  about, 267–268
  blocking, 272–273
  default subnets, 271
  defined, 822
  network prefix notation, 270
  private addresses, 273
  public addresses, 273
  rounding, 271–272
  subnet masks, 269–270
  subnets, 268–269
subscription license, 180
sudo command, 695–697, 770
SUSE, 678, 795
switches. *See also* hubs
  about, 9, 192
  considerations for, 32–34
  daisy-chaining, 51
  as Data Link layer devices, 233
  defined, 822
  installing, 50–51
  nbstate command, 344
  netstat command, 345–346, 346–348
  pathping command, 355
  ping command, 358
  virtual, 381–383
Symantec Security, 161
Synchronize permission, 565
System Fault Tolerance (SFT), 820
System Information, 127
System Properties dialog box, 26

system requirements, checking, 499–500, 677–678
System Restore, 198–200
%SYSTEMDRIVE% variable, 607
%SYSTEMROOT% variable, 607
Systems Network Architecture (SNA), 248, 821
SYSVOL share, 566

T

tables
  creating, 667–670
  defined, 660
  editing, 670
Take Ownership permission, 565
tape backups
  about, 206
  cleaning heads, 216
  reliability of, 215
  using, 206–207
tape drive, 822
tape rotation, 214
taskpads, adding, 521–527
tasks
  automating with logon scripts, 151
  defined, 822
TB (Terrazzo bytes), 822
TCP (Transmission Control Protocol), 246–247, 255
TCP/IP. *See* Transmission Control Protocol/Internet Protocol (TCP/IP)
TCP/IP Properties dialog box, 68–69
TCP/IP protocol suite
  about, 244–245
  IP, 245
  TCP, 246–247
  UDP, 247
TCP/IP tools and commands
  arp command, 339–340
  hostname command, 340
  ipconfig command
    about, 340
    displaying basic IP configuration, 341
    displaying detailed configuration information, 342

flushing local DNS cache, 343
releasing IP leases, 343
renewing IP leases, 342–343
`nbstat` command, 344–345
`netstat` command
about, 345
displaying connections, 345–346
displaying interface statistics, 346–348
`nslookup` command
about, 349
displaying DNS records, 350–352
DNS, 352–355
locating mail server for email address, 352
looking up IP addresses, 349–350
using subcommands, 350
`pathping` command, 355–356
`ping` command, 357–358
`route` command
about, 358
displaying routing table, 358–361
modifying routing table, 361–362
`tracert` command, 362–364
team site, 485
TechNet (website), 796
Technical Stuff icon, 3
Telnet, 156, 239, 256
`telnet` service, 778
`%TEMP%` variable, 607
temporary user profile, 559
10Base, 245
10Base2, 801
10Base5, 801
10BaseT, 801
Terminal Services, 407
terminator, 822
Terrazzo bytes (TB), 822
terrorism, 219
theft, 219
thin client, 407
thinnet, 801
"This is spam" feature, 176
threats, to wireless security, 105–109
Three-letter acronym (TLA), 823. *See also* Extended Three-Letter Acronym (ETLA)

time sharing, 823
Time to Live (TTL), 306, 308
`%TIME%` variable, 607
time-out, 823
`/TIMES:` parameter, 626
Tip icon, 3
TLA (Three-Letter Acronym), 823
`/tmp` directory, 691
`%TMP%` variable, 607
token, 823
Token Ring, 823
Tom's Hardware Guide (website), 793
tools
for cable, 46–47
VMware, 402–403
top-level domains
about, 294
defined, 823
generic domains, 294–295
geographic domains, 295–297
topology, 35–36, 823. *See also* bus; ring; star
`touch` command, 775–776
touchscreen, 823
tower case, 16–17
`trace` subcommand, 338
`traceroute` command, 791
`tracert` command, 127, 362–364
transceiver, 823
transitive relationships, 531
Transmission Control Protocol (TCP), 246–247, 255
Transmission Control Protocol/Internet Protocol (TCP/IP)
about, 155, 228, 249
configuration for Linux servers, 680
configuration of, 58, 502
defined, 822
diagnostic commands, 127
framework, 254–256
history of, 246
implementation, 36
ports, 155, 156
standards, 252–254
websites for, 798
Transport layer, 230, 236–237, 255–256, 823
Travan drives, 206

Traverse Folder/Execute Folder
    permission, 564
trees, 535
Trojan horse, 160, 823
troubleshooting
  about, 189, 589
  basic steps for, 190
  booting in Safe Mode, 198
  checking network connections, 192
  checking network settings, 193–194
  Computer Management console, 598–599
  documenting, 204
  error messages, 193
  event logs, 203
  Event Viewer
    about, 589
    setting event log policies, 591–592
    using, 589–591
  experimenting, 195
  fixing dead computers, 191–192
  logged on users, 196
  monitoring performance
    about, 592
    creating performance logs, 595–597
    Reliability and Performance Monitor,
      592–595
  restarting
    client computers, 196–198
    network servers, 202
    network services, 200–201
  Services console, 599–600
  using System Restore, 198–200
  using Windows Networking
    Troubleshooter, 194–195
  wireless networks, 114–118
trustee rights, 824
trusting domain, 531
trusts, 531, 823
TTL (Time to Live), 306, 308
twisted-pair cables. *See also* shielded
    twisted-pair (STP) cable; unshielded
    twisted-pair (UTP) cable
  about, 42, 192
  defined, 824
  pinouts for, 47
2600 Magazine (website), 795

2600 The Hacker Quarterly (website), 129
Type, as resource record field, 308
Type command, 338, 605
type-1 hypervisors, 368
type-2 hypervisors, 368

U

u command, 770
Ubuntu, 678, 795
UDP (User Datagram Protocol), 247, 256
Uniform Resource Locator (URL), 824
uninterruptible power supply (UPS), 504,
    824
uniquepw parameter, 611
universal scope, 553–554
Unix, location of Hosts file in, 298
unlimited parameter, 621
unmanaged switches, 34
unnecessary services, disabling, 143
unshielded twisted-pair (UTP) cable, 31,
    43, 824. *See also* 10BaseT; twisted-pair
    cable
unsubscribing, 176
up-arrow key, 603
update statement, 662
updating software, 186–188
upgrade install, 53–54, 500
upgrading, compared with installing, 500
uplink ports, 51
UPS (uninterruptible power supply), 504,
    824
URL (Uniform Resource Locator), 824
USB, 824. *See also* serial port
use statement, 662, 671
user accounts
  about, 139
  Administrator account, 142
  creating, 779
  editing in Office 365, 482–483
  managing
    about, 145, 541
    assigning permissions to groups, 150
    assigning user rights, 148
    automating tasks with logon scripts, 151

built-in accounts, 146–148
components of user accounts, 145–146
controlling user access with permissions, 149–150
creating logon scripts, 561
creating users, 542–545
deleting users, 552
disabling, 551–552
enabling, 551–552
groups, 552–558
local accounts compared with domain accounts, 541
properties, 542
resetting passwords, 550–551
setting properties, 545–550
user profiles, 150–151, 558–561
managing in Linux, 697–699
obfuscating usernames, 139
password-generator, 141–142
passwords, 140
User Datagram Protocol (UDP), 247, 256
user ID, 824. *See also* usernames
user parameter, 624, 628
user passwords, resetting, 550–551
user profiles
about, 150–151, 558–559
defined, 824
roaming, 559–561
types of, 559
user properties, setting
about, 545–546
account options, 546–548
changing contact information, 546
restricting access to certain computers, 549
specifying logon hours, 548
user's profile information, 549–550
User Properties dialog box, 561
user rights. *See also* file rights
assigning, 148
defined, 824
user subcommand, 338
useradd command, 698, 779–780
/USERCOMMENT:"text" parameter, 627
USERCTL setting, 707
userdel command, 781

%USERDOMAIN% variable, 607
usermod command, 781
username parameter, 614, 616
%username% variable, 561
USERNAME variable, 769
%USERNAME% variable, 607
usernames
about, 542
obfuscating, 139
%USERPROFILE% variable, 607
users
changing
default options for, 779–780
passwords for, 782
creating
about, 542–545
groups of, 782–783
in Office 365, 480–482
deleting, 552, 781
logged on, 196
modifying, 781
security and, 143–144
as security type in Samba, 728
Users group, 555, 824
users parameter, 619, 621
/usr directory, 691
UTF-8, 238–239
utility program, 128
UTP. *See* unshielded twisted-pair (UTP) cable
UTP (unshielded twisted-pair) cable, 31, 43, 824. *See also* 10BaseT; twisted-pair cables

V

valid users setting, 734
/var directory, 691
variables, environment, 768–769
/var/named directory, 718–721
VBScript, 824
vCenter Client, 396
vCenter Desktop, 408
vCenter Server, 395
VDI (virtual desktop infrastructure), 407

`verbose` subcommand, 338
versions, of operating systems, 26
VGA (Video Graphics Array), 824
`.vhd` format, 378
`.vhdx` format, 378
`vi` commands, 769–770
video, for server computers, 16
Video Graphics Array (VGA), 824
viewing mailboxes, 654–658
virtual consoles, 683, 690
virtual desktop infrastructure (VDI), 407
virtual disks
  about, 370–373
  creating, 384–387
  defined, 825
  Hyper-V, 378–379
Virtual Host Properties dialog box, 745–746
virtual hosts
  configuring, 742–746
    about, 742–743
    creating virtual hosts, 745–746
    default host, 743–745
  defined, 742
Virtual Local Area Network (VLAN), 825
Virtual Machine Summary pane (Hyper-V),
    381
virtual machines
  about, 680
  creating, 387–391, 398–402
  defined, 825
Virtual Machines pane (Hyper-V), 380–381
virtual memory, 825
virtual network, 373, 825
virtual private network (VPN)
  about, 114, 181, 429–430
  accessing computer remotely, 430
  defined, 825
  security, 431–432
  servers and clients, 432–433
virtual switches, creating, 381–383
virtual user, 753
virtualization
  about, 367–368
  benefits of, 373–375
  history of, 370
  hypervisors, 368–369

  network, 373
  virtual disks, 370–373
Virtualization For Dummies (Golden), 367
virtualizing desktops. *See* desktop
    virtualization
virus
  about, 159–161
  defined, 825
virus protection
  about, 159–161
  antivirus program, 161–162
  safe computing, 162
VirusScan Enterprise (McAfee), 161
Visio, 126, 825
VLAN (Virtual Local Area Network), 825
VMFS, 396
VMware
  about, 54, 395
  creating virtual machines, 398–402
  defined, 825
  installing tools, 402–403
  VMware Player, 396–398
  vSphere, 395–396
  website for, 793
VMware Infrastructure 3 For Dummies
    (Lowe), 367
VMware's Horizon View, 408
Voice over IP (VoIP), 825
voicemail, 825
volume license, 179–180
volumes, 372
VPN. *See* virtual private network (VPN)
`vsftpd`
  installing, 759
  starting, 759
vSphere, 395–396
vSphere Desktop, 408

W

`:w` command, 770
W3C (World Wide Web Consortium), 229,
    796
wall jacks, 49–50
WAN (wide area network), 13

WAP. *See* wireless access point (WAP)
Warning icon, 591
Warning! icon, 3
water, 219, 220
wavelength, 92–93
waves, 91–92
weather, 219
web browser
 defined, 825
 Hewlett-Packard, 794
Web Extras (website), 4
web interfaces, accessing network printers
  using, 84–85
web pages, creating, 747
web servers, 29
WebEx, 471–472
Webopedia (website), 797
websites
 AirWave, 109
 American National Standards Institute
   (ANSI), 796
 Android, 799
 Apache HTTP server, 795
 Apple, 799
 BarracudaWare, 208
 BIND, 795
 Bing, 797
 BlackBerry, 799
 Box, 470
 Caldera, 795
 certifications, 793
 Cheat Sheet, 4
 Cisco, 131, 793, 799
 Class A address assignments, 266
 CNET reviews, 793
 CompTIA, 130
 creating, 636–640
 default, 634–636
 Dell, 794
 D-Link, 799
 DNS lookups, 798
 Dogpile, 797
 Dropbox, 469
 EH Publishing, 794
 Exchange, 796
 Fedora, 678, 681, 795

 Firefox, 798
 Google, 141, 797
 Google Apps for Business, 462
 Google Chrome, 798
 Google Drive, 468
 GoToMeeting, 471
 GoToMyPC, 406
 hardware, 793–794
 HardwareCentral, 793
 home networking, 794
 HomePNA Alliance, 794
 HowStuffWorks, 797
 IBM, 793
 InformationWeek, 129, 795
 InfoWorld, 129, 795
 Institute of Electrical and Electronics
   Engineers (IEEE), 796
 International Organization for
   Standardization (ISO), 796
 Internet Assigned Numbers Authority, 796
 Internet Engineering Task Force (IETF),
   252, 796
 Internet Explorer, 798
 Internet Society, 796
 Internet Systems Consortium (ISC), 250,
   798
 InterNIC, 798
 iPhone, 799
 Linksys, 794, 799
 for Linux, 794–795
 Linux Journal, 795
 Linux Magazine, 795
 for magazines, 795
 Mandriva Linux, 678
 Meraki, 799
 Microsoft, 131, 795–796
 Microsoft licensing, 180
 Microsoft Office 365, 465
 Microsoft server, 796
 NETGEAR, 794, 799
 NetScout, 128
 Network Computing, 129, 795
 Network Solutions, 798
 for Network Standards Organizations, 796
 Network World, 129
 Office 365, 478, 486, 796

websites *(continued)*
Opera, 798
Oracle, 794
PowerShell, 601
Red Hat, 793, 795
for reference, 797
Register.com, 798
RFC repository, 796
Samba, 795
for search, 797
SharePoint, 796
Slackware, 678, 795
small-business networking, 794
for smartphones, 798
SMC, 799
Socialcast, 474
speed tests, 798
Spiceworks, 127
SQL Server, 796
SUSE, 678, 795
for TCP/IP and Internet, 798
TechNet, 796
Tom's Hardware Guide, 793
2600 Magazine, 795
2600 The Hacker Quarterly, 129
Ubuntu, 678, 795
VMware, 793
Web Extras, 4
WebEx, 471
Webopedia, 797
Whatis.com, 797
Wi-Fi Planet, 799
Wikipedia, 797
Windows, 795
Windows IT Pro Magazine, 795
Windows Phone, 799
Windows Software Update Services
    (WSUS), 126
Windows Update, 126
for wireless networking, 798
Wireshark, 128
World Wide Web Consortium (W3C), 796
Yahoo!, 797
Yammer, 473
Zoo, 797
WEP. *See* Wired Equivalent Privacy (WEP)

Whatis.com (website), 797
whitelisting, 171, 755
wide area network (WAN), 13
Wi-Fi, 825
Wi-Fi Planet (website), 799
Wi-Fi Protected Access (WPA)
    defined, 827
    using, 112–113
Wiki Server, 76
Wikipedia (website), 797
wildcards, 603–604, 767–768
%WINDIR% variable, 607
Windows
    defined, 825
    website, 795
Windows 7
    activating firewall in, 158–159
    booting in Safe Mode, 198
    connecting remotely with Remote
        Desktop Connection, 515–516
    defined, 826
    enabling Remote Assistance, 448–449
    starting Networking Troubleshooter in,
        195
Windows 8/8.1
    activating firewall in, 158–159
    booting in Safe Mode, 198
    defined, 826
    enabling Remote Assistance, 448–449
    location of Hosts file in, 298
    starting Networking Troubleshooter in,
        195
Windows 9x/Me, location of Hosts file in,
    298
Windows 10
    booting in Safe Mode, 198
    defined, 826
    enabling Remote Assistance, 448–449
    location of Hosts file in, 298
Windows 95, 826
Windows 98, 826
Windows 2000, location of Hosts file in, 298
Windows Action Center, 162–163
Windows Azure, 465
Windows Calculator, 260–261
Windows CE, 826

Windows clients, configuring
  about, 63
  configuring network connections, 63–69
  joining domains, 69–72
Windows commands
  about, 601
  command windows
    about, 601
    closing, 602
    Control area, 603
    editing commands, 602–603
    opening, 602
  EventCreate command, 608–609
  Net commands
    about, 609–610
    Net Accounts command, 610–611
    Net Computer command, 611
    Net Config command, 611–612
    Net Continue command, 612
    Net File command, 612–613
    Net Group command, 613–614
    Net Help command, 615
    Net Helpmsg command, 615
    Net Localgroup command, 615–617
    Net Name command, 617
    Net Pause command, 617–618
    Net Print command, 618–619
    Net Send command, 619–620
    Net Session command, 620
    Net Share command, 620–621
    Net Start command, 621–622
    Net Statistics command, 622–623
    Net Stop command, 623
    Net Time command, 623–624
    Net Use command, 624–625
    Net User command, 625–627
    Net View command, 627
  RunAs command, 627–628
  special commands
    about, 603
    batch files, 607–608
    chaining commands, 604–605
    environment variables, 606–607
    piping, 605
    redirection, 605
    wildcards, 603–604

Windows DHCP client, configuring, 287–289
Windows DNS client, configuring, 315–316
Windows DNS Server, 314–315
Windows for Workgroups, 826
Windows Group Policy, 185–186
Windows IT Pro Magazine (website), 795
Windows Millennium Edition, 826
Windows Mobile, 826
Windows Networking Troubleshooter,
  194–195
Windows NT
  defined, 826
  location of Hosts file in, 298
Windows Phone, 799
Windows Security Center, 163
Windows Server, 21, 826
Windows Server 2012, 55
Windows Server 2016
  adding server roles and features, 509–512
  enabling Group Policy Management on,
    578–579
  installing, 281–282
    checking system requirements, 499–500
    choosing workgroups or domains, 503
    licensing options, 501
    multiboot, 501
    planning partitions, 501–502
    preparing for, 503–504
    reading release notes, 500
    TCP/IP configurations, 502
    upgrading compared with installing, 500
  managing
    customizing Microsoft Management
      Console, 520–527
    using Administrator account, 513–514
    using Microsoft Management Console,
      517–520
    using Remote Desktop Connection,
      514–516
  running setup, 504–508
Windows Software Update Services
  (WSUS), 126
Windows Update, 126, 186–188
Windows user accounts, managing
  about, 541
  creating logon scripts, 561

Windows user accounts, managing *(continued)*
  creating users, 542–545
  deleting users, 552
  disabling, 551–552
  enabling, 551–552
  groups, 552–558
  local accounts compared with domain
      accounts, 541
  properties, 542
  resetting passwords, 550–551
  setting properties, 545–550
  user profiles, 558–561
Windows Vista
  booting in Safe Mode, 198
  defined, 826
  location of Hosts file in, 298
  starting Networking Troubleshooter in,
      195
Windows XP
  booting in Safe Mode, 198
  defined, 826
  location of Hosts file in, 298
  starting Networking Troubleshooter in,
      195
wire cutters, 46
wire stripper, 46
wired equivalent privacy (WEP)
  defined, 825
  enabling, 111–112
wireless, 826
wireless access point (WAP)
  about, 90, 97–99
  adding, 117–118
  configuring, 100–102
  defined, 827
  multifunction, 99
  placing outside firewall, 114
wireless bridging, 100
wireless devices, range of, 95–96
wireless local area network (WLAN), 90
wireless network adapters, 96–97
wireless networks
  about, 9, 90
  connecting to, 103–105
  security for
    about, 105

    enabling WEP, 111–112
    MAC address filtering, 113–114
    passwords, 109
    SSID, 110–111
    threats to, 105–109
    WPA/WPA2, 112–113
  setting up
    about, 89–90
    connecting to wireless networks,
        103–105
    electronics, 91–94
    range, 95–96
    roaming, 99–100
    wireless access points, 97–99, 100–102
    wireless network adapters, 96–97
    wireless network security, 105–118
    wireless networking, 90
    wireless standards, 94–95
  troubleshooting, 114–118
  websites for, 798
wireless PCI card, 97
wireless standards, 94–95
wireless USB adapter, 97
Wireshark (website), 128
wiring closet, 827
WLAN (wireless local area network), 90
workgroup setting, 733
workgroups, 58, 503
workstation parameter, 612, 618
workstations. *See* client computers; clients
/WORKSTATIONS: parameter, 627
World Wide Web (HyperText Transport
    Protocol; HTTP), 156
World Wide Web (WWW), 827
World Wide Web Consortium (W3C), 229,
    796
worm, 160–161
WPA. *See* Wi-Fi Protected Access (WPA)
:wq command, 770
Write Attributes permission, 565
Write Extended Attributes permission, 565
Write permission, 564
writeonly setting, 734
WSUS (Windows Software Update
    Services), 126
WWW (World Wide Web), 827

X

X Window System, 683, 689–690
X10, 827
XenApp (Citrix), 409–411
Xeon, 15
`xinetd.conf` file, 705, 710
XOR operator, 259–260

Y

Yahoo! (website), 797
Yammer, 473–474
yellow cable, 801
Yellowdog Updater Modified, 779
YouTube app, 427
`yum` command, 779

Z

zone files
  about, 308–309, 720–721
  A records, 309, 311, 721
  CNAME records, 309, 311–312, 721
  defined, 827
  MX records, 309, 312–313, 721
  NS records, 309, 310–311, 721
  PTR records, 309, 312, 721
  SOA records, 309–310, 721
zone transfer, 302
zones, 300–302
Zoo (website), 797

About the Author

Doug Lowe has written a whole bunch of computer books, including more than 50 *For Dummies* books, among them *Networking For Dummies*, 9th Edition; *Java All-in-One For Dummies*, 5th Edition, and *PowerPoint 2016 For Dummies*. He lives in sunny Fresno, California, where the motto is "Fres-YES." He is the Information Technology Director at Blair, Church & Flynn Consulting Engineers in nearby Clovis, CA, where the motto is "Fres-NO."

Dedication

For Kristen.

Author's Acknowledgments

I'd like to thank everyone who was involved with the sixth edition of this book, especially the most excellent project editor Elizabeth Kuball, who championed this book through all the editorial details needed to put a book of this scope together on time. Thanks also to Dan DiNicolo, who once again gave the manuscript a thorough review to ensure the technical accuracy of every sentence and in the process offered many excellent suggestions for improvements. And as always, thanks to all the behind-the-scenes people who chipped in with help I'm not even aware of.

Publisher's Acknowledgments

Acquisitions Editor: Amy Fandrei
Project Editor: Elizabeth Kuball
Copy Editor: Elizabeth Kuball
Technical Editor: Dan DiNicolo
Editorial Assistant: Matthew Lowe
Sr. Editorial Assistant: Cherie Case

Production Editor: Antony Sami
Cover Image: asharkyu/Shutterstock

Math & Science

Algebra I For Dummies,
2nd Edition
978-0-470-55964-2

Anatomy and Physiology
For Dummies, 2nd Edition
978-0-470-92326-9

Astronomy For Dummies,
3rd Edition
978-1-118-37697-3

Biology For Dummies,
2nd Edition
978-0-470-59875-7

Chemistry For Dummies,
2nd Edition
978-1-118-00730-3

1001 Algebra II Practice
Problems For Dummies
978-1-118-44662-1

Microsoft Office

Excel 2013 For Dummies
978-1-118-51012-4

Office 2013 All-in-One
For Dummies
978-1-118-51636-2

PowerPoint 2013
For Dummies
978-1-118-50253-2

Word 2013 For Dummies
978-1-118-49123-2

Music

Blues Harmonica
For Dummies
978-1-118-25269-7

Guitar For Dummies,
3rd Edition
978-1-118-11554-1

iPod & iTunes
For Dummies, 10th Edition
978-1-118-50864-0

Programming

Beginning Programming
with C For Dummies
978-1-118-73763-7

Excel VBA Programming
For Dummies, 3rd Edition
978-1-118-49037-2

Java For Dummies,
6th Edition
978-1-118-40780-6

Religion & Inspiration

The Bible For Dummies
978-0-7645-5296-0

Buddhism For Dummies,
2nd Edition
978-1-118-02379-2

Catholicism For Dummies,
2nd Edition
978-1-118-07778-8

Self-Help & Relationships

Beating Sugar Addiction
For Dummies
978-1-118-54645-1

Meditation For Dummies,
3rd Edition
978-1-118-29144-3

Seniors

Laptops For Seniors
For Dummies, 3rd Edition
978-1-118-71105-7

Computers For Seniors
For Dummies, 3rd Edition
978-1-118-11553-4

iPad For Seniors
For Dummies, 6th Edition
978-1-118-72826-0

Social Security
For Dummies
978-1-118-20573-0

Smartphones & Tablets

Android Phones
For Dummies, 2nd Edition
978-1-118-72030-1

Nexus Tablets
For Dummies
978-1-118-77243-0

Samsung Galaxy S 4
For Dummies
978-1-118-64222-1

Samsung Galaxy Tabs
For Dummies
978-1-118-77294-2

Test Prep

ACT For Dummies,
5th Edition
978-1-118-01259-8

ASVAB For Dummies,
3rd Edition
978-0-470-63760-9

GRE For Dummies,
7th Edition
978-0-470-88921-3

Officer Candidate Tests
For Dummies
978-0-470-59876-4

Physician's Assistant Exa
For Dummies
978-1-118-11556-5

Series 7 Exam For Dumm
978-0-470-09932-2

Windows 8

Windows 8.1 All-in-One
For Dummies
978-1-118-82087-2

Windows 8.1 For Dumm
978-1-118-82121-3

Windows 8.1 For Dumm
Book + DVD Bundle
978-1-118-82107-7

 Available in print and e-book formats.

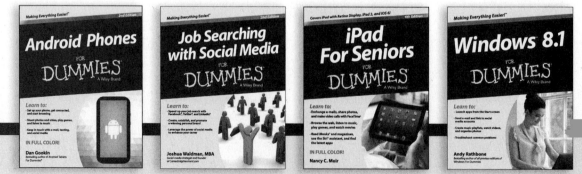

Take Dummies with you everywhere you go!

Whether you are excited about e-books, want more from the web, must have your mobile apps, or are swept up in social media, Dummies makes everything easier.

For Dummies is the global leader in the reference category and one of the most trusted and highly regarded brands in the world. No longer just focused on books, customers now have access to the For Dummies content they need in the format they want. Let us help you develop a solution that will fit your brand and help you connect with your customers.

Advertising & Sponsorships

Connect with an engaged audience on a powerful multimedia site, and position your message alongside expert how-to content.

Targeted ads • Video • Email marketing • Microsites • Sweepstakes sponsorship

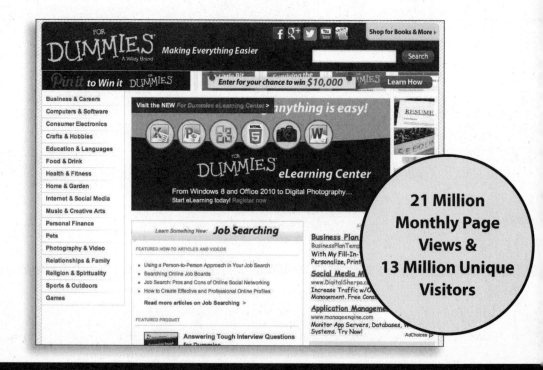

21 Million Monthly Page Views & 13 Million Unique Visitors